# Selected Papers from the pHealth 2021 Conference, Genoa, Italy, 8-10 November 2021

# Selected Papers from the pHealth 2021 Conference, Genoa, Italy, 8-10 November 2021

Editors

**Bernd Blobel**
**Mauro Giacomini**

MDPI

Basel • Beijing • Wuhan • Barcelona • Belgrade • Novi Sad • Cluj • Manchester

*Editors*

Bernd Blobel
Medical Faculty
University of Regensburg
Regensburg
Germany

Mauro Giacomini
DIBRIS
University of Genoa
Genoa
Italy

*Editorial Office*
MDPI
St. Alban-Anlage 66
4052 Basel, Switzerland

This is a reprint of articles from the Special Issue published online in the open access journal *Journal of Personalized Medicine* (ISSN 2075-4426) (available at: www.mdpi.com/journal/jpm/special_issues/pHealth_2021).

For citation purposes, cite each article independently as indicated on the article page online and as indicated below:

Lastname, A.A.; Lastname, B.B. Article Title. *Journal Name* **Year**, *Volume Number*, Page Range.

**ISBN 978-3-0365-9257-2 (Hbk)**
**ISBN 978-3-0365-9256-5 (PDF)**
**doi.org/10.3390/books978-3-0365-9256-5**

# Contents

# Preface

This reprint presents extended versions of contributions to pHealth 2021, the 18th International Conference on Wearable Micro and Nano Technologies for Personalized Health, held on 8–10 November 2021 in Genoa, Italy, selected for the related Special Issue of the Journal of Personalized Medicine. The original papers have been published in the IOS Press Studies in Health Technology and Informatics 2021, volume 285.

The 2021 edition of pHealth emphasized the interrelated aspects of advanced pHealth, i.e., personalized, participative, preventive, predictive, and precision medicine (5P medicine) in health and social services. In that context, mobile technologies, micro–nano–bio smart systems, artificial intelligence and robotics, data management and analytics, machine learning and deep learning for personalized health, the Health Internet of Things (HIoT), systems medicine, public health, and virtual care are of interest. Those new technologies create new potential risks for security, privacy, and safety, resulting in new challenges for meeting the ethical and trustworthiness requirements of systems, partners, and processes. Bernd Blobel, as the long-term Chair of the pHealth conferences' Scientific Program Committee, as well as of the pHealth Steering Committee, has checked and edited every paper invited for publication in the MDPI JPM pHealth 2021 Special Issue before giving the green flag for formal submission. Mauro Giacomini, as Chair of the pHealth 2021 Local Organizing Committee, has managed the review process performed by at least two independent international experts.

**Bernd Blobel and Mauro Giacomini**
*Editors*

Journal of *Personalized Medicine*

*Editorial*

# Selected Papers from the pHealth 2021 Conference, Genoa, Italy, 8–10 November 2021

**Bernd Blobel [1,2,3,*] and Mauro Giacomini [4]**

[1] Medical Faculty, University of Regensburg, 93053 Regensburg, Germany
[2] Faculty European Campus Rottal-Inn, Deggendorf Institute of Technology, 94469 Deggendorf, Germany
[3] First Medical Faculty, Charles University of Prague, Stare Mesto 110 00, Czech Republic
[4] DIBRIS, University of Genoa, 16145 Genoa, Italy; mauro.giacomini@dibris.unige.it
* Correspondence: bernd.blobel@klinik.uni-regensburg.de

This Special Issue of the *Journal of Personalized Medicine* presents extended versions of selected contributions to pHealth 2021, the 18th International Conference on Wearable Micro and Nano Technologies for Personalized Health, held on 8–10 November 2021 in Genoa, Italy. The original papers have been published in the IOS Press Studies in Health Technology and Informatics 2021, volume 285 (https://ebooks.iospress.nl/volume/phealth-2021-proceedings-of-the-18th-international-conference-on-wearable-micro-and-nano-technologies-for-personalized-health-810-november-2021-genoa-italy) (URL accessed on 15 June 2023).

The 2021 edition of pHealth emphasized the interrelated aspects of advanced pHealth, i.e., personalized, participative, preventive, predictive, precision medicine (5P medicine) in health and social services. In that context, mobile technologies, micro–nano–bio smart systems, artificial intelligence and robotics, data management and analytics, machine learning and deep learning for personalized health, the Health Internet of Things (HIoT), systems medicine, public health, and virtual care are of interest. Those new technologies create new potential risks for security, privacy, and safety, resulting in new challenges for meeting ethical and trustworthiness requirements of systems, partners, and processes. Bernd Blobel as the long-term Chair of the pHealth conferences' Scientific Program Committee as well as of the pHealth Steering Committee has checked and edited every paper invited for publication in the MDPI *JPM* pHealth 2021 Special Issue before giving the green flag for formal submission. Mauro Giacomini, as Chair of the pHealth 2021 Local Organizing Committee, has managed the review process, performed by at least two independent international experts.

The book starts with an introduction into the ongoing transformation of health and social care including the related organizational, methodological, and technological paradigm changes. For designing and managing ethical and intelligent transformed health ecosystems, the comprehensive and correct formal representation complex, dynamic, interdisciplinary ecosystems with their knowledge spaces is inevitable. Regarding ethical, legal, security, and privacy aspects, the system's policy domain and their aforementioned subdomains must be especially addressed. Therefore, the paper specifically discusses the deployment of ontologies for representing ecosystems and their domains, hereby also considering newly standardized ontologies for representation and management of ethically driven robotics and automation systems. Thereafter, knowledge representation and management for semantic data integration is discussed in the context of practical solutions for biobanks. As the new technologies and methodologies are not just necessary for developing and running transformed health and social care ecosystems, but are also inevitable for properly including the current and potential actors, the introductory chapter of the book concludes with a paper on didactic concepts for digital learning in care settings.

The second chapter presents two papers tackling the deployment of mobile technologies for pHealth. The first discusses and compares different approaches to learning systems

check for updates

**Citation:** Blobel, B.; Giacomini, M. Selected Papers from the pHealth 2021 Conference, Genoa, Italy, 8–10 November 2021. *J. Pers. Med.* **2023**, *13*, 1213. https://doi.org/10.3390/jpm13081213

Received: 21 July 2023
Revised: 29 July 2023
Accepted: 29 July 2023
Published: 31 July 2023

for managing ambulant stress detection. The second one studies the deployment of mobile applications for improving care processes, especially the communication between care providers in pediatrics.

The third chapter discusses the deployment of machine learning, artificial intelligence, and automation in transformed health and social care ecosystems with concrete solutions. The first paper focuses on Natural Language Processing, and the last one on unsupervised learning for automatically analyzing notes and electronic medical records. The second paper analyzes processes optimization with machine learning. The papers that follow investigate the deployment of Chatbots in the context of behavioral health, the deployment of machine learning to analyze the side effects of CVD interventions, the intelligent analysis of COVID-19 pneumonia cases using Hybrid Bayesian Networks, and, finally, the use of decision support systems.

The last chapter addresses security, privacy, safety, and trust issues changing their characteristics as well as occurrence and importance in the context of the transformation of health and social care ecosystems. First, the implementation of standard-based security and privacy in genomic information systems is discussed at length. Thereafter, a new methodology is presented for assessing privacy and trust in eHealth. The penultimate paper of this volume addresses the importance of data democratization for the advancement of data sharing at a national and European level, as well as globally, while the last paper offers a risk prediction methodology in cardiac surgery.

The editors thank all authors and reviewers for their important contribution to the success of this volume. Furthermore, they are deeply indebted to the MDPI *Journal of Personalized Medicine* and its Editorial Office, and especially to Penny Su, for the valuable continuous support. Without all those efforts, this volume would not have been possible.

**Author Contributions:** B.B. drafted this paper. All authors have reviewed and edited the article. All authors have read and agreed to the published version of the manuscript.

**Conflicts of Interest:** The author declares no conflict of interest.

Journal of *Personalized Medicine*

MDPI

*Article*

# Designing and Managing Advanced, Intelligent and Ethical Health and Social Care Ecosystems

**Bernd Blobel [1,2,3,*], Pekka Ruotsalainen [4], Mathias Brochhausen [5], Edson Prestes [6] and Michael A. Houghtaling [7]**

1 Medical Faculty, University of Regensburg, 93053 Regensburg, Germany
2 eHealth Competence Center Bavaria, Deggendorf Institute of Technology, 94469 Deggendorf, Germany
3 First Medical Faculty, Charles University of Prague, 11000 Staré Město, Czech Republic
4 Faculty of Information Technology and Communication Sciences, Tampere University, 33100 Tampere, Finland; pekka.ruotsalainen@tuni.fi
5 Department of Biomedical Informatics, University of Arkansas for Medical Sciences, Little Rock, AR 72205, USA; mbrochhausen@uams.edu
6 Informatics Institute, Federal University of Rio Grande do Sul, Porto Alegre 90040-060, Brazil; prestes@inf.ufrgs.br
7 IBM-Retired, Tucson, AZ 85750, USA; michael-h@acm.org
* Correspondence: bernd.blobel@klinik.uni-regensburg.de

**Abstract:** The ongoing transformation of health systems around the world aims at personalized, preventive, predictive, participative precision medicine, supported by technology. It considers individual health status, conditions, and genetic and genomic dispositions in personal, social, occupational, environmental and behavioral contexts. In this way, it transforms health and social care from art to science by fully understanding the pathology of diseases and turning health and social care from reactive to proactive. The challenge is the understanding and the formal as well as consistent representation of the world of sciences and practices, i.e., of multidisciplinary and dynamic systems in variable context. This enables mapping between the different disciplines, methodologies, perspectives, intentions, languages, etc., as philosophy or cognitive sciences do. The approach requires the deployment of advanced technologies including autonomous systems and artificial intelligence. This poses important ethical and governance challenges. This paper describes the aforementioned transformation of health and social care ecosystems as well as the related challenges and solutions, resulting in a sophisticated, formal reference architecture. This reference architecture provides a system-theoretical, architecture-centric, ontology-based, policy-driven model and framework for designing and managing intelligent and ethical ecosystems in general and health ecosystems in particular.

**Keywords:** health transformation; ecosystems; knowledge representation and management; architecture

check for updates

**Citation:** Blobel, B.; Ruotsalainen, P.; Brochhausen, M.; Prestes, E.; Houghtaling, M.A. Designing and Managing Advanced, Intelligent and Ethical Health and Social Care Ecosystems. *J. Pers. Med.* **2023**, *13*, 1209. https://doi.org/10.3390/jpm13081209

Academic Editor: Christine Lu

Received: 29 June 2023
Revised: 21 July 2023
Accepted: 28 July 2023
Published: 30 July 2023



## 1. Introduction

The paper at hand presents an extended version of the keynote provided to the pHealth 2021 conference [1], resulting in some inevitable similarities. This section introduces context, challenges and general solutions for transforming health and social care ecosystems.

For many years and everywhere around the globe, health and social care systems have been challenged by ongoing demographic changes towards aging, multi-diseased societies, the related development of human resources, health and social services consumerism, medical and biomedical progress, and exploding costs for health-related R&D as well as health services delivery. To overcome those problems, these systems must undergo transformations from traditional, hierarchical and regulated medicine towards an advanced health ecosystem for improving care quality and patient safety, but also efficiency and efficacy of care processes. This includes improved access to healthcare services for greater and autonomous active patient participation as well as improved decision making [2].

An ecosystem is the structural and functional unit of ecology where the living organisms interact with each other and the surrounding environment. It is the community of living organisms in conjunction with non-living components of their environment, interacting as a system [3]. The transformation towards personalized, preventive, predictive, participative precision medicine (5PM), supported by technology, is accompanied by important organizational and methodological paradigm changes, summarized in Tables 1 and 2 as follows.

**Table 1.** Organizational paradigm changes in the evolution of 5P medicine (after [4], modified).

| Care Type | Organization, Service Provision | Actors | Services | Target |
|---|---|---|---|---|
| Phenomenological medicine | Organization centered, Local services | Regulated professionals | Domain-specific general services | Humanity |
| Evidence-based medicine | Organization centered, Local services | Regulated professionals | Domain specific, group specific services | Disease-specifically defined group |
| Person-centered medicine | Cross-organizational local services | Regulated professionals | Multiple domains' services | Individual |
| Personalized medicine | Distributed local and remote services | Regulated and non-regulated, professionals, laymen, technical systems | Multiple domains' services, Telemedicine | Individual in personal disposition |
| Systems medicine | Distributed cross-domain services, Smart Healthcare | Regulated and non-regulated, professionals, laymen, technical systems | Cross-domain services, Consumerism, Telemedicine | Individual in personal, environmental, social, occupational and behavioral context |
| Ubiquitous personal health | Ubiquitous services | Regulated and non-regulated, professionals, laymen, technical systems | Integrated services, Consumerism, Ubiquitous medicine | Individual under comprehensive focus |

The described advancement of the care types from empirical to systems medicine finally results in transformed health ecosystems for ubiquitous personal health with the objectives being to provide individualized health services everywhere anytime, integrating all contributing actors and domains. This transformation must be supported by appropriate methodologies and technologies. The methodologies and technologies deployed to meet health transformation are shown in Table 3.

For designing, managing and implementing the described transformed health and social care ecosystems, new techniques and methods have to be deployed. Here, we have to mention mobile, bio-, nano- and molecular technologies, big data and analytics, virtual reality, learning algorithms as well as new computing technologies such as cloud, cognitive and edge computing. Furthermore, we also need appropriate policies and governance schemes to control the system's behavior. An overview on the technologies and methodologies enabling 5PM ecosystems is presented in Table 4.

The intrinsic nature of technology enabling transformed health ecosystems requires a philosophical and especially ethical consideration of the approach [2] to be discussed in more detail in Sections 2.3 and 3, respectively.

In the following section, we will introduce the underlying concepts of ecosystems and their management in more detail.

**Table 2.** Methodological paradigm changes in the evolution of 5P medicine (after [5], modified).

| Care Type | Way of Practicing | Justification | Representation Style | Electronic Comm./Coop | Standards |
|---|---|---|---|---|---|
| Phenomenological medicine | Observation | Pattern recognition | Data | Local data repository (inside the unit) | Data standards |
| Evidence-based medicine | Observation with objective evaluation | Statistical justification, group-specific treatment outcome | Information | Central data repositories | Information standards |
| Person-centered medicine | Managed care | Process mgmt., best medical practice guidelines | Agreed terminology, DMP best practice guidelines | Cross-organizational business process | Terminology standards; Process standards |
| Personalized medicine | Considering the pathology of disease | Clinically justified individual status and context | Disciplinary concepts in a situational context | Knowledge management | Domain ontology standards |
| Systems medicine | Understanding the pathology of disease | Scientifically justified individual status and context | Multidisciplinary concepts in a comprehensive context | Knowledge space management | Multiple ontologies guided by standards in top-level ontologies |
| Ubiquitous personal health | | Dynamically and scientifically justified individual status | | | |

**Table 3.** Transformed health ecosystems' objectives and characteristics as well as methodologies for meeting them, after [6].

| Objective | Characteristics | Methodologies/Technologies |
|---|---|---|
| Provision of health services everywhere anytime | • Openness<br>• Distribution<br>• Mobility<br>• Pervasiveness<br>• Ubiquity | • Wearable and implantable sensors and actuators<br>• Pervasive sensor, actuator and network connectivity<br>• Embedded intelligence<br>• Context awareness |
| Individualization of the system according to status, context, needs, expectations, wishes, environments, etc., of the subject of care | • Flexibility<br>• Scalability<br>• Cognition<br>• Affect and Behavior<br>• Autonomy<br>• Adaptability<br>• Self-organization<br>• Subject of care involvement<br>• Subject of care centration | • Personal and environmental data integration and analytics<br>• Service integration<br>• Context awareness<br>• Knowledge integration<br>• Process and decision intelligence<br>• Presentation layer for all actors |
| Integration of different actors from different disciplines/do-mains (incl. the participation/empowerment of the subject of care), using their own languages, methodologies, terminologies, ontologies, thereby meeting any behavioral aspects, rules and regulations | • Architectural framework<br>• End-user interoperability<br>• Management and harmonization of multiple domains including policy domains | • Terminology and ontology management and harmonization<br>• Knowledge harmonization<br>• Language transformation/translation |
| Usability and acceptability of pHealth solutions | • Preparedness of the individual subject of care Security, Privacy and Trust Framework<br>• Consumerization<br>• Subject of care empowerment<br>• Subject of care as manager<br>• Information-based assessment and selection of services, service quality and safety as well as trustworthiness<br>• Lifestyle improvement and Ambient Assisted Living (AAL) services | • Tool-based ontology management<br>• Individual terminologies<br>• Individual ontologies<br>• Tool-based enhancement of individual knowledge and skills<br>• Human-centered design of solutions<br>• User Experience Evaluation<br>• Trust calculation services |

**Table 4.** Technologies and methodologies for transforming health ecosystems (after [7], modified).

| | |
|---|---|
| • Mobile technologies, biotechnologies, nano- and molecular technologies<br>• Big data and business analytics<br>• Integration of analytics and apps<br>• Assisting technologies → robotics, autonomous systems<br>• Natural Language Processing → text analytics → intelligent media analytics<br>• Conceptualization → knowledge management (KM) and knowledge representation (KR) → artificial intelligence (AI) → artificial common (general) intelligence → intelligent autonomous systems<br>• Security and privacy, governance, ethical challenges, education → ethical AI principles<br>• Cloud computing, cognitive computing, social business | • Edge computing as a "family of technologies that distributes data and services where they best optimize outcomes in a growing set of connected assets " [8]<br>• Virtual reality and augmented reality, thereby blurring "the boundaries between the physical and digital worlds" [9]<br>• Creation of IoT platforms and APP-based ecosystems<br>• Patient-generated health data ecosystem → multiple, dynamic policies<br>• Web content management → digital experience management<br>• Databases → NoSQL technologies → data warehouses → Graph DBs → data lakes<br>• EHR extension with genomic data<br>• Specifications → implementation → tooling → testing → certification |

## 2. The 5PM Health Ecosystem

The aforementioned transformation of health systems aims at personalized, preventive, predictive, participative precision medicine (5PM), supported by technology. It considers individual health status, conditions, and genetic and genomic dispositions in personal social, occupational, environmental and behavioral contexts. In doing so, it transforms health and social care from art to science by fully understanding the pathology of diseases and turning health and social care from reactive to proactive.

The system represented by the subject of care and the processes analyzing and managing his/her health comprises all levels of granularity from elementary particles through atoms, molecules, cell components, cells, tissues, organs, bodies and communities, up to population. Regarding the functional or, in general, inter-relational aspects of that system, the relations comprise, e.g., quantum-mechanical effects in the nano-world, biochemical processes, interrelations based on classical physics and, finally, social interrelations in the macro-world.

For describing such an ecosystem, universal type theory and universal logics, formally represented using the Barendregt Cube [10], can be deployed. This approach can be advanced through system-theoretical and engineering principles by representing any ecosystem with its components, their functions and relations in the tree dimensions (Figure 1):

- The system's architectural perspective, representing the system's composition/decomposition or specialization/generalization;
- The system's domain perspective, representing the involved domains and their actors;
- The system's evolutionary or development perspective.

The described 5PM services require cooperation of many different and sovereign stakeholders from different policy domains in a multi-disciplinary approach including medicine, natural sciences, engineering, but also social, legal and political sciences and the entire systems sciences world (systems medicine, systems biology, systems pathology, etc.), performed through any type of principals (person, organization, device, application, component, object).

This requires the advancement of communication and cooperation among the business actors from different domains with their specific objectives and perspectives from data level (data sharing) to concept/knowledge level (knowledge sharing). Thereby, we have to recognize that they use different methodologies, terminologies/ontologies, education, skills and experiences.

The challenge is the understanding and the formal as well as consistent representation of the world of sciences and practices, i.e., of multidisciplinary and dynamic systems in variable context, for enabling mapping between the different disciplines, methodologies, perspectives, intentions, languages, etc., as philosophy or cognitive sciences do.

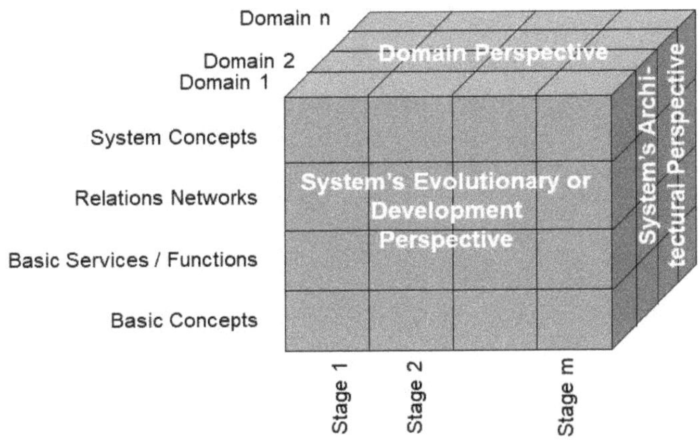


**Figure 1.** Generic model to represent ecosystems (after [11], modified).

If we do not understand components, functions and relations of the real-world ecosystem, i.e., its knowledge/concept space, we cannot properly model and formalize the integrated and interoperable ecosystem we are looking for, and thus, we cannot formulate the requirements and the design for correct solutions. Furthermore, we must keep in mind that we cannot decide on the correct integration and interoperability at data level without knowing the use case-specific context, objectives or constraints. Instead, we shall do this at the real-world business system level. The reasons for the aforementioned problems and appropriate solutions are discussed in more detail in [12,13].

### 2.1. Knowledge Representation and Management

Alter defines knowledge as "a combination of instincts, ideas, rules, and procedures that guide actions and decisions" [14]. The Merriam-Webster Online Dictionary defines knowledge as "the sum of what is known: the body of truth, information, and principles acquired by mankind" [15].

According to Davenport et al., knowledge is "information combined with experience, context, interpretation, and reflection. It is a high-value form of information that is ready to apply to decisions and actions" [16].

There are different knowledge classes such as the following:

- Classification-based knowledge;
- Decision-oriented knowledge;
- Descriptive knowledge;
- Procedural knowledge;
- Reasoning knowledge;
- Assimilative knowledge.

From the modeling perspective, three levels of knowledge representation are distinguished and must be consecutively processed:

- Epistemological level (domain-specific modeling)
- Notation level (formalization, concept representation)
- Processing level (computational, implementations)

Thereby, we have to distinguish different levels of systems representation and modeling: data, information, knowledge and decisions (Figure 2). A model is therefore defined as a representation of objects, properties, relations and interactions of a domain, enabling rational and active business in the represented domain.

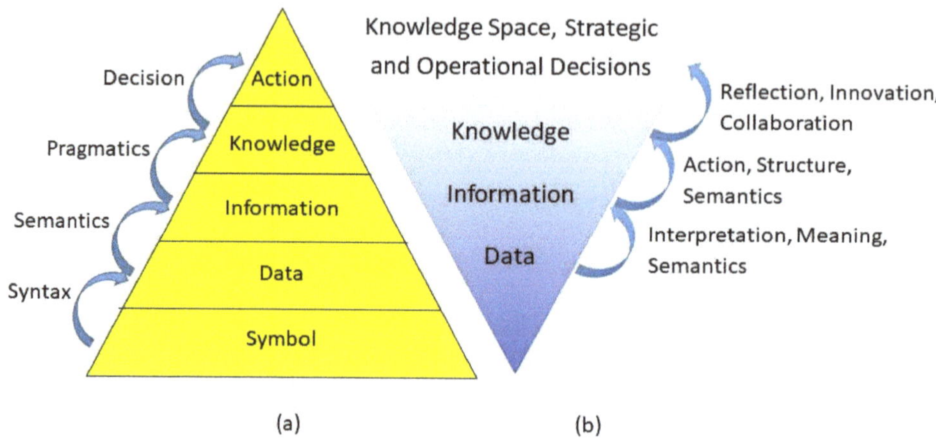


**Figure 2.** Knowledge pyramid (**a**) (after [17]) and model hierarchy (**b**) (after [18]).

The generalization of domain-specific epistemological models requires their transformation into a universal KR notation based on the aforementioned universal type theory and universal logics. The outcome must be validated on a real-world system and thereafter adopted if needed [19].

KR provides a theory of reasoning, composed of the following:

(a) The representation's fundamental conception of intelligent reasoning;
(b) The set of inferences the representation sanctions (the proof theory);
(c) The set of inferences it recommends.

Furthermore, KR supports pragmatically efficient computation by properly organizing information to facilitate making the recommended inferences. Finally, KR is a medium for human expression by defining the language to represent the world.

The dynamics of knowledge creation, especially the importance of tacit knowledge and its conversion into explicit knowledge, have been analyzed by Nonaka and Takeuchi [20]. The process of converting tacit knowledge into explicit concepts through the use of abstractions, metaphors, analogies or models is called externalization. More details on KR and KM can be found in [7].

### 2.2. *Language Theory and Classes of Languages*

A formal language is a set of words, i.e., finite strings of letters, symbols or tokens, called the alphabet, over which the language is defined. A formal language is often defined by means of a formal grammar (also called its formation rules); accordingly, words that belong to a formal language are sometimes called well-formed words (or well-formed formulas). Formal languages do not have semantics, so they are often used as the basis for richer constructs endowed with semantics. Formal languages are also used in logic and in foundations of mathematics to represent the syntax of formal theories. Logical systems can be seen as a formal language with additional constructs, like proof calculi, which define a consequence relation.

In summary, a formal language can be given as strings

- generated by some formal grammar;
- described or matched by a particular regular expression;
- accepted by some automaton, such as a Turing machine or finite state automaton, for which some decision procedure (an algorithm that asks a sequence of related YES/NO questions) produces the answer YES.

Symbols, operators and interpretation theory give sequences of symbols' *meaning* within a KR. Figure 3 classifies languages, related grammars to generate, and automata to accept them, according to the Chomsky Hierarchy Set Inclusion.

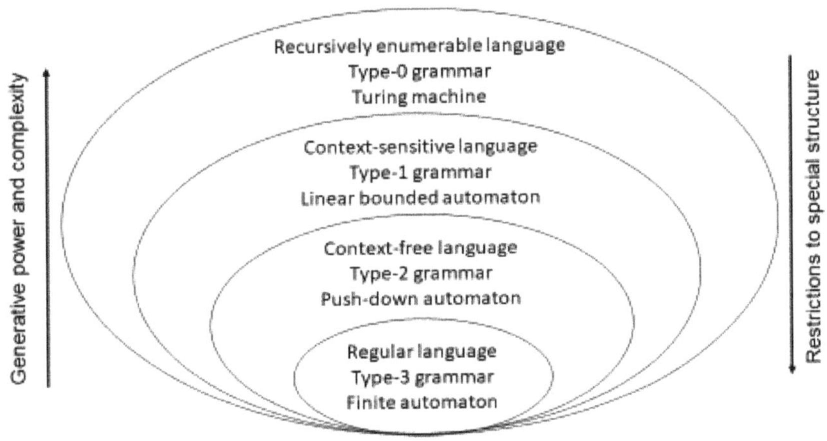


**Figure 3.** Chomsky Hierarchy Set Inclusion (after [21], modified).

### *2.3. Representation of Knowledge-Based Ecosystems*

A key parameter in choosing or creating a KR is its expressivity. The more expressive a KR, the easier and more compact it is to express a fact or element of knowledge within the semantics and grammar of that KR. However, more expressive languages are likely to require more complex logic and algorithms to construct equivalent inferences, resulting in a trade-off between expressivity and practicality [7]. A highly expressive KR is also less likely to be complete and decidable. Less-expressive KRs may be both complete and decidable [22,23]. As mentioned before, we cannot decide on the correct integration and interoperability at the data level due to its higher expressive language. Instead, we shall do this at the real-world business system level, with its less expressive and more complete and decidable languages, thereafter transforming the representations in more expressive and better-processible representation styles.

Any business system can be represented using information and communication technology (ICT) ontologies. However, the justification of the correctness and completeness of structure and behavior of the represented ecosystem can only be provided at the ecosystem's business view using the involved domains' ontologies. Justification of structure and behavior representation includes the representational components, their underlying concepts, their relations, but also the related constraints.

Therefore, natural languages are not only efficient in representing meaning, shared knowledge, skills, and experiences assumed. They also provide an optimum between restriction to special structure and generative power enabling the rich and nevertheless decidable representation of real-world concepts, supported of course by common sense knowledge.

Knowledge can be represented at different levels of abstraction and expressivity, ranging from implicit knowledge (tacit knowledge) up to fully explicit knowledge representation, i.e., from natural language up to universal logic, using different ontology types (Figure 4).

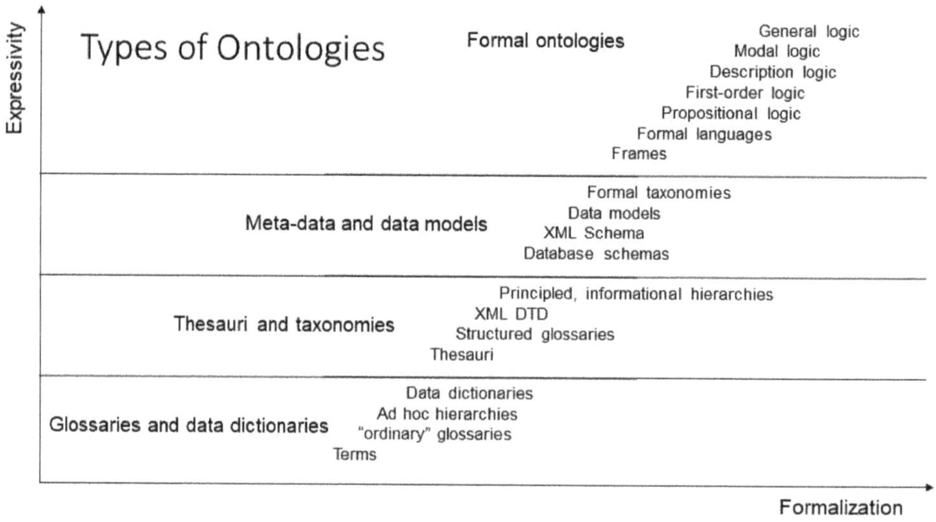


**Figure 4.** Ontology types, after [24], modified.

For representing an ICT-supported ecosystem, Figure 1 must be refined including the system development process according to ISO/IEC 19746 [25]. The result is a model with the following three dimensions: system domains, system components composition (granularity) and systems viewpoints. The representation language type from natural as well as domain languages and ontologies through Business Process Modeling Language (BPML), terminologies and Unified Modeling Language (UML) up to data models and database schemas completes the latter. Meanwhile, under the lead of the first author, this model and framework has been standardized in ISO 23903:2021 [26]. Figure 5 presents the 5PM Healthcare Ecosystem model.

In order to realize ubiquitous health, intelligent and autonomous systems (AIS) are inevitable. This includes artificial intelligence (AI) and robotics [27], using machine learning, deep learning, neural networks, big data and analytics at different levels. As described in detail in [1], intelligence is a concept in cognition theory with four foundational principles: data, information, knowledge and wisdom. During investigations and observations, organs or sensors collect data as measures or symbols describing the world, establishing the structural level of intelligence. To be able to take decisions, we must transform data into information by attaching meaning to the data, establishing the semantic level of intelligence. Knowledge enables proper actions on the represented system, supervised and evaluated by wisdom, establishing the practical level of intelligence. More background information on knowledge representation and intelligence can be found in [6].

As demonstrated, highly complex, multidisciplinary, dynamic, transformed (i.e., knowledge-driven) health and social care systems must be represented and developed using a system-theoretical, architecture-centric, ontology-based and policy-driven approach. The system-theoretical considerations shall follow the white box approach [28]. Policies and related governance schemes control the behavior of the designed, finally implemented and managed 5PM ecosystem. This includes procedural requirements expressed in procedural policies, legal requirements formulated in laws and legislations including security and privacy challenges, but also the implementation of ethical and moral principles.

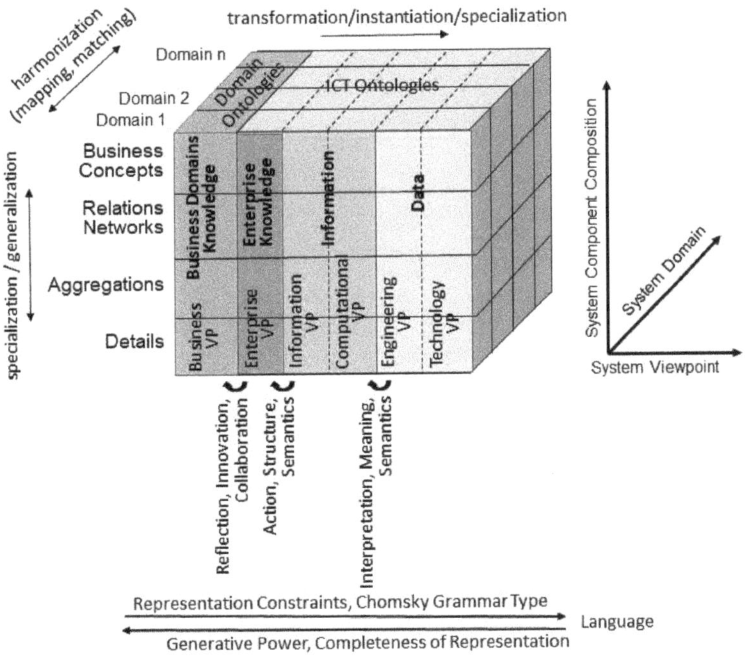


**Figure 5.** ISO 23903 mandatory framework for representing ecosystems [5].

The ecosystem shall behave ethically, e.g., by following the Seven Principles of Public Life developed by the Committee on Standards in Public Life in Great Britain: Selflessness, Integrity, Objectivity, Accountability, Openness, Honesty and Leadership. Another Code of Conduct has been established by MCI WorldCom, Ashburn, Virginia, USA. Its guiding principles are as follows: Build Trust and Credibility, Respect for the Individual, Create a Culture of Open and Honest Communication, Set Tone on the Top, Uphold the Law, Avoid Conflicts of Interest, Set Metrics and Report Results Accurately, Promote Substance over Form, Be Loyal, and Do the Right Thing. Both ethical codes have been considered in [29]. UNESCO has established a framework for ethical AI. As a global organization covering both developed and low- and middle-income countries (LMICs), each with their economic, social and environmental challenges, the code is quite generic, covering underlying values to follow, principles to be met, as well as necessary policies. The defined values are as follows: respect, protection and promotion of human rights and fundamental freedoms and human dignity; environment and ecosystem flourishing; ensuring diversity and inclusiveness; living in peaceful, just and interconnected societies. The principles are comparable with those in other codes of conduct. An aspect frequently not explicitly declared are the necessary policies, such as ethical impact assessment, ethical governance and stewardship, data policy, development and international cooperation, environment and ecosystems, gender, culture, education and research, communication and information, economy and labor, and health and social well-being [30]. The framework was adopted on 21 November 2021 at the General Conference of the United Nations Educational, Scientific and Cultural Organization (UNESCO) in Paris.

The underlying ICT technologies shall meet the Principles for Responsible Algorithmic Systems [31] defined by the Association for Computing Machinery's global Technology Policy Council (TPC). The stated instrumental principles are as follows:

- Legitimacy and Competency;
- Minimization of Harm;
- Security and Privacy;

- Transparency;
- Interpretability and Explainability;
- Maintainability;
- Contestability and Auditability;
- Accountability and Responsibility;
- Limitation of Environmental Impacts.

A similar set of ethical AI principles has been published by Adeola Adegunwa [32]. Besides the aforementioned principles, Adegunwa added the following ones:

- Respect for Human Autonomy;
- Fairness;
- Reliability and Safety;
- Inclusivity.

In order to put those ethical AI principles into practice, appropriate policies and procedures must be established, such as AI ethics policies, data governance procedures, algorithm accountability procedures, AI safety protocols and training and awareness programs. Thereby, a proactive approach to ethical challenges is inevitable. This implies ethical considerations in design and development, impact assessment, continuous monitoring and evaluation, inclusion of diverse perspectives as well as planning for future scenarios.

The pHealth 2021 keynote paper [1] discusses further ethical frameworks such as The Asimolar AI Principles of the Future of Life Institute [33]; the Congress Resolution Supporting the Development of Guidelines for the Ethical Development of Artificial Intelligence [34]; the BS 8611:2016 Robots and Robotic Devices Guide to the Ethical Design and Application of Robots and Robotic Systems [35]; and the OECD Principles for AI Research and Development presented at the Conference Toward AI Network Society, April 2015, in Japan [36]. A specific standard addressing the ethical challenges in designing ICT systems has been established by IEEE as IEEE 7000 [37]. This standard sets the framework for a series of IEEE standards [38], dealing with related issues such as security (IEEE 2933 [39]), privacy (IEEE 7012 [40]), and the representation of ethically driven robotics and automation systems (IEEE 7007 (IEEE 7007-2021 standard is freely available and accessible at https://ieeexplore.ieee.org/browse/standards/get-program/page/series?id=93 (18 December 2022)) [41]).

More information can be found in [13,42]. Table 5 summarizes the essence of those different ethical frameworks.

**Table 5.** Common A/IS principles proposed by different organizations (after [1]).

| **Guideline Originator** | **Transparency** | **Accountability** | **Controllability** | **Security** | **Value Orientation Ethics** | **Privacy** | **Safety** | **Risk** | **User Assistance** |
|---|---|---|---|---|---|---|---|---|---|
| OECD | x | x | x | x | x | x | x | | x |
| IEEE | x | x | x | | x | x | | x | x |
| Asilomar | x | x | x | x | x | x | x | x | |
| US Congress | x | x | x | x | | x | x | | x |
| World Economic Forum | | | | x | x | | | x | |

Google established the following six objectives for AI applications: be socially beneficial, avoid creating or reinforcing unfair bias, be built and tested for safety, be accountable to people, incorporate privacy design principles, and uphold high standards of scientific excellence [43].

A related and recently pushed approach addresses the so-called responsible AI. Examples can be found in [44–46]. Another approach is emotional AI, combining affective computing and artificial intelligence [47–49].

Further discussions of ethical, trustworthy, secure and safe ecosystems can be found in other papers from the authors of this paper, such as [4,42,50–54].

## 3. Representation of Intelligent and Ethical 5PM Ecosystems

As a starting point for designing and managing intelligent and ethical 5PM ecosystems, the domains including the related actors involved in the business system use case must be defined. The 5PM ecosystem policy domain (Figure 6a) can be refined to consider specific aspects such as the ethical policy, the legal policy, contextual policies, but also the service user's individual policy and the service provider's process-specific policy, as shown in Figure 6b.

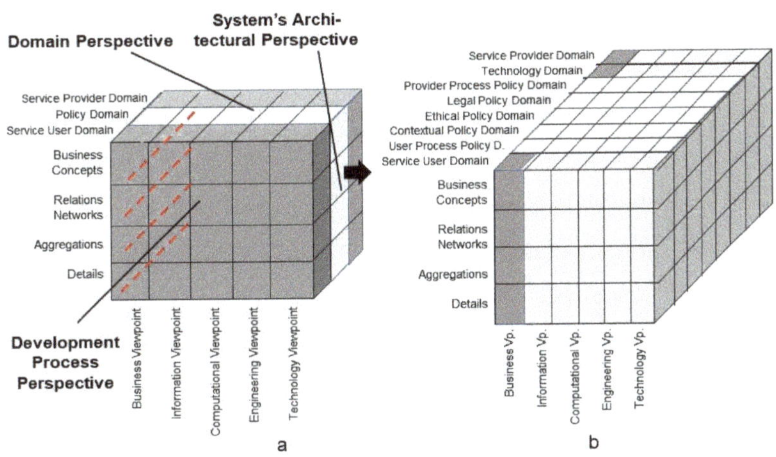


**Figure 6.** Refinement of the ISO 23903 Policy Domain.

The concepts behind the domain-specific architectural components of the business system must be represented using domain-specific languages, ontologies and methodologies. Many years ago, the first author defined a policy ontology, standardized as ISO 22600:2014 Health informatics—Privilege management and access control [55]. Figure 7 presents the ISO 22600 policy ontology.

In the next step, the sub-policy domains must be formally represented. This requires ontologies to represent the functionality or behavior of the ecosystem from the business process [56,57], the legal [58], the ethical [39] as well as the security and privacy [59,60] perspectives. Having the scope of the paper at hand in mind, in the following passages, we focus on ethical concepts including security and privacy issues.

An ontology example for legal reasoning and enforcement of security rules is PrOnto, presented in [61]. This ontology has the base components data and documents, actors and roles, processing and workflows, legal rules and deontic formula, as well as purposes and legal basis. Data categories are personal data (including pseudonymized data) and non-personal data (including anonymized data or legal person data). For more details, refer to [61]. To formally represent security requirements of ecosystems, Souag et al. defined three main dimensions and related details [60]:

- An organization with agents, assets and locations;
- Risk with severity, threat incl. threat agent, attack method and tool, vulnerability and impact;

- Treatment with security goals, requirements, criterion and control.

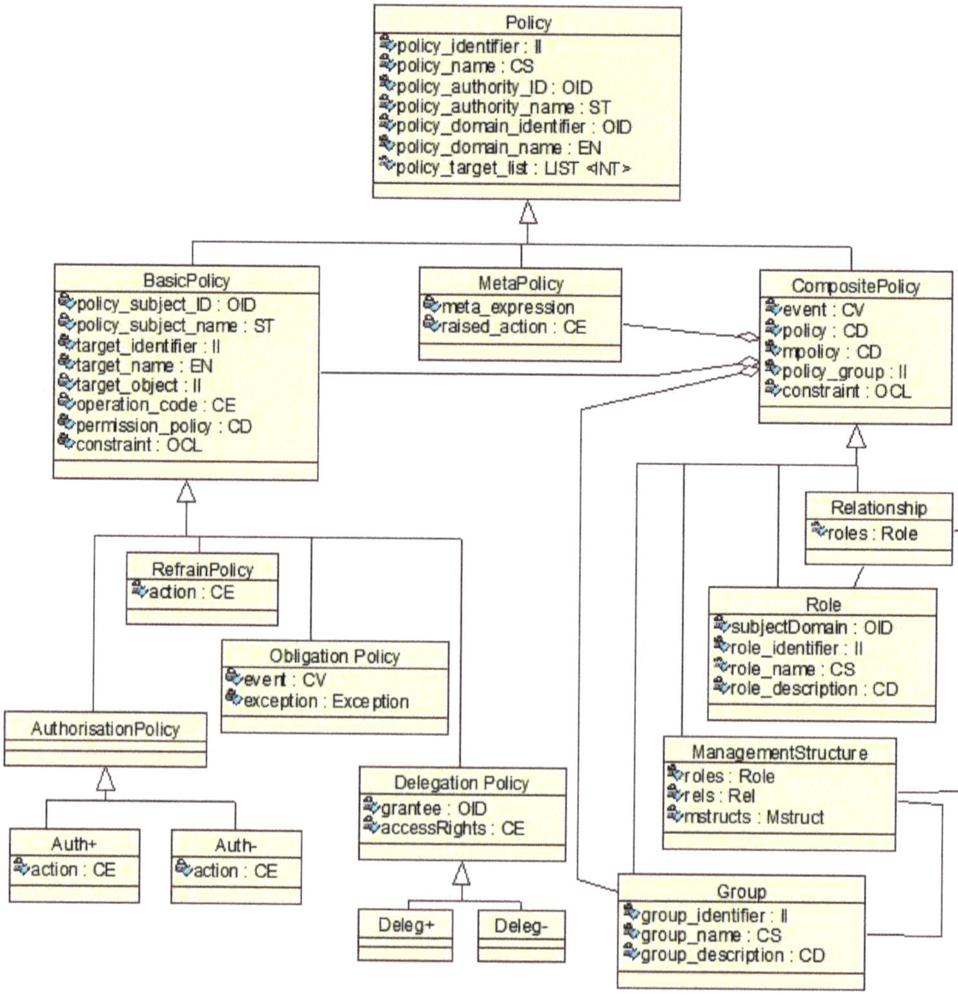


**Figure 7.** Policy ontology acc. to ISO 22600 [52].

The integration of ethical and trust aspects of autonomous and intelligent 5P medicine ecosystems has been developed at IEEE with a first global ontological standard for ethically driven robotics and automation systems (ERAS) [41] and is discussed in some detail in [62]. One foundational top-level model and four middle core subdomain models comprise the ERAS ontology. Each model defines respective semantic commitments using Common Logic Interface Format (CLIF) axioms [63]. The top-level ontology (TLO) was composed with concepts similar to other top-level ontologies such as SUMO [64], UFO [65] and BFO [66] to facilitate feasible alignment and harmonization. The ISO/IEC 21383:2020 Basic Formal Ontology (BFO) [66] conceptual taxonomy is shown in Figure 8, and the IEEE 7007:2021 ERAS TLO concepts and relationships are shown in Figure 9.

IEEE 7007:2021 specifies models and logical representations for the sub-domains Norms and Ethical Principles (NEP), Data Protection and Privacy (DPP), Transparency and Accountability (TA) and Ethical Violation Management (EVM). NEP conceptualizes principles involved in agent ethical behavior such as norms, plans and actions. DPP formalizes concepts relating to privacy and protection of agent data. TA details behaviors involved with an explanation of the agent plans and actions. EVM formalizes the concepts involved with situations where agents fail to conform with prescribed norms associated with agent plans. Figure 10 presents the IEEE 7007 ERAS norms and ethical principles ontology as a UML diagram, while Figure 11 addresses data privacy and protection.

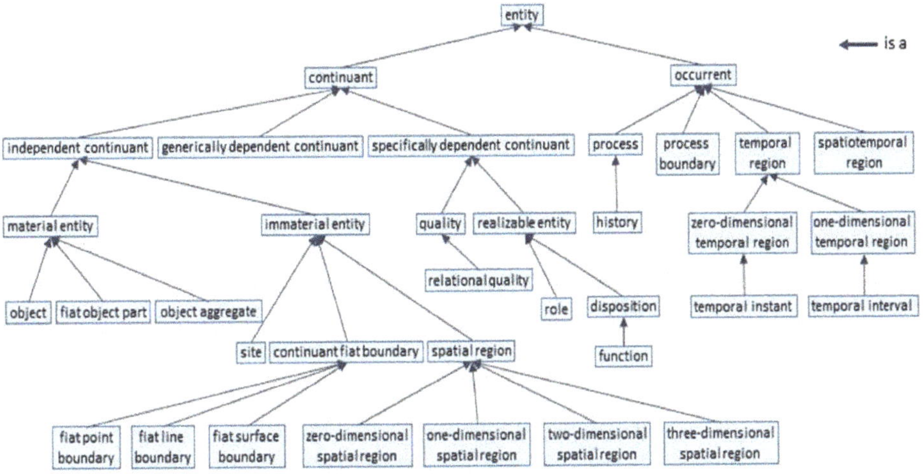


**Figure 8.** BFO is a hierarchy (after ISO/IEC 21838-2 [66]).

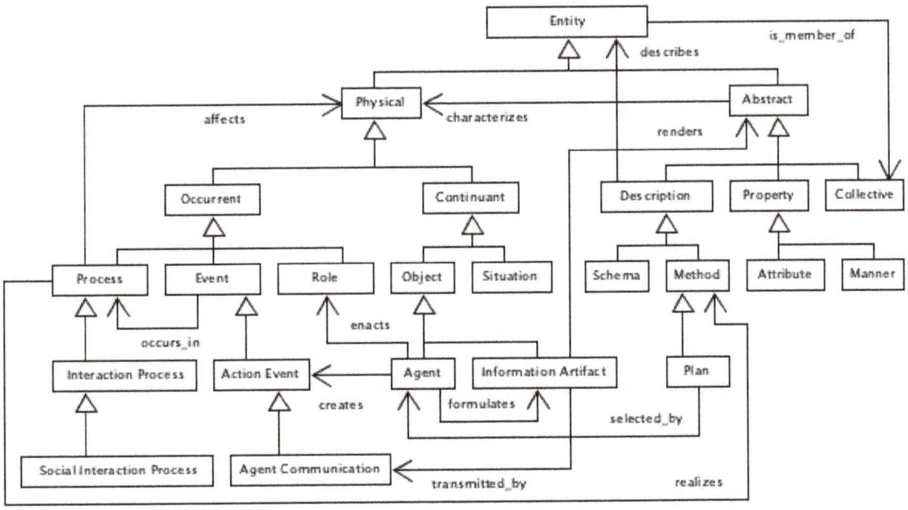


**Figure 9.** ERAS partial top-level concepts UML diagram.

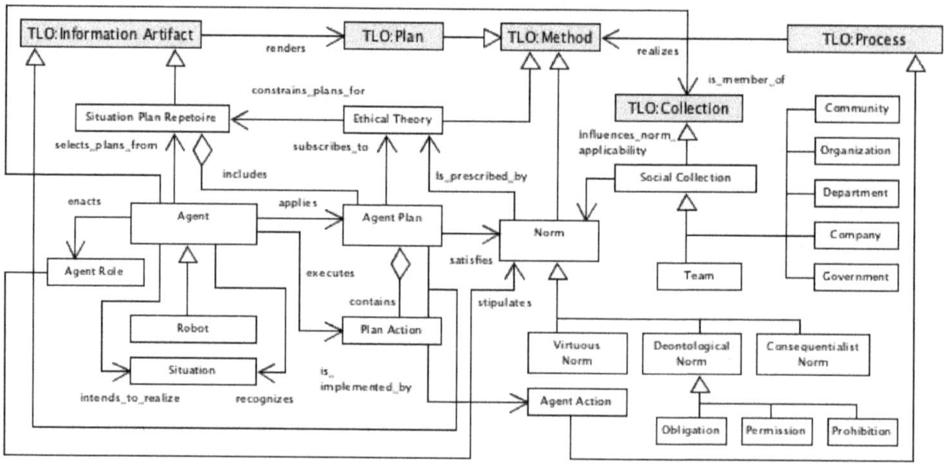


**Figure 10.** ERAS partial norms and ethical principles.

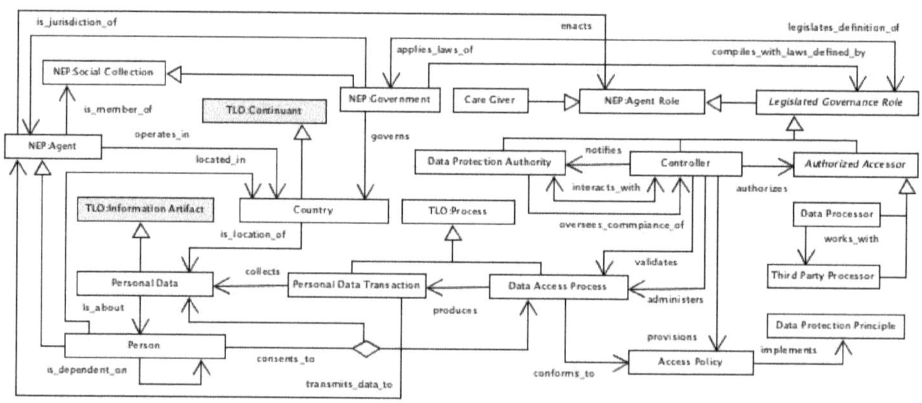


**Figure 11.** ERAS partial data privacy and protection UML diagram.

As mentioned before, the establishment, management and enforcement of an appropriate governance is inevitable to guarantee appropriate intentions and practices for developing and deploying advanced ecosystems regarding security, safety and privacy as well as ethical aspects. Those governance schemes must be properly and formally represented. While the security and privacy aspects have been addressed by the policy ontology, the ontology for managing ethical violations to realize responsible AI and its ontology is shown in Figure 12.

More information and complete UML diagrams for the ERAS ontology are available for free from the IEEE GET program.

There are also approaches to modelling such a system not from an information model perspective using UML, but representing the system with mathematical and statistical expressions. An example that deals with modeling morality using prospective logic can be found in [67].

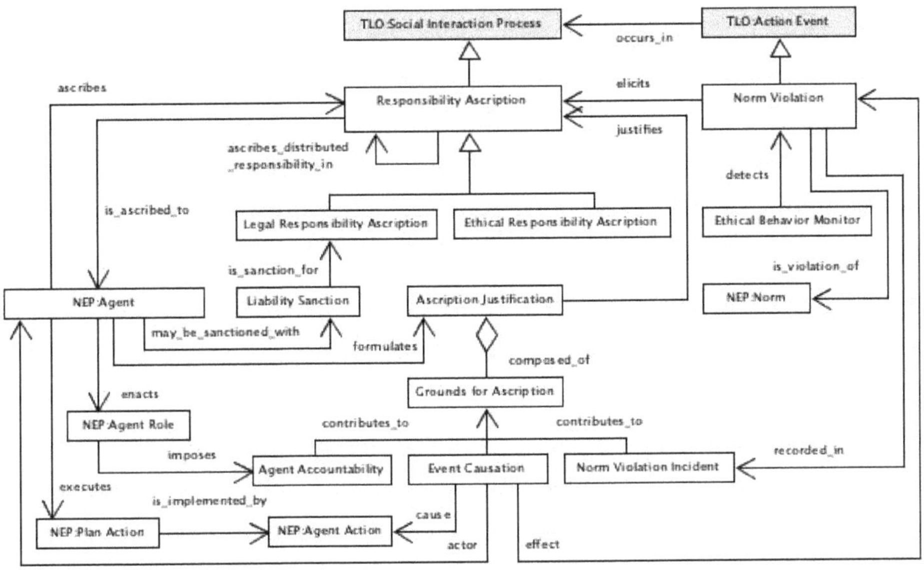


**Figure 12.** Ethical violation management UML diagram.

## 4. Conclusions

This paper addressed the challenges in designing and managing knowledge-based, policy-driven, but also ethical 5PM ecosystems. In that context, we had to formally represent the knowledge spaces of all contributing domains using approved ontologies, languages and methodologies. For clinical domains, there are several specialized sub-domain (disciplinary) ontologies. When such ontologies are missing, we can derive related ontologies from the ISO/IEC 21838 Top-level ontologies standard [66]. Referring to international standards, we exemplified the concepts for managing the behavior of health ecosystem through related policies in an ethical way.

This paper presents a foundational, sophisticated and therefore future-proof approach to advanced ecosystems. Meanwhile, the provided theoretical considerations have been widely deployed in practical projects and international standards for designing and implementing interoperable and integrable transformed health ecosystems with the essential involvement of the authors. The first author was, e.g., strongly involved in the specification of the personal privacy consent defined in IEEE 7012 [40] or the HL7 Privacy and Security Logical Data Model, Release 1, June 2021 [68]. Both standards are based on ISO 23903:2021 [26], that way guaranteeing a correct and consistent model of the ecosystem, its domains and the development process. More details about those solutions and related standards will be presented in another paper published in the MDPI JPM pHealth 2022 Special Issue [69].

Innovations in science and technology can improve the delivery of health and social services, but they can also pose risks to global health, e.g., by strengthening the digital divide between rich and low- and middle-income countries. Therefore, they are always bound to new social, moral and ethical challenges [70]. Hereby, objectives, basic principles, limitations, etc., must be carefully considered and defined in their economic, social, political and environmental contexts. A deeper discussion is provided in [1].

**Author Contributions:** B.B. drafted this paper. All authors have reviewed and edited the article. P.R. provided meaningful amendments on policies, security and privacy; E.P. and M.A.H. developed the ERAS ontology. All authors have read and agreed to the published version of the manuscript.

**Funding:** This research received no external funding.

**Institutional Review Board Statement:** Not applicable.

**Informed Consent Statement:** Not applicable.

**Data Availability Statement:** The original contributions presented in the study are included in the article. Further inquiries can be directed to the corresponding author.

**Acknowledgments:** The authors are indebted to their colleagues from IEEE, HL7, ISO TC 215 and CEN TC 251 for their kind and constructive support and cooperation.

**Conflicts of Interest:** The authors declare no conflict of interest.

## References

1. Blobel, B.; Ruotsalainen, P.; Brochhausen, M. Autonomous systems and artificial intelligence—Hype or prerequisite for P5 medicine? *Stud. Health Technol. Inf.* **2021**, *285*, 3–14.
2. Zarif, A. The ethical challenges facing the widespread adoption of digital healthcare technology. *Health Technol.* **2022**, *12*, 175–179. [CrossRef]
3. Byju's. Structure, Functions, Units and Types of Ecosystem. Available online: https://byjus.com/biology (accessed on 18 June 2023).
4. Blobel, B.; Ruotsalainen, P. Healthcare Transformation Towards Personalized Medicine—Chances and Challenges. *Stud. Health Technol. Inf.* **2019**, *261*, 3–21.
5. Blobel, B.; Ruotsalainen, P.; Giacomini, M. Standards and Principles to Enable Interoperability and Integration of 5P Medicine Ecosystems. *Stud. Health Technol. Inf.* **2022**, *299*, 3–19.
6. Blobel, B.; Ruotsalainen, P.; Lopez, D.M.; Oemig, F. Requirements and Solutions for Personalized Health Systems. *Stud. Health Technol. Inf.* **2017**, *237*, 3–21.
7. Blobel, B.; Ruotsalainen, P.; Oemig, F. Why Interoperability at Data Level Is Not Sufficient for Enabling pHealth? *Stud. Health Technol. Inform.* **2020**, *273*, 3–19. [PubMed]
8. Forrester Dictionary. Available online: https://www.forrester.com/staticassets/glossary (accessed on 18 June 2023).
9. Barrett, J. Digital Business or Automation—Is There a Difference? *Gartner Blog*, 30 July 2015. Available online: https://blogs.gartner.com/jane-barrett/2015/07/30/digitization-automation-difference/ (accessed on 18 June 2023).
10. Kamareddine, F.; Laan, T.; Nederpelt, R. *A Modern Perspective on Type Theory*; Kluwer Academic Publishers: New York, NY, USA, 2004.
11. Blobel, B. Architectural approach to eHealth for enabling paradigm changes in health. *Methods Inf. Med.* **2010**, *49*, 123–134. [CrossRef]
12. Blobel, B.; Oemig, F.; Ruotsalainen, P.; Lopez, D.M. Transformation of Health and Social Care Systems—An Interdisciplinary Approach toward a Foundational Architecture. *Front. Med.* **2022**, *9*, 802487. [CrossRef]
13. Blobel, B. Challenges and Solutions for Designing and Managing pHealth Ecosystems. *Front. Med.* **2019**, *6*, 83. [CrossRef]
14. Alter, S. *Information Systems—A Management Perspective*; Addison-Wesley: Boston, MA, USA, 1992.
15. Available online: https://www.merriam-webster.com/dictionary/knowledge#:~:text=Definitionofknowledge (accessed on 18 June 2023).
16. Davenport, T.H.; De Long, D.W.; Beers, M.C. Successful Knowledge Management Projects. In *Sloan Management Review*; ABI/INFORM Global: San Marcos, CA, USA, 1998; Volume 39, pp. 43–57.
17. Aamodt, A.; Nygard, M. Different roles and mutual dependencies of data, information and knowledge. *Data Knowl. Eng.* **1995**, *16*, 191–222. [CrossRef]
18. Krogstie, J. Business Information Systems Utilizing the Future Internet. In *Perspectives in Business Informatics Research: 10th International Conference, BIR 2011, Riga, Latvia, 6–8 October 2011; Proceedings 10*; Springer: Berlin/Heidelberg, Germany, 2011; Volume 90, pp. 1–18.
19. Doerner, H. Knowledge Representation. In *Ideas–Aspects–Formalisms*; Grabowski, J., Jantke, K.P., Thiele, H., Eds.; Foundations of Artificial Intelligence; Akademie: Berlin, Germany, 1989.
20. Nonaka, I.; Takeuchi, H. *The Knowledge Creating Company*; Oxford University Press: Oxford, UK, 1995.
21. Chomsky, N. Chomsky Hierarchy. Available online: https://en.wikipedia.org/wiki/Chomsky_hierarchy (accessed on 18 June 2023).
22. Blobel, B. Knowledge Representation and Management Enabling Intelligent Interoperability—Principles and Standards. *Stud Health Technol. Inf.* **2013**, *186*, 3–21.
23. Oemig, F.; Blobel, B. Natural Language Processing Supporting Interoperability in Healthcare. In *Text Mining—From Ontology Learning to Automated Text Processing Applications*; Biemann, C., Mehler, A., Eds.; Series Theory and Applications of Natural Language Processing; Springer GmbH: Berlin/Heidelberg, Germany, 2014; pp. 137–156.
24. Rebstock, M.; Fengel, J.; Paulheim, H. *Ontologies-Based Business Integration*; Springer: Berlin/Heidelberg, Germany, 2008.
25. *ISO/IEC 10746*; Information Technology—Reference Model—Open Distributed Processing. International Organization for Standardization (ISO): Geneva, Switzerland, 1996.

26. *ISO 23903:2021*; Health Informatics—Interoperability Reference Architecture. International Organization for Standardization (ISO): Geneva, Switzerland, 2021.
27. Denecke, K.; Baudoin, C.R. A Review of Artificial Intelligence and Robotics in Transformed Health Ecosystems. *Front. Med.* **2022**, *9*, 795957. [CrossRef]
28. Blobel, B.; Rubin, K. Defining a Reference Architecture for Transformed Health Ecosystems. *Stud. Health Technol. Inf.* **2021**, *281*, 143–147.
29. Gilman, S.C. *Ethics Codes and Codes of Conduct as Tools for Promoting an Ethical and Professional Public Service: Comparative Successes and Lessons*; World Bank: Washington, DC, USA, 2005.
30. UNECSO. *UNESCO Ethics of Artificial Intelligence*; UNESCO: Paris, France, 2022.
31. Baker, P. Status of Ethical Standards in Emerging Tech. *InformationWeek*, 24 January 2023. Available online: https://www.informationweek.com/big-data/status-of-ethical-standards-in-emerging-tech (accessed on 18 June 2023).
32. Adegunwa, A. The AI Principles to Put in Practice. *AI Time Journal*, 1 June 2023. Available online: https://www.aitimejournal.com/the-ai-principles-to-put-in-practice/44624/ (accessed on 18 June 2023).
33. Future of Life Institute. Asilomar AI Principles. Available online: https://futureoflife.org/ai-principles/ (accessed on 18 June 2023).
34. Available online: https://lawrence.house.gov/media-center/press-releases/brenda-lawrence-and-ro-khanna-introduce-resolution-calling-ethical (accessed on 18 June 2023).
35. *BS 8611:2016*; Robots and Robotic Devices. Guide to the Ethical Design and Application of Robots and Robotic Systems. British Standards Institute (BSI): London, UK, 2016.
36. Japan Science and Technology Agency; National Institute of Advanced Industrial Science and Technology; Council on Competitiveness-Nippon. 25 July 2017. Available online: https://www.soumu.go.jp/main_content/000507517.pdf (accessed on 18 June 2023).
37. *IEEE 7000:2021*; IEEE Standard Model Process for Addressing Ethical Concerns during System Design. IEEE: Piscataway, NJ, USA, 2021.
38. The IEEE Global Initiative on Ethics of Autonomous and Intelligent Systems-faq-11. 22. 2020.
39. IEEE 2933 Standard for Clinical Internet of Things (IoT) Data and Device Interoperability with TIPPSS—Trust, Identity, Privacy, Protection, Safety, Security (Running Project). Available online: https://standards.ieee.org/ieee/2933/7592/ (accessed on 18 June 2023).
40. IEEE 7012 Standard for Machine Readable Personal Privacy Terms (Running pProject). Available online: https://standards.ieee.org/ieee/7012/7192/ (accessed on 18 June 2023).
41. *IEEE 7007:2021*; IEEE Ontological Standard for Ethically Driven Robotics and Automation Systems. IEEE: Piscataway, NJ, USA, 2021.
42. Blobel, B.; Ruotsalainen, P.; Brochhausen, M.; Oemig, F.; Uribe, G.A. Autonomous Systems and Artificial Intelligence in Healthcare Transformation to 5P Medicine—Ethical Challenges. *Stud. Health Technol. Inf.* **2020**, *270*, 1089–1093.
43. Google. Artificial Intelligence at Google: Our Principles. Available online: https://ai.google/principles/ (accessed on 18 June 2023).
44. Dille, G. White House Announces New Responsible AI Efforts. *MeriTalk*, 23 May 2023. Available online: https://www.meritalk.com/articles/white-house-announces-new-responsible-ai-efforts/ (accessed on 18 June 2023).
45. Wicklund, E. Coalition Unveils Guidelines for Responsible AI Use in Healthcare. *HealthLeaders*, 6 April 2023. Available online: https://www.healthleadersmedia.com (accessed on 18 June 2023).
46. du Vignaux, M.M. Responsible and Explainable AI along the ML Pipeline with Dataiku. *Dataiku Blog*, 7 June 2021. Available online: https://blog.dataiku.com (accessed on 18 June 2023).
47. Holzer, N. *Emotion AI: Multimodale Emotionsanalyse*; Fraunhofer IIS: Erlangen, Germany, 2023; Available online: https://www.iis.fraunhofer.de (accessed on 18 June 2023).
48. Kambur, E. Emotional Intelligence or Artificial Intelligence: Emotional Artificial Intelligence. In *Florya Chronicles of Political Economy*; Istanbul Aydin University: İstanbul, Türkiye, 2021; pp. 147–168.
49. Cole, B. Emotional intelligence (EI). *TechTarget*, January 2023. Available online: https://www.techtarget.com (accessed on 18 June 2023).
50. Ruotsalainen, P.; Blobel, B. Digital pHealth—Problems and Solutions for Ethics, Trust and Privacy. *Stud. Health Technol. Inf.* **2019**, *261*, 31–46.
51. Ruotsalainen, P.; Blobel, B. Health Information Systems in the Digital Health Ecosystem—Problems and Solutions for Ethics, Trust and Privacy. *Int. J. Environ. Res. Public Health* **2020**, *17*, 3006. [CrossRef]
52. Ruotsalainen, P.; Blobel, B. Transformed Health Ecosystems—Challenges for Security, Privacy, and Trust. *Front. Med.* **2022**, *9*, 827253. [CrossRef]
53. Ruotsalainen, P.S.; Blobel, B.; Seppälä, A.; Nykänen, P. Trust Information-Based Privacy Architecture for Ubiquitous Health. *JMIR Mhealth Uhealth* **2013**, *1*, e23. Available online: http://mhealth.jmir.org/2013/2/e23/ (accessed on 18 June 2023). [CrossRef] [PubMed]
54. Ruotsalainen, P.; Blobel, B. Privacy and Trust in pHealth—Past, Present and Future. *Stud. Health Technol. Inf.* **2022**, *299*, 104–117.

55. *ISO 22600:2014*; Health Informatics—Privilege Management and Access Control. International Organization for Standardization (ISO): Geneva, Switzerland, 2014.
56. Cabral, L.; Norton, B.; Domingue, J. The business process modelling ontology. In Proceedings of the 4th International Workshop on Semantic Business Process Management (SBPM 2009), Workshop at ESWC 2009, Crete, Greece, 1 June 2009.
57. Adamo, G.; Borgo, S.; Di Francescomarino, C.; Ghidini, C.; Guarino, N.; Sanfilippo, E.M. ODD-BP—An Ontology- and Data-Driven Business Process. In Proceedings of the Conference "Lernen, Wissen, Daten, Analysen" (LWDA 2019), Berlin, Germany, 30 September–2 October 2019; Volume 2454, p. 43.
58. van Engers, T.; Boer, A.; Breuker, J.; Valente, A.; Winkels, R. Ontologies in the Legal Domain. In *Digital Government*; Springer: Berlin/Heidelberg, Germany, 2008; pp. 233–261.
59. Tsoumas, B.; Gritzalis, D. Towards an Ontology-based Security Management. In Proceedings of the 20th International Conference on Advanced Information Networking and Applications—Volume 1 (AINA'06), Vienna, Austria, 18–20 April 2006.
60. Souag, A.; Salinesi, C.; Mazo, R.; Comyn-Wattiau, I. A Security Ontology for Security Requirements Elicitation. In *Engineering Secure Software and Systems—ESSoS 2015*; Lecture Notes in Computer, Science; Piessens, F., Caballero, J., Bielova, N., Eds.; Springer: Cham, Switzerland, 2015; p. 8978. [CrossRef]
61. Palmirani, M.; Martoni, M.; Rossi, A.; Bartolini, C.; Robaldo, L. PrOnto: Privacy Ontology for Legal Reasoning. In *Electronic Government and the Information Systems Perspective—EGOVIS 2018*; Lecture Notes in Computer Science; Kő, A., Francesconi, E., Eds.; Springer: Cham, Switzerland, 2018; p. 11032. [CrossRef]
62. Prestes, E.; Houghtaling, M.A.; Goncalves, P.S.J.; Fabiano, N.; Ulgen, O.; Fiorini, S.R.; Murahwi, Z.; Olszewska, J.I.; Haidegger, T. The First Global Ontological Standard for Ethically Driven Robotics and Automation Systems. *IEEE Robot. Autom. Mag.* **2021**, *28*, 120–124. [CrossRef]
63. *ISO/IEC 24707:2018*; Information Technology—Common Logic (cl)—A Framework for a Family of Logic-Based Languages. International Organization for Standardization (ISO): Geneva, Switzerland, 2018.
64. Niles, I.; Pease, A. Towards a standard upper ontology. In Proceedings of the FOIS '01: Proceedings of the International Conference on Formal Ontology in Information Systems, Ogunquit, ME, USA, 17–19 October 2001; ACM Press: Maharashtra, India, 2001; pp. 2–9.
65. Guizzardi, G.; Benevides, A.B.; Fonseca, C.M.; Porello, D.; Almeida, J.P.A.T.P.; Sales, T.P. UFO: Unified foundational ontology. *Appl. Ontol.* **2022**, *17*, 167–210. [CrossRef]
66. *ISO/IEC 21838:2021*; Information Technology–Top-Level Ontologies (TLO). International Organization for Standardization (ISO): Geneva, Switzerland, 2021.
67. Pereira, L.M.; Saptawijaya, A. Modelling Morality with Prospective Logic. In *Progress in Artificial Intelligence*; EPIA, 2007; Lecture Notes in Computer, Science; Neves, J., Santos, M.F., Machado, J.M., Eds.; Springer: Berlin/Heidelberg, Germany, 2007; Volume 4874, pp. 99–111. [CrossRef]
68. Health Level Seven International. HL7 Privacy and Security Logical Data Model, Release 1. *Ann Arbor*. Available online: https://file://C:/Users/MDPI/Downloads/V3%20Privacy%20and%20Security%20Logical%20Data%20Model.pdf (accessed on 18 June 2023).
69. Blobel, B.; Ruotsalainen, P.; Oemig, F.; Giacomini, M.; Sottile, P.A.; Endsleff, F. Standards and Principles for Designing and Managing Integrable and Interoperable 5P Medicine Ecosystems. *J. Pers. Med.* **2023**, *13*. *submitted*. Available online: https://www.mdpi.com/journal/jpm/special_issues/36WBUZ3TG0 (accessed on 18 June 2023).
70. Watters, A. 5 Ethical Issues in Technology to Watch for in 2021. *CompTIA*, 1 July 2021. Available online: https://connect.comptia.org/blog/ethical-issues-in-technology (accessed on 18 June 2023).

Journal of
*Personalized*
*Medicine*

MDPI

*Article*

# Assessing the Need for Semantic Data Integration for Surgical Biobanks—A Knowledge Representation Perspective

**Mathias Brochhausen [1,*], Justin M. Whorton [1], Cilia E. Zayas [1], Monica P. Kimbrell [2], Sarah J. Bost [3], Nitya Singh [4,5], Christoph Brochhausen [6], Kevin W. Sexton [1,7,8,9] and Bernd Blobel [10,11,12]**

1 Department of Biomedical Informatics, University of Arkansas for Medical Sciences, Little Rock, AR 72205, USA; jmwhorton@uams.edu (J.M.W.); czayas@uams.edu (C.E.Z.); kevin.sexton@uams.edu (K.W.S.)
2 Trauma Performance Improvement Coordinator, University of Arkansas for Medical Sciences, Little Rock, AR 72205, USA; mpkimbrell@uams.edu
3 Department of Health Outcomes and Biomedical Informatics, University of Florida, Gainesville, FL 32611, USA; sarah.bost@ufl.edu
4 Department of Animal Sciences, University of Florida, Gainesville, FL 32611, USA; nitya11@epi.ufl.edu
5 Emerging Pathogens Institute, University of Florida, Gainesville, FL 32611, USA
6 Central Biobank, Institute of Pathology, University and University Clinic of Regensburg, 93053 Regensburg, Germany; christoph.brochhausen@klinik.uni-regensburg.de
7 Department of Surgery, University of Arkansas for Medical Sciences, Little Rock, AR 72205, USA
8 Institute for Digital Health & Innovation, University of Arkansas for Medical Sciences, Little Rock, AR 72205, USA
9 BioVentures LLC, Little Rock, AR 72205, USA
10 Medical Faculty, University of Regensburg, 93053 Regensburg, Germany; bernd.blobel@klinik.uni-regensburg.de
11 eHealth Competence Center Bavaria, Deggendorf Institute of Technology, 94469 Deggendorf, Germany
12 First Medical Faculty, Charles University, 11636 Prague 1, Czech Republic
* Correspondence: mbrochhausen@uams.edu



**Citation:** Brochhausen, M.; Whorton, J.M.; Zayas, C.E.; Kimbrell, M.P.; Bost, S.J.; Singh, N.; Brochhausen, C.; Sexton, K.W.; Blobel, B. Assessing the Need for Semantic Data Integration for Surgical Biobanks—A Knowledge Representation Perspective. *J. Pers. Med.* **2022**, *12*, 757. https://doi.org/10.3390/jpm12050757

Academic Editor: Theodoros Papaioannou

Received: 22 March 2022
Accepted: 30 April 2022
Published: 7 May 2022



**Abstract:** To improve patient outcomes after trauma, the need to decrypt the post-traumatic immune response has been identified. One prerequisite to drive advancement in understanding that domain is the implementation of surgical biobanks. This paper focuses on the outcomes of patients with one of two diagnoses: post-traumatic arthritis and osteomyelitis. In creating surgical biobanks, currently, many obstacles must be overcome. Roadblocks exist around scoping of data that is to be collected, and the semantic integration of these data. In this paper, the generic component model and the Semantic Web technology stack are used to solve issues related to data integration. The results are twofold: (a) a scoping analysis of data and the ontologies required to harmonize and integrate it, and (b) resolution of common data integration issues in integrating data relevant to trauma surgery.

**Keywords:** surgical biobank; post-traumatic arthritis; osteomyelitis; semantic data integration; system theory; biomedical ontologies; knowledge representation

## 1. Introduction

Trauma is the leading cause of death and disability for patients less than 45 years old [1]. Recently, the need to decrypt the post-traumatic immune response to improve patient outcomes has been identified [2–5]. One strategy proposed to achieve this is large fluidics biobanks [6]. Along with other researchers [7], we advocate for more expansive surgical biobanks, including tissue. One of the core issues when building a trauma-oriented surgical biobank is integrating patient data from other healthcare providers. This is a generic data management problem regarding biobanking [8].

Implementation, maintenance, and use of a surgical biobank are mandatory, among other things, for a better understanding of the post-traumatic immune response, for instance, in patients with multiple injuries. We aim at improving secondary data analysis to assess factors contributing to complications. Since patients with numerous injuries are frequently transferred from lower acuity facilities to a more specialized or higher-level trauma center, the data management activities of a surgical biobank need to include collecting and harmonizing data from all trauma care providers of the specimen donors. Collecting data from lower acuity facilities to trauma centers is crucial to identify potentially specific pathophysiological or new prognostic factors.

In this paper, we aim to achieve two goals:

Propose system architecture considerations for a surgical biobank against the background of crucial data needs to address post-surgical arthritis and osteomyelitis.

Demonstrate how semantic analysis guided by the generic component model (GCM) informs harmonization of clinical and clinically relevant data regarding post-traumatic arthritis and osteomyelitis in a surgical biobank. Thereby, we highlight the importance of definition, representation, and integration of the underlying concept spaces (ontologies) of the different domains involved, from which the data can be derived, represented, and implemented, but also the current context [9].

In the first step of our analysis, we will assess the patterns of complex collaborations in trauma patient triage and care using a systems theory approach. This approach will assist us in determining the scope of data collection and data harmonization across multiple healthcare providers. This research can aid in the development of IT infrastructure to support the implementation, maintenance, and management of a surgical biobank. To provide actionable information, we will suggest current domain ontologies that are applicable to our use cases.

In the second step, we will illustrate how Semantic Web technologies can resolve common data collection challenges related to surgical trauma: (a) issues created by restrictions specified in local information models, (b) issues created by the need to integrate data from heterogeneous sources, and c) issues created in the process of data entry.

## 2. Data Needs of Surgical Biobanks

Our research focuses on musculoskeletal injuries, one of the most common injury patterns leading to disability after trauma. These injuries are almost exclusively repaired surgically, making this the ideal population for creating a surgical biobank. As part of the fracture repair process, we can easily collect samples of bone, skin, subcutaneous tissue, small veins, and muscle without impact on the patients' recovery. Additionally, joint replacement is a common procedure allowing for age-matched control sample collection of similar tissues. Interestingly, the main indication for joint replacement is arthritis, a known complication of orthopedic trauma, thus allowing us to collect samples across the spectrum of life and investigate the mechanisms of post-traumatic arthritis. This is not our only outcome of interest, however, as infection, such as osteomyelitis or soft tissue infection, is the most common early complication of fracture repair. Diagnosis of both post-traumatic arthritis or osteomyelitis occurs after initial treatment for a fracture, and the reasons for the occurrences are not completely understood. Due to this, treatment for these diagnoses frequently occurs at different trauma care facilities from the initial treatment. In this context, it is desirable to establish predictive and prognostic factors for future therapeutic strategies to avoid numerous repetitive surgical interventions or amputations in complicated trauma patients. For this purpose, surgical biobanks collecting relevant biomaterials and comprehensive clinical and laboratory data are needed. The complete monitoring of laboratory, clinical, and imaging data as well as the historical information of primary care, transportation times, and duration of treatments are relevant. To reach this goal, data from different sources should be brought together with the biospecimens to curate data-rich biobank specimens.

The lack of a unified coding schema and of structured data for information relevant to address the pathogenesis of individual cases creates additional difficulty for data harmonization in this domain. While there are emerging classification systems, no widely accepted standard exists. In all likelihood, any standards set quickly, would continue to change and evolve as our understanding of precision medicine in trauma increases. Thus, the problem of lack of comparable data for mid- and long-term studies would be proliferated for years to come. Since the existence of a well-developed understanding is a requirement for creating stable standards, it is obvious that we cannot use standards to collect, curate, and maintain the data we are collecting with the goal of developing our understanding of precision medicine in trauma. Challenges in harmonizing data are frequently found regarding treatment and procedure information, demographic information, problem lists, medication lists, and organizational structures of trauma centers [10–12] or healthcare providers involved in the initial treatment.

## 3. Integration Challenges Created by Restrictions of Local Information Models

A common practice is that each trauma patient is admitted to the nearest hospital that participates in the regional or state trauma program. However, complications such as infections and prolonged or failed bone or wound healing due to complicated trauma or to known, or even unrecognized, primary diseases, such as diabetes, hypertension, or arteriosclerosis, make the transfer to a more specialized or higher-level trauma center necessary [13]. In these centers, an interdisciplinary team will review previous laboratory as well as clinical tests. Recent and earlier imaging data will be compared, and commonly, a surgical revision is necessary. With respect to the management of specimens acquired during that healthcare process, one data integration problem frequently occurs: The entry number of a specimen is commonly used as the reference number. Over the course of treatment, especially with complications, a patient may have several entries, each receiving a new entry number. These samples are identified and documented in the so-called sample history as follow-up samples for the initial injury. Typically, the sample history assignment is performed using the patient identifier. Many systems enforce that there be only one patient identifier for each patient. If the patient has all samples taken at the same healthcare institution, this does not present a problem. However, if some of the samplings are performed at another healthcare provider, tracing disease progression via the patient identifier is no longer possible because the entry number cannot be matched with the patient identifier at the location of the surgical biobank.

## 4. Integration Challenges Created by the Need to Integrate Data from Heterogeneous Sources

The University of Arkansas for Medical Sciences (UAMS) Medical Center is the only adult Level 1 Trauma Center with verification by the American College of Surgeons in Arkansas and sees over 3000 trauma-related patients annually, with admission exceeding 2000 trauma-related admissions. The medical center is the only tertiary care center in the state and has 24 trauma and surgical intensive care unit beds. In collaboration with the surgical services, the surgical critical care teams manage critically ill patients yearly across trauma surgery, burn surgery, emergency general surgery, surgical oncology, pancreas-biliary surgery, bariatric surgery, neurosurgery, orthopedics, obstetrics and gynecology, vascular surgery, otolaryngology, urology, plastic surgery, and transplantation surgery. Being the only Level 1 trauma center in the state of Arkansas, UAMS is an excellent example of a trauma care facility, receiving 560 orthopedic trauma patients annually. Additionally, they are a referral center for orthopedic patients with complications, including post-traumatic arthritis and osteomyelitis. The UAMS Trauma Database strives to collect, maintain, and store clinical data on patients in the acute care phase as well as readmission of their population within 30 days of discharge. For 2021, we had 18 readmissions within 30 days in our ortho population. This excludes patients with acute care at another hospital, who are subsequently referred for post-acute complications. Acute-phase trauma information on this selected population of Arkansas trauma patients with complications is limited to what is in the transferring records or the patient's history and physical notes. These patients are not included in the UAMS Trauma Database, thus restricting orthopedic studies to those with initial acute trauma care at UAMS.

The Arkansas Trauma Registry (ATR) might be a potential source for tying all Arkansas trauma cases together. Challenges with using data from the ATR include variability in the collection of National Trauma Data Bank (NTDB) data elements and access to the data. In Arkansas, only Level 1 and Level 2 trauma center personnel receive annual training as part of the Trauma Quality Improvement Program (TQIP) [14]. Level 3 and Level 4 programs are encouraged to use the NTDB data dictionary for applicable NTDB data elements, but training is limited to a review of data dictionary changes at the Annual ATR Conference.

Even with TQIP training, variability of data collection is suspected to be present among Level 1 and Level 2 facilities due to different interpretation of definitions. To mitigate variability, the National Trauma Data Bank (NTDB) Data Dictionary [15] work group vets the dataset annually. This process includes refinement of data element terminology, plus revision and/or additions to definitions. Additionally, TQIP provides annual education update through their annual conference, and via web training modules/quizzes. This is why the educational opportunities offered by TQIP annually are relevant to data quality.

Even with this, there remains some variation in data elements such as "unplanned OR", which has been refined from "unplanned return to the OR" to "unplanned visit to the OR" (OR stands for operation room). Another refinement includes adding exclusions to the definition. The current definition is as follows:

"Patients with an unplanned operative procedure OR patients returned to the operating room after initial operative management of a related previous procedure" [15].

This definition leaves much open to interpretation. Some users interpret this as a surgery that is unexpected or due to some untoward event and not potentially expected events such as visits to the OR due to a failed limb salvage and similar clinical situations. This is an example of a clinical situation where the possibility that the patient may require surgery is inherited. There is anecdotal evidence that there is a tendency to subsume limb salvage failure and similar examples under the unplanned OR category. This highlights the potential for different interpretations and the lack of shared understanding of the data elements in the NTDS Data Dictionary.

## 5. Integration Challenges Created during Data Entry

Besides the accurate resolution of identifiers and the ability to semantically integrate data, information about the organizational structure of trauma care providers give important insight into potential effects on patient outcomes. Curating data about organizational structures in trauma care, in particular with controlled vocabularies and ontologies, is a relatively new area of research and development. The NIH-funded CAFÉ (Comparative Assessment Framework for Environments of Trauma Care (R01GM111324)) provides a controlled vocabulary to describe and assess organizational structures of trauma care providers [11]. In addition, the project created a web-based architecture to collect, manage, and store semantically rich information about trauma care organizations via a user-friendly online questionnaire with the Ontology of Organizational Structures of Trauma centers and Trauma systems (OOSTT) automatically representing the answers in a computer-interpretable language [10,12].

For validation purposes, the CAFÉ project invited stakeholders to enter data about trauma centers and trauma systems. In the first round of this activity, we collected data on two Level 1 trauma centers and one Level 2 trauma center. Table 1 shows the extracted results for two CAFÉ questions.

The answers from trauma centers A and C looked unlikely based on the CAFÉ team's experience. Our interpretation of the situation is that the persons who entered the data for those two questions for those two centers were not certain of the difference between these two categories or they did not have access to data that provided a differentiation between board-eligible and board-certified emergency physicians. While OOSTT has a representation of both "board-certified emergency physician role" and "board-eligible emergency physician role", only the first is formally fully defined, so that at the current state of semantic representation, a disambiguation was not possible. One factor contributing to the lack of clarity is that all board-certified emergency physicians were at some point (and remain to be) board-eligible. However, the intention behind this question is to find out how many emergency physicians are board-eligible, but have not yet been board-certified, as opposed to those who are already board-certified.

**Table 1.** Example answers to CAFÉ questionnaire.

| CAFÉ Question | Trauma Center A (Level 2) | Trauma Center B (Level 1) | Trauma Center C (Level 1) |
|---|---|---|---|
| Number of emergency physicians who are board-certified in emergency medicine. | 21 | 29 | 23 |
| Number of emergency physicians who are board-eligible in emergency medicine | 21 | 2 | 23 |

## 6. Methods

### *6.1. System Architecture Methodology: The Generic Component Model*

The GCM is a top-level architectural model for any multi-domain system, formally representing the system's components, their functions, and interrelations structurally and behaviorally by a cube with three dimensions: (a) specific aspects/perspective (domains) of/on the system forming domain-specific sub-systems; (b) generic granularity levels of the system's elements enabling the composition/decomposition of the system; (c) the viewpoints within the system's development process (Figure 1). It is described and specified in ISO 23903 Interoperability and integration reference architecture—Model and framework [16,17]. For each business case, the subsystem components and their functions and interrelations are instantiated by naming and representing them using the specific terminologies and ontologies of the domains involved in that business case. For this reason, the GCM specifies a business view in addition to the five views defined by the ISO 10746 Open distributed processing—Reference model (RM-ODP) as starting point for a system development process [17]. The views prescribed by the RM-ODP are enterprise view (purpose, scope, and policies of the system), information view (information processing, semantics of information), computational view (functionality of the system, functional decomposition), engineering view (implementation, distribution of processing performed by the system), and technology view (choice of technology for the system), all represented using information and communication technology (ICT) ontologies [17,18]. Furthermore, ISO 23903 [16] introduces generic granularity levels for correctly representing and interrelating compositions/decompositions of elements, that way enabling integration of, and interoperability between, elements of different complexity. As only elements at the same granularity level can be interrelated, elements at different granularity level first have to be harmonized by composing or decomposing them. By adding the business view and granularity levels, the GCM enables the correct representation and management of multi-domain real-world systems, including supporting ICT solutions.

Applying the methods to the use case at hand first requires considering the role of the information models and the database schemata according to the views of the GCM. Both belong to the information view since their primary focus is to guide information processing within the system. Hence, they do not provide real-world knowledge, such as the fact that one person can have more than one patient ID and that sampling of tumor progression is frequently performed by different healthcare providers. More generally, due to the limitations of IT grammars, the correctness of representations of, and relations between, elements cannot be justified within this viewpoint. Notably, those aspects lie outside each electronic health record (EHR) system and are ill-fitted to be represented within the information view. However, from our database example, not accounting for those aspects of the business view may lead to errors in the system.

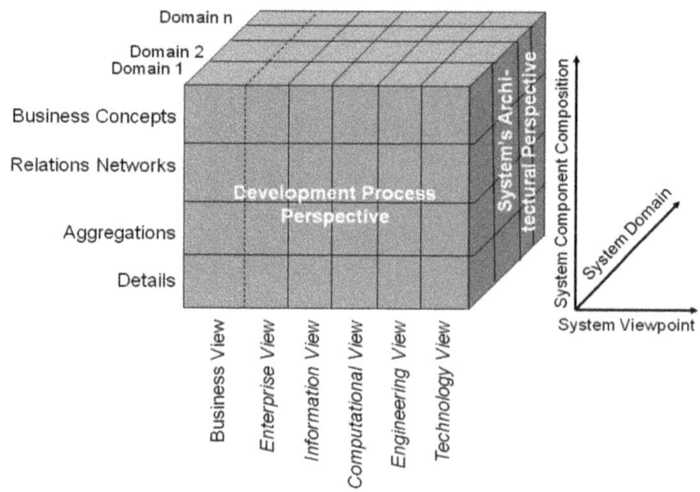


**Figure 1.** The generic component model. From: [18].

### 6.2. Semantic Integration Methods

Our challenge is to provide a semantically rich representation of clinical and clinically relevant data for a surgical biobank. This approach has been shown to be useful for integrating heterogeneous clinical data in an international cancer imaging repository, The Cancer Imaging Archive [19–21]. To create a semantically rich representation for biomedical data, we follow the recommendations outlined by Brochhausen et al. [22] The basic strategy is to use the Semantic Web stack [23] along with realism-based ontology development [24] as the general methodology to inform knowledge representation. Their approach is based on experiences with multiple implementations in biomedical informatics, which have influenced the evolution of their methodology from the beginning [25–28].

In our project, we are transforming clinical and clinically relevant data into the resource description framework (RDF) language before we load it into our RDF-based data management system of the biobank. RDF [29] is a Semantic Web standard that allows the representation of information in a machine-interpretable way. For each entity, RDF provides a unique identifier. RDF data can be annotated and used along with domain descriptions provided in the Web Ontology Language (OWL) [30]. We are using RDF representations and OWL ontologies following the methodology described by Smith and Ceusters [24] and the best-practice principles of the OBO Foundry [31,32].

In addition, we will use the GCM (Section 6.1) to assist knowledge representation. The GCM proves to be a fitting tool to help with selecting optimal knowledge representation for incoming data and guide the process of filling gaps in existing ontologies, based on the medical information models used to curate the data at the initial healthcare providers. While IT-oriented information models fulfil a crucial role in planning, defining, and describing the operational behavior of an IT system, such as an EHR system or a biobank information system, there is a lack of semantic capabilities of these models [21]. Due to the high level of abstraction and expressivity of information models, so rarely being complete and decidable, the resulting representation, especially regarding relationships, is frequently focused on data in that system alone and not on what the data represents, in our case the medical world, e.g., the patients, encounters, and prescriptions described in an EHR or the specimens, donors, and storage properties in a biobank, thereby including context and common-sense knowledge. Building an ontology or selecting from existing ontologies can lead to a mismatch between the system data model and the more holistic ontologies. In our approach, we use the GCM to overcome the implementation gap between healthcare-provider-specific information models and preexisting domain ontologies needed for the semantically rich representation of surgical biobank data.

In this paper, we follow the approach of Uribe et al. [33] used to represent a GCM-based generic model of a Type 2 diabetes mellitus care system. In parallel to their approach, we analyze the following three domains of the system: medical domain, policy domain, and resource domain.

- *Resource Domain*—represents all agents (humans, organizations, devices), means, and equipment to carry out activities (in our example, trauma care activities) in the system [33].
- *Policy Domain*—represents rules, regulations, and guidelines relevant to the system [33] (e.g., clinical guidelines, trauma system regulations, EHR regulations).
- *Medical Domain*—represents the medical and biological entities relevant to the system [33] (anatomical entities, treatments, diagnoses, etc.).

In this paper, we are not applying the GCM for a software development and implementation process, but restrict our considerations to the business view, following the approach by Uribe et al. [33].

## 7. Results

### 7.1. System Architecture Results

Using the GCM and applying it to analyze a medical care system for orthopedic trauma from the business view yields several interesting results. The findings we describe can help to inform the development of better communication and data management methods to close communication gaps that currently exist, particularly when it comes to the need for additional therapy, for osteomyelitis and post-surgical arthritis. Regarding our goal of establishing a surgical biobank to fill knowledge gaps regarding these two diagnoses, this analysis provides a survey regarding the relevant agents (healthcare providers), facilities, and guidelines. This enables a comprehensive assessment of the data needs of such a biobank.

Figure 2 shows the domains relevant to orthopedic trauma care, in accordance with the GCM. Table 2 provides a list of examples of entities relevant to the GCM business view of orthopedic trauma care. These entities are sorted into the resource domain, policy domain, and medical domain. In addition, we provide a list of OBO Foundry [31,32] ontologies that provide a semantically rich representation of entities in those domains. This analysis allows for correct modeling of the inter-domain relationships to ensure cross-domain interoperability.

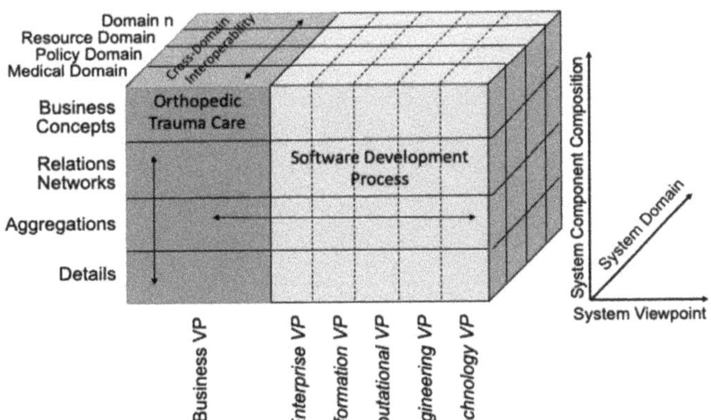


**Figure 2.** The GCM applied to analyze the business VP of orthopedic trauma care, following the approach used by Uribe et al. [33] for diabetes mellitus. Adapted from [33].

**Table 2.** Domains of orthopedic trauma care with examples of relevant entities and potential domain ontologies.

| Domain | Types of Entities in Trauma Care | Potential Ontologies |
| --- | --- | --- |
| Resource Domain | **Organization**: Trauma center, trauma system, emergency medical services (EMS), trauma team | OOSTT [10–12], OMRSE [34] |
| | **Human Individual**: Trauma patient, trauma medical director, trauma registrar, trauma surgeon, EMS personnel, plastic surgeon, infectiologist, microbiologist, surgical pathologist, endocrinologist, radiologist | |
| | **Facilities**: EMS vehicle, emergency room, trauma biobank, trauma registry | |
| Policy Domain | Resources for optimal care for injured patients; [35] EAST Practice Management Guidelines, [36] trauma system policies; triage plans; clinical guidelines | |
| Medical Domain | **Specimens**: Bone specimen; skin specimen; subcutaneous tissue specimen; small vein specimen, muscle specimen | OBIB [37], OBI [38], OMRSE [34], SNOMED-CT |
| | **Diagnosis**: Osteomyelitis, post-operative arthritis, pseudarthrosis, | |
| | **Treatment**: Resection, reconstruction, prosthesis, amputation, chronic injection therapy, nerve blocks for chronic pain | |
| | **Pathological process**: Inflammation, systemic inflammatory response syndrome, infection, necrosis, wound healing, bone regeneration, stress-induced hyperglycemia, | |

### *7.2. Semantic Integration Results*

#### 7.2.1. Overcoming Issues Created by Local Information Models—Identifiers

Applying the methods to the use case of integration issues created by restrictions on identifiers in local information models requires consideration of these information models from the perspective of the GCM (see Section 6.1).

Figure 3 shows an RDF representation of specimen donor, specimen, patient role, and the relevant identifiers. There is no restriction on the numbers of identifiers, and the graph representation allows one to trace each identifier to what it identifies, and each patient's role and each specimen to the person who is the specimen donor. The different classes and instances in our solution are modeled based on the best practice of realism-based ontology as described in Smith and Ceusters [24].

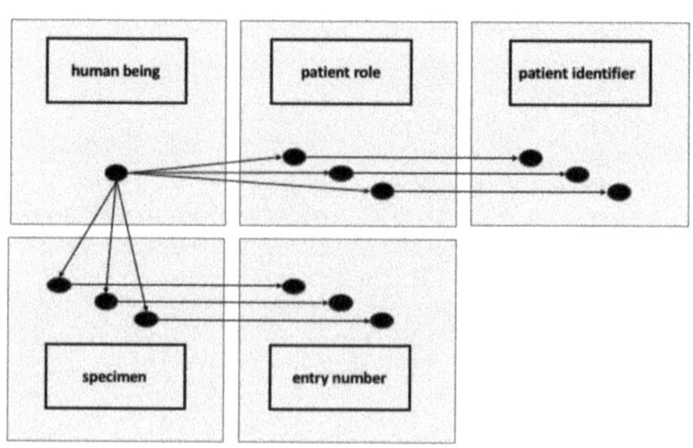


**Figure 3.** Representation of RDF individuals and OWL classes representing a human being having multiple patient roles, corresponding to multiple patient IDs and multiple specimens derived from that human being corresponding to multiple entry numbers. From: [39].

#### 7.2.2. Integration of Heterogeneous Data Sources

This problem represents the classical use case for Standard Widget Toolkits (SWTs) using the native graphical elements of the computer's operating system: existing data models, common data elements, or dictionaries are heterogeneous or ambiguous. Solving this issue using SWTs rests on the idea of using computer systems to help disambiguate the data from heterogeneous sources. Bona et al. pointed out that this rests on an agreed understanding of what it means for a computer to *understand* the content [22]. Ultimately, the level of understanding proposed by Bona et al. is the ability to sort data points into data elements using SWTs [22].

The solution we propose here is to start with providing an RDF-style representation of "unplanned visit to the OR" that formally defines whether or not ER visits such as OR due to a failed limb salvage are an instance of an unplanned visit to the OR, or similar surgical procedures, or not. The disagreement is whether or not OR visits that might not have been initially planned, but that were always a final option, belong in this category. We propose to create a new OWL class for "surgical encounter" as a subclass of "health care encounter" (OGMS_0000097) from the Ontology for General Medical Science (OGMS) [40]. For the "surgical encounter" class, we propose the following textual definition: A healthcare encounter, where the goal is to provide a patient with surgical treatment.

In addition to expanding a class from OGMS, we also propose to expand the class "plan specification" (IAO_0000104) from the Information Artifact Ontology (IAO) [41] by creating a subclass "treatment plan specification". For this class we propose the following textual definition: A plan specification that defines the objectives, actions, and healthcare encounters to treat the medical condition of one patient.

Now we can create a subclass of "surgical encounter" named "unplanned surgical encounter", which we plan to represent "unplanned visit to the OR", excluding visits such as OR due to a failed limb salvage. For this new class, we propose the following definition: A surgical encounter that does not realize the concretization of a plan specification which is part of a treatment plan.

We propose the following equivalence axiom for "unplanned surgical encounter":

"surgical encounter"

and not realizes some ('realizable entity' and concretizes some ('plan specification' and 'part of' some 'treatment plan'))

This axiom would ensure that any surgical procedures that are performed during healthcare encounters without being part of a treatment plan are not pulled into the class "unplanned surgical encounter". In the example of failed limb salvage, the amputation of the limb under treatment is already a medical option in the treatment, although certainly not the most desirable outcome. Hence, any case of failed limb salvage would not be subsumed under an unplanned surgical encounter. This would disambiguate the current situation and resolve the lack of clarity, using a computational method.

#### 7.2.3. Resolving Problem Integration Issues Created during Data Entry

The solution to the lack of clarity between board-eligible emergency physicians and board-certified physicians we detected during the data entry for the CAFÉ project begins with OOSTT. The knowledge representation requirements of the CAFÉ project did not force the previous development of a class representing the individual emergency physicians, but the following classes were sufficient: "board-eligible emergency physician role" (OOSTT_00000173) and "board-certified emergency physician role" (OOSTT_00000171). To resolve the issue surrounding potential ambiguities during data entry, we created two novel classes in a new branch of the OOSTT ontology: "board-certified emergency physician" (OOSTT_00010000) and "board-eligible emergency physician" (OOSTT_00010001). These two classes have the following equivalence axioms:

"board certified emergency physician" (OOSTT_00010000):

"Homo sapiens"

and 'bearer of" some "board-certified emergency physician role" "board-eligible emergency physician' (OOSTT_00010001):

"Homo sapiens"

and (is_specified_output_of some "emergency medicine residency program")

and (inverse ("is about") some 'compliance with state licensure requirement information content entity').

After making these changes to the class structure of OOSTT, we created 100 test individuals to represent emergency physicians in 28 virtual trauma centers, some being board-eligible, some being board-certified. Figure 4 shows an example of the RDF representation of a board-eligible emergency physician. We loaded the resulting ontology and the individuals in a GraphDB triple store using ROBOT [42] to materialize class assertions. We queried this triple store with the following SPARQL queries to query out the board-certified individuals vs. the board-eligible individuals that are not (yet) board-certified.

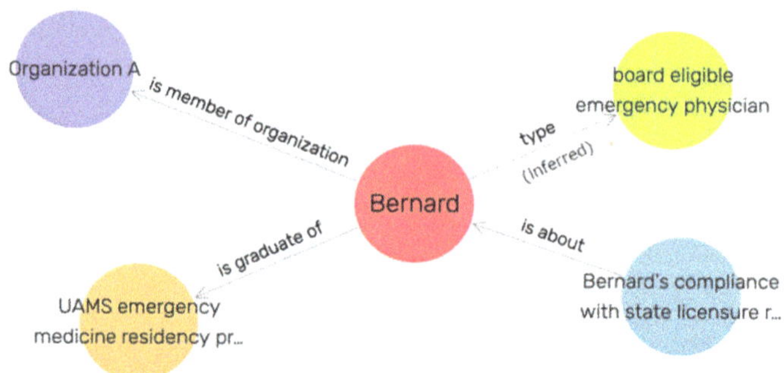


**Figure 4.** Example individual representing a human being, Bernard, who is board-eligible, but not yet board-certified.

## 8. Discussion

In applying a system architecture approach to orthopedic trauma care using the GCM, we follow Uribe et al. [33] to order the involved domains in the following sequence: medical, policy, and resource (Figure 2). This allows us to analyze and to represent the relationships between orthopedic trauma care (e.g., procedures) and the policy domain (e.g., clinical guidelines, state regulations). In placing the resource domain behind the policy domain, the focus of our analysis demonstrates how the resources (e.g., trauma centers, trauma personnel) relate to the policies, meaning which actions, requirements, and credentials the policies specify for trauma care resources. This order of the domain prioritizes the role of policy in the trauma care process, and the roles of the resources in those policies for our initial approach. This order is consistent with the accreditation practices of American College of Surgeons and state trauma systems. It is important to note that the ordering of the domains when analyzing a system is arbitrary and can be chosen according to the focus of the study. To analyze and represent how the trauma care personnel relates to the procedures, we will reorder our domains to focus on the cross-domain interoperability between the resource domain and the medical domain.

To resolve problems of data integration due to restrictions in local information models, we have applied both the GCM and methods of a realism-based ontology development. Notably, the successful deployment of ISO 23903 [17] for integrating different domains and knowledge spaces, including their specific models, has been demonstrated for the integration of HL7 privacy and security specifications [43] in ISO 13606 EHR communication [44], the harmonization of concepts from ISO 12967 [45] and ISO 13940 [46], or the mapping of open EHR (ISO 13606) archetypes [47], ISO 13972 clinical models [48], and HL7 FHIR resources [49].

The limitations of this study and the three use cases demonstrated lie in the fact that the work presented addresses issues from a knowledge representation perspective.

The solutions presented are readily available to be implemented in a data management system, but they have not yet been implemented. Thus, in this study we do not assess effects that are created by using our knowledge representation in a running medical information system, such as a biobank system.

The next step from the knowledge representation perspective is to develop computational ways to leverage the GCM system analysis and its results to immediately develop knowledge representation solutions such as OWL ontologies and RDF data. In addition, we plan to explore the deployment of the GCM to transform medical data captured with information models into computer-interpretable RDF data sources for secondary use in medicine and vice versa.

From the clinical perspective, the next step is to build a small proof-of-concept surgical biobank data management system following the knowledge representation principles demonstrated in this paper. This step, which we are currently working on, will allow validation of the functionality and usability of the proposed solutions in a clinical research setting.

## 9. Conclusions

From the results presented in this paper, we concluded that SWT is required to disambiguate and integrate data for surgical biobanks. While surgical biobanks with exclusively local data might not have the same level of need for semantic integration as those aiming to integrate data from multiple trauma care providers, we hold that integrating data from the entirety of the trauma care process is a necessity.

In addition, this paper demonstrates that the GCM is a useful tool to assess the data scope of a surgical biobank and identify relevant domain ontologies. The GCM even assists in resolving specific semantic integration problems, supplementing the SWTs.

**Author Contributions:** Conceptualization, M.B., C.B., K.W.S. and C.B.; use-cases, C.E.Z., J.M.W., M.P.K., S.J.B., N.S., C.B., K.W.S.; methodology, M.B., B.B.; virtual data set and formal analysis J.M.W.; writing—original draft preparation, M.B.; C.E.Z., J.M.W., M.P.K., C.B., K.W.S., B.B.; writing—review and editing, M.B.; C.E.Z., J.M.W., M.P.K., S.J.B., N.S., C.B., K.W.S., B.B.; visualization, M.B., J.M.W. All authors have read and agreed to the published version of the manuscript.

**Funding:** Parts of the research presented in this article are funded by the National Institute of General Medical Sciences of the National Institutes of Health under award number R01GM111324.

**Institutional Review Board Statement:** Not applicable.

**Informed Consent Statement:** Not applicable.

**Data Availability Statement:** Not applicable.

**Conflicts of Interest:** The authors declare no conflict of interest.

## References

1. Injuries and Violence Are Leading Causes of Death. 2021. Available online: https://www.cdc.gov/injury/wisqars/animated-leading-causes.html (accessed on 24 February 2022).
2. Janicova, A.; Relja, B. Neutrophil Phenotypes and Functions in Trauma and Trauma-Related Sepsis. *Shock Augusta Ga.* **2021**, *56*, 16–29. [CrossRef] [PubMed]
3. Skelton, J.K.; Purcell, R. Preclinical models for studying immune responses to traumatic injury. *Immunology* **2021**, *162*, 377–388. [CrossRef] [PubMed]
4. Recknagel, S.; Bindl, R.; Brochhausen, C.; Göckelmann, M.; Wehner, T.; Schoengraf, P.; Huber-Lang, M.; Claes, L.; Ignatius, A. Systemic inflammation induced by a thoracic trauma alters the cellular composition of the early fracture callus. *J. Trauma Acute Care Surg.* **2013**, *74*, 531–537. [CrossRef] [PubMed]
5. Kerby, J.D.; Griffin, R.L.; MacLennan, P.; Rue, L.W.I. Stress-Induced Hyperglycemia, Not Diabetic Hyperglycemia, Is Associated with Higher Mortality in Trauma. *Ann. Surg.* **2012**, *256*, 446–452. [CrossRef]
6. Yanik, E.L.; Keener, J.D.; Lin, S.J.; Colditz, G.A.; Wright, R.W.; Evanoff, B.A.; Jain, N.B.; Saccone, N.L. Identification of a Novel Genetic Marker for Risk of Degenerative Rotator Cuff Disease Surgery in the UK Biobank. *J. Bone Joint Surg. Am.* **2021**, *103*, 1259–1267. [CrossRef]
7. Hojat, A.; Wei, B.; Olson, M.G.; Mao, Q.; Yong, W.H. Procurement and Storage of Surgical Biospecimens. *Methods Mol. Biol. Clifton NJ.* **2019**, *1897*, 65–76. [CrossRef]

8. Spjuth, O.; Krestyaninova, M.; Hastings, J.; Shen, H.-Y.; Heikkinen, J.; Waldenberger, M.; Langhammer, A.; Ladenvall, C.; Esko, T.; Persson, M.-Å.; et al. Harmonising and linking biomedical and clinical data across disparate data archives to enable integrative cross-biobank research. *Eur. J. Hum. Genet. EJHG* **2016**, *24*, 521–528. [CrossRef]
9. Blobel, B.; Ruotsalainen, P.; Oemig, F. Why Interoperability at Data Level Is Not Sufficient for Enabling pHealth? *Stud. Health Technol. Inform.* **2020**, *273*, 3–20. [CrossRef]
10. Utecht, J.; Judkins, J.; Otte, J.N.; Colvin, T.; Rogers, N.; Rose, R.; Alvi, M.; Hicks, A.; Ball, J.; Bowman, S.M.; et al. OOSTT: A Resource for Analyzing the Organizational Structures of Trauma Centers and Trauma Systems. *CEUR Workshop Proc.* **2016**, *1747*. Available online: http://ceur-ws.org/Vol-1747/IT504_ICBO2016.pdf (accessed on 4 May 2022).
11. Utecht, J.; Ball, J.; Bowman, S.M.; Dodd, J.; Judkins, J.; Maxson, R.T.; Nabaweesi, R.; Pradhan, R.; Sanddal, N.D.; Winchell, R.J.; et al. Development and validation of a controlled vocabulary: An OWL representation of organizational structures of trauma centers and trauma systems. *Stud. Health Technol. Inform.* **2019**, *264*, 403–407. [CrossRef]
12. Brochhausen, M.; Ball, J.W.; Sanddal, N.D.; Dodd, J.; Braun, N.; Bost, S.; Utecht, J.; Winchell, R.J.; Sexton, K.W. Collecting data on organizational structures of trauma centers: The CAFE web service, *Trauma Surg. Acute Care Open* **2020**, *5*, e000473. [CrossRef]
13. Bradley, N.L.; Garraway, N.; Bell, N.; Lakha, N.; Hameed, S.M. Data capture and communication during transfers to definitive care in an inclusive trauma system. *Injury* **2017**, *48*, 1069–1073. [CrossRef]
14. American College of Surgeons. *Trauma Quality Improvement Program (TQIP)*; American College of Surgeons: Chicago, IL, USA; Available online: http://www.facs.org/quality-programs/trauma/tqp/center-programs/tqip (accessed on 15 February 2022).
15. American College of Surgeons. *NTDS 2021 Data Dictionary*; American College of Surgeons: Chicago, IL, USA; Available online: http://www.facs.org/quality-programs/trauma/tqp/center-programs/ntdb/ntds/data-dictionary (accessed on 15 February 2022).
16. *ISO 23903:2021*; Health Informatics—Interoperability and Integration Reference Architecture—Model and Framework. ISO: Geneva, Switzerland. Available online: https://www.iso.org/cms/render/live/en/sites/isoorg/contents/data/standard/07/73/77337.html (accessed on 17 February 2022).
17. *ISO/IEC 10746-3:2009*; Information Technology—Open distributed processing—Reference Model: Architecture—Part 3. ISO: Geneva, Switzerland. Available online: https://www.iso.org/cms/render/live/en/sites/isoorg/contents/data/standard/05/57/55724.html (accessed on 10 March 2022).
18. Blobel, B. Standardization for Mastering Healthcare Transformation—Challenges and Solutions. *Eur. J. Biomed. Inform.* **2017**, *13*, 9–15. [CrossRef]
19. Prior, F.W.; Clark, K.; Commean, P.; Freymann, J.; Jaffe, C.; Kirby, J.; Moore, S.; Smith, K.; Tarbox, L.; Vendt, B.; et al. TCIA: An information resource to enable open science. In Proceedings of the 2013 35th Annual International Conference of the IEEE Engineering in Medicine and Biology Society, Osaka, Japan, 3–7 July 2013; pp. 1282–1285. [CrossRef]
20. Sharma, A.; Tarbox, L.; Kurc, T.; Bona, J.; Smith, K.; Kathiravelu, P.; Bremer, E.; Saltz, J.H.; Prior, F. PRISM: A Platform for Imaging in Precision Medicine. *JCO Clin. Cancer Inform.* **2020**, *4*, 491–499. [CrossRef]
21. Bona, J.P.; Prior, F.W.; Zozus, M.N.; Brochhausen, M. Enhancing Clinical Data and Clinical Research Data with Biomedical Ontologies—Insights from the Knowledge Representation Perspective. *Yearb. Med. Inform.* **2019**, *28*, 140–151. [CrossRef]
22. Brochhausen, M.; Bona, J.; Blobel, B. The Role of Axiomatically-Rich Ontologies in Transforming Medical Data to Knowledge. *Stud. Health Technol. Inform.* **2018**, *249*, 38–49.
23. The Semantic Web Layer Cake. Available online: https://www.w3.org/2007/03/layerCake.svg (accessed on 16 February 2022).
24. Smith, B.; Ceusters, W. Ontological realism: A methodology for coordinated evolution of scientific ontologies. *Appl. Ontol.* **2010**, *5*, 139–188. [CrossRef]
25. Hogan, W.R.; Hanna, J.; Joseph, E.; Brochhausen, M. Towards a Consistent and Scientifically Accurate Drug Ontology. *CEUR Workshop Proc.* **2013**, *1060*, 68–73.
26. Ceusters, W.M.; Spackman, K.A.; Smith, B. Would SNOMED CT benefit from realism-based ontology evolution? *AMIA Annu. Symp. Proc. AMIA Symp.* **2007**, *2007*, 105–109.
27. Lin, Y.; Xiang, Z.; He, Y. Brucellosis Ontology (IDOBRU) as an extension of the Infectious Disease Ontology. *J. Biomed. Semant.* **2011**, *2*, 9. [CrossRef]
28. Grenon, P.; Smith, B.; Goldberg, L. Biodynamic ontology: Applying BFO in the biomedical domain. *Stud. Health Technol. Inform.* **2004**, *102*, 20–38.
29. Resource Description Framework (RDF) Primer. Available online: https://www.w3.org/TR/rdf11-concepts/ (accessed on 16 February 2022).
30. OWL 2 Web Ontology Language Primer (Second Edition). Available online: https://www.w3.org/TR/owl2-primer/ (accessed on 16 February 2022).
31. Jackson, R.; Matentzoglu, N.; Overton, J.A.; Vita, R.; Balhoff, J.P.; Buttigieg, P.L.; Carbon, S.; Courtot, M.; Diehl, A.D.; Dooley, D.M.; et al. OBO Foundry in 2021: Operationalizing open data principles to evaluate ontologies. *Database J. Biol. Databases Curation* **2021**, *2021*, baab069. [CrossRef]
32. Smith, B.; Ashburner, M.; Rosse, C.; Bard, J.; Bug, W.; Ceusters, W.; Goldberg, L.J.; Eilbeck, K.; Ireland, A.; Mungall, C.J.; et al. The OBO Foundry: Coordinated evolution of ontologies to support biomedical data integration. *Nat. Biotechnol.* **2007**, *25*, 1251–1255. [CrossRef]

33. Uribe, G.A.; Blobel, B.; López, D.M.; Schulz, S. A generic architecture for an adaptive, interoperable and intelligent type 2 diabetes mellitus care system. *Stud. Health Technol. Inform.* **2015**, *211*, 121–131.
34. Hicks, A.; Hanna, J.; Welch, D.; Brochhausen, M.; Hogan, W.R. The ontology of medically related social entities: Recent developments. *J. Biomed. Semant.* **2016**, *7*, 47. [CrossRef]
35. American College of Surgeons and Committee on Trauma. *Resources for Optimal Care of the Injured Patient*; American College of Surgeons: Chicago, IL, USA, 2014.
36. EAST Practice Management Guidelines. Available online: https://www.east.org/education-career-development/practice-management-guidelines (accessed on 15 February 2022).
37. Brochhausen, M.; Zheng, J.; Birtwell, D.; Williams, H.; Masci, A.M.; Ellis, H.J.; Stoeckert, C.J. OBIB-a novel ontology for biobanking. *J. Biomed. Semant.* **2016**, *7*, 23. [CrossRef]
38. Bandrowski, A.; Brinkman, R.; Brochhausen, M.; Brush, M.H.; Bug, B.; Chibucos, M.C.; Clancy, K.; Courtot, M.; Derom, D.; Dumontier, M.; et al. The Ontology for Biomedical Investigations. *PLoS ONE* **2016**, *11*, e0154556. [CrossRef]
39. Brochhausen, M.; Bost, S.J.; Singh, N.; Brochhausen, C.; Blobel, B. Understanding the Gap between Information Models and Realism-Based Ontologies Using the Generic Component Model. *Stud. Health Technol. Inform.* **2021**, *285*, 159–164. [CrossRef] [PubMed]
40. Ontobee: OGMS. Available online: http://www.ontobee.org/ontology/OGMS?iri=http://purl.obolibrary.org/obo/OGMS_0000029 (accessed on 31 December 2021).
41. Information Artifact Ontology (IAO). The Foundry, OBO. Available online: https://obofoundry.org/ontology/iao.html (accessed on 4 May 2022).
42. Jackson, R.C.; Balhoff, J.P.; Douglass, E.; Harris, N.L.; Mungall, C.J.; Overton, J.A. ROBOT: A Tool for Automating Ontology Workflows. *BMC Bioinform.* **2019**, *20*, 407. [CrossRef] [PubMed]
43. HL7, HL7 Standards Product Brief—HL7 Version 3 Domain Analysis Model: Composite Security and Privacy, Release 1 | HL7 International. Available online: http://www.hl7.org/implement/standards/product_brief.cfm?product_id=536 (accessed on 17 February 2022).
44. *ISO 13606-1:2019*; ISO: Health Informatics—Electronic Health Record Communication—Part 1: Reference Model. ISO: Geneva, Switzerland. Available online: https://www.iso.org/cms/render/live/en/sites/isoorg/contents/data/standard/06/78/67868.html (accessed on 10 March 2022).
45. *ISO 12967-1:2020*; ISO: Health Informatics—Service Architecture (HISA)—Part 1: Enterprise Viewpoint. ISO: Geneva, Switzerland. Available online: https://www.iso.org/cms/render/live/en/sites/isoorg/contents/data/standard/07/10/71037.html (accessed on 10 March 2022).
46. *ISO 13940:2015(en)*; Health Informatics—System of Concepts to Support Continuity of Care. ISO: Geneva, Switzerland. Available online: https://www.iso.org/obp/ui/#iso:std:iso:13940:ed-1:v1:en (accessed on 17 February 2022).
47. OpenFoundation, EHR. Available online: https://www.openehr.org/ (accessed on 16 February 2022).
48. *ISO 13972*; ISO: Health Informatics—Clinical Information Models—Characteristics, Structures, and Requirements. ISO: Geneva, Switzerland. Available online: https://www.iso.org/cms/render/live/en/sites/isoorg/contents/data/standard/07/94/79498.html (accessed on 17 February 2022).
49. HL7 International. HL7 Fast Healthcare Interoperability Resources (FHIR). Available online: http://www.hl7.org/fhir/ (accessed on 16 February 2022).

Journal of
*Personalized*
*Medicine*

MDPI

*Article*

# Towards a Didactic Concept for Heterogeneous Target Groups in Digital Learning Environments—First Course Implementation

**Matthias Katzensteiner [1,*], Stefan Vogel [2], Jens Hüsers [3], Jendrik Richter [2] and Oliver J. Bott [1]**

1 University of Applied Sciences and Arts Hanover, 30539 Hannover, Germany; oliver.bott@hs-hannover.de
2 Department for Medical Informatics, University Medical Center Göttingen, 37075 Göttingen, Germany; stefan.vogel@med.uni-goettingen.de (S.V.); jendrik.richter@med.uni-goettingen.de (J.R.)
3 Health Informatics Research Group, University AS Osnabrück, 49076 Osnabrück, Germany; j.huesers@hs-osnabrueck.de
* Correspondence: matthias.katzensteiner@hs-hannover.de

**Abstract:** In the context of the ongoing digitization of interdisciplinary subjects, the need for digital literacy is increasing in all areas of everyday life. Furthermore, communication between science and society is facing new challenges, not least since the COVID-19 pandemic. In order to deal with these challenges and to provide target-oriented online teaching, new educational concepts for the transfer of knowledge to society are necessary. In the transfer project "Zukunftslabor Gesundheit" (ZLG), a didactic concept for the creation of E-Learning classes was developed. A key factor for the didactic concept is addressing heterogeneous target groups to reach the broadest possible spectrum of participants. The concept has already been used for the creation of the first ZLG E-Learning courses. This article outlines the central elements of the developed didactic concept and addresses the creation of the ZLG courses. The courses created so far appeal to different target groups and convey diverse types of knowledge at different levels of difficulty.

**Keywords:** didactic; Healthcare IT; citizens; E-Learning; digitalization; digitization; patient empowerment; education; communication; healthcare communications

check for updates

**Citation:** Katzensteiner, M.; Vogel, S.; Hüsers, J.; Richter, J.; Bott, O.J. Towards a Didactic Concept for Heterogeneous Target Groups in Digital Learning Environments—First Course Implementation. *J. Pers. Med.* **2022**, *12*, 696. https://doi.org/10.3390/jpm12050696

Academic Editors: Bernd Blobel and Mauro Giacomini

Received: 9 March 2022
Accepted: 25 April 2022
Published: 27 April 2022



## 1. Introduction

In times of the SARS-CoV-2 pandemic and, in perspective, climate change, online formats of classic face-to-face events are becoming increasingly relevant. In terms of access to information for all, methods such as E-Learning can be used for new ways of globalization [1]. With these methods, knowledge can be shared across national borders so that developing countries can also benefit [2]. Moreover, cultural exchanges may be an additional advantage through this approach, as well as sensitivity to differences in health care systems. While a face-to-face event allows direct human contact, online events can be offered and conducted independently of location and time. Of course, online events do not lack flaws and must therefore be used in a well-considered manner.

In the information age, data and information accumulate in great abundance and high frequency, so that non-specialist viewers quickly reach a capacity limit for information processing. In the media and in politics, complex facts are often strongly abbreviated or even distorted, as frequently observed during the COVID-19 pandemic in Germany, for example [3,4].

For non-specialist consumers of these media and political reports, it is no longer easy to process and retrieve the wealth of information. Due to the fast publication time on the Internet, many reports are disseminated at an early stage. In particular, study data of untested publications are already recited and used in a variety of media, which can lead to conflicts later on [5,6].

In order to be capable of classifying this high information density and distinguishing the quality of information, media competence and certain basic knowledge are required [7]. In order to enable the general population to understand certain complex facts on their own, it is necessary to build up abilities of adequate information handling and understanding. In particular, scientific definitions of terms, the basics of good scientific practice, and competence in the use of digital tools of any kind are of great importance here [8].

### *1.1. The Research Association*

The *Lower Saxony Center for Digital Innovations* (in German: Zentrum für digitale Innovationen Niedersachsen, ZDIN) forms an interface between the Ministry of Economics and the Ministry of Science and Culture in Lower Saxony. The ZDIN is intended to promote networking and knowledge transfer between research and industry but, furthermore, make Lower Saxony's research location visible to the general public. Within the framework of the ZDIN, several *future labs* have been developed that conduct research in different sectors. These are the future labs for *agriculture, mobility, healthcare, production and society, and work.*

The *Future Lab for Healthcare* (in German: Zukunftslabor Gesundheit, ZLG) of the ZDIN is, among others, involved in the planning and implementation of E-Learning programs. For this purpose, a special didactic concept for online-exclusive teaching was developed to serve as a guideline for educators to develop and implement pure online formats.

The ZLG particularly addresses the teaching of non-specialist audiences in Healthcare IT issues to achieve patient and people empowerment. Research and the latest findings in the ZLG's research field shall be communicated to the general public. A focus should be especially on data privacy and data security, as skepticism regarding the trustworthiness of new technologies, i.e., of internet applications in general or AI technologies in particular, is widespread in society.

The ZLG is organized into three subprojects that address different aspects of Healthcare IT. Subproject 1 (TP1) is concerned with the development of a research data platform for shared data consolidation and research across site boundaries. The participating research sites of the ZLG are supposed to find the possibility to work together on research questions via this platform.

Subproject 2 (TP2) deals with the use of patient-related sensor technology for the improvement of everyday care. New sensor technology will be developed, and the use of established sensor technology will be optimized.

Subproject 3 (TP3), from which this publication arises, focuses on knowledge transfer of the research results based on E-Learning. During the project duration of the ZLG, a total of four online courses will be developed to transfer the research topics of subprojects 1 and 2. Further, TP3 is developing two demonstrators that address different aspects of online teaching.

### *1.2. Focus on Sub-Project 3 for Education, Training and Further Education*

In TP3, the first demonstrator pursues AI-assisted physiotherapy training of shoulder patients via camera technology to monitor and evaluate training at home automatically. The combination of a special depth camera and smartphone application aims to provide gamification training, which allows patients regular but adequate health sport within home health care.

The second demonstrator develops a curriculum for statistical learning and data analytics in nursing professions and studies. This curriculum aims for integration into different study programs via ECTS allocation and thus is universally applicable. Teaching in demonstrator 2 takes place almost entirely online.

In addition to the content planned throughout the project, TP3 developed another course to introduce lecturers to online teaching. The so-called "Train the Trainer" course introduces participants to different tools and methods such as video production or evaluation concepts in addition to the actual didactic concept.

The ZLG-TP3 focuses on different target groups in order to test the broadest possible applicability of the developed concepts. The target groups addressed are patients and affected persons, citizens and the interested public, medical informatics and related professions, as well as representatives of the health care professions. In particular, the target groups of citizens and patients are considered a challenge since those target groups represent the cross-section of society and thus have a very high level of heterogeneity.

In this article, we present the courses designed and developed so far and compare their implementation. The already developed courses differ strongly from each other in structure and scope as well as their target groups but are based on the same didactic concept. The universal applicability of the basic didactic core concept for online teaching shall be shown and clarified by presenting the learning offers. Based on the experiences gained, we will continuously develop the concept and optimize its quality. For this purpose, evaluations are conducted by the participants at the end of the courses.

## 2. Materials and Methods

This publication relates to the paper "*Development of a Didactic Online Course Concept for Heterogeneous Audience Groups in the Context of Healthcare IT*" at pHealth 2021 [9] and explains further development stages. In the following, the didactic methods and approaches used for the course development are explained.

To achieve the goal of developing different online courses for various target groups, a concept was developed that covers relevant didactic aspects. These aspects are covered in different chapters:

- Target group definition
- Basic concepts and scenarios of online didactics
- Topics, learning objectives, and didactic scenarios of the ZLG
- Navigation concept to the online courses
- Didactic core concepts for online course design
- Digital building blocks of learning management systems for course design
- Concept for course evaluation

To offer E-Learning, the ZLG uses and provides a learning management system (LMS) [10]. The ZLG compared and evaluated LMSs from different providers and thereafter decided to use ILIAS. The LMS serves as the central hub for the learning content, as the entire online teaching can be organized, structured, and accessed there. ILIAS stands for "Integrated Learning, Information and Work Cooperation System" in German and has been available since 2000 and was originally developed by the University of Cologne.

Overall, the basic functionalities of LMS are largely identical, so the differences lie particularly in the specific handling. Most LMSs, such as Moodle and ILIAS, support the SCORM (Sharable Content Object Reference Model) standard so that individual content can also be exchanged across LMS boundaries. The ZLG uses a shared ILIAS instance with the HiGHmed consortium teaching subproject to achieve a greater value from the collaboration [11].

The didactic concept also includes an evaluation concept that is used as a basis for iterative quality improvement of the developed E-Learning courses. Evaluation is intended to test the quality of educational programs, e.g., by surveying participants [12]. The evaluation concept of the ZLG teaching project distinguishes three dimensions: Type, method, and objects of evaluation.

The type of evaluation determines whether it is a formative or summative evaluation of the course. The evaluation method defines whether a quantitative or qualitative evaluation is to be conducted [13]. The evaluation object defines which unit is evaluated, such as course content, lecturers, or E-tivities.

From the aforementioned items, a core evaluation was designed to monitor the course quality of ZLG courses. Based on the standardized core evaluation, lecturers can extend the evaluation by individual aspects dynamically.

### 2.1. Target Group Definition

As already described in the introduction, the target groups predetermined in the project approach are characterized by great heterogeneity. In order to take this specificity into account, it must be possible to describe them as precisely as possible, using appropriate methods.

Following the system proposed in [14], the characteristics of the target groups were defined based on various criteria of socio-demographic, psychographic, and educational characteristics, as well as the expected educational behavior. The following attributes were described for each target group:

- Sociographic characteristics: Age structure, gender distribution, marital status, place of residence, area of influence, immigration background, level of education, employment status.
- Psychographic characteristics: Attitude, motivation, potential, strengths, weaknesses, aspirations, hopes.
- Educational characteristics/behavior: Previous education, media affinity, learning types, discussion types

Through the descriptions based on these characteristics, a precise differentiation of the target groups can be achieved, and the respective target group-specific communication and teaching can be designed.

For the target group of the interested public, a description based on these definitions is only possible in very general terms, as this group is characterized by the greatest possible diversity and heterogeneity. A clear description of the individual characteristics in a concise form is not feasible.

In order to at least approach an adequate description of the social structure, the ZLG didactic concept uses the marketing tool of the Sinus Milieus. This differentiates between varying subgroups, each of which has comparable attributes [15].

### 2.2. 5-Stage Model for Online Teaching by Gilly Salmon

The didactic core concept of the ZLG covers up to five phases and is essentially referring to the 5-stage model of Gilly Salmon for online teaching, which describes how online-exclusive teaching can be implemented with five successive steps (Figure 1). The model, according to Salmon, uses so-called "E-tivities", which are designed to activate the audience and lead the participants to independent and autonomous learning [16].

The stages are designed to provide the audience group with new skills and confidence so that the challenge and intensity of learning can be increased with each stage. At the same time, communication between the audience is to be strengthened in order to promote group exchange and to discuss the increasing complexity of the tasks in the group. In stage 1, 1 to 1 communication between learners is initiated, as there are few other contacts at the beginning. In phases 2–4, the ratio changes to 1:n communication so that both the number of contacts and the frequency of exchanges increase. In the final phase, 5, the level of communication is reduced again in favor of individual follow-up so that each participating person can reflect on his or her own experience.

Stage 1, "Access and motivation", is intended to enable participants to find a path around the learning environment, in this case, a learning management system (LMS). No learning context-related E-tivities and tasks are set, but low-threshold tasks are intended to motivate participation in the following work phases. Instructor support is important at this stage to resolve any access or operational issues with the LMS. Participants should perceive the course as a social environment and communicate transparently with each other.

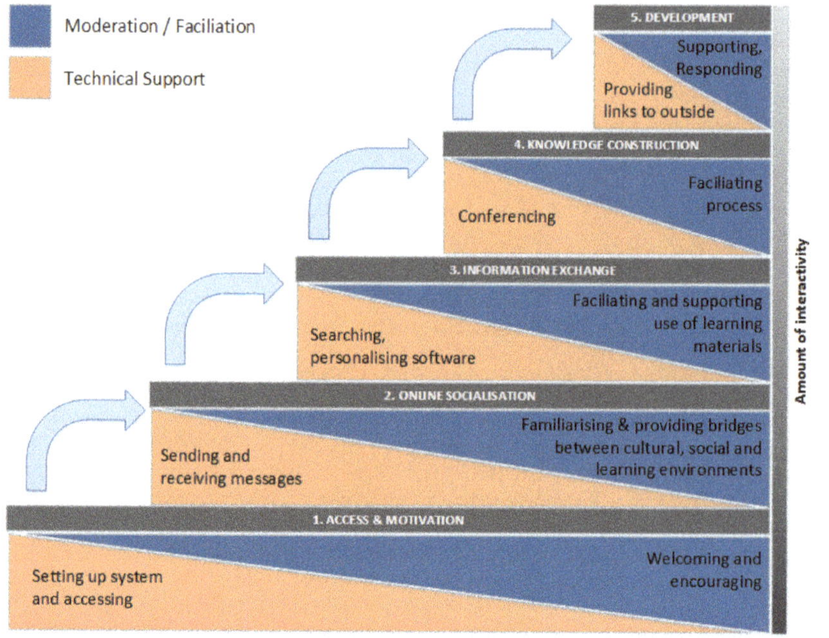


**Figure 1.** Salmon's five-stage model for online learning. Gilly Salmon–E-tivities: The key to active online learning (2013) according to [16–19]. This image is available under the Creative Commons Attribution-NonCommercial-NoDerivatives 4.0 International (CC BY-NC-ND 4.0) license as stated in the publication and on the website of the author: https://www.gillysalmon.com/contact.html (accessed on 9 March 2022).

Stage 2, "Online socialization", allows for participants to interact with each other and explore the work environment. For this purpose, Salmon recommends that participants be considered under Wenger's Communities of Practice concept [20], which includes three key components: *Shared undertaking*, such as distributed subtasks; *Reciprocity*, such as mutual acquaintance and trust; and *Shared repertoire*, which describes language, routines, or sensibilities. Socialization in the second stage is considered complete when participants communicate with each other without request.

Stage 3, "Information exchange", initiates the joint processing and critical discussion of the learning material by the participants. The knowledge gained is to be applied in practical examples in order to work on a greater complexity of E-tivities in cooperation. The group dynamics should be increased at this level so that the interaction of learners is the focus. Learners should take participation in the course for granted and enjoy being active participants. Passive content transfer, such as reading texts, should be avoided, as this is considered detrimental to learning (lurking).

Stage 4, "Knowledge Construction", should allow participants to build unconscious knowledge (tactical knowledge) to gain new perspectives. The E-tivities of this stage should demand critical, creative, and analytical thinking. Practical relevance and orientation are required in order to adequately apply the methods learned. The acquired knowledge patterns enable the learners to increase the learning effect in the long term. That way, what has been learned (theory) enters the subconscious and can be transferred to practical tasks (transfer performance).

Stage 5, "Development", is designed to allow participants to make their own decisions about the learning content. A high level of autonomy is expected in this stage, as learners independently use the knowledge they have acquired to work on more advanced tasks. The audience intuitively collaborates at a high level without discussing group composition.

By reflecting on the learning process, participants independently derive further knowledge and actions to use the knowledge in the future.

### 2.3. Didactic Core Concept for Online Learning in ZLG

A core didactic concept was developed at the ZLG to facilitate online teaching. The development and delivery of online courses are influenced by various factors. For the core concept, the focus was placed on the factors of group size, group dynamics and communication, learning and work phases, as well as the type and scope of supervision.

In relation to the factors identified, an adapted course structure was developed as a template (Figure 2), following the stage model of Gilly Salmon [16] and the HiGHmed teaching project [11,21] to support the development of online courses.

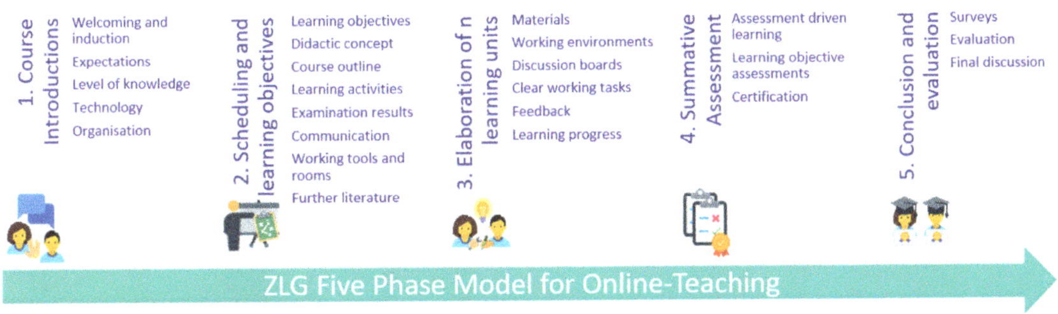


**Figure 2.** ZLG Five Phase Model for Online-Teaching based on [11,16,21].

A special feature of the template is the usage of E-tivities. E-tivities, according to Salmon, are standardized in structure and consist of an introduction, objective, task, and discussion. The E-tivities are intended to pursue a constructivist approach to learning, ranging from the pure exchange of information to knowledge construction and personal development.

For developing courses in ZLG, a 5-Phase-Model was generated. This model is characterized by five learn-phases, which can be highly associated with Salmons 5-Stage-model. It should be emphasized here, however, that Salmon's stages are not just reflections of the ZLG phase model. In particular, Salmon's 5-stage model defines the activation of learners in the online environment at a different level, while the ZLG phase model defines concrete phases of work.

Phases 1–3 of the ZLG concept can be associated with the overall 5-step model according to Salmon, as the prerequisites for successful interactive knowledge transfer are created there.

Phase 1, "Welcome and introduction", briefly introduces the course topic and the teachers in order to offer the participants a motivating introduction to the course. The expectations and level of knowledge of the participants are queried to establish an overall impression of the group. The course content should be appropriate to the level of the audience and can be supplemented with sources and references for missing knowledge. Finally, the technical and organizational issues of the participants are discussed to ensure full accessibility and usability of the Learning Management System.

Phase 2, "Scheduling and learning objectives", introduces learning contents as well as learning objectives and the general course procedure. In this phase, possible later examination achievements should also be explained, and the communication options presented. Netiquette should also be provided and explained analogously to Salmon's model.

Phase 3, "Elaboration of ***n*** learning units", represents the actual knowledge transfer in the ZLG learning phase model. In this phase, the learners are taught the learning content and competencies over several learning units, whereby this phase is characterized by discursive reflection and practical, ideally collaborative application. The learning units of this phase should be similar in sequence and structure:

1. Giving and activating input,
2. Work on one or more tasks/questions,
3. Formative assessment and feedback.

As the titles of the subdivision show, basic information introduces each learning unit on the respective focus (1). This is followed by one or more tasks and/or questions on the respective focus in order to internalize the theoretical knowledge (2). At the end of the learning unit, a formative assessment is carried out so that the learners can assess themselves, and the teachers can use the results to see whether the participants have achieved the learning objective (3).

Phase 4, "Summative assessment", plays a significant role and dictates if a certificate is to be issued for successful participation in the course. Learning objective assessments serve as proof of whether or not and to what extent participants have achieved the learning objectives and acquired or deepened new competencies. While formative assessments are primarily used for the interim assessment of learning success, summative assessments are used in particular for the final assessment of participants' performance.

Phase 5, "Conclusion and evaluation", should offer participants the opportunity to evaluate the course. The instructors can derive quality assurance or quality enhancement measures from these evaluations. The evaluations of the participants can be used to generate comparisons between the learning success and the mood of the participants. Through the combination of quantifiable learning success (assessments) and qualitative statements (evaluation), insights into the quality of the learning offer can be gained. The ZLG has developed its own evaluation concept for carrying out evaluations.

## 3. Results

The individual subproject groups of the ZLG had the task of using the didactic core concept to create learning courses that address the subprojects' research fields. The courses were created in the shared instance of the LMS ILIAS, as described above.

The following tables provide a brief overview of the created courses, regarding the criteria: Title, Content, Target Group, Learning Goals, Duration, Workload, Workload in synchronous Phase, Workload in asynchronous Phase, Amount of E-tivities, Learning Videos, other special features of the course.

### *3.1. ZLG-Metacourse "Train the Trainer"*

The ZLG Metacourse, "Train the Trainer", for knowledge transfer in ZLG, is structured by learning weeks. Each week aims for specific learning goals with intersecting topics. Following the ZLG didactic core concept, the level of difficulty increases steadily per week. The ratio between information transfer and self-learning is shifting continuously in favor of self-learning aspects (Figure 3).

The goal in the first week of the ZLG Metacourse is to enable the participants to use the learning platform for knowledge acquisition and exchange, but also to connect on a social level with other participants and the lecturers. For this reason, the E-tivities are aimed at demonstrating the features of the learning management system while introducing the individual virtually to the learning group. The introduction of the participants in the first week initially addresses the first three stages according to Gilly Salmon and the ZLG didactic core concept. The following weeks build on this preliminary work and then focus on phases three to five, not only to absorb information but also to apply it and further develop knowledge as a group.

| | | | | | | |
|---|---|---|---|---|---|---|
| Title | ZLG Metacourse: Knowledge Transfer in the ZLG "Train The Trainer" | | | | | |
| Content | In this course, participants learn the basics of knowledge transfer at the ZLG. This includes the didactic concept for online teaching of heterogeneous target groups of the ZLG, the use of a learning management system and the creation of learning videos. | | | | | |
| Target Group | Lecturers of the ZLG; scientific staff; professors; academics | | | | | |
| Learning Goals | * The participants have internalized the didactic core concept of The ZLG.<br>* The participants are aware of the Integration and addressing of different target groups.<br>* The participants can independently familiarize themselves with the use of learning management systems and create learning formats.<br>* The participants can independently create and edit learning videos. | | | | | |
| Other special features of the course | * Consultation hours offered.<br>* One synchronous learning session to learn the ILIAS platform configuration.<br>* Otherwise, all content was presented via self-paced learning or learning video. | | | | | |
| Dimensions | Duration | Workload | Workload in synchronous Phase | Workload in asynchronous Phase | E-tivities | Learning Videos |
| Units | Weeks | Hours | Hours | Hours | Amount in total | Minutes |
| Data | 4 | 12 | 3 | 9 | 11 | 80 |

**Figure 3.** Course properties for ZLG-TP3 Metacourse: "Knowledge Transfer in the TLG "Train the Trainer".

In week two, the core didactic concept of the ZLG is taught. The aim of the E-tivities is to acquire knowledge individually with the support of learning videos and literature and then to create own E-tivities along with the phase model. In a final step, the E-tivities are refined by the group of participants and improved with the help of digital building blocks with regard to the motivation of the target group.

Week 3 focuses on the administrative structure of an online course, addressing the conceptual aspects and functional possibilities, in particular, the features that support the motivation of the participants. Another aspect of week 3 is the development of learning videos to provide target group-specific content according to the didactic concept.

In the last week of the course, the core evaluation concept is taught, which can be used in the ZLG and extended for individual courses. In this way, a level of comparability between the ZLG courses is created without ignoring the individuality of the courses. The ZLG "Train the Trainer"-Metacourse is concluded by the completion of the evaluation.

### *3.2. ZLG-Course "The Learning Healthcare System: How It Learns"*

The course, "Learning Healthcare System: How it Learns—Secondary Data Use of Clinical Data for Medical Research", is particularly structured by topics. Each topic deals with a self-contained subject area. The course structure and the course sequence are not related to temporal relationship but are determined by the topics that build on one another. The complexity of this course will not be successively increased, as it addresses society as a whole in particular. The course focuses primarily on explaining the basics and clarifying simple connections in the research area (Figure 4).

The course is supplemented by two synchronous meetings. There is one synchronous online meeting for the introduction to the course and one synchronous meeting for wrapping up the learned content. The majority of the learning content is provided asynchronously.

The first synchronous online meeting gives a brief introduction to the course and explains what the audience is about to discover in the following weeks. A case study of a patient is outlined for the participants to learn the context of the knowledge imparted.

| | | | | | | |
|---|---|---|---|---|---|---|
| Title | **The Learning Healthcare System: How It Learns - Secondary Data Use of Clinical Data for Medical Research** | | | | | |
| Content | In this course, participants learn in particular basic knowledge from the field of medical informatics. The participants are introduced to the basic challenges that are dealt with in research via a realistic case study. In addition to the basics of data processing and knowledge generation, participants learn how to conduct research with clinical data. | | | | | |
| Target Group | Interested public; students | | | | | |
| Learning Goals | * Participants will be able to distinguish between data, information and knowledge.<br>* Participants will be able to distinguish between different treatment pathways.<br>* Participants understand the process of knowledge discovery.<br>* Participants will understand the differences between factual knowledge and false claims.<br>* Participants will be able to understand the purpose of research with | | | | | |
| Other special features of the course | * The asynchronous online teaching is supplemented by two synchronous online appointments for introduction and completion.<br>* The intended target group is characterized by the greatest conceivable heterogeneity, as the entire society is to be addressed. | | | | | |
| Dimensions | Duration | Workload | Workload in synchronous Phase | Workload in asynchronous Phase | E-tivities | Learning Videos |
| Units | Weeks | Hours | Hours | Hours | Amount in total | Minutes |
| Data | 4 | 5 | 2 | 3 | 7 | 60 |

**Figure 4.** Course properties for ZLG-TP1 Course: "The Learning Healthcare System: How It Learns—Secondary Data Use of Clinical Data for Medical Research".

The following lesson covers the basics concerning data itself and teaches the differentiation between data, information, and knowledge. Additionally, different kinds of data are described, such as structured and unstructured data. Different E-tivities provide the possibility to discover different datasets to learn differences and gain practical insights.

The next lesson introduces the challenge of interoperability and proposes different solutions such as terminologies or classifications. To outline the different possibilities, participants learn basics about the benefits of using standards such as ICD, OPS, or SNOMED CT.

In order to establish an overall view, the last lesson summarizes the knowledge gained beforehand in a synchronous online meeting.

### *3.3. ZLG-Course "Patient-Oriented Sensor Systems in Nursing: Application and Outlook"*

The ZLG-Course Patient-oriented Sensor Systems in Nursing: Application and Outlook focuses on introducing participants to the principles of sensor technology, the possible application of this technology in healthcare, and the fundamentals of data processing and analytics.

High school students were selected as the target audience, thus forming a subset of the interested public. Participants have the choice of taking the course as individuals or as part of a group/class involving their teacher.

The course has therefore been designed to run either in parallel with school lessons, with a duration of five weeks, or as a block course with a duration of one week. The choice of different structuring can benefit participants with lower intrinsic motivation and less experience in self-guided learning (Figure 5).

The course content covers the basics of sensing, vital sign measurement, and the underlying IT technology. This knowledge provides a background for learning selected use cases of sensing in nursing. For each use case, a reference is provided to everyday sensor interaction.

Different types of sensors are covered. Among others, sensors for motion detection such as pedometers and vital sign measurements with electrocardiography or pulse oximetry are presented. In addition, sensors for the detection of environmental parameters, such as temperature, humidity, and fine dust measurement, are also discussed.

| | | | | | | |
|---|---|---|---|---|---|---|
| Title | **Patient-oriented Sensor Systems in Nursing: Application and Outlook** | | | | | |
| Content | In this course, participants learn the basics of sensor technology and biosignal acquisition. Furthermore, sensor systems known from everyday life and established in nursing (research) for the measurement of vital signs, movement detection and recording of movement parameters and their special features as well as the associated data evaluation will be learned. | | | | | |
| Target Group | High school students; interested public | | | | | |
| Learning Goals | * The participants get to know and internalize the basics of sensor technology.<br>* Get to know and internalize the basics of biosignal acquisition.<br>* Participants learn about types of sensor technology and their areas of application and learn to better assess future potentials, developments and obstacles. | | | | | |
| Other special features of the course | * The learning process is structured and guided by learning modules.<br>* Etivities include interactive elements in the learning management system. | | | | | |
| Dimensions | Duration | Workload | Workload in synchronous Phase | Workload in asynchronous Phase | E-tivities | Learning Videos |
| Units | Weeks | Hours | Hours | Hours | Amount in total | Minutes |
| Data | 5 | 10 | - | 10 | 6 | 15 |

**Figure 5.** Course properties for ZLG-TP2 Course: "Patient-oriented Sensor Systems in Nursing: Application and Outlook".

In addition, interactive elements, such as small tests and interactive videos, are offered alongside E-tivites and learning modules to ensure the achievement of the intended learning objectives. Optional E-tivities with advanced practical tasks allow highly motivated participants to gain hands-on experience in data analysis.

### *3.4. ZLG-Demonstrator 2: "Learning Health System in Action: Clinical Data Analytics"*

The course Learning Health System in Action: Clinical Data Analytics differs from the courses for the public in that it is a classic curricular approach. The course aims to support health professionals across disciplines, such as nursing, physiotherapy, and alike, in applying and understanding analytic data procedures used for clinical data. This topic is embedded in the broader paradigm of the Learning Health System, where clinical data analytics and clinical decision support play a major role. The participants receive three ECTs when they have successfully completed the course (Figure 6).

| | | | | | | |
|---|---|---|---|---|---|---|
| Title | **Learning Health System in Action: Clinical Data Analytics** | | | | | |
| Content | In this hands-on course, participants will learn how to apply data modeling to clinical data. We will demonstrate how statistical models are used to generate clinical knowledge and evidence. We will demonstrate the transfer of this knowledge into practice (practice-based evidence), particularly through predictive models in decision making. | | | | | |
| Target Group | We recommend participation for Master's or PhD students in health care and for professionals in nursing, physical therapy, midwifery, medicine and related fields. We also invite students from health management, health sciences, business, law, engineering, computer science, and computer science to take this interdisciplinary course. | | | | | |
| Learning Goals | * The participants learn about the concept of the Learning Health System.<br>* Participants will learn about evidence generation in the learning health system.<br>* Participants learn about the importance of clinical data for evidence generation in the learning health system.<br>* Participants will explore modeling methods for clinical data, such as logistic regression.<br>* Participants practice creating their own models with data. | | | | | |
| Other special features of the course | * Course language is English | | | | | |
| Dimensions | Duration | Workload | Workload in synchronous Phase | Workload in asynchronous Phase | E-tivities | Learning Videos |
| Units | Weeks | Hours | Hours | Hours | Amount in total | Minutes |
| Data | 5 | 50 | 10 | 40 | 8 | 330 |

**Figure 6.** Course properties for ZLG-TP3-Demonstrator 2: "Learning Health System in Action: Clinical Data Analytics".

The course is designed as a hybrid course, combining online educational resources and E-tivities with a synchronous session. As such, the course starts with a two-day kick-off session, followed by an online phase. The course ends with a final workshop.

The initial kick-off session is designed to introduce the course content, the students, and the learning platform. Furthermore, lectures are given to introduce the topic, i.e., the learning health system and the role of clinical data analytics therein. This kick-off session is then followed by a seven-week online course, in which each session is built on the previous in terms of content. The complexity of the content taught increases with each learning unit. The E-tivities during the online phase comprise tasks such as video lectures, completing quizzes, applying the acquired knowledge such as data analytic exercises, and peer-reviewing the co-students' work. The course closes with a synchronous workshop, in which the focus lies on applying required data analytic skills in teamwork. This task uses realistic scenarios and clinical problems. For example, students are asked to develop a simple clinical decision system and present this system to their peers. The course closes with the course evaluation based on the concept of the ZLG, which itself is part of improving the course content and organization.

## 4. Discussion

The development of the first courses has been completed. During the set-up phase, a variety of other medical informatics fields were identified that could be taught. Based on the course evaluations, we want to evolve the developed courses longitudinally and iteratively (cf. [12,13]). Furthermore, the feedback supports the future workplan in regards to creating new courses and content, especially to address the interested public, and thus advance the transfer of knowledge from research to society. For the first rollout steps of the courses, we could learn that an essential pillar of success is the widespread advertising of the course offerings.

For very heterogeneous target groups that represent the entire spectrum of society, an efficient advertising strategy is of great value. For this reason, it is important to use a wide variety of communication channels in the future. For example, it would make sense to link up with schools in order to generate enthusiasm for exciting topics of medical informatics at an early stage and thus promote young talents. Furthermore, we see great opportunities in opening up the didactic concept and thus connecting further ZDIN labs to our course offering in order to provide a broader portfolio of research topics for potential participants.

The didactic concept developed could already be used as a guideline for the development of the four courses presented. As presented in the results chapter, various courses could be developed using the concept. Although the resulting courses differ greatly from each other both in terms of the target groups addressed, and the depth of content of the topics covered, they are based on a recognizable substantiated didactic concept.

While the "Train the Trainer" course trains lecturers, in particular, the TP1 and TP2 courses address secondary school students and the interested public. However, as the development of demonstrator 2 shows, the didactic concept can also be used to create a curricular learning offer for students.

These course developments demonstrate the adaptability and scalability of the didactic concept. The methodology is also sufficiently general that it can also be used in a research area independent of our own. The development of courses in research fields outside of health care or medical informatics should be examined to prove this thesis.

The first run of the courses could already be carried out with some participants. The quantitative impact of the evaluation results is too low at the moment, but further adaptations of the courses will follow in order to expand and optimize the course content. However, the experiences had with the implementation of the evaluation have already shown that it can be useful to position surveys very prominently and, if necessary, make them a prerequisite for certification. We expect that the number of participants will continue to scale as the courses become more established and advertising increases.

## 5. Conclusions

The developed courses address complex and eHealth-specific topics such as interoperability or data management and analysis in the healthcare sector, and the evaluation of the courses is intended to reveal the extent to which the right didactic concepts have been found. We plan to iteratively evolve the existing E-Learning courses and build additional courses incorporating eHealth research in the Future Lab for Healthcare, as it has already been started with the first courses.

At the time of publication, the didactic concept is available in version 1.0. In the project plan of the ZLG, an experience-based revision of the concept is intended so that after the implementation of the courses for TP1 and TP2, the evaluations of the participants and the experiences of the lecturers will be included in the concept.

At this point in development, the current approach appears to be well suited to fulfill the requirements for the development of E-learning courses for heterogeneous target groups.

Our approach might be helpful for other online education projects. Course design outside our own professional discipline could assess the applicability of our concepts.

As the immediate idea, the development of learning programs in the expanded ZDIN could be tested by the other future labs. This would allow to test and evaluate the scalability to other disciplines and their target audiences. The learning platform for course development is already being used by both the ZLG and the HiGHmed teaching project; thus, the integration of further future labs would be easily possible.

As explained in the introduction, knowledge transfer, in general, is facing major challenges. E-Learning opportunities are not only becoming more relevant due to crises such as the COVID-19 pandemic or climate change, but also the relevance of digital competencies of the population is increasing. Data literacy and patient empowerment are important milestones on the road to a digitally educated society.

In this context, the fifth statement of the Expert Council of the German Federal Government on COVID-19 of 30.01.2022 [22] (See Supplementary Materials for a paraphrased translation or if no longer available online.) underlines the relevance of this topic. The experts emphasize that the loss of confidence in political decisions in the context of the management of the COVID-19 pandemic has increased sharply in recent months. They point to several problems and describe various aspects that increase the uncertainty of the population and thus provide room for misinformation and disinformation. Among other aspects, the experts highlight that the decision-relevant information should be translated into target group-specific language. With a focus on the informational fairness of different educational prerequisites, cultural and linguistic backgrounds, and age-dependent differences, it should be possible to adapt the information that is conveyed individually. For this purpose, the experts demand that the communicative content should be distributed via adequate channels, such as social media, e-health, or m-health offers. In addition, it makes sense to train different multipliers so that experts can offer competent knowledge transfer in direct contact with those affected. In summary, the experts state that sustainable communication structures should be established. An infrastructure for risk and health communication is a possibility to bundle existing competencies and push the translation of professional knowledge into a language that is appropriate for the target group.

The didactic concept introduced in this contribution demonstrates the feasibility of E-learning offerings for the general public. Through the use of LMS, insights and knowledge can be passed on to society. In this context, the developed concept makes it possible to use different target group-specific methods of communication across all disciplines. We are positive that the methods presented met the Expert Council's suggestions, at least to some extent [22]. Further work progress has a high potential to meet the above-described challenges.

Complementary to this, E-Learning offerings may be factors for health and safety, as in the COVID-19 pandemic, and for sustainability, through emission avoidance.

Experienced teachers repeatedly emphasize that the E-Learning practiced today cannot completely replace traditional face-to-face teaching. Since we communicate by more means than just language, the further development of "classic" E-Learning approaches in the sense of virtualized reality is more than desirable in order to enable communication and interaction with all senses.

**Supplementary Materials:** The following are available online at https://www.mdpi.com/article/10.3390/jpm12050696/s1, Statement S1: 2022-01-30-Fifth_Statement_Expert_Council_Federal_Government_En.pdf.

**Author Contributions:** Conceptualization, M.K. and S.V.; methodology, M.K. and S.V.; resources, J.H. and J.R.; writing—original draft preparation, M.K. and S.V.; writing—review and editing, O.J.B., M.K. and S.V.; supervision, O.J.B.; project administration, O.J.B. All authors have read and agreed to the published version of the manuscript.

**Funding:** This research was funded by Lower Saxony Ministry of Science and Culture under grant number ZN3491 within the Lower Saxony "Vorab" of the Volkswagen Foundation and supported by the Center for Digital Innovations (ZDIN). This submission was funded by the Library's Publications Fund at Hanover University of Applied Sciences and Arts.

**Institutional Review Board Statement:** Not applicable.

**Informed Consent Statement:** Not applicable.

**Acknowledgments:** We thank Ursula Hübner, Dagmar Krefting, Natalia Lesniewska, Johannes Hölken, Christoph Russmann and Marcus Wuttke for their support during the development of the ZLG-DCC. We also thank Bernd Blobel for his constructive feedback during the preparation of this contribution.

**Conflicts of Interest:** The authors declare no conflict of interest. The funders had no role in the writing of the manuscript, or in the decision to publish the results.

## References

1. Amir, L.R.; Tanti, I.; Maharani, D.A.; Wimardhani, Y.S.; Julia, V.; Sulijaya, B.; Puspitawati, R. Student perspective of classroom and distance learning during COVID-19 pandemic in the undergraduate dental study program Universitas Indonesia. *BMC Med. Educ.* **2020**, *20*, 392. [CrossRef] [PubMed]
2. Lynch, M. E-Learning during a global pandemic. *Asian J. Distance Educ.* **2020**, *15*, 189–195. [CrossRef]
3. Moscadelli, A.; Albora, G.; Biamonte, M.A.; Giorgetti, D.; Innocenzio, M.; Paoli, S.; Lorini, C.; Bonanni, P.; Bonaccorsi, G. Fake News and COVID-19 in Italy: Results of a Quantitative Observational Study. *Int. J. Environ. Res. Public Health* **2020**, *17*, 5850. [CrossRef] [PubMed]
4. Naeem, S.B.; Bhatti, R.; Khan, A. An exploration of how fake news is taking over social media and putting public health at risk. *Health Inf. Libr. J.* **2021**, *38*, 143–149. [CrossRef] [PubMed]
5. Pettersson, F. On the issues of digital competence in educational contexts—A review of literature. *Educ. Inf. Technol.* **2018**, *23*, 1005–1021. [CrossRef]
6. Calvillo, J.; Román, I.; Roa, L.M. How technology is empowering patients? A literature review. *Health Expect.* **2015**, *18*, 643–652. [CrossRef] [PubMed]
7. Vuorikari, R.; Punie, Y.; Carretero Gomez, S.; Van Den Brande, G. *DigComp 2.0: The Digital Competence Framework for Citizens. Update Phase 1: The Conceptual Reference Model*; Publications Office of the European Union: Luxembourg, 2016.
8. Meskó, B.; Drobni, Z.; Bényei, É.; Gergely, B.; Győrffy, Z. Digital health is a cultural transformation of traditional healthcare. *Mhealth* **2017**, *3*, 38. [CrossRef] [PubMed]
9. Katzensteiner, M.; Vogel, S.; Hüsers, J.; Richter, J.; Hölken, J.; Lesniewska, N.; Bott, O.J. Development of a Didactic Online Course Concept for Heterogeneous Audience Groups in the Context of Healthcare IT. *Stud. Health Technol. Inform.* **2021**, *285*, 219–224. [CrossRef] [PubMed]
10. Popplow, A. Auswahl einer Lernplattform für wissenschaftliche Weiterbildung. Digitalisierung und wissenschaftliche Weiterbildung. *Z. Hochsch. Und Weit.* **2018**, *1*, 60–67. [CrossRef]
11. Education.highmed.org [Internet]. HiGHmed Teaching and Training Programme for Medical Informatics. Available online: https://www.highmed.org/en/highmed-highmeducation (accessed on 28 February 2022).
12. Baldwin, S.J.; Trespalacios, J. Evaluation instruments and good practices in online education. *Online Learn.* **2017**, *21*, 2. [CrossRef]
13. Ghislandi, P.; Raffaghelli, J.E.; Sangrà, A.; Ritella, G. The Street Lamp Paradox: Analysing Students' Evaluation of Teaching through Qualitative and Quantitative Approaches. *J. Educ. Cult. Psychol. Stud.* **2020**, *21*, 65–85. [CrossRef]
14. Köhn-Ladenburger, C. *Marketing für LOHAS*; Springer Fachmedien Wiesbaden: Wiesbaden, Germany, 2013; pp. 12–21.

15. Barth, B.; Flaig, B.B.; Schäuble, N.; Tautscher, M. *Hrsg.: Praxis der Sinus-Milieus®: Gegenwart und Zukunft Eines Modernen Gesellschafts-und Zielgruppenmodells*; Springer: Wiesbaden, Germany, 2018. [CrossRef]
16. Salmon, G. *E-Moderating: The Key to Online Teaching and Learning Paperback*, 2nd ed.; Routledge: New York, NY, USA, 2013.
17. Salmon, G. *E-Moderating: The Key to Teaching and Learning Online*, 3rd ed.; Routledge: New York, NY, USA, 2011.
18. Salmon, G. *E-Tivities: The Key to Active Online Learning*; Routledge: New York, NY, USA, 2013.
19. gillysalmon.com [Internet]. The Five Stage Model. Available online: https://www.gillysalmon.com/five-stage-model.html (accessed on 28 February 2022).
20. Wenger, E. *Communities of Practice: Learning, Meaning, and Identity*; Cambridge University Press: Cambridge, UK, 1998.
21. Witte, M.L.; Behrends, M.; Benning, N.H.; Hoffmann, I.; Bott, O.J. The HiGHmed Didactical Framework for Online Learning Modules on Medical Informatics: First Experiences. *Stud. Health Technol. Inform.* **2020**, *272*, 163–166. [CrossRef] [PubMed]
22. Bundesregierung.de [Internet]. 5. Stellungnahme des ExpertInnenrates der Bundesregierung zu COVID-19. Available online: https://www.bundesregierung.de/resource/blob/997532/2002168/ea5301f932dafa791129440858746e0a/2022-01-30-fuenfte-stellungnahme-expertenrat-data.pdf (accessed on 28 February 2022).

Journal of Personalized Medicine

Article

# Comparative Analysis Between Individual, Centralized, and Federated Learning for Smartwatch Based Stress Detection

**Muhammad Ali Fauzi [1,*,†], Bian Yang [1,†] and Bernd Blobel [2,3,4]**

1 Department of Information Security and Communication Technology, Norwegian University of Science and Technology (NTNU), 2815 Gjøvik, Norway
2 Medical Faculty, University of Regensburg, 93053 Regensburg, Germany
3 eHealth Competence Center Bavaria, Deggendorf Institute of Technology, 94469 Deggendorf, Germany
4 First Medical Faculty, Charles University Prague, 12800 Prague, Czech Republic
* Correspondence: muhammad.a.fauzi@ntnu.no
† These authors contributed equally to this work.

**Abstract:** Machine learning has been proven to provide good performances on stress detection tasks using multi-modal sensor data from a smartwatch. Generally, machine learning techniques need a sufficient amount of data to train a robust model. Thus, we need to collect data from several users and send them to a central server to feed the algorithm. However, the uploaded data may contain sensitive information that can jeopardize the user's privacy. Federated learning can tackle this challenge by enabling the model to be trained using data from all users without the user's data leaving the user's device. In this study, we implement federated learning-based stress detection and provide a comparative analysis between individual, centralized, and federated learning. The experiment was conducted on WESAD dataset by using Logistic Regression as the classifier. The experiment results show that in terms of accuracy, federated learning cannot reach the performance level of both individual and centralized learning. The individual learning strategy performs best with an average accuracy of 0.9998 and an average $F_1$-measure of 0.9996.

**Keywords:** stress detection; privacy; individual learning; centralized learning; federated learning; smartwatch; machine learning

check for updates

**Citation:** Fauzi, M.A.; Yang, B.; Blobel, B. Comparative Analysis Between Individual, Centralized, and Federated Learning for Smartwatch Based Stress Detection. *J. Pers. Med.* **2022**, *12*, 1584. https://doi.org/10.3390/jpm12101584

Academic Editor: Shang-Ming Zhou

Received: 18 August 2022
Accepted: 20 September 2022
Published: 26 September 2022



## 1. Introduction

In today's busy world, stress has become an interesting issue in recent years, gaining awareness in many countries. Stress can be defined as a unique affective state that occurs when an individual considers that their perceived resources or ability cannot cope with the perceived demand of a stimulus [1]. The latest survey by Acas in 2019 [2] about stress and anxiety at work reported that about 66% of working people have experienced work-related stress in the last 12 months. Hospital employees, who in fact are very familiar with this issue, are also exposed to high levels of work-related stress [3–5].

Stress at a low level is acceptable or maybe even positive, also called eustress. However, prolonged stress can have a negative impact on our physical, mental, and emotional health. Many studies reported that stress has a significant impact on the development of hypertension and coronary artery disease, diabetes, asthma, etc. [6]. Moreover, excessive stress also harms the employee's productivity, increases absenteeism, and plays a crucial role in mental illness development, such as generalized anxiety disorder and depression [7]. According to studies, in the hospital setting for example, a higher stress level is significantly correlated with low patient safety [8,9]. Another study also suggested that a higher stress level of hospital staff results in riskier cybersecurity practices [10]. These studies are in line with a prior study [11], reporting that stressed people will be slow in learning something new and may choose less profitable decisions.

Monitoring an individual's stress level has many advantages. Knowing their own stress level can help them in staying aware and feeling more in control of their response to situations and knowing when it is time to relax or take some actions to treat it properly [12]. Furthermore, this monitoring can help to early diagnose mental illness and disorders. The most common way to assess a stress level is the use of questionnaires (e.g., Perceived Stress Scale [13], Perceived Stress Questionnaire [14], etc.). However, this method takes time, so it is not convenient to use every day for continuous monitoring. Another approach for determining stress levels is to measure stress-related physiological reactions using sensors. The smartwatch is one of the most suitable devices to perform this stress monitoring task, especially in the working environment. A smartwatch offers a number of built-in sensors that can be used for multimodal-based stress detection including blood volume pulse, electrodermal activity, skin temperature, accelerometer, etc. Unlike many wearable devices that have very low usability and are not convenient to wear during work (e.g., chest-worn devices, finger-placed galvanic skin response (GSR) sensors, etc.), the smartwatch is well known and has a high degree of social acceptance due to their ubiquity in everyday life [15,16].

There has been a remarkable success of machine learning (ML) technologies in empowering practical artificial intelligence (AI) applications, including in medical fields. Many prior studies have used multi-modal sensor data and machine learning methods to develop stress detection systems such as Decision Tree, K-Nearest Neighbors (KNN), Random Forest, and Logistic Regression [17–20]. Machine learning techniques generally need a sufficient amount of data for training to perform well. Therefore, to create a robust method, we need to collect sensor data from several users and collect them at a central server for processing. However, the uploaded medical data may contain individual privacy-related and sensitive information. Privacy breaches can happen if the central server is compromised. Furthermore, the leakage can also happen even when well-intentioned individuals, who have access to the server, share the data for legitimate purposes. As a result, a growing number of studies place attention on safeguarding private data in analysis processes. Federated learning (FL) can be the solution to this privacy challenge. FL works by allowing each data register to train models on separate, isolated datasets while only sharing the trained models, which do not contain any personal information. The registers then send their models to a central server for aggregating them to a single, integrated model. This process is repeated for a number of iterations until a high-quality model is produced. In this work, we implement FL-based stress detection and provide a comparative analysis between individual, centralized, and federated learning.

The remainder of this paper is organized as follows. The introduction part is given in Section 1. Dataset, features, learning strategies, and evaluation methods for the stress detection task are explained in Section 2. The results and discussion of this paper are described in Sections 3 and 4, while conclusions are provided in Section 5.

## 2. Materials and Methods

### 2.1. Dataset

A public dataset called WESAD (Wearable Stress and Affect Detection) [17] was used in this study. The dataset was created in the lab by the Ubiquitous Computing research group at the University of Siegen, Germany, and was made public in 2018. The data came from 15 participants consisting of 12 males and 3 females. The demographic information of the participants in this dataset is displayed in Table 1.

**Table 1.** Participants' demographic characteristics in the WESAD dataset (N = 15).

| Characteristic | Value, Mean (SD) |
|---|---|
| Age (years) | 27.5 (2.4) |
| Height (cm) | 177.6 (6.7) |
| Weight (kg) | 73.1 (10.3) |

The data in the WESAD study were acquired using an Empatica E4 smartwatch and a RespiBAN chest band at the same time during specified tasks designed to capture three different affective states: neutral, stress, and amusement. Only Empatica E4 data are used in this study because the focus of this work is on smartwatch sensors. The built-in sensors on the smartwatch are skin temperature ($ST$), accelerometers ($ACC$), electrodermal activity ($EDA$), and blood volume pulse sensors ($BVP$). Each individual had a data collection session of at least 36.5 min, which included the neutral position for approximately 20 min, the stress situation for 10 min, and the amusement situation for around 6.5 minutes. During the neutral position, the participants were sitting/standing and neutrally reading provided magazines. During the stress situation, the participants faced the Trier Social Stress Test (TSST) [21] to induce their stress, whereas during the amusement situation, the participants watched a set of funny video clips. The neutral and relaxation sessions were combined into one non-stress class for the stress detection task in this study so that the classification problem was binary (stress and non-stress).

### 2.2. Features

In this study, we employed all the sensors' data on the smartwatch including $ST$, $ACC$, $EDA$, and $BVP$. To extract the features, the signal data were segmented by using a 60-second sliding window with a sliding step of 0.25 s following the recommendation by Kreibig et al. [22]. Furthermore, we constructed 6 different signals for each sensor's data: the original signal; its first and second derivatives; and the transformed signal data using a Discrete Wavelet Transform (DWT) with the Haar wavelet at 3 different frequencies (1 Hz, 2 Hz, and 4 Hz). Wavelet transforms can catch both frequency and time information, while immediate changes in signals can be captured by the Haar wavelet [23]. For the $ACC$ data, in addition to the 3-dimensional signal data ($x$, $y$, and $z$-axis that are represented by $ACC_x$, $ACC_y$, and $ACC_z$, respectively), we also calculated their magnitude ($ACC_{norm}$) using Equation (1). In total, we have used signals consisting of 6 $ST$ signals, 24 $ACC$ signals, 6 $EDA$ signals, and 6 $BVP$ signals as displayed in Table 2. In the last step, we extracted 10 statistical features using BioSPPy and Numpy libraries [24] in Python as displayed in Table 3. In total, 420 features were analyzed for this study.

$$ACC_{norm} = \sqrt{ACC_x^2 + ACC_y^2 + ACC_z^2} \quad (1)$$

**Table 2.** Signal data used in this study.

| Sensor | Signal |
|---|---|
| Skin temperature ($ST$) | $ST$ original signal<br>$ST$ first derivative signal<br>$ST$ second derivative signal<br>$ST$ signal with DWT with the Haar wavelet at 4 Hz<br>$ST$ signal with DWT with the Haar wavelet at 2 Hz<br>$ST$ signal with DWT with the Haar wavelet at 1 Hz |
| Accelerometers ($ACC$) | $ACC_x$ original signal<br>$ACC_x$ first derivative signal<br>$ACC_x$ second derivative signal<br>$ACC_x$ signal with DWT with the Haar wavelet at 4 Hz<br>$ACC_x$ signal with DWT with the Haar wavelet at 2 Hz<br>$ACC_x$ signal with DWT with the Haar wavelet at 1 Hz<br>$ACC_y$ original signal<br>$ACC_y$ first derivative signal<br>$ACC_y$ second derivative signal<br>$ACC_y$ signal with DWT with the Haar wavelet at 4 Hz<br>$ACC_y$ signal with DWT with the Haar wavelet at 2 Hz<br>$ACC_y$ signal with DWT with the Haar wavelet at 1 Hz |

**Table 2.** *Cont.*

| Sensor | Signal |
|---|---|
| | $ACC_z$ original signal<br>$ACC_z$ first derivative signal<br>$ACC_z$ second derivative signal<br>$ACC_z$ signal with DWT with the Haar wavelet at 4 Hz<br>$ACC_z$ signal with DWT with the Haar wavelet at 2 Hz<br>$ACC_z$ signal with DWT with the Haar wavelet at 1 Hz<br>$ACC_{norm}$ original signal<br>$ACC_{norm}$ first derivative signal<br>$ACC_{norm}$ second derivative signal<br>$ACC_{norm}$ signal with DWT with the Haar wavelet at 4 Hz<br>$ACC_{norm}$ signal with DWT with the Haar wavelet at 2 Hz<br>$ACC_{norm}$ signal with DWT with the Haar wavelet at 1 Hz |
| Electrodermal activity ($EDA$) | $EDA$ original signal<br>$EDA$ first derivative signal<br>$EDA$ second derivative signal<br>$EDA$ signal with DWT with the Haar wavelet at 4 Hz<br>$EDA$ signal with DWT with the Haar wavelet at 2 Hz<br>$EDA$ signal with DWT with the Haar wavelet at 1 Hz |
| Blood volume pulse sensors ($BVP$) | $BVP$ original signal<br>$BVP$ first derivative signal<br>$BVP$ second derivative signal<br>$BVP$ signal with DWT and the Haar wavelet at 4 Hz<br>$BVP$ signal with DWT and the Haar wavelet at 2 Hz<br>$BVP$ signal with DWT and the Haar wavelet at 1 Hz |

**Table 3.** Statistical Features.

| No. | Features |
|---|---|
| 1 | Mean of the Signal |
| 2 | Minimum value of the signal |
| 4 | Maximum value of the signal |
| 4 | Median of the signal |
| 5 | Maximum signal amplitude |
| 6 | Signal variance |
| 7 | Standard signal deviation |
| 8 | Absolute signal deviation |
| 9 | Signal kurtosis |
| 10 | Signal skewness |

### 2.3. *Learning Strategies*

In this study, three learning strategies are compared: individual learning; centralized learning; and federated learning. All those learning strategies used Logistic Regression (LR) as the machine learning model. LR is selected due to its good performance in stress detection tasks [25–27]. LR also provides relatively low computational complexity, compared to Deep Neural Networks (DNN), for example. Thus, it does not need a device with high computational power. LR in this study is implemented using the Scikit-learn library [28].

#### 2.3.1. Individual Learning

In this scheme, each user had their own model. As displayed in Figure 1, the user's data never left their device. Using this scheme, the user's device captured the sensor data, extracted the features, and then trained their individual machine learning model using their own data. In the end, each user attained a model personalized for them. Since there are 15 participants, there have been 15 separate models for each participant in this study. Like the raw sensor data, this model never left the user's device and has never been shared with other users. The model will be used later on to detect the user's stress. To be noted, this learning strategy needs a device that has enough computational power to perform the feature extraction and model training tasks.

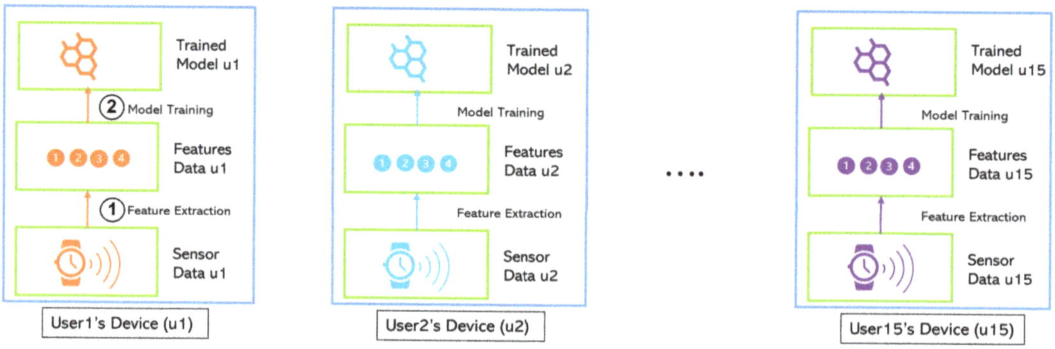


**Figure 1.** Individual Learning Scheme.

This scheme offers a very high level of privacy because no data or model left the user's device. Unlike the two other schemes, individual learning does not need a central server to combine the data or model, so it can minimize the cost. However, it prevents information sharing across users that generally can improve the performance of a machine learning model. In addition, if there is a new user, they cannot use the stress detection system right after the registration. The new user must collect their own stress data to train their individual model.

### 2.3.2. Centralized Learning

In this scheme, we only have a single integrated model. Unlike individual learning, this learning strategy needs a central server to combine the data and train the integrated model. As shown in Figure 2, each user's device captures the sensor data and then sends the raw data to the central server. Thereafter, the central server combines all the data from all users, extracts the features, and then trains a machine learning model using the combined data. As result, a single integrated model is created. This model is then sent to each user's device and is used later to detect the user's stress. Since the feature extraction and model training tasks are conducted on the central server side, this learning strategy does not need a device with high computational power. The user device only needs to do the stress detection/inference task using the model. Depending on the size of the dataset, training often takes several hours or more to complete. This stage of the process demands the greatest CPU or GPU power. The inference task on the other hand usually needs far less computing power than the training task. To minimize the computing power needed on the user's device, the integrated model in this scheme can be stored on the server. When the user needs to perform the inference task on new data, the device can send the data to the server, and the server will detect the stress level of the data using the model and send the result back. However, this strategy requires the user's device to be always online. If the integrated model is saved on each user's device, the user's device does not need to be online to predict the stress level.

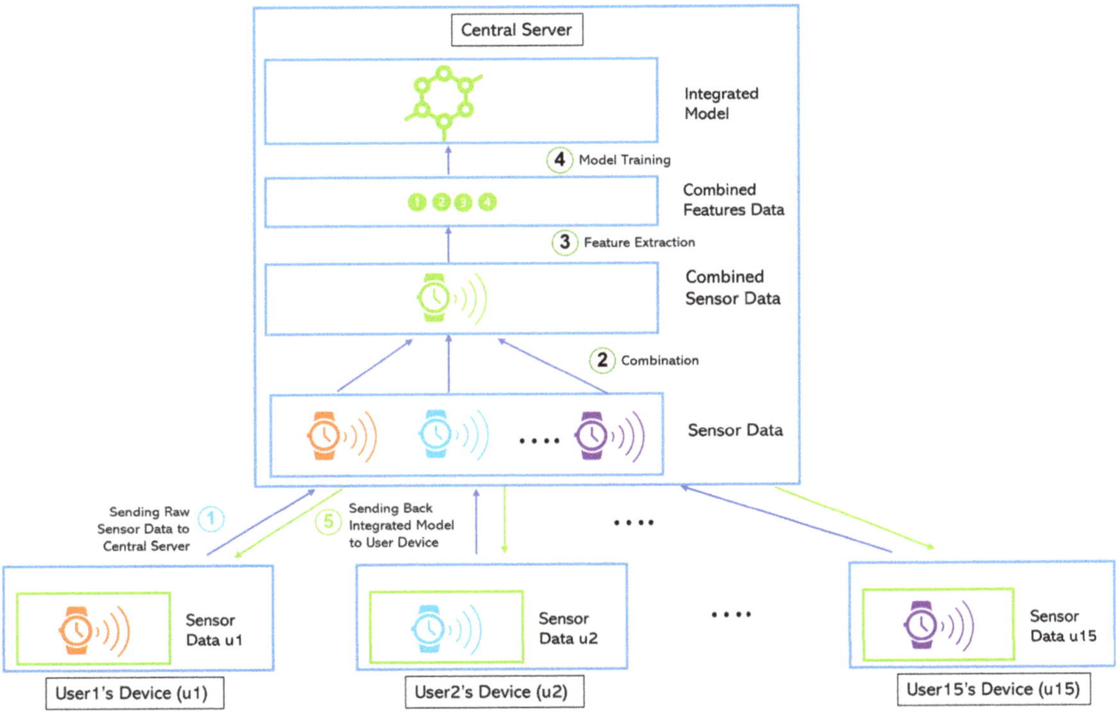


**Figure 2.** Centralized Learning Scheme.

This scheme offers a very low level of privacy because the user data leaves her/his device. This is sensitive data that can be used to disclose users' personal information and their health status. However, it enables information sharing across users that generally can increase the robustness of a machine learning model. The other advantage of using this scheme is that a new user can use the stress detection system right after the registration by deploying the integrated model. The new user does not need to collect their own stress data and do the data labeling.

### 2.3.3. Federated Learning (FL)

As displayed in Figure 3, the federated learning scheme is similar to centralized learning in terms of needing a central server and having just a single integrated model. The main difference between centralized and federated learning is that the user's data will never leave the user's device in federated learning, that way maintaining the user's privacy. Federated learning in this study is implemented using Flower [29] with FederatedAveraging (FedAvg) aggregation strategy [30].

Stress data from sensors contain sensitive information that can be used to disclose users' personal information and their health status. Therefore, the stress detection system needs to give more attention to privacy concerns. In Europe, the General Data Protection Regulation (GDPR) protects the users' privacy by limiting the exchange of sensitive data [31]. On the other hand, the use of sensor data has many potential benefits. Therefore, a new family of privacy-preserving technologies is emerging to solve this problem. The goal of privacy-preserving technologies is to make the most of the data without jeopardizing users' privacy. This technology employs strategies to reduce the amount of personal data held while maintaining the analysis operation. Several privacy-preserving methods have been proposed, and one of the techniques with high potential is Federated Learning.

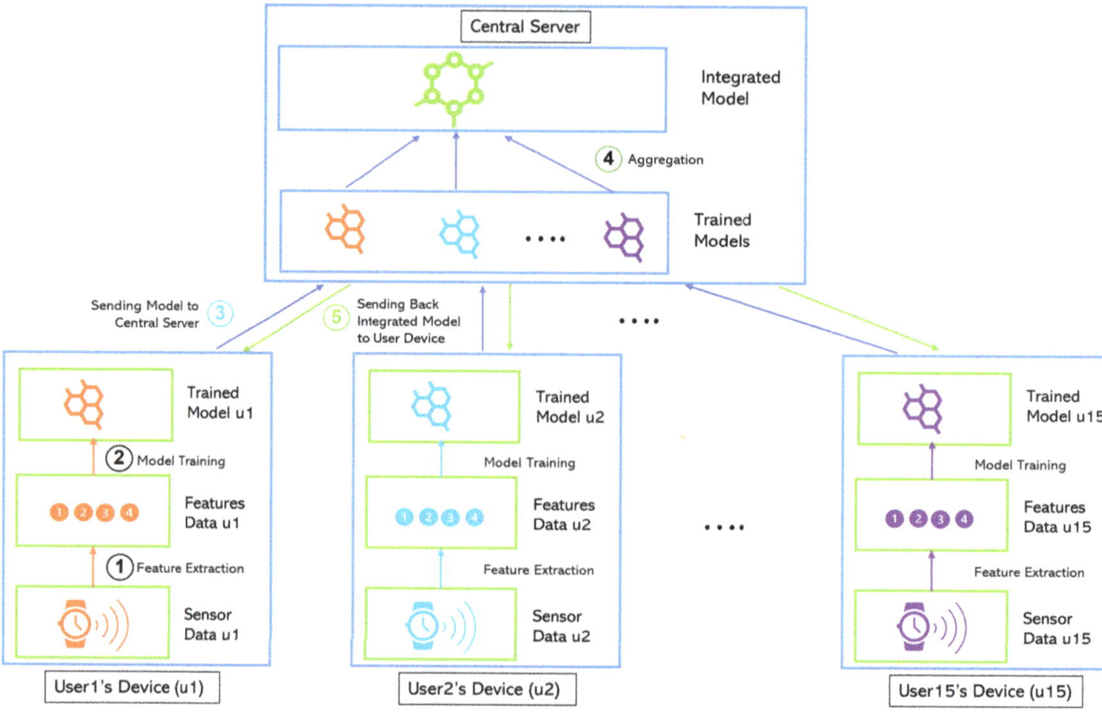


**Figure 3.** Federated Learning Scheme.

Federated learning is a learning paradigm that aims to solve the problem of data privacy by collectively training algorithms without transferring data [30]. It has recently acquired popularity in healthcare applications [32,33]. FL allows for collaboratively using datasets without transferring the raw patient data outside of the institutions' databases. As shown in Figure 3, each user's device captures the sensor data and extracts the features. Furthermore, the machine learning model is trained locally on each user's device. Next, the trained model is uploaded to the central server so that the central server can combine all the models and share the integrated model with each user's device. This model will be used later to infer the user's stress level. Some works show that models trained by FL can obtain performance levels comparable to those trained on centrally hosted data sets and exceeds models that only see isolated single-device data [34]. Successful implementation of FL could have a huge impact on enabling large-scale precision medicine, resulting in unbiased models while also respecting privacy issues [32]. To be noted, this learning strategy needs a device that has enough computational power to do the feature extraction and local model training tasks.

The federated learning scheme offers a very high level of privacy, because no data is leaving the user's device. This scheme also enables information sharing across users that generally can improve the robustness of a machine learning model. In addition, if there is a new user, she/he can use the stress detection system right after the registration by using the integrated model without doing data collection first.

### 2.4. Evaluation

In this study, each data set is divided into two parts: training and testing data with a split ratio of 80:20. All the strategies use the training data for model training and testing data to evaluate the model performance. Several measurements including Accuracy ($Acc$), Precision ($P$), Recall ($R$), and $F_1$-measure ($F_1$) were deployed for classifier performance evaluation. All measurements were calculated based on the confusion matrix displayed in Figure 4. True Positive ($TP$) and True Negative ($TN$) are the numbers of data that were correctly predicted. $TP$ represents the number of stress data that were correctly predicted as stress, while $TN$ represents the number of non-stress data that were correctly predicted as non-stress. Meanwhile, False Positive ($FP$), often called Type I Error, is the number of non-stress data that were incorrectly predicted as stress data, and False Negative ($FN$) or Type II Error represents the number of stress data that were incorrectly predicted as non-stress data.

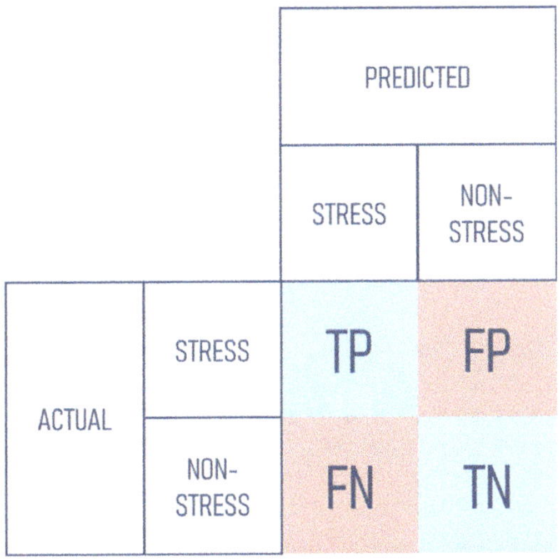


**Figure 4.** Confusion Matrix. Blue square means the data are correctly predicted while red square means the data are incorrectly predicted.

The formulas for all measurements are displayed in Equations (2)–(5) respectively.

$$Acc = \frac{TP + TN}{TP + FP + FN + TN} \quad (2)$$

$$P = \frac{TP}{TP + FP} \quad (3)$$

$$R = \frac{TP}{TP + FN} \quad (4)$$

$$F_1 = 2\frac{P \cdot R}{P + R} \quad (5)$$

## 3. Results

The results of stress detection using individual learning, centralized learning, and federated learning are presented in Tables 4–6. The experimental results show that individual learning is the most appropriate strategy for this task by obtaining an almost perfect performance with an average accuracy of 0.9998, an average precision of 0.9996, an average recall of 0.9996, and an average $F_1$-measure of 0.9996. All individual models of the participants achieved 100% accuracy and $F_1$-measure. Even the poorest individual model provided an accuracy of 0.9970 and $F_1$-measure of 0.9951, which can still be considered almost perfect.

**Table 4.** Individual Learning Result.

| Participant | Acc | P | R | $F_1$ |
|---|---|---|---|---|
| 1 | 1.0000 | 1.0000 | 1.0000 | 1.0000 |
| 2 | 1.0000 | 1.0000 | 1.0000 | 1.0000 |
| 3 | 1.0000 | 1.0000 | 1.0000 | 1.0000 |
| 4 | 1.0000 | 1.0000 | 1.0000 | 1.0000 |
| 5 | 1.0000 | 1.0000 | 1.0000 | 1.0000 |
| 6 | 1.0000 | 1.0000 | 1.0000 | 1.0000 |
| 7 | 1.0000 | 1.0000 | 1.0000 | 1.0000 |
| 8 | 1.0000 | 1.0000 | 1.0000 | 1.0000 |
| 9 | 1.0000 | 1.0000 | 1.0000 | 1.0000 |
| 10 | 1.0000 | 1.0000 | 1.0000 | 1.0000 |
| 11 | 1.0000 | 1.0000 | 1.0000 | 1.0000 |
| 12 | 0.9994 | 0.9980 | 1.0000 | 0.9990 |
| 13 | 0.9970 | 0.9960 | 0.9941 | 0.9951 |
| 14 | 1.0000 | 1.0000 | 1.0000 | 1.0000 |
| 15 | 1.0000 | 1.0000 | 1.0000 | 1.0000 |
| **Average** | **0.9998** | **0.9996** | **0.9996** | **0.9996** |

Meanwhile, centralized learning had also a good performance with an average accuracy of 0.9355, an average precision of 0.9125, an average recall of 0.8698, and an average $F_1$-measure of 0.8783. The single integrated model from the centralized learning is excellent for inferring the stress level of most of the participants. The model achieved an accuracy below 0.9 just for three participants' data (participant 5, 8, and 13). In terms of $F_1$-measure, the model achieved a value below 0.9 for six participants' data. The model best performed on the data of participant 10 with an accuracy of 0.9957, precision of 0.9880, recall of 0.9980, and $F_1$-measure of 0.9930. In contrast, the worst result was gathered when detecting the stress level of participant 8 with an accuracy of 0.8545, precision of 0.9674, recall of 0.4771, and $F_1$-measure of 0.6390.

Based on Table 6, federated learning had a relatively mediocre performance for the stress detection tasks in this study. It obtained an average accuracy of 0.8575, an average precision of 0.9892, an average recall of 0.5208, and an average of $F_1$-measure of 0.6339. The integrated model from federated learning performed quite well on most of the participants' data but performed very poorly on the data of some participants. This model achieved an $F_1$-measure below 0.5 for 5 participants (participant 2, 4, 8, 9, and 13). The integrated model achieved the best result on the data of participant 3 with an accuracy of 0.9969, precision of 1.0000, recall of 0.9887, and $F_1$-measure of 0.9943. On the contrary, the model performs the worst inferring the stress level of participant 4, with an accuracy of 0.7259, precision of 1.0000, recall of 0.0589, and $F_1$-measure of 0.1113.

The study results suggest that the individual model achieved the best stress detection performance. This scheme outperformed both centralized learning and federated learning because it offers personalization by training the model separately for each user, using the user's own data. The WESAD dataset labels the data based on the stimulus given to the participants. All the data recorded during the neutral and amusement condition, where the participants were reading magazines and watching funny videos, were labeled as non-stress, whereas all of the data recorded during the TSST session were labeled as stress. Different individuals will react to the stressors with varying intensity or duration [35]. Therefore, the personalized approach like the individual learning model surpasses the integrated model provided by centralized learning and federated learning. The integrated model aims at building a single model for all, so that it cannot adjust for each user.

**Table 5.** Centralized Learning Result.

| Participant | Acc | P | R | $F_1$ |
|---|---|---|---|---|
| 1 | 0.9414 | 0.8250 | 1.0000 | 0.9041 |
| 2 | 0.9317 | 0.9809 | 0.7809 | 0.8696 |
| 3 | 0.9660 | 0.8916 | 1.0000 | 0.9427 |
| 4 | 0.9571 | 0.8716 | 1.0000 | 0.9314 |
| 5 | 0.8833 | 0.9658 | 0.5853 | 0.7288 |
| 6 | 0.9511 | 0.8726 | 0.9720 | 0.9196 |
| 7 | 0.9772 | 0.9827 | 0.9401 | 0.9609 |
| 8 | 0.8545 | 0.9674 | 0.4771 | 0.6390 |
| 9 | 0.9244 | 1.0000 | 0.7495 | 0.8568 |
| 10 | 0.9957 | 0.9880 | 0.9980 | 0.9930 |
| 11 | 0.9475 | 0.8540 | 0.9851 | 0.9149 |
| 12 | 0.9353 | 0.8812 | 0.9127 | 0.8967 |
| 13 | 0.8837 | 0.8575 | 0.7475 | 0.7987 |
| 14 | 0.9437 | 0.8400 | 1.0000 | 0.9130 |
| 15 | 0.9404 | 0.9098 | 0.8994 | 0.9046 |
| **Average** | **0.9355** | **0.9125** | **0.8698** | **0.8783** |

**Table 6.** Federated Learning Result.

| Participant | Acc | P | R | $F_1$ |
|---|---|---|---|---|
| 1 | 0.9131 | 0.8675 | 0.8089 | 0.8372 |
| 2 | 0.7565 | 0.9872 | 0.1670 | 0.2857 |
| 3 | 0.9969 | 1.0000 | 0.9887 | 0.9943 |
| 4 | 0.7259 | 1.0000 | 0.0589 | 0.1113 |
| 5 | 0.8511 | 1.0000 | 0.4447 | 0.6156 |
| 6 | 0.8700 | 1.0000 | 0.5484 | 0.7083 |
| 7 | 0.8578 | 1.0000 | 0.5227 | 0.6866 |
| 8 | 0.7796 | 1.0000 | 0.1835 | 0.3101 |
| 9 | 0.7820 | 1.0000 | 0.2781 | 0.4352 |
| 10 | 0.9390 | 0.9950 | 0.8016 | 0.8879 |
| 11 | 0.9524 | 1.0000 | 0.8337 | 0.9093 |
| 12 | 0.9097 | 0.9917 | 0.7123 | 0.8291 |
| 13 | 0.7620 | 1.0000 | 0.2288 | 0.3724 |
| 14 | 0.8880 | 0.9967 | 0.6232 | 0.7669 |
| 15 | 0.8778 | 1.0000 | 0.6110 | 0.7585 |
| **Average** | **0.8575** | **0.9892** | **0.5208** | **0.6339** |

These results also demonstrate that some models achieved quite good accuracy on some participants, but had a very poor $F_1$-measure. To be noted, the stress dataset used in this study is imbalanced. It has more non-stress data than stress data. Therefore, accuracy is not good enough to be used as the evaluation measure. We need to perform the evaluation using precision, recall, and $F_1$-measure. High accuracy means that the model can well predict the class. However, it is important to mention that accuracy is based on True Positive ($TP$) and True Negative ($TN$). In an imbalanced dataset where the number of non-stress data is higher than stress data, high accuracy may be achieved because the value of $TN$ is very high even though the value of $TP$ is very low. As an extreme example, if we have 100 testing data containing 90 non-stress data and 10 stress data and the model predicts all of the testing data as non-stress, the model will still get very good accuracy with 0.9. In this example, the model gets 90 TN and 0 TP. This model is actually not good because it cannot predict any stress data even though the accuracy is very high. In contrast with accuracy, the $F_1$-measure of this model will be very low. Picking an example from the experimental result, the integrated model from federated learning applied to participant

4's data achieved an accuracy of 0.7259, precision of 1.0000, recall of 0.0589, and $F_1$-measure of 0.1113. The low recall with high precision means that the data predicted as stress by the model are very few, but most of the predicted labels are correct. In other words, this model mostly predicts the data as non-stress so that the $TN$ value is very high, resulting in a high-value accuracy even though the $TP$ value is very low because only a small amount of data were predicted as stress. In contrast with the accuracy, the $F_1$-measure of this model is very low. Therefore, in an imbalanced dataset, $F_1$-measure is a better measurement than accuracy.

## 4. Discussion

This paper discusses the comparison of individual learning, centralized learning, and federated learning on the WESAD stress detection dataset. Generally, more data will make the machine learning model better and more accurate, because the more information we give to the model, the more it will learn and the more cases it will be able to correctly infer [36]. Therefore, integrated models such as centralized and federated learning are expected to be more accurate than individual learning. Surprisingly, the individual model surpasses in this study both the centralized and the federated learning as depicted in Figure 5. The WESAD dataset labels the data based on the stimulus given to the participants. Different participants may react differently to each stimulus. In this case, the personalized approach such as the individual learning model can adjust the model to the user's behavior. The integrated model aims at building a single model for all so that it cannot adjust for each user. This study outcome is in line with another study about stress detection that also reported that a personalized model outperformed an integrated model [37].

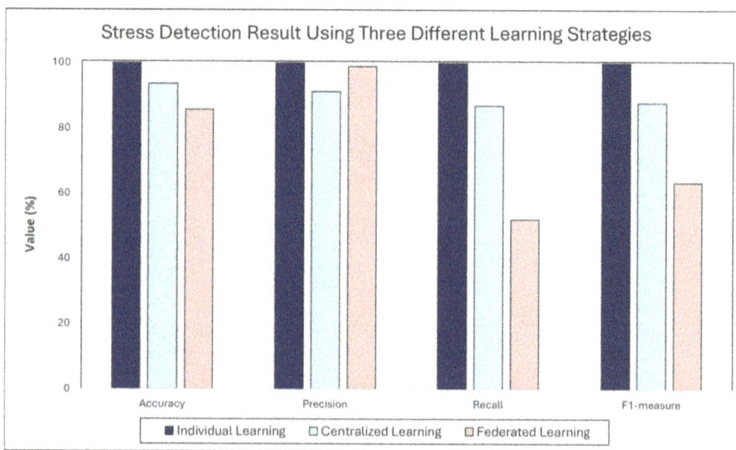


**Figure 5.** Stress Detection Results Using Three Different Learning Strategies.

Generally, federated learning is expected to perform worse than centralized learning. It is because centralized learning has direct access to all data while federated learning train the model locally and only communicates an updated model to a central server [38]. Surprisingly, the performance difference between the two strategies is very big. A more complex model such as Deep Neural Network (DNN) is needed to build a better federated learning model. Some previous work shows that federated learning with DNN can obtain performance levels comparable to those models trained using a centralized learning scheme [37,38]. Another study also suggested that less complex models perform worse than more complex models in federated learning [39]. However, a more complex model requires the user's device to have a higher computational power to train the model. Additionally, a more complex model will also lead to higher communication costs between the user's device and the central server. Thus, there will be a challenge to use a complex model for communication-sensitive applications [39].

Furthermore, since the WESAD dataset in this study is labeled based on the stimulus, there may be the possibility that the labels do not represent the participants' actual stress levels. For example, during the TSST situation, there is the possibility that the participant was not feeling stressed (e.g., because they are good at public speaking) but all their gathered data during that session will be labeled as stress. Another issue could be that a participant was feeling stressed while watching the funny videos, because it reminded them of some traumatic events, for example, but all of their data during that session will be labeled as non-stress. Therefore, it will be of interest to see the comparison between the personalized and the integrated model on the stress dataset that is labeled based on the user's subjective stress level measurement. In addition, the WESAD data collection was conducted in one session, which will make the data very similar. Thus, it is also of interest to see the comparison on the stress dataset, that is collected on multiple sessions to see how the model can perform across sessions.

Another factor that can also be considered is the usability of the three learning schemes for a new user. For centralized and federated learning, the new users can use the integrated model to predict their stress level right after the registration. For individual learning, however, the user must collect training data first. The users should record their data using the smartwatch during stress and non-stress condition. The users must also give the correct label to the data because the quality of the model heavily depends on the training data quality. This training data is used to train the personalized model for the users before they can infer their stress level automatically.

In addition, the computational cost is also different between these three schemes. Individual learning demands that a user's device has enough computing power for feature extraction, model training, and stress detection tasks. Meanwhile, centralized learning requires less computing power for a user's device, because all of the processes can be done on the central server. However, the device has to be always online since the device has to send the data to the central server. Federated learning needs a user's device that has enough computing power to do the local training as well as a communication channel to exchange data between the device and the centralized server.

Finally, stress data are considered sensitive as they can be used to disclose the user's health status. Based on a study on health data privacy, most of the interview subjects are worried about their data privacy on an individual level [40]. Therefore, the processing of this kind of data needs to pay more attention to privacy concerns. In centralized learning, all the data are collected on a centralized server. When these data are shared with the central server, privacy leaks can occur if the central server is compromised. Therefore, centralized learning can jeopardize users' privacy. On the contrary, individual and federated learning strategies offer a high level of privacy. In federated learning, only the learning model, and no raw user data, is processed centrally. Meanwhile, individual learning provides a higher level of privacy as it does not require any user data or model to leave the user's device.

## 5. Conclusions

In this study, the comparison between individual, centralized, and federated learning for smartwatch-based stress detection is discussed. In terms of accuracy, the individual learning strategy beats both centralized learning and federated learning. This is quite reasonable because different participants may react differently to stressors, so a personalized model is needed. The integrated model aims to build a single model for all so that it cannot adjust for each user. In terms of privacy, centralized learning requires all of the data to be shared with a centralized server. There is a risk of privacy breach, when the central server got compromised. In contrast, the individual learning strategy offers a very high level of privacy, since it does not require any user data or model to leave the user's device. Federated learning also offers a high level of privacy, since only the learned model, and no raw user data, is processed in the central server. The only disadvantage of individual learning is the low usability for a new user. For centralized and federated learning, the new users can use the integrated model to infer their stress level right after the registration. In contrast, for individual learning, the users must collect training data first to build the personalized model.

In future work, a more complex model such as DNN can be used to improve the federated learning scheme performance. In addition, it will be interesting to see the comparison between individual learning, centralized, and federated learning on the stress dataset that is labeled based on the user's subjective stress level measurement and collected on multi sessions, instead of only a single session.

**Author Contributions:** Conceptualization, B.Y. and M.A.F.; methodology, B.Y. and M.A.F.; software, M.A.F.; validation, M.A.F., B.Y. and B.B.; formal analysis, M.A.F.; investigation, M.A.F.; resources, B.Y. and M.A.F.; data curation, M.A.F.; writing—original draft preparation, M.A.F.; writing—review and editing, M.A.F., B.Y. and B.B.; visualization, M.A.F., B.Y. and B.B.; supervision, B.Y. and B.B.; project administration, M.A.F.; funding acquisition, B.Y. All authors have read and agreed to the published version of the manuscript.

**Funding:** This research received no external funding.

**Institutional Review Board Statement:** Not applicable.

**Informed Consent Statement:** Not applicable.

**Data Availability Statement:** The source code for individual, centralized, and federated learning in this paper can be found at https://github.com/cahkanor/WESAD-Stress-Detection-Logistic-Regression, (accessed on 17 August 2022).

**Acknowledgments:** This work is financially supported by The e-Health and Welfare Security (e-HWS) research group, Centre for Cyber and Information Security at the Norwegian University of Science and Technology (NTNU CCIS).

**Conflicts of Interest:** The authors declare no conflict of interest.

## Abbreviations

The following abbreviations are used in this manuscript:

| | |
|---|---|
| ML | Machine Learning |
| AI | Artificial Intelligence |
| KNN | K-Nearest Neighbors |
| FL | Federated learning |
| LR | Logistic Regression |
| DNN | Deep Neural Networks |
| FedAvg | Federated Averaging |
| DWT | Discrete Wavelet Transform |
| WESAD | Wearable Stress and Affect Detection |
| $ST$ | Skin temperature |
| $ACC$ | Accelerometers |
| $BVP$ | Blood Volume Pulse |
| $EDA$ | Electrodermal Activity |
| GSR | Galvanic Skin Response |
| TSST | Trier Social Stress Test |
| CPU | Central Processing Unit |
| GPU | Graphics Processing Unit |

| | |
|---|---|
| GDPR | General Data Protection Regulation |
| *Acc* | Accuracy |
| *P* | Precision |
| *R* | Recall |
| *TP* | True Positive |
| *TN* | True Negative |
| *FP* | False Positive |
| *FN* | False Negative |

## References


1. Lazarus, R.S.; Folkman, S. *Stress, Appraisal, and Coping*; Springer Publishing Company: New York, NY, USA, 1984.
2. Wakeling, A. *Stress and Anxiety at Work: Personal or Cultural?* ACAS: London, UK, 2019.
3. Marine, A.; Ruotsalainen, J.H.; Serra, C.; Verbeek, J.H. Preventing occupational stress in healthcare workers. *Cochrane Database Syst. Rev.* **2006**, *4*, 1–31.
4. Weinberg, A.; Creed, F. Stress and psychiatric disorder in healthcare professionals and hospital staff. *Lancet* **2000**, *355*, 533–537. [CrossRef]
5. Aasland, O.G.; Olff, M.; Falkum, E.; Schweder, T.; Ursin, H. Health complaints and job stress in Norwegian physicians: The use of an overlapping questionnaire design. *Soc. Sci. Med.* **1997**, *45*, 1615–1629. [CrossRef]
6. Pickering, T.G. Mental stress as a causal factor in the development of hypertension and cardiovascular disease. *Curr. Hypertens. Rep.* **2001**, *3*, 249–254. [CrossRef] [PubMed]
7. Wang, Y.; Chen, R.; Zhang, L. Reliability and validity of generalized anxiety scale-7 in inpatients in Chinese general hospital. *J. Clin. Psychiatr.* **2018**, *28*, 168–171.
8. Welp, A.; Meier, L.L.; Manser, T. Emotional exhaustion and workload predict clinician-rated and objective patient safety. *Front. Psychol.* **2015**, *5*, 1573. [CrossRef] [PubMed]
9. Tsiga, E.; Panagopoulou, E.; Montgomery, A. Examining the link between burnout and medical error: A checklist approach. *Burn. Res.* **2017**, *6*, 1–8. [CrossRef]
10. Fauzi, M.A.; Yeng, P.; Yang, B.; Rachmayani, D. Examining the Link Between Stress Level and Cybersecurity Practices of Hospital Staff in Indonesia. In Proceedings of the The 16th International Conference on Availability, Reliability and Security, Vienna, Austria, 17–20 August 2021; pp. 1–8.
11. Wemm, S.E.; Wulfert, E. Effects of acute stress on decision making. *Appl. Psychophysiol. Biofeedback* **2017**, *42*, 1–12. [CrossRef] [PubMed]
12. Liao, W.; Zhang, W.; Zhu, Z.; Ji, Q. A real-time human stress monitoring system using dynamic Bayesian network. In Proceedings of the 2005 IEEE Computer Society Conference on Computer Vision and Pattern Recognition (CVPR'05)-workshops, San Diego, CA, USA, 21–23 September 2005; p. 70.
13. Cohen, S.; Kamarck, T.; Mermelstein, R. Perceived stress scale (PSS). *J. Health Soc. Behav.* **1983**, *24*, 285.
14. Levenstein, S.; Prantera, C.; Varvo, V.; Scribano, M.L.; Berto, E.; Luzi, C.; Andreoli, A. Development of the Perceived Stress Questionnaire: A new tool for psychosomatic research. *J. Psychosom. Res.* **1993**, *37*, 19–32. [CrossRef]
15. Spagnolli, A.; Guardigli, E.; Orso, V.; Varotto, A.; Gamberini, L. Measuring user acceptance of wearable symbiotic devices: Validation study across application scenarios. In *International Workshop on Symbiotic Interaction*; Springer: Berlin/Heidelberg, Germany, 2015; pp. 87–98.
16. Lazaro, M.J.S.; Lim, J.; Kim, S.H.; Yun, M.H. Wearable technologies: Acceptance model for smartwatch adoption among older adults. In *International Conference on Human-Computer Interaction*; Springer: Berlin/Heidelberg, Germany, 2020; pp. 303–315.
17. Schmidt, P.; Reiss, A.; Duerichen, R.; Marberger, C.; Van Laerhoven, K. Introducing wesad, a multimodal dataset for wearable stress and affect detection. In Proceedings of the 20th ACM international conference on multimodal interaction, Boulder, CO, USA, 16–20 October 2018; pp. 400–408.
18. Garg, P.; Santhosh, J.; Dengel, A.; Ishimaru, S. Stress Detection by Machine Learning and Wearable Sensors. In Proceedings of the 26th International Conference on Intelligent User Interfaces, College Station, TX, USA, 14–17 April 2021; pp. 43–45.
19. Indikawati, F.I.; Winiarti, S. Stress detection from multimodal wearable sensor data. In Proceedings of the IOP Conference Series: Materials Science and Engineering, Yogyakarta, Indonesia, 16 November 2019; IOP Publishing: Bristol, UK, 2020; Volume 771, p. 012028.
20. Siirtola, P. Continuous stress detection using the sensors of commercial smartwatch. In Proceedings of the Adjunct Proceedings of the 2019 ACM International Joint Conference on Pervasive and Ubiquitous Computing and Proceedings of the 2019 ACM International Symposium on Wearable Computers, London, UK, 9–13 September 2019; pp. 1198–1201.
21. Kirschbaum, C.; Pirke, K.M.; Hellhammer, D.H. The 'Trier Social Stress Test'—A tool for investigating psychobiological stress responses in a laboratory setting. *Neuropsychobiology* **1993**, *28*, 76–81. [CrossRef] [PubMed]
22. Kreibig, S.D. Autonomic nervous system activity in emotion: A review. *Biol. Psychol.* **2010**, *84*, 394–421. [CrossRef]
23. Zhang, Y.; Haghdan, M.; Xu, K.S. Unsupervised motion artifact detection in wrist-measured electrodermal activity data. In Proceedings of the 2017 ACM International Symposium on Wearable Computers, Maui, HI, USA, 11–15 September 2017; pp. 54–57.

24. Harris, C.R.; Millman, K.J.; Van Der Walt, S.J.; Gommers, R.; Virtanen, P.; Cournapeau, D.; Wieser, E.; Taylor, J.; Berg, S.; Smith, N.J.; et al. Array programming with NumPy. *Nature* **2020**, *585*, 357–362. [CrossRef]
25. Fauzi, M.A.; Yang, B. Continuous Stress Detection of Hospital Staff Using Smartwatch Sensors and Classifier Ensemble. In *pHealth 2021*; IOS Press: Amsterdam, The Netherlands, 2021; pp. 245–250.
26. Kurniawan, H.; Maslov, A.V.; Pechenizkiy, M. Stress detection from speech and galvanic skin response signals. In Proceedings of the 26th IEEE International Symposium on Computer-Based Medical Systems, Porto, Portugal, 20–22 June 2013; pp. 209–214.
27. Zubair, M.; Yoon, C.; Kim, H.; Kim, J.; Kim, J. Smart wearable band for stress detection. In Proceedings of the 2015 5th International Conference on IT Convergence and Security (ICITCS), Kuala Lumpur, Malaysia, 24–27 August 2015; pp. 1–4.
28. Pedregosa, F.; Varoquaux, G.; Gramfort, A.; Michel, V.; Thirion, B.; Grisel, O.; Blondel, M.; Prettenhofer, P.; Weiss, R.; Dubourg, V.; et al. Scikit-learn: Machine Learning in Python. *J. Mach. Learn. Res.* **2011**, *12*, 2825–2830.
29. Beutel, D.J.; Topal, T.; Mathur, A.; Qiu, X.; Parcollet, T.; de Gusmão, P.P.; Lane, N.D. Flower: A friendly federated learning research framework. *arXiv* **2020**, arXiv:2007.14390.
30. McMahan, B.; Moore, E.; Ramage, D.; Hampson, S.; y Arcas, B.A. Communication-efficient learning of deep networks from decentralized data. In *Artificial Intelligence and Statistics*; PMLR: New York, NY, USA, 2017; pp. 1273–1282.
31. Domingo-Ferrer, J.; Blanco-Justicia, A. Privacy-preserving technologies. In *The Ethics of Cybersecurity*; Springer: Cham, Switzerland, 2020; pp. 279–297.
32. Rieke, N.; Hancox, J.; Li, W.; Milletari, F.; Roth, H.R.; Albarqouni, S.; Bakas, S.; Galtier, M.N.; Landman, B.A.; Maier-Hein, K.; et al. The future of digital health with federated learning. *NPJ Digit. Med.* **2020**, *3*, 1–7. [CrossRef] [PubMed]
33. Ahmed, S.T.; Kumar, V.V.; Singh, K.K.; Singh, A.; Muthukumaran, V.; Gupta, D. 6G enabled federated learning for secure IoMT resource recommendation and propagation analysis. *Comput. Electr. Eng.* **2022**, *102*, 108210. [CrossRef]
34. Li, W.; Milletarì, F.; Xu, D.; Rieke, N.; Hancox, J.; Zhu, W.; Baust, M.; Cheng, Y.; Ourselin, S.; Cardoso, M.J.; et al. Privacy-preserving federated brain tumour segmentation. In *International Workshop on Machine Learning in Medical Imaging*; Springer: Berlin/Heidelberg, Germany, 2019; pp. 133–141.
35. Jacoby, R.; Greenfeld Barsky, K.; Porat, T.; Harel, S.; Hanalis Miller, T.; Goldzweig, G. Individual stress response patterns: Preliminary findings and possible implications. *PLoS ONE* **2021**, *16*, e0255889. [CrossRef] [PubMed]
36. Surden, H. Machine learning and law. *Wash. L. Rev.* **2014**, *89*, 87.
37. Liu, J.C.; Goetz, J.; Sen, S.; Tewari, A. Learning from others without sacrificing privacy: Simulation comparing centralized and federated machine learning on mobile health data. *JMIR MHealth UHealth* **2021**, *9*, e23728. [CrossRef] [PubMed]
38. Nilsson, A.; Smith, S.; Ulm, G.; Gustavsson, E.; Jirstrand, M. A performance evaluation of federated learning algorithms. In Proceedings of the Second Workshop on Distributed Infrastructures for Deep Learning, Rennes, France, 10 December 2018; pp. 1–8.
39. Sozinov, K.; Vlassov, V.; Girdzijauskas, S. Human activity recognition using federated learning. In Proceedings of the 2018 IEEE Intl Conf on Parallel & Distributed Processing with Applications, Ubiquitous Computing & Communications, Big Data & Cloud Computing, Social Computing & Networking, Sustainable Computing & Communications (ISPA/IUCC/BDCloud/SocialCom/SustainCom), Melbourne, VIC, Australia, 11–13 December 2018; pp. 1103–1111.
40. De Maeyer, C.; Markopoulos, P. Are Digital Twins Becoming Our Personal (Predictive) Advisors?: 'Our Digital Mirror of Who We Were, Who We Are and Who We Will Become'. In Proceedings of the 22nd International Conference on Human-Computer Interaction'20: HCI International 2020, Copenhagen, Denmark, 19–24 July 2020; Springer: Berlin/Heidelberg, Germany, 2020; pp. 250–268.

Journal of *Personalized Medicine*

MDPI

*Article*

# Effectiveness of a Mobile App in Reducing Therapeutic Turnaround Time and Facilitating Communication between Caregivers in a Pediatric Emergency Department: A Randomized Controlled Pilot Trial

**Frederic Ehrler [1], Carlotta Tuor [2], Remy Trompier [3], Antoine Berger [3], Michael Ramusi [3], Robin Rey [2] and Johan N. Siebert [2,4,*]**

1 Division of Medical Information Sciences, Geneva University Hospitals, 1205 Geneva, Switzerland; frederic.ehrler@hcuge.ch
2 Faculty of Medicine, University of Geneva, 1205 Geneva, Switzerland; carlotta.tuor@etu.unige.ch (C.T.); robin.rey@etu.unige.ch (R.R.)
3 Information Technology Department, Geneva University Hospitals, 1205 Geneva, Switzerland; remy.trompier@hcuge.ch (R.T.); antoine.berger@hcuge.ch (A.B.); michael.ramusi@hcuge.ch (M.R.)
4 Department of Pediatric Emergency Medicine, Children's Hospital, Geneva University Hospitals, 1205 Geneva, Switzerland
* Correspondence: johan.siebert@hcuge.ch; Tel.: +41-79-55-34072



**Citation:** Ehrler, F.; Tuor, C.; Trompier, R.; Berger, A.; Ramusi, M.; Rey, R.; Siebert, J.N. Effectiveness of a Mobile App in Reducing Therapeutic Turnaround Time and Facilitating Communication between Caregivers in a Pediatric Emergency Department: A Randomized Controlled Pilot Trial. *J. Pers. Med.* **2022**, *12*, 428. https://doi.org/10.3390/jpm12030428

Academic Editors: Bernd Blobel and Mauro Giacomini

Received: 14 February 2022
Accepted: 7 March 2022
Published: 9 March 2022



**Abstract:** For maintaining collaboration and coordination among emergency department (ED) caregivers, it is essential to effectively share patient-centered information. Indirect activities on patients, such as searching for laboratory results and sharing information with scattered colleagues, waste resources to the detriment of patients and staff. Therefore, we conducted a pilot study to evaluate the initial efficacy of a mobile app to facilitate rapid mobile access to central laboratory results and remote interprofessional communication. A total of 10 ED residents and registered nurses were randomized regarding the use of the app versus conventional methods during semi-simulated scenarios in a pediatric ED (PED). The primary outcome was the elapsed time in minutes in each group from the availability of laboratory results to their consideration by participants. The secondary outcome was the elapsed time to find a colleague upon request. Time to consider laboratory results was significantly reduced from 23 min (IQR 10.5–49.0) to 1 min (IQR 0–5.0) with the use of the app compared to conventional methods (92.2% reduction in mean times, $p = 0.0079$). Time to find a colleague was reduced from 24 min to 1 min (i.e., 93.0% reduction). Dedicated mobile apps have the potential to improve information sharing and remote communication in emergency care.

**Keywords:** mobile application; mHealth; digital technology; emergency service; hospital; emergency department; clinical laboratory information systems; communication; text messaging; pediatrics

## 1. Introduction

Emergency department (ED) overcrowding is a global healthcare problem [1] that is both a source and consequence of prolonged ED length of stay (ED-LOS). Prolonged ED-LOS negatively impacts patients' waiting times by reducing the efficiency and quality of care, patient satisfaction, and willingness to return [2,3]. For a long time, it has also been recognized as a critical threat to patient safety [4]. ED-LOS is the most compelling and impactful indicator of the level of overcrowding and the organizational capacity of EDs to address this issue [5]. The entire laboratory testing process, also known as therapeutic turnaround time (TAT), is a major contributor [6,7]. It can be schematically divided into three phases (pre-, intra-, and postanalytical) that extend from the physician's request for testing to the awareness of the results (Supplementary Figure S1). There is no doubt that shortening the analytical phase can, in principle, shorten ED-LOS by allowing earlier decision making for the patient. However, it is estimated that up to 96% of the delays that contribute most to the therapeutic TAT occur in the pre- and post-analytical phases outside of the central laboratory [8,9]. In particular, caregivers' delayed awareness and review of results in the post-analytical phase have been described as the largest component of perceived TAT [10]. This makes them a prime target for interventions to mitigate their impact on ED-LOS and improve patient flow. This delay may be partially due to the fact that, while waiting for results without the support of individualized real-time laboratory prompts, caregivers are extremely busy, juggling multiple other responsibilities and multitasking, which take them away from fixed, computerized workstations and from the time the results are released. This places a cognitive burden on caregivers, who must regularly inquire about the availability of laboratory results with the risk of forgetting them. This also requires them to make incessant, time-consuming, and distracting trips to verify their availability.

Emergency care is very complex. It requires patient-centered care coordinated among multiple busy providers in a highly unpredictable and stressful environment, requiring high functional operability. Coupled with the role played by the built environment and the functional need to care for multiple patients simultaneously, this contributes to scatter caregivers, who must work as a team and in close vicinity to ensure quality care and a timely and seamless process. It also prevents accurate, synchronous communication [11] and safe collaborative emergency care [12,13]. Up to 80% of healthcare professionals' time in the ED is spent on communication in addition to any other tasks actively being performed at the same time, such as medication handling [14]. Approximately 90% of information transactions involve informal interpersonal exchanges rather than interaction with formal information sources, with 82% of synchronous face-to-face communication [14,15]. Disruption of communication in the ED therefore makes it difficult for caregivers to maintain a high level of awareness of each patient's individual situation; to follow up quickly on colleagues' requests for support, laboratory tests, radiologic examinations; or to respond to patients' demands. It has been observed that ED physicians and nurses waste nearly half of their time on indirect patient-related and non-patient-related activities. This includes traveling within the unit and locating colleagues to enable face-to-face communication and to share medical information [16–19]. Peters et al. showed that ED resident physicians walked an average 4.2 km and attending physicians 3.9 km during a typical 8.5 h shift [20]. This has a direct impact on patients, who must then wait unnecessarily in the ED when they could have been sent home or hospitalized earlier, which would have potentially reduced their LOS. Wasted time, discontinuity of care, suboptimal communication, and the omission or delay in seeking information can compromise patient outcomes and safety.

To our knowledge, no app that can be used as an interoperable mobile laboratory results viewer in the ED has been described to date [21]. Evidence demonstrating the impact of mobile apps tailored to caregivers and specifically dedicated to streamlining shared patient management in the EDs remains scarce [22–25]. In a previous study [26], we described the user-centered development and high early technology acceptance of a mobile app—the "Patients In My Pocket in my Hospital" (PIMPmyHospital) app. The app is designed to help ED caregivers automatically obtain relevant information about the patients they care for in real time, including laboratory and imaging results. The app also provides an end-to-end encrypted chat and instant messaging platform to digitally and remotely connect physicians and nurses caring for the same patients. However, the potential effectiveness of this app in mitigating ED-LOS by obtaining laboratory results in a shorter time frame than by conventional methods as well as its ability to facilitate communication in a shorter time frame among caregivers remained to be evaluated.

## 2. Materials and Methods

### *2.1. Study Design and Participants*

This prospective, single-center, non-blind, two-arm, randomized, controlled pilot trial was conducted on 6 September 2021, at the pediatric ED (PED) of the Children's Hospital in Geneva, which is part of the Geneva University Hospitals' network. It is one of the largest tertiary PED in Switzerland, with a total of approximately 33,000 visits per year for a resident population of more than 508,000 individuals, of whom 17.5% are children under 16 years of age. The present study was approved by the Geneva Cantonal Ethics Committee/SwissEthics (Req-2021-00795: date of approval, 23 July 2021) and registered at ClinicalTrials.gov (accessed on 13 February 2022) (NCT05203146, principal investigator: JNS, registration date: 24 January 2022). The trial was carried out in accordance with the principles of the Declaration of Helsinki and Good Clinical Practice guidelines [27,28] and adheres to the applicable CONSORT guidelines [29]. Written informed consent was obtained from each participant after full information disclosure prior to study participation.

We evaluated two methods for considering laboratory results (i.e., the post-analytical phase) and finding a colleague to aim for joint action during standardized, semi-simulated scenarios of everyday life in a PED. Participants were randomly assigned to undertake these two actions either with the support of the app (intervention group) or by conventional methods (control group). We hypothesized that use of the app could reduce both the time to learn about laboratory results and the time to interact with colleagues through remote communication.

Eligible participants were postgraduate residents pursuing a <6-year residency in pediatrics and registered nurses from the PED (aged > 18 years). They should have previously attended a standardized 5 min introductory course on the use of the app dispensed by the study investigators on the day of participation. Participants who had not taken the introductory course were excluded. According to Cohen's calculation, participants were recruited based on an expected effect size of 2.0, a type I error of 0.05, and a power of 80%.

### 2.2. Randomization and Blinding

Participants were randomized using a single, constant 1:1 allocation ratio determined by means of web-based software [30]. Allocation concealment was ensured with the allocation software and was not released until participants started the scenario. Participants were unaware of the scenario during recruitment to minimize preparation bias. After randomization at the beginning of the scenario, they were unblinded to the study arm. The study members (C.T., R.R., and J.N.S.) involved in the scenario and playing the assumed role of a fellow nurse to be found by participants were revealed to participants before the scenario started. Although the intervention could not be masked, all investigators remained unaware of the outcomes until all data were unlocked for analysis at the end of the trial.

### 2.3. The PIMPmyHospital App

The app was developed in an iterative way following a user-centered approach to meet end-users' needs. In a first phase, semi-structured interviews were conducted with nurses and physicians of the PED to identify their main complaints related to their daily practice. Responses were then structured and used to identify the main functionalities that a mobile app should have in order to be likely to address these grievances, namely (1) an overview of patients currently being cared for in the ED; (2) the possibility to communicate between caregivers through a secure instant messaging system; and (3) notifications when laboratory results are available. The system was implemented using a client-server architecture. The backend is composed of four microservices developed on Java Spring Boot framework. Each microservice is responsible for delivering a specific piece of information to the frontend, i.e., patient information, laboratory results, and instant messaging, and the last one is in charge of notifications. The instant messaging chat server is based on the Rocket.Chat platform installed locally on the hospital's digital infrastructure. The microservices exchange information with the frontend through a restful application programming interface. The frontend is a hybrid application developed in the Angular and Ionic frameworks. Security is enhanced by using JSON Web tokens obtained during caregiver authentication via a Keycloack identity and access management solution. Authentication on the device relies on two factors, including a login password and a specific certificate installed on the user's device. Moreover, patient medical data does not persist outside the primary system containing the source data (i.e., the patient electronic health record (EHR) located on the hospital's secure server). In other words, no data persistence is stored on the app itself.

The app runs on Google's Android and Apple's iOS operating systems. Its design and visual aspect have already been published [26]. In brief, a start screen allows caregivers to have an automatically generated view centered on the patients under their care; hence, the origin of the app is the "Patients In My Pocket" solution, referring to phone pocket carriage (Figure 1). Next to each patient, there is a clickable list of other caregivers in charge of the same patient, with whom they can be in contact remotely and collaboratively through the app via a secure instant messaging system. To make it easier to read, a color code is specifically assigned to each profession. Push notifications inform caregivers of incoming messages and whether they have been taken into account to ensure the responsiveness of the messaging system. Colored bars represent the triage level of each patient according to the five degrees of the Canadian triage and acuity scale [31]. The gender and identity of the patients are shown as well as the time elapsed since admission represented as circular radial timers. Furthermore, the geospatial localization of the patient in the department and the status of the patient (e.g., seen by a physician, waiting for results, waiting for a radiological examination, waiting for treatment, etc.) are displayed. Push notifications encourage the user to be attentive to the evolution of situations in real time. Selecting a patient on this page opens a new one containing drop-down contextual tabs with information related to laboratory results, imaging, electrocardiogram results, etc., extracted from the hospital's patient EHR. Again, push notifications indicate the availability of results. Thus, the entire patient management process is available to the caregiver in the palm of the hand and can be consulted at any time on the move.

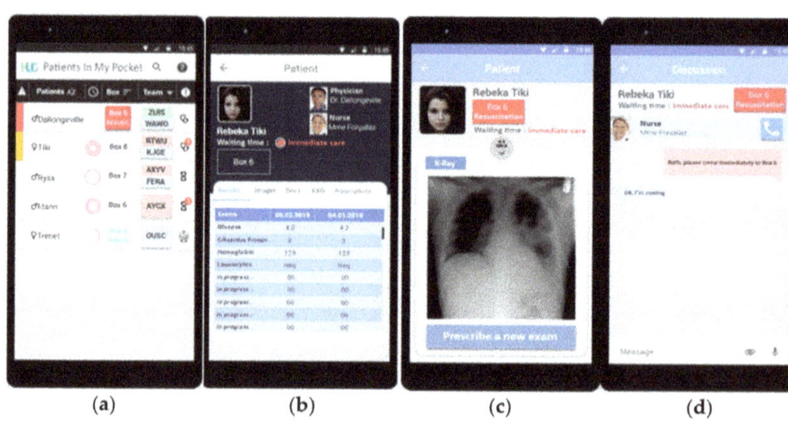


**Figure 1.** PIMPmyHospital screenshots. (**a**) Color-coded bars represent patient status on the five-level Canadian Triage and Acuity Scale [31]; patient gender and identity; time since admission as radial circular timers; patient allocation per room; color-coded box of individuals in charge of the patient; and patient status (seen by a physician, waiting for results, CT-scan in progress, etc.). Push notifications prompt the user to be aware of the situations. (**b**,**c**) Selecting a patient opens a new page with scrollable contextual tab menus containing information related to laboratory results, imaging, patient files, electrocardiograms, and prescriptions entered in the computerized institutional prescription software. (**d**) The instant messaging system. The logos at the bottom of the screen represent the possibility to also import and link documents to the conversion as well as to send voice memos. Adapted from [26].

### 2.4. Intervention

On the day of participation after randomized allocation, each participant completed a survey to collect data regarding his/her demographic characteristics. Then, they attended a standardized 5 min training session on how to use the mobile app (thus providing identical preliminary education). At this stage, this introductory course was not intended to test the usability of the app but to explain its use for the upcoming intervention. For two reasons, signage and layout of the PED were not modified for the purposes of the study. On the one hand, it is the daily working environment of the participants, who were theoretically supposed to have a similar knowledge of it after a common minimum assignment to the PED of at least 3 months. On the other hand, the study aimed at studying the impact of the app in a real PED environment during the overload period related to the coronavirus disease 2019 (COVID-19) pandemic.

Each participant was then exposed to the semi-simulated scenario about a fictitious patient mixed with the actual clinical activities of the day. They were first required to retrieve the simulated patient's laboratory results from the EHR when randomly made available. Only the indication at the beginning of the scenario that a laboratory test had just been sent to the central laboratory was provided to participants. They were then free to check the availability of the results either on the app or by using the institutional computerized system (i.e., without app support) at intervals of their choice. Once the result was obtained, participants were then asked to find a nurse (played by a study investigator: C.T., R.R., or J.N.S.) on the ward. This was done either at the prompt of a text message appearing on the app or by an oral request made by a second study investigator. Since one of the main communication problems in EDs is related to the distance between caregivers, this task aimed at determining whether remote communication via the app could generate a common and timely goal-oriented response. No information on the location of the nurse was provided. Participants were free to look for the nurse through a communication with the app for those who had it or, in both cases, to walk around to find the nurse. In all cases, participants ultimately had to physically reach the nurse and could not just make virtual contact. Procedures were standardized to follow the same chronological progression in order to ensure that each participant was exposed to exactly the same case with similar challenges in app usage and decision making. We did not organize pre-tests to minimize preparation bias so as not to influence the intervention. The app was interfaced on an Apple iPhone X with the latest version of iOS, but the app works identically on Android OS (Mountain View, CA, USA). Only the study investigators had access to the data.

### 2.5. Measurement Instruments

Time-to-goal completion was measured similarly between participants using a stop-watch. Given the pilot nature of the study, access logs on the app were not measured at this stage, similar to distances traveled using a pedometer and radio frequency identification (RFID) sensors, which will be the subject of outcomes in a subsequent larger trial. Data collection was carried out using the latest version of Prism 9 for MacOS (GraphPad software, LLC., San Diego, CA, USA).

### 2.6. Outcomes

The primary outcome was the elapsed time (in minutes) in each allocation group from the availability of the new laboratory results on either the mobile app or the institutional computerized patient data system to their consideration by the participant on the allocated medium (i.e., mobile app or EHR). The upper bound was arbitrarily set at 120 min. The secondary outcome was the elapsed time (in minutes) from the moment the participant was informed by the mobile app or a statement given by a study investigator (conventional method) that a nurse required assistance to perform a technical procedure up to the point in time when the participant reached that nurse. The upper bound was again arbitrarily set at 120 min.

### 2.7. Statistical Analysis

For the primary outcome, we first evaluated the time elapsed between the availability of the laboratory results and consideration by the participants. The Shapiro–Wilks test was used for normality analysis of the parameters. As continuous variables were non-normally distributed, the Mann–Whitney test to compare independent groups was used. No paired data were compared. Kaplan–Meier curves were estimated and compared using the log-rank (Mantel–Cox) test for bivariate survival analysis. For the secondary outcome, the same analyses were done. Statistical tests were two-tailed with a significance level of 5%. Data analysis was carried out using Prism v9.3.1 (GraphPad software, LLC., San Diego, CA, USA) for MacOS.

## 3. Results

### 3.1. Overview

A total of 10 participants (5 residents and 5 nurses) completed the scenarios, without dropouts.

Figure 2 presents the CONSORT flowchart for the present randomized, controlled trial. Table 1 summarizes participants' demographic and healthcare characteristics.

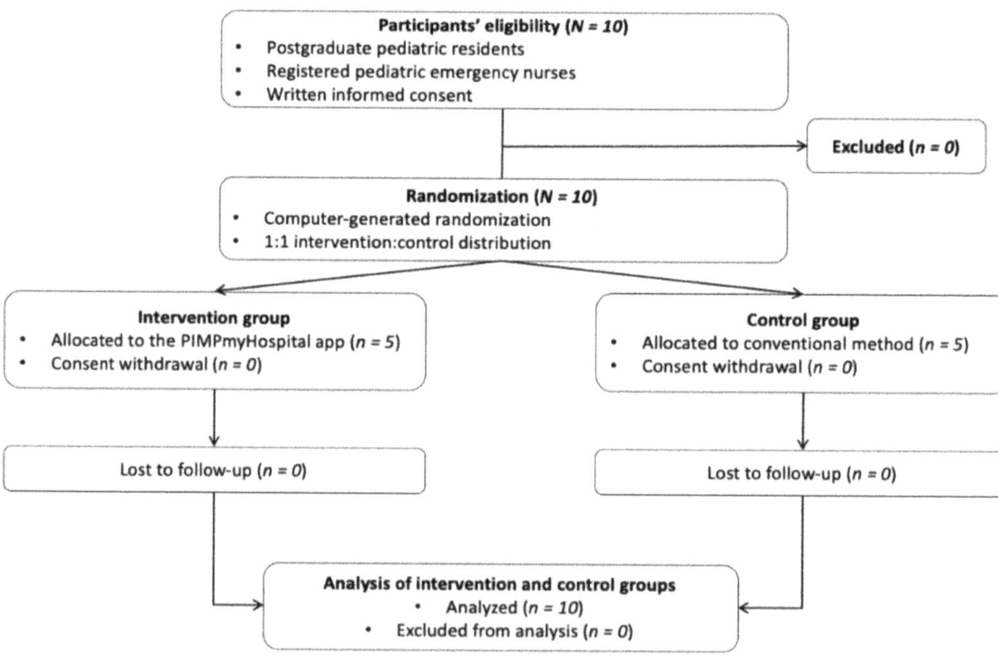


**Figure 2.** CONSORT flowchart.

### 3.2. Primary Outcome

Figure 3 shows that the median time to review laboratory results once available was significantly reduced from 23 min (interquartile range (IQR) 10.5–49.0 min) to 1 min (IQR 0–5.0 min) with the use of the app compared to the patient's EHR. All participants who used the app accessed these results at most within 7 min of their publication, whereas it took up to 58 min for participants who did not use the app (Figure 4), i.e., a 92.2% reduction in mean post-analytical time to consider the laboratory results.

**Table 1.** Baseline characteristics of participants.

| | PIMPmyHospital (*N* = 5) [a] | Control Group (*N* = 5) |
|---|---|---|
| Age in years, mean (SD) | 34.2 (8.5) | 30.8 (3.7) |
| Age in years, *n* (%) | | |
| <30 | 1 (20.0) | 2 (40.0) |
| 30–39 | 3 (60.0) | 3 (60.0) |
| ≥40 | 1 (20.0) | 0 (0) |
| Gender, *n* (%) | | |
| Female | 4 (40) | 4 (40) |
| Male | 1 (10) | 1 (10) |
| Work experience in years since certification, mean (SD) | 10.8 (9.1) | 5.8 (3.4) |
| Work experience in years since certification, *n* (%) | | |
| <5 | 1 (20.0) | 2 (40.0) |
| 5–9 | 2 (40.0) | 2 (40.0) |
| ≥9 | 2 (40.0) | 1 (20.0) |
| Work experience in months in the PED, mean (SD) | | 36.6 (26.6) |
| Work experience in months in the PED, *n* (%) | | |
| <12 | 1 (20.0) | 1 (20.0) |
| 12–24 | 1 (20.0) | 1 (20.0) |
| ≥24 | 3 (60.0) | 3 (60.0) |
| Satisfaction [b] with current timelines from laboratory report to review, mean (SD) | 4.4 (1.1) | 5.0 (3.0) |
| Satisfaction [b] with current situation to find a peer, mean (SD) | 3.6 (0.5) | 2.2 (1.8) |

[a] N, number of participants; [b] on a 10-point Likert scale (0 = not at all satisfied, 10 = extremely satisfied).

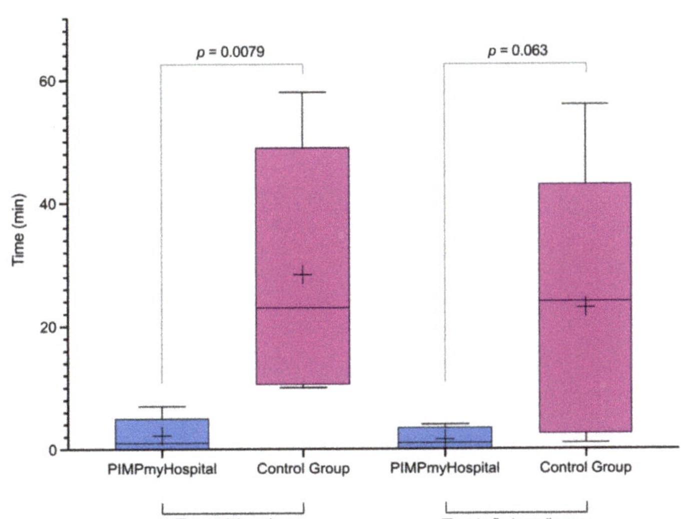


**Figure 3.** Boxplots of time to laboratory review and time to find a colleague when using the mobile app compared to conventional methods. Solid horizontal lines denote median and IQR; the endpoints of the whiskers indicate the range. The long upper whiskers show that participants were more varied among the most positive quartile groups. The cross denotes the mean.

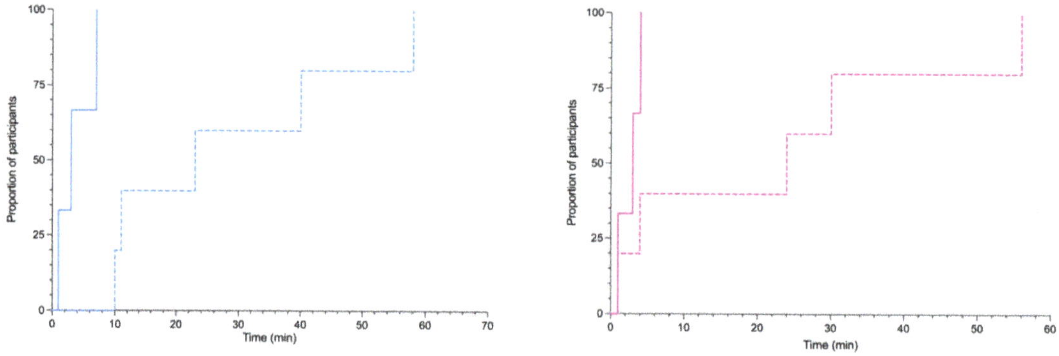


(a) (b)

**Figure 4.** Time to laboratory consideration and to find a colleague. (**a**) Kaplan–Meier curves of time elapsed from the laboratory report to consideration of results and (**b**) time from request to find a colleague to a physical connection using the PIMPmyHospital app (plain lines) vs conventional methods (dashed lines). Log-rank (Mantel–Cox) test comparing curves: $\chi^2 = 8.2$ and $p = 0.004$ for laboratory results; $\chi^2 = 2.7$ and $p = 0.1$ for finding a colleague.

### 3.3. Secondary Outcome

Median time to find a colleague was reduced almost significantly from 24 min to 1 min with the use of the app compared to the patient's EHR (Figure 3). All participants who used the app found their colleague at most within 4 min, whereas it took up to 56 min for participants who did not use the app (Figure 4), i.e., a 93.0% reduction in time wasted searching for someone.

## 4. Discussion

In this randomized pilot trial, we found that the use of a user-centered mobile app significantly reduced the time taken by pediatric emergency caregivers to consider laboratory results as well as the time needed to find colleagues. The result was borderline significant for the latter, however, likely related to the small sample size. The results of this pilot study will be used to inform the design of a future larger-scale, time-motion, randomized, controlled trial to confirm the effectiveness of PIMPmyHospital in reducing time wasted and the distance traveled to find laboratory results and colleagues.

According to the U.S. Centers for Disease Control and Prevention [32], laboratory tests are ordered in nearly 48% of ED visits, and 70% of medical decisions today are based on these [33], thus showing their important contribution in emergency care. Lack of timely follow-up of laboratory results has been widely documented as contributing to prolonged hospital LOS [34]. Their analytic phase being intrinsically linked to the incompressible speed of the measuring instruments used as well as the technological and organizational progress made in the field of centralized laboratory testing offers a limited potential for further shortening this phase [35]. This is partly at odds with the concerns of emergency physicians who are willing to sacrifice some analytical quality for a faster TAT [9]. This can explain the craze for point-of-care testing (POCT) as an alternative to provide timely results, as it speeds up clinical decision making and relieves ED congestion by expediting patient flow [36,37]. However, there is still controversy about its ability to reduce the total ED-LOS [38]. Of note, POCT does not a priori eliminate the risk that caregivers' awareness and consideration of the results will be similarly delayed, as this is a post-analytical issue. Prescribing POCT earlier in management would not necessarily change this situation and even have the unintended consequence of increasing the total number of tests [39]. Furthermore, POCTs are often more specialized and limited in their overall function compared to more advanced tests that continue to be performed in the central laboratory [40].

Our preliminary results show that in addition to being well accepted by caregivers [26], an app, such as PIMPmyHospital, could fulfill this role. Its mobile nature, supported by push notifications on their smartphones, should allow caregivers to avoid sacrificing their time to seek laboratory results but to obtain them immediately upon release wherever they are at the point of care. It has been suggested that the use of smartphones is preferable against the use of electronic whiteboard icons to communicate laboratory test results, as otherwise, this forces physicians and nurses to primarily access whiteboard information on permanent static screens also having in mind that physicians do not pay enough attention to the icons [41,42].

Real-time push notifications on mobile apps can significantly improve patient care by transforming the paradigm from the one that requires caregivers to search for information in the EHR among hundreds of data elements to the one where specific data are actively presented to frontline caregivers for timely decision making [43]. This could make a major contribution to speeding up emergency care provision and ultimately shortening the total ED-LOS whether for discharge or hospital admission. For example, push notifications of a rapid influenza test to ED physicians reduced the time to cancellation of an isolation order, the time to transfer to an inpatient unit, and the ED-LOS by approximately one hour among ED patients presenting with suspected influenza [43]. An extensive number of publications have also examined the impact of alert notifications on critical laboratory results. Although sometimes contradictory or pointing out the risk of alert fatigue potentially slowing the response to these alerts and harmful to the patient [43–45], they mostly show a significant reduction in time lag between laboratory result availability and decision making, a high degree of clinician approval, and a beneficial impact on patient care [25,46–49]. During 2018, there were an estimated 130 million ED visits in the USA. Two-thirds of patients spent more than two hours in the ED, including 34.8% between two and four hours and 29.1% with an extended ED-LOS greater than 4 h [32]. Reducing the time to interpretation of results could potentially help reduce these delays. In addition to saving time, such an app likely streamlines caregiver mobility by reducing incessant travel within the ED between the caregiver's current location and their workstation. However, this hypothesis has not yet been verified in the present study and will be the subject of the forthcoming time-motion trial.

Working in EDs requires collaboration between healthcare workers from different professions in the delivery of patient care, with frequent interaction between staff members to communicate patient and related information [50]. However, the contextual complexity of the high-risk, time-constrained ED environment segregates caregivers from one another and presents a challenge to optimal interprofessional information exchange that is often interrupted and fragmented [11,51–53]. Poor communication wastes time and is associated with inefficient patient care, loss of information, jeopardized patient safety, and lower job satisfaction [12,13,54]. The U.S. Joint Commission International has made interprofessional communication one of its main goals to improve patient safety [55]. Information and communication technologies could contribute to this goal. However, few studies have evaluated the benefits of using apps on personal mobile devices to improving communication among caregivers in the ED setting. Among these, some authors have reported the use of the popular WhatsApp app (Meta Platforms Inc., formerly known as Facebook, Menlo Park, CA, USA) [56,57], but this has raised security concerns about privacy compromises [56,58]. Moreover, WhatsApp is not primarily targeted at caregivers and was not developed in a user-centered way for this purpose, especially not for EDs and their constraints. Kentab et al. recently reported good effectiveness of using a customized, smartphone-based, push-to-talk app among ED workers for sharing instant voice messages during the COVID-19 outbreak to help optimize staff infection-control measures [59], but ED-LOS was not measured. Studies have also reported improved communication using two-way text messaging over pagers but, again, without focusing on its impact on ED-LOS [60,61]. Our preliminary findings thus add knowledge to the limited number of published studies examining the contribution of mobile apps to improve communication within an ED. This could help open up interesting prospects to reduce interprofessional communication disruptions that emergency medicine often struggles to solve with expensive and ill-suited means.

## 5. Limitations

This pilot study has some limitations. First, the sample size was small although it anticipated a large effect that was reflected in the results. Second, we did not measure the distance caregivers walked with or without the app. This will be one of the outcomes of our future trial based on a digital pedometer. Third, the quality of information exchanged during interpersonal communication was not assessed. This will also be the subject of the future larger-scale trial. Fourth, this study was conducted in a semi-simulated environment to limit potential confounders and standardize the intervention. Indeed, high-fidelity simulation is an essential method to evaluate research questions and technologies when the chaotic environment, where the intervention takes place, complicates the task [62]. Fifth, although not evaluated in this study, it might be of interest in the main study to determine whether specific alerts, such as a flashing icon or sound for flagged pathological values of laboratory findings, have an impact on outcomes. Finally, we did not weight the results obtained with respect to ED crowding between participants. Although the number of participants was modest, it is assumed that the randomized design of the study balanced this variable between the two groups, especially since the study was conducted on a single day, limiting the risk of weekly or seasonal variation. This point will be taken into account in the upcoming main study.

## 6. Conclusions

The use of a mobile app designed to automatically connect ED physicians and nurses to each other in order to collaboratively manage patients and remotely access real-time laboratory results on the move showed a reduction in caregiver turnaround times for consideration of laboratory results and a trend toward reduced time to find colleagues. Dedicated mobile apps have the potential to improve the efficiency of information sharing and emergency care by virtually reducing the distance between ED caregivers and their workstations or co-workers in a simple, lightweight, and replicable manner. This addresses one of the key ED-LOS issues, i.e., the time professionals waste searching for information and wandering around for colleagues, rather than having to painstakingly alter existing facility spatial organization and architecture. The results generated by this semi-simulated study will inform the conduct of a larger randomized, controlled trial.

**Supplementary Materials:** The following supporting information can be downloaded at: https://www.mdpi.com/article/10.3390/jpm12030428/s1, Figure S1: The therapeutic turnaround time. References [63,64] are cited in the Supplementary Materials.

**Author Contributions:** Conceptualization, F.E. and J.N.S.; data curation, J.N.S.; formal analysis, J.N.S.; investigation, C.T., R.R. and J.N.S.; methodology, F.E., C.T., R.R. and J.N.S.; project administration, J.N.S.; resources, J.N.S.; software, F.E., R.T., A.B. and M.R.; supervision, J.N.S.; validation, J.N.S.; visualization, J.N.S.; writing—original draft, F.E. and J.N.S.; writing—review and editing, J.N.S. All authors have read and agreed to the published version of the manuscript.

**Funding:** This research received no external funding.

**Institutional Review Board Statement:** The study was conducted in accordance with the Declaration of Helsinki and approved by the Geneva Cantonal Ethics Committee/SwissEthics, Switzerland (protocol code Req-2021-00795: date of approval 23 July 2021).

**Informed Consent Statement:** Informed consent was obtained from all subjects involved in the study.

**Data Availability Statement:** The data presented in this study are available in deidentified form on request from the corresponding author. The data are not publicly available due to privacy restrictions.

**Acknowledgments:** We are grateful to Rosemary Sudan (freelance technical editor) for providing editorial assistance. This person was compensated for her work.

**Conflicts of Interest:** F.E. and J.N.S. are the owners of the PIMPmyHospital mobile app. The app is currently not available on the commercial Google Play Store or App Store (Apple). F.E. and J.N.S. declare no support from commercial entities for the submitted work and no financial relationships with any commercial entities that might have an interest in the submitted work in the previous years. F.E. and J.N.S. declare no other relationships or activities that could appear to have influenced the submitted work. The rest of the authors declare no potential conflict of interests in connection with the app, research, authorship, and/or publication of this article.

## References

1. Javidan, A.P.; Hansen, K.; Higginson, I.; Jones, P.; Lang, E. The International Federation for Emergency Medicine report on emergency department crowding and access block: A brief summary. *Int. J. Emerg. Med.* **2021**, *14*, 4. [CrossRef] [PubMed]
2. Franklin, B.J.; Li, K.Y.; Somand, D.M.; Kocher, K.E.; Kronick, S.L.; Parekh, V.I.; Goralnick, E.; Nix, A.T.; Haas, N.L. Emergency department provider in triage: Assessing site-specific rationale, operational feasibility, and financial impact. *J. Am. Coll. Emerg. Physicians Open* **2021**, *2*, e12450. [CrossRef] [PubMed]
3. Driesen, B.; van Riet, B.H.G.; Verkerk, L.; Bonjer, H.J.; Merten, H.; Nanayakkara, P.W.B. Long length of stay at the emergency department is mostly caused by organisational factors outside the influence of the emergency department: A root cause analysis. *PLoS ONE* **2018**, *13*, e0202751. [CrossRef] [PubMed]
4. Trzeciak, S.; Rivers, E.P. Emergency department overcrowding in the United States: An emerging threat to patient safety and public health. *Emerg. Med. J.* **2003**, *20*, 402–405. [CrossRef] [PubMed]
5. Andersson, J.; Nordgren, L.; Cheng, I.; Nilsson, U.; Kurland, L. Long emergency department length of stay: A concept analysis. *Int. Emerg. Nurs.* **2020**, *53*, 100930. [CrossRef]
6. Yoon, P.; Steiner, I.; Reinhardt, G. Analysis of factors influencing length of stay in the emergency department. *Can. J. Emerg. Med.* **2003**, *5*, 155–161. [CrossRef]
7. Van der Veen, D.; Remeijer, C.; Fogteloo, A.J.; Heringhaus, C.; de Groot, B. Independent determinants of prolonged emergency department length of stay in a tertiary care centre: A prospective cohort study. *Scand. J. Trauma Resusc. Emerg. Med.* **2018**, *26*, 81. [CrossRef]
8. Mwogi, T.; Mercer, T.; Tran, D.N.T.; Tonui, R.; Tylleskar, T.; Were, M.C. Therapeutic turnaround times for common laboratory tests in a tertiary hospital in Kenya. *PLoS ONE* **2020**, *15*, e0230858. [CrossRef]
9. Steindel, S.J.; Howanitz, P.J. Changes in emergency department turnaround time performance from 1990 to 1993: A comparison of two College of American Pathologists Q-probes studies. *Arch. Pathol. Lab. Med.* **1997**, *121*, 1031–1041.
10. Hawkins, R.C. Laboratory turnaround time. *Clin. Biochem. Rev.* **2007**, *28*, 179–194.
11. Tindle, K.; David, A.; Carlisle, S.; Faircloth, B.; Fields, J.M.; Hayden, G.; Ku, B. Relationship of the built environment on nursing communication patterns in the emergency department: A task performance and analysis time study. *J. Emerg. Nurs.* **2020**, *46*, 440–448. [CrossRef] [PubMed]
12. Bekkink, M.O.; Farrell, S.E.; Takayesu, J.K. Interprofessional communication in the emergency department: Residents' perceptions and implications for medical education. *Int. J. Med. Educ.* **2018**, *9*, 262–270. [CrossRef] [PubMed]
13. Ong, Z.H.; Tan, L.H.E.; Ghazali, H.Z.B.; Ong, Y.T.; Koh, Y.T.; Ang, R.Z.E.; Bok, C.; Chiam, M.; Lee, A.S.I.; Chin, A.M.C.; et al. A systematic scoping review on pedagogical strategies of interprofessional communication for physicians in emergency medicine. *J. Med. Educ. Curric. Dev.* **2021**, *8*, 23821205211041794. [CrossRef] [PubMed]
14. Coiera, E.W.; Jayasuriya, R.A.; Hardy, J.; Bannan, A.; Thorpe, M.E. Communication loads on clinical staff in the emergency department. *Med. J. Aust.* **2002**, *176*, 415–418. [CrossRef] [PubMed]
15. Woloshynowych, M.; Davis, R.; Brown, R.; Vincent, C. Communication patterns in a UK emergency department. *Ann. Emerg. Med.* **2007**, *50*, 407–413. [CrossRef]
16. Weng, S.J.; Tsai, M.C.; Tsai, Y.T.; Gotcher, D.F.; Chen, C.H.; Liu, S.C.; Xu, Y.Y.; Kim, S.H. Improving the efficiency of an emergency department based on activity-relationship diagram and radio frequency identification technology. *Int. J. Environ. Res. Public Health* **2019**, *16*, 4478. [CrossRef]
17. Hollingsworth, J.C.; Chisholm, C.D.; Giles, B.K.; Cordell, W.H.; Nelson, D.R. How do physicians and nurses spend their time in the emergency department? *Ann. Emerg. Med.* **1998**, *31*, 87–91. [CrossRef]
18. Weigl, M.; Handl, T.; Wehler, M.; Schneider, A. Time-allocation study of nurse and physician activities in the emergency department. *Med. Klin. Intensivmed. Notfmed.* **2021**, *116*, 229–237. [CrossRef]
19. Mamykina, L.; Vawdrey, D.K.; Hripcsak, G. How do residents spend their shift time? A time and motion study with a particular focus on the use of computers. *Acad. Med.* **2016**, *91*, 827–832. [CrossRef]
20. Peters, G.A.; Wong, M.L.; Sanchez, L.D. Pedometer-measured physical activity among emergency physicians during shifts. *Am. J. Emerg. Med.* **2020**, *38*, 118–121. [CrossRef]
21. Raymond, L.; Pare, G.; Maillet, E.; de Guinea, A.O.; Trudel, M.C.; Marsan, J. Improving performance in the ED through laboratory information exchange systems. *Int. J. Emerg. Med.* **2018**, *11*, 15. [CrossRef] [PubMed]

22. Alhejily, W.A. Implementing "chest pain pathway" using smartphone messaging application "WhatsApp" as a corrective action plan to improve ischemia time in "ST-Elevation Myocardial Infarction" in primary PCI capable center "WhatsApp-STEMI Trial". *Crit. Pathw. Cardiol.* **2021**, *20*, 179–184. [CrossRef] [PubMed]
23. Noone, M.L.; Moideen, F.; Krishna, R.B.; Kumar, V.G.P.; Karadan, U.; Chellenton, J.; Salam, K.A. Mobile app based strategy improves door-to-needle time in the treatment of acute ischemic stroke. *J. Stroke Cerebrovasc. Dis.* **2020**, *29*, 105319. [CrossRef] [PubMed]
24. Ehrler, F.; Sahyoun, C.; Manzano, S.; Sanchez, O.; Gervaix, A.; Lovis, C.; Courvoisier, D.S.; Lacroix, L.; Siebert, J.N. Impact of a shared decision-making mHealth tool on caregivers' team situational awareness, communication effectiveness, and performance during pediatric cardiopulmonary resuscitation: Study protocol of a cluster randomized controlled trial. *Trials* **2021**, *22*, 277. [CrossRef]
25. Boillat, T.; Siebert, J.N.; Alduaij, N.; Ehrler, F. GOFlow: Smartwatch app to deliver laboratory results in emergency departments—A feasibility study. *Int. J. Med. Inform.* **2020**, *134*, 104034. [CrossRef]
26. Ehrler, F.; Tuor, C.; Rey, R.; Siebert, J.N. A mobile app to improve patient management in emergency departments: Caregiver needs analysis, design and early technology acceptance assessment. *Stud. Health Technol. Inform.* **2021**, *285*, 233–238.
27. Cheng, A.; Kessler, D.; Mackinnon, R.; Chang, T.P.; Nadkarni, V.M.; Hunt, E.A.; Duval-Arnould, J.; Lin, Y.; Cook, D.A.; Pusic, M.; et al. Reporting guidelines for health care simulation research: Extensions to the CONSORT and STROBE statements. *Simul. Healthc.* **2016**, *11*, 238–248. [CrossRef]
28. Eysenbach, G.; Consort-Ehealth Group. Consort-Ehealth: Improving and standardizing evaluation reports of Web-based and mobile health interventions. *J. Med. Internet Res.* **2011**, *13*, e126. [CrossRef]
29. Schulz, K.F.; Altman, D.G.; Moher, D.; Consort Group. CONSORT 2010 statement: Updated guidelines for reporting parallel group randomised trials. *BMJ* **2010**, *340*, c332. [CrossRef]
30. Sealed Envelope Ltd. Simple Randomisation Service. 2021. Available online: https://www.sealedenvelope.com/simple-randomiser/v1 (accessed on 7 February 2022).
31. Beveridge, R. CAEP issues. The Canadian Triage and Acuity Scale: A new and critical element in health care reform. Canadian Association of Emergency Physicians. *J. Emerg. Med.* **1998**, *16*, 507–511.
32. Cairns, C.; Kang, K.; Santo, L. National Hospital Ambulatory Medical Care Survey: 2018 Emergency Department Summary Tables. 2018. Available online: https://www.cdc.gov/nchs/data/nhamcs/web_tables/2018-ed-web-tables-508.pdf (accessed on 7 February 2022).
33. Rohr, U.P.; Binder, C.; Dieterle, T.; Giusti, F.; Messina, C.G.; Toerien, E.; Moch, H.; Schafer, H.H. The value of in vitro diagnostic testing in medical practice: A status report. *PLoS ONE* **2016**, *11*, e0149856. [CrossRef] [PubMed]
34. Ong, M.S.; Magrabi, F.; Coiera, E. Delay in reviewing test results prolongs hospital length of stay: A retrospective cohort study. *BMC Health Serv. Res.* **2018**, *18*, 369. [CrossRef] [PubMed]
35. Schimke, I. Quality and timeliness in medical laboratory testing. *Anal. Bioanal. Chem.* **2009**, *393*, 1499–1504. [CrossRef] [PubMed]
36. Wilson, S.; Bohn, M.K.; Adeli, K. POCT: An inherently ideal tool in pediatric laboratory medicine. *EJIFCC* **2021**, *32*, 145–157.
37. Goyder, C.; Tan, P.S.; Verbakel, J.; Ananthakumar, T.; Lee, J.J.; Hayward, G.; Turner, P.J.; Van Den Bruel, A. Impact of point-of-care panel tests in ambulatory care: A systematic review and meta-analysis. *BMJ Open* **2020**, *10*, e032132. [CrossRef]
38. Alter, D.N. Point-of-care testing for the emergency department patient: Quantity and quality of the available evidence. *Arch. Pathol. Lab. Med.* **2021**, *145*, 308–319. [CrossRef]
39. Gottlieb, M.; Farcy, D.A.; Moreno, L.A.; Vilke, G.M.; Guittard, J.A. Triage nurse-ordered testing in the emergency department setting: A review of the literature for the clinician. *J. Emerg. Med.* **2021**, *60*, 570–575. [CrossRef]
40. Larsson, A.; Greig-Pylypczuk, R.; Huisman, A. The state of point-of-care testing: A European perspective. *Ups. J. Med. Sci.* **2015**, *120*, 1–10. [CrossRef]
41. Á Torkilsheyggi, A.; Hertzum, M.; From, G. Evaluating the impact of electronic whiteboard icons: An observational study of the work with blood tests in an emergency department. *Scand. J. Trauma Resusc. Emerg. Med.* **2013**, *1*. [CrossRef]
42. Hertzum, M.; Simonsen, J. Effects of electronic emergency-department whiteboards on clinicians' time distribution and mental workload. *Health Inform. J.* **2016**, *22*, 3–20. [CrossRef]
43. Salmasian, H.; Landman, A.B.; Morris, C. An electronic notification system for improving patient flow in the emergency department. *AMIA Jt Summits Transl. Sci. Proc.* **2019**, *2019*, 242–247. [PubMed]
44. Chopra, V.; McMahon, L.F., Jr. Redesigning hospital alarms for patient safety: Alarmed and potentially dangerous. *JAMA* **2014**, *311*, 1199–1200. [CrossRef] [PubMed]
45. Winters, B.D.; Slota, J.M.; Bilimoria, K.Y. Safety culture as a patient safety practice for alarm fatigue. *JAMA* **2021**, *326*, 1207–1208. [CrossRef] [PubMed]
46. Slovis, B.H.; Nahass, T.A.; Salmasian, H.; Kuperman, G.; Vawdrey, D.K. Asynchronous automated electronic laboratory result notifications: A systematic review. *J. Am. Med. Inform. Assoc.* **2017**, *24*, 1173–1183. [CrossRef]
47. Verma, A.; Wang, A.S.; Feldman, M.J.; Hefferon, D.A.; Kiss, A.; Lee, J.S. Push-alert notification of troponin results to physician smartphones reduces the time to discharge emergency department patients: A randomized controlled trial. *Ann. Emerg Med.* **2017**, *70*, 348–356. [CrossRef] [PubMed]
48. Trotzky, D.; Posner, L.; Mosery, J.; Cohen, A.; Avisar, S.; Pachys, G. Do automatic push notifications improve patient flow in the emergency department? analysis of an ED in a large medical center in Israel. *PLoS ONE* **2021**, *16*, e0258169. [CrossRef]

49. Koziatek, C.; Swartz, J.; Iturrate, E.; Levy-Lambert, D.; Testa, P. Decreasing the lag between result availability and decision-making in the emergency department using push notifications. *West. J. Emerg Med.* **2019**, *20*, 666–671. [CrossRef]
50. Creswick, N.; Westbrook, J.I.; Braithwaite, J. Understanding communication networks in the emergency department. *BMC Health Serv. Res.* **2009**, *9*, 247. [CrossRef]
51. Pun, J.K.; Chan, E.A.; Murray, K.A.; Slade, D.; Matthiessen, C.M. Complexities of emergency communication: Clinicians' perceptions of communication challenges in a trilingual emergency department. *J. Clin. Nurs.* **2017**, *26*, 3396–3407. [CrossRef]
52. Weigl, M.; Catchpole, K.; Wehler, M.; Schneider, A. Workflow disruptions and provider situation awareness in acute care: An observational study with emergency department physicians and nurses. *Appl. Ergon.* **2020**, *88*, 103155. [CrossRef]
53. Weigl, M.; Beck, J.; Wehler, M.; Schneider, A. Workflow interruptions and stress at work: A mixed-methods study among physicians and nurses of a multidisciplinary emergency department. *BMJ Open* **2017**, *7*, e019074. [CrossRef] [PubMed]
54. Pun, J.K.; Matthiessen, C.M.; Murray, K.A.; Slade, D. Factors affecting communication in emergency departments: Doctors and nurses' perceptions of communication in a trilingual ED in Hong Kong. *Int. J. Emerg. Med.* **2015**, *8*, 48. [CrossRef] [PubMed]
55. The Joint Commission. 2022 National Patient Safety Goals. 2022. Available online: https://www.jointcommission.org/standards/national-patient-safety-goals/-/media/131f1a35ea9743eca04b9858b73b0a93.ashx (accessed on 7 February 2022).
56. Dungarwalla, M.; Chapireau, D.; Bentley, R. Use of WhatsApp in an oral and maxillofacial surgery department at a major trauma centre and its role during major incidents: Our experience. *Br. J. Oral Maxillofac. Surg.* **2019**, *57*, 449–453. [CrossRef] [PubMed]
57. Johnston, M.J.; King, D.; Arora, S.; Behar, N.; Athanasiou, T.; Sevdalis, N.; Darzi, A. Smartphones let surgeons know WhatsApp: An analysis of communication in emergency surgical teams. *Am. J. Surg.* **2015**, *209*, 45–51. [CrossRef] [PubMed]
58. Watson, L.; Pathiraja, F.; Depala, A.; O'Brien, B.; Beyzade, S. Ensuring safe communication in health care: A response to Johnston et al on their paper "Smartphones let surgeons know WhatsApp: An analysis of communication in emergency surgical teams". *Am. J. Surg.* **2016**, *211*, 302–303. [CrossRef] [PubMed]
59. Kentab, O.; Soliman, K.; Al Ibrahim, A.A.; Alresseeni, A.; Aljohani, K.; Aljahany, M. A Push-to-talk Application as an interprofessional communication tool in an emergency department during the COVID-19 pandemic. *Open Access Emerg. Med.* **2021**, *13*, 189–199. [CrossRef]
60. Hansen, J.E.; Lazow, M.; Hagedorn, P.A. Reducing interdisciplinary communication failures through secure text messaging: A quality improvement project. *Pediatr. Qual. Saf.* **2018**, *3*, e053. [CrossRef]
61. Pourmand, A.; Roberson, J.; Gallugi, A.; Sabha, Y.; O'Connell, F. Secure smartphone application-based text messaging in emergency department, a system implementation and review of literature. *Am. J. Emerg. Med.* **2018**, *36*, 1680–1685. [CrossRef]
62. Cheng, A.; Auerbach, M.; Hunt, E.A.; Chang, T.P.; Pusic, M.; Nadkarni, V.; Kessler, D. Designing and conducting simulation-based research. *Pediatrics* **2014**, *133*, 1091–1101. [CrossRef]
63. Lundberg, G.D. Acting on significant laboratory results. *JAMA* **1981**, *245*, 1762–1763. [CrossRef]
64. Pati, H.P.; Singh, G. Turnaround Time (TAT): Difference in Concept for Laboratory and Clinician. *Indian J. Hematol. Blood Transfus.* **2014**, *30*, 81–84. [CrossRef] [PubMed]

Journal of *Personalized Medicine*

MDPI

*Article*

# A NLP Pipeline for the Automatic Extraction of a Complete Microorganism's Picture from Microbiological Notes

**Sara Mora [1], Jacopo Attene [1], Roberta Gazzarata [2,3], Daniele Roberto Giacobbe [4,5], Bernd Blobel [6,7,8], Giustino Parruti [9] and Mauro Giacomini [1,*]**

[1] Department of Informatics, Bioengineering, Robotics and System Engineering (DIBRIS), University of Genoa, 16145 Genoa, Italy
[2] Healthropy, Corso Italia 15/6, 17100 Savona, Italy
[3] HL7 Europe, 1000 Brussels, Belgium
[4] Infectious Diseases Unit, IRCCS San Martino Polyclinic Hospital, 16132 Genoa, Italy
[5] Department of Health Sciences (DISSAL), University of Genoa, 16132 Genoa, Italy
[6] Medical Faculty, University of Regensburg, 93053 Regensburg, Germany
[7] eHealth Competence Center Bavaria, Deggendorf Institute of Technology, 94469 Deggendorf, Germany
[8] First Medical Faculty, Charles University Prague, 12800 Prague, Czech Republic
[9] Department of Infectious Diseases, AUSL Pescara, 65124 Pescara, Italy
* Correspondence: mauro.giacomini@unige.it

**Abstract:** The Italian "Istituto Superiore di Sanità" (ISS) identifies hospital-acquired infections (HAIs) as the most frequent and serious complications in healthcare. HAIs constitute a real health emergency and, therefore, require decisive action from both local and national health organizations. Information about the causative microorganisms of HAIs is obtained from the results of microbiological cultures of specimens collected from infected body sites, but microorganisms' names are sometimes reported only in the notes field of the culture reports. The objective of our work was to build a NLP-based pipeline for the automatic information extraction from the notes of microbiological culture reports. We analyzed a sample composed of 499 texts of notes extracted from 1 month of anonymized laboratory referral. First, our system filtered texts in order to remove nonmeaningful sentences. Thereafter, it correctly extracted all the microorganisms' names according to the expert's labels and linked them to a set of very important metadata such as the translations into national/international vocabularies and standard definitions. As the major result of our pipeline, the system extracts a complete picture of the microorganism.

**Keywords:** hospital-acquired infections; international coding system; laboratory information systems; natural language processing; information extraction



**Citation:** Mora, S.; Attene, J.; Gazzarata, R.; Giacobbe, D.R.; Blobel, B.; Parruti, G.; Giacomini, M. A NLP Pipeline for the Automatic Extraction of a Complete Microorganism's Picture from Microbiological Notes. *J. Pers. Med.* **2022**, *12*, 1424. https://doi.org/10.3390/jpm12091424

Academic Editor: Norman R. Williams

Received: 10 July 2022
Accepted: 26 August 2022
Published: 31 August 2022



## 1. Introduction

The recent COVID-19 pandemic highlighted even more the worrying and widespread increasing circulation of pathogenic microorganisms in hospitals, sheltering for elderly, and assisted residences. The Italian "Istituto Superiore di Sanità" (ISS) [1] identifies hospital-acquired infections (HAI) as the most frequent and serious complications of healthcare. A possible definition of HAI is "infections that first appear 48 h or more after hospital admission or no later than 30 days after discharge following inpatient care" [2]. HAIs constitute a real health emergency and require decisive action from both local and national health organizations. The main objective is to build stable and automatic systems dedicated to reporting and epidemiological surveillance. When a pathogenic microorganism responsible for HAI is identified, the information can allow targeted antibiotic treatment, as well as the prompt adoption of specific infection-control measures for multidrug-resistant (MDR) bacteria.

This information is obtained from microbiological cultures of specimens collected from infected body sites, and the outcomes are usually reported in the results of laboratory exams [3,4]. MDR bacteria are defined as those organisms that show resistance to one or more agents in at least three antimicrobial categories during in vitro antimicrobial susceptibility tests [5,6].

MDR organisms are a world health problem causing about 33,000 deaths per year in Europe [7] and 35,000 in the United States [8]. It becomes even more serious when the infection affects critically ill patients, e.g., those admitted to intensive care units (ICUs) [9,10], because it is associated with increased mortality [11]. However, this is not only a human-related problem, because MDR bacteria are frequently found in the environment [12], especially in intensive farming both in agriculture (livestock and poultry) [13–15] and in aquaculture [16–18].

Although for more than 20 years modern laboratory information systems (LISs) [19,20] managed laboratory analyses, individual centers created their own vocabulary. This is mainly due to the fact that the development of information systems has been non-simultaneous and strongly localized. The resulting need to make results coming out of the single laboratories comparable led to the development of international coding systems and standards devised for the management of terminologies. An example of an international vocabulary applicable in this field is the Logical Observations Identifiers Names and Codes (LOINC). The Common Terminology Service Release 2 (CTS2) [21] is a standard dedicated to terminology management, whose specifications result from the collaboration between the Object Management Group (OMG) [22] and Health Level 7 (HL7) [23].

One of the fields where computerized systems faced many problems was the management of microbiology. This resulted from the high variability of the discipline and the strict link to the habits of individual laboratories (i.e., the coding system on which the nomenclature of bacteria relies, how sensitivity analyses are performed, etc.). Therefore, a contrast arose between the need for more variability and the mandatory use of LISs, imposed by national laws, whose structure in some specific cases may be considered too stiff. Therefore, because of the lack of ad hoc and appropriate fields for representing and managing microbiological-related information, the staff instead preferred exploiting clinical notes written as natural text. Accordingly, clinical notes became an important source of information for biomedical research, patient management, and care, while the necessity of manual inspection made their use expensive in terms of personnel effort and time. The limitations of data/information collection in LIS, on the one hand, and the advantage of concept representations using domain-specific languages instead of data/information representation, on the other hand, are discussed in more detail in Section 4.

This kind of problem can be addressed using artificial intelligence (AI) tools, especially with natural language processing (NLP). It is a branch of computer science that deals with the processing of natural human language by computers, studying the problems connected to the learning, understanding and automatic generation of human language both in written and in spoken form [24–26].

The objective of our work was to build a NLP-based pipeline for automatic information extraction from the notes of microbiological culture reports.

This could represent a first step toward the development of a system able to monitor antibiotic prescriptions at a hospital and territorial level in the Abruzzo Region [27].

This paper is an extension of work originally presented at the 18th International Conference on Wearable, Micro, and Nano Technologies for Personalized Health (pHealth 2021) titled "A NLP pipeline for the automatic extraction of microorganisms names from microbiological notes" [28]. The extended version addresses the problem of managing the national and international terminology systems linked to the project and of filtering clinical notes in order to exclude nonsignificant sentences.

## 2. Materials and Methods

The complete schema of the developed pipeline is presented in Figure 1, and it can be divided into four main sections (discussed in detail below). "Data preparation" prepares the inputs values, explaining how we build the vocabulary database, and it loads and preprocesses the clinical notes. "Pattern recognition" takes as input the textual data, converting them into a numerical representation, and it builds three ML-based models that predict if the specific pattern is contained or not in a clinical note. "Pattern removal" takes as input the sentences identified by the model as containing the specific pattern and removes it. "Microorganism detection" takes as input both the filtered and the nonfiltered sentences and first performs the "Genus extension" process before extracting from the clinical notes meaningful information such as the microorganism name and if it belongs to the group of dangerous microorganisms.

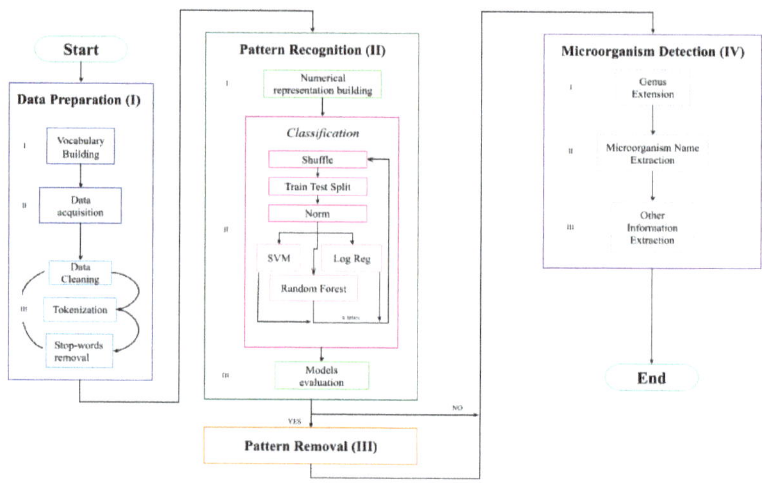


**Figure 1.** Complete schema of the pipeline. It can be divided into 4 main sections: data preparation, pattern recognition and removal, and microorganism detection.

### 2.1. *Characteristics of the Sample*

The collected sample was derived from the LIS of the main hospital of Pescara in Abruzzo Region and was obtained from clinical notes extracted from a 1 month collection of anonymized laboratory referral. It was composed of 499 texts from culture reports, classified as follows:

- 276 (55.3%) texts containing the name of a microorganism where an expert from the hospital confirmed its presence;
- 56 (11.2%) texts needing to be filtered because they contained a pattern that is not useful for our analysis and was, thus, removed. An example of a sentence belonging to that pattern is the following: "Integration of the preliminary report sent on ... ". Indeed, we considered the use of synonyms, e.g., "provisional" instead of "preliminary", and the presence of orthographic errors, e.g., missing letters. Therefore, we decided not to use regular expressions alone as first attempt.

We are waiting for the authorization from Abruzzo region to access the entire LIS system at a regional level to massively test the proposed system with notes produced by a wide range of persons.

### 2.2. *Environment and Libraries*

We completely developed the pipeline in Python language, and we used the Jupyter Notebook environment. The Python libraries used within this project were as follows:

Pandas: This is an open-source Python library containing data analysis and manipulation tools [29].

Pyodbc: This is an open-source module developed in Python that allows accessing databases through the ODBC (Open DataBase Connectivity).

Natural Language Toolkit (NLTK): This is a worldwide used library to perform text analysis in multiple languages; therefore, it is popular in both academia and research [30]. Some of the operations supported by the NLTK are tokenization, stemming, part of speech tagging (POS tagging), and disambiguation.

SpaCy: This is an open-source library for NLP in Python supporting different languages [31].

Re: This is a Python module that provides operations useful to work with regular expressions [32].

Scikit-learn: This is an open-source library that contains several machine learning algorithms, e.g., classification, regression, and clustering [33].

Seaborn, matplotlib: These are libraries used to produce graphics [34,35].

FuzzyWuzzy: This is a Python library used to manage the comparisons between strings. In detail, it is used to compute the distance between two strings with the same number of characters or not, taking into account the order of words and the allowed maximum frequency of a string. This comparison is based on the Levenshtein distance.

$$lev_{a,b}(i,j) = \begin{cases} \max(i,j) & if \ \min(i,j) = 0, \\ \min \begin{cases} lev_{a,b}(i-1,j) + 1 \\ lev_{a,b}(i,j-1) + 1 \\ lev_{a,b}(i-1,j-1) + 1_{(a_i \neq b_j)} \end{cases} & otherwise \end{cases}$$

where $i$ and $j$ constitute the indices of the last character of the two substrings [36].

### 2.3. Data Preparation (I)

Vocabulary building (I.I): We built a vocabulary containing the names of microorganisms (bacteria, fungi, yeasts, and viruses) from the "National Healthcare Safety Network organism list", including the current taxonomic subdivision which was proposed by Carl Woase in 1990. We mapped the microorganism's genus and specie into three standard coding systems, at national and/or international level: Italian Clinical Microbiologists Association (AMCLI), Systematized Nomenclature of Medicine—Clinical Terms (SNOMED-CT), and National Healthcare Safety Network (NHSN). Together with the name of the microorganism, we retrieved other metadata, such as the microorganism's definitions according to Medical Subject Headings (MSH) and the National Cancer Institute (NCI). We stored all the information in an SQL Server database, and we loaded them using the pyodbc tool.

Data acquisition (I.II): We used the pandas library to import data.

Data cleaning, tokenization, and stopword removal (I.III): We cleaned the clinical notes first by removing punctuation and substituting patterns that could be dates with the word "data". Then, we divided them into minimal text units of analysis, which we called tokens. Then, we proceeded with stopword removal, but considering only words longer than one character in order to exclude from the analysis strings belonging to the class of prepositions, articles, and adverbs, while keeping single letters that could be the abbreviation of a genus name.

### 2.4. Pattern Recognition (II)

Once we loaded and cleaned data, we needed to convert text into a numerical representation that could be used as input for ML algorithms, and we adopted the bag of words technique. This choice was guided by the structure of the sentences that was fragmentary and did not respect any strict syntactic rules. Therefore, we preferred to use a context-free representation.

Numerical representation building (II.I): Bag of words (BoW) is a numerical representation of text that describes the occurrence of words within a document. It involves two main issues: a vocabulary of known words (or n-grams of characters) and a measure of their presence in the text. BoW representation does not keep any information about the structure or order of words in the document. The possibility to add grouped words (called n-grams of words) to the vocabulary allows capturing a little of the meaning from the document. The resulting numerical representation was composed of both n-grams of characters and n-grams of words following the proportion of 70:30. We decided to select more features composed by n-grams of characters in order to deal with misspellings, abbreviations, and limited syntactic rules. We tested the model performance considering 10 possible total numbers of selected features from 10 to 100 with a step size of 10. We obtained the best performance with a total number of features equal to 90.

Classification (II.II): We used the aforementioned numerical representation to learn a supervised binary classifier to predict whether the observed pattern was present in the clinical note or not. Specifically, we compared the performances of three classifiers, as described below.

SVM is a supervised learning method that can be used to perform classification analysis on both linear and nonlinear data [37]. The main aim of SVM is to find a line or a hyperplane that maximizes the distance between the classes (support vectors) when placed between them [38]. If data are not linearly separable, then they can be transformed using a kernel function from a low-dimensional to a high-dimensional structure to make the data separable.

Logistic regression (LR) is a method of statistical analysis used to estimate the relationship between a dependent variable and at least one independent variable, minimizing the Euclidean distance between the true label and the model output. Specifically, for binary classification, the output variable is modeled by a sigmoid ranging between 0 and 1. We introduced model sparsity adding an $L_1$ penalty term [39].

Random forest (RF) is an ensemble of K decision tree classifiers created from a different bootstrap sample. The trees are built by sampling a random subset of the attributes at each internal node in the decision tree. The random sampling of the attributes reduces the correlation between the trees in the ensemble [40].

We split the dataset into a learning and a testing set with the proportion of 80:20. On the learning set, we performed the hyperparameter search through a tenfold cross-validation, which iteratively split the learning set into a training and validation set. They were respectively used to learn the model with all the possible combinations of hyperparameters and to evaluate the performances thereafter. Then, we learned the three models with the selected set of best hyperparameters, and we evaluated the model performances on the testing set. We repeated the classification 20 times, shuffling the data each time. In order to guarantee reproducibility of results, we set the random state equal to the loop index.

Models Evaluation (II.III): We evaluated the performance of the three ML models in terms of accuracy.

### 2.5. Pattern Removal (III)

Once the algorithm classified the clinical notes as "containing"/"not containing" the pattern, we used regular expressions to remove the uninformative pattern from the identified notes.

The schema of the regular expression was as follows: \b[Ii]\w.+?\bdata\b.

The elements of the expression are defined below.

\b asserts the position of a word boundary. In this case, we want the pattern beginning with 'I' (the first letter of the word 'Integrazione' (integration), which can be abbreviated and/or can be uppercase or lowercase in the notes).

\w matches any word character and ends with 'data' (the word that we substituted for all dates in the data cleaning phase).

. matches any character (e.g., letters, numbers, and punctuation) except for line terminators.

+? matches the previous token between one and unlimited times, the fewest times possible, but expanding as needed.

### 2.6. Microorganism Detection (IV)

Genus Extension (IV.I): We stored the microorganism names using the binomial nomenclature originating from the Linnaeus classification [41]. It is composed of two terms: the first is the genus name with the first letter capitalized; the second is the species name in lower case. Usually, after a microorganism's name is written once in a text, then it can be substituted with its first capital letter, followed by a period, in subsequent mentions. However, considering the brevity of the clinical notes, a shared agreement is to always write the abbreviated form, despite the entire genus having not yet been introduced. This binomial nomenclature does not allow the use of an abbreviation composed of two letters for the genus. Nevertheless, even though the microorganisms should be written according to this strict rule, we decided to keep words composed of only one character and not to use a regular expression, because we considered that abbreviations may be not written correctly, e.g., by using abbreviations that are not followed by a period, or where uppercase letters are followed by a period but not followed by lowercase letters. Hence, we performed the extension of the microorganism genus. Specifically, we compared the "$n$ + 1" token with each species of the vocabulary. If the similarity index between the two tokens was greater than or equal to 98, then we checked the token $n$". If the token "$n$" began with the same letter of the genus of the species in position "$n$ + 1", we substituted the token "$n$" with the genus name found in the vocabulary. The schema of the treatment is presented in Figure 2.

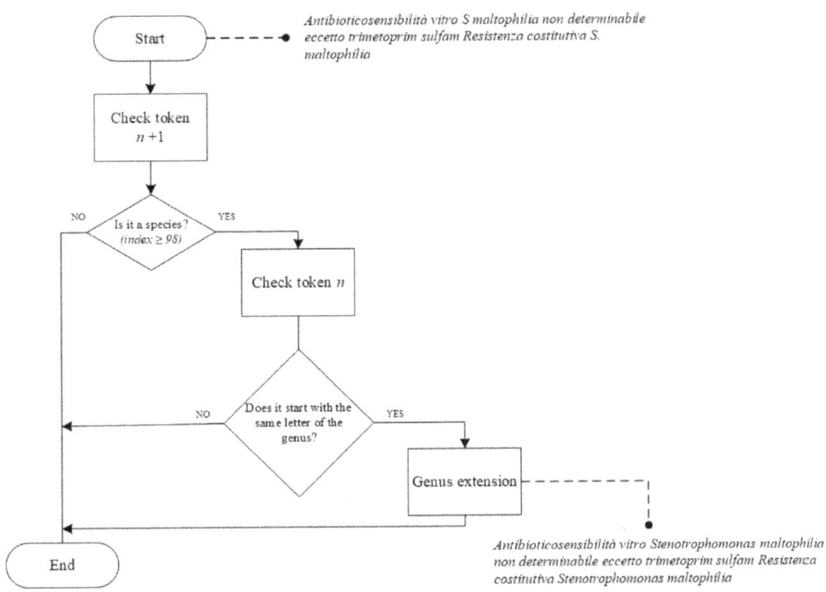


**Figure 2.** Genus extension decision flow. The figure also includes an example. In the upper part of the figure, there is a sentence already preprocessed but before the genus extension phase, whereas, in the lower part, we can see the extended version. First, the maltophilia species is identified, while "S" as the first letter of genus Stenotrophomonas is extended.

Microorganism name extraction (IV.II): Initially, we tried to carry out a lexical and morphological analysis, but the lack of morphological structure of the clinical notes resulted in no good results. Therefore, we extracted the microorganism name by comparing each token "$n$" of the preprocessed clinical notes and the genera in the vocabulary using the FuzzyWuzzy library. The complete workflow of the microorganism name extraction phase is shown in Figure 3.

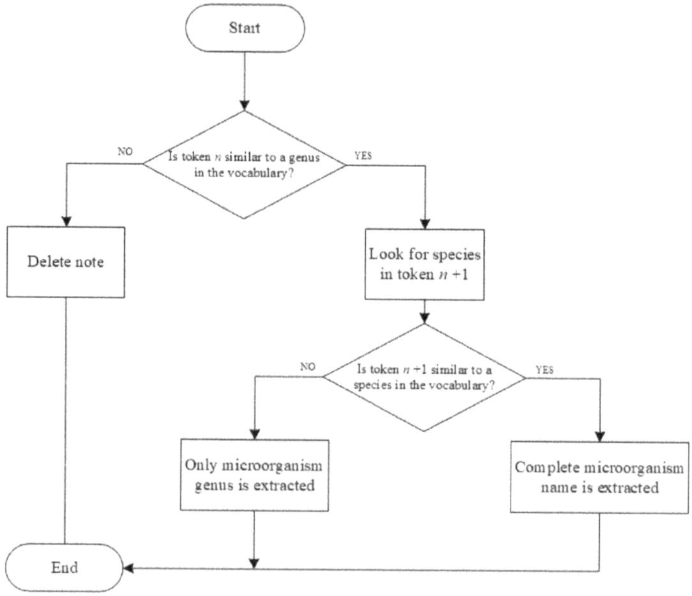


**Figure 3.** Microorganism name extraction decision flow. In contrast to the genus extension phase, in this process, the token "$n$" is first considered, and it is compared to the genera listed in the vocabulary. Only if a match is found (with a high similarity index) is the token "$n + 1$" considered and compared to the list of species in the vocabulary that belong to the identified genus.

In particular, considering the genus extraction, we set the threshold of the similarity index at 75, while we set the threshold of the species index as 85 (as they were typically written correctly).

Other Information Extraction (IV.III): Together with the identification of the genus and species, in order to highlight microorganisms that could be potentially dangerous, we also searched the clinical notes for the keyword "alert", which is an explicit indication of microbiologists regarding the danger of the identified microorganism. Similarly, but much less frequently, the "non-alert" bi-gram, with which the microbiologists indicate the harmlessness of the microorganism, may be present. To address both cases, we performed a search at the token level for the keyword "alert". If identified at the n position, we checked if token $n - 1$ matched the negation "non".

## 3. Results

### *3.1. Identification and Removal of a Specific Pattern*

In the process of information extraction from the microbiological notes, it is useful to identify nonmeaningful sentences, e.g., "integration of the provisional report of . . . ". The lack of morphological structure in the sentences led us to use a count-based method to build a numerical representation of the clinical notes.

Figure 4 summarizes the mean values of accuracy obtained using the three classifiers over the 20 iterations per each total number of features, shuffling the data each time.

We obtained best results in terms of mean accuracy across classifiers (99.06%) with a total number of features equal to 90. The SVM classifier with a Gaussian kernel obtained a mean accuracy of 98.99%, logistic regression obtained a mean accuracy of 98.99%, and random forest obtained a mean accuracy of 99.19%.

This means that the pattern was correctly identified using all classifiers, and it can be securely removed from the specific clinical notes.

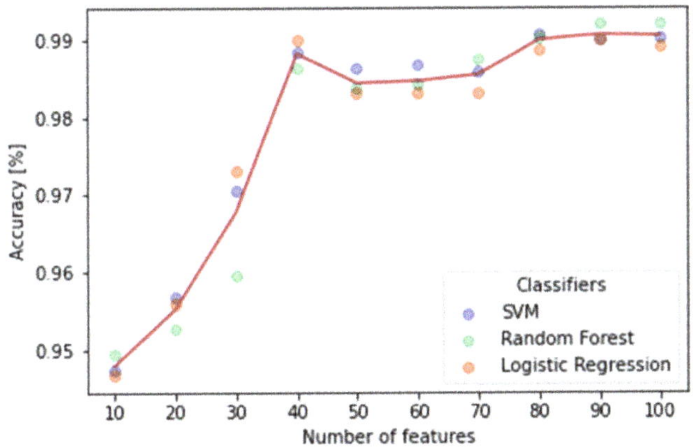


**Figure 4.** Mean accuracy performances of the three classifiers displayed for each value of the total number of features. Each data point is the mean value of 20 values obtained by shuffling the data.

### 3.2. Genus Extension

Our sample of clinical notes contained a total number of 107 abbreviated genera followed by their species. After the system elaboration process of the notes, all 107 genera were extended, and they completely matched with the expert indications.

### 3.3. Microorganism Detection

Our sample of clinical notes was composed of 499 texts, and 276 (55.3%) of them actually presented the name of a microorganism. We performed two tests.

First, we introduced the entire sample into the module for microorganism extraction.

Then, we introduced only those notes that actually contained the name of the microorganisms.

The system correctly identified all microorganism names in both cases. In detail, it found 416 genera, and, as shown in Figure 5a, the majority of them (321) had a similarity index of 100. This was also a consequence of the genus extension process.

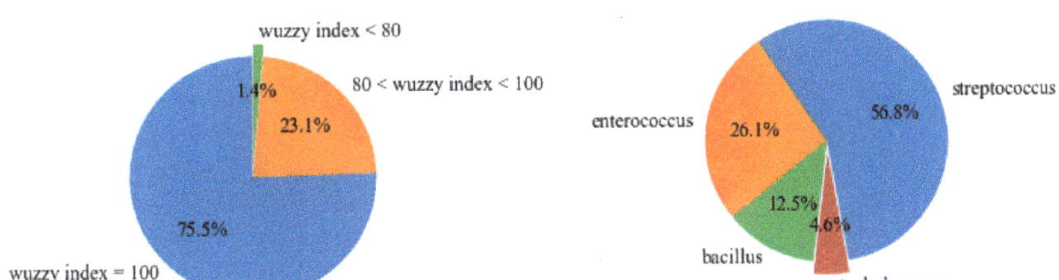


**Figure 5.** System performance for genus extraction. (**a**) Similarity index percentage distribution of genera. (**b**) Percentage distribution of genera found with low indices.

Figure 5b shows that '*Staphylococcus*' was the genus name with the lowest score; in particular, it usually presented a very low similarity index, between 76 and 80, if a species was not specified. Indeed, we frequently found not only the strictly scientific term, but also the Italian term in the notes, because *Staphylococcus* is among the most widespread bacteria and is frequently mentioned in the common discourse.

This behavior affected the similarity index; in particular, *Staphylococcus* and 'stafilococco/stafilococchi' (Italian terms referring to the *Staphylococcus* genus) have 14 and 12 letters, respectively, within which only nine coincide, representing a Levenshtein distance of 5 (i.e., five changes are needed to transform the first word into the other). On the other hand, species never showed a Wuzzy index lower than 88.

Lastly, we introduced a weight, which was a decimal parameter ranging between 0 and 1. It could be associated with the genus–species couple or only with the genus, if present alone. As the same word (genus and/or species) could be associated with more than one genus/species, this process was necessary to highlight the maximum Wuzzy indices. An example of the system output is shown in Table 1; the similarity index of the two genera *Acinetobacter* and *Acetobacter* was 92, which is quite high. Thus, in order to identify the correct genus without any doubt, we compared the following token with all species of that specific genus present in the vocabulary. If a match was found (with a Wuzzy index over 98), then we assigned to that genus–species couple a weight parameter equal to 1, while the others received a weight of 0.

**Table 1.** Example of the system output returned when the input was "Gram negativi profilo proteomico riferibile ad *A baumannii*. Propensione di *A baumannii* alla pan-resistenza eccetto colistina (Microorganismo alert)". The displayed columns correspond to the genus from the vocabulary, the specific word or character in text which the genus matches to, the genus Wuzzy similarity index, the species from the vocabulary, the word in text which the species matches to, the species Wuzzy similarity index, the clinical note divided into tokens, and the weight parameter.

| Genus | Match Genus | Wuzzy Index Genus | Species | Match Species | Wuzzy Index Species | Clinical Notes | Weight |
|---|---|---|---|---|---|---|---|
| *Acinetobacter* | *A* | 100.0 | *baumannii* | *baumannii* | 100.0 | [94,'propensione','NaN','Acinetobacter','b ... | 1 |
| *Acetobacter* | *A* | 92.0 | NaN | NaN | NaN | [94,'propensione','NaN','Acinetobacter','b ... | 0 |
| *Aminobacter* | *A* | 83.0 | NaN | NaN | NaN | [94,'propensione','NaN','Acinetobacter','b ... | 0 |
| *Citrobacter* | *A* | 83.0 | NaN | NaN | NaN | [94,'propensione','NaN','Acinetobacter','b ... | 0 |

Otherwise, if the clinical note did not contain any species, and the two genera that could correspond to the same word had an identical Wuzzy index, e.g., as a consequence of a spelling error, then the algorithm would assign to both genera an equal weight of 0.5.

### 3.4. Other Information Extraction

The whole sample included 48 clinical notes that contained the keyword "alert". Our algorithm was able to correctly discriminate between the notes that contained the bi-gram "non-alert" ($N = 9$) and those that contained the keyword alone ($N = 39$).

## 4. Discussion

In general, the pattern recognition and the genus extension phases led to good results. The first achieved a mean accuracy value of 99.06% considering all three classifiers, while the second extracted all the names of microorganisms reported by the experts from the hospital. We should consider, however, that some ambiguities could be found during this second phase. Indeed, there are a few microorganisms with identical species and whose genera begin with the same letter. If one such case appears, then the system will duplicate the clinical note and it will extract both microorganisms, but both notes will be associated with a weight equal to 0.5. However, we should specify that, luckily, these kinds of ambiguities are quite rare. A well-known example is the *intermedius* species, which can belong to both the *Staphylococcus* genus and the *Streptococcus* genus. *Staphylococcus intermedius* is quite frequent in animals; however, it is reported as a human pathogen in very few cases, most of which are associated with exposure to animals, especially dogs. On the contrary, *Streptococcus intermedius* is one of the major causes of brain abscesses, but very few cases of this condition are documented annually in Italy, with an incidence that is less than 0.1% per year. Therefore, we can affirm that the probability that such ambiguity is present in the report notes of the microbiological laboratory is extremely rare.

The major result of our pipeline is that we can extract a wider picture of the microorganism, because each microorganism is stored together with other metadata in the build vocabulary, such as the definition according to MeSH and its translation into national and international vocabularies. Furthermore, the pipeline also extracts the property of the microorganism under healthcare surveillance. Therefore, we can say that the system returns an object with its main characteristics. Once we accurately describe the microorganism, we can consider its identification in the clinical note as a trigger event of a series of messages and communications in accordance with the management policies of resistant microorganisms. Thus, it is possible to build a path to safeguard the patient and the community against the resistant microorganism [42]. The above-described system should be integrated in a multidisciplinary context. Correctly integrating objects from any viewpoint of the system in question requires its formal representation and management using the ISO 23903 Interoperability and Integration Reference Architecture [43]. ISO 23903 standardizes a model and framework for representing any type of system from the perspectives of the involved domains, its architectural composition/decomposition, and the related development process of implementable information and communications technology (ICT) solutions.

A limitation of the presented work is the low number of samples considered due to the fact that, to be delivered to researchers outside the laboratory, all these notes were checked individually and manually in order to avoid the illicit dissemination of personal data. In the near future, the correct structuring of electronic health records (which enables in constitutive law the reuse of clinical data for the purposes of scientific research) and greater awareness of the health risk that antibiotic-resistant bacteria constitute will result in a much higher number of notes to be analyzed. The more important methodological limitations of our project and ways to overcome them are discussed in the next section.

## 5. Future Work—Challenges and Solutions

Collecting, as well as storing and retrieving, representational objects of facts, systems, and processes is always a matter of the language and related grammar used to perform those actions. A simpler and more constrained language and ruling grammar, which is equivalent to the expressivity of languages/ontologies, facilitates processing of the outcome. However, highly expressive languages are less complete. This is a crucial challenge of knowledge representation in any business system including health and its special domains such as microbiology or infectious diseases.

Any business system can be represented using ICT ontologies. This holds for data stored in LIS databases, information models to represent the system's objects, and business process models representing the business processes needed to meet the intended business objectives. However, the justification of correctness and completeness of structure and behavior of the represented ecosystem can only be provided from the ecosystem's business view using the involved domains' ontologies. Justification of structure and behavior representation includes the representational components, their underlying concepts, their relations, and the related constraints. Figure 6 illustrates the related business system according to ISO 23903. The domains involved are clinical domains, managing patient care, and supporting facilities such as laboratories and microbiological departments to provide diagnostic services, as well as regulatory domains (policy domains) such as legal affairs, administration, security, and privacy management. Within the development process, the real-world system is then transformed into the different viewpoints of the intended ICT solution from the business process modeling (enterprise view) through the informational representation of all entities involved (information view) up to implementable artifacts (engineering view) and their management (technology view). The views in that order are represented by languages/grammars with increasing constraints and decreasing generative power, as well as decidability.

The technology view and engineering view are represented by data, while the computational view and information view are represented by information using related presentation styles such as programming languages or UML, respectively. The enterprise view represents the enterprise knowledge using business process modeling languages, and the business view represents the domain knowledge using domain ontologies (Figure 7). The different levels in the model hierarchy allow for different actions necessary for designing and running the business process according to Krogstie [45].

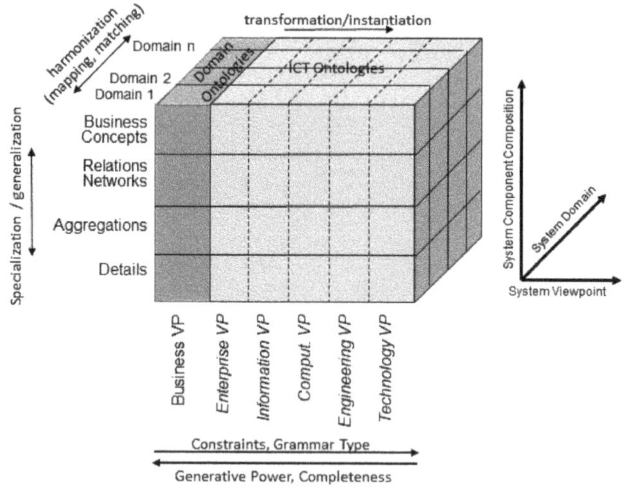


**Figure 6.** Generic business system representation according to ISO 23903, including the language/grammar characterization according to Chomsky [44].

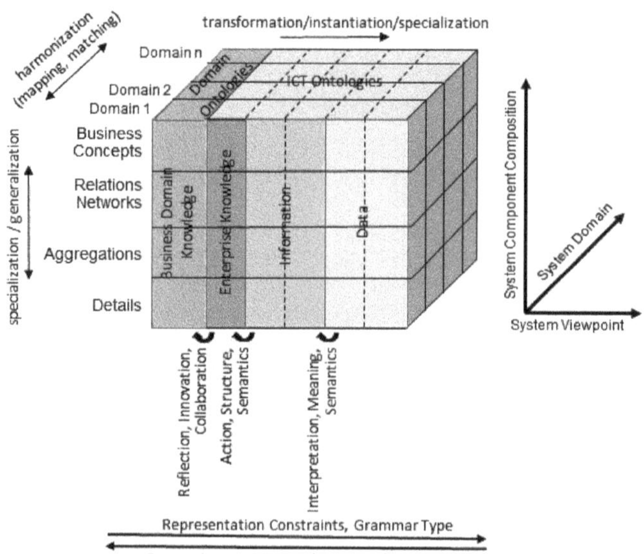


**Figure 7.** Generic business system representation according to ISO 23903 from the perspective of the knowledge pyramid after Aamodt and Nygard [46] and the model hierarchy after Krogstie [45].

For performing process-related actions, the enterprise view is necessary. For taking strategic and operational decisions, driving innovations, and enabling comprehensive collaboration, the representation of the business system in its comprehensive context using the ontologies of the directly and indirectly involved domains, guided by top-level ontologies according to ISO 21838 [47], is inevitable. In other words, the taxonomies used to analyze the business system must be replaced by ontologies, thereby not just considering the domain knowledge, but also the knowledge space in question. This involves not only the naming of entities, but also the underlying concepts and comprehensive relations. More details on the challenges and solutions can be found, e.g., in [48] or [49], as well as in the introductory paper to this volume.

## 6. Conclusions

The main aim of this work was to develop an NLP pipeline to support the automatic extraction of the microorganisms' names and important information contained in microbiological notes of culture reports. We decided to preprocess the notes before the extraction process by removing not meaningful sentences, such as "integration of the provisional report of ... ". We performed this task by applying machine learning methods to the numerical representation of the texts obtained using the bag of words technique. All the microorganisms present were extracted correctly; hence, the main goal was achieved. Lastly, considering that our vocabulary is based on international nomenclature standards, the presented pipeline can be applied to similar laboratory notes from other hospitals across the nation.

A next step of this project will be to also automatically extract from the same clinical notes the antibiogram data. In particular, key information that should be considered is the sensitivity of the specific microorganism to each single antibiotic tested. In the context of healthcare transformation toward pHealth or even 5P medicine (personalized, preventive, predictive, participative, and precision medicine), we have to advance the system further.

**Supplementary Materials:** The following supporting information can be downloaded at: https://www.mdpi.com/article/10.3390/jpm12091424/s1.

**Author Contributions:** Conceptualization, M.G., B.B. and R.G.; methodology, S.M.; software, J.A. and S.M.; validation, S.M.; formal analysis, S.M.; investigation, S.M.; resources, S.M.; data curation, G.P., J.A. and S.M.; writing—original draft preparation, S.M.; writing—review and editing, S.M., D.R.G., M.G. and B.B.; visualization, S.M.; supervision, M.G.; project administration, R.G.; funding acquisition, G.P. All authors have read and agreed to the published version of the manuscript.

**Funding:** This research received no external funding.

**Institutional Review Board Statement:** Not applicable.

**Informed Consent Statement:** Not applicable.

**Data Availability Statement:** Data used in this project are available as Supplementary Materials.

**Acknowledgments:** The authors want to thank the technical staff of the AUSL Pescara who contributed to the collection of the data used in the project.

**Conflicts of Interest:** Outside of the submitted work, D.R.G. reports investigator-initiated grants from Pfizer, Gilead Italia, and Shionogi, and speaker/advisory board fees from Pfizer and Tillotts Pharma. The other authors declare no conflict of interest.

## References

1. Available online: https://www.epicentro.iss.it/ (accessed on 25 August 2022).
2. Angela, R. Healthcare–associated infections: A public health problem. *Niger. Med. J. Niger. Med. Assoc.* **2012**, *53*, 59.
3. Huys, G.; Cnockaert, M.; Bartie, K.; Oanh, D.; Phuong, N.; Somsiri, T.; Chinabut, S.; Yussoff, F.; Shariff, M.; Giacomini, M.; et al. Intra- and interlaboratory performance of antibiotic disk-diffusion-susceptibility testing of bacterial control strains of relevance for monitoring aquaculture environments. *Dis. Aquat. Org.* **2005**, *66*, 197–204. [CrossRef] [PubMed]
4. Adamu, J.Y.; Raufu, A.I.; Chimaroke, F.C.; Ameh, J.A. Antimicrobial susceptibility testing of Staphylococcus aureus isolated from apparently healthy humans and animals in Maiduguri, Nigeria. *Int. J. Biomed. Health Sci.* **2021**, *6*, 4.
5. Magiorakos, A.-P.; Srinivasan, A.; Carey, R.B.; Carmeli, Y.; Falagas, M.E.; Giske, C.G.; Harbarth, S.; Hindler, J.F.; Kahlmeter, G.; Olsson-Liljequist, B.; et al. Multidrug-resistant, extensively drug-resistant and pandrug-resistant bacteria: An international expert proposal for interim standard definitions for acquired resistance. *Clin. Microbiol. Infect.* **2012**, *18*, 268–281. [CrossRef]
6. Basak, S.; Singh, P.; Rajurkar, M. Multidrug Resistant and Extensively Drug Resistant Bacteria: A Study. *J. Pathog.* **2016**, *2016*, 1–5. [CrossRef] [PubMed]

7. Organisation for Economic Co-operation and Development, European Centre for Disease Prevention and Control. *Antimicrobial Resistance—Tackling the Burden in the European Union—Briefing Note for EU/EEA Countries*; OECD: Paris, France, 2019. Available online: https://www.oecd.org/health/health-systems/AMR-Tackling-the-Burden-in-the-EU-OECD-ECDC-Briefing-Note-2019.Pdf (accessed on 25 August 2022).
8. Centers for Disease Control and Prevention. 2019. Available online: https://www.cdc.gov/drugresistance/pdf/threats-report/2019-ar-threats-report-508.pdf (accessed on 25 August 2022).
9. Timsit, J.-F.; Ruppé, E.; Barbier, F.; Tabah, A.; Bassetti, M. Bloodstream infections in critically ill patients: An expert statement. *Intensive Care Med.* **2020**, *46*, 266–284. [CrossRef]
10. Giacobbe, D.R.; Roberts, J.A.; Abdul-Aziz, M.H.; de Montmollin, E.; Timsit, J.F.; Bassetti, M. Treatment of ventilator-associated pneumonia due to carbapenem-resistant Gram-negative bacteria with novel agents: A contemporary, multidisciplinary ESGCIP perspective. *Expert Rev. Anti Infect* **2022**, *20*, 963–979. [CrossRef]
11. Bassetti, M.; Poulakou, G.; Ruppe, E.; Bouza, E.; Van Hal, S.J.; Brink, A. Antimicrobial resistance in the next 30 years, humankind, bugs and drugs: A visionary approach. *Intensive Care Med.* **2017**, *43*, 1464–1475. [CrossRef]
12. Costa, D.; Martins, P.; Loureiro, L.; Matos, A.J.F. Transfer of multidrug-resistant bacteria between intermingled ecological niches: The interface between humans, animals and the environment. *Int. J. Environ. Res. Public Health* **2013**, *10*, 278–294. [CrossRef]
13. Saud, B.; Paudel, G.; Khichaju, S.; Bajracharya, D.; Dhungana, G.; Awasthi, M.S.; Shrestha, V. Multidrug-Resistant Bacteria from Raw Meat of Buffalo and Chicken, Nepal. *Vet. Med. Int.* **2019**, *2019*, 7960268. [CrossRef]
14. Rahman, M.; Husna, A.; Elshabrawy, H.A.; Alam, J.; Runa, N.Y.; Badruzzaman, A.T.M.; Banu, N.A.; Al Mamun, M.; Paul, B.; Das, S.; et al. Isolation and molecular characterization of multidrug-resistant Escherichia coli from chicken meat. *Sci. Rep.* **2020**, *10*, 21999. [CrossRef] [PubMed]
15. Jeżak, K.; Kozajda, A. Occurrence and spread of antibiotic-resistant bacteria on animal farms and in their vicinity in Poland and Ukraine—review. *Environ. Sci. Pollut. Res.* **2021**, *29*, 9533–9559. [CrossRef]
16. Huys, G.; Bartie, K.; Cnockaert, M.; Oanh, D.T.H.; Phuong, N.T.; Somsiri, T.; Chinabut, S.; Yusoff, F.M.; Shariff, M.; Giacomini, M.; et al. Biodiversity of chloramphenicol-resistant mesophilic heterotrophs from Southeast Asian aquaculture environments. *Res. Microbiol.* **2007**, *158*, 228–235. [CrossRef]
17. Pham, T.T.H.; Rossi, P.; Dinh, H.D.K.; Pham, N.T.A.; Tran, P.A.; Ho, T.T.K.M.; Dinh, Q.T.; De Alencastro, L.F. Analysis of antibiotic multi-resistant bacteria and resistance genes in the effluent of an intensive shrimp farm (Long An, Vietnam). *J. Environ. Manag.* **2018**, *214*, 149–156. [CrossRef] [PubMed]
18. Higuera-Llantén, S.; Vásquez-Ponce, F.; Barrientos-Espinoza, B.; Mardones, F.; Marshall, S.H.; Olivares-Pacheco, J. Extended antibiotic treatment in salmon farms select multiresistant gut bacteria with a high prevalence of antibiotic resistance genes. *PLoS ONE* **2018**, *13*, e0203641. [CrossRef] [PubMed]
19. Grimson, W.; Brender, J.; Grimson, J.; Groth, T.; Hermanson, B.; Yearworth, M.; Wade, V. Specifying an open clinical laboratory information system. *Comput. Methods Programs Biomed.* **1996**, *50*, 95–109. [CrossRef]
20. Aller, R.D. Software standards and the laboratory information system. *Am. J. Clin. Pathol.* **1996**, *105*, S48–S53.
21. Gazzarata, R.; Monteverde, M.E.; Vio, E.; Saccavini, C.; Gubian, L.; Borgo, I.; Giacomini, M. A Terminology Service Compliant to CTS2 to Manage Semantics within the Regional HIE. *Eur. J. Biomed. Inform.* **2017**, *13*. [CrossRef]
22. Available online: https://www.omg.org/ (accessed on 25 August 2022).
23. Available online: https://www.hl7.org/ (accessed on 25 August 2022).
24. Matheny, M.E.; Fitzhenry, F.; Speroff, T.; Hathaway, J.; Murff, H.J.; Brown, S.H.; Fielstein, E.M.; Dittus, R.S.; Elkin, P.L. Detection of blood culture bacterial contamination using natural language processing. *AMIA Annu. Symp. Proc. AMIA Symp.* **2009**, *2009*, 411–415.
25. Maganti, N.; Tan, H.; Niziol, L.M.; Amin, S.; Hou, A.; Singh, K.; Ballouz, D.; Woodward, M.A. Natural Language Processing to Quantify Microbial Keratitis Measurements. *Ophthalmology* **2019**, *126*, 1722–1724. [CrossRef]
26. Fu, S.; Wyles, C.C.; Osmon, D.R.; Carvour, M.L.; Sagheb, E.; Ramazanian, T.; Kremers, W.K.; Lewallen, D.G.; Berry, D.J.; Sohn, S.; et al. Automated Detection of Periprosthetic Joint Infections and Data Elements Using Natural Language Processing. *J. Arthroplast.* **2020**, *36*, 688–692. [CrossRef] [PubMed]
27. Gazzarata, R.; Monteverde, M.E.; Bonetto, M.; Savini, V.; Polilli, E.; Corridoni, S.; Costantini, A.; Santoleri, F.; Rapacchiale, G.; Palmieri, D.; et al. A SOA based solution for MDRO surveillance and improved antibiotic pre-scription in the Abruzzo region. *pHealth* **2019**, *2019*, 49–54.
28. Mora, S.; Attene, J.; Gazzarata, R.; Parruti, G.; Giacomini, M. A NLP Pipeline for the Automatic Extraction of Microorganisms Names from Microbiological Notes. *Stud. Health Technol. Inform.* **2021**, 153–158. [CrossRef]
29. Pandas. Available online: https://pandas.pydata.org/ (accessed on 25 August 2022).
30. Steven, B. NLTK: The natural language toolkit. In Proceedings of the COLING/ACL 2006 Interactive Presentation Sessions, Sydney, Australia, 17-21 July 2006.
31. Honnibal, M.; Montani, I. spaCy 2: Natural language understanding with Bloom embeddings, convolutional neural networks and incremental parsing. *Appear* **2017**, *7*, 411–420.
32. Van Rossum, G. *The Python Library Reference, Release 3.8.2*; Python Software Foundation: Fredericksburg, Virginia, 2020.
33. Pedregosa, F.; Varoquaux, G.; Gramfort, A.; Michel, V.; Thirion, B.; Grisel, O.; Blondel, M.; Prettenhofer, P.; Weiss, R.; Dubourg, V.; et al. Scikit-learn: Machine learning in Python. *J. Mach. Learn. Res.* **2011**, *12*, 2825–2830.

34. Waskom, M.L. seaborn: Statistical data visualization. *J. Open Source Softw.* **2021**, *6*, 3021. [CrossRef]
35. Hunter, J.D. Matplotlib: A 2D graphics environment. *Comput. Sci. Eng.* **2007**, *9*, 90–95. [CrossRef]
36. Available online: https://github.com/seatgeek/thefuzz (accessed on 25 August 2022).
37. Ghosh, S.; Dasgupta, A.; Swetapadma, A. A Study on Support Vector Machine based Linear and Non-Linear Pattern Classification. In Proceedings of the 2019 International Conference on Intelligent Sustainable Systems (ICISS), IEEE, Palladam, India, 21–22 February 2019; pp. 24–28. [CrossRef]
38. Chapelle, O.; Haffner, P.; Vapnik, V. Support vector machines for histogram-based image classification. *IEEE Trans. Neural Netw.* **1999**, *10*, 1055–1064. [CrossRef]
39. Kleinbaum, D.G.; Dietz, K.; Gail, M.; Klein, M.; Klein, M. *Logistic Regression*; Springer: New York, NY, USA, 2002.
40. Leo, B. Random forests. *Mach. Learn.* **2001**, *45*, 5–32.
41. Linnaeus, C. Systema naturae. *Stockh. Holmiae (Laurentii Salvii)* **1758**, *10*, 551.
42. Mondain, V.; Secondo, G.; Guttmann, R.; Ferrea, G.; Dusi, A.; Giacomini, M.; Courjon, J.; Pradier, C. A toolkit for the management of infection or colonization by extended-spectrum beta-lactamase producing Enterobacteriaceae in Italy: Implementation and outcome of a European project. *Eur. J. Clin. Microbiol.* **2018**, *37*, 987–992. [CrossRef]
43. *ISO 23903:2021*; Interoperability and Integration Reference Architecture–Model and Framework. ISO: Geneva, Switzerland, 2021.
44. Chomsky Hierarchy in Theory of Computation. Available online: https://www.geeksforgeeks.org/chomsky-hierarchy-in-theory-of-computation/ (accessed on 25 August 2022).
45. Krogstie, J. Business Information Systems Utilizing the Future Internet. *Data Knowl. Eng.* **2011**, *90*, 1–18. [CrossRef]
46. Aamodt, A.; Nygård, M. Different roles and mutual dependencies of data, information, and knowledge—An AI perspective on their integration. *Data Knowl. Eng.* **1995**, *16*, 191–222. [CrossRef]
47. *ISO/IEC 21838:2021*; Information Technology–Top-Level Ontologies (TLO). ISO: Geneva, Switzerland, 2021.
48. Blobel, B.; Ruotsalainen, P.; Oemig, F. Why Interoperability at Data Level Is Not Sufficient for Enabling pHealth? In *pHealth*; IOS Press: Amsterdam, The Netherlands, 2020; Volume 273, pp. 3–20. [CrossRef]
49. Blobel, B.; Oemig, F.; Ruotsalainen, P.; Lopez, D.M. Transformation of Health and Social Care Systems—An Interdisciplinary Approach Toward a Foundational Architecture. *Front. Med.* **2022**, *9*, 802487. [CrossRef]

Journal of *Personalized Medicine*

MDPI

*Article*

# Application of Machine Learning Methods for Epilepsy Risk Ranking in Patients with Hematopoietic Malignancies Using

**Iaroslav Skiba [1], Georgy Kopanitsa [2,3,*], Oleg Metsker [2], Stanislav Yanishevskiy [2] and Alexey Polushin [1]**

[1] Department of Chemotherapy and Stem Cell Transplantation for Cancer and Autoimmune Diseases, First Pavlov State Medical University of St. Peterburg, 197022 Saint Petersburg, Russia
[2] Almazov National Medical Research Centre, 197341 Saint Petersburg, Russia
[3] National Center for Cognitive Research, ITMO University, 49 Kronverskiy Prospect, 197101 Saint Petersburg, Russia
* Correspondence: georgy.kopanitsa@gmail.com

**Abstract:** Machine learning methods to predict the risk of epilepsy, including vascular epilepsy, in oncohematological patients are currently considered promising. These methods are used in research to predict pharmacoresistant epilepsy and surgical treatment outcomes in order to determine the epileptogenic zone and functional neural systems in patients with epilepsy, as well as to develop new approaches to classification and perform other tasks. This paper presents the results of applying machine learning to analyzing data and developing diagnostic models of epilepsy in oncohematological and cardiovascular patients. This study contributes to solving the problem of often unjustified diagnosis of primary epilepsy in patients with oncohematological or cardiovascular pathology, prescribing antiseizure drugs to patients with single seizure syndromes without finding a disease associated with these cases. We analyzed the hospital database of the V.A. Almazov Scientific Research Center of the Ministry of Health of Russia. The study included 66,723 treatment episodes of patients with vascular diseases (I10–I15, I61–I69, I20–I25) and 16,383 episodes with malignant neoplasms of lymphoid, hematopoietic, and related tissues (C81-C96 according to ICD-10) for the period from 2010 to 2020. Data analysis and model calculations indicate that the best result was shown by gradient boosting with mean accuracy cross-validation score = 0.96. f1-score = 98, weighted avg precision = 93, recall = 96, f1-score = 94. The highest correlation coefficient for G40 and different clinical conditions was achieved with fibrillation, hypertension, stenosis or occlusion of the precerebral arteries (0.16), cerebral sinus thrombosis (0.089), arterial hypertension (0.17), age (0.03), non-traumatic intracranial hemorrhage (0.07), atrial fibrillation (0.05), delta absolute neutrophil count (0.05), platelet count at discharge (0.04), transfusion volume for stem cell transplantation (0.023). From the clinical point of view, the identified differences in the importance of predictors in a broader patient model are consistent with a practical algorithm for organic brain damage. Atrial fibrillation is one of the leading factors in the development of both ischemic and hemorrhagic strokes. At the same time, brain infarction can be accompanied both by the development of epileptic seizures in the acute period and by unprovoked epileptic seizures and development of epilepsy in the early recovery and in a longer period. In addition, a microembolism of the left heart chambers can lead to multiple microfocal lesions of the brain, which is one of the pathogenetic aspects of epilepsy in elderly patients. The presence of precordial fibrillation requires anticoagulant therapy, the use of which increases the risk of both spontaneous and traumatic intracranial hemorrhage.

**Keywords:** oncohematology; risk factors; machine learning; epilepsy risk; epilepsy modeling

check for updates

**Citation:** Skiba, I.; Kopanitsa, G.; Metsker, O.; Yanishevskiy, S.; Polushin, A. Application of Machine Learning Methods for Epilepsy Risk Ranking in Patients with Hematopoietic Malignancies Using. *J. Pers. Med.* **2022**, *12*, 1306. https://doi.org/10.3390/jpm12081306

Academic Editors: Bernd Blobel and Mauro Giacomini

Received: 22 June 2022
Accepted: 8 August 2022
Published: 11 August 2022



## 1. Introduction

Malignant diseases of the hematopoietic system, despite their relatively low prevalence in the population, remain a socially significant group of diseases. Neurological complications in this cohort of patients occur in correlation with disease or with ongoing treatment. These complications may affect patient survival and may determine whether a therapy protocol can be fully implemented [1]. Acute symptomatic seizure (ASS) is one of the most significant neurological complications because of its high incidence and impact on survival [2]. A number of studies have evaluated the risk of ASS in this cohort of patients [3,4], while assessment of the risks of epilepsy is virtually unreported in the research to date [5,6].

Arterial hypertension is a cardiovascular complication in oncohematological patients that develops due to both disease-related and treatment-related factors [7,8]. Arterial hypertension has also been identified as one of the risk factors for the late-onset epilepsy in the general population [9].

Posterior reversible encephalopathy syndrome (PRES) is a brain disease associated with hypertension, which may determine the risk of epilepsy by indirect (in relation to arterial hypertension itself) mechanisms [10]. In the general population of patients with PRES syndrome, ACS occurs in 77% of cases [11]. In the cohort of oncohematological patients, the development of PRES syndrome may be accompanied by ASS in 97% of cases [12]. In the general population, arterial hypertension is the main etiological factor in the development of PRES syndrome (72%) [13]. It is a high-risk factor for the development of this complication in oncohematological patients as well (HR 14.466, 95% CI 7.107–29.443, $p < 0.001$) [12]. The risk of epilepsy in patients with PRES syndrome is considered low but may increase significantly in the presence of signs of cytotoxic edema and ASS in the debut of PRES syndrome [14].

The use of machine learning methods to predict the risk of complications in oncohematological patients has proven to be promising [15]. These methods are actively used in epilepsy, for example, to predict the pharmacoresistant epilepsy [16], to predict surgical treatment outcomes [17], to determine the epileptogenic zone [18] and to determine functional neural systems in patients with epilepsy [19], to develop new classification approaches [20,21], and to perform other tasks [22]. Machine learning models are actively used in decision support systems to treat patients with various forms of epilepsy [23,24]. At the same time, classical statistical methods of analysis are usually used to identify factors associated with the development of epilepsy within a typical case-control study design. However, factors related to the presence of epilepsy and prognostic tools that substantiate the optimal model for determining the risk of epilepsy in oncohematological patients are not fully understood now [25]. Currently, there exist no risk stratification models for epilepsy in oncohematological patients. The causes of symptomatic epilepsy are heterogeneous and require different approaches in the prevention of new foci of altered electrogenesis (e.g., brain infarcts in atrial fibrillation) [26].

The main goal of the study is to improve algorithms for diagnosing the cause of epilepsy in a group of patients without a previous history of epilepsy.

The groups of patients under consideration are patients with oncohematological diseases and cardiovascular pathology.

The main problem is the often-unjustified diagnosis of primary epilepsy in patients with oncohematological or cardiovascular pathology, prescribing antiseizure drugs to patients with single seizure syndromes without finding a disease associated with these episodes.

This paper presents the results of applying machine learning to analyzing data and developing diagnostic models of presence of epilepsy in oncohematological and cardiovascular patients.

We evaluate factors associated with the presence of epilepsy in oncohematological patients and the effect of arterial hypertension and the number of transplanted hematopoietic stem cells on the risk of epilepsy.

## 2. Materials and Methods

A single-center retrospective study was conducted. We analyzed the hospital database of the V.A. Almazov Scientific Research Center of the Ministry of Health of Russia. The study included 35,634 patients with 66,723 inpatient treatment cases (Dataset II) and

3723 patients with 16,383 inpatient treatment cases (Dataset I) of patients with malignant neoplasms of lymphoid, hematopoietic, and related tissues (C81–C96 according to ICD-10) for the period from the 27 January 2010 to the 5 January 2020. Laboratory parameters were chosen according to their clinical relevance and available data from real clinical practice. We considered their potential role in metabolism, systemic inflammation, and hemostasis and in the development of epileptic syndromes. Cerebrovascular factors were chosen according to the evidence on the increasing role of cardiovascular complications in predicting long-term outcomes in patients with oncohematological diseases.

### 2.1. Study Datasets

**Dataset I** was formed to develop a detailed descriptive and prognostic model of epilepsy for clinical, anamnestic, and laboratory patient factors in patients with oncohematology.

**Inclusion criteria**

- Age: 1–90 years old;
- Diagnosis: verified malignant neoplasms of lymphoid, hematopoietic, and related tissues;
- Case type: inpatient treatment.

**Exclusion criteria**

1. Absence of oncohematological or cardiac disease. Outpatient treatment was an exclusion criterion;
2. A history of Acute symptomatic seizures (ASS) without a verified diagnosis of epilepsy (G40.0–G40.8);
3. Outpatient treatment.

A total of 356 factors were extracted for each patient, including genetic sex and constitutional factors, presence of comorbid pathology, factors for hematopoietic stem cell transplantation, and laboratory parameters.

The patients had the following clinical parameters:

1. Comorbidities: 14% of I60–I69, fibrillation—6%, epilepsy (G40.0–G40.8)—1.5%, hypertension—20%;
2. Genetic sex: females—49%, males—51%;
3. Age: mean age—52.5 (min—1, max—90, 25%—40, 50%—57, 75%—66).

As an endpoint, we analyzed whether the patient developed epilepsy (presence of ICD-10 G40.0–G40.8 diagnoses).

**Dataset II** was formed to develop a descriptive and prognostic model of epilepsy in patients with cardiovascular disease to identify vascular factors in the development of epilepsy. Therefore, a group of patients with epilepsy both with and without oncohematological diagnosis was selected for this stage of the analysis to identify the contribution of the presence of oncohematological diagnosis to epilepsy. A second dataset was generated to analyze epilepsy in a wider patient group of 35,634 patients with 66,723 treatment episodes with 285 parameters among which: Age mean—55 (min—1, max 99, 25%—46, 50%—60, 75%—69), presence of comorbid diseases (hypertension, cerebral vascular disease, infarcts, atrial fibrillation and congenital heart disease (CHD), blood pressure, fibrillation (13%), G40—8%, males—44%, females—56%, BMI mean—1.87 (std—0.33, min—0.17, max—6.06, 25%—1.73, 50%—1.9, 75%—2.06).

**Inclusion criteria:**

1. Age: 1–99 years old;
2. Diagnosis: hypertension, acute coronary syndrome (ACS), strokes, coronary artery disease (CAD),congenital heart disease (CHD), verified malignant neoplasms of lymphoid, hematopoietic, and related tissues;
3. Case type: inpatient treatment.

**Exclusion criteria:**

1. Absence of cardiovascular disease and oncological disease;
2. Outpatient treatment was an exclusion criterion;

3. A history of Acute symptomatic seizures (ASS) without a verified diagnosis of epilepsy (G40.0–G40.8).

The following data preparation procedure was performed for both datasets. We removed the patients with the insufficient amount of data (<80% of parameters). We also removed 1% of values having the highest z-score to filter out some obvious outliers.

After that, we applied two strategies of dealing with missing values to ensure that all patients have the same set of variables:

Replacement of missing data with the medians of the corresponding parameters;

Deletion of parameters that have too many missing values and removal of all patients that have any missing values in the remaining parameters.

## 2.2. Correlation Analysis

The Pearson coefficient was used to assess the correlation of the G40.0–G40.8 with the analyzed factors. The chi-squared criterion was applied to the binary values.

## 2.3. Machine Learning Methods

Gradient boosting and random forest models were applied.

Parameters of the model are XGBClassifier (base_score = 0.5, booster = None, colsample_bylevel = 1, colsample_bynode = 1, colsample_bytree = 0.6, gamma = 2, gpu_id = −1, importance_type = 'gain', interaction_constraints = None, learning_rate = 0.300000012, max_delta_step = 0, max_depth = 5, min_child_weight = 2, missing = nan, monotone_constraints = None, n_estimators = 100, n_jobs = 0, num_parallel_tree = 1, random_state = 0, reg_alpha = 0, reg_lambda = 1, scale_pos_weight = 1, subsample = 0.8, tree_method = None, validate_parameters = False, verbosity = None).

The parameters of the random forest were taken by default.

We also searched for optimal hyperparameters of the model using the greedy search method, Randomized Search CV, GridSearchCVwith params = { 'min_child_weight': [1, 2, 3, 4, 5, 6, 7, 8, 9, 10], 'gamma': [0.5, 1, 1.5, 2, 5]

'subsample': [0.1, 0.2, 0.3, 0.4, 0.5, 0.6, 0.8, 0.9, 1.0], 'colsample_bytree': [0.1, 0.2, 0.3, 0.4, 0.5, 0.6, 0.8, 0.9, 1.0], 'max_depth': [2, 3, 4, 5, 6, 7, 8, 9, 10, 15] }

We applied a stratified K-fold crossvalidation with 5 splits:

results = cross_val_score(rfc, X, y, cv = skf)

skf = StratifiedKFold(n_splits = 5, shuffle = True, random_state = 42)

The experiments were performed using the following hardware:

Intel Core i3-8109U CPU (3.00 GHz);

8 GM of Ram;

64-bit Windows 10 operating system.

The average times of the experiments were:

Dataset I: 01 min 19 s;

Dataset II: 52 min 18 s.

## 2.4. Importance of Predictors

Using the Shapley index, predictor significance factors were calculated in a model on an epilepsy class in patients with oncohematology and in a sample of patients with cerebrovascular disease.

## 2.5. Cerebrovascular Disease

After the first stage of data analysis, we detailed the parameters of cerebrovascular pathology I60–I69 as a significant factor associated with the presence of epilepsy. The detailing was carried out according to ICD-10 classification subheadings and included a search for specific nosological forms, including that within I67 and I65nosologies, which showed the greatest significance in the model for the "epilepsy" class.

The ranking of predictors for the presence of an epilepsy diagnosis on Dataset II was performed using the built-in method of predictor significance according to the Gini criterion in sklearn (also known as skikit-learn) with the setting of "balanced_subsample" weights autobalancing. The weight of each subsample varied according to the class distribution in that subsample. The built-in method provided an estimate of the significance of each individual feature in the model, in contrast to the Shapley index.

## 3. Results

Demographic details of the patients are presented in the Table 1.

**Table 1.** Demographic details of the study population.

| Dataset | Males | Females | Mean Age | Age 25% | Age 50% | Age 75% | Comorbidities |
|---|---|---|---|---|---|---|---|
| Dataset I | 51% | 49% | 52.5 | 40 | 57 | 66 | 14% of I60–I69, Fibrillation—6%, epilepsy (G40.0–G40.8)—1.5%, hypertension—20% |
| Dataset II | 44% | 56% | 55 | 46 | 60 | 69 | presence of comorbid diseases (hypertension, cerebral vascular disease, infarcts, atrial fibrillation and congenital heart disease (CHD), blood pressure, fibrillation (13%), G40—8% |

### 3.1. Dataset I

As a result of data analysis and model calculations, the best result was shown by gradient boosting (Table 2) with mean accuracy cross-validation score = 0.96, f1-score = 0.98, weighted avg precision = 0.93, recall = 0.96.

**Table 2.** Model evaluation for the Dataset I.

| Method | Accuracy | Precision | Recall | F1-Score | AUC of ROC |
|---|---|---|---|---|---|
| Gradient Boosting | 0.96 | 0.93 | 0.96 | 0.98 | 0.94 |
| Random forest | 0.92 | 0.89 | 0.93 | 0.94 | 0.91 |

The highest correlation coefficient for the presence of epilepsy and recurrent seizures (G40) was achieved with stenosis or occlusion of the precerebral arteries (0.16), cerebral sinus thrombosis (0.089), arterial hypertension (0.17), age (0.03), non-traumatic intracranial hemorrhage (0.07), atrial fibrillation (0.05), delta absolute neutrophil count (0.05), platelet count at discharge (0.04), transfusion volume for stem cell transplantation (0.023). The discriminative ability of the model calculated as AUC of ROC is 0.94.

The results of the Shapley index analysis of factors associated with the development of epilepsy in oncohematological patients are presented in the Figure 1 that contains the following predictors:

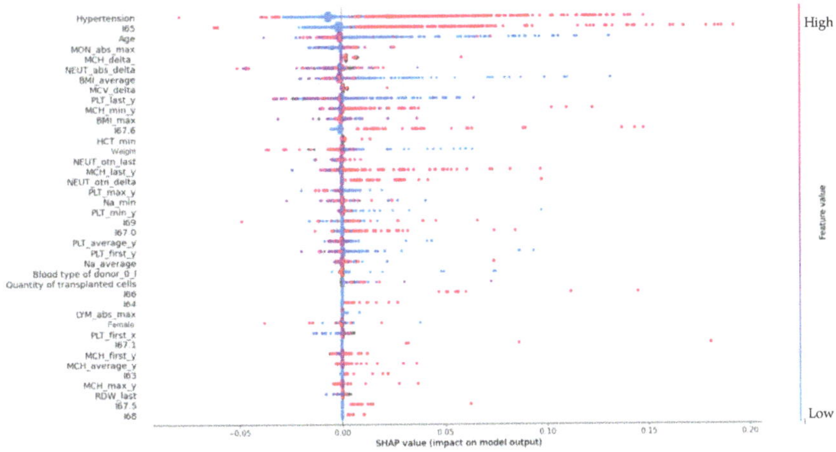


**Figure 1.** Factors associated with the development of epilepsy in oncohematological patients.

Hypertension—arterial hypertension;
I65—Occlusion and stenosis of precerebral arteries, not resulting in cerebral infarction;
MON—monocytes, maximum absolute number;
MCH—average concentration of hemoglobin in the erythrocyte;
NEUT—absolute neutrophil count;
BMI—body mass index;
MCV—mean erythrocyte volume;
PLT—platelets;
MCH min—minimum mean content of hemoglobin in an erythrocyte;
BMI max—maximum body mass index;
I67.6—Nonpyogenic thrombosis of intracranial venous system;
HCT—hematocrit;
NEUT otn—neutrophils, fraction in %;
PLT max—maximum platelet count;
Na—natrium;
I69—Sequelae of cerebrovascular disease;
I67.0—Other cerebrovascular diseases;
PLT average y—Platelets, mean per year;
Na average—mean sodium;
Bood type—blood group;
Quantity of transplanted cells—Quantity of transplanted cells;
I66—Occlusion and stenosis of cerebral arteries, not resulting in cerebral infarction;
I64—Stroke, not specified as hemorrhage or infarction;
Lym_abs_max—absolute lymphocyte count;
Female-woman—Female gender;
PLT_first_x—platelets, first measurement;
I67.1–Cerebral aneurysm, nonruptured;
MCH_first_y—Mean concentration of hemoglobin in an erythrocyte in the first blood test;
MCH_average_y—Mean concentration of hemoglobin in an erythrocyte
I63–Cerebral infarction;
MCH_max_y—maximum mean concentration of hemoglobin in the erythrocyte;
RDW—erythrocyte size distribution;
I67.5—Moyamoya disease;
I68—Cerebrovascular disorders in diseases classified elsewhere.

The effect of cerebral venous sinus thrombosis and arterial hypertension on the risk of epilepsy is shown in Figure 2.

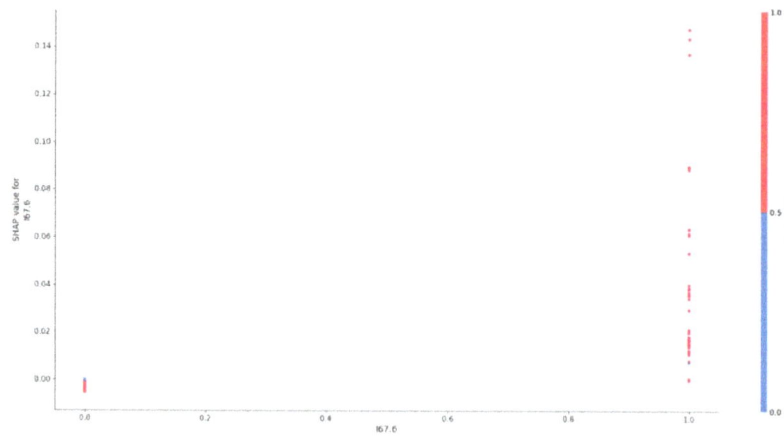


**Figure 2.** Effect of cerebral venous sinus thrombosis and arterial hypertension on the risk of epilepsy.

The effect of the number of transplanted hematopoietic stem cells on the risk of epilepsy is shown in Figure 3.

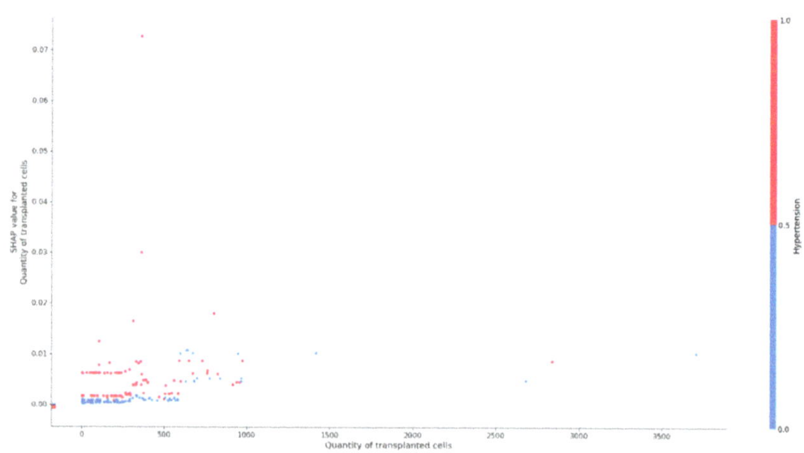


**Figure 3.** Dependency of the number of transplanted hematopoietic stem cells on hypertension in the model of an epilepsy class.

### 3.2. Dataset II

For the next stage of the analysis, a group of patients with epilepsy with and without the oncohematological diagnosis was selected to identify the contribution of the presence of oncohematological diagnosis on epilepsy (see Table 3 for the evaluation).

**Table 3.** Model evaluation for the Dataset II.

| Method | Cross-Validation Score | Precision | Recall | F1-Score | AUC of ROC |
|---|---|---|---|---|---|
| Gradient Boosting | 0.93 | 0.91 | 0.94 | 0.94 | 0.94 |
| Random forest | 0.89 | 0.82 | 0.91 | 0.90 | 0.90 |

Figure 4 shows that children (1–17 years old) are characterized by a slight increase in the risk of epilepsy in the presence of oncohematological disease, but the absence of oncological disease significantly increases the risk of epilepsy.

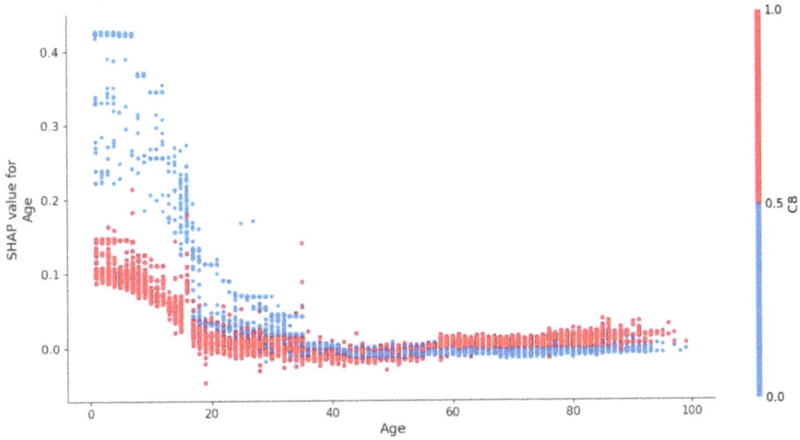


**Figure 4.** Dependency of epilepsy on age and presence of oncohematological diagnosis.

Figure 5 demonstrates the plot of dependence of oncohematological diagnosis on the presence of epilepsy and age.

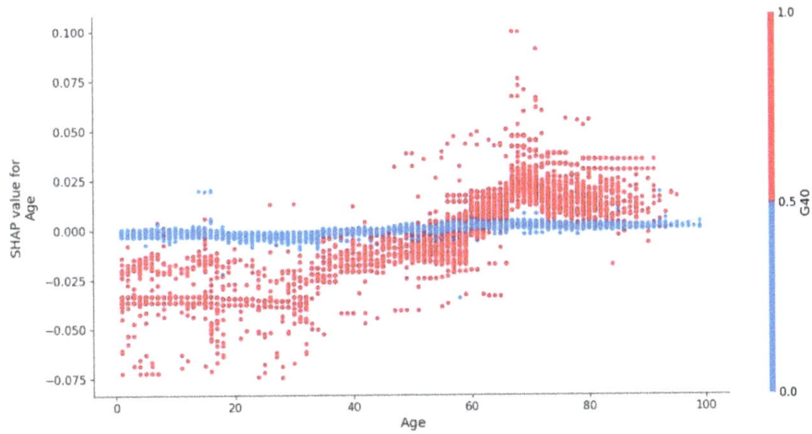


**Figure 5.** Dependency of oncohematological diagnosis on the presence of epilepsy and age.

In the age group of 18–40 years old, there was a gradual decrease in the influence of the "oncohematological disease" factor on the risk of epilepsy (Figure 6). In the age range of 40–60 years old, the presence/absence of oncohematological disease had almost no effect on the risk of epilepsy. At the same time, after the age of 60, the presence of such disease increased the risk of epilepsy in patients.

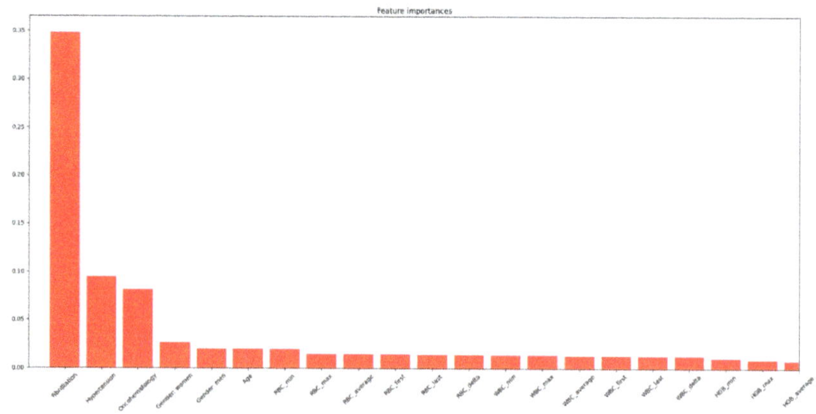


**Figure 6.** Predictor ranking for the onset of epilepsy in Dataset II.

When ranking the features associated with the presence of epilepsy, atrial fibrillation was found to have the highest weight, and oncohematological disease was the third most important feature (Figure 6).

## 4. Discussion

### *4.1. General*

A number of factors (clinical, gender, and laboratory) have been associated with the development of epilepsy in oncohematological patients. These factors can be grouped as follows:

- vital signs (age, body mass index, patient weight);
- cardiovascular pathology, cerebrovascular pathology (arterial hypertension, stenosis or occlusion, occlusion and stenosis of precerebral arteries, cerebral sinus thrombosis, cerebral artery dissection without rupture, cerebral aneurysmatic disease, cerebral infarction);
- laboratory parameters (maximum absolute monocyte count, average hemoglobin content of red blood cells, neutrophil count, platelet count at hospital discharge, minimum hematocrit value, minimum and average blood sodium levels);
- hematopoietic stem cell transplantation parameters (donor blood group, number of transplanted cells).

A number of factors had no significant effect on the risk of epilepsy. Demographic characteristics such as sex, age, and body weight were generally not significant. In spite of the known features of the age distribution of epilepsy, this relationship was not detected in the group of oncohematological patients. This fact may be related to the peculiarities of etiological factors in this cohort of patients, but further studies are needed to clarify the influence of various factors in different age groups.

The inclusion criteria in the first stage were limiting patients with oncohematological pathology and checking that possible structural or functional brain changes in oncohematological pathology would be associated with the development of epilepsy (more for secondary epilepsy).

In fact, there was a study of oncology-epilepsy and a high incidence of epilepsy was confirmed. The inclusion of patients with cardiovascular diseases in the second stage expanded the patient base due to a higher incidence of cardiovascular diseases, and the rank of nosological form (specific disease) in the development of comorbid epilepsy was determined.

### 4.2. Study Population

In the first dataset, the proportions of males and females were comparable, and the incidence of epilepsy was 1.5%. This prevalence of epilepsy in the first dataset was significantly higher than in the general population (1%) [27]. The incidence of atrial fibrillation (6%) at a mean age of 52.5 years (lower in comparison to other studies in the general population) was also comparable to that in the general population [28], including in the Russian Federation (5.8% for men and 7.4% for women) [29]. In the second dataset, the prevalence of atrial fibrillation was more than twice as high as in the first dataset. This may be associated with high comorbidity of this variant of rhythm disturbance and cardiovascular diseases [30]. Despite the lower proportion of males in dataset II (male gender is generally associated with a higher incidence of epileptic syndromes) [31]. The prevalence of epilepsy was significantly higher (8%) than in the first dataset.

### 4.3. Risk Factors

Among the laboratory parameters, both granulocytic and erythrocytic hematopoiesis parameters and platelet levels were found to be significant factors influencing the presence of epilepsy in oncohematological patients. Changes in these parameters are influenced by both the blood disease itself and its complications, as well as the administered therapy. A higher neutrophil count may indirectly indicate infectious complications or a more severe/prolonged course. In this regard, we can assume that factors such as infectious complications and hypofunction of the transplant, which are accompanied by significant laboratory changes, may explain the presence of these factors among the parameters influencing the epilepsy in this group of patients. Thrombocytopenia may be a risk factor for primarily intracranial hemorrhages in oncohematological patients [32–34]. These complications can lead to the formation of an epileptogenic substrate in the brain. In addition, the lower platelet count could be due to the antiseizure therapy being taken. Although epidemiological data on the development of epilepsy in patients with cerebral sinus thrombosis are not available, our results concerning the role of this factor in the development of epilepsy are more significant. Unfortunately, extrapolation to the general population is not possible given the sample of patients in our study (oncohematological patients). Thrombocytopenia was not previously considered a risk factor for epilepsy in the general population, as well as in the population of patients with other neurological [35–37] or general pathology [38].

The relationship between the development of cerebral venous sinus thrombosis (CVST) and oncology in general, and oncohematology in particular, has been investigated in a number of scientific papers [39]. Patients with oncohematologic diseases have a higher risk of CVST (aOR, 25.14; 95% CI, 11.64–54.30) than patients with solid cancer (aOR, 3.07; 95% CI, 2.03–4.65) [40]. Risks are even more severe in the first year after the cancer has been diagnosed (oncohematological OR, 85.57; 95% CI, 19.70–371.69; solid cancer aOR, 10.50; 95% CI, 5.40–20.42) [40]. CVST can account for up to 31.5% of all venous thromboembolic complications, for example, in a cohort of adult patients with acute myeloblastic leukemia [41].

Dimethyl sulfoxide as a factor is considered in the studies and can provoke the development of ASS. It can cause cardiovascular complications including ischemic stroke in the early post-transplant period [42–44]. In this regard, it is important to emphasize the contribution of the number of cells injected during transplantation in the risk of epilepsy that we identified in patients with arterial hypertension. This emphasizes the possible cardiovascular mechanisms of this effect.

The significance of the factor of presence of I67.6 (Nonpyogenic thrombosis of intracranial venous system) including in young patients could be due to indirect mechanisms of stroke development. Epidemiological data on the development of epilepsy in patients with cerebral sinus thrombosis are not available. This emphasizes the significance of our findings regarding the role of this factor in the development of epilepsy.

### 4.4. Arterial Hypertension

Arterial hypertension contributed the most to the presence of epilepsy in oncohematological patients (Figure 1). This, along with the presence of less significant vascular factors (extracranial arteries stenosis/occlusion, cerebral sinus thrombosis, cerebral artery dissection without rupture, cerebral aneurysmatic disease, cerebral infarction), may indicate a significant role of cerebrovascular pathology in the presence of epilepsy in this group of patients [45]. Younger age may be related to a known peak of higher prevalence of epilepsy specifically in young people in the general population [46]. This fact may be associated with a higher incidence of complications associated with arterial hypertension at a young age, for example, PRES. The presence of arterial hypertension in younger patients (18–23 years old) significantly increased the likelihood of epilepsy, while in older patients (including the elderly, over 65 years of age), its presence had the opposite effect: it reduced the likelihood of epilepsy.

Interestingly, the combined presence or absence of cerebral venous sinus thrombosis and arterial hypertension altered the likelihood of epilepsy in patients.

### 4.5. Cerebral Sinus Thrombosis

As shown in the Figure 7, in the absence of Cerebral venous sinus thrombosis (CVST), the presence/absence of arterial hypertension had no significant effect on the risk of epilepsy. While during the development of CVST, arterial hypertension sharply increased its significance as a factor in the presence of epilepsy in the patient.

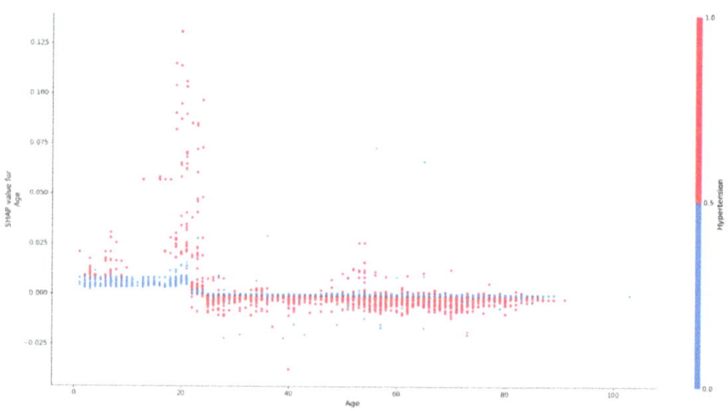


**Figure 7.** Effect of arterial hypertension on the risk of epilepsy depending on the age of patients.

CVST itself is a well-known risk factor for the development of acute symptomatic epileptic seizures and epilepsy [47–49]. Meanwhile, the relationship between CVST and arterial hypertension in terms of epilepsy risk has been described for the first time and may reflect the presence of combined mechanisms of these conditions in oncohematological patients.

A number of hematologic factors can determine the risk of CVST. The development of this complication may be associated with a higher platelet count ($p < 0.001$) and a higher platelet/neutrophil index ($p < 0.001$) [50]. The incidence of ASS in the acute phase of CVST is up to 34% in the general adult population. The incidence of ASS in CVST in children is 37.5% to 57%. This is often the main manifestation of the development of thrombosis [51,52]. The results of a study of the risk of epilepsy in young patients and children show that systemic inflammation, a reflection of which may be the fact of increased platelets, may play a significant role. This role can be both direct and mediated through the development of complications involving the CNS) in the development of epilepsy [53]. Given the heterogeneity of causes leading to the development of elevated neutrophil levels, unambiguous interpretation is difficult and the role of systemic inflammation in the development of epilepsy requires further study.

### 4.6. Transplanted Hematopoietic Stem Cells

Among the factors associated with hematopoietic stem cell transplantation, a higher volume of transplanted cells was associated with the presence of epilepsy (Figure 4). This factor increased its weight in patients with arterial hypertension. This may indicate a possible influence of the volume of a donor cell infusion, and the volume of injected cryopreservative on the development acute arterial hypertension and other complications, including ASS [54].

### 4.7. Age Factor

The factor of age for predicting the presence of epilepsy in oncohematological patients had different significance depending on the age group (Figure 5). In patients under 18 years old, the presence of a malignant neoplasm of the blood system reduced the likelihood of epilepsy. This may be related to the debut of hereditary genetically determined forms of epilepsy syndromes with no etiological and pathogenetic connection to oncohematological diseases [55]. At the age of 18–20 years, there was an increase in the prognostic significance of the presence of C81–C96 on the risk of epilepsy. This may be related to the transition of patients to adult inpatient care, changes in neoplasm treatment protocols, and possible disruption of continuity between specialists [56]. This leads to a possible increase in the risk of complications. In the age group of 60 years and older, the presence of C81–C96 diseases increased the likelihood of a patient having epilepsy. This is associated with an increased number of complications leading to damage of the brain substance due to the presence of other comorbid pathology (primarily, pathology of the cardiovascular system) and its decompensation against the background of oncological disease therapy [55].

At the same time, in the same sample of patients, when analyzing the importance of predictors for the oncohematological diagnosis class, we can see that the absence of epilepsy is in no way related and does not contribute to the model for the oncohematological diagnosis class, as opposed to the presence of epilepsy (Figure 6).

### 4.8. Dataset I vs. Dataset II Patients

When performing a features-engineering of a model of epilepsy in oncohematological patients, a model development cycle should include a step to compare the importance of the features with the model that considers a wider group of patients. If differences in the importance of predictors are found, validation and interpretation of the results, and adjustment of the initial narrow model with the identified limitations are necessary.

From the clinical point of view, the identified differences in the importance of predictors (Figure 7) in a broader patient model are consistent with a practical algorithm for organic brain damage. Atrial fibrillation is one of the leading factors in the development of both ischemic and hemorrhagic strokes. At the same time, brain infarction can be accompanied both by the development of epileptic seizures in the acute period and by unprovoked epileptic seizures and development of epilepsy in the early recovery and in a longer period [57]. In addition, microembolism of the left heart chambers can lead to multiple microfocal lesions of the brain, which is considered to be one of the pathogenetic aspects of epilepsy in elderly patients. The presence of precordial fibrillation requires anticoagulant therapy, the use of which increases the risk of both spontaneous and traumatic intracranial hemorrhage. Which, in the case of involvement of the brain substance, forms an epileptogenic substrate in the form of hemosiderin zones [58].

### 4.9. Clinical Implications

Alongside identifying of the risk factors and the ability of the model to rate the risks of individual patients, our results have other practical clinical meaning. It is important that in patients with a cardiovascular history, the development of seizures is not always associated with primary epilepsy. It is structural changes in the brain of acute or chronic genesis can be inducers of seizures and secondary epilepsy. Moreover, given that the most frequent diagnosis of "epilepsy" was eventually found in patients with atrial fibrillation, in the absence of electroencephalogram changes and the presence of sinus rhythm on electrocardiogram, and the absence of gross structural changes in the brain, long-term cardiac rhythm monitoring should be conducted to look for a paroxysmal form of atrial fibrillation.

From a clinical point perspective, our results may be useful for classifying and ranking the causes of epileptic seizures, especially in the group of patients with no history of epilepsy as the primary pathology. The developed prognostic model made it possible to identify factors associated with epilepsy in patients with oncohematological diseases. Further study of the causal relationship between these factors and the development of epilepsy will allow for the creation of an algorithm for its timely prevention.

### 4.10. Study Limitation

The limitations of this study are related to the neurotoxicity of a number of chemotherapy drugs used to treat oncohematological patients, which increase the risk of ASS (acute symptomatic seizure) and other neurological complications. This can lead to structural damage to the brain substance (e.g., ischemic stroke and intracranial hemorrhage).

The inclusion and exclusion criteria we selected and the parameters chosen for analysis did not take into account the stage of the disease and the protocol of the patient's therapy, nor did we consider the reason for the patient's admission to the hospital and its urgency.

In our study, we considered the presence of epilepsy, coded as a competing, comorbid disease or complication, in patients with oncohematological (dataset 1) and cardiovascular diseases (dataset 2) during the contraction time (period of admission); however, the fact of epilepsy in dynamics and the risk factors of such an event, were not assessed. We focused on finding factors associated with the presence of epilepsy rather than its development (predictors of its development) in the future.

## 5. Conclusions

Patients with oncohematological pathology have a number of clinical and laboratory factors that correlate with the presence of epilepsy. In addition, age and a number of factors associated with hematopoietic cell transplantation also correlate with the presence of epilepsy in patients with malignant neoplasms of lymphoid, hematopoietic and related tissues. This study shows how age characteristics influence the significance of other predictors. Patient age and shelf life of the transplanted cells change the significance. The obtained results of the thrombosis factor in the development of epilepsy have a meaningful effect because this issue has been poorly described in previous studies. Further research should be aimed at creating a prognostic model for the development of ASS in this group of patients. We proposed to include ASS as a risk factor to the prognostic model of epilepsy development in oncohematological patients. In addition, the identified association between platelet levels and epilepsy requires a study of the effect of the use of antiepileptic drugs in patients with malignant blood neoplasms.

**Author Contributions:** G.K. and O.M. were responsible for a literature review, setting up the concept and methods and writing the manuscript. I.S. was responsible for the data analysis. S.Y. and A.P. were responsible for clinical interpretations. G.K. and O.M. were responsible for writing and reviewing of the manuscript. All authors have read and agreed to the published version of the manuscript.

**Funding:** This work was financially supported by the Ministry of Science and Higher Education of the Russian Federation (Agreement No. 075-15-2022-301).

**Institutional Review Board Statement:** The study was conducted in accordance with the Declaration of Helsinki, and approved by the Institutional Review Board (or Ethics Committee) of Almazov National Medical Research Centre in Saint Petersburg, Russian Federation.

**Informed Consent Statement:** Patient consent was waived due to the use of anonymized medical data without any possibility to identify patients.

**Data Availability Statement:** The datasets used and/or analysed during the current study are available from the corresponding author on reasonable request.

**Conflicts of Interest:** The authors declare no conflict of interest.

## Abbreviations

| | |
|---|---|
| ACS | Acute coronary seizure |
| ICD-10 | International Classification of Diseases, 10th revision |
| PRES | Posterior reversible encephalopathy syndrome |
| ASS | acute symphtomatic seizure |
| CVST | Cerebral venous sinus thrombosis |
| CI | confidence indicator |
| BMI | Body mass index |
| CAD | coronary artery disease |
| CHF | congestive heart failure |
| CHD | congenital heart disease |
| ANN | artificial neuron network |
| DT | decisions tree |
| AUC | Area under the Curve |
| ROC | receiver operating characteristic curve |
| PDW | platelet distribution width |
| SVM | support vector machine |
| HGB | Hemoglobin |
| LEU | Leukocytes |
| PLT | Platelets |
| MPW | Mean platelet volume |
| MCH | Mean cell hemoglobin |
| NEUT | Neutrophils |
| MCV | Mean corpuscular volume |
| PCT | Procalcitonin |
| RDW | Red blood cell distribution width |
| ALT | Alanine transaminase |
| PDW | Platelet distribution width |
| HDL | High-density lipoprotein |
| AST | Aspartate aminotransferase |
| WBC | White blood count |
| RBC | Red blood cell count |
| HCT | Hematocrit |
| LDL | Low-density lipoproteins |
| BLD | Blood in urine |

## References


1. Kang, J.M.; Kim, Y.J.; Kim, J.Y.; Cho, E.J.; Lee, J.H.; Lee, M.H.; Lee, S.H.; Sung, K.W.; Koo, H.H.; Yoo, K.H. Neurologic Complications after Allogeneic Hematopoietic Stem Cell Transplantation in Children: Analysis of Prognostic Factors. *Biol. Blood Marrow Transplant.* **2015**, *21*, 1091–1098. [CrossRef]
2. Khan, R.B.; Morris, E.B.; Pui, C.H.; Hudson, M.M.; Zhou, Y.; Ledet, D.S.; Howard, S.C. Long-Term Outcome and Risk Factors for Uncontrolled Seizures after a First Seizure in Children with Hematological Malignancies. *J. Child Neurol.* **2014**, *29*, 774–781. [CrossRef] [PubMed]
3. Cordelli, D.M.; Masetti, R.; Zama, D.; Gueraldi, D.; Rondelli, R.; Cottone, C.; Prete, A.; Pession, A.; Franzoni, E. Etiology, Characteristics and Outcome of Seizures after Pediatric Hematopoietic Stem Cell Transplantation. *Seizure* **2014**, *23*, 140–145. [CrossRef] [PubMed]
4. Zhang, X.H.; Xu, L.P.; Liu, D.H.; Chen, H.; Han, W.; Chen, Y.H.; Wang, F.R.; Wang, J.Z.; Wang, Y.; Zhao, T.; et al. Epileptic Seizures in Patients Following Allogeneic Hematopoietic Stem Cell Transplantation: A Retrospective Analysis of Incidence, Risk Factors, and Survival Rates. *Clin. Transplant.* **2013**, *27*, 80–89. [CrossRef]
5. Yam, K.M.K.; Leung, W.K.A.; Zhu, X.L.; Fung, L.W.E. Drug Resistant Epilepsy with Mesial Temporal Sclerosis as Possible Late Neurological Complication in Two AML Survivors after Stem Cell Transplantation. *Epilepsy Behav. Case Rep.* **2018**, *10*, 71–77. [CrossRef]
6. Leng, Y.; Yu, T.; Li, Y.; Chen, W. Surgical Treatment of Refractory Epilepsy after Chemotherapy in Two Children with Leukemia. *Epilepsy Behav. Case Rep.* **2013**, *1*, 32–34. [CrossRef] [PubMed]

7. Steegmann, J.L.; Baccarani, M.; Breccia, M.; Casado, L.F.; García-Gutiérrez, V.; Hochhaus, A.; Kim, D.W.; Kim, T.D.; Khoury, H.J.; Le Coutre, P.; et al. European LeukemiaNet Recommendations for the Management and Avoidance of Adverse Events of Treatment in Chronic Myeloid Leukaemia. *Leukemia* **2016**, *30*, 1648–1671. [CrossRef]
8. Armenian, S.H.; Chemaitilly, W.; Chen, M.; Chow, E.J.; Duncan, C.N.; Jones, L.W.; Pulsipher, M.A.; Remaley, A.T.; Rovo, A.; Salooja, N.; et al. National Institutes of Health Hematopoietic Cell Transplantation Late Effects Initiative: The Cardiovascular Disease and Associated Risk Factors Working Group Report. *Biol. Blood Marrow Transplant.* **2017**, *23*, 201–210. [CrossRef]
9. Johnson, E.L.; Krauss, G.L.; Lee, A.K.; Schneider, A.L.C.; Dearborn, J.L.; Kucharska-Newton, A.M.; Huang, J.; Alonso, A.; Gottesman, R.F. Association between Midlife Risk Factors and Late-Onset Epilepsy: Results from the Atherosclerosis Risk in Communities Study. *JAMA Neurol.* **2018**, *75*, 1375–1382. [CrossRef]
10. Gasparini, S.; Ferlazzo, E.; Sueri, C.; Cianci, V.; Ascoli, M.; Cavalli, S.M.; Beghi, E.; Belcastro, V.; Bianchi, A.; Benna, P.; et al. Hypertension, Seizures, and Epilepsy: A Review on Pathophysiology and Management. *Neurol. Sci.* **2019**, *40*, 1775–1783. [CrossRef]
11. Sha, Z.; Moran, B.P.; McKinney, A.M.; Henry, T.R. Seizure Outcomes of Posterior Reversible Encephalopathy Syndrome and Correlations with Electroencephalographic Changes. *Epilepsy Behav.* **2015**, *48*, 70–74. [CrossRef]
12. Chen, Q.; Zhao, X.; Fu, H.X.; Chen, Y.H.; Zhang, Y.Y.; Wang, J.Z.; Wang, Y.; Wang, F.R.; Mo, X.D.; Han, W.; et al. Posterior Reversible Encephalopathy Syndrome (PRES) after Haploidentical Haematopoietic Stem Cell Transplantation: Incidence, Risk Factors and Outcomes. *Bone Marrow Transplant.* **2020**, *55*, 2035–2042. [CrossRef]
13. Datar, S.; Singh, T.; Rabinstein, A.A.; Fugate, J.E.; Hocker, S. Long-Term Risk of Seizures and Epilepsy in Patients with Posterior Reversible Encephalopathy Syndrome. *Epilepsia* **2015**, *56*, 564–568. [CrossRef] [PubMed]
14. Heo, K.; Cho, K.H.; Lee, M.K.; Chung, S.J.; Cho, Y.J.; Lee, B.I. Development of Epilepsy after Posterior Reversible Encephalopathy Syndrome. *Seizure* **2016**, *34*, 90–94. [CrossRef] [PubMed]
15. Gupta, V.; Braun, T.M.; Chowdhury, M.; Tewari, M.; Choi, S.W. A Systematic Review of Machine Learning Techniques in Hematopoietic Stem Cell Transplantation (HSCT). *Sensors* **2020**, *20*, 6100. [CrossRef] [PubMed]
16. An, S.; Malhotra, K.; Dilley, C.; Han-Burgess, E.; Valdez, J.N.; Robertson, J.; Clark, C.; Westover, M.B.; Sun, J. Predicting Drug-Resistant Epilepsy—A Machine Learning Approach Based on Administrative Claims Data. *Epilepsy Behav.* **2018**, *89*, 118–125. [CrossRef] [PubMed]
17. Park, S.C.; Chung, C.K. Postoperative Seizure Outcome-Guided Machine Learning for Interictal Electrocorticography in Neocortical Epilepsy. *J. Neurophysiol.* **2018**, *119*, 2265–2275. [CrossRef]
18. Nissen, I.A.; Stam, C.J.; van Straaten, E.C.W.; Wottschel, V.; Reijneveld, J.C.; Baayen, J.C.; Hamer, P.C. de W.; Idema, S.; Velis, D.N.; Hillebrand, A. Localization of the Epileptogenic Zone Using Inter-ictal MEG and Machine Learning in a Large Cohort of Drug-Resistant Epilepsy Patients. *Front. Neurol.* **2018**, *9*, 647. [CrossRef]
19. Bharath, R.D.; Panda, R.; Raj, J.; Bhardwaj, S.; Sinha, S.; Chaitanya, G.; Raghavendra, K.; Mundlamuri, R.C.; Arimappamagan, A.; Rao, M.B.; et al. Machine Learning Identifies "RsfMRI Epilepsy Networks" in Temporal Lobe Epilepsy. *Eur. Radiol.* **2019**, *29*, 3496–3505. [CrossRef]
20. Rudie, J.D.; Colby, J.B.; Salamon, N. Machine Learning Classification of Mesial Temporal Sclerosis in Epilepsy Patients. *Epilepsy Res.* **2015**, *117*, 63–69. [CrossRef]
21. Del Gaizo, J.; Mofrad, N.; Jensen, J.H.; Clark, D.; Glenn, R.; Helpern, J.; Bonilha, L. Using Machine Learning to Classify Temporal Lobe Epilepsy Based on Diffusion MRI. *Brain Behav.* **2017**, *7*, e00801. [CrossRef] [PubMed]
22. Abbasi, B.; Goldenholz, D.M. Machine Learning Applications in Epilepsy. *Epilepsia* **2019**, *60*, 2037–2047. [CrossRef]
23. Chiang, S.; Vannucci, M.; Goldenholz, D.M.; Moss, R.; Stern, J.M. Epilepsy as a Dynamic Disease: A Bayesian Model for Differentiating Seizure Risk from Natural Variability. *Epilepsia Open* **2018**, *3*, 236–246. [CrossRef] [PubMed]
24. Chiang, S.; Goldenholz, D.M.; Moss, R.; Rao, V.R.; Haneef, Z.; Theodore, W.H.; Kleen, J.K.; Gavvala, J.; Vannucci, M.; Stern, J.M. Prospective Validation Study of an Epilepsy Seizure Risk System for Outpatient Evaluation. *Epilepsia* **2020**, *61*, 29–38. [CrossRef]
25. Kalin, F.; Akinci, T.C.; Türkpence, D.; Seker, S.; Korkmaz, U. Detection of Epileptic Seizure Using STFT and Statistical Analysis. In *Advances in Neural Signal Processing*; Intech Open: London, UK, 2020. [CrossRef]
26. Frolov, N.S.; Grubov, V.V.; Maksimenko, V.A.; Lüttjohann, A.; Makarov, V.V.; Pavlov, A.N.; Sitnikova, E.; Pisarchik, A.N.; Kurths, J.; Hramov, A.E. Statistical Properties and Predictability of Extreme Epileptic Events. *Sci. Rep.* **2019**, *9*, 7243. [CrossRef]
27. Fiest, K.M.; Sauro, K.M.; Wiebe, S.; Patten, S.B.; Kwon, C.-S.; Dykeman, J.; Pringsheim, T.; Lorenzetti, D.L.; Jetté, N. Prevalence and Incidence of Epilepsy: A Systematic Review and Meta-Analysis of International Studies. *Neurology* **2017**, *88*, 296. [CrossRef]
28. Schnabel, R.B.; Yin, X.; Gona, P.; Larson, M.G.; Beiser, A.; McManus, D.D.; Newton-Cheh, C.; Lubitz, S.A.; Magnani, J.W.; Ellinor, P.; et al. 50 Year Trends in Atrial Fibrillation Prevalence, Incidence, Risk Factors, and Mortality in the Fram-ingham Heart Study: A Cohort Study. *Lancet* **2015**, *386*, 154–162. [CrossRef]
29. Shkolnikova, M.A.; Jdanov, D.A.; Ildarova, R.A.; Shcherbakova, N.V.; Polyakova, E.B.; Mikhaylov, E.N.; Shalnova, S.A.; Shkolnikov, V.M. Atrial Fibrillation among Russian Men and Women Aged 55 Years and Older: Prevalence, Mortality, and Associations with Biomarkers in a Population-Based Study. *J. Geriatr. Cardiol. JGC* **2020**, *17*, 74. [CrossRef] [PubMed]
30. Börschel, C.S.; Schnabel, R.B. The Imminent Epidemic of Atrial Fibrillation and Its Concomitant Diseases—Myocardial Infarction and Heart Failure—A Cause for Concern. *Int. J. Cardiol.* **2019**, *287*, 162–173. [CrossRef]
31. Chen, C.-C.; Chen, L.-S.; Yen, M.-F.; Chen, H.-H.; Liou, H.-H. Geographic Variation in the Age- and Gender-Specific Prevalence and Incidence of Epilepsy: Analysis of Taiwanese National Health Insurance-Based Data. *Epilepsia* **2012**, *53*, 283–290. [CrossRef]

32. Tichy, E.; Lam, S.; Militano, U.; Bessmertny, O. A Case of Severe Thrombocytopenia and Antiepileptic Hypersensitivity Syndrome. *J. Pediatric Pharmacol. Ther.* **2003**, *8*, 29–33. [CrossRef] [PubMed]
33. Basith, M.; Francis, A.; Bellon, A. Reversible Thrombocytopenia after Gabapentin in an HIV-Positive Patient. *Case Rep. Psychiatry* **2018**, *2018*, 5927065. [CrossRef] [PubMed]
34. Nasreddine, W.; Beydoun, A. Valproate-Induced Thrombocytopenia: A Prospective Monotherapy Study. *Epilepsia* **2008**, *49*, 438–445. [CrossRef] [PubMed]
35. Chi, N.F.; Kuan, Y.C.; Huang, Y.H.; Chan, L.; Hu, C.J.; Liu, H.Y.; Chiou, H.Y.; Chien, L.N. Development and Validation of Risk Score to Estimate 1-Year Late Poststroke Epilepsy Risk in Ischemic Stroke Patients. *Clin. Epidemiol.* **2018**, *10*, 1001–1011. [CrossRef] [PubMed]
36. Spatola, M.; Dalmau, J. Seizures and Risk of Epilepsy in Autoimmune and Other Inflammatory Encephalitis. *Curr. Opin. Neurol.* **2017**, *30*, 345–353. [CrossRef]
37. Burneo, J.G.; Antaya, T.C.; Allen, B.N.; Belisle, A.; Shariff, S.Z.; Saposnik, G. The Risk of New-Onset Epilepsy and Refractory Epilepsy in Older Adult Stroke Survivors. *Neurology* **2019**, *93*, E568–E577. [CrossRef]
38. Kurien, M.; Ludvigsson, J.F.; Sanders, D.S.; Zylberberg, H.M.; Green, P.H.; Sundelin, H.E.K.; Lebwohl, B. Persistent Mucosal Damage and Risk of Epilepsy in People with Celiac Disease. *European J. Neurol.* **2018**, *25*, 592-e38. [CrossRef]
39. Pinto, M.J.; Medeiros, P.B.; Príncipe, F.; Carvalho, M. Cerebral Venous Thrombosis in Hematological Malignancy: Balancing the Risks. *J. Stroke Cerebrovasc. Dis.* **2020**, *29*, 104683. [CrossRef]
40. Silvis, S.M.; Hiltunen, S.; Lindgren, E.; Jood, K.; Zuurbier, S.M.; Middeldorp, S.; Putaala, J.; Cannegieter, S.C.; Tatlisumak, T.; Coutinho, J.M. Cancer and Risk of Cerebral Venous Thrombosis: A Case–Control Study. *J. Thromb. Haemost.* **2018**, *16*, 90–95. [CrossRef]
41. Underwood, B.; Zhao, Q.; Walker, A.R.; Mims, A.S.; Vasu, S.; Long, M.; Haque, T.Z.; Blaser, B.W.; Grieselhuber, N.R.; Wall, S.A.; et al. Incidence of Venous Thrombosis after Peg-Asparaginase in Adolescent and Young Adults with Acute Lymphoblastic Leukemia. *Int. J. Hematol. Oncol.* **2020**, *9*, IJH28. [CrossRef]
42. Bauwens, D.; Hantson, P.; Laterre, P.F.; Michaux, L.; Latinne, D.; De Tourtchaninoff, M.; Cosnard, G.; Hernalsteen, D. Recurrent Seizure and Sustained Encephalopathy Associated with Dimethylsulfoxide-Preserved Stem Cell Infusion. *Leuk. Lymphoma* **2005**, *46*, 1671–1674. [CrossRef] [PubMed]
43. Maral, S.; Albayrak, M.; Pala, C.; Yildiz, A.; Sahin, O.; Ozturk, H.B. Dimethyl Sulfoxide-Induced Tonic-Clonic Seizure and Cardiac Arrest During Infusion of Autologous Peripheral Blood Stem Cells. *Cell Tissue Bank.* **2018**, *19*, 831–832. [CrossRef]
44. Chen-Plotkin, A.S.; Vossel, K.A.; Samuels, M.A.; Chen, M.H. Encephalopathy, Stroke, and Myocardial Infarction with DMSO Use in Stem Cell Transplantation. *Neurology* **2007**, *68*, 859–861. [CrossRef] [PubMed]
45. Argañaraz, G.A.; Konno, A.C.; Perosa, S.R.; Santiago, J.F.C.; Boim, M.A.; Vidotti, D.B.; Varella, P.P.V.; Costa, L.G.; Canzian, M.; Porcionatto, M.A.; et al. The Renin-Angiotensin System Is Upregulated in the Cortex and Hippocampus of Patients with Temporal Lobe Epilepsy Related to Mesial Temporal Sclerosis. *Epilepsia* **2008**, *49*, 1348–1357. [CrossRef] [PubMed]
46. Berg, A.T.; Zelko, F.A.; Levy, S.R.; Testa, F.M. Age at Onset of Epilepsy, Pharmacoresistance, and Cognitive Outcomes: A Prospective Cohort Study. *Neurology* **2012**, *79*, 1384. [CrossRef] [PubMed]
47. Mahale, R.; Mehta, A.; John, A.A.; Buddaraju, K.; Shankar, A.K.; Javali, M.; Srinivasa, R. Acute Seizures in Cerebral Venous Sinus Thrombosis: What Predicts It? *Epilepsy Res.* **2016**, *123*, 1–5. [CrossRef]
48. Ferro, J.M.; Canhão, P.; Bousser, M.G.; Stam, J.; Barinagarrementeria, F. Early Seizures in Cerebral Vein and Dural Sinus Thrombosis: Risk Factors and Role of Antiepileptics. *Stroke* **2008**, *39*, 1152–1158. [CrossRef]
49. Uluduz, D.; Midi, I.; Duman, T.; Yayla, V.; Karahan, A.Y.; Afsar, N.; Goksu, E.O.; Mengulluoglu, N.; Aytac, E.; Sungur, M.A.; et al. Epileptic Seizures in Cerebral Venous Sinus Thrombosis: Subgroup Analysis of VENOST Study. *Seizure* **2020**, *78*, 113–117. [CrossRef]
50. Xian, Z.; Chen, Y.; Chen, L.; Lu, Q.; Huang, G.; Qin, Q.; Zeng, J.; Liang, Z. A Clinical Research on the Potential Pathogenesis of Somatic Cancer Related Cerebral Venous Sinus Thrombosis. *Medicine* **2019**, *98*, e15134. [CrossRef]
51. Mineyko, A.; Kirton, A.; Billinghurst, L.; Tatishvili, N.N.; Wintermark, M.; deVeber, G.; Fox, C.; Abdalla, A.; Zafeiriou, D.; Friedman, N.; et al. Seizures and Outcome One Year After Neonatal and Childhood Cerebral Sinovenous Thrombosis. *Pediatric Neurol.* **2020**, *105*, 21–26. [CrossRef]
52. Fitzgerald, K.C.; Williams, L.S.; Garg, B.P.; Carvalho, K.S.; Golomb, M.R. Cerebral Sinovenous Thrombosis in the Neonate. *Arch. Neurol.* **2006**, *63*, 405–409. [CrossRef] [PubMed]
53. Ahlers, F.S.; Benros, M.E.; Dreier, J.W.; Christensen, J. Infections and Risk of Epilepsy in Children and Young Adults: A Nationwide Study. *Epilepsia* **2019**, *60*, 275–283. [CrossRef]
54. Skiba, Y.B.; Polushin, A.Y.; Prokudin, M.Y.; Vladovskaya, M.D.; Kulagin, A.D. Acute Symptomatic Seizures during Haematopoietic Stem Cell Transplantation. *Epilepsy Paroxysmal Cond.* **2021**, *13*, 65–82. [CrossRef]
55. Gesche, J.; Christensen, J.; Hjalgrim, H.; Rubboli, G.; Beier, C.P. Epidemiology and Outcome of Idiopathic Generalized Epilepsy in Adults. *Eur. J. Neurol.* **2020**, *27*, 676–684. [CrossRef] [PubMed]
56. Schröder, H.; Kjeldahlk, M.; Boesen, A.M.; Nielsen, O.J.; Schmidt, K.; Johnsen, H.E.; Gregersen, H.; Heyman, M.; Gustafsson, G. Acute Lymphoblastic Leukemia in Adolescents Betweeen 10 and 19 Years of Age in Denmark—Secondary Publication. *Dan. Med. Bull.* **2006**, *53*, 76–79.

57. Yang, H.; Rajah, G.; Guo, A.; Wang, Y.; Wang, Q. Pathogenesis of Epileptic Seizures and Epilepsy after Stroke. *Neurol. Res.* **2018**, *40*, 426–432. [CrossRef]
58. Dammann, P.; Schaller, C.; Sure, U. Should We Resect Peri-Lesional Hemosiderin Deposits When Performing Lesionectomy in Patients with Cavernoma-Related Epilepsy (CRE)? *Neurosurg. Rev.* **2017**, *40*, 39–43. [CrossRef]

Journal of *Personalized Medicine*

MDPI

*Article*

# Usability Testing of a Social Media Chatbot for Increasing Physical Activity Behavior

**Dillys Larbi [1,2,*], Kerstin Denecke [3] and Elia Gabarron [1,4]**

1 Norwegian Centre for E-Health Research, 9019 Tromso, Norway; elia.gabarron@ehealthresearch.no
2 Department of Clinical Medicine, Faculty of Health Sciences, UiT The Arctic University of Norway, 9037 Tromso, Norway
3 Institute for Medical Informatics, Bern University of Applied Sciences, 3012 Bern, Switzerland; kerstin.denecke@bfh.ch
4 Department of Education, ICT and Learning, Østfold University College, 1757 Halden, Norway
* Correspondence: dla011@uit.no or dillys.larbi@ehealthresearch.no; Tel.: +47-909-497-60

**Abstract:** Digital interventions for increasing physical activity behavior have shown great potential, especially those with social media. Chatbots, also known as conversational agents, have emerged in healthcare in relation to digital interventions and have proven effective in promoting physical activity among adults. The study's objective is to explore users' experiences with a social media chatbot. The concept and the prototype development of the social media chatbot MYA were realized in three steps: requirement analysis, concept development, and implementation. MYA's design includes behavior change techniques effective in increasing physical activity through digital interventions. Participants in a usability study answered a survey with the Chatbot Usability Questionnaire (CUQ), which is comparable to the Systems Usability Scale. The mean CUQ score was below 68, the benchmark for average usability. The highest mean CUQ score was 64.5 for participants who thought MYA could help increase their physical activity behavior. The lowest mean CUQ score was 40.6 for participants aged between 50 and 69 years. Generally, MYA was considered to be welcoming, very easy to use, realistic, engaging, and informative. However, some technical issues were identified. A good and diversified user experience promotes prolonged chatbot use. Addressing identified issues will enhance users' interaction with MYA.

**Keywords:** social media; physical activity; chatbot; health; participatory health; usability; conversational agent; behavior change

check for updates

**Citation:** Larbi, D.; Denecke, K.; Gabarron, E. Usability Testing of a Social Media Chatbot for Increasing Physical Activity Behavior. *J. Pers. Med.* **2022**, *12*, 828. https://doi.org/10.3390/jpm12050828

Academic Editors: Bernd Blobel and Mauro Giacomini

Received: 6 April 2022
Accepted: 16 May 2022
Published: 20 May 2022



## 1. Introduction

Decades of research show that physical activity interventions can reduce the risk of chronic conditions such as obesity, heart disease, type 2 diabetes, or depression, among others [1,2], and help reduce healthcare costs [3]. The increasing levels of adult inactivity in recent years highlight a clear challenge with developing interventions capable of engaging the adult population in physical activity [4].

There is a positive association between the use of digital technologies as interventions and an increase in physical activity behavior. The use of digital interventions for increasing adult physical activities has shown great improvement and potential [4–8]. In a review by Petersen et al. [9], digital interventions for physical activity incorporating a social media element were more engaging to adults and therefore more effective than those without social media. Chatbots, also known as conversational agents or virtual agents, have emerged in the health sector in relation to digital interventions. The psychological and pedagogical effect of spoken opinions vs. written recommendations is evident, establishing effective relationships. In this sense, computer software programs simulating a human conversation via text or voice have been used to either manage chronic conditions or promote healthy behaviors including physical activity behavior [4,10,11].

According to Luo et al. [4], chatbots are effective in promoting physical activity among adults. The popularity of social media platforms and the intuitive nature of chatbots suggest a potentially effective means of promoting physical activity if these tools are combined. One of the benefits of a social media-based chatbot for behavior change is that users are already familiar with communicating with friends via social media platforms on a regular basis. We have developed a prototype of a social media-based chatbot that aims to motivate users to be more physically active, that is, to increase their number of steps per day. The chatbot acts as a friend and contacts users via a social media platform with physical activity-related information mainly for inspiration.

The objective of this study is to explore users' experiences with the social media chatbot and to assess its potential to change physical activity behavior. User evaluation of digital health interventions at an early stage of the development process is essential to ensure that the resulting tool is acceptable and useful to the target population. For this reason, we focused our study on the assessment of user experiences when using the first version of the social media chatbot.

## 2. Materials and Methods

### 2.1. System Development and Requirement Analysis

The concept and the prototype development of the social media chatbot were realized in three steps: requirement analysis, concept development, and implementation. Requirements were collected in close collaboration with experts in health informatics and psychology. Additional requirements were obtained by reviewing relevant literature for behavior change strategies to motivate individuals. Further details about the development process can be found in Larbi et al. [12].

A chatbot called MYA, integrated into an existing social media platform (Telegram Messenger), was developed for the following reasons: (1) A user can easily add the chatbot to the Telegram application and start communicating with it; (2) no additional app has to be installed; (3) since most people can interact via a social media messenger, interacting with the chatbot will be intuitive and understandable.

### 2.2. Behavior Change Techniques and Functionalities

MYA's design includes behavior change techniques that have been proven to be effective in increasing physical activity behavior in digital interventions [7]: goals and planning; feedback and monitoring; social support (unspecified); associations (prompts/cues); and reward and threat (social reward) [13]. In more detail, MYA allows the user to set a personal step goal and review this goal. The chatbot is designed to compare the user's current number of steps (simulated number of steps in this prototype) with the set goal and inform the user of discrepancies between current behavior and goal. In this context, MYA gives feedback on the user's behavior. The chatbot also encourages users (if they achieve their goals or are about to achieve them), and it sends prompts, reminding the user about his/her commitment to increasing physical activity.

MYA is a rule-based chatbot developed using FlowXo [14], which is a platform to create chatbot flows. Table 1 shows the nine conversation flows implemented in MYA. With the trigger word "menu", a flow is activated where the user can choose whether he/she wants to set goals or challenges, check his/her current step count, or hear a fun fact about exercising. When a user sends MYA a message, a distinction is made between the "First Encounter" when MYA is used for the very first time and a "Further Encounter" flow for each subsequent use. MYA encourages the user to complete his/her specified number of steps per day by sending motivational messages in the chat.

The entire conversation flow of MYA was designed using the Business Process Model and Notation standard (BPMN). The BPMN models were then translated into conversation streams within FlowXo. To enable personalization of step goals and challenges, Google Sheets was used to collect and store unencrypted non-personal data during conversations with MYA, including current challenge, daily step goal, and first encounter status.

**Table 1.** Implemented conversation flows of MYA.

| Conversation Flow | Description |
|---|---|
| First encounter | Started only the first time MYA is used. Collects basic information on the user and explains the usage of the chatbot. A daily step goal is specified. |
| Further encounter | Greeting for any other than the first encounter. MYA asks the user about his well-being and tries to encourage the user. |
| Menu | Offers access to the four functions: goals, challenges, steps, and facts. |
| Goals | Allows the user to specify a goal for long-time encouragement. |
| Challenges | Out of a set of user-tailored challenges, one is selected. |
| Steps today | Checks the number of steps (simulated step count). This function compares the set goal with current number of steps. If the step goal is not achieved, MYA encourages the user to take more steps. |
| Facts | Presentation of a randomly selected fact on health and activity behavior. |
| Chatting | Allows out-of-topic chatting with the bot. Current version of MYA is not designed to start out-of-topic discussions. |
| Help | Provides help on the various functions. |

### 2.3. Preliminary Study on MYA's Usability

We carried out a study to get feedback on the usability and acceptability of the social media chatbot MYA and to identify issues for improvement. Holmes et al. [15] proposed 26 as a reliable number of participants for studies on chatbot usability. Colleagues of the co-authors aged 18 years and above were invited via a link on social media or email to participate in the study. Study participants had the option to use either the mobile or desktop version of the Telegram application. The participants interacted with the chatbot at their convenience, and then answered a survey that included the Chatbot Usability Questionnaire (CUQ), see Table A1 in Appendix A.

The CUQ is a chatbot-specific usability questionnaire that is comparable to the Systems Usability Scale (SUS)—a commonly used tool for assessing usability that has a benchmark score of 68 out of a total score of 100 [15]. The 16 CUQ items are ranked out of five, the scores are calculated out of 160 and then normalized to 100. The CUQ assesses aspects related to a chatbot's personality, onboarding, user experience, and error handling. Using SUS is not recommended for usability testing of conversation-driven systems since they exploit other design principles [15]. A CUQ Calculation Tool—a Microsoft Excel spreadsheet—is available for the easy calculation of CUQ scores for each participant, the mean CUQ score, and the median score [16]. Further details about the usability study are published in Larbi et al. [12].

The CUQ scores were further analyzed using Microsoft Excel and SPSS (version 25; IBM Corp) to create graphs and group statistics. The participants' gender and age groups were analyzed using Crosstabulation. Bar charts were used to display the participants' ratings of the positive and negative aspects of the CUQ, and a scatter plot was used to display the participants' age groups and CUQ scores. NVivo 12 Pro was used to conduct an inductive thematic analysis of participants' open-ended answers. Each participant's feedback was read through thoroughly and coded. The generated codes were then categorized into themes and/or subthemes.

### 2.4. Ethics

No personal data were collected for this study. All data were treated confidentially and only used for this usability study. This study was approved by the Institutional Review Board Cantonal Ethics Committee in Bern (BASEC-Nr: Req-2021-00244).

## 3. Results

### 3.1. Participant Characteristics

The survey was answered by 30 adult volunteers between 17 and 26 March 2021. Nine of the 30 study participants were aged between 18 and 29 years, 18 participants were aged between 30 and 49 years, and 3 participants were aged between 50 and 69 years. The self-reported gender and age group of the respondents are listed in Table 2.

**Table 2.** Characteristics of the survey respondents ($n$ = 30).

| Age Group | Gender | | Total |
|---|---|---|---|
| | Female | Male | |
| 18–29 years | 3 (10%) | 6 (20%) | 9 (30%) |
| 30–49 years | 12 (40%) | 6 (20%) | 18 (60%) |
| 50–69 years | 0 | 3 (10%) | 3 (10%) |
| Total | 15 (50%) | 15 (50%) | 30 (100%) |

Of the 30 participants, 63.3% (19/30) interacted with MYA for between 5 to 15 min, 16.7% (5/30) had a 15 to 30 min interaction, 13.3% (4/30) interacted for less than 5 min, and 6.7% (2/30) interacted with the chatbot for more than 60 min.

### 3.2. Average Ranking of Chatbot Usability Questionnaire

The odd question numbers of the CUQ have statements that relate to the positive aspects of the chatbot. On a scale of 1—Strongly Disagree to 5—Strongly Agree to the positive statements about MYA's usability, Question 3, which states 'The chatbot was welcoming during initial setup' had the highest average ranking of 4.1 corresponding to Agree. The lowest average ranking was 2.6 for Question 9 which states 'The chatbot understood me well' (See Figure 1).

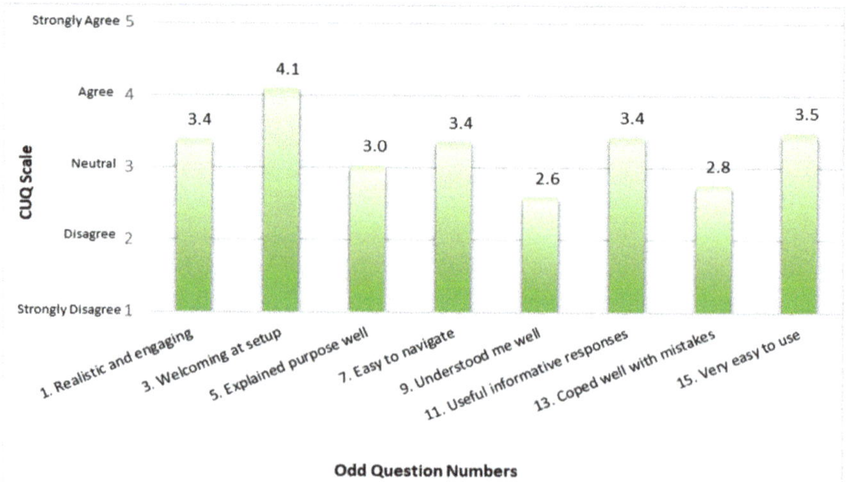


**Figure 1.** Average ranking for the positive aspects of MYA's usability.

In Figure 2, the average ranking on a scale of 1—Strongly Disagree to 5—Strongly Agree of the CUQ even question numbers with statements related to the negative aspects of the chatbot are shown. Question 10, which states 'The chatbot failed to recognize a lot of my inputs' had the highest average ranking of 3.4. With an average ranking of 1.8, Question 4, which states 'The chatbot seemed very unfriendly' had the lowest ranking.

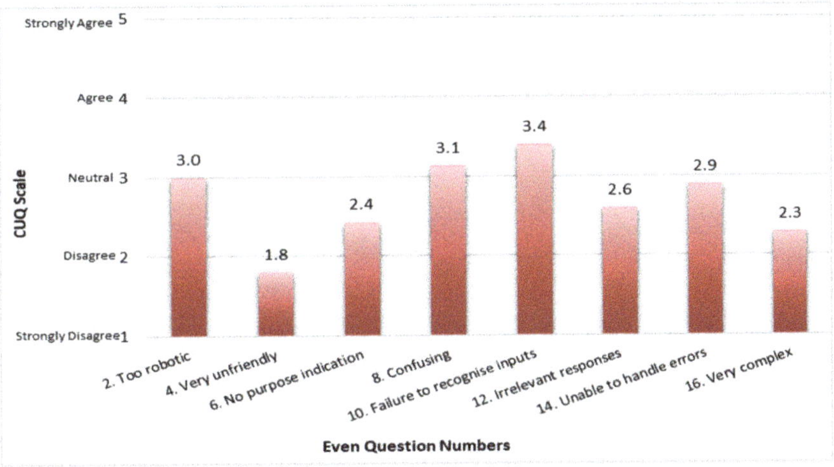


**Figure 2.** Average ranking for the negative aspects of MYA's usability.

### 3.3. Usability Study Results (According to CUQ Calculator)

In Figure 3, the chatbot usability scores for MYA, the prototype of a physical activity social media chatbot by each participant are illustrated. The highest score was 92.2 and the lowest was 29.7. The mean score was 57.4 ± 16.7 and the median was 60.2. Compared with the benchmark score of 68, the usability of MYA is below average.

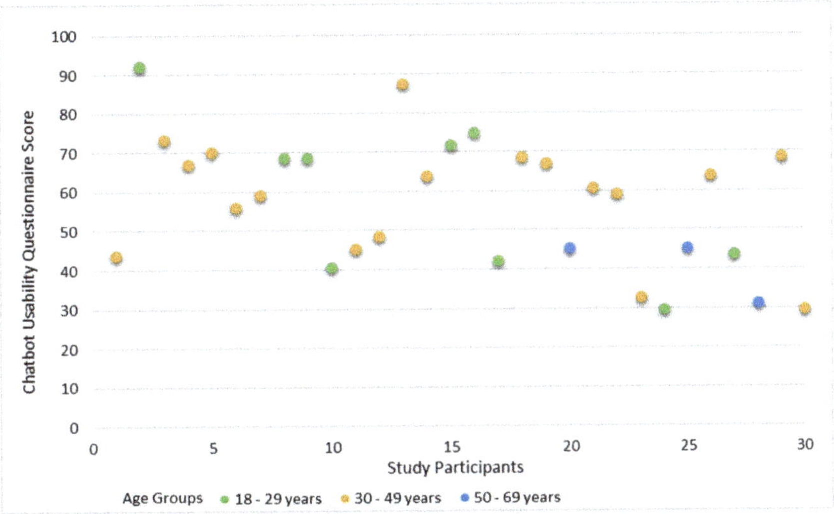


**Figure 3.** Chatbot Usability Questionnaire (CUQ) Scores for MYA.

Female participants' median CUQ score was 60.9, and male respondents' CUQ median was 56.3 (See Table 3). Participants aged 18–29 years reported the highest usability CUQ scores, with a median of 68.8; participants aged 50–69 years had the lowest CUQ scores, with a median of 45.3 (See Table 3).

**Table 3.** Chatbot Usability Questionnaire (CUQ) Scores for study participants ($n = 30$) according to participant characteristics.

| Participant Characteristic | Mean CUQ Score | Median CUQ | Lowest Score | Highest Score |
|---|---|---|---|---|
| **Gender** | | | | |
| Female | 59.9 ± 18.06 | 60.9 | 29.7 | 92.2 |
| Male | 54.9 ± 15.5 | 56.3 | 29.7 | 75.0 |
| **Age Group** | | | | |
| 18 and 29 years | 59.2 ± 20.7 | 68.8 | 29.7 | 92.2 |
| 30 and 49 years | 59.3 ± 14.6 | 62.5 | 29.7 | 87.5 |
| 50–69 years | 40.6 ± 8.1 | 45.3 | 31.3 | 45.3 |
| **MYA's ability to increase physical activity behavior** | | | | |
| Maybe | 57.9 ± 16.2 | 60.2 | 29.7 | 92.2 |
| No | 49.1 ± 15.5 | 43.8 | 31.3 | 71.9 |
| Yes | 64.5 ± 17.7 | 68.8 | 29.7 | 87.5 |
| **Mode of Interaction** | | | | |
| Telegram desktop app | 52.6 ± 21.1 | 43.8 | 29.7 | 92.2 |
| Telegram mobile app | 59.5 ± 14.6 | 64.1 | 29.7 | 87.5 |
| Android phone | 61.5 ± 14.8 | 64.1 | 29.7 | 87.5 |
| iPhone | 56.9 ± 15.7 | 60.9 | 31.3 | 73.4 |

Of the 30 study participants, 9 used the Telegram desktop app and 21 used the Telegram mobile app. A total of 12 out of the 21 Telegram mobile app users used an Android phone, 7 used an iPhone, and 2 did not specify the type of phone used to chat with MYA. Participants who used the Telegram desktop app had a mean CUQ score of 52.6 and a median score of 43.8 (range 29.7–92.2).

In general, participants who used the Telegram mobile app had a mean CUQ score of 59.5 and a median score of 64.1 (range 29.7–87.5). Regarding the type of phone, participants who used an Android phone to interact with MYA had a mean CUQ score of 61.5; and iPhone users had a mean CUQ score of 56.9 (see Table 3).

### 3.4. Additional Feedback from Study Participants

Three themes emerged from the analysis of the feedback from the participants. These included:

- Identified issues: *"The only thing was that the app got stuck at times, and it wasn't clear how to proceed or if this behavior was intended"*
- Preferred chatbot features: *"The random challenge is my favorite feature because it really distinguishes this bot from fitness trackers, and motivates me to do some activity"*
- Suggestions for improvements: "A weekly activity challenge would be interesting, like a schedule with the desired level", and *"More inputs so that it can talk about everyday subjects like weather and answer some questions"*.

Additionally, some subthemes were identified. A detailed analysis of the comments from the participants is given in Table A2 in Appendix A.

## 4. Discussion

In this study, we aimed to explore users' experiences with the physical activity social media chatbot, including identified usability issues. The mean Chabot Usability Questionnaire score was below 68, the benchmark for average usability. The highest mean CUQ score was 64.5, recorded for participants who thought MYA could help increase their physical activity behavior. The lowest mean CUQ score was 40.6 for participants aged between 50 and 69 years.

### 4.1. Social Media Chatbot Features

The results show that the social media chatbot MYA still has potential for improvement: the clarity of the chatbot's comments and its communication skills should be extended and error handling has to be integrated (i.e., dealing with unexpected user input). In its current prototype stage, MYA's conversation capabilities are very limited. Extending the small talk functionality and including more variety in the motivational comments or features would be required to ensure user acceptance [17]. Unlike artificial intelligence (AI) chatbot modules that may invoke hesitancy among potential users [18], MYA is a non-AI-based social media chatbot module that interacts with users as a friend and can therefore be effective in increasing and sustaining physical activity among users. It has also been suggested that social rewards that entail active peer-on-peer interactions, such as a chatbot interaction, are effective for sustaining habits [19].

Integrating MYA into a social media messenger instead of a stand-alone version of the chatbot also has limitations. Data privacy and data security cannot be guaranteed; the Telegram messenger has—similar to other social media messengers—been criticized with respect to data security [20]. In a stand-alone application, this could be avoided. However, the user would have to install an app which could have negative effects on acceptance. Even though MYA is not supposed to store the real name of a user, users might enter their real names or even a unique username that could make them identifiable.

### *4.2. Can a Social Media Chatbot Help Increase Physical Activity?*

In a brief review conducted by Zhang et al. [21] that involved 7 studies on chatbot-based behavior interventions for physical activity and diet, it was found that chatbots can be effective in changing the activity behavior of users. Users of these chatbots, among other things, increased their step-goal achievements [22], physical activity [23,24], and weight loss [25].

In our study, we had mixed opinions on MYA's potential to impact an individual's activity behavior, which might be due to the early prototype status of the chatbot that was tested. Furthermore, the maximum duration of participants' interaction with MYA was 60 min, which limits the chatbot experience and therefore participants' ability to determine the effect of using it. Our chatbot is still under development so there were few and/or limited functionalities, for example, the integration with an activity tracker was simulated at the time of this study. Some of the study participants realized this and it might have impacted their perception of the chatbot. In addition, the communication skills of MYA were restricted. Another usability and acceptability study will be carried out before testing its efficacy in a clinical trial.

### *4.3. Study Limitations*

This study has some limitations. The chatbot did not have a step-counter integrated when the usability test was carried out; the number of steps was randomly generated, which was not appreciated by some participants as it did not reflect the effort made that day. However, we believe it is important to run a usability test at an early stage of system development to ensure a well-accepted system is developed, and in this way, the time spent developing the software is maximized.

The anonymous online survey involved volunteers, mostly students and researchers in the field of digital health or computer science. Therefore, the findings of this study might not be comparable to the general population, nor to other social media chatbots for increasing physical activity behavior. Our study does not provide much insight into the functionality and utility of the chatbot as the focus of the study was on the chatbot prototype's usability.

## 5. Conclusions

In this paper, we introduced MYA, a social-media-based chatbot for behavior change. Our study indicates that the social media chatbot MYA is welcoming, very easy to use, has a realistic and engaging personality, and provides useful, appropriate, and informative responses. However, some technical issues that need to be fixed were identified and suggestions for improvement were also made.

Further research on the use of chatbots for increasing physical activity could explore the impact of integrating event databases or gadgets and including additional or different behavior change techniques. In addition, future research should investigate the role of different functionalities and the utility of a social media chatbot for increasing physical activity behavior.

It is only when the user experience is good and diversified that the chatbot will be used for a longer period. By integrating the suggested functionalities, we will be able to achieve a wide variation in the way future users interact with MYA.

**Author Contributions:** Conceptualization: D.L., E.G. and K.D.; Methodology: D.L., E.G. and K.D.; Software: K.D.; Validation: D.L., E.G. and K.D.; Formal Analysis and data curation: D.L., E.G. and K.D.; Writing—Original Draft Preparation: D.L., E.G. and K.D.; Writing—Review and Editing: D.L., E.G. and K.D. All authors have read and agreed to the published version of the manuscript.

**Funding:** This research received no external funding.

**Institutional Review Board Statement:** The study was conducted according to the guidelines of the Declaration of Helsinki, and approved by the Institutional Review Board Cantonal Ethics Committee in Bern (BASEC-Nr: Req-2021-00244).

**Informed Consent Statement:** Informed consent was waived due to the study being anonymous. No personal information was obtained during the study.

**Data Availability Statement:** Further details from the usability questionnaire can be obtained from the corresponding author (dillys.larbi@ehealthresearch.no).

**Acknowledgments:** The chatbot was developed within a student project at the Bern University of Applied Sciences, Switzerland by Patricia Romao, Stefanie Neuenschwander, and Apiwat-David Gaupp, who are Medical Informatics students. We are grateful to all the study participants for their contributions.

**Conflicts of Interest:** The authors declare no conflict of interest.

## Appendix A

**Table A1.** MYA Usability Testing Survey.

1. What is your gender? ☐ Female ☐ Male ☐ Diverse ☐ Prefer not to say
2. What is your age group? ☐ 18–29 years ☐ 30–49 years ☐ 50 – 69 years ☐ ≥70 years
3. How often do you do physical activity? ☐ Less than 30 min per day ☐ More than 30 min per day ☐ Less than 30 min per week ☐ More than 30 min per week ☐ Monthly ☐ Never ☐ Other:
4. How did you interact with MYA? ☐ Telegram desktop app ☐ Telegram mobile app (Android) ☐ Telegram mobile app (iPhone) ☐ Other:
5. Do you think MYA could help you in increasing your physical activity/change your current activity behavior? ☐ Yes ☐ No ☐ Maybe ☐ Other:
6. For approximately how long did you interact with MYA? ☐ Less than 5 min ☐ 5–15 min ☐ 15–30 min ☐ 30–60 min ☐ More than 60 min ☐ Other:
7. **Chatbot Usability Questionnaire** (Holmes et al. 2019)

| | 1 -Strongly Disagree | 2 -Disagree | 3 -Neutral | 4 -Agree | 5 -Strongly Agree |
|---|---|---|---|---|---|
| Q1 The chatbot's personality was realistic and engaging | ☐ | ☐ | ☐ | ☐ | ☐ |
| Q2 The chatbot seemed too robotic | ☐ | ☐ | ☐ | ☐ | ☐ |
| Q3 The chatbot was welcoming during initial setup | ☐ | ☐ | ☐ | ☐ | ☐ |
| Q4 The chatbot seemed very unfriendly | ☐ | ☐ | ☐ | ☐ | ☐ |
| Q5 The chatbot explained its scope and purpose well | ☐ | ☐ | ☐ | ☐ | ☐ |
| Q6 The chatbot gave no indication as to its purpose | ☐ | ☐ | ☐ | ☐ | ☐ |
| Q7 The chatbot was easy to navigate | ☐ | ☐ | ☐ | ☐ | ☐ |
| Q8 It would be easy to get confused when using the chatbot | ☐ | ☐ | ☐ | ☐ | ☐ |
| Q9 The chatbot understood me well | ☐ | ☐ | ☐ | ☐ | ☐ |
| Q10 The chatbot failed to recognise a lot of my input | ☐ | ☐ | ☐ | ☐ | ☐ |
| Q11 Chatbot responses were useful, appropriate, and informative | ☐ | ☐ | ☐ | ☐ | ☐ |
| Q12 Chatbot responses were not relevant | ☐ | ☐ | ☐ | ☐ | ☐ |
| Q13 The chatbot coped well with any errors or mistakes | ☐ | ☐ | ☐ | ☐ | ☐ |
| Q14 The chatbot seemed unable to handle any errors | ☐ | ☐ | ☐ | ☐ | ☐ |
| Q15 The chatbot was very easy to use | ☐ | ☐ | ☐ | ☐ | ☐ |
| Q16 The chatbot was very complex | ☐ | ☐ | ☐ | ☐ | ☐ |

8. Any other comments (including suggestions for improvement)?

**Table A2.** Identified themes from the comments of respondents of the chatbot usability testing survey.

| Theme (Subtheme) | Examples of Statements |
| --- | --- |
| | Identified Issues |
| Interaction Difficulties | Many reverse-coded questions—A bit difficult to answer:)<br>If I type in 'challenge' in a layer where it fits, but apparently not to the Chatbot, it is overwhelmed |
| Incomplete app design | It's very inaccurate when it comes to counting steps<br>The chatbot makes an "unfinished" impression, e.g., the menu below is not always visible and sometimes it is shown with icons and sometimes with / text |
| Spelling errors | Some spelling mistakes (e.g., writte (write), smartes (smartest), reapeat (repeat), etc.<br>A lot of spelling errors (reapeat instead of repeat, smartes instead of smartest, etc) |
| Unresponsive/frozen app | The only thing was that the app got stuck at times, and it wasn't clear how to proceed or if this behavior was intended<br>If you want to create a new goal and have him help you with it, he hangs himself up |
| | Preferred Chatbot features |
| Challenge feature | The random challenge is my favorite feature because it really distinguishes this bot from fitness trackers, and motivates me to do some activity |
| Goal feature | I also like the functionality for checking the user-defined goals |
| | Suggestions for Improvement |
| Challenge related suggestions | |
| Avoid repeating challenge | When the user does not accept the proposed challenge and asks for a different one, the chatbot should avoid suggesting the same one again |
| Personalize challenges | It may be nice for the user to be able to personalize the types of challenges (e.g., in the one-time welcome phase, ask the user to select the types of exercise he/she is never going to accept, that can be excluded from the suggestions) |
| Weekly activity challenge | A weekly activity challenge would be interesting, like a schedule with the desired level. |
| Interaction related suggestions | |
| More facts and input | The idea of a chatbot is cool, but it would need to be connected to services and give more inputs. For example, find activities near you that you can do and suggest them<br>The *chat* is too fixed. Would have been much better if it could take varied answers.<br>More facts should be linked to the chatbot.<br>More inputs so that that it can talk about everyday subjects like weather n answer some questions<br>It could be useful if it answered at least a generic sentence, or if it prompted the initial menu again. |
| More empathy and motivation | Finally, she congratulates that I did 2294 steps even though I did not set a goal and she does not motivate me to set one. I would prefer if she could be more empathic and encourage me to set a goal. |
| Options always available | The second time I tried the chatbot was a bit weird. The chatbot was in a kind of "stand by" mode, in order to discuss goals/steps/etc... again, you need to remember to type "/menu". Perhaps the different options should be shown all the time.<br>Entries should be checked for their meaningfulness. If menu suggestions are made, then these should also work |

## References


1. Ding, D.; Lawson, K.D.; Kolbe-Alexander, T.L.; Finkelstein, E.A.; Katzmarzyk, P.T.; van Mechelen, W.; Pratt, M. The economic burden of physical inactivity: A global analysis of major non-communicable diseases. *Lancet* **2016**, *388*, 1311–1324. [CrossRef]
2. World Health Organization. Global Action Plan on Physical Activity 2018–2030. *More Active People for a Healthier World.* 2018. Available online: https://apps.who.int/iris/bitstream/handle/10665/272722/9789241514187-eng.pdf (accessed on 4 August 2021).
3. Guillon, M.; Rochaix, L.; Dupont, J.-C.K. Cost-effectiveness of Interventions Based on Physical Activity in the Treatment of Chronic Conditions: A systematic literature review. *Int. J. Technol. Assess Health Care* **2018**, *34*, 481–497. [CrossRef] [PubMed]
4. Luo, T.C.; Aguilera, A.; Lyles, C.R.; Figueroa, C.A. Promoting Physical Activity Through Conversational Agents: Mixed Methods Systematic Review. *J. Med. Internet Res.* **2021**, *23*, e25486. [CrossRef] [PubMed]
5. Kongstad, M.B.; Valentiner, L.S.; Ried-Larsen, M.; Walker, K.C.; Juhl, C.B.; Langberg, H. Effectiveness of remote feedback on physical activity in persons with type 2 diabetes: A systematic review and meta-analysis of randomized controlled trials. *J. Telemed Telecare* **2019**, *25*, 26–34. [CrossRef] [PubMed]
6. Kramer, L.L.; Ter Stal, S.; Mulder, B.; de Vet, E.; Van Velsen, L. Developing Embodied Conversational Agents for Coaching People in a Healthy Lifestyle: Scoping Review. *J. Med. Internet Res.* **2020**, *22*, e14058. [CrossRef] [PubMed]

7. Laranjo, L.; Ding, D.; Heleno, B.; Kocaballi, B.; Quiroz, J.C.; Tong, H.L.; Chahwan, B.; Neves, A.L.; Gabarron, E.; Dao, K.P.; et al. Do smartphone applications and activity trackers increase physical activity in adults? Systematic review, meta-analysis and metaregression. *Br. J. Sports Med.* **2021**, *55*, 422–432. [CrossRef] [PubMed]
8. Tsoli, S.; Sutton, S.; Kassavou, A. Interactive voice response interventions targeting behaviour change: A systematic literature review with meta-analysis and meta-regression. *BMJ Open* **2018**, *8*, e018974. [CrossRef] [PubMed]
9. Petersen, J.M.; Prichard, I.; Kemps, E. A Comparison of Physical Activity Mobile Apps With and Without Existing Web-Based Social Networking Platforms: Systematic Review. *J. Med. Internet Res.* **2019**, *21*, e12687. [CrossRef] [PubMed]
10. Gabarron, E.; Larbi, D.; Denecke, K.; Årsand, E. What Do We Know About the Use of Chatbots for Public Health? *Stud Health Technol. Inf.* **2020**, *270*, 796–800. [CrossRef]
11. Kramer, J.-N.; Tinschert, P.; Scholz, U.; Fleisch, E.; Kowatsch, T. A Cluster-Randomized Trial on Small Incentives to Promote Physical Activity. *Am. J. Prev. Med.* **2019**, *56*, e45–e54. [CrossRef] [PubMed]
12. Larbi, D.; Gabarron, E.; Denecke, K. Social Media Chatbot for Increasing Physical Activity: Usability Study. *Stud. Health Technol. Inf.* **2021**, *285*, 227–232. [CrossRef]
13. Michie, S.; Richardson, M.; Johnston, M.; Abraham, C.; Francis, J.; Hardeman, W.; Eccles, M.P.; Cane, J.; Wood, C.E. The Behavior Change Technique Taxonomy (v1) of 93 Hierarchically Clustered Techniques: Building an International Consensus for the Reporting of Behavior Change Interventions. *Ann. Behav. Med.* **2013**, *46*, 81–95. [CrossRef] [PubMed]
14. Flow XO LLC. Create a Chatbot with Zero Coding Skills Required. 2020. Available online: https://flowxo.com (accessed on 15 January 2021).
15. Holmes, S.; Moorhead, A.; Bond, R.; Zheng, H.; Coates, V.; McTear, M. Usability testing of a healthcare chatbot: Can we use conventional methods to assess conversational user interfaces? In Proceedings of the 31st European Conference on Cognitive Ergonomics; ECCE: Belfast, UK, 2019; pp. 207–214.
16. Research & Impact. Ulster University. Available online: https://www.ulster.ac.uk/research/topic/computer-science/artificial-intelligence/projects/cuq (accessed on 15 January 2022).
17. De Cicco, R.; Iacobucci, S.; Aquino, A.; Romana Alparone, F.; Palumbo, R. Understanding Users' Acceptance of Chatbots: An Extended TAM Approach. In *Chatbot Research and Design, CONVERSATIONS 2021, Lecture Notes in Computer Science*; Følstad, A., Araujo, T., Papadopoulos, S., Law, E.L.-C., Luger, E., Goodwin, M., Brandtzaeg, P.B., Eds.; Springer: Cham, Switzerland, 2022; Volume 13171, pp. 3–22.
18. Nadarzynski, T.; Miles, O.; Cowie, A.; Ridge, D. Acceptability of artificial intelligence (AI)-led chatbot services in healthcare: A mixed-methods study. *Digit Health* **2019**, *5*, 2055207619871808. [CrossRef] [PubMed]
19. Piao, M.; Kim, J.; Ryu, H.; Lee, H. Development and Usability Evaluation of a Healthy Lifestyle Coaching Chatbot Using a Habit Formation Model. *Healthc Inform Res.* **2020**, *26*, 255–264. [CrossRef] [PubMed]
20. Greenberg, A. Fleeing WhatsApp for Better Privacy? *Don't Turn to Telegram.* 2021. Available online: https://www.wired.com/story/telegram-encryption-whatsapp-settings/ (accessed on 2 March 2022).
21. Zhang, J.; Oh, Y.J.; Lange, P.; Yu, Z.; Fukuoka, Y. Artificial Intelligence Chatbot Behavior Change Model for Designing Artificial Intelligence Chatbots to Promote Physical Activity and a Healthy Diet: Viewpoint. *J. Med. Internet Res.* **2020**, *22*, e22845. [CrossRef] [PubMed]
22. Kramer, J.-N.; Künzler, F.; Mishra, V.; Smith, S.N.; Kotz, D.; Scholz, U.; Fleisch, E.; Kowatsch, T. Which Components of a Smartphone Walking App Help Users to Reach Personalized Step Goals? Results From an Optimization Trial. *Ann. Behav. Med.* **2020**, *54*, 518–528. [CrossRef] [PubMed]
23. Kocielnik, R.; Xiao, L.; Avrahami, D.; Hsieh, G. Reflection Companion: A Conversational System for Engaging Users in Reflection on Physical Activity. *Proc. ACM Interact. Mob. Wearable Ubiquitous Technol.* **2018**, *2*, 1–26. [CrossRef]
24. Piao, M.; Ryu, H.; Lee, H.; Kim, J. Use of the Healthy Lifestyle Coaching Chatbot App to Promote Stair-Climbing Habits Among Office Workers: Exploratory Randomized Controlled Trial. *JMIR Mhealth Uhealth* **2020**, *8*, e15085. [CrossRef] [PubMed]
25. Maher, C.A.; Davis, C.R.; Curtis, R.G.; Short, C.E.; Murphy, K.J. A Physical Activity and Diet Program Delivered by Artificially Intelligent Virtual Health Coach: Proof-of-Concept Study. *JMIR Mhealth Uhealth* **2020**, *8*, e17558. [CrossRef] [PubMed]

Journal of Personalized Medicine

*Article*

# Application of Machine Learning Methods to Analyze Occurrence and Clinical Features of Ascending Aortic Dilatation in Patients with and without Bicuspid Aortic Valve

Olga Irtyuga [1,*], Georgy Kopanitsa [1,2], Anna Kostareva [1], Oleg Metsker [1], Vladimir Uspensky [1], Gordeev Mikhail [1], Giuseppe Faggian [3], Giunai Sefieva [1], Ilia Derevitskii [2], Anna Malashicheva [1] and Evgeny Shlyakhto [1]

[1] Almazov National Medical Research Centre, 197341 Saint Petersburg, Russia; georgy.kopanitsa@gmail.com (G.K.); akostareva@hotmail.com (A.K.); olegmetsker@gmail.com (O.M.); vladimiruspenskiy@gmail.com (V.U.); mlgordeev@mail.ru (G.M.); gunaj4143@icloud.com (G.S.); amalashicheva@gmail.com (A.M.); e.shlyakhto@almazovcentre.ru (E.S.)

[2] Department of Cardiac Surgery, Medical School, ITMO University, 49 Kronverskiy Prospect, 197101 Saint Petersburg, Russia; ivderevitckii@itmo.ru

[3] Department of Cardiac Surgery, Medical School, University of Verona, 37126 Verona, Italy; giuseppe.faggian@univr.it

* Correspondence: olgir@yandex.ru

check for updates

**Citation:** Irtyuga, O.; Kopanitsa, G.; Kostareva, A.; Metsker, O.; Uspensky, V.; Mikhail, G.; Faggian, G.; Sefieva, G.; Derevitskii, I.; Malashicheva, A.; et al. Application of Machine Learning Methods to Analyze Occurrence and Clinical Features of Ascending Aortic Dilatation in Patients with and without Bicuspid Aortic Valve. *J. Pers. Med.* **2022**, *12*, 794. https://doi.org/10.3390/jpm12050794

Academic Editors: Bernd Blobel and Mauro Giacomini

Received: 17 April 2022
Accepted: 8 May 2022
Published: 14 May 2022



**Abstract:** Aortic aneurysm (AA) rapture is one of the leading causes of death worldwide. Unfortunately, the diagnosis of AA is often verified after the onset of complications, in most cases after aortic rupture. The aim of this study was to evaluate the frequency of ascending aortic aneurysm (AscAA) and aortic dilatation (AD) in patients with cardiovascular diseases undergoing echocardiography, and to identify the main risk factors depending on the morphology of the aortic valve. We processed 84,851 echocardiographic (ECHO) records of 13,050 patients with aortic dilatation (AD) in the Almazov National Medical Research Centre from 2010 to 2018, using machine learning methodologies. Despite a high prevalence of AD, the main reason for the performed ECHO was coronary artery disease (CAD) and hypertension (HP) in 33.5% and 14.2% of the patient groups, respectively. The prevalence of ascending AD (>40 mm) was 15.4% (13,050 patients; 78.3% (10,212 patients) in men and 21.7% (2838 patients) in women). Only 1.6% ($n$ = 212) of the 13,050 patients with AD knew about AD before undergoing ECHO in our center. Among all the patients who underwent ECHO, we identified 1544 (1.8%) with bicuspid aortic valve (BAV) and 635 with BAV had AD (only 4.8% of all AD patients). According to the results of the random forest feature importance analysis, we identified the eight main factors of AD: age, male sex, vmax aortic valve (AV), aortic stenosis (AS), blood pressure, aortic regurgitation (AR), diabetes mellitus, and heart failure (HF). The known factors of AD-like HP, CAD, hyperlipidemia, BAV, and obesity, were also AD risk factors, but were not as important. Our study showed a high frequency of AscAA and dilation. Standard risk factors of AscAA such as HP, hyperlipidemia, or obesity are significantly more common in patients with AD, but the main factors in the formation of AD are age, male sex, vmax AV, blood pressure, AS, AR, HF, and diabetes mellitus. In males with BAV, AD incidence did not differ significantly, but the presence of congenital heart disease was one of the 12 main risk factors for the formation of AD and association with more significant aortic dilatation in AscAA groups.

**Keywords:** ascending aortic dilatation; aneurysm; risk factors; echocardiography

## 1. Introduction

According to different systematic reviews, the incidence of thoracic aortic aneurysms (TAA) in the general population is increasing in frequency from 5 to 10.4 per 100,000 patients [1–3]. However, there are no recommendations for screening for thoracic aortic aneurysms

(TAAs) [4]. Only few studies have illustrated the role of different risk factors in the onset and progression of ascending aortic dilatation [5,6] The majority of them have shown that the prevalence of ascending aortic aneurysm increases with age and depends on sex and body surface area. It is also known that occurrences of ascending aorta aneurysm in males is twice higher than in females. Other recognized risk factors were arterial hypertension, atherosclerosis, tobacco smoking, dyslipidemia, and diabetes mellitus [2,5–7]. Dyslipidemia is a weaker risk factor, whereas diabetes generally reduces the risk of abdominal aortic aneurysm [8]. Furthermore, it has been shown that antihypertensive therapy and smoking cessation can modify the dimension of the aorta in patients with abdominal aortic aneurysms [9–11]. Only family history of AA, increase of the ascending aortic diameter over 3 mm per year, aortic coarctation and history of arterial hypertension are powerful predictors of aortic aneurysm [12]. On the other hand, it is known that BAV is currently one of the most common congenital heart defects. Its detectability according to various data in the general population varies from 0.5% to 2% of cases also associated with aortic pathology [13,14].

Recent ESC guidelines on the diagnosis and treatment of aortic diseases recommended beta blockers and ACE inhibitors to control hypertension, but still no pharmacological treatment is available to effectively reduce ascending aortic dilatation. Currently, open-heart surgery is the only effective treatment for patients with ascending aortic aneurysms and the main measurement to recommend intervention for aortic aneurysms for surgeons is aortic diameter [9]. It is the best predictor for operation, but there are many articles which demonstrate that complications occur frequently with small aortic sizes and the cause of this is unknown [15,16].

Furthermore, the progression of ascending aortic dilation to aortic dissection is well known. Incidence of aortic dissection is still estimated to range between 2.49 and 2.78 cases per 100,000 persons a year, and 85% of all cases are still undiagnosed before death [12].

Therefore, estimation of the individual risk profile, early diagnosis of ascending aortic dilatation (AscAD) in high-risk patients, and elective surgery are crucial to prevent AD and its potential progression to aortic dissection, rupture, and sudden death.

Over the years, medical centers have accumulated a significant amount of information about patient observations [17]. This information can be used for the statistical analysis and identification of characteristics of patients with diseases. This can be especially applicable for asymptomatic diseases. A significant number of disparate changes in indicators allows to identify the progression of diseases in the early stages.

This study describes clinical features and pathology patterns of a population of Russian patients with AscAA with the aim of identifying risk factors for early diagnosis of "silent" AscAD and aneurysm using machine learning methods, and characterizing their association with valve morphology and patient characteristics.

## 2. Materials and Methods

The study protocol was approved by the local ethics committee at the Almazov National Medical Research Centre in Saint Petersburg, Russian Federation, before the initiation of the study according to the principles of the Declaration of Helsinki.

### *2.1. Study Cohort*

We retrospectively analyzed the ECHO database in the Almazov National Medical Research Centre to identify patients with aneurysms.

Furthermore, original methods of natural language processing were applied to extract the characteristics of BAV and tricuspid aortic valve (TAV) from electronic medical records including anamnesis, epicrisis, and results of instrumental tests [18,19].

This database included results of 145,454 ECHOs of outpatients and hospitalized patients, who were observed and treated in the centre between January 2010 and November 2018.

We used the following criteria to include and exclude patients in the study:

Inclusion criteria:

1. Patient from the ECHO database whose treatment started after the 1st of January 2010 and ended before the 30th of November 2018;
2. Diameter of the ascending aorta > 40 mm;
3. For patients who underwent ECHO examination more than once during this period, only the first results of verified AD were included in the study. ECHO was most commonly performed in the following clinical situations: suspected cardiac etiology based on symptoms, signs or other testing; evaluation and follow-up of subjects with cardiovascular disease;
4. Age ≥ 18 years old.

Exclusion criteria:

5. Patients whose treatment started before the 1st of January 2010 or ended after the 30th of November 2018;
6. Patients who did not have a complete data set.

The data set contained 50 predictors and 1 function with the following values: 1 for the patients with AD and 0 for the patients with no AD. A total of 84,851 cases that met the inclusion and exclusion criteria were analyzed retrospectively.

Detailed information including demographic characteristics, characteristics obtained through ECHO, and comorbidities were extracted from outpatient clinic physical exams, as well as from hospital charts related to hospitalizations occurring within a year before index echocardiography was performed. Comorbid diseases were similarly extracted from outpatient clinic and/or hospital admissions.

All patients were divided into 2 subgroups: patients with TAV, and patients with BAV. Demographic characteristics of all patients are presented in Table 1, subgroups in Table 2.

**Table 1.** Demographic and clinical characteristics of all patients.

| Variables | N | All Patients | Min/Max |
|---|---|---|---|
| Age, years (median; quartiles) | 84,851 | 59 (34; 68) | 18; 107 |
| Aortic diameter at the sinus of the Valsalva, mm, median; quartiles | 84,851 | 34 (31; 37) | 8; 90 |
| Aortic diameter at the proximal ascending aorta, mm, median; quartiles | 84,851 | 33 (30; 36) | 12; 98 |
| BMI, kg/m$^2$, median; quartiles | 27,362 | 27.3 (21.4; 31.0) | 12.5; 97.7 |
| AS dpmax, mmHg, median; quartiles | 84,851 | 7.0 (5.0; 10.0) | 0.36; 424 |
| EF LV (%), median; quartiles | 76,800 | 63.9 (56.9; 68.9) | 7.0; 91.5 |
| SBP office, mmHg, median; quartiles | 84,851 | 130 (120; 142) | 55; 270 |
| DBP office, mmHg, median; quartiles | 84,851 | 80 (80; 87) | 20; 140 |
| AR, *n* (%) | 84,757 | 4460 (5.26) | - |
| AS, *n* (%) | 84,851 | 11,252 (13.26) | - |
| Diabetes mellitus, *n* (%) | 84,851 | 8426 (9.93) | - |
| Hypertension, *n* (%) | 84,851 | 59,711 (70.37) | - |
| CAD, *n* (%) | 84,851 | 28,440 (33.52) | - |
| COPD, *n* (%) | 84,851 | 6818 (8.04) | - |
| Asthma, *n* (%) | 84,851 | 2207 (2.60) | - |
| Obesity, (BMI > 30), *n* (%) | 27,362 | 8420 (30.77) | - |
| Hyperlipidemia, *n* (%) | 84,851 | 21,087(24.85) | - |
| Heart failure, *n* (%) | 84,851 | 35,194 (41.48) | - |

BMI—body mass index; SBP—systolic blood pressure; DBP—diastolic blood pressure; AS dpmax—antegrade gradient across the narrowed aortic valve; AR—aortic regurgitation; AS—aortic stenosis; COPD—chronic obstructive pulmonary disease; CAD—coronary artery disease.

**Table 2.** Demographic and clinical characteristics of all patients depend on valve morphology.

| Variables | BAV, $n$ = 1544<br>N; Median; Quartiles | TAV, $n$ = 83,317<br>N; Median; Quartiles | $p$ |
|---|---|---|---|
| Age, years (median and bounds) | 40.5 (18; 104) | 59 (18; 88) | <0.0001 |
| Aortic diameter at the sinus of the Valsalva, mm | 35 (32; 39) | 34 (31; 37) | <0.0001 |
| Aortic diameter at the proximal ascending aorta, mm | 36 (32; 42) | 33 (30; 36) | <0.0001 |
| BMI, $kg/m^2$ | 25.5 (22.8; 28.6) | 27.3 (24.2; 31.1) | <0.0001 |
| AS dpmax, mmHg | 18 (11; 34) | 7 (5; 10) | <0.0001 |
| EF LV (%), ΦB | 65.0 (59.7; 70.1) | 63.9 (56.9; 68.9) | <0.0001 |
| SBP office, mmHg | 130 (120; 140) | 130 (120; 143) | 0.008 |
| DBP office, mmHg | 80 (73.5; 83.5) | 80 (80; 88) | 0.0006 |
| AR, $n$ (%) | 333 (21.72) | 4127 (4.96) | <0.0001 |
| AS, $n$ (%) | 901 (58.77) | 10,351 (12.42) | <0.0001 |
| Diabetes mellitus, $n$ (%) | 77 (5.02) | 8349 (10.02) | <0.0001 |
| Hypertension, $n$ (%) | 861 (56.13) | 58,850 (70.63) | <0.0001 |
| CAD, $n$ (%) | 249 (16.23) | 28,191 (33.84) | <0.0001 |
| COPD, $n$ (%) | 101 (6.58) | 6717 (8.06) | 0.03 |
| Asthma, $n$ (%) | 46 (3.00) | 2161 (2.59) | 0.32 |
| Obesity, (BMI > 30), $n$ (%) | 133 (18.68) | 8287 (31.10) | <0.0001 |
| Hyperlipidemia, $n$ (%) | 305 (19.88) | 20,782 (24.94) | <0.0001 |
| Heart failure, $n$ (%) | 750 (48.89) | 34,444 (41.34) | <0.0001 |

BMI—body mass index; SBP—systolic blood pressure; DBP—diastolic blood pressure; AS dpmax—antegrade gradient across the narrowed aortic valve; AR—aortic regurgitation; AS—aortic stenosis; COPD—chronic obstructive pulmonary disease; CAD—coronary artery disease.

### 2.2. Echocardiography

All patients underwent comprehensive 2-dimensional and Doppler transthoracic echocardiography according to current echocardiography guidelines, using the Vivid 7.0 system (GE, Philadelphia, PA, USA) [10–12]. Aortic root planimetry (including diameters of the ascending aorta at different levels) was comprehensively assessed. Internal diameter was measured perpendicular to the axis of blood flow routinely obtained through the parasternal long-axis view.

Measurements of aortic diameters, ventricular sizes and function, and valve performance were conducted according to current recommendations on echocardiography [18,20,21]. Absolute value of the maximal aortic diameter was indexed to body surface area [22]. Diagnosis of BAV was based on short-axis imaging of the aortic valve, demonstrating the existence of only 2 commissures, delimiting only 2 aortic valve cusps. For each ECHO case, we also analyzed the reason why ECHO was ordered. ECHO was performed in patients with coronary artery disease (CAD) and hypertension in 33.5% and 14.2% of cases, respectively.

### 2.3. Statistical Methods

Statistical analysis was performed using STATISTICA v. 10.0 (StatSoft Inc., Tulsa, OK, USA). Baseline characteristics of the study population are given as percentages for qualitative variables, and medians and quartiles for quantitative variables (not normally distributed), as appropriate, by sex and aortic dilatation status. The $p$-test was applied to obtain the probability for the distribution of characteristic values of different groups of patients with BAV aneurysms compared to observed patients with TAV. Because of the demonstration of significant differences between sexes in terms of demographic characteristics, all the analyses were separately reported for men and women.

### 2.4. Data Preprocessing

We removed 1% of values having the highest z-score to filter out some obvious outliers. Furthermore, we applied the min and max normalization to the remaining values.

### 2.5. Classification Model and Feature Importance

Each experiment ran in the setting of stratified 5-fold cross-validation (i.e., randomly 80% of patients were used for training and 20% for testing, target class ratios in the folds were preserved). A random forest algorithm was applied to calculate the feature importance. The algorithm was implemented using Python 3.6.3 and the scikit-learn 0.19.1 (https://scikit-learn.org/stable/ (accessed on 12 May 2022)) library. A random forest (RF) is an ensemble of machine-learning algorithms, which is best defined as a "combination of tree predictors such that each tree depends on the values of a random vector sampled independently and with the same distribution for all trees in the forest".

As an additional performance assessment score, we used the area under the curve (AUC) of the receiver operating characteristic (ROC), which represents the trade-off between sensitivity and specificity of the model. The AUC was calculated based on an average of 5 curves (one curve per fold in the setting of 5-fold cross-validation). All the measurements were performed separately per dataset and per model parameter value to determine the best parameters for classifiers as well as optimal data preprocessing. The hyperparameters optimization was performed and the results were obtained based on having hyperparameters tuned.

The $p$-value was calculated using the following methods: for each sample of the dead (<1, 1–3, 4–10), the $p$-value of the corresponding test was calculated for each column. Chi-square criterion was applied for categorical features, and Kolmogorov–Smirnov test was deployed for continuous features.

The experiments were conducted with Python 3 packages: scikit-learn [23] and Catboost [24] for machine-learning models implementation, seaborn [25] and matplotlib [26] for data visualization, smote [27] for dataset balancing, and SHapley Additive exPlanations (SHAP) [28] for the black-box results interpretation. The discrimination was evaluated using ROC curves.

Table 3 lists the machine learning models and parameters used in the research.

**Table 3.** Models and parameters.

| Model | Parameters |
|---|---|
| LR * (imp. feat.) | 'C': 2.83, 'solver': 'newton-cg' |
| LR + SMOTE (imp. feat.) | 'C': 0.5, 'solver': 'newton-cg' |
| LR + SMOTE (all feat.) | 'C': 4.0, 'solver': 'liblinear' |
| RF (imp. feat.) | 'criterion': 'gini', 'max_features': 'auto' |
| RF + SMOTE (imp. feat.) | 'criterion': 'gini', 'max_features': 'auto' |
| RF + SMOTE (all feat.) | 'criterion': 'gini', 'max_features': 'log2' |
| CC * (all. feat.) | 'depth': 4, 'l2_leaf_reg': 3, 'learning_rate': 0.6 |
| CC + SMOTE (imp. feat.) | 'depth': 5, 'l2_leaf_reg': 2, 'learning_rate': 0.9 |
| CC + SMOTE (all feat.) | 'depth': 4, 'l2_leaf_reg': 1, 'learning_rate': 0.2 |

* LR—logistic regression; SMOTE—Synthetic Minority Oversampling Technique; RF—random forest; CC—catboost classifier; imp. feat.—the model is composed using only important features; all feat.—the model is composed using all available features.

## 3. Results

The population size of the study was 84,851 patients screened by ECHO.

The main reason to apply ECHO were CAD, suspected hypertension or known valvular heart disease (VHD), different variants of arrhythmia, and other reasons (Figure 1). Only 212 (0.25%) of patients had been aware of their aortic aneurysm before ECHO was performed in the Centre.

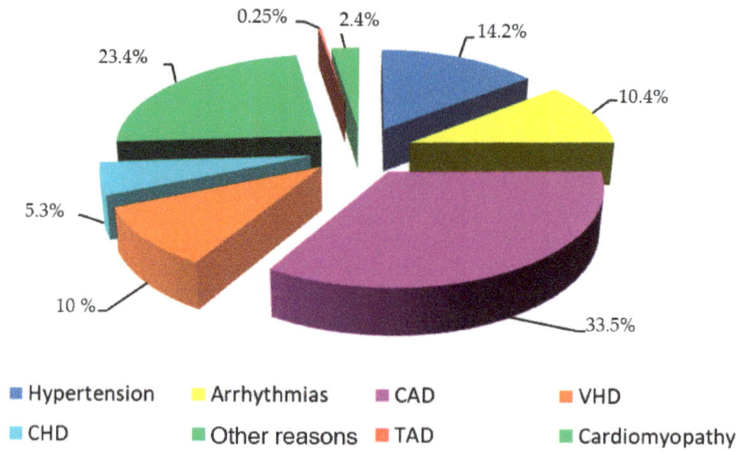


**Figure 1.** The pipeline for medical risk model development.

However, 13,050 (15.4%) patients undergoing ECHO were diagnosed with aortic dilatations. Demographic and clinical characteristics of all patients, who underwent ECHO, are outlined in Table 1. The average age of all included patients was 55.8 (34:68) years. HF, CAD, HP, and obesity were more common in the cohort than dyslipidemia or VHD. Average EF of LV, BP, were normal. The main characteristics of 13,050 patients with aortic dilation are shown in Table 2. Among them, the majority were male (10,202 patients, representing 78.2%). Tables 4 and 5 present demographic and clinical characteristics of all the patients.

**Table 4.** Demographic and clinical characteristics of female patients.

| Variables | BAV | | TAV | |
|---|---|---|---|---|
| | **With AD, *n* = 150** | **Without AD, *n* = 400** | **With AD, *n* = 2688** | **Without AD, *n* = 40,925** |
| Age, years | 54.5 | 35 | 67 | 59 |
| Aortic diameter (sinus Valsalva) | 36 | 31 | 38 | 32 |
| Aortic diameter proximal ascending aorta | 44 (41; 47) | 33 (30; 4) | 41 (40; 44) | 31 (29; 34) |
| BMI, kg/m$^2$ | 26.7 | 24.5 | 28.7 | 27.2 |
| ASdpmax, mm Hg. | 22 (14; 44) | 22 (12; 42.5) | 10 (6; 19) | 7 (6; 10) |
| EF LV (%), | 66.2 | 66.9 | 64.2 | 65.8 |
| SBP office, mm Hg. | 122.5 | 120 | 135 | 130 |
| DBPoffice, mm Hg. | 80 | 80 | 80 | 80 |
| AR, *n* (%) | 24 (16.0) | 67 (16.75) | 372 (13.9) | 1691 (4.1) |
| AS, *n* (%) | 105 (70.0) | 260 (65.0) | 824 (30.7) | 5104 (12.5) |
| Diabetes mellitus, *n* (%) | 8 (5.33) | 21 (5.25) | 305 (11.4) | 4389 (10.7) |
| CAD, *n* (%) | 25 (16.67) | 51 (12.75) | 1041 (38.7) | 11,110 (27.2) |
| COPD, *n* (%) | 5 (3.33) | 15 (3.75) | 205 (7.6) | 2365 (5.8) |
| Asthma, *n* (%) | 5 (3.33) | 10 (2.50) | 122 (4.5) | 1219 (2.9) |
| Obesity, *n* (%) | 24 (30.77) | 28 (13.93) | 392 (42.2) | 4496 (32.2) |
| Hyperlipidemia, *n* (%) | 51 (34.0) | 62 (15.50) | 856 (31.9) | 9695 (23.7) |
| Heart failure, *n* (%) | 26.7 (24.5; 32.1) | 24.5 (21.5; 27.5) | 28.7 (25.1; 32.9) | 27.2 (23.7; 31.2) |

**Table 5.** Demographic and clinical characteristics of male patients.

| Variables | BAV | | TAV | |
|---|---|---|---|---|
| | **With AD, $n$ = 495** | **Without AD, $n$ = 499** | **With AD, $n$ = 9717** | **Without AD, $n$ = 29,987** |
| Age, years, | 50 | 29 | 63 | 56 |
| Aortic diameter (sinus Valsalva) | 41 | 34 | 41 | 35 |
| Aortic diameter proximal ascending aorta | 42 (40; 46) | 33 (30; 36) | 40 (37; 42) | 33 (31; 36) |
| BMI, kg/m$^2$, | 27.1 | 24.3 | 28.4 | 27.0 |
| ASdpmax, mm Hg. | 20 (12; 39) | 14,5 (9; 26) | 7 (5; 11) | 6 (5; 8) |
| EF LV (%), | 62.9 | 64.9 | 59.4 | 61.6 |
| SBP office, mm Hg. | 135 | 130 | 130 | 130 |
| DBPoffice, mm Hg. | 80 | 80 | 80 | 80 |
| AR, $n$ (%) | 129 (26.6) | 113 (22.7) | 1029 (10.6) | 1035(3.4) |
| AS, $n$ (%) | 302 (62.3) | 234 (46.9) | 1661 (17.1) | 2762 (9.2) |
| Diabetes mellitus, $n$ (%) | 24 (4.95) | 24 (4.8) | 953 (9.8) | 2702 (9.0) |
| CAD, $n$ (%) | 119 (24.54) | 54 (10.8) | 4454 (45.8) | 11,586 (38.6) |
| COPD, $n$ (%) | 52 (10.7) | 29 (5.8) | 1045 (10.8) | 3102 (10.3) |
| Asthma, $n$ (%) | 16 (3.3) | 15 (3.0) | 230 (2.4) | 590 (1.9) |
| Obesity, $n$ (%) | 53 (24.31) | 28 (13.0) | 1046 (36.9) | 2353 (26.5) |
| Hyperlipidemia, $n$ (%) | 122 (25.2) | 70 (14.0) | 2901 (29.9) | 7330 (24.4) |
| Heart failure, $n$ (%) | 282 (58.1) | 195 (39.1) | 4854 (49.9) | 12248 (40.8) |

Feature importance: According to the analysis of the significance of predictors by the random forest method, the greatest contribution to the development of aortic aneurysm is made by age and male sex (cut off = 0.25). Less significant contributions were provided by Vmax AV, AS, blood pressure, AR, HF (cut off = 0.025), and other factors such as diabetes mellitus, HP, CAD, fibrillation, asthma, obstructive pulmonary disease (COPD), hyperlipidemia, stroke, thyroid disorders, cholecystitis, congenital heart disease (CHD), BAV, and obesity (Figure 2).

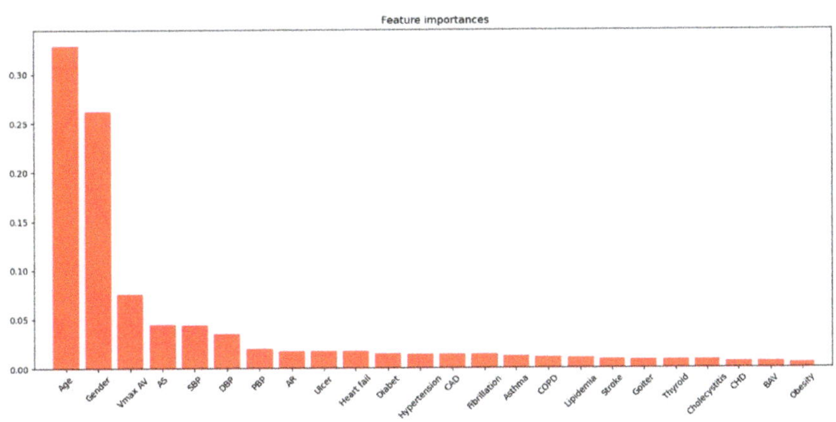


**Figure 2.** Features importance analysis.

AUC of ROC was calculated with a value of 0.92. The resulting ROC curve is presented in Figure 3.

Among all patients who underwent ECHO, we identified 1544 (1.8%) with BAV, and 645 patients with BAV had AD (only 4.9% of all patients with AD).

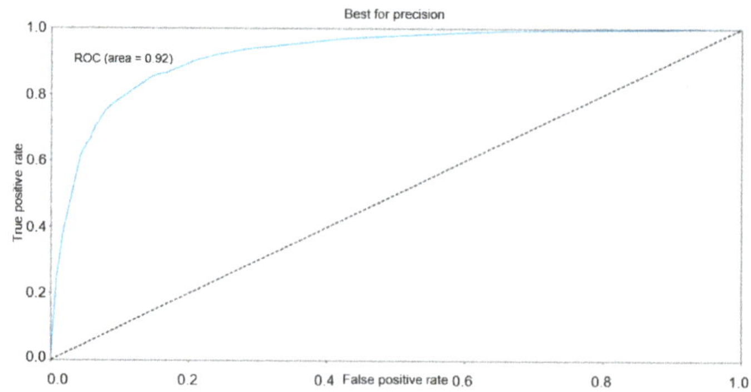


**Figure 3.** ROC for the classification model.

According to the results of the analysis of all patients who underwent ECHO dependent on valve morphology, a more significant aortic dilatation was observed in the group with BAV (Table 2). Besides, AS and AR verification happened in BAV patients four times more often compared to patients without CHD. The latter were younger and had HF more frequently ($p < 0.0001$), while HP, CAD, obesity, hyperlipidemia, and diabetes mellitus were more frequently registered in patients with TAV ($p < 0.0001$).

All patients with AD (Table 3), regardless of valve morphology, were older, and rates of obesity, hyperlipidemia, and HF were higher ($p < 0.003$).

Aortic regurgitation (AR) is more often diagnosed in TAV patients with AD (Figure 4). Aortic stenosis (AS) was frequently verified in all AD patients besides women with BAV (Figure 4). Furthermore, in the group of men with BAV and AD, CAD and COPD were more frequently registered than in patients without AD (Table 3) ($p < 0.0001$).

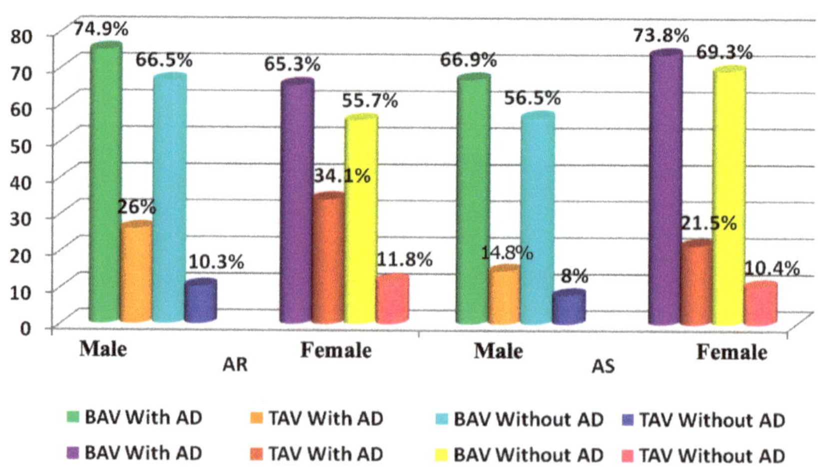


**Figure 4.** The frequency of the AR and AS in patients with/without AD and BAV; AR—aortic regurgitation; AS—aortic stenosis.

In the TAV group with AD rates of CAD, asthma (Table 3) was more frequent than in the group without AD regardless of sex ($p < 0.02$). Besides, patients from the TAV group with AD had higher blood pressure (BP) than patients without AD, also regardless of sex ($p < 0.0001$). Hypotensive and lipid-reducing therapy was more common in patients with aortic aneurysm according to our register. Table 3 shows the best performances for each classification target.

## 4. Discussion

The present study demonstrates that the prevalence of aortic ascending dilatation is 15.4% over 84,851 individuals in our region, a proportion higher than the average incidence of thoracic aortic aneurysm (5–10.4 per 100,000 population) reported in the general population [19]. Compared with epidemiological studies in other countries, our study showed a relatively higher prevalence. This discrepancy of risk in ascending aneurysms compared with the general population might be explained in part by the nature of individuals in the current study. The study subjects were not selected incidentally from the general population, but they initially underwent elective TTE due to a cardiologic clinical indication. We compared our data with another retrospective study, which was also based on a medical center's database. Wang et al. showed that the average incidence among the elderly was 56.1 per 100,000 [29,30]. Unfortunately, our study showed that only 1.6% (n = 212) of 13,050 patients with AD diagnosed by ECHO were aware of their disease. Indeed, in the majority of cases, the disease was accidentally diagnosed during examinations of other diseases, given that the main indication for echocardiography examination was CAD and HP.

The previous study as well as our analysis revealed that women are less likely to have aortic aneurysms compared to men, but women with abdominal aortic aneurysms are at higher risks of aneurysmal dissection, rupture, and complications-related mortality than men [17,18].

In our study, we identified significant risk factors associated with ascending aortic dilatation. According to our results, patients with AD were older than patients without AD, suffered more often from obesity, and had hyperlipidemia and HF more often. However, only males with AD in BAV patients have more often shown CAD, COPD, and AS. Besides, TAV patients with AD were older than TAV patients without AD, had higher BP, suffered more often from obesity, and had hyperlipidemia, CAD, HF, AR, and AS more often. Low prevalence of CAD, HP, and COPD in patients with BAV can reflect another mechanism of the formation and a possible influence of genetic factors [31].

We also observed a higher prevalence of aortic regurgitation and AS in all groups with AD besides the frequency of AS in females with BAV. During the analysis, both men and women had an AS and AR frequency four times higher in patients with BAV.

However, given that the number of females with BAV and AD is less than that of other patients, this did not affect the results of the machine learning analysis of the significance of AD development predictors. According to the results of the machine learning analysis, it is AS that has the greatest impact on the development of AD. On the one hand, the data we obtained contradicts the analysis conducted by Boudoulas et al., which demonstrated that aortic pathology in combination with AS was mostly found in patients with BAV, while only 3% of cases were found in patients with TAV [32].

On the other hand, the results of this analysis once again confirm the contribution of the hemodynamic role of AD formation called "post-stenotic aortic dilatation" due to the influence of the high-velocity turbulent transaortic jet on the aortic wall. An interesting fact is the contribution of diabetes mellitus, CAD, asthma, and COPD to the formation of AD. In general, the understanding of the formation of these diseases follows an inflammatory theory. In particular, Liu. et al. demonstrated a possible mechanism for increasing the size of the abdominal aortic aneurysm in the presence of a lung asthma allergic disease through the activation of an immuno-inflammatory pathway in mice. Intraperitoneal administration of an anti-IgE antibody suppressed AAA lesion formation and reduced lesion inflammation, plasma IgE, and bronchioalveolar inflammation [33]. Rosa et al. showed an inverse association of soluble IL6R with abdominal aortic aneurysm [34]. As for diabetes mellitus, there is currently conflicting data from some authors about its protective effect on patients with AD [35–37]. The results of other studies confirm the negative role of diabetes mellitus for patients with AD [38,39]. Furthermore, Ortega et al. demonstrated that inhibition of SGLT-2 by empagliflozin inhibits AAA formation and can represent a promising therapeutic strategy to prevent AAA progression [40].

In conclusion, our data confirms the importance of echocardiography screening in patients with a known risk factor for aortic dilation. In addition to patients with a known diagnosis of AS, AR, and CAD, ECHO should be performed in patients with diabetes mellitus and asthma, especially in older males. Similarly, if BAV was diagnosed, but aortic dilatation or another pathology was not verified, it is necessary to repeat a control echocardiography, especially if age exceeds 40 years. For example, the risk of aneurysm is 26% at 25 years after the initial diagnosis of BAV at echocardiography, with an incidence of approximately 85 cases per 10 000 patient–years, which represents 80 times the risk of aneurysm formation of the general population [41]. However, the follow-up time interval between BAV diagnosis and aneurysm formation is unpredictable in a single patient. Therefore, a strong recommendation for annual follow-up shall be made for ascending aortic diameters > 45 mm. Large clinical registries based on electronic health records (EHRs) may be used to assess different treatment strategies, to evaluate multiple risk factors and/or outcomes simultaneously, to test associations in subpopulations, to analyze longitudinal outcomes and adverse effects for large cohorts of diverse patients, and to capture uncommon diseases or conditions that are rarely examined in traditional clinical trials. However, analyzing these data is not easy due to differences in EHR encoding systems and data fragmentation across practices and institutions.

*Study Limitation*

This study is based on a retrospective analysis of clinically obtained patient data derived from a single center. It is not truly a population-based research. All patients were admitted and followed-up in a tertiary referral center. This may have led to a selection bias of a higher risky population of patients. Both biases can be minimized by the inclusion of all consecutive patients undergoing echocardiography between 2010 and 2018. Another limitation of this study was the selection of patients based only on the performance of an echocardiographic study.

## 5. Conclusions

Our study showed a high prevalence of ascending aortic dilatation, most of which is completely asymptomatic. This fact puts these patients at great risk of severe aortic-related complications. Recognition of risk factors for aortic dilatation can lead to individualized screening programs. AS, AR, diabetes mellitus, CAD, and asthma are established major risk factors for echocardiography screening in order to identify unknown ascending aorta aneurysms, especially if the patient has other risk factors for AD such as COPD, obesity, hyperlipidemia, HP, BAV, age, and male sex.

The need for such ultrasound screening in patients with ascending aorta aneurysm is confirmed by the results of a similar survey of patients with abdominal aneurysm, which demonstrated a reduction in aneurysm-related mortality in men older than 65 years [42,43].

We have identified the main risk factors, the commonality of which results in the activation of the immuno-inflammatory system, which can help in finding therapeutic targets for the treatment of thoracic aortic dilation.

**Author Contributions:** Conceptualization, O.I. and O.M.; methodology, G.K. and A.K.; validation, V.U.; formal analysis, G.M., G.F., G.S. and I.D.; investigation, O.M.; data curation, O.M.; writing—original draft preparation, O.I. and G.K.; writing—review and editing, A.K. and G.K; visualization, O.M. and A.M.; supervision, E.S.; project administration, A.K. All authors have read and agreed to the published version of the manuscript.

**Funding:** This work was financially supported by the Ministry of Science and Higher Education of the Russian Federation (Agreement No. 075-15-2022-301 of 20 April 2022).

**Institutional Review Board Statement:** The study was conducted in accordance with the Declaration of Helsinki, and approved by the Institutional Review Board (or Ethics Committee) of Almazov National Medical Research Centre in Saint Petersburg, Russian Federation (protocol code 181 of 16 October 2013).

**Informed Consent Statement:** Patient consent was waived due to the use of anonymized medical data without any possibility to identify patients.

**Data Availability Statement:** Not applicable.

**Conflicts of Interest:** The authors declare no conflict of interest.

## Abbreviations

| | |
|---|---|
| AA | aortic aneurysm |
| AscAA | ascending aortic aneurysm |
| AS dpmax | antegrade gradient across the narrowed aortic valve, |
| AD | aortic dilatation |
| AR | aortic regurgitation, |
| AS | aortic stenosis, |
| AV | aortic valve |
| BAV | bicuspid aortic valve |
| BMI | body mass index, |
| CAD | coronary artery disease |
| CHD | congenital heart disease |
| COPD | chronic obstructive pulmonary disease, |
| DBP | diastolic blood pressure, |
| ECHO | echocardiographic |
| HF | heart failure |
| HP | hypertension |
| SBP | systolic blood pressure, |
| TAA | thoracic aortic aneurysms |
| VHD | valvular heart disease |

## References


1. Sampson, U.K.A.; Norman, P.E.; Fowkes, F.G.R.; Aboyans, V.; Song, Y.; Harrell, F.E.; Forouzanfar, M.H.; Naghavi, M.; Denenberg, J.O.; McDermott, M.M.; et al. Global and Regional Burden of Aortic Dissection and Aneurysms: Mortality Trends in 21 World Regions, 1990 to 2010. *Glob. Heart* **2014**, *9*, 171–180.e10. [CrossRef] [PubMed]
2. Devereux, R.B.; De Simone, G.; Arnett, D.K.; Best, L.G.; Boerwinkle, E.; Howard, B.V.; Kitzman, D.; Lee, E.T.; Mosley, T.H.; Weder, A.; et al. Normal Limits in Relation to Age, Body Size and Gender of Two-Dimensional Echocardiographic Aortic Root Dimensions in Persons >15 Years of Age. *Am. J. Cardiol.* **2012**, *110*, 1189–1194. [CrossRef] [PubMed]
3. Senser, E.M.; Misra, S.; Henkin, S. Thoracic Aortic Aneurysm: A Clinical Review. *Cardiol. Clin.* **2021**, *39*, 505–515. [CrossRef] [PubMed]
4. Gaudry, M.; Barral, P.A.; Blanchard, A.; Palazzolo, S.; Bolomey, S.; Omnes, V.; De Masi, M.; Carcopino-Tusoli, M.; Meyrignac, O.; Rousseau, H.; et al. Prevalence of Thoracic Aortic Aneurysms in Patients with Degenerative Abdominal Aortic Aneurysms: Results from the Prospective ACTA Study. *Eur. J. Vasc. Endovasc. Surg.* **2021**, *61*, 930–937. [CrossRef]
5. Kälsch, H.; Lehmann, N.; Möhlenkamp, S.; Becker, A.; Moebus, S.; Schmermund, A.; Stang, A.; Mahabadi, A.A.; Mann, K.; Jöckel, K.H.; et al. Body-Surface Adjusted Aortic Reference Diameters for Improved Identification of Patients with Thoracic Aortic Aneurysms: Results from the Population-Based Heinz Nixdorf Recall Study. *Int. J. Cardiol.* **2013**, *163*, 72–78. [CrossRef]
6. Rogers, I.S.; Massaro, J.M.; Truong, Q.A.; Mahabadi, A.A.; Kriegel, M.F.; Fox, C.S.; Thanassoulis, G.; Isselbacher, E.M.; Hoffmann, U.; O'Donnell, C.J. Distribution, Determinants, and Normal Reference Values of Thoracic and Abdominal Aortic Diameters by Computed Tomography (from the Framingham Heart Study). *Am. J. Cardiol.* **2013**, *111*, 1510–1516. [CrossRef]
7. Lam, C.S.P.; Xanthakis, V.; Sullivan, L.M.; Lieb, W.; Aragam, J.; Redfield, M.M.; Mitchell, G.F.; Benjamin, E.J.; Vasan, R.S. Aortic Root Remodeling over the Adult Life Course: Longitudinal Data from the Framingham Heart Study. *Circulation* **2010**, *122*, 884–890. [CrossRef]
8. Lenivtceva, I.; Panfilov, D.; Kopanitsa, G.; Kozlov, B. Aortic Risks Prediction Models after Cardiac Surgeries Using Integrated Data. *J. Pers. Med.* **2022**, *12*, 637. [CrossRef]
9. Brady, A.R.; Thompson, S.G.; Fowkes, F.G.R.; Greenhalgh, R.M.; Powell, J.T. Abdominal Aortic Aneurysm Expansion: Risk Factors and Time Intervals for Surveillance. *Circulation* **2004**, *110*, 16–21. [CrossRef]
10. Norman, P.; Spencer, C.A.; Lawrence-Brown, M.M.; Jamrozik, K. C-Reactive Protein Levels and the Expansion of Screen-Detected Abdominal Aortic Aneurysms in Men. *Circulation* **2004**, *110*, 862–866. [CrossRef]
11. Golledge, J.; Muller, J.; Daugherty, A.; Norman, P. Abdominal Aortic Aneurysm: Pathogenesis and Implications for Management. *Arterioscler. Thromb. Vasc. Biol.* **2006**, *26*, 2605–2613. [CrossRef] [PubMed]

12. Erbel, R.; Aboyans, V.; Boileau, C.; Bossone, E.; Di Bartolomeo, R.; Eggebrecht, H.; Evangelista, A.; Falk, V.; Frank, H.; Gaemperli, O.; et al. 2014 ESC Guidelines on the diagnosis and treatment of aortic diseases: Document covering acute and chronic aortic diseases of the thoracic and abdominal aorta of the adult The Task Force for the Diagnosis and Treatment of Aortic Diseases of the European Society of Cardiology (ESC). *Eur. Heart J.* **2014**, *35*, 2873–2926. [PubMed]
13. Siu, S.C.; Silversides, C.K. Bicuspid Aortic Valve Disease. *J. Am. Coll. Cardiol.* **2010**, *55*, 2789–2800. [CrossRef] [PubMed]
14. Agnese, V.; Pasta, S.; Michelena, H.I.; Minà, C.; Romano, G.M.; Carerj, S.; Zito, C.; Maalouf, J.F.; Foley, T.A.; Raffa, G.; et al. Patterns of Ascending Aortic Dilatation and Predictors of Surgical Replacement of the Aorta: A Comparison of Bicuspid and Tricuspid Aortic Valve Patients over Eight Years of Follow-Up. *J. Mol. Cell. Cardiol.* **2019**, *135*, 31–39. [CrossRef] [PubMed]
15. Koechlin, L.; Macius, E.; Kaufmann, J.; Gahl, B.; Reuthebuch, O.; Eckstein, F.; Berdajs, D.A. Aortic Root and Ascending Aorta Dimensions in Acute Aortic Dissection. *Perfusion* **2020**, *35*, 131–137. [CrossRef] [PubMed]
16. Zafar, M.A.; Chen, J.F.; Wu, J.; Li, Y.; Papanikolaou, D.; Abdelbaky, M.; Vinholo, T.F.; Rizzo, J.A.; Ziganshin, B.A.; Mukherjee, S.K.; et al. Natural History of Descending Thoracic and Thoracoabdominal Aortic Aneurysms. *J. Thorac. Cardiovasc. Surg.* **2021**, *161*, 498–511.e1. [CrossRef]
17. Kopanitsa, G. Integration of Hospital Information and Clinical Decision Support Systems to Enable the Reuse of Electronic Health Record Data. *Methods Inf. Med.* **2017**, *56*, 238–247. [CrossRef]
18. Baumgartner, H.; Hung, J.; Bermejo, J.; Chambers, J.B.; Evangelista, A.; Griffin, B.P.; Iung, B.; Otto, C.M.; Pellikka, P.A.; Quiñones, M. Echocardiographic Assessment of Valve Stenosis: EAE/ASE Recommendations for Clinical Practice. *J. Am. Soc. Echocardiogr.* **2009**, *22*, 1–23. [CrossRef]
19. Clouse, W.D.; Hallett, J.W.; Schaff, H.V.; Gayari, M.M.; Ilstrup, D.M.; Melton, L.J. Improved Prognosis of Thoracic Aortic Aneurysms. A Population-Based Study. *J. Am. Med. Assoc.* **1998**, *280*, 1926–1929. [CrossRef]
20. Hiratzka, L.F.; Bakris, G.L.; Beckman, J.A.; Bersin, R.M.; Carr, V.F.; Casey, D.E.; Eagle, K.A.; Hermann, L.K.; Isselbacher, E.M.; Kazerooni, E.A.; et al. 2010 ACCF/AHA/AATS/ACR/ASA/SCA/SCAI/SIR/STS/SVM Guidelines for the Diagnosis and Management of Patients With Thoracic Aortic Disease. *Circulation* **2010**, *55*, e27–e129. [CrossRef]
21. Lang, R.M.; Bierig, M.; Devereux, R.B.; Flachskampf, F.A.; Foster, E.; Pellikka, P.A.; Picard, M.H.; Roman, M.J.; Seward, J.; Shanewise, J.; et al. Recommendations for Chamber Quantification. *Eur. J. Echocardiogr.* **2006**, *7*, 79–108. [CrossRef] [PubMed]
22. Mosteller, R.D. Simplified Calculation of Body-Surface Area. *N. Engl. J. Med.* **1987**, *317*, 1098. [PubMed]
23. Pedregosa FABIANPEDREGOSA, F.; Michel, V.; Grisel OLIVIERGRISEL, O.; Blondel, M.; Prettenhofer, P.; Weiss, R.; Vanderplas, J.; Cournapeau, D.; Pedregosa, F.; Varoquaux, G.; et al. Scikit-Learn: Machine Learning in Python. *J. Mach. Learn. Res.* **2011**, *12*, 2825–2830.
24. Prokhorenkova, L.; Gusev, G.; Vorobev, A.; Dorogush, A.V.; Gulin, A. CatBoost: Unbiased Boosting with Categorical Features. *NIPS'18 Adv. Neural Inf. Process. Syst.* **2018**, *31*, 6639–6649. [CrossRef]
25. Waskom, M.L. Seaborn: Statistical Data Visualization. *J. Open Source Softw.* **2021**, *6*, 3021. [CrossRef]
26. Hunter, J.D. Matplotlib: A 2D Graphics Environment. *Comput. Sci. Eng.* **2007**, *9*, 90–95. [CrossRef]
27. Chawla, N.V.; Bowyer, K.W.; Hall, L.O.; Kegelmeyer, W.P. SMOTE: Synthetic Minority over-Sampling Technique. *J. Artif. Intell. Res.* **2002**, *16*, 321–357. [CrossRef]
28. Lundberg, S.M.; Lee, S.-I. A Unified Approach to Interpreting Model Predictions. *NIPS'17 Adv. Neural Inf. Process. Syst.* **2017**, *30*, 4768–4777. [CrossRef]
29. Wang, S.W.; Huang, Y.B.; Huang, J.W.; Chiu, C.C.; Lai, W.T.; Chen, C.Y. Epidemiology, Clinical Features, and Prescribing Patterns of Aortic Aneurysm in Asian Population from 2005 to 2011. *Medicine* **2015**, *94*, e1716. [CrossRef]
30. McPhee, J.T.; Hill, J.S.; Eslami, M.H. The Impact of Gender on Presentation, Therapy, and Mortality of Abdominal Aortic Aneurysm in the United States, 2001–2004. *J. Vasc. Surg.* **2007**, *45*, 891–899. [CrossRef]
31. Nigam, V.; Srivastava, D. Notch1 Represses Osteogenic Pathways in Aortic Valve Cells. *J. Mol. Cell. Cardiol.* **2009**, *47*, 828–834. [CrossRef] [PubMed]
32. Boudoulas, K.D.; Wolfe, B.; Ravi, Y.; Lilly, S.; Nagaraja, H.N.; Sai-Sudhakar, C.B. The Aortic Stenosis Complex: Aortic Valve, Atherosclerosis, Aortopathy. *J. Cardiol.* **2015**, *65*, 377–382. [CrossRef] [PubMed]
33. Liu, C.L.; Wang, Y.; Liao, M.; Wemmelund, H.; Ren, J.; Fernandes, C.; Zhou, Y.; Sukhova, G.K.; Lindholt, J.S.; Johnsen, S.P.; et al. Allergic Lung Inflammation Aggravates Angiotensin II-Induced Abdominal Aortic Aneurysms in Mice. *Arterioscler. Thromb. Vasc. Biol.* **2016**, *36*, 69–77. [CrossRef] [PubMed]
34. Rosa, M.; Chignon, A.; Li, Z.; Boulanger, M.C.; Arsenault, B.J.; Bossé, Y.; Thériault, S.; Mathieu, P. A Mendelian Randomization Study of IL6 Signaling in Cardiovascular Diseases, Immune-Related Disorders and Longevity. *NPJ Genom. Med.* **2019**, *4*, 23. [CrossRef]
35. Nienaber, C.A. Diabetes Mellitus and Thoracic Aortic Disease: Are People With Diabetes Mellitus Protected From Acute Aortic Dissection? *J. Am. Heart Assoc.* **2012**, *1*, e001404. [CrossRef]
36. Jiménez-Trujillo, I.; González-Pascual, M.; Jiménez-Garća, R.; Hernández-Barrera, V.; Miguel-Yanes, J.M.; Méndez-Bailón, M.; De Miguel-DIez, J.; Ángel Salinero-Fort, M.; Perez-Farinos, N.; Carrasco-Garrido, P.; et al. Type 2 Diabetes Mellitus and Thoracic Aortic Aneurysm and Dissection an Observational Population-Based Study in Spain from 2001 to 2012. *Medicine* **2016**, *95*, e3618. [CrossRef]

37. Liu, H.; Shi, L.; Zeng, T.; Ji, Q.; Shi, Y.; Huang, Y.; Zhang, L.; Xiao, T.; Ye, J.; Lin, Y.; et al. Type 2 Diabetes Mellitus Reduces Clinical Complications and Mortality in Stanford Type B Aortic Dissection after Thoracic Endovascular Aortic Repair: A 3-Year Follow-up Study. *Life Sci.* **2019**, *230*, 104–110. [CrossRef]
38. Takagi, H.; Umemoto, T. Negative Association of Diabetes with Thoracic Aortic Dissection and Aneurysm. *Angiology* **2017**, *68*, 216–224. [CrossRef]
39. Avdic, T.; Franzeán, S.; Zarrouk, M.; Acosta, S.; Nilsson, P.; Gottsäter, A.; Svensson, A.M.; Gudbjörnsdottir, S.; Eliasson, B. Reduced Long-Term Risk of Aortic Aneurysm and Aortic Dissection Among Individuals With Type 2 Diabetes Mellitus: A Nationwide Observational Study. *J. Am. Heart. Assoc.* **2018**, *7*, e007618. [CrossRef]
40. Ortega, R.; Collado, A.; Selles, F.; Gonzalez-Navarro, H.; Sanz, M.-J.; Real, J.T.; Piqueras, L. SGLT-2 (Sodium-Glucose Cotransporter 2) Inhibition Reduces Ang II (Angiotensin II)-Induced Dissecting Abdominal Aortic Aneurysm in ApoE (Apolipoprotein E) Knockout Mice. *Arter. Thromb. Vasc. Biol.* **2019**, *39*, 1614–1628. [CrossRef]
41. Michelena, H.I.; Khanna, A.D.; Mahoney, D.; Margaryan, E.; Topilsky, Y.; Suri, R.M.; Eidem, B.; Edwards, W.D.; Sundt, T.M.; Enriquez-Sarano, M. Incidence of Aortic Complications in Patients with Bicuspid Aortic Valves. *JAMA—J. Am. Med. Assoc.* **2011**, *306*, 1104–1112. [CrossRef] [PubMed]
42. Guirguis-Blake, J.M.; Beil, T.L.; Senger, C.A.; Whitlock, E.P. Ultrasonography Screening for Abdominal Aortic Aneurysms: A Systematic Evidence Review for the U.S. Preventive Services Task Force. *Ann. Intern. Med.* **2014**, *160*, 321–329. [CrossRef] [PubMed]
43. Sidloff, D.; Stather, P.; Dattani, N.; Bown, M.; Thompson, J.; Sayers, R.; Choke, E. Aneurysm Global Epidemiology Study Public Health Measures Can Further Reduce Abdominal Aortic Aneurysm Mortality. *Circulation* **2014**, *129*, 747–753. [CrossRef] [PubMed]

Journal of
*Personalized
Medicine*

*Article*

# Hybrid Bayesian Network-Based Modeling: COVID-19-Pneumonia Case

**Ilia Vladislavovich Derevitskii *, Nikita Dmitrievich Mramorov, Simon Dmitrievich Usoltsev and Sergey V. Kovalchuk**

National Center for Cognitive Research, ITMO University, 199034 Saint-Petersburg, Russia
* Correspondence: ilyaderevitskiy@gmail.com; Tel.: +7-(919)-3207725

**Abstract:** The primary goal of this paper is to develop an approach for predicting important clinical indicators, which can be used to improve treatment. Using mathematical predictive modeling algorithms, we examined the course of COVID-19-based pneumonia (CP) with inpatient treatment. Algorithms used include dynamic and ordinary Bayesian networks (OBN and DBN), popular ML algorithms, the state-of-the-art auto ML approach and our new hybrid method based on DBN and auto ML approaches. Predictive targets include treatment outcomes, length of stay, dynamics of disease severity indicators, and facts of prescribed drugs for different time intervals of observation. Models are validated using expert knowledge, current clinical recommendations, preceding research and classic predictive metrics. The characteristics of the best models are as follows: MAE of 3.6 days of predicting LOS (DBN plus FEDOT auto ML framework), 0.87 accuracy of predicting treatment outcome (OBN); 0.98 F1 score for predicting facts of prescribed drug (DBN). Moreover, the advantage of the proposed approach is Bayesian network-based interpretability, which is very important in the medical field. After the validation of other CP datasets for other hospitals, the proposed models can be used as part of the decision support systems for improving COVID-19-based pneumonia treatment. Another important finding is the significant differences between COVID-19 and non-COVID-19 pneumonia.

**Keywords:** COVID-19; pneumonia; dynamical Bayesian networks; treatment trajectories; auto ML



**Citation:** Derevitskii, I.V.; Mramorov, N.D.; Usoltsev, S.D.; Kovalchuk, S.V. Hybrid Bayesian Network-Based Modeling: COVID-19-Pneumonia Case. *J. Pers. Med.* **2022**, *12*, 1325. https://doi.org/10.3390/jpm12081325

Academic Editors: Bernd Blobel and Mauro Giacomini

Received: 17 May 2022
Accepted: 8 August 2022
Published: 17 August 2022



## 1. Introduction

### *1.1. Background*

The COVID-19 pandemic has affected the world for over two years. According to [1], over six million people have died and almost half a billion people have been infected during the pandemic. New mutated strains, such as the Omicron variant, spread around the globe and produce an immune escape, with a higher risk of reinfection than the Beta and Delta variants. It not only invades the respiratory system but also causes other organ injuries in severe cases, such as kidney injury, liver injury, myocardial injury, coagulation dysfunction, and gastrointestinal symptoms [2].

Symptoms of respiratory system failure are highly frequent in COVID-19 cases [3]. Over 15% of hospitalized COVID-19 patients develop acute respiratory distress syndrome (ARDS). The mortality of the critically ill group of COVID-19 patients is comparable with that of severe ARDS, reaching approximately 40% at day 30 after admission to the intensive care unit [4]. Most frequent reasons of ARDS are different types of pneumonia [5]. Therefore, the research of COVID-19 pneumonia is an essential and urgent task.

A disease trajectory modeling approach might be used for proper COVID-19 pneumonia diagnosis and treatment. Kim et al. claim that monitoring the early trajectory of pneumonia extent on chest radiographs could further stratify patients at risk for worse outcomes beyond the baseline tests [6]. Other studies provide new ideas to understand the heterogeneous etiopathology of COVID-19 patients and the associations of distinct trajectories with disease severity, which is essential to improve early risk assessment, patient monitoring, and follow-up schedules [7].

The outlined studies underscore the necessity of pneumonia disease trajectory modeling. In this article, we propose our own approach, using both ordinary and dynamic Bayesian Networks, but also modern auto ML approaches.

### 1.2. Related Works

There are many methods described in the literature that have been used for predictive modeling of disease trajectory. The most frequent approaches are hidden Markov models (HMM), deep learning, expert-based modeling, and Bayesian networks (BN). Hereinafter, we call these approaches as A, B, C, and D, respectively.

Approach A is a standard tool for disease modeling [8,9]. Yusuf A Amrulloh et al. presented a cough model based on the HMM. With data collected from a pediatric population diagnosed as pneumonia and asthma, the model achieved an accuracy of 82.7% for a pneumonia prediction task [8]. Ozonoff et al. proposed an approach based on HMMs, and demonstrated it on pneumonia and influenza (P&I) mortality data [9]. The paper shows that hidden Markov models are intuitively motivated and demonstrate improvements in goodness-of-fit, when applied to retrospective P&I mortality data. However, approach A does not consider "past" states of variables and relies on the current state of the presented variable. Furthermore, this approach cannot provide an approximation of difficult relationships between medical indicators.

Unlike approach A, deep learning approach B uses more sophisticated algorithms for constructing the model [10–12]. Artificial neural networks (ANN) have been used for pneumonia predictions [10]. Using a backpropagation algorithm, the feedforward ANN was trained on sociodemographic, symptom, sign, comorbidity, and radiographic outcome data. Among adults suffering from acute respiratory disease, the model accurately discovered patients with and without pneumonia [11] in a retrospective study for testing the ability of a deep learning algorithm at extracting features from chest x-rays (CXR) to track and predict radiological evolution. CXR deep learning features showed promise for classifying disease trajectory and may inform triage decisions after validation. CXR data have been used differently by Hoon Ko et al. [12], to develop an artificial intelligence technique to diagnose COVID-19 pneumonia in CT images and differentiate it from non-COVID-19 pneumonia and non-pneumonia diseases. Their fast-track COVID-19 classification network (FCONet), a simple 2D deep learning framework based on a single chest CT image, provided excellent diagnostic performance in detecting COVID-19 pneumonia. Despite the great performance of the deep learning approach in a large variety of tasks, it lacks interpretability, which is an essential part of disease modeling.

This disadvantage was eliminated by approach C, which nowadays is frequently used together with approach D [13,14]. For example, Shaochong Lin et al. aimed to develop a machine-learning model that identifies future high-cost patients with chronic obstructive pulmonary disease (COPD) and to ensure that such a model incorporates expert knowledge about causal relationships [13]. The learning BN structure was later used for model creation and showed considerable improvement compared with the baseline machine-learning methods. An application of expert knowledge towards learning BN structure is covered in [14]. Using multiple kinds of expert knowledge, it was shown that such an approach facilitates the knowledge engineering process and allows us to perform hybrid structure learning algorithms. Expert-based modeling could be used as a starting point of research or as a facilitation for some other methods, such as approach B. However, it has many limitations, such as the frequent lack of sufficiently evidence-based conclusions and statistically confirmed patterns of disease development [15].

Approach D is widely used in studies on COVID-19. Bayesian networks are known for underlying causal assumptions and interpretability and are widely used in disease modeling. For example, in our previous work, we compared BN and HMM built on COVID-19 pneumonia patients' clinical data [16].

Nowadays, the continuous time Bayesian network (CTBN) and dynamic Bayesian network models have become an object of interest for many researchers in disease modeling. For example, Gatti et al. created a CTBN that was used to diagnose cardiogenic heart failure and to anticipate its likely evolution [17]. The proposed model managed to overcome the strong modeling and computational limitations of dynamic Bayesian networks (DBN) and allowed the direct representation of time, offering valid computational machinery for medical inference. For COVID-19 pneumonia, we propose a new approach, which facilitates the advantages of time period modeling and Bayesian networks and allows us to build complex and more realistic models for a COVID-19 pneumonia disease trajectory prediction task.

### 1.3. The Research Question

In the Introduction, we described reasons for researching COVID-19-pneumonia. In a short version of this paper, we investigated differences between CP and ordinary pneumonia [16]. Using these differences, we created models for automatically distinguishing different types of pneumonia. This model showed a prediction quality of more than 85 for the F1 score (best model: hidden Markov model, with 95% F1 score on the test samples). After validations using other COVID-19 datasets, it could be deployed in practice. However, using this model, we cannot improve the treatment process. These models do not support finding an optimal treatment strategy for new patients. Thus, we need to upgrade our approach.

To find an optimal treatment strategy for new CP cases, medical specialists need high-quality predictions about the future dynamics of important patients' condition indicators. Here and below, we refer to predictions with a quality of more than 0.85 in terms of F1 score or accuracy on cross-validation for the test samples (that were not used for training models) as "high-quality predictions" and "high-quality models".

These predictions should consider specifics of each treatment case and use all important history for the approximation of future indicators. Predictions should include treatment results, length of stay (for optimal planning of hospitals resources, which is especially important during a pandemic), and dynamics of all condition indicators as time-sequences for early prevention of critical conditions.

For solving the problem, we can use methods listed in the section Related Work. HMM models, according to approach A, are high-interpretations tools [18]. However, they cannot investigate the complex relationships between medical indicators. Neural networks, according to approach B, cannot be used, because predictions by this tool are hard to interpret. Moreover, validations using expert knowledge could be difficult. The literature overview on approaches B and C, as well as our experience with real COVID-19 data, show that Bayesian networks can make approximations with high enough quality (92% precision in a task of defining type of pneumonia [16]) of statistical influence from patients' conditions to the targets.

Specifics of real data have many gaps for important indicators. For aggregated data, we divided the length of stay into several time intervals and aggregated values from this interval (the method is described in Sections 2.1 and 2.2). We used a set of ordinary BN to find statistical relationships between the indicators from each treatment time interval. Then, we deployed DBN to find relationships between the indicators from different intervals and to predict all the values for the next interval using the last interval. Finally, we applied hybrid methods (auto ML and DBN together) for improving the prediction quality. Thus, we can predict full future sequences of values for each medical indicator using only information from the first interval.

## 2. Materials and Methods

Figure 1 shows a chart of the procedure.

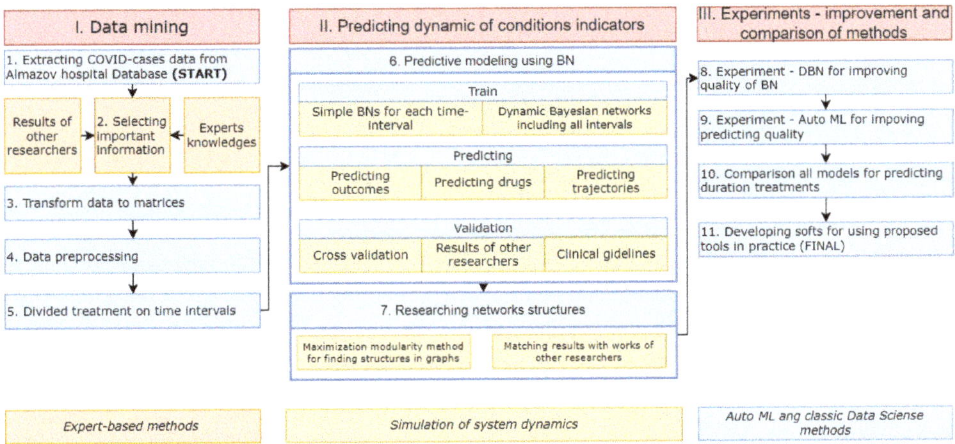


**Figure 1.** Procedure. Research includes 3 stages and 11 steps.

The first stage is data mining. In the first step, 6,302,049 electronic medical records from 2445 cases of COVID-19-based pneumonia were extracted from the Almazov Medical Research Database. The data are described in detail in Section 2.3. In the second step, we selected important features, using knowledge from the following three sources: clinical recommendations, experts' knowledge, and works of other researchers. We selected 160 medicals indicators that are important in predicting treatment dynamics and treatment outcomes. Then, we performed data pre-processing. To overcome the problem of gaps, we used the MICE algorithm [19]. For coding categorical features, we applied the one-hot-encoding method. In the fifth step, we divided each treatment interval into several time intervals. Then, information for each interval of several days was aggregated and each interval was considered as a discrete time point. Patients' conditions do not change every day, and for high-quality modeling of the trajectory of changing important indicators (in terms of metrics and experts' opinion), we need aggregated time points.

In the second stage, patient condition indicators' dynamics were predicted; this includes steps 6–7. In the 6th step, we trained OBN and DBN models using real data. These steps are described in detail in Sections 2.1 and 2.2. Thereafter, we investigated statistical relationships between the indicators at each time interval using OBN. Furthermore, we tried using these networks to predict the treatment results. Then, we researched probabilistic relationships between the indicators at different time intervals using DBN. Based on trained DBN, we created tools for predicting sequences of all important indicators and treatment duration. Indicators included therapy. Therefore, we can predict future therapy effects in terms of changing important indicators for all time intervals. We validated models using classical metrics for predictive tasks and results of other researchers.

The third step included experiments for comparing and improving models from the second step. In step 8, we created DBN for improving prediction quality by ordinary BN for some time intervals. In step 9, we used the modern auto ML method for predicting length of stay (LOS) for CP-patients in hospitals and used a hybrid of the auto ML method and DBN approaches to achieve better predictive quality. Then, we compared methods (step 10) using cross-validation and classical metrics. Finally, we developed software for using the proposed models as part of medical decision support systems.

### 2.1. Simple Bayesian Networks

A BN is a directed acyclic graph, whose nodes represent random variables, and links express dependencies between the nodes. Each node is a random variable, i.e.,

$N_i \in N(1 \le i \le n)$. Each edge is a link, $E \subseteq N \times N$, and P is joint probability distribution, described as

$$P(N) = \prod_{N_i \in N} P(N_i|\pi(N_i)) \quad (1)$$

where $\pi(N_i)$ is the set of parent nodes of $N_i$. In this article, we use hybrid Bayesian networks that contain both discrete variables and continuous variables [20].

Training Bayesian networks is a process of estimating parameters P that best represent the given data set D and creating a Bayesian directed acyclic graph (DAG). Several quality metrics of Bayesian networks exist, such as Bayesian information criterion (BIC) [21], maximum description length (MDL) [22], or Akaike information criterion (AIC) [23]. One of the most common metric of quality for created BN is log-likelihood (LL) [24], which is as follows:

$$LL(B|D) = \sum_{N_i} \log(P(N_i|P(N_i|\pi_B(N_i)))) \quad (2)$$

where B is the Bayesian network over D, and $|\pi_B(N_i)$ is the parent node of $N_i$ in B.

This metric is often used for creating predictive Bayesian networks in medical tasks [25,26] and results in high performance of the created models. For example, in the paper [25], BN showed 0.89 AUC-ROC quality in a task of medical classification. This result was better than the results of a logistic regression model and naive Bayesian classifier. In task [26], the Bayesian network and regression method were implicated in treatment cost prediction. This model showed 89.14 accuracy, which is better than the second result (by locally weighted LASSO regression model) by 4%.

Furthermore, the authors empirically evaluated the capability of various scoring functions of Bayesian networks for recovering true underlying structures [22]. Z. Liu and colleagues explained that MLD and BIC methods consistently outperform other scoring functions, such as Akaike's information criterion (AIC), Bayesian Dirichlet equivalence score (BDeu), and factorized normalized maximum likelihood (fNML). In the current paper, we use BIC to find the optimal DAG structure for Bayesian dynamical networks.

We train Bayesian networks to carry out the following tasks:

- Find statistical patterns between patients' condition indicators.
- Select dynamical predictors (indicators and time of its measurement) of treatment outcomes.
- Predict treatment outcomes.

The algorithm for training the network includes the following five steps:

1. The dataset is separated by 5 time periods—each period lasts 7 days. Patients' conditions do not change every day. For researching statistically significant patterns, we, therefore, aggregate information for each interval.
2. Learning the DAG. There are two approaches for finding the structure of the BN graph, score-based structure learning algorithms and constraint-based algorithms. We try to use two methods from the first approach—hillclimb search and Chow-liu and one method from the second approach—constraint-based search [27]. Hillclimb search performs a greedy local search that begins with default DAG without edges and proceeds by iteratively performing single-edge manipulations that maximally increase the score (BIC). Chow-liu is based on the hypothesis that networks have a tree structure. The tree structure shows the best metric, given that each node has at most one parent. The constraint-based approach identifies probabilistic dependencies in the data set based on hypothesis tests, such as chi-square.
3. Learning the network parameters using the maximum likelihood estimation method [28].
4. Visualizing Bayesian networks as graphs. Nodes were clustered using the modularity maximization method. This method is based on the widely-used objective function to determine communities from a given network [29].
5. Estimating the predictive quality of each network in terms of predicting treatment outcomes by using the classical metric of predictive tasks, including F1 score for the classification problem and mean absolute error (MSE) for regression.

### 2.2. Dynamic Bayesian Networks

In this research, we went beyond ordinary Bayesian networks by using dynamical Bayesian networks (DBN). A DBN is a Bayesian network that relates variables to one another over adjacent time steps. Figure 2 demonstrates the visualization of an example DBN, which includes three states A, B, C and four time periods (0–3). By states, we mean any components of an object (patient) condition in a dynamical discrete system, which may be related to one another within one-time intervals and between different time intervals, as shown in Figure 2. Processes of learning parameters and structures, as well as making inferences, are similar to ordinary BN. The structure of DBN is described in more detail in [30].

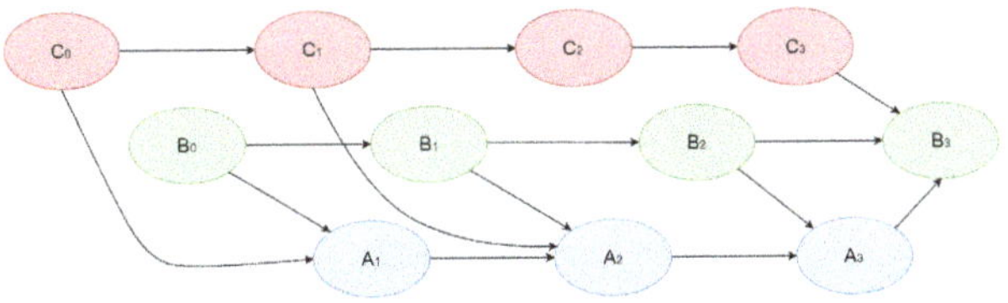


**Figure 2.** DAG-example of a dynamic Bayesian network.

In this paper, we use DBN for the following tasks:

- Research of dynamical statistical patterns of treatment trajectories.
- Predicting the full future trajectory of important patients' indicators
- Predicting the therapy effect in terms of treatment outcomes and length of stay (therapy included in factors of networks)

The algorithm for training DBN is described in the chart below (Figure 3).

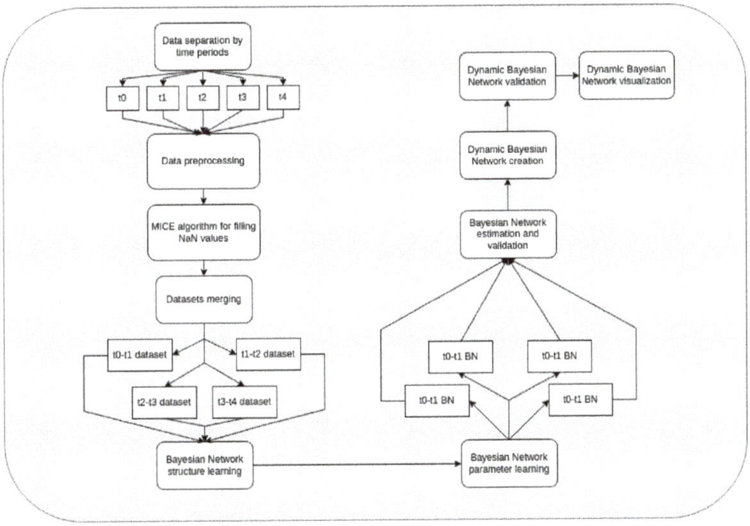


**Figure 3.** Dynamic Bayesian network modeling algorithm.

The algorithm comprises the following steps:

1. The dataset is separated into 5 time periods, each of them with a 7-day length.
2. The MICE algorithm is applied to fill the missing data, since real clinical data might contain missing values. Features without data are dropped.

3. Information from day t to day t +1 is merged and used for the creation of Bayesian networks. Data are separated into train and test datasets for every time.
4. Learning DAG and parameters of joint probability distribution are similar to learning for ordinary BN (algorithm in the item 2.2). All networks learn using the BAMT python package [31,32].
5. We validate DBN using only test samples. Using models, we made predictions of the treatment outcomes and a series of important patient condition indicators using the following algorithm: using initial data from t-0 interval, we provide predictions of all the medical indicators for t-1 interval; using predicted indicators, we make predictions for the t-2-time interval, and so on. When we have predictions of the patients′ condition indicators, we predict the treatment outcomes.
6. For analyzing structures of trained DBN, we visualize it as a graph; we deploy the method of modularity maximization to divide networks into clusters and to analyze the model's structure.

### 2.3. Data

The study is based on a dataset including 6,302,049 medical records for 2445 patients who were treated for COVID-19 pneumonia at the Almazov National Medical Research Centre, St. Petersburg, Russia, in 2020–2021. There are several entries and exclusion criteria for a patient to be included in dataset. The criteria are shown in Table 1.

**Table 1.** Entry and exclusion criteria for including a patient in the dataset.

| Entry Criteria | Exclusion Criteria |
|---|---|
| 1. COVID-19-based pneumonia<br>2. Minimum length of stay is three days<br>3. Treatment outcomes include lethal outcome and hospital discharge<br>4. Treatment process was inpatient | 1. Observation period less than three days |

For analysis, we used electronic medical records that fully describe each treatment cases. Information includes results of laboratory tests (blood, urine, cerebrospinal fluid, etc.); results of diagnostic procedures, such as CT scans of the lungs, x-rays, clinical parameters, such as heart rate, blood pressure, anthropometric parameters; symptoms; vaccination information; physical measurements; lifestyle; medication and many more. The time interval for each treatment case is described using a set of more than 160 indicators. Table 2 describes these data in more detail.

**Table 2.** Medical indicators for treatment cases.

| Feature's Group | Features |
|---|---|
| Anthropometrics parameters | Height, weight, gender, body mass index, body surface area. |
| Simple measurements | Systolic blood pressures (SBP), diastolic blood pressure; (DBP), heart rate, temperature, saturation (SPO2), respiratory rate. |
| Laboratory results | 101 indicators: different type of laboratory tests: venous and arterial blood tests, urine tests, cerebrospinal fluid tests, etc. |
| COVID-19 symptoms | Headache, unconsciousness, cough, sore throat, pus in the throat, feeling of congestion in the chest, type of breathing, weakness, decreased consciousness. |
| Results of diagnostic procedures | The presence of clinical manifestations of severe pneumonia, the percentage of lung tissue damage, the severity of the course, the patient's condition, NEWS score, etc. |
| Vaccination | Flu, pneumonia, COVID-19 vaccination. |
| Complications | Multiple organ failure, septic shock, febrile fever, unstable hemodynamics. |
| COVID-19 therapy | Information of prescribed therapy for COVID-19 treatment drugs from clinical recommendations, including glucocorticosteroids, monoclonal antibodies, anticoagulants, antivirals, non-steroidal anti-inflammatory drugs and other drugs from current clinical recommendations. |

## 3. Results

### *3.1. Simple Bayesian Network-Based Analysis*

We trained four BN (for each period) using the algorithm described in Section 2.1. One of the main goals of training BN is to research statistical relationships between medical indicators, and to analyze the dynamics of these relationships. For that purpose, we presented BN as graphs and applied the method of modularity maximization for analyzing the graph's structure. We considered how the relationships and graph structure changed in the models for the first- and last-time interval (graphs in Figure 4).

**Figure 4.** Graphs of trained BN for two-time intervals—first-time interval (top) and last-time interval (bottom). The colors represent nodes' modularity maximization clustering. The size of each node is weighted degree.

We can observe that these two graphs have different structures. Table 3 describes those clusters and our conclusions in some detail.

**Table 3.** Description of the resulting network for the first-time interval.

| Time Interval | Cluster | Description | Count of Nodes | Nodes with the Highest Power | Weighted Average Degree |
|---|---|---|---|---|---|
| First week of treatment | Purple | Includes predictors of treatment outcomes, and two outcome indicators—treatment outcomes and length of stay. | 21 | Duration of hospital stay (treatment outcome) | 19 |
| Fourth week of treatment | Purple | Includes predictors of treatment outcomes, and two outcome indicators—treatment results and length of stay. | 28 | Length of stay (treatment outcome) | 10 |
| First week of treatment | Orange | Some laboratory test results. Cluster does not include nodes with link to treatment outcomes. | 4 | PCT-plateletcrit | 8 |
| Fourth week of treatment | Orange | Some laboratory test results. Cluster includes nodes with link to treatment outcomes—monocyte% and saturation. | 18 | Saturation (link to treatment results) | 8 |
| First week of treatment | Green | C-reactive protein, RBC, basophils—indicators that have links to treatment outcomes (length of stay); however, they are not included in purple clusters. In the graph of the last period, this cluster joins with purple, part of indicators lose the link with treatment outcome. | 12 | C-reactive protein | 10 |
| First week of treatment | Blue | Patient condition and features that influence it—age, severity according to CT scan, bilirubin total, information of vaccination. In the fourth interval cluster, nodes transfer to purple cluster. | 7 | PLT | 15 |

Bayesian network graphs show different relationships between indicators and different set of nodes with links to treatment outcomes for different time intervals. We also analyzed the graphs for other time intervals and made conclusions from the statistical relationships and their changes over time. The lists of dependencies and joint probability distributions are important findings for fundamental medicine. We analyzed clusters with treatment outcomes for first-time and last-time intervals in detail. Subgraphs are shown in Figures 5 and 6.

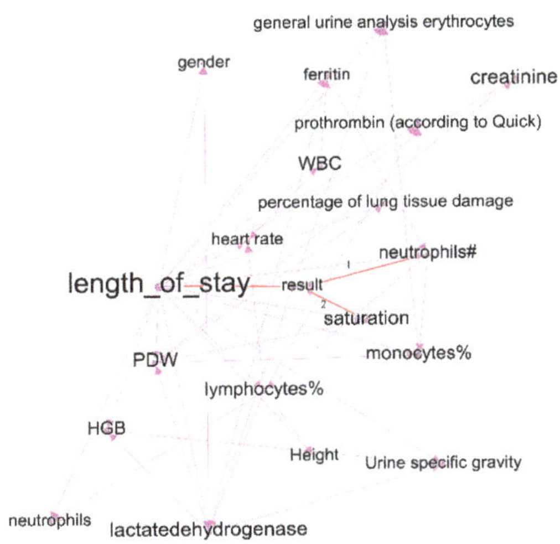


**Figure 5.** Cluster from DAG for the first-time interval, which includes the variable length of stay and treatment outcomes.

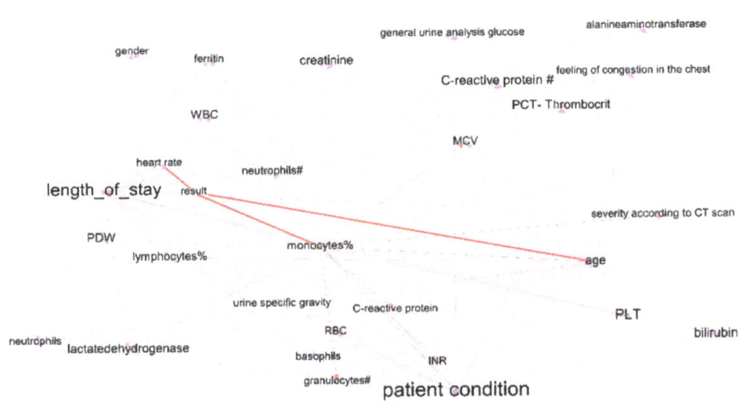


**Figure 6.** Cluster from DAG for fourth time interval, including length of stay and treatment results.

The first target is the length of stay, which has links to all indicators of the purple clusters. These indicators include blood and urine laboratory results, level of saturation, percentage of lung tissue damage, heart rate, and gender. Other researchers confirmed parts of these relationships, e.g., the influence of lymphocytes [33] on treatment outcomes. Node results (the binary indicator of treatment outcome—fatal or recovered) have three links (marked red) to saturation (matched to the results of other researchers [34]), neutrophils (matched to results in [35]) and length of stay (the dependency is evident).

The purple cluster of the graph was based on medical indicators from the fourth time interval (from day 21 to day 29 of the patient's stay in the hospital) and has many similarities with the cluster for the first interval. The length of stay was connected to all indicators of the clusters. Most indicators match for these two graphs, which demonstrates the stability and significance of the discovered relationships in the two graphs. The graph in Figure 6 shows a link between the length of stay and C-reactive protein (its link with COVID-19 outcome has been proven in many studies [36]) on the one hand and PLT (which influences COVID-19-related length of stay as described in [37]) on the other hand.

Similarly, predictors of treatment outcomes were identified for the graph of each interval. The statistical connections found, as well as some references to the work of other researchers who obtained similar results, are shown in Table 4.

Upon training, four BN were validated. For the test samples, we predicted treatment outcomes and estimated the predictive metrics. For the variable of treatment result, the metrics are accuracy and F1 score (classification problem). For the variable of length of stay, the metric is the mean absolute error (MAE). We state that the proposed hybrid Bayesian network can predict categorical and continuous variable simultaneously. In addition, its advantage in comparison to some ML models is that they solve only one type of task (classification or regression). To solve two tasks, we need to train two ML models. Table 5 shows the metrics for each interval and variables. All metrics have been calculated using cross validation with 5 folds.

The metrics show that the predictive quality of the treatment results increases from the t-0 to the t-2 interval. As for the t-3 interval, it decreases significantly. Many patients leave the hospital before the beginning of this interval (recovery or fatal outcome). Therefore, there were fewer precedents, which explains the deterioration in the quality of the prognosis.

The quality of prediction of treatment outcomes is more than 0.8 (quality improves as new information becomes available, as observed in Table 5), for a length of stay MAE near one week. Figure 7 presents violin plots with real and predictive distributions of length of stay. We can observe that, for all intervals, the probability distribution is similar. Therefore, we can use this model for predicting the length of stay for a large patient population. However, the MAE metric is more than 10 for the t-3 intervals. For one patient, the error could be significant. We improve the quality for this interval using dynamical Bayesian networks further.

Using ordinary BN, we found statistical patterns and selected predictors for each treatment outcome for each time interval. Furthermore, we used information for creating more complex predictive models.

### 3.2. Dynamical Bayesian Network-Based Analysis

For improving the prediction quality of length of stay, we developed dynamical Bayesian networks (DBN) that consider dynamical relationships between indicators and make better approximations than ordinary BN. Algorithms used for creating DBN are described in Section 2.2. We use the BIC metric for finding the DAG structure, and the log-likelihood metric for parameters learning. Furthermore, we use modern soft BAMT for working with DBN [32]. We selected features for DBN to be considered for detecting dependencies, as described in Section 3.1. The DAG of the created model is presented in Figure 8.

The results of modularity maximization clustering are four clusters within the graph. The investigation of the graph structure reveals that the model considers the age variable to be the most essential one for all patients and allows the consideration of a large variety of symptoms (including severe ones) every time. Using this network, we can predict length of stay. The quality of prediction is estimated using the MAE score. DBN improved the results of predicting the length of stay using information from the t-3 interval. DBN shows 8.12 MAE against 10.22 by using the simple Bayesian network from the 3.1 item. The major advantage of DBN is its good interpretability, as well as the increased confidence of doctors.

**Table 4.** Predictors of treatment outcome from four-time intervals.

| Outcome Feature | t0 | t1 | t2 | t3 |
|---|---|---|---|---|
| Treatment outcomes | Saturation | Lymphocytes [38] | Monocytes | Age |
| Treatment outcomes | Neutrophils [39] | Red blood cells [40] | Age | Patient condition |
| Length of stay | Feeling of congestion in the chest | Urea | MCV mean corpuscular volume [41] | C-reactive protein |
| Length of stay | PCT-plateletcrit | MCV mean corpuscular volume [41] | Alanineaminotransferase [39] | Lactatedehydrogenase [42] |
| Length of stay | Neutrophils | C-reactive protein [43] | C-reactive protein | PDW—platelet distribution width [44] |

**Table 5.** Metrics of BN models.

| | t0 | t1 | t2 | t3 |
|---|---|---|---|---|
| Treatment outcomes—accuracy | 0.87 | 0.94 | 0.95 | 0.84 |
| Treatment outcomes—F1-score | 0.84 | 0.93 | 0.95 | 0.82 |
| Length of stay | 8.61 | 7.3 | 9.18 | 10.22 (needs improvement) |

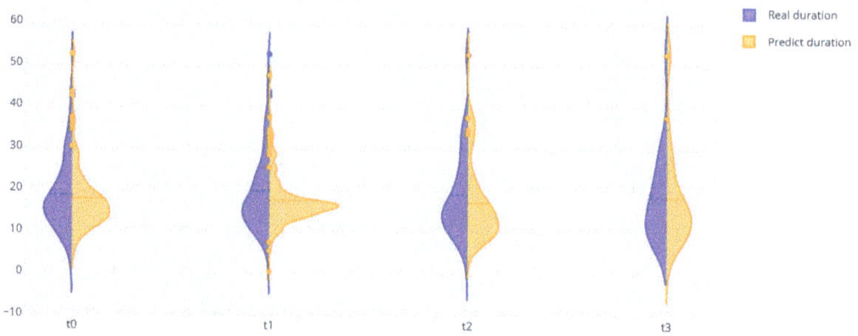


**Figure 7.** Real and predicted probability distributions of length of stay for predictions using information from different time intervals.

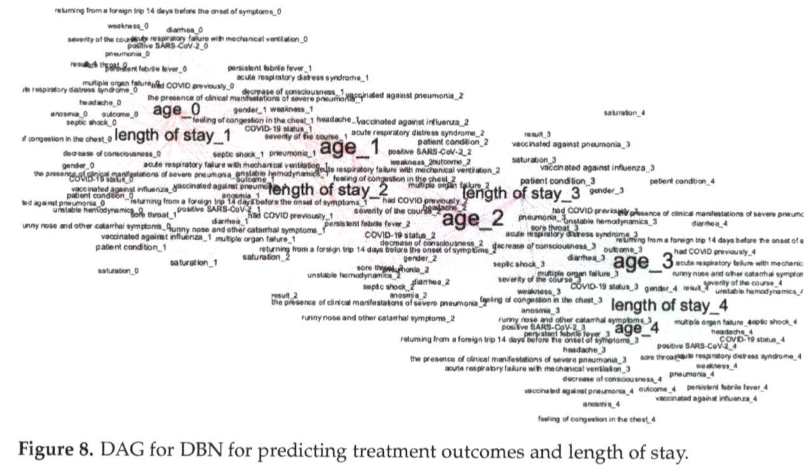


**Figure 8.** DAG for DBN for predicting treatment outcomes and length of stay.

Next, we created a separate DBN for predicting time series of variables that are important for treatment outcomes. We selected a set of variables based on the conclusions from Section 3.1. The created model has been visualized in a graph form, applying the modularity analysis to locate clusters and to obtain insights about the model's inner structure (see Figure 9). This model uses information from the patients' blood tests (such as PLT) and lung tissue damage data to predict a set of features, which would directly affect the future condition of the patient. Using initial data from blood tests at the t0 period and data about vaccination or general health state, it evaluates the severity of lung tissue damage for every period, mostly relying on blood test data.

The modularity analysis divided nodes into four clusters with different structures than those in the previous DAG. We trained networks and predicted all variables (from the graph) using only real values from the first time. The violin plots showed similarities in the probability distributions of the real and predicted variables (Figures 10 and 11).

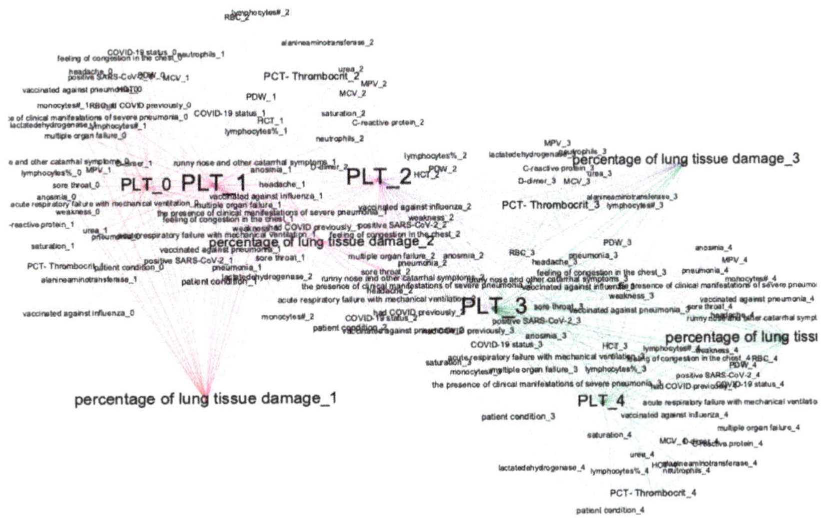


**Figure 9.** DBN for predicting time series of patient condition indicators.

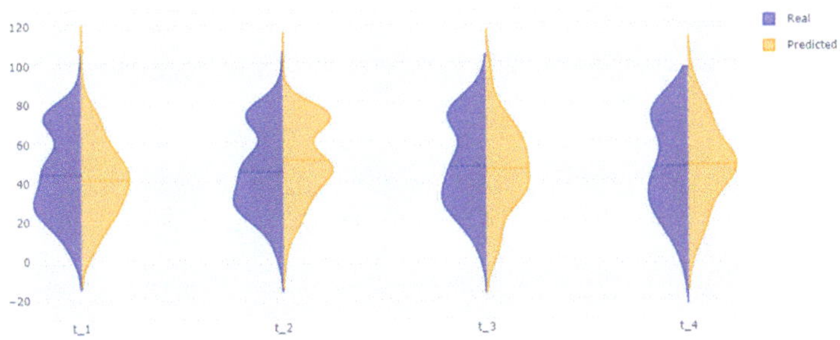


**Figure 10.** Real and predicted distribution of percentage of lung tissue damage.

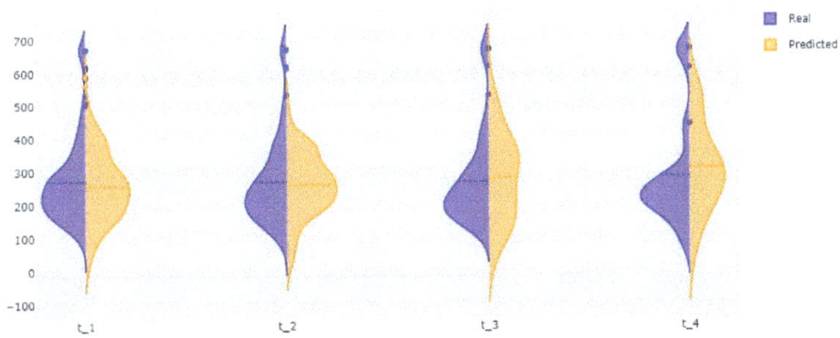


**Figure 11.** Real and predicted distribution of PCT.

After validation using classic predictive metrics and comparisons of distributions, we concluded that the quality of the model is sufficient for deploying DBN in combination with auto ML methods to predict the length of stay (Section 3.3).

One of the main goals of this research is the prediction of future therapy trajectories for CP patients. Using the created DBN, we provided predictions of therapy trajectories in terms of sequences of prescribed CP drugs. The learning process is similar to the models described above. Nodes include a list of anti-CP-drugs that are most frequently applied in Russian hospitals at different time periods, including the following: ambroxol, dexamethasone, bisoprolol, azithromycin, etc. We assessed the therapy frequency in different intervals. Thereby, patients with and without applied therapy were in our training data for further estimation. Table 6 shows the quality metrics of proposed DBN.

**Table 6.** Metrics of DBN predictions facts of prescribing drugs in different time intervals.

| | t-1 | t-2 | t-3 | t-4 |
|---|---|---|---|---|
| F1-score—dexamethasone | 0.8421 | 0.8666 | 0.9 | 0.8333 |
| F1-score—ambroxol | 0.6516 | 0.6538 | 0.6136 | 0.998 |
| F1-score—azithromycin | 0.7481 | 0.8461 | 0.8421 | 0.4166 |
| F1-score—bisoprolol | 0.743 | 0.74 | 0.5133 | 0.909 |

The created DBN is capable of predicting therapy trajectories and combines both therapy and patient clinical data. The model enables the prediction of therapy trajectories every time (see Figure 12). We achieved the best overall f1-score (higher than 0.8) with the drug dexamethasone. For ambroxol, we observed the best score of 0.998 for the t4 period; however, metrics for the t1–t3 periods state that the model needs more fine-tuning to predict such therapy successfully and thoroughly. The model performed well with the azithromycin prediction. However, the prediction quality was significantly decreased for the last period. The root cause of this problem lies in the lack of training data for the later periods, which affects both the t3 and the t4 intervals.

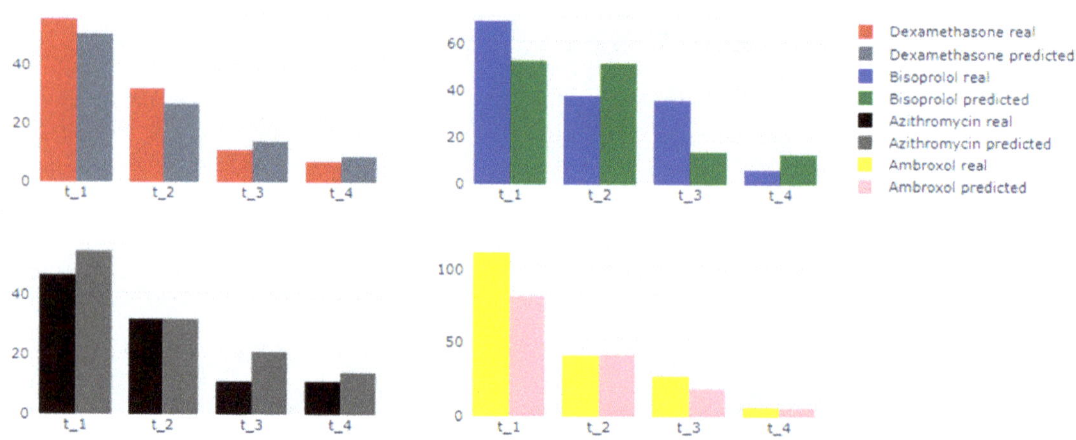


**Figure 12.** Comparison of real and predictive counts of drug prescribing.

From Table 6, with enough training data available, the model could provide decent scores, but therapy predictions for later periods were not as precise as for the t1 and t2 periods. However, with enough training data provided, the model increased its performance for the later time periods. The metrics for t1–t2 demonstrated good quality for approximations of relationships between patients' condition indicators and prescribing therapy. After validation by medical specialists, this model could, therefore, be used for simulating the process of therapy prescribing, and for supporting decision-making in the COVID-19-pneumonia treatment process.

### 3.3. Hybrid Approach

In modern bioinformatics literature, authors often use various machine learning methods for creating predictive models. In specific practical settings, results of BN can upgrade the quality of ML models, and CP outcome prediction is one of these tasks.

We provided such an outcome by using FEDOT [45] for predicting the length of stay and the output of DBN for improving the quality of FEDOT's results. FEDOT is an open-source framework for automated modeling and machine learning (auto ML). It can build custom modeling pipelines for different real-world processes in an automated way using an evolutionary approach. FEDOT supports binary and multiclass classification, regression, clustering, and time series prediction tasks [46]. We deployed it for predicting the length of stay and compared results of the FEDOT method with the hybrid method, combining FEDOT and DBN to predict future series of medical indicators. The FEDOT algorithm includes the following steps: feature selection using the tree-based features importance method; developing the structure of FEDOT model, including modeling the process pipeline as sequences of the methods for preprocessing and prediction; cross-validations with the MAE metric. The hybrid method included just one extra step. Before we selected the features for each sample, we trained DBN, and we predicted the future time-series of indicators that were important in terms of treatment outcome predictions. For feature selection, we chose features from two sets, real indicators and predictions of future dynamics of treatment outcomes predictors (the feature list is provided in Section 3.1). That way, we expanded the dataset with new variables. Table 7 compares the quality of the following three methods: results of ordinary BNs (Section 3.1), FEDOT, and the hybrid method combining FEDOT and DBN.

**Table 7.** Metrics of three methods in the task of predicting length of stay.

| Methods | t-0 | t-1 | t-2 | t-3 |
|---|---|---|---|---|
| Set of ordinary BNs | 8.61 | 7.3 | 9.18 | 10.22 (8.12) |
| FEDOT framework | 4.12 | <u>2.81</u> | 2.65 | 3.95 |
| FEDOT + DBN | <u>3.6</u> | 2.45 | <u>2.88</u> | <u>3.39</u> |

In three of the four intervals, the hybrid method combining FEDOT and DBN presents the best quality. Pipelines of the three best models are shown in Figure 13.

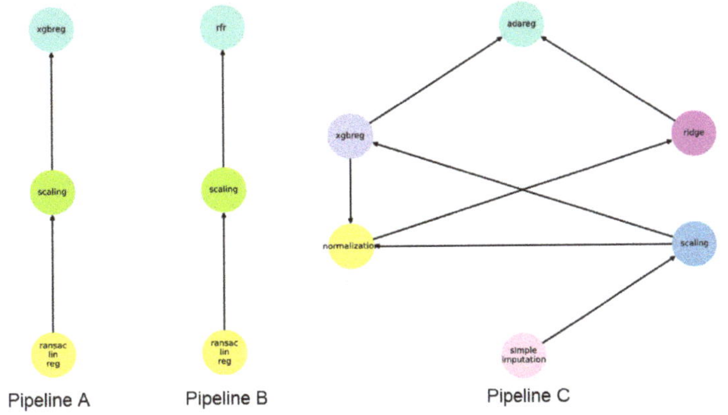


**Figure 13.** Pipelines of created predictive models for three-time intervals.

Pipeline A is used for the (t-0) and (t-1) intervals, pipeline B is used for the (t-2) intervals, and the last interval (t-3) is modeled by the more complex pipeline C. Each pipeline includes a data-scaling step. Pipelines for the three best models include a XGB regressor. The pipeline for the t-2 interval includes a random forest regressor instead of XGB. It could explain the deterioration in the quality of the hybrid method compared with conventional FEDOT. Metrics from Table 7 show that the approach provides a small error (MAE near 3 for all time intervals). The model could be useful for predicting the length of stay for patient flow in a hospital. It can support decision-making in optimization management of hospital resources, which is especially important in a pandemic.

## 4. Discussion

The outcomes of this paper are twofold. First, the research contributes to the evidence base of medicine with information about the course of COVID-19 pneumonia. Secondly, this paper proposes practical tools for predicting important indicators of future conditions of patients with COVID-19-based pneumonia and new algorithms (or new pipelines of using existed algorithms) for modelling the course of the disease in the hospital. The first outcome is presented in items 3.1–3.2. We suggested a Bayesian network-based method for identifying the following three types of probabilistic relationships: factor-to-factor within time interval, factor-to-factor between time interval, and factor-to-target. The extracted probabilistic relationships inform evidence-based knowledge on the course of COVID-19 pneumonia with inpatient treatment. Some of these relationships matched with the results of other researchers [38–44]. However, other extracted results are new, such as the influence of monocytes from the third time interval (10–17 days) to lethality. Our models show that this is one of the main predictors of treatment outcomes from this interval.

Moreover, the novelty of this research is the study of the course of COVID-19 pneumonia as a dynamic process using graph-probabilistic models. Probabilistic discrete-time models are often used for modelling dynamics of the COVID-19 epidemic [47,48], but almost never used to model the course of the disease in the hospital on the macrolevels. Abhinav Vepa and colleagues used Bayesian networks to extract probabilistic relationships and predict treatment outcomes [49]; however, their work does not research the course of the disease as a dynamic process with the analysis of all types of relationships.

The second outcome of the paper includes four approaches for predicting important disease indicators. Three approaches are based on sets of Bayesian networks, dynamic Bayesian networks, and the state-of-the-art auto ML framework FEDOT. The fourth approach is based on a new algorithm that uses the DBN and framework together. The quality of the developed tools for predicting CP length of stay is shown in Tables 5 and 7. The best quality of cross-validation (mean for all test samples) was shown by the hybrid algorithm, which we associate with using temporal information extracted from data using the DBN, together with linear and nonlinear patterns extracted from data using auto ML. The results also include a tool to predict facts of different prescribed CP therapy drugs, which is a high-interpretability tool that supports the selection of therapy. Table 6 shows that for some drug models, the quality is more than 0.8 in terms of F1 score (e.g., dexamethasone), while for other drugs, the mean quality is less than 0.7 (e.g., azithromycin). This variability can be attributed to the different rigidity of rules for including drugs in the treatment strategy, and the consequently different difficulties of extracting this rule from data. In addition, we propose tools for predicting future multidimensional time series of patient condition indicators based on DBN. The violin plots in Figures 10 and 11 show that the distributions of the predictive indicators are similar to the real distributions.

One of the main advantages of BN-based approaches is high interpretability. By "high-interpretability", we mean that the predictions of the DBN algorithm are more understandable in comparison with other popular machine learning algorithms, such as neural networks, random forests and other. Each prediction of DBN can be interpreted using an understandable graph representation of causal probabilistic relationships between the indicators. For each case, we can extract an algorithm reasoning sequence using Bayesian probabilistic inference [50]. This increases the confidence of doctors and contributes to the implementation of the solution in practice.

## 5. Conclusions

In this paper, we proposed Bayesian network-based approaches for solving the following four problems: prediction of treatment outcomes for inpatient cases; prediction of the dynamics of patient conditions indicators; simulation of doctor's therapy choice; upgrading the quality of the ML method for treatment outcome prediction.

All methods were applied on real practice tasks to optimize the COVID-19-based pneumonia treatment process. The developed practice tools have been validated using real cases that are different from those deployed in the model learning process, and they demonstrated high metrics of predictive quality (Tables 5–7). Furthermore, all the results have been matched with results of other researchers (Table 4) and modern clinical guidelines. In addition, dynamical Bayesian networks are a high-interpretability tool ("high interpretability" is explained in detail in the previous section), and this will increase the confidence of doctors and contribute to the implementation of the tool in practice.

Finally, we found statistical relationships in the dynamics of the COVID-19 pneumonia treatment process. High metrics of approximation (Table 5 for treatment outcomes and Table 7 for length of stay) demonstrates the reliability of these relationships. Thus, this paper contributes to evidence-based medicine and could be the basis for developing other models for CP patients.

The software developed for predictive modeling could be used as part of decision support systems in caring for COVID-19-based pneumonia patients.

Future work will include research on creating modules that include knowledge from fundamental medicine and developing a new hybrid approach, combining data-driven models and expert-based models for improving the quality of predictive modeling of treatment dynamics.

**Author Contributions:** Conceptualization, I.V.D., S.V.K.; methodology, I.V.D., N.D.M.; software, I.V.D., N.D.M., S.D.U.; validation, I.V.D., S.V.K.; formal analysis, I.V.D., N.D.M., S.D.U.; investigation, I.V.D., N.D.M., S.D.U.; resources, I.V.D.; data curation, I.V.D.; writing—original draft preparation, I.V.D., N.D.M., S.D.U.; writing—review and editing, I.V.D.; visualization, I.V.D., N.D.M., S.D.U.; supervision, I.V.D., S.V.K.; project administration, S.V.K. All authors have read and agreed to the published version of the manuscript.

**Funding:** This research is financially supported by the Ministry of Science and Higher Education, Agreement #075-15-2020-808.

**Institutional Review Board Statement:** Not applicable for studies not involving humans or animals.

**Informed Consent Statement:** Not applicable.

**Data Availability Statement:** Not applicable.

**Acknowledgments:** We thank to Ministry of Science and Higher Education, Agreement #075-15-2020-808, for financial support.

**Conflicts of Interest:** The authors declare no conflict of interest.

## References

1. COVID Live—Coronavirus Statistics—Worldometer. Available online: https://www.worldometers.info/coronavirus/ (accessed on 10 April 2022).
2. Cummings, M.J.; Baldwin, M.R.; Abrams, D.; Jacobson, S.D.; Meyer, B.J.; Balough, E.M.; Aaron, J.G.; Claassen, J.; Rabbani, L.R.E.; Hastie, J.; et al. Epidemiology, clinical course, and outcomes of critically ill adults with COVID-19 in New York City: A prospective cohort study. *Lancet* **2020**, *395*, 1763–1770. [CrossRef]
3. Shi, N.; Huang, C.; Zhang, Q.; Shi, C.; Liu, F.; Song, F.; Hou, Q.; Shen, J.; Shan, F.; Su, X.; et al. Longitudinal trajectories of pneumonia lesions and lymphocyte counts associated with disease severity among convalescent COVID-19 patients: A group-based multi-trajectory analysis. *BMC Pulm. Med.* **2021**, *21*, 233. [CrossRef] [PubMed]
4. Symptoms of Coronavirus: Early Signs, Serious Symptoms and More. Available online: https://www.webmd.com/lung/covid-19-symptoms#1 (accessed on 10 April 2022).
5. Bauer, T.T.; Ewig, S.; Rodloff, A.C.; Müller, E.E. Acute respiratory distress syndrome and pneumonia: A comprehensive review of clinical data. *Clin. Infect. Dis.* **2006**, *43*, 748–756. [CrossRef]
6. Kim, J.Y.; Ji Jung, K.; Yoo, S.J.; Yoon, S.H. Stratifying the early radiologic trajectory in dyspneic patients with COVID-19 pneumonia. *PLoS ONE* **2021**, *16*, e0259010. [CrossRef] [PubMed]
7. Tian, D.; Sun, Y.; Xu, H.; Ye, Q. The emergence and epidemic characteristics of the highly mutated SARS-CoV-2 Omicron variant. *J. Med. Virol.* **2022**, *94*, 2376–2383. [CrossRef]

8. Amrulloh, Y.A.; Triasih, R.; Setyati, A. Hidden markov model of cough from pediatric patients with respiratory infections. In Proceedings of the 2016 International Seminar on Application for Technology of Information and Communication (ISemantic), Semarang, Indonesia, 5–6 August 2016; pp. 341–345. [CrossRef]
9. Ozonoff, A.; Sukpraprut, S.; Sebastiani, P. Modeling seasonality of influenza with Hidden Markov Models. *Proc. Am. Stat. Assoc.* **2006**. Available online: https://www.researchgate.net/publication/267206133 (accessed on 4 May 2015).
10. Heckerling, P.S.; Gerber, B.S.; Tape, T.G.; Wigton, R.S. Prediction of community-acquired pneumonia using artificial neural networks. *Med. Decis. Mak.* **2003**, *23*, 112–121. [CrossRef] [PubMed]
11. Duchesne, S.; Gourdeau, D.; Archambault, P.; Chartrand-Lefebvre, C.; Dieumegarde, L.; Forghani, R.; Gagné, C.; Hains, A.; Hornstein, D.; Le, H.; et al. Tracking and predicting COVID-19 radiological trajectory using deep learning on chest X-rays: Initial accuracy testing. *medRxiv* **2020**. [CrossRef]
12. Ko, H.; Chung, H.; Kang, W.S.; Kim, K.W.; Shin, Y.; Kang, S.J.; Lee, J.H.; Kim, Y.J.; Kim, N.Y.; Jung, H.; et al. COVID-19 pneumonia diagnosis using a simple 2d deep learning framework with a single chest CT image: Model development and validation. *J. Med. Internet Res.* **2020**, *22*, e19569. [CrossRef]
13. Lin, S.; Zhang, Q.; Chen, F.; Luo, L.; Chen, L.; Zhang, W. Smooth Bayesian network model for the prediction of future high-cost patients with COPD. *Int. J. Med. Inform.* **2019**, *126*, 147–155. [CrossRef]
14. Julia Flores, M.; Nicholson, A.E.; Brunskill, A.; Korb, K.B.; Mascaro, S. Incorporating expert knowledge when learning Bayesian network structure: A medical case study. *Artif. Intell. Med.* **2011**, *53*, 181–204. [CrossRef] [PubMed]
15. Derevitskii, I.V.; Savitskaya, D.A.; Babenko, A.Y.; Kovalchuk, S.V. Hybrid predictive modelling: Thyrotoxic atrial fibrillation case. *J. Comput. Sci.* **2021**, *51*, 101365. [CrossRef]
16. Mramorov, N.; Derevitskii, I.; Kovalchuk, S. Predictive Modeling of COVID and non-COVID Pneumonia Trajectories. *Stud. Health Technol. Inform.* **2021**, *285*, 112–117. [CrossRef] [PubMed]
17. Gatti, E.; Luciani, D.; Stella, F. A continuous time Bayesian network model for cardiogenic heart failure. *Flex. Serv. Manuf. J.* **2012**, *24*, 496–515. [CrossRef]
18. Awad, M.; Khanna, R. Hidden Markov Model. *Effic. Learn. Mach.* **2015**, *263*, 81–104. [CrossRef]
19. van Buuren, S.; Groothuis-Oudshoorn, K. Mice: Multivariate imputation by chained equations in R. *J. Stat. Softw.* **2011**, *45*, 1–67. [CrossRef]
20. Puga, J.L.; Krzywinski, M.; Altman, N. Points of Significance: Bayesian networks. *Nat. Methods* **2015**, *12*, 799–800. [CrossRef]
21. Schwarz, G. Estimating the Dimension of a Model. *Ann. Stat.* **1978**, *6*, 461–464. [CrossRef]
22. Liu, Z.; Malone, B.; Yuan, C. Empirical evaluation of scoring functions for Bayesian network model selection. *BMC Bioinform.* **2012**, *13* (Suppl. 1), 1–16. [CrossRef]
23. De Campos, C.P.; Ji, Q. Efficient structure learning of Bayesian networks using constraints. *J. Mach. Learn. Res.* **2011**, *12*, 663–689.
24. Park, E.; Chang, H.J.; Nam, H.S. A Bayesian network model for predicting post-stroke outcomes with available risk factors. *Front. Neurol.* **2018**, *9*, 699. [CrossRef] [PubMed]
25. Van Der Gaag, L.C.; Renooij, S.; Feelders, A.; De Groote, A.; Eijkemans, M.J.C.; Broekmans, F.J.; Fauser, B.C.J.M. Aligning bayesian network classifiers with medical contexts. In *Lecture Notes in Computer Science (Including Subseries Lecture Notes in Artificial Intelligence and Lecture Notes in Bioinformatics)*; Springer: Berlin/Heidelberg, Germany, 2009; Volume 5632 LNAI, pp. 787–801. [CrossRef]
26. Tong, L.L.; Gu, J.B.; Li, J.J.; Liu, G.X.; Jin, S.W.; Yan, A.Y. Application of Bayesian network and regression method in treatment cost prediction. *BMC Med. Inform. Decis. Mak.* **2021**, *21*, 284. [CrossRef] [PubMed]
27. Package 'bnlearn' Type Package Title Bayesian Network Structure Learning, Parameter Learning and Inference. 2022. Available online: https://www.bnlearn.com/ (accessed on 10 April 2022).
28. Ji, Z.; Xia, Q.; Meng, G. A Review of Parameter Learning Methods in Bayesian Network. In *Lecture Notes in Computer Science (Including Subseries Lecture Notes in Artificial Intelligence and Lecture Notes in Bioinformatics)*; Springer: Berlin/Heidelberg, Germany, 2015; Volume 9227, pp. 3–12. [CrossRef]
29. Tsung, C.K.; Lee, S.L.; Ho, H.J.; Chou, S.K. A modularity-maximization-based approach for detecting multi-communities in social networks. *Ann. Oper. Res.* **2021**, *303*, 381–411. [CrossRef]
30. Łupińska-Dubicka, A. Modeling dynamical systems by means of dynamic Bayesian networks. *Sci. Bull. Bialystok Univ. Technol. Inform.* **2012**, *9*, 77–92.
31. Bubnova, A.V.; Deeva, I.; Kalyuzhnaya, A.V. MIxBN: Library for learning Bayesian networks from mixed data. *Procedia Comput. Sci.* **2021**, *193*, 494–503. [CrossRef]
32. ITMO-NSS-Team/BAMT: Repository of a Data Modeling and Analysis Tool Based on Bayesian Networks. Available online: https://github.com/ITMO-NSS-team/BAMT (accessed on 12 April 2022).
33. Tan, L.; Kang, X.; Ji, X.; Li, G.; Wang, Q.; Li, Y.; Wang, Q.; Miao, H. Validation of Predictors of Disease Severity and Outcomes in COVID-19 Patients: A Descriptive and Retrospective Study. *Med* **2020**, *1*, 128–138.e3. [CrossRef]
34. Mukhtar, A.; Rady, A.; Hasanin, A.; Lotfy, A.; El Adawy, A.; Hussein, A.; El-Hefnawy, I.; Hassan, M.; Mostafa, H. Admission SpO2 and ROX index predict outcome in patients with COVID-19. *Am. J. Emerg. Med.* **2021**, *50*, 106–110. [CrossRef]
35. Zeng, Z.Y.; Feng, S.D.; Chen, G.P.; Wu, J.N. Predictive value of the neutrophil to lymphocyte ratio for disease deterioration and serious adverse outcomes in patients with COVID-19: A prospective cohort study. *BMC Infect. Dis.* **2021**, *21*, 80. [CrossRef]

36. Lentner, J.; Adams, T.; Knutson, V.; Zeien, S.; Abbas, H.; Moosavi, R.; Manuel, C.; Wallace, T.; Harmon, A.; Waters, R.; et al. C-reactive protein levels associated with COVID-19 outcomes in the United States. *J. Osteopath. Med.* **2021**, *121*, 869–873. [CrossRef]
37. Mahboub, B.; Bataineh, M.T.A.; Alshraideh, H.; Hamoudi, R.; Salameh, L.; Shamayleh, A. Prediction of COVID-19 Hospital Length of Stay and Risk of Death Using Artificial Intelligence-Based Modeling. *Front. Med.* **2021**, *8*, 592336. [CrossRef]
38. Lai, K.-L.; Hu, F.-C.; Wen, F.-Y.; Chen, J.-J. Lymphocyte count is a universal predictor to the health status and outcomes of patients with coronavirus disease 2019 (COVID-19): A systematic review and meta-regression analysis. *medRxiv* **2021**. [CrossRef]
39. Zhao, Y.; Chen, Q.; Liu, T.; Luo, P.; Zhou, Y.; Liu, M.; Xiong, B.; Zhou, F. Development and Validation of Predictors for the Survival of Patients With COVID-19 Based on Machine Learning. *Front. Med.* **2021**, *8*, 683431. [CrossRef] [PubMed]
40. Ramachandran, P.; Gajendran, M.; Perisetti, A.; Elkholy, K.O.; Chakraborti, A.; Lippi, G.; Goyal, H. Red Blood Cell Distribution Width in Hospitalized COVID-19 Patients. *Front. Med.* **2022**, *8*, 2531. [CrossRef] [PubMed]
41. Kilercik, M.; Demirelce, Ö.; Serdar, M.A.; Mikailova, P.; Serteser, M. A new haematocytometric index: Predicting severity and mortality risk value in COVID-19 patients. *PLoS ONE* **2021**, *16*, e0254073. [CrossRef] [PubMed]
42. Henry, B.M.; Aggarwal, G.; Wong, J.; Benoit, S.; Vikse, J.; Plebani, M.; Lippi, G. Lactate dehydrogenase levels predict coronavirus disease 2019 (COVID-19) severity and mortality: A pooled analysis. *Am. J. Emerg. Med.* **2020**, *38*, 1722–1726. [CrossRef]
43. Tomasiuk, R.; Dabrowski, J.; Smykiewicz, J.; Wiacek, M. Predictors of COVID-19 Hospital Treatment Outcome. *Int. J. Gen. Med.* **2021**, *14*, 10247–10256. [CrossRef]
44. Bommenahalli Gowda, S.; Gosavi, S.; Ananda Rao, A.; Shastry, S.; Raj, S.C.; Menon, S.; Suresh, A.; Sharma, A. Prognosis of COVID-19: Red Cell Distribution Width, Platelet Distribution Width, and C-Reactive Protein. *Cureus* **2021**, *13*, e13078. [CrossRef]
45. Nikitin, N.O.; Vychuzhanin, P.; Sarafanov, M.; Polonskaia, I.S.; Revin, I.; Barabanova, I.V.; Maximov, G.; Kalyuzhnaya, A.V.; Boukhanovsky, A. Automated evolutionary approach for the design of composite machine learning pipelines. *Future Gener. Comput. Syst.* **2022**, *127*, 109–125. [CrossRef]
46. nccr-itmo/FEDOT: Automated Modeling and Machine Learning Framework FEDOT. Available online: https://github.com/nccr-itmo/FEDOT (accessed on 11 April 2022).
47. Probabilistic and Mean-Field Model of COVID-19 Epidemics with User Mobility and Contact Tracing | Semantic Scholar. Available online: https://www.semanticscholar.org/paper/Probabilistic-and-mean-field-model-of-COVID-19-with-Akian-Ganassali/9c8b962fb4ee58cb5cc3c25cbb29cbc30e2d583b (accessed on 28 July 2022).
48. Alguliyev, R.; Aliguliyev, R.; Yusifov, F. Graph modelling for tracking the COVID-19 pandemic spread. *Infect. Dis. Model.* **2020**, *6*, 112–122. [CrossRef]
49. Vepa, A.; Saleem, A.; Rakhshan, K.; Daneshkhah, A.; Sedighi, T.; Shohaimi, S.; Omar, A.; Salari, N.; Chatrabgoun, O.; Dharmaraj, D.; et al. Using Machine Learning Algorithms to Develop a Clinical Decision-Making Tool for COVID-19 Inpatients. *Int. J. Environ. Res. Public Health* **2021**, *18*, 6228. [CrossRef]
50. Mihaljević, B.; Bielza, C.; Larrañaga, P. Bayesian networks for interpretable machine learning and optimization. *Neurocomputing* **2021**, *456*, 648–665. [CrossRef]

Journal of Personalized Medicine

Article

# A Decision Support Framework for Periprosthetic Joint Infection Treatment: A Cost-Effectiveness Analysis Using Two Modeling Approaches †

Vasiliy N. Leonenko [1,*], Yulia E. Kaliberda [1], Yulia V. Muravyova [2] and Vasiliy A. Artyukh [2]

[1] Faculty of Digital Transformation, ITMO University, Kronverksky Pr. 49A, 197101 St. Petersburg, Russia; julia.kaliberda@gmail.com
[2] Russian Scientific Research Institute of Traumatology and Orthopedics Named after R.R. Vreden, Akademika Baykova St., 8, 195427 St. Petersburg, Russia; julia-muraveva@yandex.ru (Y.V.M.); artyukhva@mail.ru (V.A.A.)
* Correspondence: vnleonenko@itmo.ru

† This article is an extended version of the conference paper published in Leonenko V. N., Kaliberda Y. E., Artyuk V. A. A Modeling Framework for Decision Support in Periprosthetic Joint Infection Treatment. *Stud. Health Technol. Inform.* **2021**, *285*, 106–111.

**Abstract:** Today, periprosthetic joint infection (PJI) is one of the leading indications for revision surgery and the most ominous complication in artificial joint patients. The current state of the art for treating PJI requires the development of methods for planning the costs at different scales to facilitate the selection of the best treatment methods. In this paper, we perform a cost-effectiveness assessment for strategies related to the treatment of PJI using a composite decision support modeling framework. Within the framework, two models are implemented: a detailed discrete-event probabilistic model based on the decision tree approach and a dynamic Markov model with generalized states. The application of the framework is demonstrated on the dataset which was provided by the Russian Scientific Research Institute of Traumatology and Orthopedics named after R.R. Vreden. The analyzed dataset contains 600 patient records divided into two groups (retrospective group, based on old records, and prospective group, based on real-time follow-up). The cost-effectiveness of treatment methods was compared based on associated costs and QALY units gained, with the mentioned two indicators calculated using two models independently from each other. As a result, two comparative rankings of cost-effectiveness of PJI treatment methods were presented based on the model output.

**Keywords:** Markov model; periprosthetic joint infection; revision arthroplasty; total hip replacement; decision trees



**Citation:** Leonenko, V.N.; Kaliberda, Y.E.; Muravyova, Y.V.; Artyukh, V.A. A Decision Support Framework for Periprosthetic Joint Infection Treatment: A Cost-Effectiveness Analysis Using Two Modeling Approaches. *J. Pers. Med.* **2022**, *12*, 1216. https://doi.org/10.3390/jpm12081216

Academic Editors: Bernd Blobel and Mauro Giacomini

Received: 15 June 2022
Accepted: 20 July 2022
Published: 26 July 2022



## 1. Introduction

### 1.1. Periprosthetic Joint Infection

Due to the advancement of public health and medicine, we see a stable increase in life span throughout the world. As a consequence, the diseases of the elderly are becoming more widespread and require more attention. Particularly, joint arthroplasty, also known as joint replacement, aimed at restoring the function of joints, is increasingly performed. The replacement of the affected joints with artificial ones creates a need for revision arthroplasty. Today, periprosthetic joint infection (PJI) is one of the leading indications for revision surgery and the most ominous complication in artificial joint patients [1,2]. Periprosthetic infection is associated with high morbidity, because the implant, as a foreign body, increases the pathogenicity of bacteria and the presence of a biofilm makes the diagnosis and treatment problematic [3]. As a result, complex strategies are required to treat PJI, including multiple surgical revisions and long-term antimicrobial treatment. The widespread use of antibiotics, the enhanced technical equipment of operating rooms and the development of surgical techniques made it possible to reduce the number of infectious complications from 9% in the early years of arthroplasty to 1.25% in recent decades [4]. Nevertheless, the number of cases of PJI is expected to increase in the near future and will double by 2030 [5]. It is also worth mentioning that the cost of PJI treatment is several times higher than of the primary endoprosthesis and places a significant financial burden both on the family budget of patients and on the state health care system. In 2005, the cost of revision hip arthroplasty related to PJI in the United States was 2.8 times higher than the revision arthroplasty related to aseptic instability and 4.8 times more expensive than primary total hip replacement [6]. In addition, the researchers found an increase in the cost of revision arthroplasty for infectious complications between 1997 and 2006.

During a large period of time, there was no firm, generally accepted understanding of PJI in the orthopedic community and supervising healthcare structures. Therefore, it was not possible to interpret data on the number of disease cases, the variants of disease course, the outcomes, and the economic effect of treatment strategies. The situation changed in 2011, when the Musculoskeletal Infection Society (MSIS) PJI Diagnostic Standards were first proposed [7]. Based on the analysis of the dynamics of changes in the modern theory of PJI, Haddad F. et al. believe that research in the next decade will be critical to further develop the understanding of PJI and to establish the most cost-effective treatment methods [4].

### 1.2. PJI Treatment Methods

Currently, a number of researchers consider the two-stage revision total joint replacement method as the most effective from the infection eradication point of view [3,8]. The leading indications for a two-stage revision total joint replacement (re-TJR) are cases of PJI, where the pathogen was not identified before surgery, the microflora is highly resistant, and there are bone or soft tissue defects [9,10]. Among the unsolved problems of two-stage re-TJR are: high costs, long period of disability, necessity of prolonged antibiotic therapy, blood loss, dislocation of spacers, and high mortality among patients between the stages [11].

An alternative method of treating PJI is the one-stage re-TJR. The long-standing discussion about the role and effectiveness of one-stage re-TJR in the treatment of chronic PJI is now almost overcome. The end of the discussion was initiated by the publication Zahar A. et al. in 2019, in which the authors reported long-term (10-year) results of a one-stage revision total hip arthroplasty (re-THR) [12]. They found that 94% of patients did not have a recurrence of PJI, 75% of patients did not require re-THR, and good and excellent functional results were found in 57% of cases. In studies with patients carefully selected before surgery, the success rate of one-stage re-THR was even higher, up to 100% [13].

Another possible way to improve the results of treatment with PJI is to shorten the time interval between the re-TJR stages. According to the results of the discussion in the International Consensus Meeting in 2018, it was found that there were currently no data indicating the optimal time interval between the stages of re-EP. Nowadays, the waiting period between operations can range from a week to several years. Most surgeons consider the period after wound healing, the end of antibiotic therapy, and the appearance of data on the positive dynamics of serological markers the optimal time for reimplantation [14]. However, the recommended time interval between re-EP stages is still unclear.

Last but not least, up to this date the experience related to re-TJR with partial preservation of stable endoprosthesis structures is still accumulating. Despite the fact that nowadays there are no generally accepted recommendations, in some cases, partial re-TJR can be the best alternative as it allows to avoid significant bone defects, reduce the degree of surgical aggression and problems with the choice of components of the endoprosthesis in the future [15]. Researchers also emphasize the importance of careful patient selection for partial re-TJR [16,17].

### 1.3. Cost-Effectiveness Analysis

It is known that the decision of surgeons to choose the method of treatment for individual patients with PJI is increasingly dependent on economic considerations, which is constraining and often not optimal [18]. Moreover, the cost of re-THR, missing generally accepted standards, differs significantly in national health systems. In 2012–2013, e.g., a two-stage re-THR for each case of PJI cost USD 90–100,000 in the USA [19], USD 57,000 (GDP 44,000) in the UK [5], and USD 53,000 (AUD 70,000 ) in Australia [20]. The current state of the art treating PJI requires systematization of costs and the development of methods for planning the costs at different scales—for separate individuals, on the level of healthcare units, and on the city level.

A state-of-the-art approach to medical practice requires justification of efficacy and safety of treatment methods. The methods of treating PJI should be selected based on evidence-based medicine, the means of which allow comparison, generalization, and wide practical application of the data obtained [21]. Thus, the need for a clinical and economic analysis of PJI treatment from the standpoint of evidence-based medicine seems to be very relevant, especially due to the lack of corresponding quality studies [22,23].

In addition to the problem of finding the best PJI treatment method in general, relying on both direct (a chance of successful PJI elimination) and indirect treatment outcomes (such as resulting increase in quality of life of the patients who underwent the treatment), there is an arising challenge of finding an optimal treatment strategy in advance for the particular patient based on his individual characteristics [24]. This challenge became an actual part of the personalized medicine concept and requires research based on a multidisciplinary approach, relying on statistical analysis, mathematical modeling, and machine learning [25].

### *1.4. Problem Statement*

In this paper, we present a framework which compares the cost-effectiveness of PJI treatment methods. The patient dataset used in the study was provided by Russian Scientific Research Institute of Traumatology and Orthopedics named after R.R. Vreden, it contains records of the patients with PJI after total hip arthroplasty (THA). The methods of the cost-effectiveness analysis of treatment strategies are discussed and the method comparison is performed based on associated costs and QALY units gained. The ultimate objective of that direction of research consists in developing a computational tool to predict the consequences of a fixed treatment strategy for a given patient. Such a tool, when applied by healthcare professionals, will help enhancing the quality of PJI treatment both in terms of cost-effectiveness and the quality of life of individuals undergoing treatment.

## 2. Related Works

One study with objectives similar to ours has been published in [26]. The overall goal of the research was to estimate the effect of PJI treatment using contemporary treatment methods. The model of a hypothetical patient of working age with a PJI after a re-THR was built as a Markov state-transition model with the help of TreeAge Pro 2009 software. The algorithm accounts for a fixed percentage of patients undergoing one of three initial treatments: irrigation and debridement, single-stage exchange, or two-stage exchange based on available studies of current practices. The outcomes of these treatments were defined as septic/aseptic failures or successes. In addition, age-specific yearly mortality rates were used to predict transitions between the states. Patients who received successful treatment according to the model entered a state of being healthy which they might leave with a fixed annual rate related to repeated septic failure. Patients with failed treatment due to sepsis undergo a second procedure (two-stage exchange). The output of the model contains incidence and cost estimates associated with common medical complications. Each health state is assigned a cost for a fixed period of time (1 year). Transition probabilities determine the likelihood that a patient will either transition to the next health state or remain in the current one. For cost estimation by different rates of THA reinfection, the authors conducted a one-way sensitivity analysis (during the first year of treatment and beyond the first year). The main outcome of the research was to demonstrate that accounting for indirect costs and failures of treatment options dramatically increases the estimated overall treatment costs of PJI after total hip replacement. Thus, it seems to be much higher than it was thought in similar previous studies.

An example of a specific economic analysis based on data from one particular setting was presented in [27], where researchers considered the problem of PJI in low-middle-income countries. The aim of the study was to evaluate the incidence and economic burden of PJIs in a university hospital in Turkey. The costs in the model were set according to the information from hospital's accounting system and included, among others, the cost of antibiotics, laboratory, radiology, prosthesis, operation, and total bed stay.

The research connected with PJI after Total Elbow Arthroplasty (TEA) was observed in [28]. The study aimed at investigating the risk factors which are associated with periprosthetic elbow infection, the incidence of infection after TEA and the acuteness of these infections. The importance of the study lies in the fact that compared to the knowledge regarding hip, knee, and shoulder PJI, research on prosthetic elbow infections is very limited and as a rule relies on data drawn from small case series. Authors used frequency tables to calculate the incidence of PJI among patients undergoing TEA. Frequency tables were also used to describe the details of patient presentation and management during admission for PJI. A logistic regression was used for each variable to determine the significance of each demographic variable as an independent predictor of PJI following TEA. As a result of the study, additional prognostic data were presented which, as the authors stated, could be used for patient selection and risk profile analysis.

A comprehensive review of the publications about PJI treatment cost-effectiveness analysis was performed in [22]. The aim of the researchers was to report the less costly and more effective procedures. The study highlighted existing problems in finding the best treatment method due to ambiguity of assessment techniques and data uncertainty.

The closest to the presented work is the article [29], where the investigators compare the effectiveness of 1-stage and 2-stage strategies for Total Knee Revision. Decision trees were built and subsequent Monte-Carlo simulations were used to calculate QALYs and costs. Sensitivity analysis was also performed to measure the influence of particular parameters on the outcome. Compared to this study, our research has an advantage of using unique patient data, while in the paper [29] all the parameters are taken from open sources.

## 3. Methods

### *3.1. Data*

The analyzed dataset contains the records of patients who were subjected to revision total hip replacement (re-THR) in the period of 2000–2020. The patient records were collected in two different ways.

The first part of the disease histories was taken from the archives. The corresponding patient group is named 'the retrospective group'. Initially the group contained 603 patients with PJI. The collection of information was started by personal examination and questioning of patients in the polyclinic of the Vreden's Russian Scientific Research Institute of Traumatology and Orthopedics (25 (4.1%) patients). Patients who did not have the opportunity to come for examination were interviewed by phone (356 (59.03%) cases). In a number of observations, information about the condition of patients was obtained as a result of correspondence by mail (53 (8.8%) observations). In 169 (28.02%) cases, it was not possible to establish the results of PJI treatment and they were excluded from the study. The final list of patients in the retrospective part contained 434 patients with chronic PJI.

The prospective group of records included 166 patients with chronic PJI who were treated in the Department of Purulent Surgery of Vreden's Russian Scientific Research Institute of Traumatology and Orthopedics in the period from 2016 to 2020. The record list contains those patients who were not subjected to exclusion from the study. Among the criteria of the latter were the following:

- Systemic inflammatory response syndrome, sepsis;
- Infectious inflammation of soft tissues of an unlimited form (phlegmon) or extensive purulent streaks to the neurovascular bundles;

- A soft tissue defect that does not allow the wound to be sutured;
- Implant-associated osteomyelitis IV (diffuse) anatomical type, patient's physiological class C (Cierny-Mader classification);
- Recurrent course of PJI, when the number of reEP with implantation of an antibacterial spacer was equal of more than 3;
- Defects of the acetabulum not less than 3B and of the femur not less than 4 according to Paprosky classification, which were identified before surgery or formed as a result of surgical treatment.

All the patients were being observed for the possible PJI relapse till the end of 2020. In the retrospective group, the following treatment methods were applied: resection arthroplasty (RA), revision operation with the preservation of endoprosthesis (re-THR-PE) and two-stage revision total hip replacement with the two consecutive interventions separated by more than 2 months.

In the prospective group, new treatment methods were presented, namely, one-stage re-THR and partial re-THR (both 1-stage and 2-stage). The patients in the prospective group who underwent two-stage re-THR were divided into two subgroups based on their waiting time: 2–3 weeks and 6–8 weeks correspondingly.

The quantities of groups of patients of a certain age and gender in the records database are presented in Table 1. The description of treatment methods regarded in this study is presented in Table 2. As it can be seen the group '1-stage retro' has extremely small sample size. Due to that reason it was excluded from this study.

**Table 1.** Demographic characteristics of study participants.

| Treatment | Age/Sex | <20 | 21–30 | 31–40 | 41–50 | 51–60 | 61–70 | 71–80 | 81–90 | >90 | Total |
|---|---|---|---|---|---|---|---|---|---|---|---|
| 2-stage > 2 mth | M | | 3 | 20 | 33 | 59 | 50 | 26 | 5 | | 196 |
| | F | 1 | 2 | 17 | 17 | 46 | 46 | 36 | 6 | | 171 |
| 1-stage retro | M | | | | | | | | 1 | | 1 |
| | F | | | | | | | 1 | 1 | | 2 |
| 2-stage 2–3 wk | M | | | 2 | 4 | 1 | 3 | 1 | | | 11 |
| | F | | | | | 1 | 1 | 1 | | | 3 |
| 2-stage 6–8 wk | M | | | 8 | 8 | 9 | 6 | | 1 | | 32 |
| | F | | | | 2 | 5 | 10 | 2 | | | 19 |
| 1-stage | M | | | 1 | 4 | 4 | 11 | 9 | 3 | 1 | 33 |
| | F | | | | 1 | 6 | 14 | 13 | 11 | | 45 |
| RA | M | | | | 1 | 2 | 4 | | 1 | | 8 |
| | F | | | | 1 | | 2 | 2 | | | 5 |
| re-THR-PE | M | | 1 | 4 | 2 | 5 | 3 | 3 | 2 | | 20 |
| | F | | | 1 | 3 | 10 | 9 | 8 | | | 31 |
| Partial-I | M | | | | | | | | | | |
| | F | | | 1 | 1 | 3 | 2 | 1 | 3 | | 11 |
| Partial-II | M | | | 2 | 3 | | | 2 | | | 7 |
| | F | | | 1 | 2 | | 2 | | | | 5 |
| **Total** | | 1 | 6 | 57 | 82 | 151 | 163 | 105 | 34 | 1 | 600 |

Each patient record in the dataset contains their ID, birthdate, dates of registered health issues (manifestation dates), operation dates, types, and costs, the resulting state of the patient measured during his/her last attendance to healthcare services (PJI relapse or no PJI), and death date, if the patient died.

In case of the optimal treatment outcome, the resulting number of operations performed on each patient is defined solely by the PJI treatment method (for instance, two-stage re-THR assumes two interventions, with the installation of antibiotic-impregnated cement spacer and its subsequent removal, whereas the one-stage method is a single surgery). However, in many cases additional operations are required due to the relapse of PJI or other issues (postoperative wound hematomas, spacer dislocations, etc.). The recorded data we worked with contain 15 different types of operations, which were divided into three groups: operations which have no connection with PJI, first case of PJI, or PJI relapse. The full list of operations is presented in Table 3.

**Table 2.** Description of treatment methods.

| Abbreviation | Full Name | Description |
|---|---|---|
| re-THR-PE | Revision operation with the preservation of endoprosthesis | The joint is opened and washed. The parts of the artificial joint, which can be easily removed, are replaced with the new ones, and the wound is closed. |
| 2-stage re-THR | Two-stage total hip replacement with > 2 months (2–3 weeks, 6–8 weeks) between the stages | The joint is opened and cleaned up, an antibacterial spacer is placed, and the wound is closed. After a certain time period, the joint is opened again, the spacer is removed, the prosthesis is installed and the joint is closed. |
| RA | Resection arthroplasty | The joint is opened, everything is removed, the hole in the tissues is filled with a muscle cut from the thigh, and the wound is closed. |
| 1-stage | One-stage total hip replacement | The joint is opened, everything is removed, a new endoprosthesis is installed and the wound is closed. |
| Partial-I | Partial one-stage total hip replacement | Equal to one-stage re-THR, but with partial preservation of the endoprosthesis. |
| Partial-II | Partial two-stage total hip replacement | Equal to two-stage re-THR, but with partial preservation of the endoprosthesis. |

**Table 3.** Operations performed and their relation to PJI.

| No PJI | First Case of PJI or PJI Relapse | PJI Relapse |
|---|---|---|
| Endoprosthesis (EP) installation + spacer removal;<br>EP installation (no spacer);<br>Non-infectious: spacer dislocation;<br>Other: (suturing, etc.);<br>Non-infectious: periprosthetic fracture case; | Debridement + spacer installation;<br>Debridement;<br>EP components replacement + debridement;<br>Debridement + full EP replacement;<br>Joint drainage + long-term suppressive antibiotic therapy (ABT); | Debridement + spacer reinstallation;<br>Disarticulation;<br>Spacer removal + support osteotomy;<br>Debridement + support osteotomy + muscle plastic;<br>Joint drainage |

### 3.2. *Models*

#### 3.2.1. Decision Tree

A tree-based imitational model was first used by the authors to study PJI treatment methods in [30]. In that context, a generalized model was introduced, relating the states of the tree to the total number of operations for a given patient, which was considered as a factor for the PJI relapse. It was shown that the functional capacity of a patient is badly affected by repetitive operations, independent of the treatment method. However, the correlation of PJI relapse chance and the number of operations performed were not supported by the data. Following that approach, we developed an algorithm to create and to verify detailed decision trees which distinguish different operation types.

A decision tree describes transitions between the states, which are attributed to different medical interventions. Each state is one of the registered interventions from the patient records database (see Table 3). Each transition signifies the change in patient's functional capacity and is associated with the treatment costs. The time passed between the transition is not explicitly considered.

An algorithm was developed to build a tree for a given treatment method based on the sample of records for the patients who were treated using this method. The procedure uses a recursive approach and has the following structure:

- For each patient record:
  - Collect the sequence of operations performed;
  - Add the resulting outcome at the end of the sequence as a last patient state, based on death date (if available) and on the PJI status checked during the last observation. Patients who died with confirmed PJI are marked by the state 'Death'. Those, who had PJI and were alive by the end of the study, are marked by the state 'Failure' (of treatment). Finally, those who did not have PJI have the state 'Success';
  - Assume that the first state of the decision tree (the root) coincides with the name of the applied treatment strategy, and the second, third, ..., $n+1$-th states are related to the first, second, ..., $n$-th registered interventions taken from the patient records ($n \leq 10$). The $n+2$-th state is related to the treatment outcome assigned at the previous step of the algorithm.
- Starting from $i = 1$:
  - Gather the list $L_i$ of all recorded intervention types which correspond to the intervention #$i$ in the patient records;
  - Calculate the ratios of occurrence for each operation type $l_j^{(i)} \in L_i$;
  - For each $l_j^{(i)} \in L_i$:
    * Gather the list $L_{i+1}$ of all recorded intervention types which correspond to the intervention #$i+1$ in the patient records which had intervention #$i$ equal to $l_j^{(i)}$;
    * Calculate the ratios of occurrence for each operation type $l_j^{(i+1)} \in L_{i+1}$;
    * For each $l_j^{(i+1)} \in L_{i+1}$:
    * ...
    * If $L_k = \emptyset$, break.

A fragment of a decision tree for partial re-THR is shown in Figure 1. The data, which could be derived from the decision tree, include generated individual trajectories and probability distributions for the treatment states calculated via repetitive simulation runs.

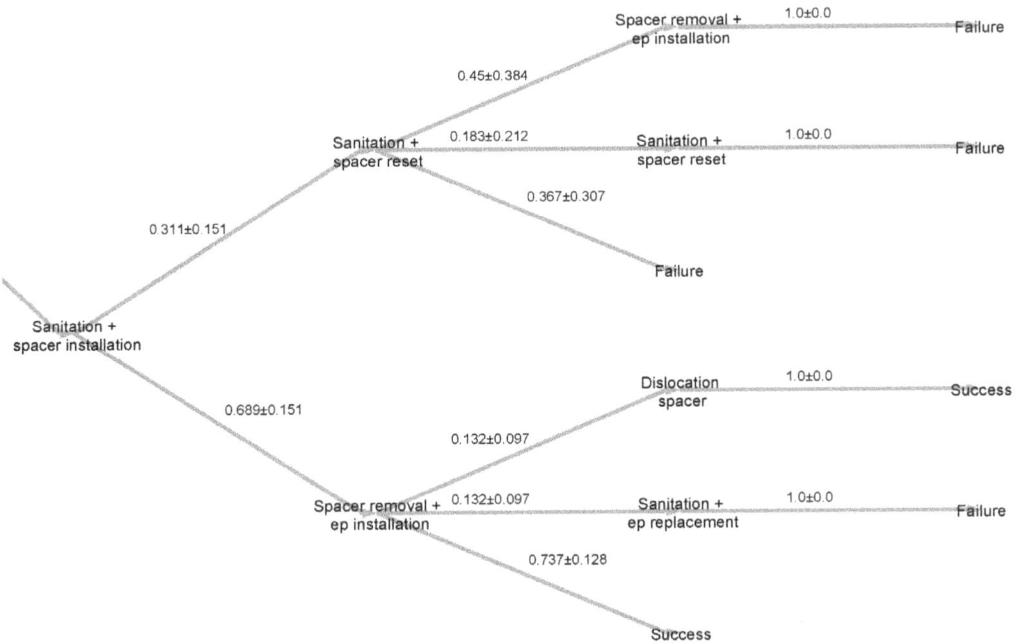


**Figure 1.** A fragment of the decision tree partial re-THR with confidence intervals for transition probabilities.

### 3.2.2. Markov Model

A decision tree approach is prone to some issues, particularly:

- It can become intractable if the number of different states and transitions in the patient records is too big;
- It does not consider the time passed between the transitions from state to state.

To address this issues, we developed a Markov model with generalized states as an alternative approach. The detailed description of the model is provided in [31], the major highlights of it are given below.

- To create the model states, the classification described in Table 3, Section 3.1 is used. In addition to the PJI-related interventions (PJI or PJI relapse) and the interventions not related to PJI, a separate intervention type is introduced, which is a second stage intervention for two-stage treatment methods ('Endoprosthesis installation + spacer removal');
- The resulting model states are: (a) PJI (waiting for the treatment), (b) second stage (no PJI, waiting for the spacer removal in two-stage treatment methods), (c) additional surgeries (waiting for the treatment of a non-PJI issue), (d) observation (no PJI), and (e) death. The situations of a first PJI case and a recurrent PJI are not distinguished due to the lack of corresponding data in the records;
- The time in the model is discrete, with the time step equal to one month;
- The simulation starts with the state 'PJI'. The state 'death' is an absorbing state.

The general scheme of state transitions for the model is shown in Figure 2.

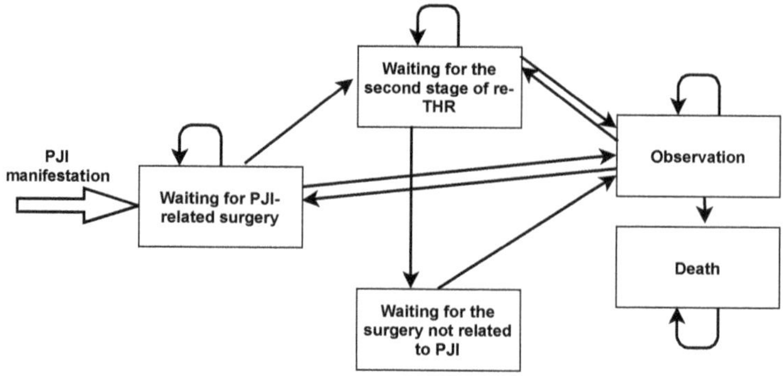


**Figure 2.** Markov model states and transitions.

The transitional probabilities are calculated based on the available patient records. The calibration procedure consists of the following steps:

- Form a subset of records of patients who were treated using a fixed treatment strategy;
- For each patient, form a list of his subsequent states with the step size of one month, starting from the first manifestation date (i.e., when he was first observed at the hospital with PJI) till the present moment or until he dies. The manifestation dates and intervention dates are used in this process. If the states were changed several times during one month, the last state is taken as the current one at the end of the regarded month;
- Calculate the overall number of transitions between the model states;
- Estimate the transition probabilities via dividing the number of transitions of particular type by the total number of transitions.

The model enables the generation of individual patient trajectories with the consideration of time, which is useful for the calculation of the expected amount of observation time and the hospitalization time.

*3.3. Model Uncertainty*

The accuracy of mathematical modeling depends on how well the mathematical model reflects the properties of the object. The question of special interest is, to what extent a model calibrated on a particular sample is able to predict results for new data. In general, the smaller the training sample is, the bigger is the uncertainty in the model output, and this uncertainty should be quantified to understand the model limitations. In this work, we used a bootstrapping technique to assess the confidence intervals for the transitional probabilities of the models. The procedure of assessing the intervals was the following:

- Draw a random subsample from the patient records database;
- Use the selected subsample to obtain possible model states and calculate the transitional probabilities between them;
- Repeat the procedure $n$ times using different subsamples each time;
- Based on obtained samples of size $n$, calculate the confidence interval for each transitional probability using the formula:

$$\overline{x} - t_{\alpha/2,n-1} \cdot \frac{S}{\sqrt{n}}, \overline{x} + t_{\alpha/2,n-1} \cdot \frac{S}{\sqrt{n}},$$

where $\overline{x}$ is the sample mean, $S$ is the sample standard deviation, and $t_{\alpha/2,n-1}$ is a quantile of Student's $t$-distribution.

### 3.4. Cost-Effectiveness Analysis

To assess and compare the cost-effectiveness of different treatment methods, we implemented algorithms to calculate the statistics of expenses and the overall QALY (quality-adjusted life-years, a generic measure of disease burden), related to different treatment stages. Since the decision trees and the Markov models have different structures, the calculation algorithms, although conceptually similar, differ in some details. The resulting value to measure cost-effectiveness, which is used as an output of the framework, is average cost per QALY for the particular PJI treatment method.

#### 3.4.1. Decision Trees

Since, in a decision tree, each state matches exactly with the particular intervention from the patient record, the intervention costs could be assessed in an easy and straightforward way. At the same time, the time is not tracked in this model type, which makes it complicated to compare time-dependent costs. As it was described in [31], the framework supports the assignments of parameters, related to the impact of the intervention, to each branch of the tree. To assess the cost-effectiveness of the treatment methods, we measured intervention costs in rubles and measured utility of the patient calculated in QALY units. The quantitative outcomes of the treatment in terms of healthcare costs and QALY units gained by the patient might be derived from the decision tree using the following formula:

$$C = \sum_i p_i \cdot c_i, \quad (1)$$

where $p_i$ is the probability of selecting the branch, obtained by cross-validation, $c_i$ is the impact measured in either of the two units. The interval assessment of $C$ can be calculated using the same formula with left and right boundaries for $p_i$ used instead of their mean assessments.

The resulting values of $C_{rubl}$ and $C_u$ are used to calculate the costs of one QALY unit and analyze them for different treatment strategies. To calculate QALY units and costs for particular tree branches, we relied on the data provided by Russian Scientific Research Institute of Traumatology and Orthopedics named after R.R. Vreden. The operation costs were taken from the disease histories, and the QALY units were assessed based on the EQ-5D indices for each particular patient measured between the subsequent operations according to the methodology described in [32].

#### 3.4.2. Markov Models

The treatment impact for a fixed individual patient trajectory is calculated according to the formula

$$C(t) = \sum_i t_i \cdot \overline{c_i}, \quad (2)$$

where $\overline{c_i}$ are the monthly costs or QALY units associated with the patient state $i$ in the model, and $t_i$ is the expected average patient's time of staying in a state $i$ (the number of months). Due to the fact that in the Markov model we use generalized patient conditions which are not tied to particular intervention types, the accurate values for $\overline{c_i}$ (both in rubles and QALY units) cannot be found in records. The expenses for every model state were assessed by averaging the costs of all possible interventions associated with that particular state, and the QALY units gained were found based on the experts' opinion. We assumed that the patient gains maximum QALY units when he is in the 'Observation' status. The lowest QALY values correspond to 'PJI'. The quality of life of a patient waiting for the second stage or additional surgeries is higher than in case of PJI, but lower than in the 'Observation' state due to corresponding health issues (particularly, the patients waiting for the second stage of the treatment have limited mobility due to spacer installation which badly affects their QALY count). Under the expert assumption, we assumed the QALY for the 'PJI' state equal to 0.35, for 'Second stage' equal to 0.7, for 'Non-PJI operation' equal to 0.5, for 'Observation' equal to 0.85, and for 'Death' equal to 0.

As an example, we consider a patient who undergoes a two-stage therapy with a three-month interval between stages. The model presents the chain of states 'Waiting for surgery related to PJI (month 1)', 'Waiting for the second stage of therapy' (month 2), 'Waiting for the second stage of therapy' (month 3), 'Waiting for the second stage of therapy' (month 4), and 'Observation' (month 5). When searching for the average QALY values obtained with various methods of therapy, based on the Markov model, the length of stay in each state is multiplied by the QALY units characteristic of it. In our example, we have to sum $1 \times 0.35$ (QALY for PJI condition, 1 month duration), $3 \times 0.7$ (QALY for the period of waiting for the second stage, 3 months duration) and $1 \times 0.85$ (observation, 1 month duration).

For calculating costs, along with the cost of staying in a model state during a certain amount of time (as in QALY calculation), the cost of operations should also be considered. In the setting of generalized Markov model operations are attributed to transitions between states. For instance, a transition from 'Waiting for the second stage of therapy' to 'Observation' implies a performed operation with spacer removal and endoprosthesis installation. Consequentially, in the above example, the total cost will consist of the following terms:

- The cost of a month of inpatient stay awaiting surgery related to PJI (state of the model);
- Cost of the PJI operation (the transition of the model from "Waiting for surgery with PJI" to "Waiting for the second stage of therapy with PJI");
- Cost of three months of waiting for the second stage of therapy (state of the model);
- Cost of the operation of the second stage of therapy with PJI (transition of the model from "Waiting for the second stage of therapy with PJI" to "Observation");
- The cost of a month in the "Observation" state.

The results of assessing cost-effectiveness of PJI treatment using two described modeling approaches are presented in the following section.

## 4. Results

An algorithm for model calibration and cost-effectiveness assessment was implemented using Python programming language, with *numpy*, *pandas*, and *scipy* libraries employed for data management and *python-igraph* library employed to draw decision trees. For each considered treatment method, a separate decision tree and a Markov model were built. In both cases all possible disease states related to a particular treatment were established and transition probabilities between the model states were assessed in a form of confidence intervals for mean values. Confidence intervals were calculated through bootstrapping based on 10 subsamples from the patient record database, with a size of every subsample equalled 80% of the whole database. For the sake of saving space, we omitted resulting decision trees. Resulting Markov models for all the treatment methods with calculated transitional probabilities are presented in Appendix A.

The values of QALY and costs were calculated as sums during a fixed period of time after the first case of PJI (24 months for decision trees and 30 months for Markov models). The results along with the costs per QALY are shown in Tables 4 and 5 (for retrospective methods) and Tables 6 and 7 (for prospective methods). The optimal values (higher QALY, lower costs) are marked in bold.

It is important to mention that due to differences in assessing both QALY and costs, the corresponding values of these characteristics cannot be compared between the two employed models (decision trees and Markov models). The comparison that could however be made is related to the ranks of treatment types related to their cost-effectiveness (smallest cost per QALY, second smallest, etc.). From this perspective, different modeling methods agree on the fact that RA (resection arthroplasty) is the optimal treatment method among the retrospective methods. In case of comparing treatment methods used for the prospective cohort of patients, the results are not so consistent, as the tables clearly demonstrate.

**Table 4.** Average costs for treatment methods in the retrospective group according to the decision trees.

| | re-THR-PE | 2-Stage > 2 Months | RA |
|---|---|---|---|
| QALY | 2.08 | 4.19 | **6.30** |
| Cost, rubles | 142,367 | 239,770 | **90,220** |
| Costs per QALY, rubles | 68,411.22 | 57,200.29 | **14,323.45** |
| Rank of effectiveness | 3 | 2 | **1** |

**Table 5.** Average costs for treatment methods in the retrospective group according to the Markov model simulations.

| | re-THR-PE | 2-Stage > 2 Months | RA |
|---|---|---|---|
| QALY | 1.88 | **1.92** | 1.79 |
| Cost, rubles | 117,634 | 243,670 | **105,920** |
| Costs per QALY, rubles | 62,571.27 | 126,911.46 | **59,173.18** |
| Rank of effectiveness | 2 | 3 | **1** |

**Table 6.** Average costs for treatment methods in the prospective group according to the decision trees.

| | 2-Stage 2–3 wk | 2-Stage 6–8 wk | 1-Stage | Partial-I | Partial-II |
|---|---|---|---|---|---|
| QALY | 8.16 | **8.89** | 3.21 | 4.59 | 8.6 |
| Cost, rubles | 314,771 | 289,315 | **144,815** | 158,484 | 264,606 |
| Costs per QALY, rubles | 38,596.55 | 32,562.1 | 45,095.1 | 34,546.21 | **30,766.29** |
| Rank of effectiveness | 4 | 2 | 5 | 3 | **1** |

**Table 7.** Average costs for treatment methods in the prospective group according to the Markov model simulations.

| Treatment Method | 2-Stage 2–3 wk | 2-Stage 6–8 wk | 1-Stage | Partial-I | Partial-II |
|---|---|---|---|---|---|
| QALY | 1.925 | **2.055** | 1.99 | 1.83 | 2.0 |
| Cost, rubles | 288,507 | 300,471 | 147,687 | **135,370** | 267,436 |
| Costs per QALY, rubles | 149,874.77 | 146,214.6 | 74,214.57 | **73,972.68** | 133,718 |
| Rank of effectiveness | 5 | 4 | 2 | **1** | 3 |

## 5. Discussion

In this paper, a modeling framework is presented which aims at facilitating the decision-making for the healthcare professionals in the area of periprosthetic joint infection treatment. By using two different approaches within one framework, one can obtain a detailed static analysis of the prospected patient treatment trajectories, depending on the selected strategy (decision tree approach), or, alternatively, perform a dynamic simulation of a patient trajectory of transitions between the generalized states in an imitational model (Markov modeling approach). The former helps to calculate detailed total operational costs and quality of life obtained, e.g., their average values and their distributions, whereas the latter offers an opportunity to dynamically monitor and forecast the dynamics of costs and QALY units. In the current study, we demonstrated how the framework could be used to compare different treatment methods based on the following indicators:

- Total/average treatment impact related to the increase in quality of life for the patient (in QALY units) and the operational costs for the healthcare unit (in rubles);
- Proportions between the costs in rubles and the utility gained for one average patient or a group of patients (costs of one QALY unit, or costs per QALY).

Both model types within the framework demonstrate a compromise between the explanatory and predictive power of the model. Particularly:

- The approach connected with the decision trees makes it possible to trace the sequence of operations in high detail, thus making it easier to accurately calculate average QALY and costs per model state, since one state is easily interpreted as an actual medical procedure. At the same time, detailed states make it harder to use the model for prediction purposes. The limited sample sizes for particular treatment methods dramatically increase the uncertainty in transition probabilities assessment and the nomenclature of possible states themselves. Lastly, since the model is event-based and does not include time, it is not suitable for dynamic time-explicit prediction of the health outcomes. Only the ultimate result for the patient might be established (PJI-related death or death from other causes).
- In comparison with decision trees, the Markov model is better suitable for handling treatment processes based on small patient samples due to its generalized states. Additionally, it is more suitable for prediction of individual patient trajectories. Since the Markov model includes time, it allows to monitor time-related costs and expenses. The drawbacks of the model include complications in calculating QALY and costs per state. The generalized states have somewhat abstract interpretation and, therefore, some form of averaging is inevitable in calculating $\overline{c_i}$ (Formula (2)), which increases the calculation uncertainty.

We assume that for thorough cost-effectiveness analysis, both modeling methods could be applied in parallel to mutually compensate their weak spots.

It is also important to mention that the cost-effectiveness analysis results in an outcome demonstrated in Tables 4–7, which cannot serve as a direct guide to action related to the selection of the treatment method for the particular patients, because the regarded treatment methods cannot be considered totally interchangeable. In addition to the cost-effectiveness, there are other factors that influence method selection, among which are individual conditions of the regarded PJI case and personal characteristics of patients which might favor one or another treatment method. To compensate this drawback, we suggest using more patient parameters from the database and developing the treatment models based on patients' individual characteristics (age, gender, body mass index) as parameters affecting the transition probabilities. In this case, a calculation of individual treatment trajectories becomes possible, which converts the described framework into a more powerful software tool within the personalized medicine approach.

In addition to the mentioned framework modification, we consider another way of framework development which includes the changing of the modeling scale. We propose a framework evolution towards a geographically explicit prediction of dynamics of PJI cases in time at a city level, using synthesized populations as a model input [33,34]. The modified modeling framework for the PJI treatment can be fed by synthetic data coming from a demographic model for the urban population and a statistical model of PJI occurrence in that population. As a result, it will become possible to assess the hospital occupancy, the long-term consequences of PJI treatment, and the prospected potential years of life lost in the urban population depending on the prevalent treatment methods.

**Author Contributions:** Conceptualization, V.N.L. and V.A.A.; Methodology, V.N.L. and V.A.A.; Software, V.N.L. and Y.E.K.; Validation, Y.V.M. and V.A.A.; Investigation, V.N.L., Y.V.M. and V. A.A.; Writing—original draft preparation, V.A.L.; Writing—review and editing, Y.V.M. and V.A.A.; Visualization, V.N.L. All authors have read and agreed to the published version of the manuscript.

**Funding:** This research was supported by Priority 2030 Federal Academic Leadership Program.

**Institutional Review Board Statement:** Not applicable.

**Informed Consent Statement:** Informed consent was obtained from all subjects involved in the study.

**Data Availability Statement:** Data available upon request.

**Conflicts of Interest:** The authors declare no conflict of interest.

## Appendix A. Model Schemes with Transition Probabilities

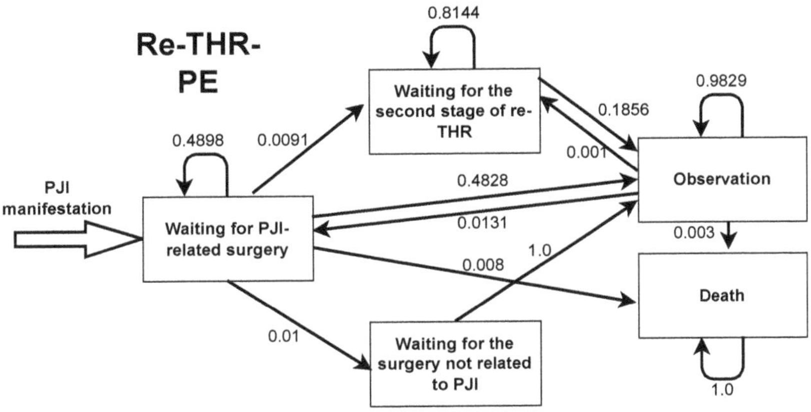


**Figure A1.** Markov model transition probabilities for revision operation with the preservation of endoprosthesis.

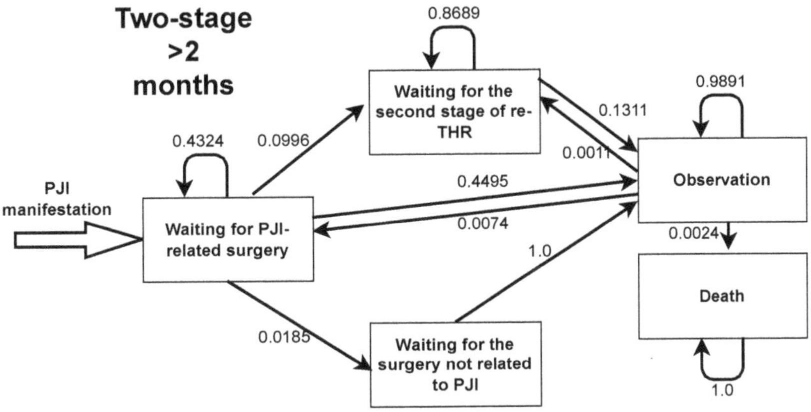


**Figure A2.** Markov model transition probabilities for two-stage total hip replacement with > 2 months between the stages.

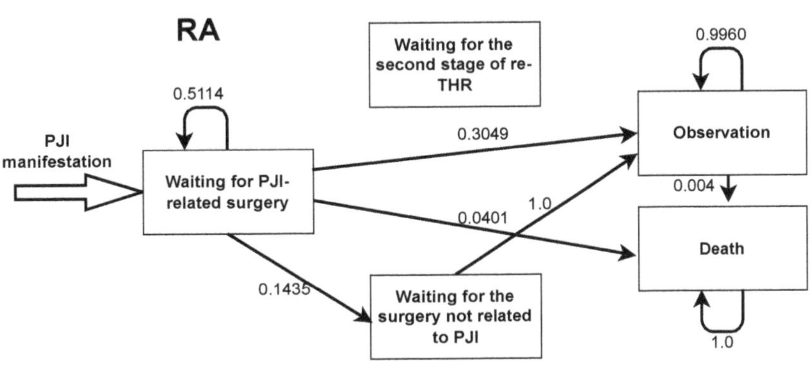


**Figure A3.** Markov model transition probabilities for resection arthroplasty.

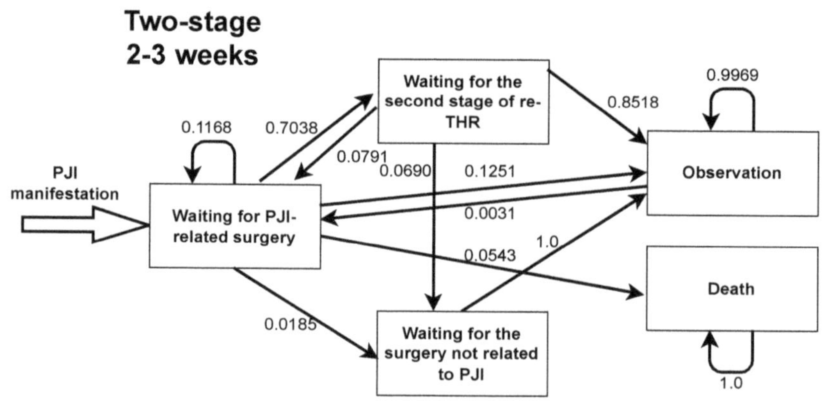


Figure A4. Markov model transition probabilities for two-stage total hip replacement with 2–3 weeks between the stages.

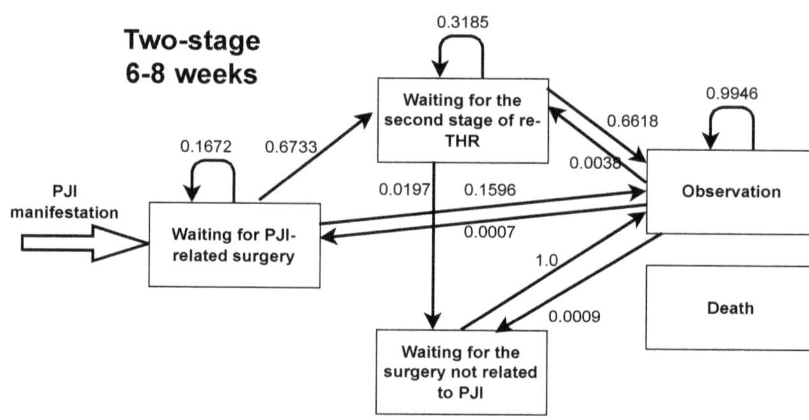


Figure A5. Markov model transition probabilities for two-stage total hip replacement with 6–8 weeks between the stages.

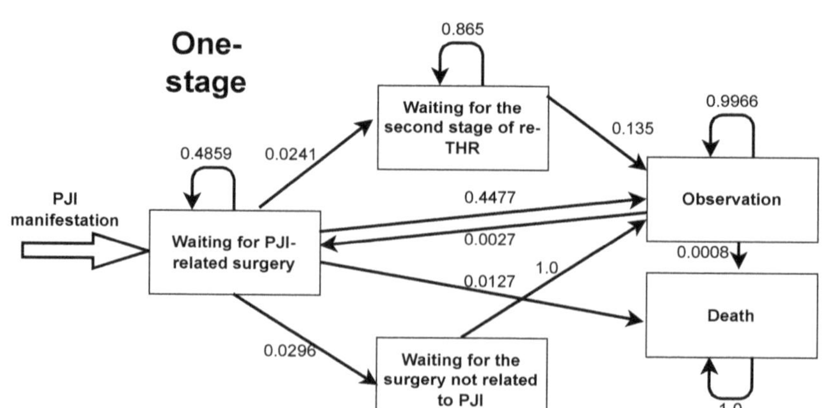


Figure A6. Markov model transition probabilities for one-stage total hip replacement.

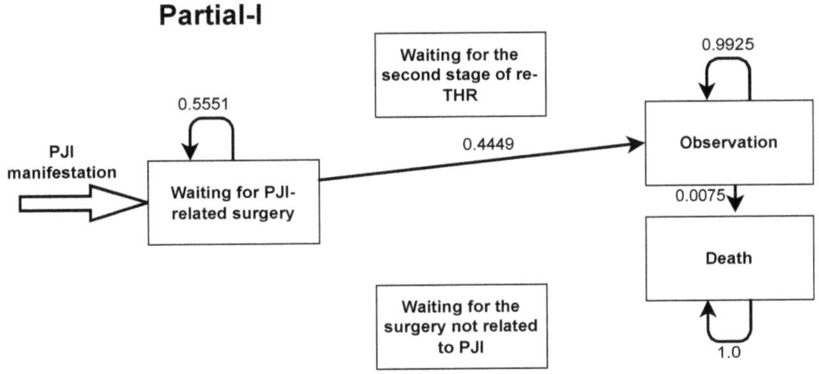


**Figure A7.** Markov model transition probabilities for partial one-stage total hip replacement.

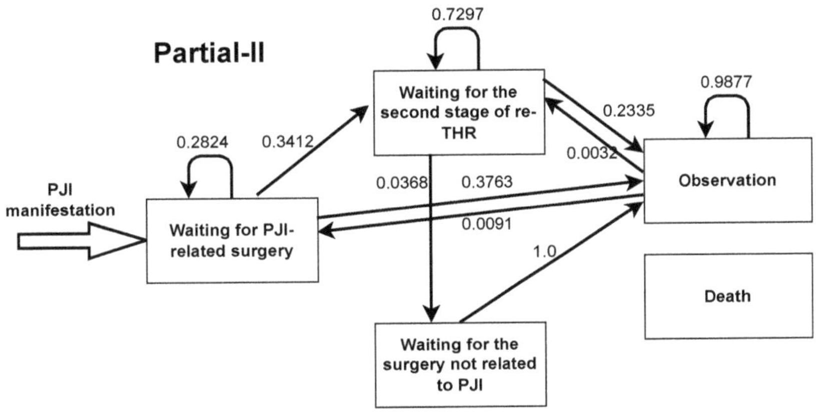


**Figure A8.** Markov model transition probabilities for partial two-stage total hip replacement.

## References


1. Boelch, S.P.; Jakuscheit, A.; Doerries, S.; Fraissler, L.; Hoberg, M.; Arnholdt, J.; Rudert, M. Periprosthetic infection is the major indication for TKA revision–experiences from a university referral arthroplasty center. *BMC Musculoskelet. Disord.* **2018**, *19*, 1–6. [CrossRef] [PubMed]
2. Meyer, J.A.; Zhu, M.; Cavadino, A.; Coleman, B.; Munro, J.T.; Young, S.W. Infection and periprosthetic fracture are the leading causes of failure after aseptic revision total knee arthroplasty. *Arch. Orthop. Trauma Surg.* **2021**, *141*, 1373–1383. [CrossRef] [PubMed]
3. Masters, E.A.; Trombetta, R.P.; de Mesy Bentley, K.L.; Boyce, B.F.; Gill, A.L.; Gill, S.R.; Muthukrishnan, G. Evolving concepts in bone infection: Redefining "bio-film", "acute vs. chronic osteomyelitis", "the immune proteome" and "local antibiotic therapy". *Bone Res.* **2019**, *7*, 1–18. [CrossRef] [PubMed]
4. Haddad, F.S.; Ngu, A.; Negus, J.J. Prosthetic joint infections and cost analysis? In *A Modern Approach to Biofilm-Related Orthopaedic Implant Infections*; Springer: Berlin/Heidelberg, Germany, 2017; Volume 971, 93–100.
5. Vanhegan, I.S.; Malik, A.K.; Jayakumar, P.; Ul Islam, S.; Haddad, F.S. A financial analysis of revision hip arthroplasty: The economic burden in relation to the national tariff. *J. Bone Joint Surg. Br.* **2012**, *94*, 619–623. [CrossRef]
6. Bozic, K.J.; Ries, M.D. The impact of infection after total hip arthroplasty on hospital and surgeon resource utilization. *J. Bone Joint Surg.* **2005**, *87*, 1746–1751.
7. Parvizi, J.; Zmistowski, B.; Berbari, E.F.; Bauer, T.W.; Springer, B.D.; Della Valle, C.J.; Garvin, K.L.; Mont, M.A.; Wongworawat, M.D.; Zalavras, C.G. New definition for periprosthetic joint infection: From the workgroup of the Musculoskeletal Infection Society. *Clin. Orthop. Relat. Res.* **2011**, *469*, 2992–2994. [CrossRef]
8. Shanmugasundaram, S.; Ricciardi, B.F.; Briggs, T.W.; Sussmann, P.S.; Bostrom, M.P. Evaluation and management of periprosthetic joint Infection–an international, multicenter study. *HSS J.* **2014**, *10*, 36–44. [CrossRef] [PubMed]
9. Ibrahim, M.S.; Twaij, H.; Haddad, F.S. Two-stage revision for the culture-negative infected total hip arthroplasty: A comparative study. *Bone Jt. J.* **2018**, *100*, 3–8. [CrossRef]

10. Kuo, F.C.; Goswami, K.; Shohat, N.; Blevins, K.; Rondon, A.J.; Parvizi, J. Two-stage exchange arthroplasty is a favorable treatment option upon diagnosis of a fungal periprosthetic joint infection. *J. Arthroplast.* **2018**, *33*, 3555–3560. [CrossRef]
11. Goel, R.; Buckley, P.; Sterbis, E.; Parvizi, J. Patients with Infected Total Hip Arthroplasty Undergoing 2-Stage Exchange Arthroplasty Experience Massive Blood Loss. *J. Arthroplast.* **2018**, *33*, 3547–3550. [CrossRef] [PubMed]
12. Zahar, A.; Klaber, I.; Gerken, A.M.; Gehrke, T.; Gebauer, M.; Lausmann, C.; Citak, M. Ten-year results following one-stage septic hip exchange in the management of periprosthetic joint infection. *J. Arthroplast.* **2019**, *34*, 1221–1226. [CrossRef]
13. Klouche, S.; Sariali, E.; Mamoudy, P. Total hip arthroplasty revision due to infection: A cost analysis approach. *Orthop. Traumatol. Surg. Res.* **2010**, *96*, 124–132. [CrossRef]
14. Toulson, C.; Walcott-Sapp, S.; Hur, J.; Salvati, E.; Bostrom, M.; Brause, B.; Westrich, G.H. Treatment of infected total hip arthroplasty with a 2-stage reimplantation protocol: Update on "our institution's" experience from 1989 to 2003. *J. Arthroplast.* **2009**, *24*, 1051–1060. [CrossRef] [PubMed]
15. Ji, B.; Xu, B.; Guo, W.; Rehei, A.; Mu, W.; Yang, D.; Cao, L. Retention of the well-fixed implant in the single-stage exchange for chronic infected total hip arthroplasty: An average of five years of follow-up. *Int. Orthop.* **2017**, *41*, 901–909. [CrossRef]
16. El-Husseiny, M.; Haddad, F.S. The role of highly selective implant retention in the infected hip arthroplasty. *Clin. Orthop. Relat. Res.* **2016**, *474*, 2157–2163. [CrossRef] [PubMed]
17. Fukui, K.; Kaneuji, A.; Ueda, S.; Matsumoto, T. Should well-fixed uncemented femoral components be revised in infected hip arthroplasty? *Rep. Five Trial Cases. J. Orthop.* **2016**, *13*, 437–442.
18. Crowe, J.F.; Sculco, T.P.; Kahn, B. Revision total hip arthroplasty: Hospital cost and reimbursement analysis. *Clin. Orthop. Relat. Res.* **2003**, *413*, 175–182. [CrossRef]
19. Kurtz, S.M.; Lau, E.; Watson, H.; Schmier, J.K.; Parvizi, J. Economic burden of periprosthetic joint infection in the united states. *J. Arthroplast.* **2012**, *27*, 61–65. [CrossRef]
20. Peel, T.N.; Dowsey, M.M.; Buising, K.L.; Liew, D.; Choong, P.F.M. Cost analysis of debridement and retention for management of prosthetic joint infection. *Clin. Microbiol. Infect.* **2013**, *19*, 181–186 [CrossRef]
21. Guyatt, G.; Cairns, J.; Churchill, D.; Cook, D.; Haynes, B.; Hirsh, J.; Irvine, J.; Levine, M.; Levine, M.; Nishikawa, J.; et al. Evidence-based medicine: A new approach to teaching the practice of medicine. *JAMA* **1992**, *268*, 2420–2425. [CrossRef] [PubMed]
22. Hernández-Vaquero, D.; Fernández-Fairen, M.; Torres, A.; Menzie, A.M.; Fernández-Carreira, J.M.; Murcia-Mazon, A.; Guerado, E.; Merzthal, L. Treatment of periprosthetic infections: An economic analysis. *Sci. World J.* **2013**, *2013*, 821650. [CrossRef] [PubMed]
23. Li, C.; Renz, N.; Trampuz, A. Management of Periprosthetic Joint Infection. *Hip Pelvis* **2018**, *30*, 138–146. [CrossRef] [PubMed]
24. Kovalchuk, S.V.; Funkner, A.A.; Metsker, O.G.; Yakovlev, A.N. Simulation of patient flow in multiple healthcare units using process and data mining techniques for model identification. *J. Biomed. Inform.* **2018**, *82*, 128–142. [CrossRef]
25. Kovalchuk, S.V.; Knyazkov, K.V.; Syomov, I.I.; Yakovlev, A.N.; Boukhanovsky, A.V. Personalized clinical decision support with complex hospital-level modelling. *Procedia Comput. Sci.* **2015**, *66*, 392–401. [CrossRef]
26. Parisi, T.J.; Konopka, J.F.; Bedair, H.S. What is the Long-term Economic Societal Effect of Periprosthetic Infections After THA? A Markov Analysis. *Clin. Orthop. Relat. Res.* **2017**, *475*, 1891–1900. [CrossRef] [PubMed]
27. Alp, E.; Cevahir, F.; Ersoy, S.; Guney, A. Incidence and economic burden of prosthetic joint infections in a university hospital: A report from a middle-income country. *J. Infect. Public Health* **2016**, *9*, 494–498. [CrossRef]
28. Somerson, J.S.; Boylan, M.R.; Hug, K.T.; Naziri, Q.; Paulino, C.B.; Huang, J.I. Risk factors associated with periprosthetic joint infection after total elbow arthroplasty. *Shoulder Elb.* **2019**, *11*, 116–120. [CrossRef]
29. Srivastava, K.; Bozic, K.J.; Silverton, C.; Nelson, A.J.; Makhni, E.C.; Davis, J.J. Reconsidering strategies for managing chronic periprosthetic joint infection in total knee arthroplasty: Using decision analytics to find the optimal strategy between one-stage and two-stage total knee revision. *JBJS* **2019**, *101*, 14–24. [CrossRef]
30. Kaliberda, Y.E.; Leonenko, V.N.; Artyukh, V.A. Towards cost-effective treatment of periprosthetic joint infection: From statistical analysis to Markov models. In Proceedings of the International Conference on Computational Science, Krakow, Poland, 16–18 June 2021; pp. 494–505.
31. Leonenko, V.N.; Kaliberda, Y.E.; Artyuk, V.A. A Modeling Framework for Decision Support in Periprosthetic Joint Infection Treatment. *Stud. Health Technol. Inform.* **2021**, *285*, 106–111.
32. Dolan, P. Modeling valuations for EuroQol health states. *Med. Care* **1997**, *35*, 1095–1108. [CrossRef] [PubMed]
33. Bates, S.; Leonenko, V.; Rineer, J.; Bobashev, G. Using synthetic populations to understand geospatial patterns in opioid related overdose and predicted opioid misuse. *Comput. Math. Organ. Theory* **2019**, *25*, 36–47. [CrossRef]
34. Leonenko, V.N. Analyzing the spatial distribution of acute coronary syndrome cases using synthesized data on arterial hypertension prevalence. In Proceedings of the International Conference on Computational Science, Amsterdam, The Netherlands, 3–5 June 2020; Springer: Cham, Switzerland, 2020; pp. 483–494.

Journal of
*Personalized
Medicine*

*Article*

# An Unsupervised Approach to Structuring and Analyzing Repetitive Semantic Structures in Free Text of Electronic Medical Records

**Varvara Koshman [1,2], Anastasia Funkner [1,2] and Sergey Kovalchuk [1,2,*]**

1 Federal Almazov North-West Medical Research Centre, Center for Artificial Intelligence Development in Medicine, 197341 Saint Petersburg, Russia; koshman.varia@gmail.com (V.K.); funkner.anastasia@gmail.com (A.F.)
2 National Center for Cognitive Research, ITMO University, 49 Kronverksky Pr., 197101 Saint Petersburg, Russia
* Correspondence: sergey.v.kovalchuk@gmail.com

**Abstract:** Electronic medical records (EMRs) include many valuable data about patients, which is, however, unstructured. Therefore, there is a lack of both labeled medical text data in Russian and tools for automatic annotation. As a result, today, it is hardly feasible for researchers to utilize text data of EMRs in training machine learning models in the biomedical domain. We present an unsupervised approach to medical data annotation. Syntactic trees are produced from initial sentences using morphological and syntactical analyses. In retrieved trees, similar subtrees are grouped using Node2Vec and Word2Vec and labeled using domain vocabularies and Wikidata categories. The usage of Wikidata categories increased the fraction of labeled sentences 5.5 times compared to labeling with domain vocabularies only. We show on a validation dataset that the proposed labeling method generates meaningful labels correctly for 92.7% of groups. Annotation with domain vocabularies and Wikidata categories covered more than 82% of sentences of the corpus, extended with timestamp and event labels 97% of sentences got covered. The obtained method can be used to label EMRs in Russian automatically. Additionally, the proposed methodology can be applied to other languages, which lack resources for automatic labeling and domain vocabulary.

**Keywords:** syntactical parsing; natural language processing; electronic health records; Node2Vec; automatic text labeling; graph algorithms



**Citation:** Koshman, V.; Funkner, A.; Kovalchuk, S. An Unsupervised Approach to Structuring and Analyzing Repetitive Semantic Structures in Free Text of Electronic Medical Records. *J. Pers. Med.* **2022**, *12*, 25. https://doi.org/10.3390/jpm12010025

Academic Editor: Shang-Ming Zhou

Received: 18 November 2021
Accepted: 30 December 2021
Published: 1 January 2022



## 1. Introduction

It has been previously shown that the performance of language machine learning models significantly increases when textual content of EMRs is included in the model's training data [1]. However, at this point, it is barely possible to use it when working with the Russian language due to the lack of labeled datasets available. The main reason is that manual labeling requires significant effort and time by domain experts. On the other hand, an automatic annotation system can save experts' time and promptly provide researchers with labeled data. Unfortunately, though, the idea of automatic annotation faces significant challenges for many languages, such as a lack of ready-to-use medical terminologies (e.g., terminologies of signs and symptoms, diseases, diagnosis, medications, vocabularies of medical abbreviations, etc.). Additionally, a specific syntactic structure with free word order missing conjunctions and omitting subject naming complicates the process of automatic annotation.

For clinical text processing in English, one may find extensive medical resources such as structured medical vocabularies (e.g., Unified Medical Language System (UMLS) [2], SNOMED CT), systems for clinical information extraction (e.g., cTAKES [3]), or search engines (e.g., PubMed, MetaMap [4]) are available. However, any other language except English has fewer resources to integrate into the research process. Thus, scientists search for various ways to reduce this limitation. In a project with a similar goal to automate the process of clinical text annotation in the Spanish language [5] an analogous tool to MetaMap was implemented from scratch. The tool performed the mapping of medical terms in EMRs to concepts in UMLS Metathesaurus and utilized Spanish-specific biomedical resources such as vocabularies of health acronyms and abbreviations. Researchers working with EMRs in Russian implemented a similar instrument to MetaMap on their own using MeSH, the only available vocabulary from UMLS for the Russian language [6]. However, the focus of the study was disease linking, and automatic annotation was not performed.

In case the language lacks analogous medical resources, one may use the Wikipedia-based approach to annotation which is being researched. For example, a recent study successfully applied DBpedia to link words in Arabic to their English translations in textual data [7]. To this end, researchers used morphological parsing and DBpedia's multilingual word mapping. Wikipedia was also successfully applied in a bilingual entity linking for both Chinese and English language systems, which showed state-of-the-art performance on the task [8]. The application of a Wiki-based approach to Russian was studied by Sysoev A., who used a Russian Wikidata graph for training word embeddings to improve the performance of entity linking [9]. There are numerous studies outside the biomedical domain on this approach to annotation, for which ideas can be applied in a clinical context. For instance, J. Raiman assigned categories to words in a text using Wikidata graph's parental relations in an entity disambiguation task [10]. This approach of labeling with Wikidata's categories has not been applied yet for the annotation of EMRs. An attempt to extract deterministic characteristics from EMRs in Russian was proposed by A. Funkner [11]. However, results contained incorrect and unnecessary constructions, so it was concluded that syntactic and morphological parsing should be used to discover sentence structure.

A recent study on Chinese EMRs suggested an unsupervised approach linking symptoms to the ICD10 classification [12]. Faced with the same issue of a lack of structured data in a corresponding language, authors pre-compiled a vocabulary of signs and symptoms crawling data from Chinese medical websites (more than 12 k terms in size). Additionally, they utilized word embeddings pre-trained with Word2Vec to compare a mention with a term in a vocabulary in terms of semantic similarity. However, most often, embeddings are trained separately to convey the context of the study. When working with graphical structures, a Node2Vec [13] method is commonly used in fields including biomedical [14,15]. Its random sampling strategy helps to preserve hierarchical relations between nodes in word embeddings. Node2Vec method for training word embeddings was also applied to syntactic trees for text generation [16]. However, it has not been used yet for text clustering, which is the focus of the current study. Tree similarity-based text clustering was suggested for relation extraction beyond the clinical domain [17]. Using cosine similarity was rejected mainly because the relationships between words might differ in different contexts. This way, a similarity function was proposed, and the retrieved clusters were then labeled with the most frequent head of a tree. However, with Node2Vec, the mentioned limit can be overcome by incorporating syntactic relations between words in word embeddings.

This paper aims to design and develop a method for automatic detection of repetitive semantic constructions in unstructured text data of EMRs. First, we utilize morphological and syntactic parsing to get structural representations of sentences. Then we train word embeddings using the Node2Vec method and group words with similar embeddings together; we find groups of similar syntactic trees and label them with Wiki-data categories.

To the best of our knowledge, we are the first to apply Node2Vec on syntactic trees in the task of text clustering. An approach of labeling with Wikidata concepts using categorical relations is firstly applied for labeling medical text data. Additionally, this is the first tool for automatic annotation of EMRs in Russian. A significant advantage of the proposed approach is that it is universal and can easily be adapted to another language regardless of the variety of biomedical resources available for this language.

## 2. Methods

The variety of mentioned drugs, signs, and symptoms terms is not usually covered by vocabularies, as it is hard to make them complete. Additionally, EMRs usually include specific language features (e.g., word abbreviations, typos), which are hard to correct with no additional medical vocabulary of acronyms. Therefore, we group similar semantic constructions to put similar symptom terms, word abbreviations, and drug names. With this done, when we perform automatic labeling, some of the words not presented in the knowledge base get relevant labels as members of a labeled group.

The detailed method schema is depicted in Figure 1. First, we split textual data of EMRs into sentences and have made morphological and syntactic analyses. With these means, we get a hierarchical structure for each sentence. Then, we applied Word2Vec [18] and Node2Vec [13] methods to train word embeddings on a corpus of syntactic trees. We have picked the most similar ones for each word and added them as new nodes on the same level to the initial tree. Cosine distance was used as a similarity metric. After these modifications to initial parsed trees, they were joined together to form one merged tree. We suggested an algorithm for finding equal subtrees, resulting in groups with similar semantic constructions. Eventually, a labeling module uses the medical knowledge base to assign labels to groups. The knowledge base is a Wikidata-based language-specific base set once before labeling.

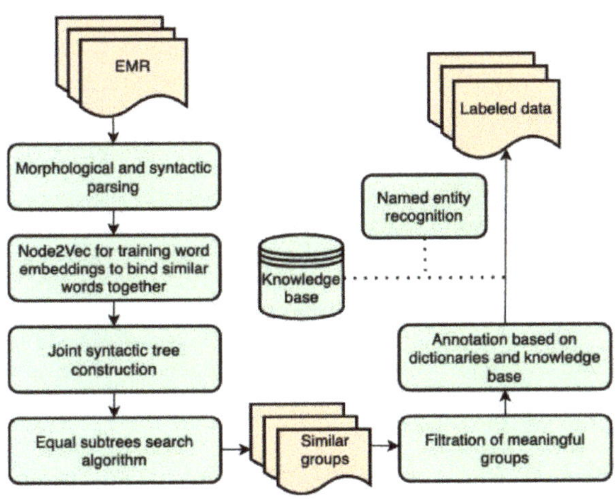


**Figure 1.** Method schema of sequential modules with EMR as input and labeled groups as output.

### 2.1. Morphological and Syntactic Parsing

Syntactic and morphological analyzers are used to extract information about sentence structure. This procedure ensures that groups with similar semantic constructions share the same structural meaning. In this research, we use a neural model for morphological tagging, as it showed promising results before [19]. We utilized a high performant graph-based parser with neural attention suggested by [20] for syntactic parsing. Both approaches were implemented for the Russian language by the DeepPavlov project [21]. Several studies proved that parsing of medical text is better with a model that is also trained on medical data [22,23]. However, we did not have labeled data for re-training, so we used a model already trained on a UD Russian SynTagRus corpus (version 2.3).

We use pos-tags provided by a morphological analyzer to ensure similar words have the same part of speech. An example of a resulting syntactic tree in a CoNLL-U format used further in analyses has a structure shown in Figure 2. Word's initial form, lemma, and a pos-tag are stored in a tree's node. Syntactic relations connect semantically dependent nodes.

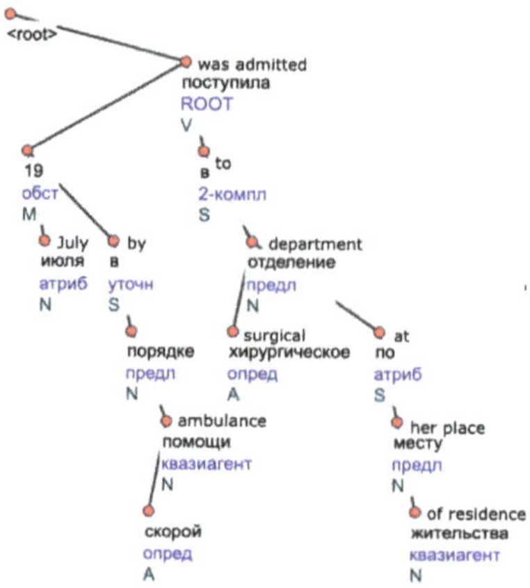


**Figure 2.** An example of a syntactic tree of a sentence "On 19 July, she was admitted by ambulance to the surgical department at her place of residence" in a CoNLL-U format.

### 2.2. Node2Vec on Syntactic Trees

The received syntactic trees commonly contained phrases with similar meanings yet said in different words. We aimed to cluster these similar fragments of trees and apply labeling to groups instead of single ones to let the annotation cover more text. To compare words in terms of similarity, we utilize the capabilities of Word2Vec [18]. Word2Vec is a set of neural network algorithms for computing words' continuous vector representations. Word embeddings are based on context similarity, meaning that textually close words should locate close in the vector space. Word2Vec comprises two models: Skip-gram and a continuous bag of words (CBOW). However, both models have a one-layer neural network as a core of different architectures. Skip-gram follows the text with a given window and learns to predict the nearest context from the current word. CBOW, on the contrary, predicts the central word as the average of neighboring context words' representations. Weights of the trained model are then used to predict word embedding. This way, for any two words from the training vocabulary, a semantic affinity can be calculated using the cosine distance between their embeddings. Equation 1 shows this metric for word embeddings A and B from the vocabulary.

$$\cos(A,\ B) = \frac{A \times B}{\parallel A \parallel \times \parallel B \parallel}, \tag{1}$$

A word embedding computed with Word2Vec is based on the surrounding words in a sentence. However, while working with free word order in sentences, one may face a situation when words next to each other do not have semantic proximity, and related words are found in different parts of a sentence. Therefore, to retrieve word embeddings that preserve meaningful relations between words obtained with syntactic parsing, we use a Node2Vec method [13].

To utilize a network's non-linear structure, Node2Vec for each node generates random samplings in its neighborhood. This way, instead of one linear sequence of words, a set of neighboring sequences are used for training a model. The objective function of a method maximizes the log probability of observation of a node u of its neighborhood $N_s(\mathrm{u})$, where $S$—a sampling strategy conditioned on feature representation f (Equation (2)).

$$\max_{f} \sum\nolimits_{\mathrm{u} \in V} \log(P(N_s(\mathrm{u})|\mathrm{f}(\mathrm{u})), \tag{2}$$

Node2Vec is based on parametrized random walks with parameters $p$ and $q$, which allow adjusting the probability of jumping to new unvisited nodes ($q$) and the probability of returning to a node already visited ($p$). With this setting, there is a trade-off between exploring the network's local structure in a breadth-first search (BFS) manner and discovering long-distance connections in a depth-first search (DFS) manner. The probability of visiting node $x$ from node $v$ is defined by Equations (3) and (4).

$$P(c_i = x | c_{i-1} = v) = \begin{cases} \alpha_{pq}, (v,\ x) \in E \\ 0 \end{cases}, \tag{3}$$

$$\alpha_{pq} = \begin{cases} \frac{1}{p},\ d_{tx} = 0 \\ 1, d_{tx} = 1 \\ \frac{1}{q},\ d_{tx} = 2 \end{cases}, \tag{4}$$

In the current work, we use a Node2Vec method to train a CBOW model. For preprocessing, we have removed stop words and normalized words before training. We have created the joined tree by connecting the roots of all syntactic trees with a virtual node considering syntactic relations as weights. Node2Vec was executed with non-normalized probabilities $p = 2$, $q = 3$, with five random walks per root and five words in one walk at most. When $q$ is higher than $p$, the algorithm's behavior is similar to the local search. Such behavior is beneficial when dealing with syntactic relations in a tree. The resulting vector space contains embeddings trained on medical data and 50 k embeddings pre-trained on the Russian fiction dataset.

### *2.3. Algorithm for Search of Similar Subtrees in a Tree*

The motivation behind searching for similar subtrees in syntactic trees is forming semantic groups conveying the same meaning. We aimed to join synonymous verbs, adjectives, and nouns.

Our algorithm for grouping similar subtrees in a tree is inspired by an equal subtree search [24,25]. Before we define the main ideas of the base algorithm, pointed out its drawbacks for the current task, and introduced our modifications, it is reasonable to give definitions of several terms used further. A repeat is a subtree encountered more than once in a tree. There are two types of repeats: a full and a partial. A full repeat is a repeat which includes all nodes and edges reachable from a root of a repeat, while a partial repeat is a repeat which might not include all nodes and edges from a subtree. By group, we mean a set of unique repeats which is a result of an algorithm. Two trees are considered equal if they have equal string representations (i.e., a sorted sequence of child nodes' labels).

Algorithm 1 with pseudocode illustrates the main idea of the base algorithm [24]. An algorithm takes as input a set of trees, searches for full repeats, and outputs groups of equal subtrees. To reduce the algorithm's computational complexity, the authors of [24] suggested mapping all strings to numerical representations. While the algorithm searches for full repeats, it iteratively looks for repeating subtrees on each height separately. By the end, a group consists of roots of repeats.

This algorithm takes care of free word order among closest words (the subtree representation does not depend on the order of child nodes) within a syntactic tree. However, a crucial drawback is that it searches for full repeats. Figure 3 depicts the difference between a full and a partial repeat on a clinical syntactic tree example. The idea behind the search for partial repeats is that the chance of finding more groups is higher in this case.

**Algorithm 1:** Main idea of the base algorithm of an equal subtree search in pseudocode. The base algorithm of an equal subtree search

```
H ← {} – a height dictionary
T – a joint tree
groups ← {} – a result set
for each v ∈ V do:          // compute heights and map all strings to numbers
  mapStringLabelToNumeric(v.label)
  H[h(v)] ← H[h(v)] ∪ v
for each height h in H do:
  representations ← {} // compute string representations of subtrees for each node
  for each v ∈ V do:
        representations ← representations ∪ computeRepresentation(v)
    // group equal subtrees together and add to result set
  groups ← groups ∪ groupSubtrees(representations)
```

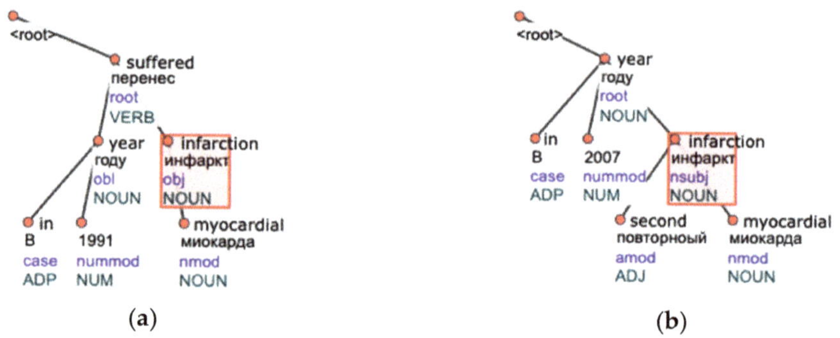


**Figure 3.** Tree examples of sentences where the algorithm for full repeat search will not find any repeating subtrees: (**a**) A tree contains a mention of disease: "infarction myocardial"; (**b**) Another tree containing "infarction myocardial" but with an extra child node with the word "second", making it a partial repeat.

The replacement of a single height with multiple ones is desirable, as it means that it allows a subtree (a phrase) to occur in different parts of a tree (a sentence) instead of a fixed position. It is especially suitable for languages with a free word order like Russian. Restrictions of the base approach are clear from the examples shown in Figure 4. Figure 4a illustrates the case when the repeating subtree "assigned a diagnosis diabetes mellitus" (literal translation from Russian) encountered in both trees will not be found by the algorithm because roots of these subtrees have different heights (3 and 4 accordingly). This situation may happen as they are checked on separate iterations. Even if the second tree in Figure 4b does not have a node "II" and has a height equal to 3, repeats will not be found either, as trees do not fully match. These situations are commonly encountered in free text, so we change the algorithm's behavior accordingly.

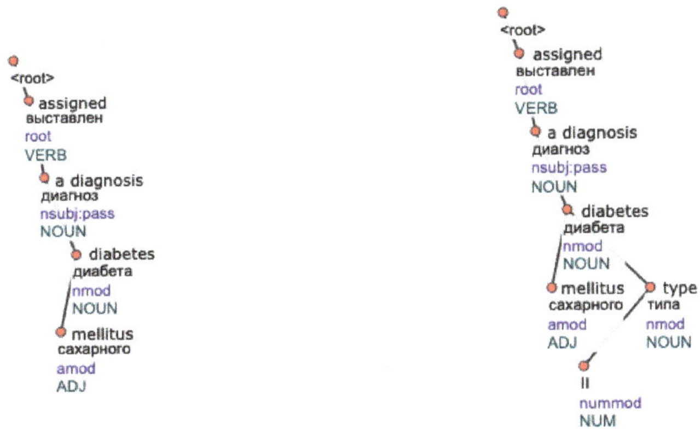


(a) (b)

**Figure 4.** Tree examples of sentences where a repeat "assigned a diagnosis diabetes mellitus" will not be found by the base algorithm, as trees are checked for equality on separate iterations: (**a**) A tree with the word "assigned" as a root of height 3 is checked with trees of height 3; (**b**) A second tree with an obvious repeat is not grouped with the first one, as it has a height 4.

Fully equal word sequences are rare in text data. The reason is that different words can convey the same meaning, some of which can also be often omitted. To this end, in the context of syntactic trees, we made modifications to achieve two things. First, replace equality with similarity by application of machine learning technologies. Second, search for partial repeats instead of full ones on multiple heights instead of a one to be consistent with the free structure of the text. Figure 5 depicts one of the repeats examples found by the modified version of the algorithm. Most of the words are not equal, although, have a very close meaning, which captures a Word2Vec model.

(a) (b)

**Figure 5.** Tree examples of sentences that form a repeat by our algorithm: (**a**) A tree of a sentence about a patient's hospitalization; (**b**) Another tree with similar information about a patient said in other words.

The modifications mentioned above produce a new version of the algorithm, for which main steps are described in pseudocode in Algorithm 2.

**Algorithm 2:** Main idea of a similar subtree search algorithm. The subtree search algorithm

```
H ← {} – a height dictionary
T – a joint tree
groups ← {} – a result set
extendTree(T)                 // create new nodes in T for synonymous words
for each v ∈ V do:            // compute heights and map all strings to numbers
    mapStringLabelToNumeric(v.label)
    H[h(v)] ← H[h(v)] ∪ v
for each height h in H do:
    representations ← {} // compute string representations of subtrees for each node
    for each v ∈ V do:
        representations ← representations ∪ computeRepresentation(v)
    // generate possible subtree combinations C_n^k, n– number of children, k = 1..n
    combinations ← generateCombinations(representations)
    // group equal subtrees together and add to result set
    groups ← groups ∪ groupSubtrees(combinations)
stringGroups ← DFS(T, groups) // traverse tree T to restore initial word sequences
```

The first key difference is that a tree gets extended with new nodes before the repeats search. Having a vector space produced by a Word2Vec model, each word can be linked with its most similar ones. This way, for each word, we found its most similar ones by picking those with a cosine distance higher than 0.75. These new nodes were created on the same level as an initial word and are linked with other nodes with the same edges. Concretely, if a word has k similar words, then k new nodes are created in the same place in a tree. Figure 6 shows how a syntactic tree looks after these additions are made. By doing this, our problem of finding similar subtrees reduces to a problem of finding equal subtrees.

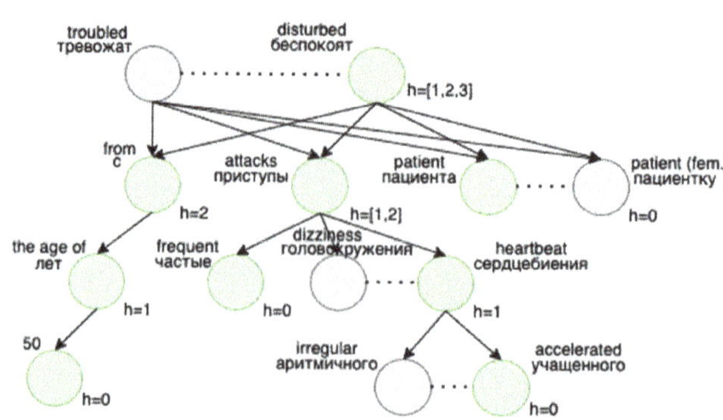


**Figure 6.** Syntactic tree representation with initial nodes colored in green and added similar nodes colored in grey.

Firstly, heights are calculated for all initial nodes. A second key difference is that a node is assigned not a single height but an array of heights. Concretely, each of the heights in an array corresponds to one of the child subtrees. Each value shows what height a root has if all the other subtrees are excluded. It is intended to make particular text patterns searchable in different parts of a sentence. Analogically to the base version, words are not straightforwardly compared in the algorithm. Initial words are lemmatized and then mapped to numerical representations in the interest of performance. The core idea of the algorithm is iterating through all heights and searching for partial repeats. For all nodes with equal lemmas, $C_n^k$ combinations of possible partial repeats were computed. If a subtree repeats several times on one height, then in all sentences where it is encountered, a new vertex is created with the new class label as a lemma. Incoming edges (the same ones that enter the original vertex) and outgoing edges (those that lead to child vertices of this particular repetition) are created. Creating new vertices for each repetitive combination simplifies the reconstruction of a path when traversing the initial tree with DFS at the end of the algorithm. The matching subtrees are grouped and added to the result set. By the end, a result set contains groups of roots of similar subtrees, and as the final step, all of them are traversed with DFS for restoring repeating word sequences.

### 2.4. Labeling Process

#### 2.4.1. Usage of Wikidata for Labeling

Aiming to assign meaningful categories to the retrieved groups of similar semantic structures, we utilized the capabilities of knowledge graphs. Concepts in knowledge graphs were associated with typified relationships in which parental relationships were categorical. These relationships were then used for labeling terms in received groups.

Knowledge graph combines entities (facts, events, named entities) by semantic relations into a graph structure. Examples of knowledge graphs are DBpedia [26], Freebase, Wikidata, which are actively used in question-answering systems, machine learning tasks related to named entities recognition and linking, and other natural language processing tasks. For English, there are systems for annotating and linking entities to knowledge bases, such as MetaMap, BabelFly, TagMe, which successfully work with medical texts [27]. However, such systems are available for English. For Russian, only BabelFly has an implementation able to find the word and link it to the entity's name and an article in the DBpedia.

However, the above information about an entity's name in the knowledge graph seems insufficient for meaningful annotation. For example, when annotating the word "hospitalization", its free-form definition may not be as valuable as its category "medical procedure". Furthermore, the mentioned systems do not include inheritance relationships. Given this, and the limited options available for languages other than English, a centralized structured multidisciplinary multilingual knowledge base, Wikidata, has become actively used for annotation. Wikidata was created to support the Wikipedia ontology, and therefore also contains a great deal of medical information, such as names of diseases, signs and symptoms, medical procedures, medical organizations, body organs, medications, etc.

The Wikidata knowledge graph comprises two types of entities: objects and properties. Properties reflect the relationships between objects, building relationships also to strings, dates, geographic locations, images, and so on, depending on the nature of the property. Objects have an identifier with the prefix "Q", properties with "P". To categorize multi-domain entities, the Wikidata knowledge graph [10] extracted inheritance relations by type for each entity: "instance of", "subclass of", "part of", as they are most defining.

Wikidata, being a secondary knowledge base, aggregates many others, including medical ones. If an item is found in a specific knowledge base, it has a corresponding property. In [28], the authors analyzed this potential of Wikidata as a medical knowledge base and, in particular, made a list of knowledge bases included in it. Each has a corresponding property identifier, meaning that an object is indexed in the following knowledgebase. By the presence of these properties, an object can be related to the medical field. The complete list contains about a hundred knowledge bases identifiers. However, most of them were filtered out due to their specificity (e.g., database with physician names, brain structure database, etc.). We left only the most general ones (i.e., eMedicine, Drugbank, Disease Ontology, MeSH, etc.). The resulting full list of properties consisted of 32 entries: "P636", "P673", "P486", "P715", "P699", "P780", "P923", "P924", "P2452", "P1748", "P557", "P2892", "P4338", "P3550", "P3841", "P4495", "P5270", "P1694", "P1693", "P1554", "P1550", "P1323", "P696", "P595", "P494", "P1692", "P1461", "P667", "P2275", "P4250", "P2176", "P1995". The presence of one of these properties in a Wikidata entity's properties indicates that this entity belongs to the medical domain.

We have fetched only Wikidata entities with the specified properties for compiling the database. Interaction with the knowledge graph and fetching entities was done with queries in the specialized query language SPARQL and the public MediaWiki interaction interface. Then, only those entities remained that have their names available in Russian translation, leaving only about a third of initially fetched. For these entities, synonyms and names associated with each other with inheritance relationships are found on the Wikidata graph (as mentioned, inheritance relations are: "instance of", "subclass of", "part of"). In addition to the data obtained from Wikidata, we also normalized entities' names, as the algorithm for searching similar partial repeats works with the normal forms of words. Figure 7 depicts the resulting database schema, where we have aggregated all fetched and filtered categorical information from Wikidata. We stored entities with hierarchical relations in one table and linked synonyms to existing entities in another table.

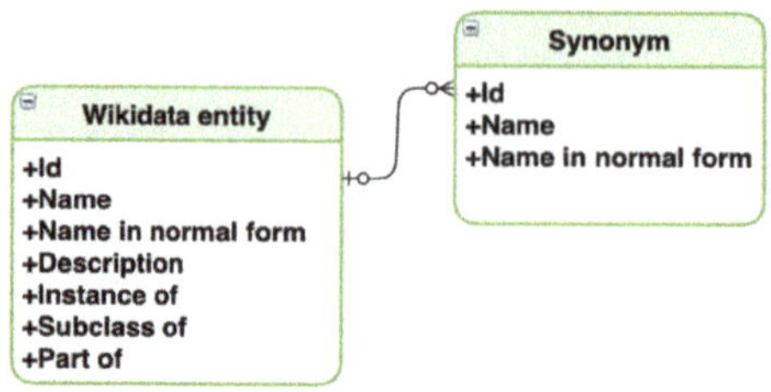


**Figure 7.** Medical database schema.

A concrete example of an entity "electrocardiogram" is shown in Figure 8. According to Wikidata, this entity has a medical property "P486" (MeSH descriptor ID), synonyms "EKG" and "ECG"; and categories "medical test type" ("instance of"), "medical test" ("subclass of"), and "electrophysiology" (part of). This way, a mention of "EKG" gets a "medical test type" label as the closest parental relation.

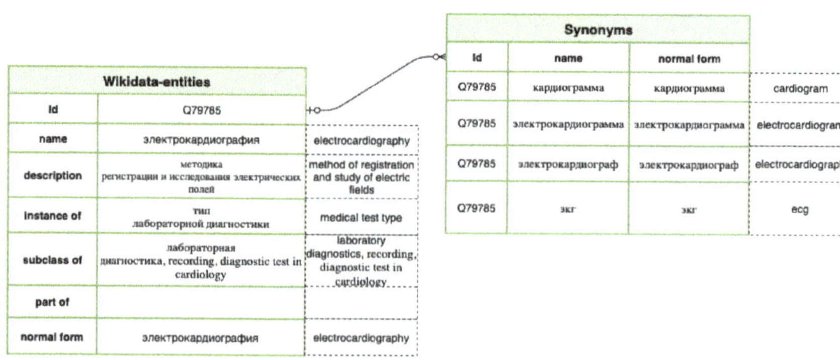


**Figure 8.** Wikidata entity "electrocardiogram" representation in a database.

### 2.4.2. Usage of Domain Vocabularies for Labeling

Medical knowledge bases can cover most medical terms. However, some serious gaps remain. Several essential databases were compiled in English and are relevant only for English. Concretely, fundamental differences exist in the drugs' names and most active substances' names, which are not translated in other languages. Thus, vocabularies of Russian-language terms are needed to supplement the knowledge bases in cases where their data are insufficient. There are no such pre-compiled vocabularies for the Russian language, and their compilation is done as a subtask. We compiled a vocabulary of drugs containing a parsed set of names listed in the Vidal.ru reference book (6360 names).

We also compiled vocabularies, as there are cases where no Russian translations exist for some terms (e.g., diseases, sign and symptoms names) crucial for EMR labeling. The resulting vocabularies of disease names (4657), signs and symptoms names (355), physician specializations names (41) were crawled from Russian medical websites.

A significant disadvantage of labeling with vocabularies is that even if the text specifies the exact name of the entity, the group still gets the general label "Disease", even though it can be matched with a more specific category. For example, "Atherosclerosis of the carotid arteries" will be labeled with vocabulary as "Disease", while this disease is categorized more specifically as "chronic arterial disease" according to the Wikidata. Additionally, unlike the Wikidata knowledge base, vocabularies do not contain synonyms and the most common abbreviations for domain terms.

#### 2.4.3. Labels Assignment

The received groups of semantic constructions are labeled with structured medical resources. Firstly, groups are labeled with compiled domain vocabularies. Groups get labels "Disease", "Sign and symptom", "Medication", and "Physician specialization" if a word is present in the corresponding vocabulary. Additionally, groups containing any date designations get a "Timestamp" label. Additionally, a group with a verb in passive voice (i.e., "was hospitalized", "was appointed", "was discharged") indicates some event in a patient's EMR, so it gets labeled "Event".

Afterward, in each group, adjectives and nouns are picked, their possible permutations are matched against names of entries in a retrieved database. If a word or a combination of words is matched with one of the entities' names or synonyms, a group gets a label equal to the category linked by "instance of" relation. If a Russian translation for "instance of" entity does not exist, then a "subclass of" relation is followed. Likewise, "subclass of" and "part of". The reason is that "instance of" is considered the closest category, while "part of" is the most abstract of them.

### *2.5. Entity Linking in a New Knowledge Base*

There were examples of words relating to more than one label in a knowledge base during the labeling process. In these cases, a simple decision rule was applied to pick the most relevant. Cosine similarity between vector representation of a label and a term being labeled defined the decision rule.

The proximity of vector representations links words from the text with corresponding words from knowledge bases. The proposal was made in [29] to represent a graph using vector representations of low dimensionality encoding the graph's topology. The advantage of this approach is that such representations can include information about related concepts embedded in the knowledge graph structure, in contrast to other means of analysis. The core idea behind this approach is using Node2Vec [13] or DeepWalk [30] methods to generate samples and train a skip-gram model Word2Vec [18]. In [29], authors conduct experiments on the whole DBpedia, implement a custom random walk procedure, and suggest a candidate ranking metric, which uses cosine distance between embeddings to select a relevant candidate.

However, entity linking in the current study's context is much easier, as we have already selected a medical part of a Wikidata. Most non-medical terms simply do not participate in the labeling process. Unfortunately, though, a few hundred names point to multiple entities. As ambiguous cases are rare, it was set to define a rule that prefers those entities closer to the context of a corpus being annotated. Concretely, a skip-gram model was trained with Node2Vec on a database graph and a forest of initial syntactic trees (Node2Vec parameters: $p = 1$, $q = 2$, number of walks per root = 3, walk length = 5). A decision between possible entities was made in favor of the one with the highest cosine similarity score.

The ambiguous example is shown in Figure 9 with an entity with the label "pain" and an entity with the label "nociception". The last one is an alias and is referenced additionally by the "pain" label. In this situation, it is indefinite which category to pick—a "livelihood" (which "nociception" is an instance of) or a "negative emotion" (which "pain" is an instance of). Having trained embeddings of nodes of a knowledge graph, we compute cos(*pain, negative emotion*) = 0.75 and cos(*pain, livelihood*) = 0.31. This way, "negative emotion" is selected as a label, with the highest score.

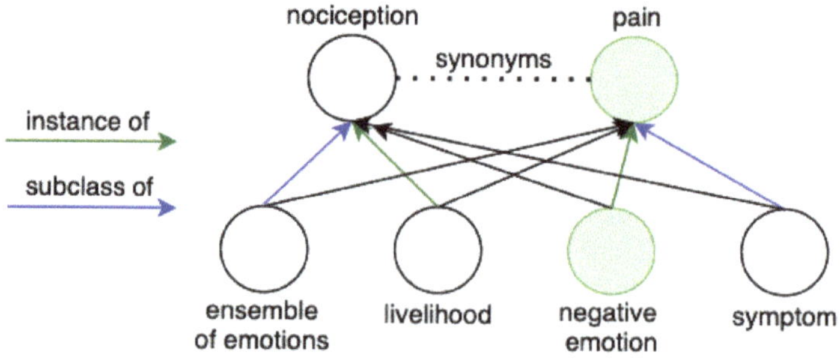


**Figure 9.** Example of ambiguous choice of labels in case of a presence of multiple synonymous entities.

## 3. Results

### 3.1. Data

Experiments were conducted on a corpus of 5 k sentences with time constructions in the Russian language. Sentences were taken from a set of anonymous histories included in EMRs of patients with acute coronary syndrome under observation in Almazov National Medical Research Centre (Almazov Centre) in 2010–2015.

### 3.2. Method's Implementation Details

Labeling was performed on a personal computer with a 1.8 GHz Dual-Core Intel Core i5 processor and 8 GB RAM taking 6.2 min for the whole process on average. The implementation of the described method was written in the Python programming language. Software technologies used in this research, besides standard ones, included Gensim [31] and StellarGraph [32] libraries for training embeddings and DeepPavlov [21] for text parsing.

### 3.3. The Resulting Medical Database

The resulting number of medical entities retrieved by the specified algorithm is 18.9 k entities and 17.1 k synonyms. From the compiled database, the appearance of the knowledge graph in Wikidata can be partially reconstructed, although greatly simplified, which uses only inheritance relations as links. Figure 10 shows the knowledge base graph, where the "name" field from both tables and category names are the vertices and inheritance relations are the edges. There are many sets with a small number of vertices that are specific and have few related entities. At the same time, in the center, extensive concepts such as "cure", "disease", and "chemical compound" link many entities together.

Figure 11 shows examples of how entities and relationships in the constructed database look at closer inspection. Random samples from the database were taken for the construction.

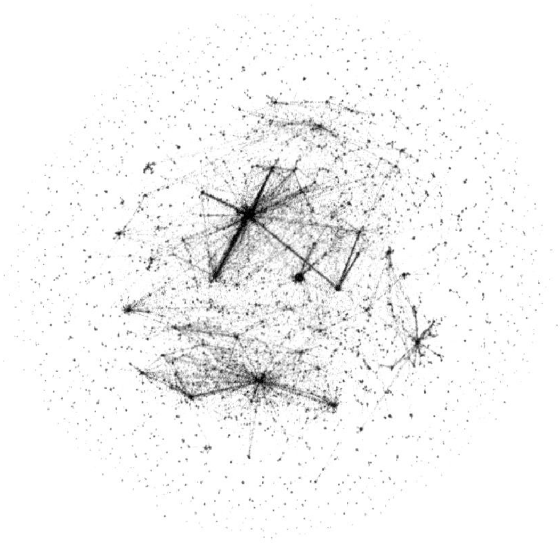

**Figure 10.** Graph of the compiled medical knowledge base.

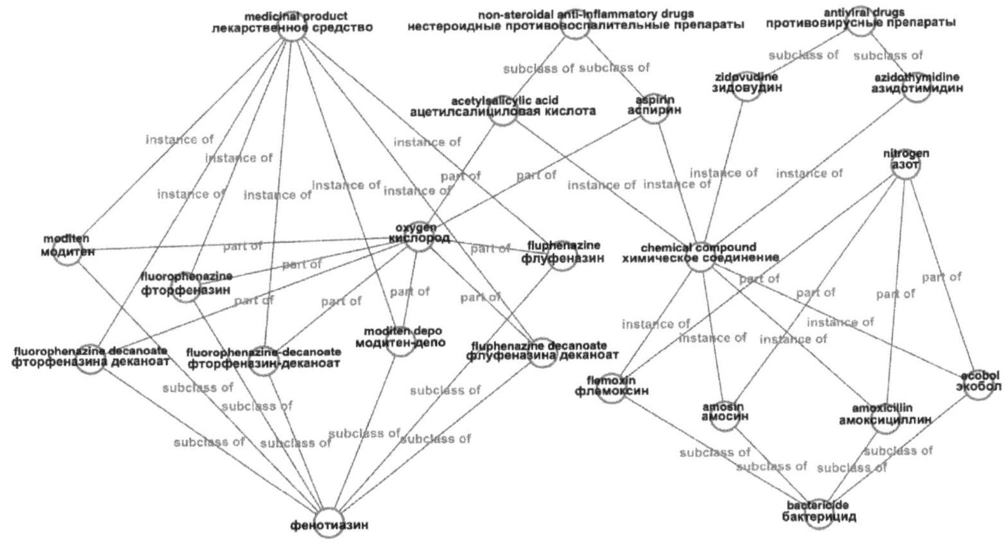


**Figure 11.** Examples of entities and their relationships in a medical knowledge base at close examination.

### 3.4. Embeddings Trained with Node2Vec

Figure 12 shows medical terms in the text of EMRs marked after labeling with vocabularies. First, the embedding of each word was obtained from the resulting vector spaced received by training a CBOW model with the Node2Vec method. Then, they are visualized with a t-SNE method.

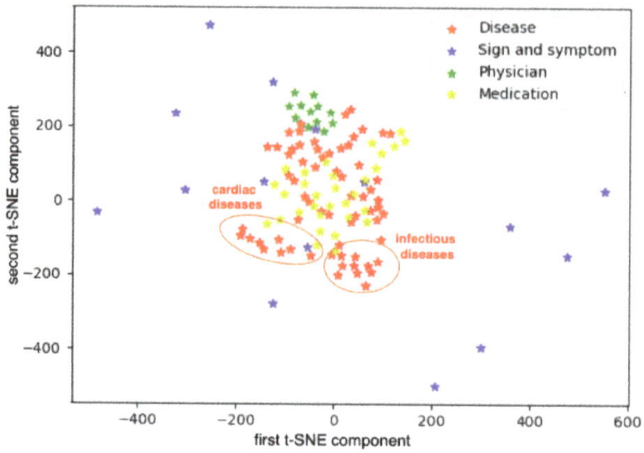


**Figure 12.** Space of vector word representations, labeled with vocabularies, obtained by the Node2Vec method.

Physician specializations clustered together, cardiac and infectious diseases groups are also noticeably separated from others. On the other hand, similar medications and the diseases for which they are prescribed are located closely. We provide examples below of the most similar words according to the obtained vector space. Table 1 compares similar words retrieved with the Node2Vec method and a plain Word2Vec method. The last one linked many unrelated by common sense words, whereas the Node2Vec focused more on meaningful relations between words rather than a local neighborhood.

**Table 1.** Comparison of words similar by cosine distance defined by Node2Vec and Word2Vec.

| Russian Word | English Word | Russian Synonyms Node2Vec | English Synonyms Node2Vec | Russian Synonyms Word2Vec | English Synonyms Word2Vec |
|---|---|---|---|---|---|
| бедренный | femoral | латеральный<br>малоберцовый<br>суставный | lateral<br>peroneal<br>articular | дистальный<br>височный<br>паховый | distal<br>temporal<br>inguinal |
| преднизолон | prednisone | верошпирон<br>новокаинамид<br>фуросемид | verospiron<br>novokainamide<br>furosemide | в/в<br>мг/сут<br>фуросемид | intravenously<br>mg/day<br>furosemide |
| нии | nii (national research institute) | кб<br>окб | ch (clinical hospital)<br>lch (local clinical hospital) | кб<br>окб<br>приёмный<br>хлснрс | ch<br>lch<br>emergency<br>surgical treatment of complex cardiac arrhythmias |
| фельдшер | paramedic | врач | physician | врач<br>медсанчасть | physician<br>medical unit |
| нагноение | suppuration | сепсис<br>воспаление<br>гной<br>рубцевание<br>инфекция | sepsis<br>inflammation<br>pus<br>scarring<br>infection | абсцесс<br>опухоль<br>инфекция<br>гематома<br>кровотечение | abscess<br>tumor<br>infection<br>hematoma<br>bleeding |

Even though in some cases, words in both vector spaces are close, in a one retrieved by Word2Vec, relatively distant words are grouped (i.e., diseases and symptoms). Additionally, some designations have a high cosine distance with medication names. For example, as per Table 1, the abbreviation for national research institute is redundantly close to emergency and paramedic to a medical unit. In some cases, completely different words are correlated: "cardio dispensary" with "child", "accounting" with "lung", "appointment" with "intravenously", and "arrhythmologist". Additionally, big typos in words, which are hard to relate to initial forms, are unreasonably close to each other. Embeddings trained with the Node2Vec method avoid these problems and provide a significantly more meaningful vector space. Several selected examples of similar words are listed in Table 2.

**Table 2.** Examples of words similar by cosine distance defined by Node2Vec.

| Russian Word | English Word | Russian Synonyms Node2Vec | English Synonyms Node2Vec |
|---|---|---|---|
| црб | cch (central clinical hospital) | стационар<br>диспансер | hospital<br>dispensary |
| мрт | mri | гастроскопия<br>оэкт<br>экг<br>рентгенография | gastroscopy<br>spect<br>ecg<br>radiography |
| гкмп | hcm (hypertrophic cardiomyopathy) | пролапс<br>поликистоз<br>кардиомиопатия | prolapse<br>polycystic<br>cardiomyopathy |
| искуственный | atificial | искусственный | artificial |
| отсутсвие | absense | отсутствие | absence |
| тошнота | nausea | головокружение<br>жжение<br>рвота | dizziness<br>burning<br>vomit |

With examples in Table 2, symptoms, medications, medical test types, and diseases with several abbreviations were grouped. Additionally, names of cities, names of relatives (i.e., "grandmother", "mother", "brother", "relative", etc.), physician specializations, medical institutions, body parts, text numbers (i.e., "one", "two", "twenty", etc.), words with minor typos and similar non-medical words (i.e., verbs "occur", "form", "manifest" in relation to the beginning of the disease) got together.

### 3.5. Extracted Groups

Our algorithm extracted nearly 8.2 k groups in total. Frequency statistics of the size of groups are shown with bar charts in Figure 13. It is noticeable that groups are most commonly small and consist of up to 10 repeated phrases. Therefore, the maximum repeat length was limited to five words to keep groups short and informative.

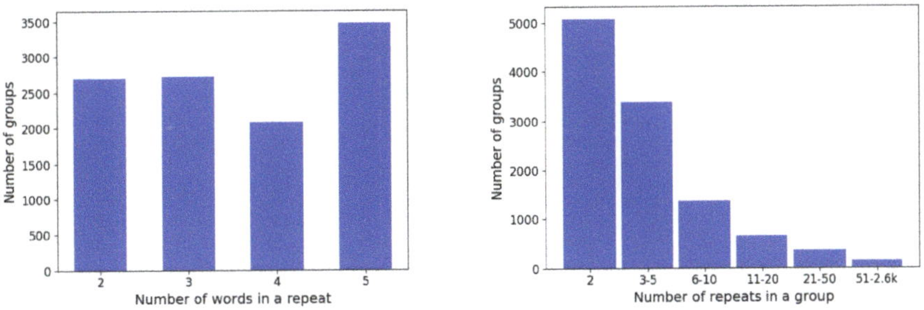


(a) (b)

**Figure 13.** Bar charts with frequency statistics: (**a**) A bar chart with a number of groups with an equal number of words in a repeat; (**b**) A bar chart with a number of groups with an equal number of repeats.

### 3.6. Labeling Groups

Utilizing domain vocabularies of diseases, symptoms, medications, and physician specializations got only 700 groups labeled. This number is low, as full names of terms are seldom found in free texts. Labeling with Wikidata increased the annotated number of groups to 3.8 k, adding labels "Timestamp" and "Event" the number grew to 6.6 k annotated groups. This way, 4844 out of 5 k sentences got labeled, 3877 of which are labels from Wikidata and domain vocabularies.

Table 3 represents several examples of repeats in groups and their corresponding labels.

**Table 3.** Examples of labeled semantic groups.

| Group Russian | Group English | Label Russian | Label English |
|---|---|---|---|
| выявили в2009 году<br>зарегистрирован в1995 г<br>обнаружена в2004 году<br>зафиксированы в2009 г | identified in 2009<br>registered in 1995<br>discovered in 2004<br>recorded in 2009 | временная метка, событие | timestamp, event |
| ухудшение состояния | deterioration | характеристика заболевания | disease characteristic |
| переломы костей | bone fractures | тип класса анатомическойструктуры, повреждение организма, болезнь | anatomical structure class type, body injury, disease |
| приступы тахикардии<br>пароксизм тахикардии | bouts of tachycardia<br>paroxysm of tachycardia | медицинское заключение, болезнь, обострение | medical report, disease, exacerbation |

Thirty of the most common results from the assigned labels are displayed in Figure 14. Except a few, all of them are related to the biomedical domain.

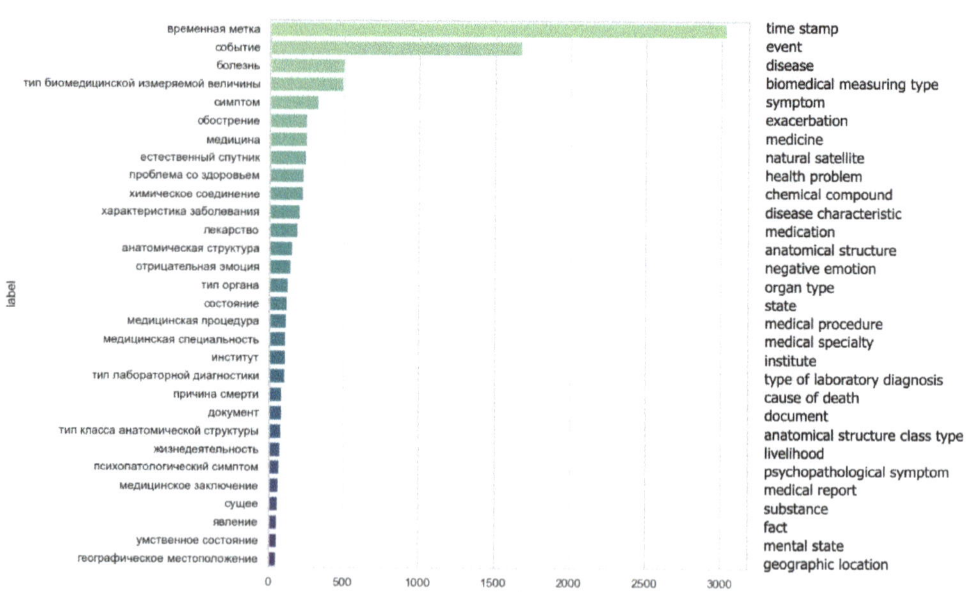


**Figure 14.** The 30 most common labels sorted by their frequency in a result set.

We randomly generated a validation set of 500 sentences assigned labels with Wikidata and domain vocabularies. Manually validating, we decided whether a label is relevant to the context or not. As expected, classes of diseases, symptoms, laboratory tests, and anatomical structures are covered in most cases by this labeling, making labeling correct in more than 92.7% of cases.

## 4. Discussion

The proposed algorithm extracted nearly 8.2 k groups of similar semantic constructions from a corpus of 5 k sentences. Using medical vocabularies, only 700 groups got annotated, whereas, with the use of Wikidata's categorical concepts, this number grew to 3.8 k, making a significant improvement. These labeled groups covered 82% of sentences of a corpus with annotation. Validation established that 92.7% of the labels assigned with Wikidata and vocabularies were meaningful. When labels were extended with "Time construction" and "Event", the coverage of the corpus with annotation grew to 97%. These results show that the designed method can be successfully applied to label medical text data.

The method we developed succeeded in joining semantically close phrases: some common abbreviations (for example, ones for medical organizations and lab tests), word reductions (for example, 'department' and 'dep' in Russian), and minor typos. Diseases, organs, body parts, and geographical places were grouped by the system. To the best of our knowledge, this is a first attempt at grouping medical free text by semantic similarity before automatic annotation intending to cover more words.

In addition to the positive results, several limitations discovered should also be mentioned. Firstly, even though the database used is mostly medical-related, some non-medical terms got included (for example, together with a geographical knowledge base containing names of medical organizations) and caused incorrect labeling. Concretely, the word "pool" (relating to "middle cerebral artery pool") is incorrectly linked to "sports facility", a word "month" (relating to some point in time)—to "natural satellite" referring to the Moon, a word "work" (relating to "heart work")—to "geographic location". Additionally, "infarction", "myocardial infarction", and "stroke" are assigned labels "cause of death", but in the text there were described cases of patients who survived. This label is considered the closest category as it is linked with "instance of" relation, however "subclass of" relation leads to more meaningful in these case categories: "necrosis", "coronary insufficiency", and "cerebrovascular diseases", respectively.

Nevertheless, these exclusive cases relate to 97 out of 2047 assigned labels, making labeling correct, as mentioned, in more than 95% of cases. Secondly, many articles do not yet have a translation of the name or individual properties into Russian in Wikidata. However, it is reassuring that this knowledge base is updated daily and constantly expanding, making it a more comprehensive resource.

In the nearest future, it is planned to improve the decision process of Wikidata labels. In this work, we picked "instance of", "subclass of", and "part of" categorical relations as most descriptive in the Wikidata graph and considered them to be in descending order of closeness. Though, closeness does not always follow this rule and often is dependent on the context of the whole semantic construction. We apply exact matching with Wikidata terms and rely entirely on groups to join similar concepts together. A way to improve can be to assume that similar words have similar Wikidata categories. Doing this can cover more information with labels. Additionally, a method currently uses a uniform way of choosing a category for an entity in a Wikidata graph. However, each time the best option is dependent on the context. It is planned to avoid this limitation and incorporate similarity in this decision process.

## 5. Conclusions

The key contributions of this work are a design of a new methodology for automatic annotation of EMRs, a proposed method for finding similar subtrees in a tree, a successful application of a classic Node2Vec algorithm to syntactic trees, and a creation of a medical Wikidata-based database for labeling in Russian. The whole pipeline can be adapted to other languages by changing the language-specific preprocessing module. Additionally, a corresponding database can be created by changing a language code. For Russian, a graphic interface was implemented for annotating new datasets with statistical representation.

The developed tool can generally increase the number of labeled datasets available, which researchers can use in machine learning problems related to the medical domain. Availability of such tools, in turn, can broaden the scope of problems and save time for domain experts, saving them time engaged in searching and for researchers who get their data labeled quickly.

**Author Contributions:** Conceptualization, S.K. and A.F.; Methodology, V.K., A.F. and S.K.; Software, V.K.; Validation, V.K.; Formal analysis, A.F.; Investigation, V.K. and A.F.; Writing—original draft preparation, V.K.; Writing—review and editing, A.F. and S.K.; Visualization, V.K.; Supervision, A.F. and S.K. All authors have read and agreed to the published version of the manuscript.

**Funding:** This work was supported financially by the Ministry of Science and Higher Education of the Russian Federation, agreement no. 075-15-2021-1013 (8 October 2021) (Internal project number 13.2251.21.0067).

**Institutional Review Board Statement:** Not applicable.

**Informed Consent Statement:** All data of patients' electronic medical records were fully depersonalized from the hospital to the data controller. The Institutional Review Board waived the requirement for the informed consent.

**Data Availability Statement:** The data presented in this study are available on request from the authors.

**Conflicts of Interest:** The authors declare no conflict of interest.

## References


1. Liu, J.; Zhang, Z.; Org, N.R. Deep EHR: Chronic Disease Prediction Using Medical Notes. In Proceedings of the 3rd Machine Learning for Healthcare Conference, Palo Alto, CA, USA, 17–18 August 2018.
2. Bodenreider, O. The Unified Medical Language System (UMLS): Integrating biomedical terminology. *Nucleic Acids Res.* **2004**, *32*, D267–D270. [CrossRef] [PubMed]
3. Savova, G.K.; Masanz, J.J.; Ogren, P.V.; Zheng, J.; Sohn, S.; Kipper-Schuler, K.C.; Chute, C.G. Mayo clinical Text Analysis and Knowledge Extraction System (cTAKES): Architecture, component evaluation and applications. *J. Am. Med. Inform. Assoc.* **2010**, *17*, 507–513. [CrossRef] [PubMed]
4. Aronson, A.R. Effective mapping of biomedical text to the UMLS Metathesaurus: The MetaMap program. In Proceedings of the AMIA Annual Symposium, Washington, DC, USA, 3–7 November 2001; pp. 17–21.
5. Oronoz, M.; Casillas, A.; Gojenola, K.; Perez, A. Automatic annotation of medical records in spanish with disease, drug and substance names. In Proceedings of the Lecture Notes in Computer Science (Including Subseries Lecture Notes in Artificial Intelligence and Lecture Notes in Bioinformatics), Tokyo, Japan, 29–31 October 2013; Volume 8259 LNCS.
6. Shelmanov, A.O.; Smirnov, I.V.; Vishneva, E.A. Information extraction from clinical texts in Russian. *Komp'juternaja Lingvist. i Intell. Tehnol.* **2015**, *1*, 560–572.
7. Bouziane, A.; Bouchiha, D.; Doumi, N. Annotating Arabic Texts with Linked Data. In Proceedings of the ISIA 2020—Proceedings, 4th International Symposium on Informatics and its Applications, M'sila, Algeria, 15–16 December 2020.
8. Zhang, J.; Cao, Y.; Hou, L.; Li, J.; Zheng, H.T. Xlink: An unsupervised bilingual entity linking system. In Proceedings of the Lecture Notes in Computer Science (Including Subseries Lecture Notes in Artificial Intelligence and Lecture Notes in Bioinformatics), Thessaloniki, Greece, 22–24 November 2017; Volume 10565 LNAI.
9. Sysoev, A.A.; Andrianov, I.A. Named entity recognition in Russian: The power of Wiki-based approach. In Proceedings of the International Conference "Dialogue 2016", Moscow, Russia, 1–4 June 2016.
10. Raiman, J.; Raiman, O. DeepType: Multilingual entity linking by neural type system evolution. In Proceedings of the 32nd AAAI Conference on Artificial Intelligence, AAAI 2018, New Orleans, LA, USA, 2–7 February 2018.
11. Funkner, A.A.; Kovalchuk, S.V. *Time Expressions Identification without Human-Labeled Corpus for Clinical Text Mining in Russian*; Springer International Publishing: Berlin/Heidelberg, Germany, 2020; ISBN 9783030504236.
12. Yan, C.; Zhang, Y.; Liu, K.; Zhao, J.; Shi, Y.; Liu, S. Enhancing unsupervised medical entity linking with multi-instance learning. *BMC Med. Inform. Decis. Mak.* **2021**, *21*, 317. [CrossRef] [PubMed]
13. Grover, A.; Leskovec, J. Node2vec: Scalable feature learning for networks. In Proceedings of the ACM SIGKDD International Conference on Knowledge Discovery and Data Mining, San Francisco, CA, USA, 13–17 August 2016.
14. Kim, M.; Baek, S.H.; Song, M. Relation extraction for biological pathway construction using node2vec. *BMC Bioinform.* **2018**, *19*, 75–84. [CrossRef] [PubMed]

15. Shen, F.; Liu, S.; Wang, Y.; Wang, L.; Wen, A.; Limper, A.H.; Liu, H. Constructing Node Embeddings for Human Phenotype Ontology to Assist Phenotypic Similarity Measurement. In Proceedings of the 2018 IEEE International Conference on Healthcare Informatics Workshops, ICHI-W 2018, New York, NY, USA, 4–7 June 2018.
16. Bhardwaj, S. Syntree2Vec-An Algorithm to Augment Syntactic Hierarchy into Word Embeddings. *arXiv* **2018**, arXiv:1808.05907.
17. Zhang, M.; Su, J.; Wang, D.; Zhou, G.; Tan, C.L. Discovering relations between named entities from a large raw corpus using tree similarity-based clustering. In Proceedings of the Lecture Notes in Computer Science (Including Subseries Lecture Notes in Artificial Intelligence and Lecture Notes in Bioinformatics), Tallinn, Estonia, 12–15 September 2005; Volume 3651 LNAI.
18. Mikolov, T.; Chen, K.; Corrado, G.; Dean, J. Efficient estimation of word representations in vector space. In Proceedings of the 1st International Conference on Learning Representations, ICLR 2013-Workshop Track Proceedings, Scottsdale, AZ, USA, 2–4 May 2013.
19. Heigold, G.; Neumann, G.; Van Genabith, J. An Extensive Empirical Evaluation of Character-Based Morphological Tagging for 14 Languages. In Proceedings of the 15th Conference of the European Chapter of the Association for Computational Linguistics, EACL 2017-Proceedings of Conference, Valencia, Spain, 3–7 April 2017; Volume 1.
20. Dozat, T.; Manning, C.D. Deep biaffine attention for neural dependency parsing. In Proceedings of the 5th International Conference on Learning Representations, ICLR 2017-Conference Track Proceedings, Toulon, France, 24–26 April 2017.
21. Burtsev, M.; Seliverstov, A.; Airapetyan, R.; Arkhipov, M.; Baymurzina, D.; Bushkov, N.; Gureenkova, O.; Khakhulin, T.; Kuratov, Y.; Kuznetsov, D.; et al. DeepPavlov: Open-Source library for dialogue systems. In Proceedings of the 56th Annual Meeting of the Association for Computational Linguistics-System Demonstrations, Melbourne, Australia, 15–20 July 2018; pp. 122–127. [CrossRef]
22. Kara, E.; Zeen, T.; Gabryszak, A.; Budde, K.; Schmidto, D.; Roller, R. A domain-adapted dependency parser for German clinical text. In Proceedings of the KONVENS 2018—Conference on Natural Language Processing/Die Konferenz zur Verarbeitung Naturlicher Sprache, Vienna, Austria, 19–21 September 2018.
23. Fan, J.w.; Yang, E.W.; Jiang, M.; Prasad, R.; Loomis, R.M.; Zisook, D.S.; Denny, J.C.; Xu, H.; Huang, Y. Syntactic parsing of clinical text: Guideline and corpus development with handling ill-formed sentences. *J. Am. Med. Inform. Assoc.* **2013**, *20*, 1168–1177. [CrossRef] [PubMed]
24. Christou, M.; Crochemore, M.; Flouri, T.; Iliopoulos, C.S.; Janoušek, J.; Melichar, B.; Pissis, S.P. Computing all subtree repeats in ordered ranked trees. In Proceedings of the Lecture Notes in Computer Science (Including Subseries Lecture Notes in Artificial Intelligence and Lecture Notes in Bioinformatics), Virtual Event, 3–5 December 2011; Volume 7024.
25. Christou, M.; Crochemore, M.; Flouri, T.; Iliopoulos, C.S.; Janoušek, J.; Melichar, B.; Pissis, S.P. Computing all subtree repeats in ordered trees. *Inf. Process. Lett.* **2012**, *112*, 958–962. [CrossRef]
26. Bizer, C.; Lehmann, J.; Kobilarov, G.; Auer, S.; Becker, C.; Cyganiak, R.; Hellmann, S. DBpedia—A crystallization point for the Web of Data. *J. Web Semant.* **2009**, *7*, 154–165. [CrossRef]
27. Thorne, C.; Faralli, S.; Stuckenschmidt, H. Cross-evaluation of entity linking and disambiguation systems for clinical text annotation. In Proceedings of the ACM International Conference Proceeding Series, Indianapolis, IN, USA, 24–28 October 2016.
28. Turki, H.; Shafee, T.; Hadj Taieb, M.A.; Ben Aouicha, M.; Vrandečić, D.; Das, D.; Hamdi, H. Wikidata: A large-scale collaborative ontological medical database. *J. Biomed. Inform.* **2019**, *99*, 103292. [CrossRef] [PubMed]
29. Parravicini, A.; Patra, R.; Bartolini, D.B.; Santambrogio, M.D. Fast and accurate entity linking via graph embedding. In Proceedings of the ACM SIGACT-SIGMOD-SIGART Symposium on Principles of Database Systems, Amsterdam, The Netherlands, 30 June–5 July 2019.
30. Perozzi, B.; Al-Rfou, R.; Skiena, S. DeepWalk: Online learning of social representations. In Proceedings of the ACM SIGKDD International Conference on Knowledge Discovery and Data Mining; New York, New York, NY, USA, 24–27 August 2014.
31. Rehurek, R.; Sojka, P. *Gensim—Python Framework for Vector Space Modelling*; NLP Centre, NLP Centre, Faculty of Informatics, Masaryk University: Brno, Czech Republic, 2011; p. 3.
32. CSIRO's Data61. StellarGraph Machine Learning Library. GitHub Repository. Available online: https://github.com/stellargraph/stellargraph (accessed on 30 December 2021).

Journal of *Personalized Medicine*

MDPI

Article

# Implementation of Privacy and Security for a Genomic Information System Based on Standards

**Silvia Llorente *** and **Jaime Delgado ***

Information Modeling and Processing (IMP) Group—DMAG (Distributed Multimedia Applications Group), Computer Architecture Department, Universitat Politècnica de Catalunya · BarcelonaTech, 08034 Barcelona, Spain
* Correspondence: silvia.llorente@upc.edu (S.L.); jaime.delgado@upc.edu (J.D.)

**Abstract:** Genomic information is a very sensitive type of digital information as it not only applies to a person, but also to close relatives. Therefore, privacy provision is key to protecting genomic information from unauthorized access. It is worth noting that most of the current genomic information formats do not provide specific mechanisms by which to secure the stored information. In order to solve, among other things, the privacy provision issue, we proposed the GIPAMS (Genomic Information Protection And Management System) modular architecture, which is based on the use of standards such as ISO/IEC 23092 and a few GA4GH (Global Alliance for Genomics and Health) initiatives. Some of the GIPAMS modules have already been implemented, mainly based on ISO/IEC 23092 features, and we are conducting work on the complete version of the architecture, and other standards are also considered. One of the objectives of GIPAMS is to enable the management of different formats of genomic information in a unique and interoperable way, providing privacy and security for formats that do not currently support them.

**Keywords:** genomics; privacy; security; modular architecture; GIPAMS; standards



**Citation:** Llorente, S.; Delgado, J. Implementation of Privacy and Security for a Genomic Information System Based on Standards. *J. Pers. Med.* **2022**, *12*, 915. https://doi.org/10.3390/jpm12060915

Academic Editors: Bernd Blobel and Mauro Giacomini

Received: 25 April 2022
Accepted: 30 May 2022
Published: 31 May 2022



## 1. Introduction

Genomic information is a very sensitive type of digital information. If it is leaked, it becomes public "forever". However, this is not the worst of the potential consequences; if some genomic information is leaked, not only will one person's information be revealed, but her close relatives' information is also impacted. So, it is key to define mechanisms for providing privacy and security related to genomic information.

Genomic information is currently stored in different file formats and locations, making it difficult for researchers, and, in general, health professionals to access it. Moreover, file sizes may be up to several hundreds of GB, complicating its transmission and manipulation. Finally, researchers need to follow strict authorization procedures to access some genomic studies, hindering possible research advances due to the complexity of such an authorization process.

In order to solve some of these issues, we present our proposal for a secure modular system in this paper, called GIPAMS (Genomic Information Protection And Management System) [1]. With this system, we attempt to provide a solution to the problem of privacy protection of genomic information. It implements mechanisms for providing privacy as well as secure storage, search and access to genomic information. We already described a preliminary version of this system in [1], but it is still under improvement, as we explain in this paper. Although the proposed system architecture is standards-agnostic, most of the modules implemented in this version are based on the ISO/IEC 23092 standard, also known as MPEG-G (Genomic Information Representation) [2,3], as we further describe in the following sections.

Nevertheless, ISO/IEC 23092 is not the only way of representing genomic information. The Global Alliance for Genomics and Health (GA4GH) [4] also defines protected genomic information representation formats, such as Crypt4GH [5], and ways of authorizing and authenticating access to genomic information, such as GA4GH Passports [6,7] and Authentication and Authorization Infrastructure (AAI) [8,9]. Moreover, they embrace some of the most relevant genomic file formats such as SAM/BAM [10] or CRAM [11] for the representation and storage of genomic information. Based on this, we also describe how GA4GH standards can help us in improving GIPAMS.

The aim of the work presented in this paper is to describe how genomic information can be managed in a secure way using a modular architecture (GIPAMS [1]) based on standardized information formats, specifically ISO/IEC 23092 [2,3]. Moreover, we explain some implementation details (programming languages, tools, etc.) of the GIPAMS architecture together with improvements we plan to apply to the current version. These improvements include, among other things, the use of other secure standardized formats, such as Crypt4GH [5], or authorization technologies such as AAI [8,9] and GA4GH Passports [6,7], all coming from GA4GH [4]. To do so, we propose the "duplication" of some modules of the architecture in order to support the different file formats and protection and authorization mechanisms. Other possible improvement is the implementation of a federation of GIPAMS to facilitate communication and interoperability between different organizations in charge of genomic information storage and management.

In the rest of this section, we briefly describe ISO/IEC 23092, as it will be further developed in Sections 1.1 and 2.2. Moreover, we describe some GA4GH mechanisms for the provision of privacy and security for genomic information.

### 1.1. ISO/IEC 23092 (Genomic Information Representation)

ISO/IEC 23092 Information Technology - Genomic Information Representation [2,3] is a standard devoted to the representation of compressed genomic information including appropriate security and privacy features [12–14] since its inception following a Security and Privacy by Design approach [15]. It is composed of six parts, most of them already published. Some of them are even under revision for new editions [16–20], and one of them is still under development [21]. Part 1 is devoted to the Transport and Storage of Genomic Information. Part 2 describes the Coding of Genomic Information. Part 3 is more relevant for this work, as it defines Genomic Information Metadata and Application Programming Interfaces (APIs). Part 4 specifies the Reference Software. Part 5 addresses Conformance, and Part 6 defines the coding of genomic annotations.

The ISO/IEC 23092-3 is devoted to protection [18]. Amongst other security features, it defines the selective encryption of sequencing data and metadata, and enforces privacy with the definition of privacy rules that can also be applied to genomic data and associated metadata. In addition to privacy rules and encryption, digital signatures can be applied to the information to assure integrity by preventing tampering. However, signatures are not the only mechanism to prevent the tampering of genomic data, as fingerprinting has also been considered [22].

These protection mechanisms can be applied at different levels inside ISO/IEC 23092 conformant files, providing high granularity when securing genomic data [12,13]. Each identifiable portion of the coded file can be encrypted to protect confidentiality or signed to protect integrity. In order to provide access control to the protected information, encryption and privacy rules have to be combined, ensuring that only authorized users can perform an action on the information.

ISO/IEC 23092 provides a syntax expressed in XML language [23], to support different strategies for encrypting and signing genomic information. For instance, we could define encryption and access control with privacy rules for data and only signature for metadata. Another scenario could be the encryption and application of privacy rules associated with just metadata, leaving out genomic information. Possible protection strategies also provide support for key retrieval, key derivation, key wrappers and, as already mentioned, signatures [18]. Some of these ideas are described in more detail in [24]. In Section 2, we describe ISO/IEC 23092 standard features and how we used them to design and implement GIPAMS.

### 1.2. Global Alliance for Genomics and Health (GA4GH)

The Global Alliance for Genomics and Health (GA4GH) [4] defines itself as "a policy-framing and technical standards-setting organization, seeking to enable responsible genomic data sharing within a human rights framework".

As mentioned before, there are several initiatives within GA4GH that manage security, privacy, authentication and the authorization of access to genomic content, at different levels, such as Passports [6,7], Authentication and Authorization Infrastructure (AAI) [8,9] and Crypt4GH [5]. GA4GH also defines communication protocols to interchange genomic information, such as the htsget API [25,26]. htsget defines a data retrieval application programming interface (API) based on well-known standards and recommendations such as HTTP(S), JSON [27] and OAuth 2.0 [28]. It supports the retrieval of data for different genomic data formats, such as SAM/BAM [10] or CRAM [11].

We briefly describe some of these initiatives in the following Section.

#### 1.2.1. GA4GH Passports

GA4GH Passports [6,7] define a mechanism by which to determine whether a researcher can access some genomic information based on the data contained in her passport. The structure of a GA4GH Passport is sketched in Figure 1. Objects and tokens are grouped together as presented. There are two separate sections inside the passport, one for the Access Token and the other for the Passport Claim, where different Passport Visas can be found. Each Passport Visa can be issued by a different organization, whose signature is included to provide integrity and authentication to the issued visa.

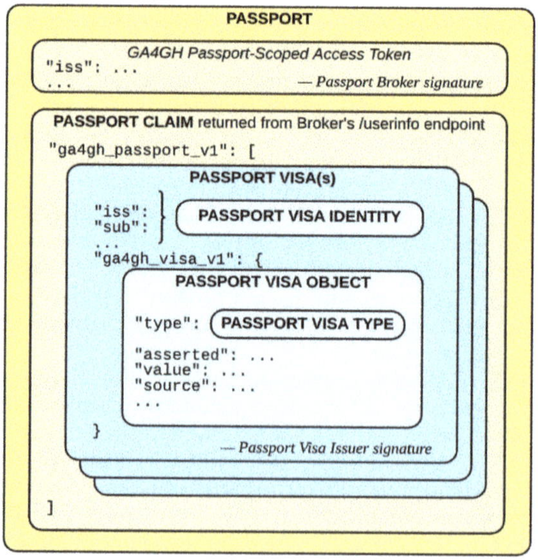


**Figure 1.** The composition of objects and tokens within a Passport. Source [7].

The basic flow of data from the Passport Visa Assertion Source to Passport Clearinghouse Service is shown in Figure 2. As it can be seen, there are different services involved in the process. Some of the steps are completely defined by GA4GH in [7], such as the one between Passport Broker and Passport Clearinghouse services. Other services just need to be compliant, such as the ones involved with Passport Visa, and others remain unspecified, such as the communication between services until reaching the Passport Broker.

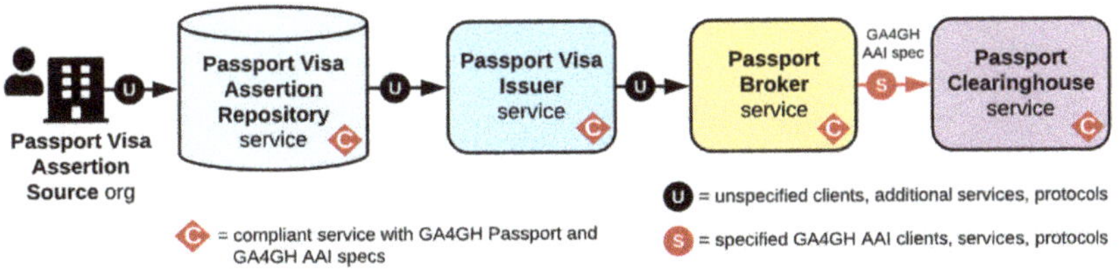


**Figure 2.** Basic flow of data from Passport Visa Assertion Source to Passport Clearinghouse. Source [7].

Some limitations of the first version of GA4GH Passport led to the development of version 1.2, which will allow for the separation of Passport visas from other personal information, and 2.0, which attempts to solve more sophisticated security issues in the token interchange process.

#### 1.2.2. GA4GH Authorization and Authentication Infrastructure (AAI)

GA4GH Authorization and Authentication Infrastructure (AAI) [8,9] defines mechanisms for authenticating an individual and authorizing access to a dataset, independent of being genomic or not, as GA4GH AAI claims to be "domain agnostic". It makes use of the OpenID Connect standard [29] to introduce the concept of the "access token".

In particular, AAI profiles the OpenID Connect protocol to provide a federated authentication and authorization infrastructure between genomics institutions in order to facilitate interoperability, especially when, but not limited to, sharing restricted datasets.

The relationship between GA4GH Passports and AAI is that AAI provides a method for identifying users and transporting claims related to them, whilst Passports provide the data format for converting user claims into permissions associated with datasets, user roles, resources and more.

In this way, an AAI access token can be included in the Passport to transport a researcher's digital identity and permissions. Then, these permissions can be mapped to the specific organizations, tools and environments, favoring federation handling, as it can manage different organizations, tools and environments.

#### 1.2.3. Crypt4GH File Format

Crypt4GH [5] is the file format defined by GA4GH [4] used to encrypt genomic files to provide them with confidentiality, integrity and authentication. To do so, the use of several encryption keys is defined, both symmetric and asymmetric, which are used to protect both header packets and genomic data.

Figure 3 shows the file structure. It can be seen that the first level of this structure consists of Header and Data Blocks. Inside the Header, we can find Header Packets containing encryption information, which are basically the keys and encryption methods needed to decrypt the genomic data for the different users with access to the file. A combination of asymmetric reader and writer keys is used to obtain the symmetric key used for encrypting data blocks. Both header packets and data blocks contain a Message Authentication Code (MAC), to ensure its authentication.

To process the file, the reader first has to read the Header, checking that the magic number and version provided match the expected values. Then, she should attempt to decode all header packets, ignoring those whose MAC cannot be verified, as this means that this specific header packet was not intended for this reader. If no header packet has been verified after processing all of them, an error has to be reported. If there is more than one header packet verified, the reader must store all the keys decoded in order to process the corresponding data blocks.

The data blocks decoding process involves the authentication and decryption of the segment(s) enclosing the data range required by the reader, expressed by two numbers, P and Q, where $P < Q$.

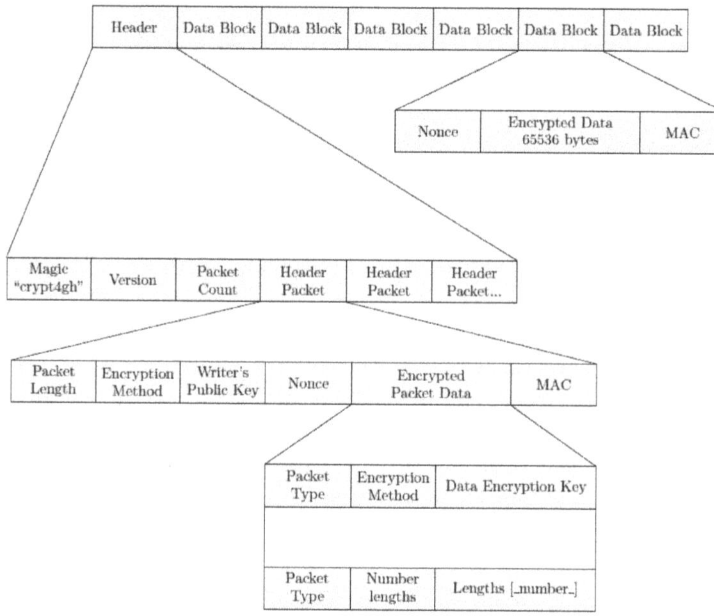


**Figure 3.** Crypt4GH file structure. Source [5].

To decrypt the required data range, the initial segment, including the Nonce and the MAC, is read. After that, an authentication tag is calculated over the cipher-text and compared with the MAC read from the file. The cipher-text is authenticated if and only if both tags match. If there is more than one key for decrypting data in the header, each one has to be checked until one authenticates the segment or no keys are left. In case no key authenticates the cipher-text, an error should be reported.

To effectively decrypt the cipher-text, the key authenticating the MAC and the Nonce are used, returning the corresponding plain text. The process is repeated for the subsequent segments, until the segment containing position Q is reached.

Ref. [5] defines the encryption and authentication methods accepted together with some considerations on how to improve the decryption process after keys are decoded from the header packets.

## 2. Materials and Methods

This section describes in detail the development and set-up of the Genomic Information Protection And Management System (GIPAMS) [1]. Some of the proposed modules have an initial implementation that can be accessed at [30]. It is worth noting that this is not an outline of the complete implementation of the system, as it is currently under development as further explained in the following subsections. Moreover, we also describe how GIPAMS follows some of ISO/IEC 23092 features.

### 2.1. *Genomic Information and Protection Management System (GIPAMS)*

The Genomic Information Protection And Management System, GIPAMS, is an evolution of our original Multimedia Information Protection And Management System, MIPAMS [31]. It transitioned from managing multimedia content to genomic content, but the underlying concepts remain, i.e., providing a secure standards-based modular architecture for managing the information and its associated metadata. To achieve this, we used the features defined in the different parts of the ISO/IEC 23092 GIPAMS architecture and structure, as depicted in Figure 4.

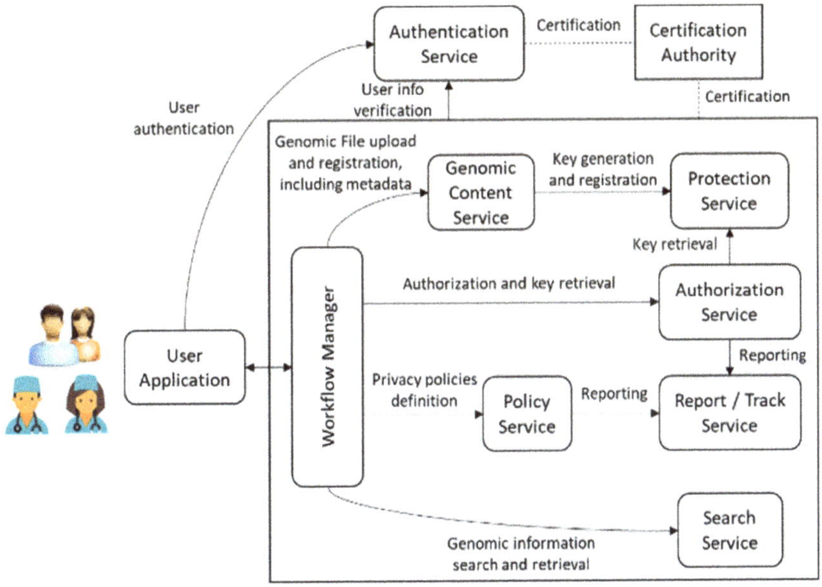


**Figure 4.** GIPAMS architecture.

We already performed a partial pilot implementation [1] of the architecture mainly based on ISO/IEC 23092 features. Nevertheless, this is the expected final complete picture, where other standardization initiatives may be considered, as further described in Section 4.1. The functionality of the different modules is as follows:

- User Application (UA): Access point to the whole system. It sends all requests to the Workflow Manager, which redirects to the corresponding module based on the action requested by the user. An access token is required, which is provided by the Authentication Service. Communication between this application and the rest of the architecture is performed through a secure channel. It is currently implemented as a web application but it could be a desktop application or even a mobile application.
- Workflow Manager (WM): Intermediate module that acts as a unique entry point to the system to facilitate interactions with the other modules, making them transparent to the final user. Before redirecting to the module in charge of an operation coming from the User Application, it checks if this operation is authorized using the information inside the access token.
- Authentication Service (ATS): Server in charge of user identification. It provides authentication features using OAuth 2.0 [28] and JSON Web Tokens [32]. Its implementation is currently based on Keycloak [33], although other providers may be considered, such as FusionAuth [34] or Gluu [35].
- Genomic Content Service (GCS): Module in charge of genomic archives management, both in reading and writing operations. In case genomic data has to be protected (encrypted or signed), it may connect with the Protection Service to obtain the required keys. It also manages metadata storage.
- Authorization Service (AS): Module which validates authorization rules. It is currently based on WSO2 Balana [36]. Authorization requests are usually sent from the Workflow Manager responding to user actions, but other modules may also interact with it to request the authorization of internal operations.
- Search Service (SS): Module which performs searches over genomic information (especially metadata). In order to provide extra filtering features, it uses a relational database

where metadata fields are stored. It must be checked by means of authorization rules so that the returned results can be seen by the user requesting them.
- Policy Service (PS): Module in charge of the creation of the authorization rules. In the current version of this module, which makes use of eXtensible Access Control Markup Language (XACML) [37], they are organized into XACML policies and rules.
- Protection Service (PTS): Module which creates protection information metadata associated with genomic information. It applies the defined mechanisms (i.e., encryption, signature, etc.) to the corresponding genomic data or metadata.
- Report/Track Service (RTS): Module in charge of reporting the operations implemented in the system, especially those not authorized. It helps in keeping track of illegal/unusual operations that may indicate an attempt to attack the system.
- Certification Authority (CA): This is not a real module of the system, but something required for its proper functioning. It provides the certificates needed to establish secure connections between the different system components.

### 2.2. ISO/IEC 23092 Relationship with GIPAMS

As already mentioned throughout this paper, ISO/IEC 23092 was adopted as a starting point for the implementation of GIPAMS (Genomic Information Protection And Management System) architecture as it provides different features that can be separated into interconnected modules to provide the complete picture. Some of these features are outlined below.

- Hierarchical organization of the genomic information thanks to the file structure defined in the standard [16].
- Compression of genomic information, by means of standardized compression algorithms [18].
- Metadata at different levels of the hierarchy using the corresponding metadata box at the information level it applies, such as file, dataset group, dataset or access unit [18].
- Privacy rules used for access control on both genomic data and metadata, are stored in the corresponding protection box at the information level and apply to dataset groups or datasets [18]. This structure is described in Section 2.3.
- Encryption and protection mechanisms both for genomic data and metadata, stored in the corresponding protection box at the information level it applies to, with dataset groups, datasets or access units [18].
- Integrity by means of digital signatures, which can be applied to genomic data and metadata, stored in the corresponding protection box at the information level it applies to, including dataset groups, datasets or access units [18].

### 2.3. ISO/IEC 23092 File Structure

In order to support the security strategies proposed in ISO/IEC 23092, a hierarchical file format was defined, as shown in Figure 5. This file format combines protection and metadata elements with the genomic data. It is worth noting the security and privacy using the design approach taken into account in the definition of this file format.

Figure 5 shows the standardized format of an ISO/IEC 23092 file when working in an Access Unit Container (AUC) mode. When using AUC, genomic information is stored as access units, which are sets of coded genomic information that can be independently accessed and inspected. There is another mode, called the Descriptor Stream Container (DSC), where genomic information is organized in a different way, specifically, as descriptor streams. Both modes may contain the same base genomic information, although the difference lies in how it is organized, which depends on how and when genomic information has to be generated, processed and accessed. We will focus on the AUC mode for the description of the features presented.

The file is structured in hierarchical boxes, with the File as the root element, which has a header element, including basic file information. Inside the file structure, we can find Dataset Groups, which also have an associated header as well as metadata and protection information. The Dataset Group may contain one or more Datasets, which, in turn, may contain information boxes or other container boxes. The last level of the hierarchy may be organized in Access Units (AUC mode), as shown in Figure 5, or in Descriptor Streams (DSC mode), depending on how genomic information needs to be accessed. In the end, genomic information is stored in Blocks, regardless of the use of Access Units or Descriptor Streams. Figure 5 shows an example of a Dataset Group containing several Datasets, as well as support for protection and metadata. The indexation information appearing at the Dataset level supports direct access to different parts of the genomic information.

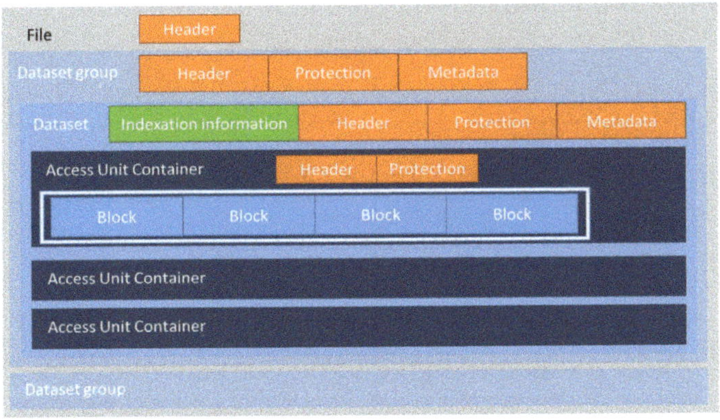


**Figure 5.** ISO/IEC 23092 basic file structure.

The advantages of the ISO/IEC 23092 file structure include the hierarchical organization and the fact that metadata and protection information are stored together with the genomic information itself, as described in Sections 2.4 and 2.5. Moreover, other advantages include the existence of an API for accessing information and the availability of authorization policies and rules also included inside the file. Finally, indexes can be defined to provide direct access to specific regions of the genomic information. The main current disadvantage is that it is not widely accepted for the moment, as there are well established genomic information formats used both in genomic research and clinical practice.

### *2.4. ISO/IEC 23092 Metadata*

The hierarchy defined in ISO/IEC 23092 attempts to represent the metadata structures for different organizations, such as the European Genome-Phenome Archive (EGA) [38] and the National Center for Biotechnology Information (NCBI) [39], among others. The Dataset Group represents concepts such as Study in EGA or BioProject in NCBI. Analogously, each dataset corresponds to a dataset in EGA or BioSample in NCBI.

ISO/IEC 23092 part 3 [18] stores metadata in the information boxes Dataset Group Metadata (dgmd) and Dataset Metadata (dtmd) using Extensible Markup Language (XML) [23]. We created some mappings in order to check that the metadata coming from EGA and NCBI are compatible with the developments required for GIPAMS architecture. The results of this mapping were diverse for different reasons, briefly outlined in the following section.

EGA uses a similar structure, so the mapping is direct, as represented in Table 1. For NCBI, the mapping was not as easy to achieve, as there are some differences. For example, the Abstract field is not present in NCBI metadata and their Type is not identical in both cases. This mapping is represented in Table 2.

On the other hand, ISO/IEC 23092 provides a mechanism by which to store additional information inside metadata fields. To test this mechanism, we defined some extensions for the NCBI metadata, represented in Table 3 and briefly described next. The field StudyDesign indicates an epidemiological or omics research design context in which a sample was used.

BodySite stores information about the type of tissue the sample was taken from. AnalyteType represents the biological specimen sampled from a subject (e.g., DNA from blood). The IsTumor indicates whether the sample corresponds to a tumor or not. These mappings have their corresponding XML representation according to ISO/IEC 23092 part 3 [18].

**Table 1.** EGA metadata mapping.

| MPEG-G Field | EGA Field |
|---|---|
| Title | Study-STUDY_TITLE |
| Type | Study-STUDY_TYPE |
| Abstract | Study-STUDY_ABSTRACT |
| ProjectCentre | Study-CENTER_PROJECT_NAME |
| Description | Study-STUDY_DESCRIPTION |
| Sample-TaxonId | Assembly-TAXON_ID |
| Sample-Title | Assembly-TITLE |

**Table 2.** NCBI metadata mapping.

| MPEG-G Field | NCBI Field |
|---|---|
| Title | BioProject-Title |
| Type | BioProject-ProjectTypeSubmission |
| Abstract | Non existent |
| ProjectCentre | BioProject-Organization |
| Description | BioProject-Description |
| Sample-TaxonId | BioSample-TAXON_ID |
| Sample-Title | BioSample-TITLE |

**Table 3.** Attribute extension fields.

| Attribute Extension | NCBI Field |
|---|---|
| StudyDesign | BioSample-Attribute-study design |
| BodySite | BioSample-Attribute-body site |
| AnalyteType | BioSample-Attribute-analyte type |
| IsTumor | BioSample-Attribute-is tumor |

### 2.5. ISO/IEC 23092 Privacy Rules

In current version of ISO/IEC 23092, privacy rules are expressed in the eXtensible Access Control Markup Language (XACML) standard [37], from OASIS [40]. XACML defines several information structures in order to support authorization mechanisms.

Regarding the definition of policies and rules, it describes the elements PolicySet, Policy and Rule. A PolicySet may have some Policy elements, which, in turn, may contain some Rule elements. XACML defines some algorithms to combine policies and rules when authorizing some action.

On the other hand, in order to ask for authorization, the XACML Request concept is required. These requests include the attributes that are sent to the XACML authorization mechanism, which attempts to match with the existing policies and rules in order to return an authorization decision.

Inside XACML rules, different information elements can be defined, as presented in [12–14]:

1. Who is able to access to the genomic information (user roles or individuals);
2. Wat information can be accessed (the complete file, a chromosome, etc.);
3. When it can be accessed;
4. With which purpose (genetic analysis, anonymized study, etc.) it can be accessed;
5. Whether the data provider has to be informed when information is accessed; and
6. Which specific permission is provided.

In our approach, the privacy rules are represented using XACML and the possible actions are defined in the ISO/IEC 23092 Application Programming Interface (API) [18]. We convey privacy rules only at the Dataset Group and the Dataset levels, as there are no specific actions for Access Unit level. An XACML policy element is included in the ISO/IEC 23092 protection XML schema. In this way, each protection element inside the file may have its corresponding privacy policy, which, in turn, may have several privacy rules, controlling access to different parts of the file.

The methods defined in the API also use other attributes. For example, in GetDataBySimpleFilter, the user can select whether multiple alignments [41] should be considered in the returned result. Filtering can be relevant to the privacy rules (most notably when used to delimit the returned region of the genome); therefore, in our proposal, this should also be included in the request. This translates, for example, into an attribute with its ID equal to presence_of_multiple_alignments.

The rule shown in Figure 6 allows for the execution of the operation GetDataBySimpleFilter by the role practitioner under some conditions intended to protect regions helping to identify Alzheimer's disease predisposition (it is not an exhaustive list, as some conditions are missing):

- Under an emergency situation.
- For a read count of 5000.
- Without multiple alignments.
- For reference sequence equal to 4, considering a range between 40,810,027 and 41,216,714, with both extremes included.

```
<Rule RuleId="urn:oasis:names:tc:xacml:2.0:ejemplo:RuleGen" Effect="Permit">
  <Description>
    Get Data by Simple Filter from Dataset for practitioner under Emergency situation
  </Description>
  <Target>
    <AnyOf>
      <AllOf>
       <!-- Which kind of user: practitioner -->
       <Match MatchId="urn:oasis:names:tc:xacml:1.0:function:string-equal">
         <AttributeValue DataType="http://www.w3.org/2001/XMLSchema#string">
           practitioner
         </AttributeValue>                                              Role
         <AttributeDesignator MustBePresent="true"
           Category="urn:oasis:names:tc:xacml:1.0:subject-category:access-subject"
           AttributeId="urn:oasis:names:tc:xacml:3.0:example:attribute:role"
           DataType="http://www.w3.org/2001/XMLSchema#string"/>
       </Match>
       <!-- Which action  -->
       <Match MatchId="urn:oasis:names:tc:xacml:1.0:function:string-equal">
         <AttributeValue DataType="http://www.w3.org/2001/XMLSchema#string">
           GetDataBySimpleFilter
         </AttributeValue>                                           Action
         <AttributeDesignator MustBePresent="true"
           Category="urn:oasis:names:tc:xacml:3.0:attribute-category:action"
           AttributeId="urn:oasis:names:tc:xacml:1.0:action:action-id"
           DataType="http://www.w3.org/2001/XMLSchema#string"/>
       </Match>
      </AllOf>
    </AnyOf>
  </Target>
  <Condition> <!-- Which conditions  -->
    <Apply FunctionId="urn:oasis:names:tc:xacml:1.0:function:and">
      <Apply FunctionId="urn:oasis:names:tc:xacml:1.0:function:string-equal">
       <Apply FunctionId="urn:oasis:names:tc:xacml:1.0:function:string-one-and-only">
         <AttributeDesignator MustBePresent="true"
           Category="urn:oasis:names:tc:xacml:3.0:string" AttributeId="situation"
           DataType="http://www.w3.org/2001/XMLSchema#string"/>
       </Apply>
       <AttributeValue DataType="http://www.w3.org/2001/XMLSchema#string">
         Emergency
       </AttributeValue>                            Emergency condition
      </Apply>
```

**Figure 6.** *Cont.*

```
<Apply FunctionId="urn:oasis:names:tc:xacml:1.0:function:
                integer-less-than-or-equal">
 <Apply FunctionId="urn:oasis:names:tc:xacml:1.0:function:integer-one-and-only">
   <AttributeDesignator MustBePresent="true" Category="count"
                        AttributeId="read_count"
                        DataType="http://www.w3.org/2001/XMLSchema#integer"/>
 </Apply>
 <AttributeValue DataType="http://www.w3.org/2001/XMLSchema#integer">
   5000
 </AttributeValue>                                  Read count condition
</Apply>
<Apply FunctionId="urn:oasis:names:tc:xacml:1.0:function:boolean-equal">
 <Apply FunctionId="urn:oasis:names:tc:xacml:1.0:
                function:boolean-one-and-only">
   <AttributeDesignator MustBePresent="true" Category="alignment"
                        AttributeId="presence_of_multiple_alignments"
                        DataType="http://www.w3.org/2001/XMLSchema#boolean"/>
 </Apply>
 <AttributeValue DataType="http://www.w3.org/2001/XMLSchema#boolean">
   False                          Multiple alignments condition
 </AttributeValue>
</Apply>
<Apply FunctionId="urn:oasis:names:tc:xacml:1.0:function:and">
 <Apply FunctionId="urn:oasis:names:tc:xacml:1.0:function:integer-equal">
   <Apply FunctionId="urn:oasis:names:tc:xacml:1.0:function:
                  integer-one-and-only">
     <AttributeDesignator MustBePresent="true" Category="sequence"
                          AttributeId="reference_sequence"
                          DataType="http://www.w3.org/2001/XMLSchema#integer"/>
   </Apply>
   <AttributeValue DataType="http://www.w3.org/2001/XMLSchema#integer">
     4                              Reference sequence condition
   </AttributeValue>
 </Apply>

    <Apply FunctionId="urn:oasis:names:tc:xacml:1.0:function:
                   integer-greater-than-or-equal">
     <Apply FunctionId="urn:oasis:names:tc:xacml:1.0:function:
                    integer-one-and-only">
       <AttributeDesignator MustBePresent="true"
                            Category="urn:oasis:names:tc:xacml:3.0:integer"
                            AttributeId="position"
                            DataType="http://www.w3.org/2001/XMLSchema#integer"/>
     </Apply>
     <AttributeValue DataType="http://www.w3.org/2001/XMLSchema#integer">
       40810027
      </AttributeValue>                Positions in the reference condition
    </Apply>
    <Apply FunctionId="urn:oasis:names:tc:xacml:1.0:function:
                   integer-less-than-or-equal">
     <Apply FunctionId="urn:oasis:names:tc:xacml:1.0:function:integer-one-and-only">
       <AttributeDesignator MustBePresent="true"
                            Category="urn:oasis:names:tc:xacml:3.0:integer"
                            AttributeId="position"
                            DataType="http://www.w3.org/2001/XMLSchema#integer"/>
     </Apply>
     <AttributeValue DataType="http://www.w3.org/2001/XMLSchema#integer">
       41216714
     </AttributeValue>
    </Apply>
   </Apply>
  </Apply>
 </Condition>
</Rule>
```

**Figure 6.** XACML Genomic rule example.

For the particular case of ISO/IEC 23092 file elements, the definition of the resource is not required as the rule applies to the Dataset or Dataset Group where it is contained. So, the ISO/IEC 23092 file structure already provides the relationship between the rule and the data to which it refers (either a Dataset Group or a Dataset). Therefore, there is no need to link both in the rule, as the resource is implicitly associated with the policy.

Figure 6 shows the rule constructed to represent this information. First of all, it represents the role, practitioner, indicating that it is an attribute called role, defined in XACML version 3 [37], which is of category access-subject (defined in XACML version 1, as indicated by urn:oasis:names:tc:xacml:1.0:subject-category:access-subject). Then, the permitted action, GetDataBySimpleFilter, is defined as an action-id attribute of category action. Then, the Emergency condition is defined, using the attribute situation, specific for this rule. The rest of the conditions, the read count, the presence of multiple alignments, reference and positions in the reference, are also defined for this rule, not belonging to any XACML standardized category. It is worth noting the flexibility provided by XACML, as it helps to define the required attributes and categories for a specific use case such as ours.

Figure 7 shows an example of an XACML request considering some attributes such as role, date and action. The authorization result of this XACML request according to the XACML rule is Deny, as the role is not the same as the one defined in the rule shown in Figure 6.

```
<Request>
    <Attributes Category="urn:oasis:names:tc:xacml:1.0:subject-category:access-subject">
        <Attribute AttributeId="urn:oasis:names:tc:xacml:3.0:example:attribute:role"
            IncludeInResult="true">
            <AttributeValue DataType="http://www.w3.org/2001/XMLSchema#string">
                researcher                                                    Role
            </AttributeValue>
        </Attribute>
    </Attributes>
    <Attributes Category="urn:oasis:names:tc:xacml:3.0:date">
        <Attribute AttributeId="accessDate" IncludeInResult="true">
            <AttributeValue DataType="http://www.w3.org/2001/XMLSchema#date">
                2022-02-22
            </AttributeValue>                                                 Date
        </Attribute>
    </Attributes>
    <Attributes Category="urn:oasis:names:tc:xacml:3.0:attribute-category:action">
        <Attribute AttributeId="urn:oasis:names:tc:xacml:1.0:action:action-id"
            IncludeInResult="true">
            <AttributeValue DataType="http://www.w3.org/2001/XMLSchema#string">
                GetDataBySimpleFilter                                         Action
            </AttributeValue>
        </Attribute>
    </Attributes>
</Request>
```

**Figure 7.** XACML Genomic request example.

On the other hand, it is also possible to protect the privacy of other parts of the ISO/IEC 23092 files, such as metadata. In this case, the rule indicates the operation that can be performed over metadata (contained in the Dataset or the Dataset Group). Then, the rule(s) should be checked before a user or role performs any operation over metadata.

*2.6. Authorization Based on ISO/IEC 23092 Hierarchy*

The Application Programming Interface (API) methods defined for Dataset Group and Dataset in ISO/IEC 23092 are very similar. For instance, a user can request data with the GetDataBySimpleFilter method to retrieve information either from a Dataset Group or a Dataset. In the end, they are different methods, as each apply to a different data structure, but the privacy rule may have the same syntax. This may lead to multiple rules for the same method, applied to different levels of the hierarchy.

However, we can expect certain homogeneity when providing permissions. For example, in a Dataset Group for research purposes on Alzheimer's, we can expect all requests to Alzheimer's related regions of the genome to be granted. To simplify the privacy rules that need to be defined, we would ideally use a mechanism that delegates the permission for the dataset(s) to the container dataset group. Nevertheless, this mechanism should not impede on one dataset so as to diverge from the rules applied to the container dataset group. In other words, the permission for a dataset must be able to rely on a default dataset group-wide policy, but the dataset group-wide policy should not hide specificities of the dataset.

To manage this situation, we propose the following two algorithms: one for asking for access to a specific dataset and another one for asking for access to the complete dataset group. They are described in detail in the rest of the section, but they were originally introduced in Daniel Naro's PhD Thesis [24].

Figure 8 represents a case where the user makes a data request of information contained in a Dataset. In this case, only dataset-specific rules are checked. If permission is granted, then the corresponding data is returned. If not, the algorithm checks whether the equivalent request to the dataset group is granted, that is, the rules in the upper level are checked. If so, an additional attribute granted by the dataset group is added to the original request for the dataset.

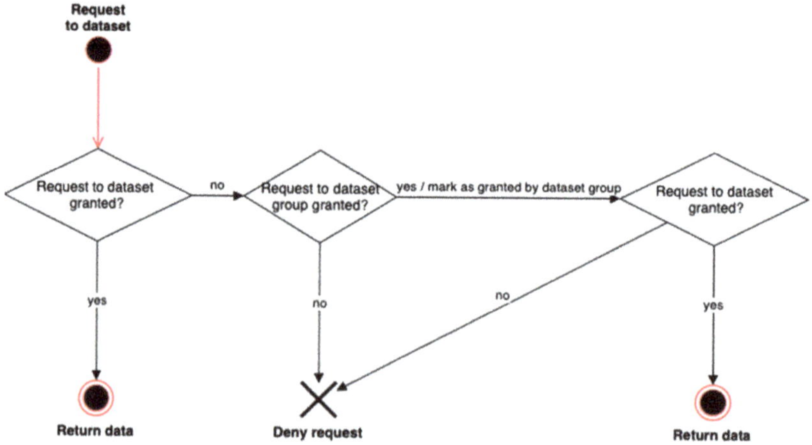


**Figure 8.** Privacy rules inheritance. Granting access to dataset from dataset group.

On the other hand, we want to prevent those denied access from accessing information. The process is shown in Figure 9, where it can be seen that, if access to the dataset group is granted, access to the specific datasets should be reviewed one by one to ensure that there are no different access rules for any of them. So, we navigate in the structure, going down in the hierarchy. In that case, specific rules for Datasets are checked, blocking the return of the data associated with this Dataset, if it is not granted by the corresponding rules. The granted results have to be stored during the process, in order to return the data coming from the granted Datasets to the user.

It is worth noting that, from the user perspective, it is required to build a, XACML Request containing some attributes that will be checked against the rules contained in the genomic file. As already explained in Section 2.5, these rules may be inside a dataset or dataset group, depending on the requested data and the authorization process required (going up or going down for the processing of the rules), as shown in Figures 8 and 9.

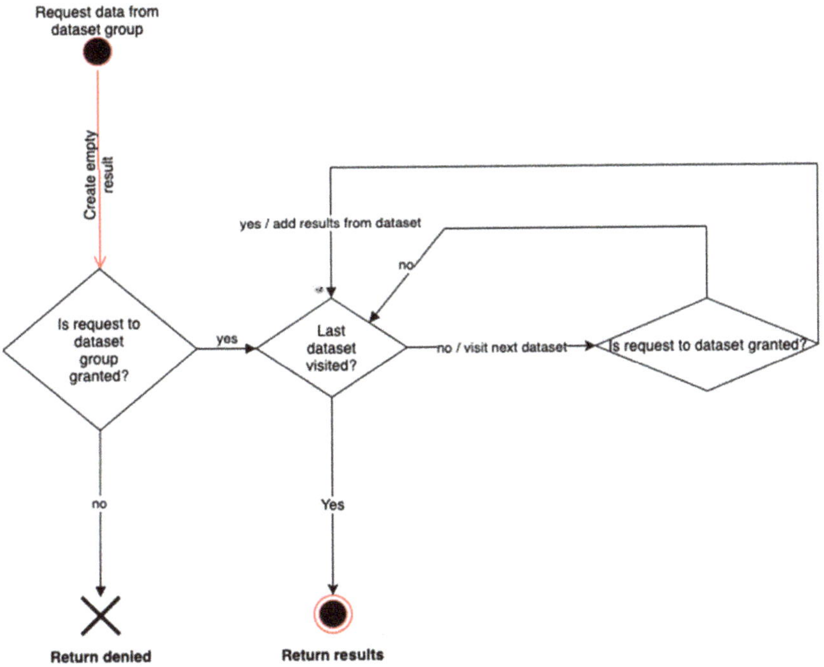


**Figure 9.** Privacy rules combining data from multiple structures. Check that dataset group rules are compatible with dataset rules.

## 3. Results

This section describes the research findings of this work. Some preliminary results were already sketched in [1]. Its source code can be found in [30].

Section 3.1 describes our implementation of the hierarchical ISO/IEC 23092 file structure to manipulate it in an easier way. It is worth noting that an ISO/IEC 23092 file size could reach up to several hundreds of GB, so, maintaining it in memory to perform different operations, such as accessing encrypted information, is a "hard" task for any program. In this way, splitting the file into several smaller files facilitates the creation and modification of the internal structure. Once the complete structure is created and protected, one can generate the MPEG-G file following the ISO/IEC 23092 structure.

Section 3.2 describes how the different modules are implemented, including details on programming language and architecture.

Some specific details of the implementation process are also described in the rest of this section.

### *3.1. File Structure Implementation*

As explained in Section 2.3, ISO/IEC 23092 files are structured in hierarchical boxes forming a single file. As already mentioned, the size of this file could be up to several hundreds of GB. To avoid having to deal with such large files and for the sake of testing, we used an alternative approach to simulate this structure, which consists of using the file system (folders and files) to represent the box hierarchy, as shown in Figure 10. In the end, the storage space used by our approach could be even greater than the ISO/IEC 23092 file. The point here is that we can access and manipulate all the information in an easier way, navigating through the folders and files.

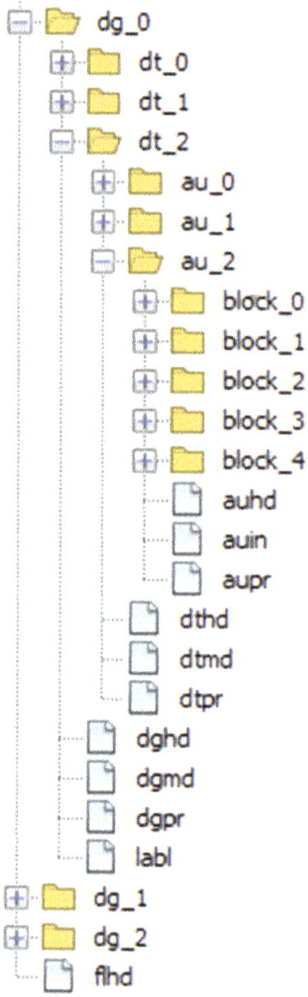


**Figure 10.** File structure example.

In this approach, every box is represented by a directory, which may have several files inside containing the header, metadata or protection information, depending on the elements present in a specific box according to the corresponding hierarchy level. Moreover, some subdirectories representing the inner boxes, that is, datasets inside dataset groups and so on, are also created. Each subdirectory may contain files associated with its hierarchy level. It is worth noting that some elements are optional, such as metadata or protection, so, they may not be present. So, in Figure 10, dataset groups are contained in dg_X folders, datasets are contained in dt_X folders, Access Units are contained in au_X folders and block_X folders contain the different Blocks inside an Access Unit.

Header files present in the boxes follow the pattern xxhd, where xx may be au for access units, dt for datasets, dg for dataset groups and fl for the complete file. Protection files follow a similar naming pattern, but using xxpr. Metadata files use the naming convention xxmd. The other files appearing in Figure 10 are labl, which represents the label element at the dataset level and auin, which stands for access unit information. The complete file structure can be found in [16].

The information files still need to be manipulated at the bit level, so we developed a Python script [30] that can generate this whole directory structure and create the information files for each hierarchy level using valid data. The script can also integrate real metadata and protection policies into the files, using the data provided by users in the form of XML files. Once the file system structure is created, the complete ISO/IEC 23092 file can be constructed from the directories and files stored in disk, in case it needs to be shared with some other researcher or organization.

*3.2. Modules Implementation*

GIPAMS modules [1] use the Java programming language [42] by implementing J2EE (Java 2 Platform Enterprise Edition) [43] compliant web applications. This is the base for User Application (UA), Workflow Manager (WM), Genomic Content Service (GCS), Authorization Service (AS) and Search Service (SS) modules. Some implementation details are provided in the following.

Keycloack [33] is used as the authentication provider. It is an open source software used by the UA to obtain a JSON Web Token (JWT) [32]. Then, this JWT is used to authenticate the user in front of the rest of services through the WM. An Nginx [44] reverse proxy is also needed to provide secure connections (through HTTPS) to Keycloack as it does not support it natively.

It is worth noting that, in our current implementation, only the UA is accessible from the Internet, while the rest of the services are only accessed locally. As already mentioned, it connects with the Keycloack service to achieve user authentication via the WM. As already mentioned, we implemented UA as a web application, but the UA could be implemented as a desktop application or even a mobile one.

The database used is MySQL [45], a well-known open source relational database where metadata is stored following the ISO/IEC 23092 hierarchical structure. This database is used by WM, GCS and SS, in order to find the information associated with the files stored in the system together with the user who created them and the corresponding metadata.

WM is the entry point to GIPAMS services, in this case, from the UA. We would like to highlight the fact that UA is implemented as a web application, but any application (mobile, desktop-based, etc.) could access GIPAMS services via the WM. WM confirms user authentication by means of JWT and, depending on the operation requested by the UA (file creation, dataset group or dataset creation or modification, metadata management, etc.), it also requests authorization before calling to the corresponding service. In this way, if the operation is not authorized in the first place, the service is never invoked, minimizing unauthorized operations as soon as possible. WM communication is implemented using REST (REpresentational State Transfer) [46] endpoints. Figure 11 shows an example of the operation calls workflow between UA, WM, AS and GCS.

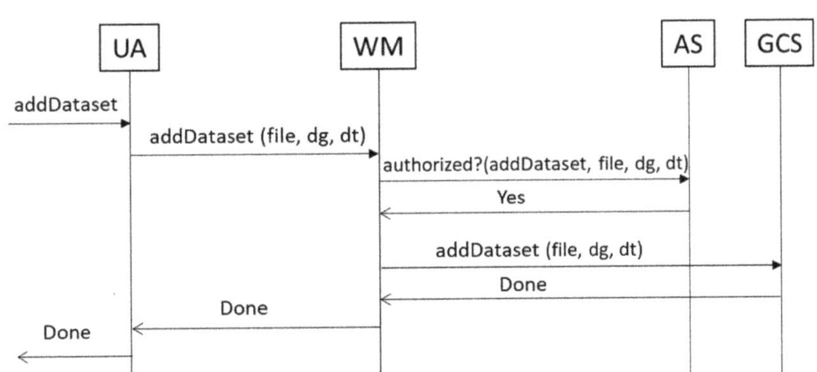


**Figure 11.** Example of operation workflow: addDataset.

AS does not require database access as it authorizes user actions based on XACML requests and rules. To do so, it uses WSO2 Balana [36], an open source implementation of XACML authorization mechanisms. The different modules request authorization for AS before genomic information (including metadata) can be accessed. The rules are stored as XML files in the ISO/IEC 23092 hierarchy as shown in Figure 10, inside dgpr or dtpr files. Apart from XACML policies and rules, these files may contain other protection information such as signatures or protection keys.

GCS manages ISO/IEC 23092 file hierarchy creation and management. The hierarchy is also stored in the database, to support searches over file structure and metadata. It also manages XML information derived from metadata and protection files. For the specific case of XML metadata files, their content is parsed and inserted in the database, so searches can be performed with SS. AS is used in order to authorize operations. Only the file creation operation does not require authorization, as it creates a new file, but the rest of the operations modifying the hierarchy (for instance, addDatasetGroup, editAnyElement or deleteAnyElement) should be authorized before they can be performed. In this case, several checks should be implemented, including file ownership.

SS provides a search interface for metadata stored inside the system database. Authorization is also required in this case, to ensure that the returned results are available for the user requesting them.

## 4. Discussion

A standards-based modular architecture such as GIPAMS has several advantages when providing security and privacy mechanisms to protect genomic information. The first one is that using standardized mechanisms favors interoperability, as implementation is based on published specifications. If there are other implementations dealing with the same standard genomic information format, GIPAMS should be able to support them. The second one is that, as each feature is implemented as an independent module, a module can be changed or updated without affecting the complete system. This provides support for new standard features in an easier way. It would even be possible to support different versions of a standard by replicating a module, as explained in Section 4.1, with GIPAMS extended architecture.

We are currently working on the complete implementation of GIPAMS, by integrating the encryption and signature features provided by the Protection Service (PTS) with the Genomic Content Service (GCS). Moreover, we aim to implement some of the improvements proposed in this paper with modules not only based on ISO/IEC 23092 but also with GA4GH features. One implementation we plan to achieve is to combine security features from both ISO/IEC 23092 and GA4GH in the Protection Service, using protection features derived from Crypt4GH into PTS, following the path described in Section 4.1. In this way, we can achieve the integration of different standardization initiatives into GIPAMS. The next modules to implement are the Policy Service and, finally, the Reporting/Track Service modules. It is worth noting that these are not core modules for the system, but accessory ones that provide extra features to support privacy and security provisions.

Furthermore, we also plan to account for GA4GH features when implementing new modules, i.e., to use several Genomic Content Services to support different file formats or alternatives to Authorization Service using other authorization technologies, as described further in the following section.

Finally, in Section 4.2, we describe the future work we foresee in different aspects related to GIPAMS, such as implementing different versions of the modules, search functionalities or a possible GIPAMS federation.

### 4.1. Alternatives for GIPAMS Modules Implementation Using Other Standards

GIPAMS was designed with ISO/IEC 23092 features in mind. Nevertheless, other standardized alternatives exist for some of the defined modules, as explained next.

Genomic Content Service (GCS) design is based on the ISO/IEC 23092 hierarchy. However, it is not difficult to define other GCS in order to support different genomic formats, such as Crypt4GH [5], SAM/BAM [10] or CRAM [11]. The most difficult part is the fact that these formats do not have all the features provided by ISO/IEC 23092 such as metadata, protection, hierarchy or indexing, and the connection with other modules will be more complex to achieve.

Authorization Service (AS) could also be implemented using GA4GH Passports [6]. Nevertheless, the use of XACML rules to provide privacy can be extended to other file formats, due to XACML authorization rules and requests for flexibility. In this way, a two way interoperability mechanism could be provided, combining both format and authorization mechanisms coming from different standardization initiatives, for example, by authorizing Crypt4GH or BAM files using XACML or authorizing access to GCS using GA4GH passports. Other combinations could be also defined and implemented, especially if public API specifications are provided.

Furthermore, a Search Service (SS) could be implemented as a beacon interface [47] to perform searches of genomic information stored inside GIPAMS. This module does not currently follow any standardized mechanism. It is worth noting that the AS is contacted to check that the query is authorized.

Policy Service (PS) relates to the AS, so the use of GA4GH Passports could be also indicated for this case. Again, XACML can be used to implement privacy rules over different genomic formats, not necessarily ISO/IEC 23092. We already have experience of the privacy protection of eHealth-related information using XACML, as described in [48,49]. Moreover, GA4GH was used to produce the Data Use Ontology (DUO) [50], which provides matching between data use restrictions on genomic data and intended research use requested by researchers. DUO could act as an alternative to XACML privacy policies when dealing with the definition of data usage restrictions. Nevertheless, an authorization mechanism is required to be as powerful as XACML currently is.

Protection Services (PTS) is currently based on the protection of information defined in ISO/IEC 23092. Again, the solution proposed for GCS, i.e., the implementation of protection methods coming from other standards, such as the ones in Crypt4GH [5], could be a feasible solution. In this case, the inclusion of encryption algorithms used in Crypt4GH in the ISO/IEC 23092 protection XML schema is a first step to extend security and protection features. On the other hand, defining more encryption algorithms into Crypt4GH data structures could also be performed. In the end, the implementation of different PTS depending on the file formats supported by GIPAMS could be also a feasible solution.

Report/Track Service (RTS) mainly derives from the need to track illegal/unusual operations. It is not really defined (at least with a formal structure and API) in ISO/IEC 23092, but it is required, as it is in other formats, as defined in [51]. The idea of defining such a module comes from MIPAMS, where a specific standard for reporting multimedia content operations was used, namely MPEG-21 Event Reporting [52].

Figure 12 shows how GIPAMS could be extended to support more standards, offering new and extended modules, providing additional functionality. Genomic Content Service (GCS) module may be replicated to support different genomic content formats. Each GCS may need a different Protection Service (PTS), as shown in Figure 12, depending on the file format and its security and protection mechanisms. Furthermore, Policy and Authorization Services (PS, AS) modules may be replicated to support different authorization mechanisms coming, for example, from ISO/IEC 23,092 or GA4GH. Finally, the Search Service (SS) could be implemented using the metadata stored in the database, as it is now, or by providing a Beacon-such as [47] SS.

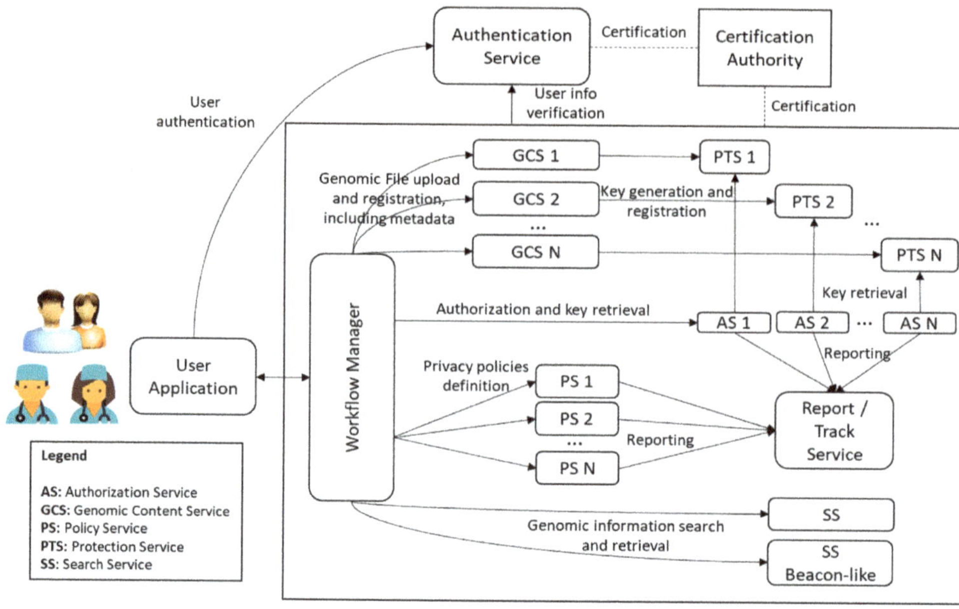


**Figure 12.** GIPAMS extended architecture.

### 4.2. Future Work

After completing GIPAMS implementation, we will integrate other standardization initiatives as alternate versions of the modules, as shown in Figure 12 This will lead us to GIPAMS version 2, where different genomic formats and related standards may interoperate. The complete implementation of PTS integrating ISO/IEC 23092 and the GA4GH mechanisms provides proof of concept that standards interoperability can really be achieved. We have already performed some testing on that direction, so we are confident that we will achieve complete PTS soon.

Furthermore, several GIPAMS instances could be established at different locations, providing a federated system. The definition of global access rules over metadata stored at the different locations may allow for the provision of a federated search whilst guaranteeing the privacy and security of the results. Having such a system, that is, GIPAMS federation, provides several advantages. The first is that each location only manages their own genomic information, so less storage and transmission is required. This is better than having several copies of the complete system. The second one is that although each location only contains its own metadata, the federated metadata search provides each location with the possibility of accessing the complete metadata describing other genomic studies that may be relevant. Discovering relevant information through the federated search may provide researchers with the opportunity requesting request access to genomic data (or part of it) in a secure and controlled way, as they may find genomic studies of interest in an easier way. In any case, rules for metadata should be checked before returning the results, as is already performed in one GIPAMS. Once a GIPAMS federation is established, new services and opportunities for researchers may arise, based on the federated search.

In order to facilitate relevant genomic information discovery, a metadata search may also include information on whether the genomic data associated with some metadata can be accessed partially or completely and how this access can be requested. This can be controlled by means of the access rules defined for genomic metadata and data and of course supported by the encryption/decryption of the information. This could be very useful for rare diseases, where a few cases are available and the privacy and security standards should be maximal in order to not to reveal patient identity, but, at the same time, provide the maximum visibility to find a treatment thanks to research results.

Finally, the application of different security mechanisms provides privacy protection for the genomic information managed inside GIPAMS. First of all, the communication between the user application and the rest of the modules/services is conducted through a secure channel. Moreover, tracking of user actions and unique user identification are also implemented. For the protection of the genomic data and metadata, different encryption techniques can be applied. To control which actions users can perform in the system, privacy protection rules can be defined with a high level of granularity. Although information could be leaked from the user's application, we should be aware of two relevant facts: (1) users are identified and "trustable" and (2) all actions related to the information are tracked.

## 5. Conclusions

This paper presents how we can provide security and privacy to genomic information using standards in a modular architecture. This is the basic idea of GIPAMS, a modular architecture for the secure management of genomic information, as introduced in Section 2.

For its purpose, we mainly focused on ISO/IEC 23092 features [2,3], as this is a genomic information format which has been developed using privacy by design principles since its inception. Such features, among others, are as follows: protection of information and privacy rules associated with genomic information, including metadata, a hierarchical structuring of the information, starting from the complete file and finishing on the blocks containing genomic information itself, and the possibility of associating security information with a high level of granularity.

Taking these features as a starting point, we developed a first implementation of GIPAMS, as a continuation of previous preliminary work [1].

Therefore, inside GIPAMS, we used the ISO/IEC 23092 hierarchical structure as a base point to facilitate the integration of other existing genomic information formats. In this way, search and linkage between different genomic formats could be easily achieved with the implementation of differentiated modules for each genomic content format. The Workflow Manager (WM) may orchestrate calls to the corresponding modules. Related to this, the extension metadata mechanism defined in ISO/IEC 23092 also assists in the inclusion and integration of new metadata, facilitating the implementation of more specific and accurate searches, thereby providing access to more research results with a common interface.

The idea of describing a modular architecture for managing content comes from MIPAMS [31], which was defined for the secure management of multimedia content. Some of the modules have evolved, but the underlying ideas remain, i.e., the provision of different modules in charge of the content creation and management, protection, governance and access control (by means of licenses) of multimedia content.

Therefore, by combining MIPAMS with ISO/IEC 23092, we defined GIPAMS module functionalities, how the communication among them should be performed and ways in which to implement a first version. In this paper, we went a step forward, as we did not only use ISO/IEC 23092 to support genomic information, but we also included GA4GH security mechanisms and authentication features, as explained before.

To integrate GA4GH standards into GIPAMS, we firstly identified the initiatives that can be included in current (or an evolved version of) GIPAMS modules. One of them is Crypt4GH [5], as it defines a file encryption standard and it involves both GCS and PTS modules. Another GA4GH initiative identified is Passports [6,7] and Authentication and Authorization Infrastructure (AAI) [8,9]. Both of them could be integrated or used as an alternative to the AS module. There are other initiatives inside GA4GH, such as Phenopackets [53,54], that we are also considering for its inclusion and support as part of GIPAMS. It is worth noting that Phenopackets is also an ISO standard [54].

**Author Contributions:** Conceptualization, J.D. and S.L.; methodology, J.D. and S.L.; software, S.L.; validation, J.D.; formal analysis, J.D. and S.L.; investigation, J.D. and S.L.; resources, J.D. and S.L.; data curation, J.D. and S.L.; writing—original draft preparation, S.L.; writing—review and editing, J.D. and S.L.; visualization, S.L.; supervision, J.D.; project administration, J.D.; funding acquisition, J.D. All authors have read and agreed to the published version of the manuscript.

**Funding:** This research has been partially supported by the Spanish Government under the project GenClinLab-Sec (Mechanisms for secure and efficient management of genomic information tailored to clinical laboratories: Security Aspects, PID2020-114394RB-C31) funded by MCIN/AEI/10.13039/501100011033 and by the Generalitat de Catalunya (2017 SGR 1749).

**Institutional Review Board Statement:** Not applicable.

**Informed Consent Statement:** Not applicable.

**Data Availability Statement:** Not applicable.

**Conflicts of Interest:** The authors declare no conflict of interest.

## References

1. Delgado, J.; Llorente, S.; Reig, G. Implementation of privacy and security for a genomic information system. In *pHealth 2021—Proceedings of the 18th International Conference on Wearable Micro and Nano Technologies for Personalized Health—Genoa, Italy, 8–10 November 2021*; Blobel, B., Giacomini, M., Eds.; Studies in Health Technology and Informatics Series; IOS Press: Amsterdam, The Netherlands, 2021; Volume 285, pp. 253–258. Available online: https://ebooks.iospress.nl/doi/10.3233/SHTI210609 (accessed on 8 February 2022).
2. *ISO/IEC 23092*; Information Technology—Genomic Information Representation. ISO/IEC: Geneva, Switzerland, 2020. Available online: https://www.mpeg.org/standards/MPEG-G/ (accessed on 8 February 2022).
3. Voges, J.; Hernaez, M.; Mattavelli, M.; Ostermann, J. An Introduction to MPEG-G: The First Open ISO/IEC Standard for the Compression and Exchange of Genomic Sequencing Data. *Proc. IEEE* **2021**, *109*, 1607–1622. [CrossRef]
4. Global Alliance for Genomics and Health (GA4GH). Available online: https://www.ga4gh.org/ (accessed on 8 February 2022).
5. GA4GH, GA4GH File Encryption Standard. Available online: https://www.ga4gh.org/wp-content/uploads/crypt4gh.pdf (accessed on 8 February 2022).
6. GA4GH, GA4GH Passports and the Authorization and Authentication Infrastructure. Available online: https://www.ga4gh.org/ga4gh-passports/ (accessed on 8 February 2022).
7. GA4GH, GA4GH Passport. Available online: https://github.com/ga4gh-duri/ga4gh-duri.github.io/blob/master/researcher_ids/ga4gh_passport_v1.md (accessed on 8 February 2022).
8. GA4GH, Introduction to the GA4GH Authentication and Authorization Infrastructure (AAI). Available online: https://github.com/ga4gh/data-security/tree/master/AAI (accessed on 8 February 2022).
9. GA4GH, Introduction to the GA4GH Authentication and Authorization Infrastructure (AAI) OpenID Connect Profile. Available online: https://github.com/ga4gh/data-security/blob/master/AAI/AAIConnectProfile.md (accessed on 10 March 2022).
10. Li, H.; Handsaker, B.; Wysoker, A.; Fennel, T.; Ruan, J.; Homer, N.; Marth, G.; Abecasis, G. The sequence alignment/map format and samtools. *Bioinformatics* **2009**, *25*, 2078–2079. [CrossRef] [PubMed]
11. Hsi-Yang Fritz, M.; Leinonen, R.; Cochrane, G.; Birney, E. Efficient storage of high throughput DNA sequencing data using reference-based compression. *Genome Res.* **2011**, *21*, 734–740. [CrossRef] [PubMed]
12. Delgado, J.; Llorente, S.; Naro, D. Adding Security and Privacy to Genomic Information Representation. In *ICT for Health Science Research*; Shabo, A., Madsen, I., Prokosch, H.-U., Häyrinen, K., Wolf, K.-H., Martin-Sanchez, F., Löbe, M., Deserno, T.M., Eds.; Studies in Health Technology and Informatics; IOS Press: Amsterdam, The Netherlands, 2019; Volume 258, pp. 75–79. Available online: http://ebooks.iospress.nl/publication/51356 (accessed on 8 February 2022).
13. Delgado, J.; Llorente, S.; Naro, D. Protecting privacy of genomic information. In *Informatics for Health: Connected Citizen-Led Wellness and Population Health*; Randell, R., Cornet, R., McCowan, C., Peek, N., Scott, P.J., Eds.; Studies in Health Technology and Informatics; IOS Press: Amsterdam, The Netherlands, 2017; Volume 235, pp. 318–322. Available online: http://ebooks.iospress.nl/volumearticle/46354 (accessed on 8 February 2022).
14. Delgado, J. Privacy, metadata and APIs in compressed genomic information: The MPEG-G case. In Proceedings of the GA4GH & MPEG Genome Compression Workshop, Basel, Switzerland, 3 October 2018. Available online: https://drive.google.com/file/d/14Y7qK5TmRM5b_5_F5x8UZfwJX3tDS11d/view?usp=sharing (accessed on 8 February 2022).
15. Cavoukian. Privacy by Design. Available online: https://www.ipc.on.ca/wp-content/uploads/resources/7foundationalprinciples.pdf (accessed on 8 February 2022).
16. *ISO/IEC 23092-1*; Information Technology—Genomic Information Representation—Part 1: Transport and Storage of Genomic Information. 3rd ed. ISO/IEC: Geneva, Switzerland, 2020. Available online: https://www.iso.org/standard/83526.html (accessed on 8 February 2022).

17. *ISO/IEC 23092-2;* Information Technology—Genomic Information Representation—Part 2: Coding of Genomic Information. 3rd ed. ISO/IEC: Geneva, Switzerland, 2020. Available online: https://www.iso.org/standard/83527.html (accessed on 8 February 2022).
18. *ISO/IEC 23092-3;* Information Technology—Genomic Information Representation—Part 3: Metadata and Application Programming Interfaces (APIs). 2nd ed. ISO/IEC: Geneva, Switzerland, 2020. Available online: https://www.iso.org/standard/82725.html (accessed on 8 February 2022).
19. *ISO/IEC 23092-4;* Information Technology—Genomic Information Representation—Part 4: Reference Software. 1st ed. ISO/IEC: Geneva, Switzerland, 2020. Available online: https://www.iso.org/standard/75859.html (accessed on 8 February 2022).
20. *ISO/IEC 23092-5;* Information Technology—Genomic Information Representation—Part 5: Conformance. 1st ed. ISO/IEC: Geneva, Switzerland, 2020. Available online: https://www.iso.org/standard/73668.html (accessed on 8 February 2022).
21. *ISO/IEC 23092-6;* Information Technology—Genomic Information Representation—Part 6: Coding of Genomic Annotations. 1st ed. ISO/IEC: Geneva, Switzerland, *under development*. Available online: https://www.iso.org/standard/78478.html (accessed on 8 February 2022).
22. Naro, D.; Delgado, J.; Llorente., S. Reversible fingerprinting for genomic information. *Multimed. Tools Appl.* **2020**, *79*, 8161–8180. [CrossRef]
23. W3C. *Extensible Markup Language (XML)*, version 1.1. 2nd ed. W3C: Cambridge, MA, USA. Available online: https://www.w3.org/TR/xml11/(accessed on 8 February 2022).
24. Naro, D. Security Strategies in Genomic Files. Ph.D. Thesis, Polytechnic University of Catalonia, Barcelona, Spain, 2020. Available online: http://hdl.handle.net/10803/669108 (accessed on 8 February 2022).
25. *Htsget Retrieval API*; spec v1.2.0; GA4GH: Toronto, ON, Canada, 2019. Available online: http://samtools.github.io/hts-specs/htsget.html (accessed on 8 February 2022).
26. Kelleher, J.; Lin, M.; Albach, C.H.; Birney, E.; Davies, R.; Gourtovaia, M.; Glazer, D.; Gonzalez, C.Y.; Jackson, D.K.; Kemp, A.; et al. Htsget: A protocol for securely streaming genomic data. *Bioinformatics* **2019**, *35*, 119–121. [CrossRef] [PubMed]
27. IETF. *The JavaScript Object Notation (JSON) Data Interchange Format*; IETF: Fremont, CA, USA, 2017. Available online: https://datatracker.ietf.org/doc/html/rfc8259 (accessed on 8 February 2022).
28. IETF. *The OAuth 2.0 Authorization Framework*; IETF: Fremont, CA, USA, 2012. Available online: https://datatracker.ietf.org/doc/html/rfc6749 (accessed on 8 February 2022).
29. OpenID Foundation. OpenID Connect. Available online: https://openid.net/connect/ (accessed on 8 March 2022).
30. Llorente, S. *GIPAMS v1*; GitHub: San Francisco, CA, USA, 2022. Available online: https://github.com/silvia-llorente/gipams-v1 (accessed on 8 March 2022).
31. Llorente, S.; Rodriguez, E.; Delgado, J.; Torres-Padrosa, V. Standards-based architectures for content management. *IEEE Multimed.* **2012**, *20*, 62–72. [CrossRef]
32. IETF. JSON Web Token (JWT). Available online: https://datatracker.ietf.org/doc/html/rfc7519 (accessed on 8 February 2022).
33. Keycloak. Open Source Identity and Access Management. Available online: https://www.keycloak.org/ (accessed on 8 February 2022).
34. FusionAuth. Available online: https://fusionauth.io/ (accessed on 8 February 2022).
35. Gluu. Available online: https://gluu.org/ (accessed on 8 February 2022).
36. WSO2. WSO2 Balana. Available online: https://github.com/wso2/balana (accessed on 8 February 2022).
37. OASIS. *eXtensible Access Control Markup Language (XACML)*, v3.0; OASIS: Woburn, MA, USA, 2017. Available online: http://docs.oasis-open.org/xacml/3.0/errata01/os/xacml-3.0-core-spec-errata01-os-complete.html(accessed on 8 February 2022).
38. European Genome-Phenome Archive (EGA). Available online: https://ega-archive.org/ (accessed on 8 February 2022).
39. National Center for Biotechnology Information (NCBI). Available online: https://www.ncbi.nlm.nih.gov/ (accessed on 8 February 2022).
40. OASIS. Available online: https://www.oasis-open.org/ (accessed on 8 February 2022).
41. Chowdhury, B.; Garai, G. A review on multiple sequence alignment from the perspective of genetic algorithm. *Genomics* **2017**, *109*, 419–431. [CrossRef] [PubMed]
42. Oracle, Oracle Java. Available online: https://www.oracle.com/java/ (accessed on 14 February 2022).
43. Oracle, Java 2 Platform Enterprise Edition (J2EE). Available online: https://www.oracle.com/java/technologies/appmodel.html (accessed on 21 February 2022).
44. Nginx. Nginx Reverse Proxy. Available online: https://www.nginx.com/ (accessed on 16 February 2022).
45. MySQL. MySQL Relational Database. Available online: https://www.mysql.com/ (accessed on 16 February 2022).
46. Fielding, R.T. Architectural Styles and the Design of Network-based Software Architectures. Dissertation Thesis, University of California, Irvine, CA, USA, 2000. Available online: https://www.ics.uci.edu/~{}fielding/pubs/dissertation/fielding_dissertation.pdf (accessed on 17 February 2022).
47. GA4GH. GA4GH Beacon Project. Available online: https://beacon-project.io/ (accessed on 8 February 2022).
48. Delgado, J.; Llorente, S. Privacy provision in eHealth using external services. In *Digital Healthcare Empowering Europeans*; Cornet, R., Stoicu-Tivadar, L., Hörbst, A., Calderón, C.L.P., Andersen, S.K., Hercigonja-Szekeres, M., Eds.; Studies in Health Technology and Informatics; IOS Press: Amsterdam, The Netherlands, 2015; Volume 210, pp. 823–827. Available online: https://ebooks.iospress.nl/publication/39463 (accessed on 8 March 2022).

49. Delgado, J.; Llorente, S.; Pamies, M.; Vilalta, J. Security and Privacy in a DACS. In *Exploring Complexity in Health: An Interdisciplinary Systems Approach*; Hoerbst, A., Hackl, W.O., de Keizer, N., Prokosch, H.-U., Hercigonja-Szekeres, M., de Lusignan, S., Eds.; Studies in Health Technology and Informatics; IOS Press: Amsterdam, The Netherlands, 2016; Volume 228, pp. 122–126. Available online: https://ebooks.iospress.nl/publication/44584 (accessed on 8 March 2022).
50. GA4GH. Data Use Ontology (DUO). Available online: https://github.com/EBISPOT/DUO (accessed on 10 March 2022).
51. GA4GH. GA4GH Data Privacy and Security Policy. Available online: https://www.ga4gh.org/wp-content/uploads/GA4GH-Data-Privacy-and-Security-Policy_FINAL-August-2019_wPolicyVersions.pdf (accessed on 8 February 2022).
52. *ISO/IEC 21000-15:2006*; Information Technology—Multimedia Framework (MPEG-21)—Part 15: Event Reporting. ISO/IEC: Geneva, Switzerland, 2006. Available online: https://www.iso.org/standard/41837.html (accessed on 8 February 2022).
53. Jacobsen, J.O.B.; Baudis, M.; Baynam, G.S.; Beckmann, J.S.; Beltran, S.; Callahan, T.J.; Chute, C.G.; Courtot, M.; Danis, D.; Elemento, O.; et al. The GA4GH Phenopacket schema: A computable representation of clinical data for precision medicine. *medRxiv*, 2021; *preprint*. Available online: https://www.medrxiv.org/content/10.1101/2021.11.27.21266944v1(accessed on 8 February 2022).
54. *ISO/TC 215/SC 1. ISO/DIS 4454*; Genomics Informatics—Phenopackets. ISO/IEC: Geneva, Switzerland, *under development*. Available online: https://www.iso.org/standard/79991.html (accessed on 8 February 2022).

Journal of *Personalized Medicine*

MDPI

*Article*

# Privacy and Trust in eHealth: A Fuzzy Linguistic Solution for Calculating the Merit of Service

**Pekka Ruotsalainen [1,*], Bernd Blobel [2] and Seppo Pohjolainen [1]**

1 Faculty of Information Technology and Communication Sciences (ITC), Tampere University, 33100 Tampere, Finland; seppo.pohjolainen@tuni.fi
2 Medical Faculty, University of Regensburg, 93953 Regensburg, Germany; bernd.blobel@klinik.uni-regensburg.de
* Correspondence: pekka.ruotsalainen@tuni.fi

**Abstract:** The use of eHealth and healthcare services are becoming increasingly common across networks and ecosystems. Identifying the quality and health impact of these services is a big problem that in many cases it is difficult determine. Health ecosystems are seldom designed with privacy and trust in mind, and the service user has almost no way of knowing how much trust to place in the service provider and other stakeholders using his or her personal health information (PHI). In addition, the service user cannot rely on privacy laws, and the ecosystem is not a trustworthy system. This demonstrates that, in real life, the user does not have significant privacy. Therefore, before starting to use eHealth services and subsequently disclosing personal health information (PHI), the user would benefit from tools to measure the level of privacy and trust the ecosystem can offer. For this purpose, the authors developed a solution that enables the service user to calculate a Merit of Service (Fuzzy attractiveness rating (FAR)) for the service provider and for the network where PHI is processed. A conceptual model for an eHealth ecosystem was developed. With the help of heuristic methods and system and literature analysis, a novel proposal to identify trust and privacy attributes focused on eHealth was developed. The FAR value is a combination of the service network's privacy and trust features, and the expected health impact of the service. The computational Fuzzy linguistic method was used to calculate the FAR. For user friendliness, the Fuzzy value of Merit was transformed into a linguistic Fuzzy label. Finally, an illustrative example of FAR calculation is presented.

**Keywords:** privacy; trust; modelling; antecedents; Fuzzy attractiveness rating

check for updates

**Citation:** Ruotsalainen, P.; Blobel, B.; Pohjolainen, S. Privacy and Trust in eHealth: A Fuzzy Linguistic Solution for Calculating the Merit of Service. *J. Pers. Med.* **2022**, *12*, 657. https://doi.org/10.3390/jpm12050657

Academic Editor: Amir Hajjam El Hassani

Received: 21 March 2022
Accepted: 14 April 2022
Published: 19 April 2022

**Publisher's Note:** MDPI stays neutral with regard to jurisdictional claims in published maps and institutional affiliations.



## 1. Introduction

Nowadays, people use digital services such as e-commerce, online shopping and, increasingly, eHealth services, nearly every day. These services are often built on platforms that—together with different stakeholders—form an ecosystem, where transactions take place without physical contact [1,2]. Although information privacy, security and trust are major concerns in digital markets, researchers have observed that digital information systems are seldom designed with privacy in mind [2]. Tan found that digital information systems are unreliable, unsecure and risky, and service providers deploying them have the power, tools and intention to manipulate their users' (a person or patient) trusting beliefs [3]. The assumption that a user can control the use of their personal information on the Internet and in ecosystems is only an illusion. In fact, we simply do not have privacy [4–6]. In real life, it is nearly impossible for the service user (SerU) to prevent unnecessary data collection, and to know to whom data is disclosed [7]. Often, the SerU is unaware and lacks understanding of actual privacy threats and their possible consequences [8]. Unfortunately, she/he cannot expect that domain-specific laws guarantee privacy and trust [9]. Instead, personal information is often disclosed and distributed to other stakeholders across health ecosystems without the user's consent or an awareness of privacy policies [10]. Frequently, the only choice for a SerU is to blindly trust the service provider (SerP) or to reject the service [11].

Today's eHealth services and applications offer many health promises, but to be beneficial they require a large amount of personal health information (PHI), such as vital signs, lifestyle, psychological characteristics and personal health beliefs. The SerU's education and socioeconomic status are also often exploited [12]. The ongoing transition towards personalized, participative, preventive, predictive and precision health and social care requires even more PHI, such as personal behaviors, social relations and environmental data [12]. A significant privacy concern is that PHI is not collected and used just by regulated healthcare organizations, but also by commercial web service providers and social web applications. PHI is also shared across eHealth ecosystems between stakeholders following different business models. These facts raise meaningful privacy and trust concerns. They result from the insufficiency of security-oriented privacy protection tools currently used in eHealth, such as access control, consent, and data anonymization. Furthermore, data encryption has limited power, as eHealth applications frequently need PHI in plain form [13].

From a privacy and trust point of view, the current situation is unsatisfactory. To enjoy the health benefits offered by eHealth, personal health apps and precise health services, the SerU has to maintain information privacy and know how much trust to place in a service provider and in the ecosystem, and what the level of actual offered privacy is. To meet this challenge, the authors have developed a solution that enables the SerU to calculate the level of trust and privacy to place in online eHealth ecosystems.

## 2. Definitions

Many of the terms used in this research do not have clear meaning. In this paper, the following definitions are used:

- Attitude is an opinion based on beliefs. It represents our feelings about something and the way a person expresses beliefs and values [10];
- Belief is the mental acceptance that something exists or is true without proof. Beliefs can be rational, irrational or dogmatic [14];
- eHealth is the transfer and exchange of health information between health service consumers (subject of care), health professionals, researchers and stakeholders using information and communication networks, and the delivery of digital health services [15];
- Harm is a potential direct or indirect damage, injury or negative impact of a real or potential economic, physical or social (e.g., reputational) action [11];
- Perception refers to the way a person notices something using his or her senses, or the way a person interprets, understands or thinks about something. It is a subjective process that influences how we process, remember, interpret, understand and act on reality [16]. Perception occurs in the mind and, therefore, perceptions of different people can vary;
- Reputation is a related but distinct concept of trust. It can be considered as a collective measure (a common opinion or recommendation) of a community about a trustee [17,18];
- Risk is a subjective expectation of loss, and the probability, likelihood or possibility of something that people fear as negative [19]. Consequently, risk perception is a feeling, impression, judgement and subjective evaluation about the likelihood of negative occurrences [20].

## 3. Methods

This study drew from existing privacy, trust, e-commerce, Internet shopping, and eHealth literature. Instead of defining separate privacy and trust scores, a Merit of Service as a combination of privacy, trust and expected health impact was calculated for the service used as a whole. Figure 1 shows the different phases of this study. Methods such as literature analysis, system analysis, modelling, Fuzzy mathematics and heuristics were used.

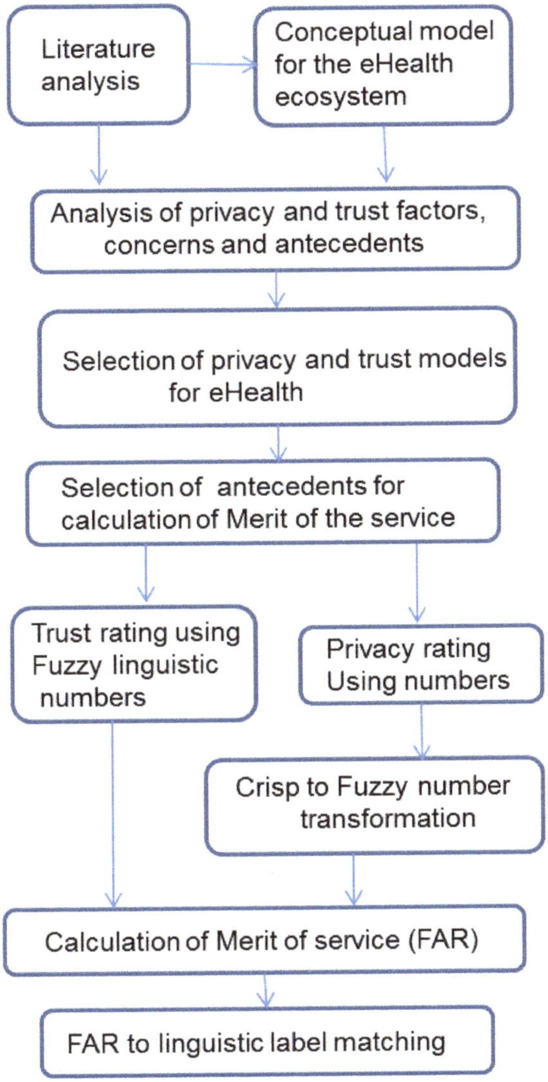


**Figure 1.** Phases of the study.

In this study, the first step was a deep literature analysis followed by the development of a conceptual model for the eHealth ecosystem. Up to 480 research articles covering different views on e-commerce, Internet shopping, privacy, trust and eHealth published in major journals were reviewed in detail. Because e-commerce, Internet shopping and eHealth build on the same format of ICT architecture and technology, concerns researchers have found in e-commerce and Internet shopping were also expected to exist in eHealth services that are modelled ecosystems. Appropriate privacy and trust models for eHealth, and privacy and trust attributes for calculating the Merit of Service, were selected using a heuristic method and findings were obtained from the literature analysis.

The Fuzzy attractiveness rating (FAR) method was used for calculating the Merit of eHealth service. The value of Merit was calculated using a linguistic Fuzzy approximation method, where the input attributes were Fuzzy trust rating, linguistic privacy value, and expected quality of service. Personal weights for attributes were also supported. To make the result (a linguistic FAR number) user-friendly, it was finally transformed into a Fuzzy linguistic label.

## 4. Related Research

Privacy is an elusive concept that has been studied as a philosophical, psychological, sociological, behavioral, economical and legal concept [19,21]. Traditionally, privacy is understood as an interpersonal concept, but today we understand that it exists in person–computer, computer–computer, and person–organization contexts. Two basic modes of privacy are general privacy and contextual privacy. Basic approaches for general privacy are value-based (e.g., human rights) or cognate-based, where privacy is related to the individual's mind, perception and cognition [19,22]. Privacy violations involve harm to individuals that can also take place in the future [21].

Widely used privacy approaches include privacy as an individual's right to control; privacy as a commodity, property, contextual integrity, a behavioral concept and social good; privacy as a concern or legal construct; risk-based privacy; and privacy as a fiducial duty [23,24]. The focus of control theory is self-determination regarding personal information. Modern control approaches see privacy as the ability to control access to the self [22,23]. In Pertronio's boundary theory, people control information flow through boundaries [23]. According to Lilien, privacy is "the right of an entity acting on its own behalf, to determine the degree to which it will interact with its environment, including the degree to which the entity is willing to share information about itself with others" [25].

The concept of privacy as a commodity understands privacy as economic good that can be traded for other goods or services [22,26]. In the model of privacy as personal property, the person has data ownership [27,28]. Privacy as a concern refers to individuals' anxiety regarding data collectors' and processors' information practices [20]. Privacy as a regulative (legal) construct tries to regulate the disclosure and use of information in a context, and to protect individuals [27]. The risk-based approach to privacy focuses on risk (e.g., social discrimination, negative impacts of data misuse, surveillance and behavioral manipulation) caused by data collection, use and disclosure [19]. Risk includes uncertainty, and in real life it is difficult or impossible for the SerU to measure the actual level of privacy risk at play [19].

Consumer privacy and online privacy are contextual privacy approaches used in consumer-to-business relationships (e.g., in e-commerce and Internet shopping) [29]. Online privacy can be understood as the level of privacy a user has on the Internet and social networks.

The vague and context-dependent nature of privacy and the lack of reliable information available make the measurement of actual (objective) privacy challenging [30]. Therefore, different proxies such as disposition, belief, expectation, perception, service-level agreements, contracts, external third-party seals, service provider's privacy policy documents, reputation, audit trails, direct observations, and degree of compliance with standards and risk are widely used [25,31,32]. Unfortunately, all of these have weaknesses. Belief is a personal trait, disposition is a psychological prerequisite, and neither can be measured [33]. In real life, a SerU has almost no chance to negotiate a service-level agreement (SLA) or to make a contract with the service provider. Third-party seals and certification are seldom available for the eHealth user, and the current security-oriented access-control solutions are ineffective. Privacy damage frequently takes place after the incident, and risks and perceptions are often only opinions [13].

Researchers have developed many methods for calculating or estimating levels of privacy, such as privacy calculus, risk evaluation and assessments, privacy threat analysis, regulatory compliance analysis, the evaluation of privacy documents and privacy policy compliance, and the privacy level of an information system [25]. In these calculations, the SerP's privacy features and user's privacy concerns are typically used. Regarding the privacy calculus method, it assumed that individuals can rationally estimate and weigh risks, and maximize benefits. According to Kruthoff, the assumption that people are aware of the risk is seldom true; therefore, the privacy calculus is not a good solution [34]. According to Mitchell, objective risk is a good proxy for privacy but, unfortunately, it cannot be measured in real life [35].

Similarly to privacy, trust is a vague concept that is defined in various ways in different cultures and contexts [9]. Trust exists in the relationship between a trustor and trustee, and it is widely understood as a subjective feature, psychological state, and personal trait, and it is the prerequisite of an action [9,36,37]. Trust has been studied from the viewpoints of philosophy, psychology, social sciences, information science, and economy. Basic trust types are general trust that has no relation to features of the trustee, and domain-specific trust [38]. Interpersonal trust takes place between humans, but the trustor/trustee can be any entity, such as an organization, institution or artefact [39]. Typically, trust is needed in situations where the trustor has insufficient information about the features and behaviors of the trustee [39]. Disposition (propensity) to trust is the tendency to trust others [40]. Trust is also widely understood as a belief, expectancy or feeling [41]. According to Castelfranchi, trust is, at the same time, a mental attitude towards another agent and a simple disposition to rely upon the other [42]. Chen defined trust as an intention to accept vulnerability under the conditions of risk caused by a trustee's actions [36]. A widely used definition of trust is "The willingness of a party to be vulnerable to the actions of another party based on the expectation that the other will perform a particular action important to the trustor, irrespective of the ability to monitor or control that other party." [38,41,43]. For Gambetta, "trust is a particular level of the subjective probability with which an agent will perform a particular action, both before one can monitor such action and in a context in which it affects own action" [9]. Economic perceptions of trust are based on calculations, i.e., rational choice mechanisms [38]. Trust and risk are interrelated concepts, i.e., trust is only needed if risk is involved. For Mayer, trust in fiduciary relationships is based on belief in the professional's competence and integrity [44].

Trust (or lack of trust) is one of the major problems in digital environments, e.g., in information systems, computer–computer and human–computer interactions, e-commerce, Internet shopping, social networks, smart physical environments, mobile networks and eHealth [45]. Computational trust imitates the human notion of trust, and it is widely used to substitute mental trust models [18]. It helps the SerU to estimate the degree of trust in a situation. Methods such as intuitive formula, simple mathematics (e.g., mean value, weighted average, weighted rank), probabilistic approaches, cost/benefit calculations, risk evaluations, recommender systems, game theory, utility theory, entropy, belief calculus, subjective logic, collaborative filtering, calculations using linguistic variables, analytic hierarchy processes, use of regression models, and machine learning are widely used for computational trust [18,38,46–54]. According to Nefti and Liu, major challenges with computational methods regard how to quantify trust, the lack of sufficient and reliable (direct) information, and uncertainty in attributes [48,55].

The Fuzzy nature of trust makes it logical to use Fuzzy logic in presenting and calculating levels of trust. This process has many advantages: Fuzzy logic is a computational method that is capable of using imprecise data and quantifying uncertainty [55]. Furthermore, Fuzzy logic is able to present measurement values and results in linguistic terms, such as "low", "high" and "good" [56].

For modelling and calculation, Fuzzy trust methods such as simple arithmetical operations (e.g., Fuzzy mean, simple additional weighting, and Fuzzy weighted average), Fuzzy distance measurement, Fuzzy multicriteria decision making, the Fuzzy analytic hierarchy process, and Fuzzy attractiveness ratings [57–59] are used. Truong et al. developed a reputation and knowledge-based Fuzzy trust service platform for the calculation of personal trust in IoT environments using utility theory [56]. Mahalle et al. used a utility function to calculate the overall trust value for a service using attributes such as experience and knowledge [60]. In a solution developed by Nefti et al., Fuzzy trust was used to evaluate a merchant's trust in e-commerce. Thereby, attributes such as the existence of a provider, policy fulfilment, and affiliation were deployed [55]. Lin et al. used linguistic terms describing weights of criteria and values of ratings to calculate Fuzzy attractiveness ratings (FARs) for different bids [61].

According to Herrera et al., there are situations where information cannot be presented in crisp numbers. Instead, a qualitative linguistic approach should be used where values of variables are described with words. The value of a variable is characterized by a label (a word), and the meaning is presented as a Fuzzy membership function [62].

Fuzzy logic-based trust solutions have also been used in health care in topics such as medical decision-making, patient monitoring, supporting diagnosis, the analysis of medical (big) data, the quality evaluation of health care services, the analysis of personal health and the creation of Fuzzy healthcare systems [63–67].

## 5. Solution to Calculate the Merit of eHealth Services

### *5.1. Conceptual Model for the eHealth Ecosystem*

People use eHealth services and disclose their PHI for applications to obtain personal health benefits. At the same time, they intend to maintain privacy, and to trust in the service provider and in the ICT technology used. Nowadays, eHealth services are increasingly offered via eHealth ecosystems. To understand how this functions and which trust and privacy relations and challenges exist in eHealth ecosystems, a conceptual model has been developed (Figure 2). Typical stakeholders in the eHealth ecosystem are the SerU (a primary source of PHI), health service providers, secondary users of PHI, computational service providers, communication service providers, the service platform operator, and regulators. The platform orchestrates health applications and information sharing in the network. The Internet and mobile networks are typically used for communication. According to Vega et al., typical eHealth websites include portal sites, support groups, charity sites, governmental sites, pharmaceutical sites, sales sites, personal sites, medical databases, media sites and clinical sites [32]. Health services offered by them include health promotion (e.g., nutrition, personal activity), self-care, and self-assessment, forecasting of future disease risk, and different test-, disease- and health-specific information services [68]. The delivery of health services needs large amount of PHI, such as information about conditions, treatments, symptoms, outcomes, laboratory results, genetic information, and health survey responses [6]. An eHealth application collects, processes and stores PHI, and it can also share PHI with other partners in the ecosystem.

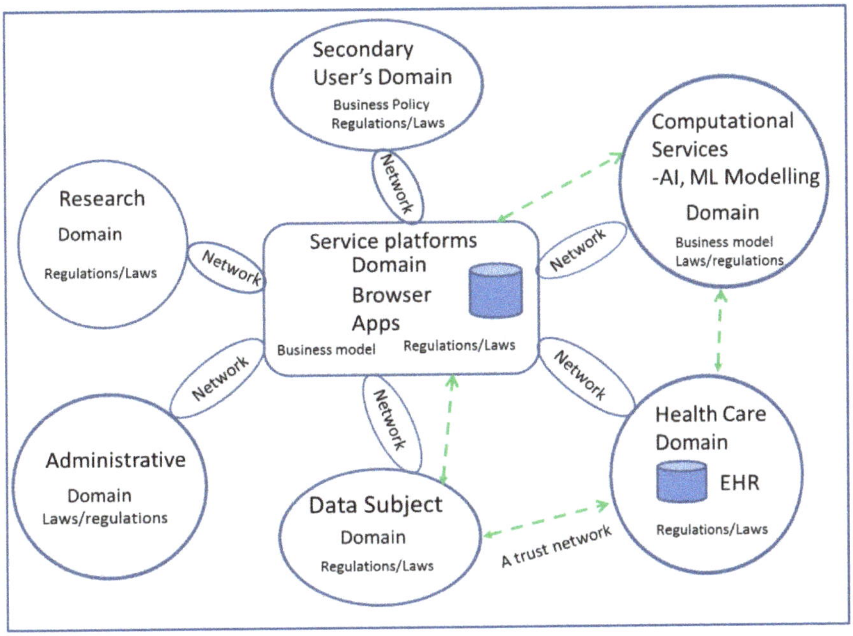


**Figure 2.** A conceptual model of the eHealth ecosystem.

*5.2. Privacy and Trust Challenges in eHealth Ecosystems*

In an ecosystem, stakeholders can locate different domains, having their own business models and domain-specific laws/regulations with their own privacy policies and trust features. The main features which separate eHealth ecosystems from e-commerce ecosystems are summarized in Table 1.

**Table 1.** Specific features of eHealth ecosystems.

| |
|---|
| Highly sensitive health-related data (e.g., diseases, symptoms, social behavior, and psychological features) are collected, used and shared |
| Healthcare-specific laws regulate the collection, use, retention and disclosure of PHI |
| To use services, the user must disclose sensitive PHI |
| Misuse of PHI can cause serious discrimination and harm |
| Service provided is often information, knowledge or recommendations without quality guarantee or return policy |
| The service provider can be a regulated or non-regulated healthcare service provider, wellness-service provider or a computer application |
| Service user can be a patient, and there exists a fiducial patient–doctor relationship |

The SerU's challenge is to find answers to the questions: "How shall I trust the faceless and the intangible?" [39] Who are the stakeholders in the system? Who are the data sharers? Who else can see and use my data? Who has control over my data, and how long it is stored? Furthermore, he or she needs to know the level of trust and privacy of the whole ecosystem, what kind of actual privacy risks exist, and what the harmful future effects of data misuse are. The SerU's concerns are linked to the lack of reliable and precise privacy and trust information, such as: to which unknown partners and purposes PHI is disclosed; data ownership; whether the SerP and other stakeholders will behave as expected and follow ethical rules and regulatory requirements; whether PHI is sold for direct marketing purposes; and the legitimacy and presence of the vendor, and the quality of the health services offered [58,68–70]. Furthermore, it is difficult for the SerU to know which laws and regulations are applied by a certain stakeholder [71]. Often, the SerP's privacy policy document does not explain which protection tools and procedures required by law are actually implemented [19]. Furthermore, tamper-proof audit trails are seldom available, and even if policy documents are available, they do not explain precisely how PHI is processed [72].

In real life, service providers often expect that the SerU's privacy needs can be balanced with the providers' business needs [73,74]. SerU's and providers can also have contradictorily opinions concerning who "owns" the user's data. Additionally, often, a service provider assumes the right to use PHI for their own purposes, and share or sell it to business partners [75]. Gomez et al. found that most websites use personal information for customized advertising, and many "trusted" firms share data with their affiliated companies [22]. Furthermore, commercial service providers often have minimal incentives to enforce strong privacy policies [76], and they do not always do what they promise in their policy documents and trust promises. In eHealth, the situation is not much better. Huckvale et al. found poor information privacy practices in health apps [68]. According to Papageorgiou et al., many eHealth service providers failed to provide even basic privacy protection. According to their review, 80% of health apps transmit users' health-related data, and 50% of apps send data to third parties without encryption [77].

### 5.3. *Privacy and Trust Models for eHealth*

The different privacy and trust approaches discussed in Chapter 4 present different views on privacy and trust, with different factor weights. Therefore, for the calculation of the level of privacy and trust in eHealth ecosystems, it is necessary to choose appropriate models. In this research work, a heuristic method was deployed.

As eHealth services are used in specific contexts, the general privacy approach cannot be successful. Researchers have found (Chapter 4) that a control approach is only an illusion, and from the SerU's point of view, privacy as commodity, social good, and contextual integrity approaches are insufficient [13]. Because the SerU is unable to utilize information systems and program codes, he or she cannot know the actual privacy risks or estimate the impacts of possible harm. Furthermore, risk perception and probabilities are only subjective opinions and, for the user, it is impossible to know to what extent they represent the actual risks. Therefore, the privacy as risk approach is not suitable for eHealth. According to Kosa, information privacy is about legislation and compliance [78], and because Internet users often have limited knowledge of the SerP's privacy features and no power to protect their data, they must rely on laws and regulations [79]. Based on the analysis performed above, the authors' state that, in eHealth ecosystems, a good privacy model is to understand privacy as a personal property [27], and to use legal norm (law) responsibilities and privacy policies as proxy. A benefit to this approach is that both laws and organization's privacy policy documents are often publicly available, and the privacy as property approach enables the SerU to decide what PHI to disclose and what to protect.

Dispositional trust and trusting belief models are widely used in e-commerce. McKnight has proposed a human disposition to trust technology, as well as trusting beliefs and trusting intentions for information systems [80]. The authors' state that reducing trust to a personal trait (i.e., propensity to trust) and belief has meaningful weaknesses. Both are strong personal feelings without connection to actual trust in information systems and data processing, and user's beliefs and feelings are easy to be manipulated by the service provider. Therefore, disposition and trusting beliefs cannot be used in eHealth. The approach comprising willingness to be vulnerable to the actions of another party (Chapter 4) also does not work, because it is based on belief or feelings [81]. Furthermore, trust as subjective probability is not useful, because it is only an opinion, and the definition of realistic probability is frequently impossible. The economistic rational choice model approach also fails because of the limited capacity of humans to make rational choices.

Based on the aforementioned analysis, the authors' selected a computational trust model. It has many advantages, such as imitating human trust and enabling the service user to compute the level of trust in a context using measurable attributes, such as direct experiences, historical (past) information of the SerP's features and behaviors, and it also takes into account the SerU's perceptions [48]. Computational methods are mathematically formulated algorithms which can be quite easily programmed and implemented. As the computational linguistic Fuzzy trust approach has the power to manage uncertainty and the ability to present both attributes and results in an easily understandable linguistic form, it was used in this research.

### *5.4. A Method for Calculating the Value of Merit of eHealth Services*

The solution developed by the authors can be used by the SerU to calculate a contextual value of Merit (Fuzzy attractiveness rating, FAR) for a selected health service and other participating stakeholders (Figure 3). The SerU can use the calculated value of Merit in the decision to use or not to use the service.

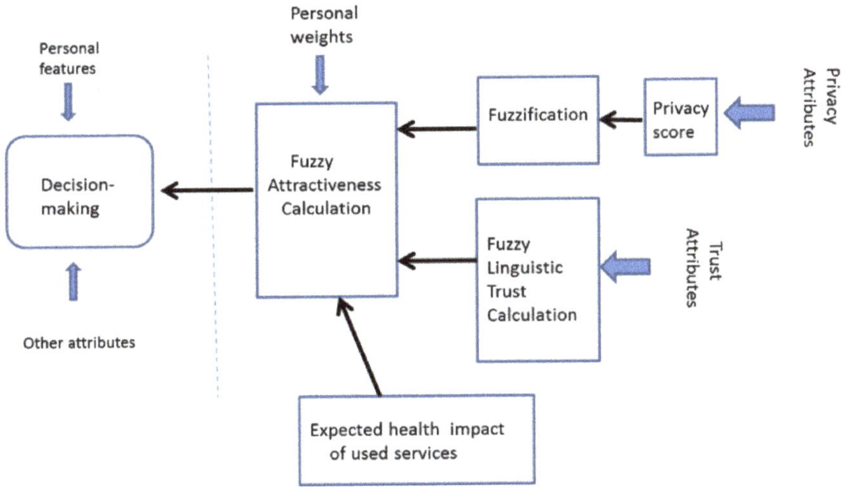


**Figure 3.** Calculation of the Merit of eHealth service.

In this research, the computational Fuzzy linguistic method, developed by Lin at al., was used for FAR calculation, and the formative measurement approach for the selection of attributes was applied in the calculation [61,82]. FAR was calculated using Equation (1) [56]. In the calculation, three variables were deployed: the service computational privacy score, trust rating, and expected health impact of service (EXPHI). The SerU's psychological and personal factors and impacts of marketing were not included because these are difficult or impossible to measure. To simplify the calculation, the Fuzzy triangular membership function was used. The privacy score was calculated as the numeric (crispy) average of selected attributes, and it was transformed into a linguistic Fuzzy number using a method proposed by Delgado et al. [83–85]. The Fuzzy trust number is a simple Fuzzy average of the linguistic values of the trust attributes.

$$\mathrm{FAR} = \sum_{j=1}^{n} (\mathrm{Wj} \otimes \mathrm{Rj}) / \sum_{j=1}^{n} \mathrm{Wj} \quad (1)$$

where $W_j$ is the personal weight for j's attribute and $R_j$ is the Fuzzy linguistic rating for j's attribute.

The calculated FAR was itself a Fuzzy number. To make its meaning easily understandable for a human it was matched to the linguistic labels used earlier for trust. Additionally, the label whose meaning was closest to the meaning of the FAR number was selected for the proxy for FAR. Different methods such as the Fuzzy similarity measurement and Fuzzy set distance measurement can be used for this transformation [61,86,87]. As the Euclidian method requires the use of alpha cuts, a mathematically easier method using center-of-gravity points of Fuzzy numbers was deployed in this paper. According to Zhang, the value of full similarity of two Fuzzy sets in this method is "1" [86].

### 5.5. Information Sources and Quantification of Privacy and Trust

The main challenge in FAR calculation is the availability and usability of attributes. Furthermore, the attributes used should be easy to use and to understand for a human, and the number of attributes should be kept low. Furthermore, attributes should be, if possible, directly measurable, matching both SerU's privacy and trust concerns, and be in line with previously selected trust models (Chapter 5). Based on our performed literature analysis, a summary of available sources for privacy and trust attributes is shown in Table 2.

**Table 2.** Typical sources for privacy and trust attributes from [7,54,88–97].

| |
|---|
| Direct measurements, experiences, interactions and observations |
| Service provider's privacy policy document |
| Content of privacy certificate or seal for the medical quality of information, content of certificate for legal compliance (structural assurance), andaudit trial (transparency). |
| Past experiences, transaction history, previous expertise |
| Information available on service provider's website |
| Provider's promises and manifestations |
| Others recommendations and ratings, expected quality of services |
| Information of service provider's properties and information system |
| Vendor's type or profile (similarity information) |

The optimal solution is to measure the level of actual privacy. As mentioned earlier, this is nearly impossible for the SerU. Therefore, proxy variables (legal norm responsibilities and privacy policies) are used instead (Chapter 5.3). Their attributes can be extracted from available sources such as policy documents, certificates and audit documents (Table 2). Third party seals and the use of data encryption in communication can be also exploited. The literature analysis performed by the authors resulted in a summary of eHealth user's privacy needs and how they are expressed in privacy policy documents and privacy law (Appendix A).

Researchers have intensively studied the privacy policy documents of organizations. Wilson et al. found that privacy policies vary in length, complexity, legal sophistication, and coverage of services, and the majority of them are unstructured, making their analysis difficult for a human [98]. In real life, privacy policies are usually long narrative documents written in legalese [99]. According to Pollach, the primary goal of policy documents is to protect companies against privacy lawsuits [100]. Iwaya et al. noted that policy documents are commonly publicly available on the service provider's website, and a level of communication privacy can be estimated from their content [101]. Oltramari et al. note that privacy policies are legally binding documents [102]. Researchers have found that the main challenge for the content analysis of policy documents is to select a useful granularity. According to Harkous et al., researchers have proposed the use of 10 classes for privacy policy analysis; however, in his Polisis solution, 122 privacy classes were used. For a human, such a large number of factors can be confusing. However, computer-based automatic analysis seems to be a promising solution [103].

Based on the performed literature analysis and previous discussions, the authors state that policy document analysis is a suitable tool to identify privacy attributes. In this research work, privacy attributes for eHealth services were selected using heuristic analysis. The findings are shown in Appendix A, and the proposals made by Egger, Oltamari, Harkous, Costance, and Beke [102–105] were used to select the privacy attributes applied (Table 3).

**Table 3.** Selected privacy attributes and their possible values.

| Name | Meaning of Attribute | Value = 2 | Value = 1 | Value = 0 |
|---|---|---|---|---|
| P1 | PHI disclosed to third parties | No data disclosed to third parties | Only anonymous datais disclosed | Yes/no information |
| P2 | Regulatory Compliance | Compliance certified by experts third-party privacy seals | Demonstrated regulatory complianceAvailable | Manifesto or no information |
| P3 | PHI Retention | Kept no longer than necessary for purposes of collection | Stored in encrypted form for further use | No retention time expressed |
| P4 | Use of PHI | Used only for presented purposes | Used for other named purposes | Purposes defined by the vendor |
| P5 | User access to collected PHI | Direct access via network | Vendor made document of collected PHI is available on request | No access or no information available |
| P6 | Transparency | Customer has access to audit trail | No user access to audit trail | No audit trail or no information |
| P7 | Ownership of the PHI | PHI belongs to DS (user) | Shared ownership of PHI | Ownership of PHI remains at vendor or no information |
| P8 | Support of SerU's privacy needs | SerU's own privacy policy supported | Informed consent supported | No support of DS' privacy policies or no information |
| P9 | Presence of organisation | Name, registered office address, e-mail address and contact address of privacy officer available | Name, physical address, e-mail address available | Only name and e-mail address available |
| P10 | Communication privacy | End-to-end encryption for collected PHI | HTTPS is supported | Raw data collected or no information |

Encryption is applied as proxy for communication privacy, and audit trails as proxy for transparency. To support the privacy as property approach discussed earlier, the SerU can present their own privacy needs (i.e., how PHI should be processed) by selecting one of three possible values shown in Table 4.

**Table 4.** Selected trust attributes for FAR calculation.

| Name | Attribute | Meaning | Sources |
|---|---|---|---|
| T1 | Perceived Credibility | How SerP keeps promises, type of organisation, external seals, ownership of organisation | Previous experiences, website information |
| T2 | Reputation | General attitude of society | Websites, other sources |
| T3 | Perceived competence and professionalism of the service provider | Type of organisation, qualification of employees/experts, similarity with other organisations | Website information, external information |
| T4 | Perceived quality and professionalism of health information | General information quality and level of professionalism, quality of links and scientific references | Own experience, third party ratings, other's proposals, website information, |
| T5 | Past experiences | Overall quality of past experiences | Personal past experiences |
| T6 | Regulatory compliance | Type and ownership of organisation. Experiences how the SerP keeps its promises | Websites, oral information, social networks and media. Previous experiences |
| T7 | Website functionality and ease of use | Easy to use, usability, understandability, look of the website, functionality | Direct experiences |
| T8 | Perceived quality of the information system | Functionality, helpfulness, structural assurance, reliability (system operates properly) | Own experiences, others recommendations |

Researchers have proposed a huge amount of trust attributes for e-commerce, Internet shopping and online services, such as personality-based, sociological, provider-specific, technology- and IT-system-specific, institutional, structural, information, service type and quality-based features. Pennanen presented 49 different antecedents in 3 categories: interpersonal (22); institutional (8); and consumer-specific (19) [38]. Hussin et al. classified trust attributes in 7 groups: information-based (25 attributes); function-based (6); merchant-based (15); content-based (4); product-based (4); process-based (4); and others (36). He mentioned that a company's information, such as address, e-mail address, privacy policy, third-party seals for secure transactions for personal data protection, and third-party recommendations were the most important factors [106]. For organizations, Söllner found 53 attributes: 6 for institutions and 11 for IT [107]. Beldad et al. classified trust attributes in online services into 10 categories (e.g., customer-/client-based, website-based, and company-/organization-based) [39]. Rocs et al. found that perceived ease of use, perceived usefulness, and perceived security are important determinants for trust in online systems [108]. In a review made by Arifim et al., 34 trust antecedents were identified. Most commonly cited were expertise, reputation, experience, frequency of interactions, confidential communication, similarity, integrity, dependability, length of relationship, and firm size [109]. Tamini et al. found that factors such as reliability, assurance, credibility, product type, experience, reputation, personality type, and cultural background were main drivers for e-trust [110]. In a literature analysis, Ruotsalainen et al. found 58 trust attributes classified into the following groups: customer perception and experiences, characteristic of the service provider, service features, and information-based features and infrastructural factors [111]. McKnight el. al. proposed structural assurance and situational normality of an organization as trust attributes [80].

The authors' literature analysis of eHealth publications found 38 different trust attributes in 5 categories: personal elements and individual antecedents (5); website-related antecedents (9); service provider-related elements (20); informational elements, i.e., design and content factors (9); and information sources (5) (Appendix B). A meaningful finding was that informational elements were the most meaningful attributes in eHealth [112]. According to Liu et al., direct experience is the most reliable information factor for trust measurement [18]. In the case of unavailability of that information, second-hand knowledge and perceptions [113], as well as existing knowledge and evidence [114], can be used. Chen et al. noted that customer's expectations of a seller's future behavior are determined by an evaluation of the seller's past behavior, intentions, capabilities, and values [36].

As discussed in Chapter 5.3, a computational trust approach was used in this research. Considered trust attributes included direct measurements, past personal experiences, observed information, transaction ratings, public knowledge (reputation), experts' recommendations and reports, and users' perceptions [9,17,88,97,115–117]. In real life, perceptions describing the relationship between a trustor and a trustee are widely used as a proxy for trust [43]. A challenge with perceptions is that their sources can remain unclear, and it can be difficult for a person to separate perceptions from beliefs. Furthermore, perceptions do not fully guarantee the service provider's actual trust features and trust behaviors. In spite of these limitations, according to Li et al., perceptions and second-hand knowledge (e.g., reputation and expert opinions) can be used as proxy for trust in situations where direct and previous information are not available [113].

A heuristic method using the content of Appendix B and the findings discussed above were deployed in the selection of five trust attributes for FAR calculation (Table 4).

The third variable used in FAR calculation, i.e., the expected health impact of services (EXPHI), can be understood as an estimate of expected quality of service (QoS).

*5.6. Case Study*

In a case study, a SerU found an interesting website of a health service that seemed to offer personal health benefits. For the calculation of trust and EXPHI, the following linguistic labels and triangular membership functions (set S) were used (Figure 4).

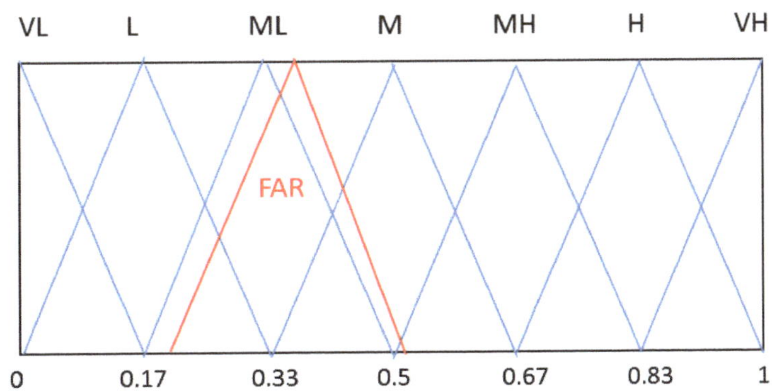


**Figure 4.** Used membership function and labels.

For the Set S, the following values were selected: Very low (VL) (0, 0, 0.17); Low (L) (0, 0.17, 0.33); Lower than average (ML) (0.7, 0.33, 0.5); Average (M)(033, 0.5, 0.67); Higher than average (MH) (0.5, 0.67, 0.83); High (H) (0.67, 0.83, 1); Very High (VH) (0.83, 1, 1). For personal weights (W) for privacy, trust and EXPHI, the following labels were selected: Very Low (VL) (0, 0, 0.4); Low (L) (0, 0.4, 0.6); Average (M) (0.4, 0.6, 0.8); High (0.6, 0.8, 1); and Very High (VH) (0.8, 1, 1).

In this case, the user selected the following privacy ("P") and trust ("T") ratings for the eHealth website studied ($P_i$ is i privacy rating and $T_j$ is j trust value). Furthermore, the linguistic value "M" was selected for the expected health impact (EXPHI) (Table 5).

**Table 5.** Privacy and trust ratings and EXPHI value example.

| P1 = 0. | P2 = 0 | P3 = 0 | P4 = 1 | P5 = 0 | P6 = 0 | P7 = 0 | P8 = 0 | P9 = 1 | P10 = 1 |
|---|---|---|---|---|---|---|---|---|---|
| T1 = M | T2 = MH | T3 = ML | T4 = M | T5 = H | T6 = L | T7 = H | T8 = M | | EXPHI = M |

The average of the privacy attributes had the value 0.15. This crisp number was transformed into a Fuzzy number using the method presented by Herrera et al. [79]. The two tuples that represent the information of 0.15 are shown in set S→(L, −12). This indicates that linguistic level L (Low) in set S is an acceptable approach for the number 0.15. In this use case, the user selected the following linguistic weights: privacy = VH; Trust = H; and EXPHI = M. The calculated Fuzzy numbers and their corresponding weights used in the FAR calculation are shown in Table 6. Using Equation (1) for FAR calculation (Chapter 5.4.1), the Fuzzy value for FAR was (0.198, 0.376, 0.56) (Table 6).

**Table 6.** Linguistic values for calculation of FAR.

| Factor | Fuzzy Value | Fuzzy Weight |
|---|---|---|
| Privacy | L (0.0, 0.17, 0.33) | VH (0.8, 1, 1) |
| Trust | (0.375, 0.54, 0.71) | H (0.6, 0.8, 1) |
| EXPHI | M (0.33, 0.5, 0.67) | M (0.4, 0.6, 0.8) |
| **FAR** | **(0.198, 0.376, 0.562)** | |

To present FAR in set S, a similarity calculation using the center-of-gravity method (i.e., similarity of two Fuzzy numbers) was performed [86]. It produced the following similarities: $S_{COG}$ (FAR, L) = 0.70, $S_{COG}$ (FAR, ML) = 0.92 and $S_{COG}$ (FAR,M) = 0.77. Therefore, the Fuzzy label "ML" is a good linguistic estimate for the Merit of Service (see Figure 4).

## 6. Discussions

Millions of people use the Internet and mobile eHealth services and applications. Furthermore, an increasing number of regulated healthcare organizations are moving part of their services to digital networks and ecosystems. To be effective, these services require the availability of an extensive amount of PHI. These, and situations where eHealth services are part of an ecosystem, raise many security and trust concerns. The disclosure of sensitive PHI requires that the SerU knows in advance the level of privacy in the ecosystem, and why and how much she or he can trust the SerP and the other stakeholders in the ecosystem. Trust requires data about the other partners [118] and knowledge of the ecosystem's privacy features. In real life, it is difficult for the SerU to know the actual level of privacy and trust offered by the ecosystem, and to make informed decisions. There is often a lack of reliable and directly measurable privacy and trust information. In this situation, humans are subject to psychological deviations from rationality, and individuals often mispredict their own preferences, derive inaccurate conclusions, or make inappropriate decisions [119].

To help SerUs in making information-based decisions regarding whether or not to use eHealth services, the authors developed a solution that calculates the Merit of Service value for the eHealth service and the surrounding ecosystem. The solution uses available information and perceptions concerning the SerP's and ecosystem's privacy and trust features and behaviors. For calculation, a Fuzzy linguistic method that used available or measurable attributes was deployed. Privacy attributes were derived from the service provider's privacy policy documents, and trust was estimated from the available trust-related information and from user's trust perceptions. Personal weights were also supported. The solution was user friendly, as linguistic labels were applied for trust attributes and for the value of Merit. The solution was automated, i.e., it can be given by a computer application that autonomously collects most/all data needed for the calculation. The solution was also flexible, so different privacy and trust models and context-specific attributes can be used. The service user can use the FAR value as an input to the final decision-making process to use or not to use the offered eHealth service. In this way, the FAR is—from the service user's point of view—a step forward from the current unsatisfactory situation. Considering the possible dissemination of the developed method, the next step might be the development of an open-source application, made freely available for testing in real-life situations.

The solution has also weaknesses. Caused by the lack of reliable information of actual privacy and trust, proxies were used. The availability of the service provider's privacy documents and trust promises does not fully guarantee that the provider keeps their promises. Furthermore, privacy documents are often high-level documents which do not explain the level of situational normality (i.e., which privacy safeguards are in place). E-commerce research has shown that a user's trust in service providers can be manipulated in many ways. For example, the appearance of a website impacts a user's trust, and the recommendations of others can be manipulated [120]. A weakness of the current solution is also that, currently, a SerU has to analyze the SerP's privacy documents manually, which can be time consuming, difficult and frustrating. Policy analysis using artificial intelligence (AI) and machine learning is a promising solution to this problem [102–104].

Two remaining barriers to this solution are: firstly, the lack of reliable and accurate privacy and trust information available; secondly, regulators' low willingness to force service providers and other stakeholders of the ecosystem to make reliable and detailed information concerning their privacy and trust features freely available. This unsatisfactory situation will continue as long as service providers do not have incentives to publish this information to enable the measurement of actual levels of privacy and trust.

The question as to whether there are risks when using FAR values (i.e., the possibility that physical, social or economic harm can be caused) also needs attention. The FAR value is generated by a computational algorithm that can be voluntarily used in decision-making. It differs from machine learning algorithms because, in the FAR method, the user defines personal weights. Based on these features, the authors consider it unlikely to cause harm to the service user.

The authors' solution is a step towards the trustworthy and privacy-enabled use of eHealth services. It highlights the development of new intelligent tools for the SerU in managing information privacy and creating trust in eHealth and in other digital services offered in ecosystems. Political will is needed to change the current regime that enables the collection and use of PHI against a user's personal preferences and privacy laws [11].

**Author Contributions:** P.R. is the main writer of the original draft; author B.B. participated in the development of the draft and made meaningful work in reviewing and editing the article. S.P. validated the mathematical methods used in this article. All authors have read and agreed to the published version of the manuscript.

**Funding:** This research received no external funding.

**Institutional Review Board Statement:** Not relevant in this study.

**Informed Consent Statement:** This study did not involve humans.

**Data Availability Statement:** Not applicable.

**Conflicts of Interest:** The authors declare no conflict of interest.

## Appendix A

**Table A1.** Privacy Needs and Requirements In Policy Documents and Law from [95,102–105,121].

| Privacy Needs/Questions | Meaning in a Privacy Policy Document | Requirements Exressed by Law (General Data Protection Regulation, EU GDPR) [1] |
|---|---|---|
| PHI used only for purposes defined by the service provider | How and why a service provider collects and uses PHI | Limited by what is necessary in relation to purpose. Explicit purpose |
| PHI not disclosed to third parties | What data and how PHI is shared with third party | Personal policiesTransparency |
| Regulatory compliance | Level Regulatory compliance | Lawfully processing Demonstrate regulatory compliance |
| What is the content of a personal privacy policy? | Edit and deletion | Erase, right to become forgotten, right to object processing, explicit purpose |

**Table A1.** *Cont.*

| Privacy Needs/Questions | Meaning in a Privacy Policy Document | Requirements Exressed by Law (General Data Protection Regulation, EU GDPR) [1] |
|---|---|---|
| What are the service provider's characteristics? | Type of organisation address | |
| Encryption | Communication privacy | Encryption |
| How PHI is stored for future use | Data retention (stored as long as needed to perform the requested service/indefinitely) | Retention no longer than necessary for purpose |
| User access to audit trail | What data is shared/transparency | Lawfully processing and transparency |
| User access to own PHI | User access, rights to view records | Access to collected PHI. Right to erase and object processing |
| How personal privacy needs are supported | User choice/control (consent, Opt in/opt out, purpose) | Accept personal privacy policies/explicit consent |
| Does PHI belongs to the customer? | Ownership of data | The individual owns the rights to their data |
| Does a registered office and address exist? | Contact information | |
| Privacy guarantees | Third-party seals or certificates | |
| Transparency | Transparency | Right to become informed |

[1] The General Data Protection Regulation (GDPR) is an EU-wide privacy and security law put into effect on 25 May 2018.

## Appendix B. Trust Attributes for eHealth

**Personal elements and individual antecedents** from [32,49,112,122]

- General trust of the health website;
- Personality;
- Privacy concerns;
- Subjective belief of suffering a loss;
- Beliefs in ability, integrity and benevolence.

**Website-related antecedents** from [32,49,112,122–124]

- Website design and presence, website design for easy access and enjoyment;
- System usability, perceived as easy to use;
- Technical functionality;
- Website quality (being able to fulfil the seekers' needs);
- Perceived information quality and usefulness;
- Quality (familiarity) that allows better understanding;
- Simple language used;
- Professional appearance of the health website;
- Integrity of the health portal policies with respect to privacy, security, editorial, and advertising.

**Service provider (institution, non-profit organisation, private business)-related elements** from [32,49,112,122–126]

- Credibility and impartiality;
- Reputation;
- Ability to perform promises made;
- Accountability of misuse;
- Familiarity;
- Branding, brand name and ownership;
- System quality (functionality flexibility), quality of systems, stability;
- Professional expertise;
- Similarity with other systems, ability, benevolence, integrity of the health portal with the same brand;
- Transparency, oversight;
- Privacy, security;

- Privacy and security policies, strategies implemented;
- Regulatory compliance.

**Informational elements (design and content factors)** from [49,112,122,124]

- Quality of links;
- Information quality and content (accuracy of content, completeness, relevance, understandable, professional, unbiased, reliable, adequacy and up-to-date), source expertise, scientific references;
- Information source credibility, relevant and good information, usefulness, accuracy, professional appearance of a health website;
- Information credibility;
- Information impartiality.

**Information sources** from [49,67,112,122,127]

- Personal interactions;
- Personal experiences;
- Past (prior) experiences;
- Presence of third-party seals (e.g., HONcode, Doctor Trusted™, TrustE).

## References


1. Kangsberger, R.; Kunz, W.H. Consumer trust in service companies: A multiple mediating analysis. *Manag. Serv. Qual.* **2010**, *20*, 4–25. [CrossRef]
2. Gupta, P.; Akshat Dubey, A. E-Commerce-Study of Privacy, Trust and Security from Consumer's Perspective. *Int. J. Comput. Sci. Mob. Comput.* **2016**, *5*, 224–232.
3. Tan, Y.-H.; Thoen, W. Toward a Generic Model of Trust for Electronic Commerce. *Int. J. Electron. Commer.* **2000**, *5*, 61–74.
4. Taviani, H.T.; Moor, J.M. Privacy Protection, Control of Information, and Privacy-Enhancing Technologies. *ACM SIGCAS Comput. Soc.* **2001**, *31*, 6–11. [CrossRef]
5. Fairfield, J.A.T.; Engel, C. Privacy as a public good. *Duke Law J.* **2015**, *65*, 3. Available online: https://scholarship.law.duke.edu/cgi/viewcontent.cgi?article=3824&context=dlj (accessed on 11 April 2022).
6. Li, J. Privacy policies for health social networking sites. *J. Am. Med. Inform. Assoc.* **2013**, *20*, 704–707. [CrossRef]
7. Corbitt, B.J.; Thanasankit, T.; Yi, H. Trust and e-commerce: A study of consumer perceptions. *Electron. Commer. Res. Appl.* **2003**, *2*, 203–215. [CrossRef]
8. Gerber, N.; Reinheimer, B.; Volkamer, M. Investigating People's Privacy Risk Perception. *Proc. Priv. Enhancing Technol.* **2019**, *3*, 267–288. [CrossRef]
9. Yan, Z.; Holtmanns, S. Trust Modeling and Management: From Social Trust to Digital Trust. In *Computer Security, Privacy and Politics;* Current Issues, Challenges and Solutions; IGI Global: Hershey, PA, USA, 2007. [CrossRef]
10. Weitzner, D.J.; Abelson, H.; Berners-Lee, T.; Feigenbaum, J.; Hendler, J.; Sussman, G.J. *Information Accountability*; Computer Science and Artificial Intelligence Laboratory Technical Report, MIT-CSAIL-TR-2007-034; Massachusetts Institute of Technology: Cambridge, UK, 2007.
11. Richards, N.; Hartzog, W. Taking Trust Seriously in Privacy Law. *Stanf. Tech. Law Rev.* **2016**, *19*, 431. [CrossRef]
12. Pravettoni, G.; Triberti, S. *P5 eHealth: An Agenda for the Health Technologies of the Future*; Springer Open: Berlin/Heidelberg, Germany, 2020. [CrossRef]
13. Ruotsalainen, P.; Blobel, B. Health Information Systems in the Digital Health Ecosystem—Problems and Solutions for Ethics, Trust and Privacy. *Int. J. Environ. Res. Public Health* **2020**, *17*, 3006. [CrossRef]
14. Kimi, A.; Choobineh, J. Trust in Electronic Commerce: Definition and Theoretical Considerations. In Proceedings of the Thirty-First Hawaii International Conference on System Sciences, Kohala Coast, HI, USA, 9 January 1998; Volume 4, pp. 51–61. [CrossRef]
15. World Health Organization. Available online: https://who.int/trade/glossary/story021/en/ (accessed on 11 April 2022).
16. LEXICO. Available online: https://www.lexico.com/definition/perception (accessed on 11 April 2022).
17. Jøsang, A.; Ismail, R.; Boyd, C. A Survey of Trust and Reputation Systems for Online Service Provision. *Decis. Support Syst.* **2007**, *43*, 618–644. [CrossRef]
18. Liu, X.; Datta, A.; Lim, E.-P. *Computational Trust Models and Machine Learning*; Chapman & Hall/CRC Machine Learning & Pattern Recognition Series, 2015 Taylor and Francis Group; CRC Press: New York, NY, USA, 2015; ISBN 978-1-4822-2666-9.
19. Bhatia, J.; Breaux, T.D. Empirical Measurement of Perceived Privacy Risk. *ACM Trans. Comput.-Hum. Interact.* **2018**, *25*, 1–47. [CrossRef]
20. Chang, L.Y.; Lee, H. Understanding perceived privacy: A privacy boundary management model. In Proceedings of the 19th Pacific Asia Conference on Information Systems (PACIS 2015), Singapore, 5–9 July 2015.
21. Solove, D.J. A Taxonomy of Privacy. *Univ. Pa. Law Rev.* **2006**, *154*, 2. [CrossRef]

22. Smith, H.J.; Dinev, T.; Xu, H. Information privacy research: An interdisciplinary review. *MIS Q.* **2011**, *35*, 989–1015. [CrossRef]
23. Marguilis, S.T. Privacy as a Social Issue and Behavioral Concept. *J. Soc. Issues* **2003**, *59*, 243–261. [CrossRef]
24. Kasper, D.V.S. Privacy as a Social Good. *Soc. Thought Res.* **2007**, *28*, 165–189. [CrossRef]
25. Lilien, L.; Bhargava, B. *Trading Privacy for Trust in Online Interactions*; Center for Education and Research in Information Assurance and Security (CERIAS), Purdue University: West Lafayette, IN, USA, 2009. [CrossRef]
26. Kehr, F.; Kowatsch, T.; Wentzel, D.; Fleish, E. Blissfully Ignorant: The Effects of General Privacy Concerns, General Institutional Trust, and Affect in the Privacy Calculus. *Inf. Syst. J.* **2015**, *25*, 607–635. [CrossRef]
27. Zwick, D. *Models of Privacy in the Digital Age: Implications for Marketing and E-Commerce*; University of Rhode Island: Kingston, RI, USA, 1999; Available online: https://www.researchgate.net/profile/Nikhilesh-Dholakia/publication/236784823_Models_of_privacy_in_the_digital_age_Implications_for_marketing_and_e-commerce/links/0a85e5348ac5589862000000/Models-of-privacy-in-the-digital-age-Implications-for-marketing-and-e-commerce.pdf?origin=publication_detail (accessed on 11 April 2022).
28. Ritter, J.; Anna Mayer, A. Regulating Data as Property: A New Construct for Moving Forward. *Duke Law Technol. Rev.* **2018**, *16*, 220–277. Available online: https://scholarship.law.duke.edu/dltr/vol16/iss1/7 (accessed on 11 April 2022).
29. Goodwin, C. Privacy: Recognition of consumer right. *J. Public Policy Mark.* **1991**, *10*, 149–166. [CrossRef]
30. Dinev, T.; Xu, H.; Smith, J.H.; Hart, P. Information privacy and correlates: An empirical attempt to bridge and distinguish privacy-related concepts. *Eur. J. Inf. Syst.* **2013**, *22*, 295–316. [CrossRef]
31. Fernández-Alemán, J.L.; Señor, I.C.; Pedro Lozoya, Á.O.; Toval, A. Security and privacy in electronic health records. *J. Biomed. Inform.* **2013**, *46*, 541–562. [CrossRef] [PubMed]
32. Vega, L.C.; Montague, E.; DeHart, T. Trust between patients and health websites: A review of the literature and derived outcomes from empirical studies. *Health Technol.* **2011**, *1*, 71–80. [CrossRef]
33. Li, Y. A model of individual multi-level information privacy beliefs. *Electron. Commer. Res. Appl.* **2014**, *13*, 32–44. [CrossRef]
34. Kruthoff, S. Privacy Calculus in the Context of the General Data Protection Regulation and Healthcare: A Quantitative Study. Bachelor's Thesis, University of Twente, Enschede, The Netherlands, 2018.
35. Mitchell, V.-M. Consumer perceived risk: Conceptualizations and models. *Eur. J. Mark.* **1999**, *33*, 163–195. [CrossRef]
36. Chen, C.C.; Dhillon, G. Interpreting Dimensions of Consumer Trust in E-Commerce. *Inf. Technol. Manag.* **2003**, *4*, 303–318. [CrossRef]
37. Schoorman, F.D.; Mayer, R.C.; Davis, J.H. An integrative model of organizational trust: Past, present, and future. *Acad. Manag. Rev.* **2007**, *32*, 344–354. [CrossRef]
38. Pennanen, K. *The Initial Stages of Consumer Trust Building in E-Commerce*; University of Vaasa: Vaasa, Finland, 2009; ISBN 978–952–476–257–1.; Available online: https://www.uwasa.fi/materiaali/pdf/isbn_978-952-476-257-1.pdf (accessed on 11 April 2022)ISBN 978.
39. Beldad, A.; de Jong, M.; Steehouder, M. How shall I trust the faceless and the intangible? A literature review on the antecedents of online trust. *Comput. Hum. Behav.* **2010**, *26*, 857–869. [CrossRef]
40. Wanga, S.W.; Ngamsiriudomb, W.; Hsieh, C.-H. Trust disposition, trust antecedents, trust, and behavioral intention. *Serv. Ind. J.* **2015**, *35*, 555–572. [CrossRef]
41. Grabner-Kräuter, S.; Kaluscha, E.A. *Consumer Trust in Electronic Commerce: Conceptualization and Classification of Trust Building Measures*; Chapter in 'Trust and New Technologies'; Kautonen, T., Karjaluoto, H., Eds.; Edward Elgar Publishing: Cheltenham, UK, 2008; pp. 3–22.
42. Castelfranchi, C. Trust Mediation in Knowledge Management and Sharing. In *Lecture Notes in Computer Science*; Trust Management. iTrust 2004; Jensen, C., Poslad, S., Dimitrakos, T., Eds.; Springer: Berlin/Heidelberg, Germany, 2004; Volume 2995. [CrossRef]
43. Wiedmann, K.-P.; Hennigs, N.; Dieter Varelmann, D.; Reeh, M.O. Determinants of Consumers' Perceived Trust in IT-Ecosystems. *J. Theor. Appl. Electron. Commer. Res.* **2010**, *5*, 137–154. [CrossRef]
44. Mayer, R.C.; Davis, J.H.; Schoorman, F.D. An Integrative Model of Organizational Trust. *Acad. Manag. Rev.* **1995**, *20*, 709–734. Available online: http://www.jstor.org/stable/258792.137-154 (accessed on 11 April 2022). [CrossRef]
45. Medic, A. P2P Appliance Calculation Method for Trust between Nodes within a P2P Network. *Int. J. Comput. Sci. Issues* **2012**, *9*, 125–130.
46. Sabater, J.; Sierra, C. Review on computational trust and reputation models. *Artif. Intell. Rev.* **2005**, *24*, 33–60. [CrossRef]
47. Braga, D.D.S.; Niemann, M.; Hellingrath, B.; Neto, F.B.D.L. Survey on Computational Trust and Reputation Models. *ACM Comput. Surv.* **2019**, *51*, 1–40. [CrossRef]
48. Liu, X.; Datta, A.; Rzadca, K. Stereo Trust: A Group Based Personalized Trust Model. In Proceedings of the 18th ACM Conference on Information and Knowledge Management (CIKM'09), Hong Kong, China, 2–6 November 2009. ACM978-1-60558-512-3/09/1. [CrossRef]
49. Kim, Y. Trust in health information websites: A systematic literature review on the antecedents of trust. *Health Inform. J.* **2016**, *22*, 355–369. [CrossRef]
50. Vu, L.-H.; Aberer, K. Effective Usage of Computational Trust Models in Rational Environments. *ACM Trans. Auton. Adapt. Syst.* **2011**, *6*, 1–25. [CrossRef]

51. Nafi, K.W.; Kar, T.S.; Hossain Md, A.; Hashem, M.M.A. A Fuzzy logic based Certain Trust Model for e-commerce. In Proceedings of the 2013 International Conference on Informatics, Electronics and Vision (ICIEV), Dhaka, Bangladesh, 17–18 May 2013; pp. 1–6. [CrossRef]
52. Jøsang, A. Computational Trust. In *Subjective Logic. Artificial Intelligence: Foundations, Theory, and Algorithms*; Springer: Cham, Switzerland, 2016. [CrossRef]
53. Ries, S. Certain Trust: A Model for Users and Agents. In Proceedings of the 2007 ACM Symposium on Applied Computing, Seoul, Korea, 11–15 March 2007.
54. Skopik, F. Dynamic Trust in Mixed Service-Oriented Systems Models, Algorithms, and Applications. Ph.D. Thesis, Technischen Universität Wien, Fakultät für Informatik, Austria, 2010.
55. Nefti, S.; Meziane, F.; Kasiran, K. A Fuzzy Trust Model for E-Commerce. In Proceedings of the Seventh IEEE International Conference on E-Commerce Technology (CEC'05), Munich, Germany, 19–22 July 2005. ISBN 0-7695-2277-7. [CrossRef]
56. Truong, N.B.; Lee, G.M. A Reputation and Knowledge Based Trust Service Platform for Trustworthy Social Internet of Things. In Proceedings of the 19th International Conference on Innovations in Clouds, Internet and Networks (ICIN 2016), Paris, France, 1–3 March 2016.
57. Nguyen, H.-T.; Md Dawal, S.Z.; Nukman, Y.; Aoyama, H.; Case, K. An Integrated Approach of Fuzzy Linguistic Preference Based AHP and Fuzzy COPRAS for Machine Tool Evaluation. *PLoS ONE* **2015**, *10*, e0133599. [CrossRef]
58. Keshwani, D.R.; Jones, D.D.; Meyer, G.E.; Brand, R.M. Ruke-based Mamdani-type fuzzy modeling of skin permeability. *Appl. Soft Comput.* **2008**, *8*, 285–294. [CrossRef]
59. Afshari, A.R.; Nikolić, M.; Ćoćkalo, D. Applications of Fuzzy Decision Making for Personnel Selection Problem-A Review. *J. Eng. Manag. Compet. (JEMC)* **2014**, *4*, 68–77. [CrossRef]
60. Mahalle, P.N.; Thakre, P.A.; Prasad, N.R.; Prasad, R. A fuzzy approach to trust based access control in internet of things. In Proceedings of the 3rd International Conference on Wireless Communication, Vehicular Technology, Information Theory and Aerospace & Electronic Systems Technology (Wireless ViTAE) 2013, Atlantic City, NJ, USA, 24–27 June 2013. [CrossRef]
61. Lin, C.-T.; Chen, Y.-T. Bid/no-bid decision-making–A fuzzy linguistic approach. *Int. J. Proj. Manag.* **2004**, *22*, 585–593. [CrossRef]
62. Herrera, T.; Herrera-Viedma, E. Linguistic decision analysis: Steps for solving decision problems under linguistic information. *Fuzzy Sets Syst.* **2000**, *115*, 67–82. [CrossRef]
63. Mishaand, S.; Prakash, M. Study of fuzzy logic in medical data analytics, supporting medical diagnoses. *Int. J. Pure Appl. Math.* **2018**, *119*, 16321–16342.
64. Gürsel, G. Healthcare, uncertainty, and fuzzy logic. *Digit. Med.* **2016**, *2*, 101–112. [CrossRef]
65. de Medeiros, I.B.; Machadoa, M.A.S.; Damasceno, W.J.; Caldeira, A.M.; Santos, R.C.; da Silva Filho, J.B. A Fuzzy Inference System to Support Medical Diagnosis in Real Time. *Procedia Comput. Sci.* **2017**, *122*, 167–173. [CrossRef]
66. Hameed, K.; Bajwa, I.S.; Ramzan, S.; Anwar, W.; Khan, A. An Intelligent IoT Based Healthcare System Using Fuzzy Neural Networks. *Hindawi Sci. Program.* **2020**, *2020*, 8836927. [CrossRef]
67. Athanasiou, G.; Anastassopoulos, G.C.; Tiritidou, E.; Lymberopoulos, D. A Trust Model for Ubiquitous Healthcare Environment on the Basis of Adaptable Fuzzy-Probabilistic Inference System. *IEEE J. Biomed. Health Inform.* **2018**, *22*, 1288–1298. [CrossRef] [PubMed]
68. Huckvale, K.; Prieto, J.T.; Tilney, M.; Benghozi, P.-J.; Car, J. Unaddressed privacy risks in accredited health and wellness apps: A cross-sectional systematic assessment. *BMC Med.* **2015**, *13*, 214. [CrossRef]
69. Bellekens, X.; Seeam, P.; Franssen, Q.; Hamilton, A.; Nieradzinska, K.; Seeam, A. Pervasive eHealth services a security and privacy risk awareness survey. In Proceedings of the 2016 International Conference On Cyber Situational Awareness, Data Analytics And Assessment (CyberSA), London, UK, 13–14 June 2016; pp. 1–4. [CrossRef]
70. Krasnova, H.; Günther, G.; Spiekermann, S.; Koroleva, K. Privacy concerns and identity in online social networks. *IDIS* **2009**, *2*, 39–63. [CrossRef]
71. Abe, A.; Simpson, A. Formal Models for Privacy. In *Proceedings of the Workshop Proceedings of the EDBT/ICDT 2016 Joint Conference, Bordeaux, France, 15 March 2016*; ISSN 1613-0073. Available online: CEUR-WS.org (accessed on 11 April 2022).
72. Baldwin, A.; Jensen, C.D. *Enhanced Accountability for Electronic Processes*; iTrust 2004, LNCS 2995; Jensen, C., Poslad, S., Dimitrakos, T., Eds.; Springer: Berlin/Heidelberg, Germany, 2004; pp. 319–332.
73. Culnan, M.J.; Bies, R.J. Consumer Privacy: Balancing Economic and Justice Considerations. *J. Soc. Issues* **2003**, *59*, 323–342. [CrossRef]
74. Lanier, C.D., Jr.; Saini, A. Understanding Consumer Privacy: A Review and Future Directions. *Acad. Mark. Sci. Rev.* **2008**, *12*, 2. Available online: https://www.amsreview.org/articles/lanier02-200 (accessed on 11 April 2022).
75. Wetzels, M.; Ayoola, I.; Bogers, S.; Peters, P.; Chen, W.; Feijs, L. Consume: A privacy-preserving authorization and authentication service for connecting with health and wellbeing APIs. *Pervasive Mob. Comput.* **2017**, *43*, 20–26. [CrossRef]
76. Wanigasekera, C.P.; Feigenbaum, J. Trusted Systems Protecting Sensitive Information through Technological Solutions. Sensitive Information in a Wired World Course (CS457) Newhaven, Yale University, 12 December 2003, 16p. Available online: http://zoo.cs.yale.edu/classes/cs457/backup (accessed on 11 April 2022).
77. Papageorgiou, A.; Strigkos, M.; Politou, E.; Alepis, E.; Solanas, A.; Patsakis, C. Security and Privacy Analysis of Mobile Health Applications: The Alarming State of Practice. *IEEE Access* **2018**, *6*, 9390–9403. [CrossRef]
78. Kosa, T.A.; El-Khati, K.; Marsh, S. Measuring Privacy. *J. Internet Serv. Inf. Secur.* **2011**, *1*, 60–73.

79. Škrinjarić, B. Perceived quality of privacy protection regulations and online privacy concern. *Econ. Res.-Ekon. Istraživanja* **2019**, *32*, 982–1000. [CrossRef]
80. McKnight, D.H. Trust in Information Technology. In *The Blackwell Encyclopedia of Management*; Management Information Systems; Davis, G.B., Ed.; Blackwell: Malden, MA, USA, 2005; Volume 7, pp. 329–333.
81. McKnigth, H.D.; Choundhury, V.; Kacmar, C. Developing and Validating Trust Measures for e-Commerce: An Integrative Typology. *Inf. Syst. Res.* **2002**, *13*, 334–359. [CrossRef]
82. Coltman, T.; Devinney, T.M.; Midgley, D.F.; Venaik, S. Formative versus reflective measurement models: Two applications of formative measurement. *J. Bus. Res.* **2008**, *61*, 1250–1262. [CrossRef]
83. Herrera, F.; Martinez, L.; Sanchez, P.J. Integration of Heterogeneous Information in Decision-Making Problems. Available online: https://sinbad2.ujaen.es/sites/default/files/publications/Herrera2000b_IPMU.pdf (accessed on 11 April 2022).
84. Andayani, S.; Hartati, S.; Wardoyo, R.; Mardapi, D. Decision-Making Model for Student Assessment by Unifying Numerical and Linguistic Data. *Int. J. Electr. Comput. Eng.* **2017**, *7*, 363–373. [CrossRef]
85. Delgado, M.; Herrera, F.; Herrera-Viedma, E.; Marffnez, L. Combining numerical and linguistic information in group decision making. *J. Inf. Sci.* **1998**, *107*, 177–194. [CrossRef]
86. Zhang, X.; Ma, W.; Chen, L. New Similarity of Triangular Fuzzy Numbers and its applications. *Hindawi Sci. World J.* **2014**, *2014*, 215047. [CrossRef]
87. Luo, M.; Cheng, Z. The Distance between Fuzzy Sets in Fuzzy Metric Space. In Proceedings of the 12th International Conference on Fuzzy Systems and Knowledge Discovery 2015 (FSKD'15), Zhangjiajie, China, 15–17 August 2015; pp. 190–194. [CrossRef]
88. Abdul-Rahman, A.; Hailes, S. Supporting Trust in Virtual Communities. In Proceedings of the 33rd Annual Hawaii International Conference on System Sciences, Maui, HI, USA, 4–7 January 2000; Volume 1, pp. 1–9. [CrossRef]
89. Jøsang, A.; Presti, S.L. Analysing the Relationship between Risk and Trust. In *Lecture Notes in Computer Science*; Trust Management. iTrust 2004.; Jensen, C., Poslad, S., Dimitrakos, T., Eds.; Springer: Berlin/Heidelberg, Germany, 2004; Volume 2995. [CrossRef]
90. Pinyol, I.; Sabater-Mir, J. Computational trust and reputation models for open multi-agent systems: A review. *Artif. Intell. Rev.* **2013**, *40*, 1–25. [CrossRef]
91. Wang, G.; Chen, S.; Zhou, Z.; Liu, J. Modelling and Analyzing Trust Conformity in E-Commerce Based on Fuzzy Logic. *Wseas Trans. Syst.* **2015**, *14*, 1–10.
92. Meziane, F.; Nefti, S. Evaluating E-Commerce Trust Using Fuzzy Logic. *Int. J. Intell. Inf. Technol.* **2007**, *3*, 25–39. [CrossRef]
93. Guo, G.; Zhang, J.; Thalmann, D.; Basu, A.; Yorke-Smith, N. From Ratings to Trust: An Empirical Study of Implicit Trust in Recommender Systems. In Proceedings of the 29th Annual ACM Symposium on Applied Computing (SAC'14), Gyeongju Korea, 24–28 March 2014; pp. 248–253. [CrossRef]
94. Patel, G.N. Evaluation of Consumer Buying Behaviour for Spefic Food Commodity Using FUZZY AHP Approach. In Proceedings of the International Symposium on the Analytic Hierarchy Process, London, UK, 4–7 August 2016. [CrossRef]
95. Egger, F.N. *From Interactions to Transactions: Designing the Trust Experience for Business-to-Consumer Electronic Commerce*; Eindhoven University of Technology: Eindhoven, The Netherlands, 2003; ISBN 90-386-1778-X.
96. Manchala, D. E-Commerce Trust Metrics and Models. *IEEE Internet Comput.* **2000**, *4*, 36–44. [CrossRef]
97. Kim, Y.A.; Ahmad, M.A.; Srivastava, J.; Kim, S.H. Role of Computational Trust Models in Service Science. 5 January 2009; Journal of Management Information Systems, Forth-coming, KAIST College of Business Working Paper Series No. 2009-002, 36 pages. Available online: https://ssrn.com/abstract (accessed on 11 April 2022).
98. Wilson, S.; Schaub, F.; Dara, A.A.; Liu, F.; Cherivirala, S.; Leon, P.G.; Andersen, M.S.; Zimmeck, S.; Sathyendra, K.M.; Russell, N.C.; et al. The Creation and Analysis of a Website Privacy Policy Corpus. In Proceedings of the 54th Annual Meeting of the Association for Computational Linguistics (Volume 1: Long Papers), Berlin, Germany, 7–12 August 2016. [CrossRef]
99. Mazmudar, M.; Goldberg, I. Mitigator: Privacy policy compliance using trusted hardware. *Proc. Priv. Enhancing Technol.* **2020**, *2020*, 204–221. [CrossRef]
100. Pollach, I. What's wrong with online privacy policies? *Commun. ACM* **2007**, *50*, 103–108. [CrossRef]
101. Iwaya, L.H.; Fischer-Hubner, S.; Åhlfeldt, R.-M.; Martucci, L.A. mHealth: A Privacy Threat Analysis for Public Health Surveillance Systems. In Proceedings of the 2018 IEEE 31st International Symposium on Computer-Based Medical Systems (CBMS), Karlstad, Sweden, 18–21 June 2018; pp. 42–47. [CrossRef]
102. Oltramari, A.; Piraviperumal, D.; Schaub, F.; Wilson, S.; Cherivirala, S.; Norton, T.; Russell, N.C.; Story, P.; Reidenberg, J.; Sadeh, N. PrivOnto: A Semantic Framework for the Analysis of Privacy Policies. *Semant. Web* **2017**, *9*, 185–203. [CrossRef]
103. Harkous, H.; Fawaz, K.; Lebret, R.; Schaub, F.; Shin, K.G.; Aberer, K. Polisis: Automated Analysis and Presentation of Privacy Policies Using Deep Learning. In Proceedings of the 27th USENIX Security Symposium, Baltimore, MD, USA, 15–17 August 2018. [CrossRef]
104. Costance, E.; Sun, Y.; Petkovic, M.; den Hartog, J. A Machine Learning Solution to Assess Privacy Policy Completeness. In Proceedings of the 2012 ACM Workshop on Privacy in the Electronic Society (WPES '12), Raleigh North, CA, USA, 15 October 2012; pp. 91–96. [CrossRef]
105. Beke, F.; Eggers, F.; Verhof, P.C. Consumer Informational Privacy: Current Knowledge and Research Directions. *Found. Trends Mark.* **2018**, *11*, 1–71. [CrossRef]
106. Hussin, A.R.C.; Macaulay, L.; Keeling, K. The Importance Ranking of Trust Attributes in e-Commerce Website. In Proceedings of the 11th Pacific-Asia Conference on Information Systems, Auckland, New Zealand, 4–6 July 2007; 2007.

107. Söllner, M.; Leimeister, J.M. What We Really Know About Antecedents of Trust: A Critical Review of the Empirical Information Systems Literature on Trust. In *Psychology of Trust: New Research Gefen, D., Ed.*; Nova Science Publishers: Hauppauge, NY, USA, 2013; pp. 127–155. ISBN 978-1-62808-552-5.
108. Rocs, J.C.; Carcia, J.J.; de la Bega, J. The importance of perceived trust, security and privacy in online trading systems. *Inf. Manag. Comput. Secur.* **2009**, *17*, 96–113. [CrossRef]
109. Arifin, D.M. Antecedents of Trust in B2B Buying Process: A Literature Review. In Proceedings of the 5th IBA Bachelor Thesis Conference, Enschede, The Netherlands, 2 July 2015.
110. Tamini, N.; Sebastinelli, R. Understanding eTrust. *J. Inf. Priv. Secur.* **2007**, *3*, 3–17. [CrossRef]
111. Ruotsalainen, P.; Blobel, B. How a Service User Knows the Level of How a Service User Knows the Level of Privacy and to Whom Trust in pHealth Systems? *Stud. Health Technol. Inf.* **2021**, *285*, 39–48. [CrossRef]
112. Sillence, E.; Bruggs, P.; Fishwick, L.; Harris, P. Trust and mistrust of Online Health Sites. In Proceedings of the 2004 Conference on Human Factors in Computing Systems, CHI 2004, Vienna, Austria, 24–29 April 2004. [CrossRef]
113. Li, X.; Hess, T.J.; Valacich, J.S. Why do we trust new technology a study of initial trust formation with organizational information systems. *J. Strateg. Inf. Syst.* **2008**, *17*, 39–71. [CrossRef]
114. Seigneur, J.-M.; Jensen, C.D. Trading Privacy for Trust, Trust Management. In Proceedings of the Second International Conference, iTrust 2004, Oxford, UK, 29 March–1 April 2004; Volume 2995, pp. 93–107. [CrossRef]
115. Jøsang, A.; Ismail, R. The Beta Reputation System. In Proceedings of the 15th Bled Conference on Electronic Commerce, Bled, Slovenia, 17–19 June 2002.
116. Wang, Y.; Lin, E.-P. The Evaluation of Situational Transaction Trust in E-Service Environments. In Proceedings of the 2008 IEEE International Conference on e-Business Engineering, Xi'an, China, 22–24 October 2008; pp. 265–272. [CrossRef]
117. Matt, P.-A.; Morge, A.; Toni, F. Combining statistics and arguments to compute trust. In Proceedings of the 9th International Conference on Autonomous Agents and Multiagent Systems (AAMAS 2010), Toronto, ON, Canada, 10–14 May 2010; Volume 1–3. [CrossRef]
118. Fuchs, C. Toward an alternative concept of privacy. *J. Commun. Ethics Soc.* **2011**, *9*, 220–237. [CrossRef]
119. Acquisti, A.; Grossklags, J. Privacy and Rationality in Individual Decision Making. *IEEE Secur. Priv.* **2005**, *3*, 26–33. Available online: https://ssrn.com/abstract=3305365 (accessed on 11 April 2022). [CrossRef]
120. Lankton, N.K.; McKnight, D.H.; Tripp, J. Technology, Humanness, and Trust: Rethinking Trust in Technology. *J. Assoc. Inf. Syst.* **2015**, *16*, 880–918. [CrossRef]
121. EU-GDPR. Available online: htpps://eur-lex.europa.eu/legal-content/EN/TXT/?uri=CELEX%3A02016R0679-2016950&qid=1532348683434 (accessed on 11 April 2022).
122. Luo, W.; Najdawi, M. Trust-building Measures: A Review of Consumer Health Portals. *Commun. ACM* **2004**, *47*, 109–113. [CrossRef]
123. Adjekum, A.; Blasimme, A.; Vayena, E. Elements of Trust in Digital Health Systems: Scoping Review. *J. Med. Internet Res.* **2018**, *20*, e11254. [CrossRef]
124. Boon-itt, S. Quality of health websites and their influence on perceived usefulness, trust and intention to use: An analysis from Thailand. *J. Innov. Entrep.* **2019**, *8*, 4. [CrossRef]
125. Geissbuhler, A.; Safran, C.; Buchan, I.; Bellazzi, R.; Labkoff, S.; Eilenberg, K.; Leese, A.; Richardson, C.; Mantas, J.; Murray, P.; et al. Trustworthy reuse of health data: A transnational perspective. *Int. J. Med. Inf.* **2013**, *82*, 1–9. [CrossRef]
126. Esmaeilzadeh, P. The Impacts of the Perceived Transparency of Privacy Policies and Trust in Providers for Building Trust in Health Information Exchange: Empirical Study. *JMIR Med. Inf.* **2019**, *7*, e14050. [CrossRef]
127. Vega, J.A. Determiners of Consumer Trust towards Electronic Commerce: An Application to Puerto Rico. *Esic Mark. Econ. Bus. J.* **2015**, *46*, 125–147. [CrossRef]

Journal of *Personalized Medicine*

*Article*

# Reinforcing Health Data Sharing through Data Democratization

**Yuhang Wang [1,*], Bernd Blobel [2,3,4] and Bian Yang [1]**

1 Department of Information Security and Communication Technology, Norwegian University of Science and Technology, 2815 Gjøvik, Norway
2 Medical Faculty, University of Regensburg, 93053 Regensburg, Germany
3 First Medical Faculty, Charles University, 12800 Prague, Czech Republic
4 eHealth Competence Center Bavaria, Deggendorf Institute of Technology, 94469 Deggendorf, Germany
* Correspondence: yuhang.wang@ntnu.no

**Abstract:** In this paper, we propose a health data sharing infrastructure which aims to empower a democratic health data sharing ecosystem. Our project, named Health Democratization (HD), aims at enabling seamless mobility of health data across trust boundaries through addressing structural and functional challenges of its underlying infrastructure with the core concept of data democratization. A programmatic design of an HD platform was elaborated, followed by an introduction of one of our critical designs—a "reverse onus" mechanism that aims to incentivize creditable data accessing behaviors. This scheme shows a promising prospect of enabling a democratic health data-sharing platform.

**Keywords:** eHealth; data democratization; health data infrastructure; privacy-enhancing technologies

check for updates

**Citation:** Wang, Y.; Blobel, B.; Yang, B. Reinforcing Health Data Sharing through Data Democratization. *J. Pers. Med.* **2022**, *12*, 1380. https://doi.org/10.3390/jpm12091380

Academic Editor: Enrico Capobianco

Received: 13 June 2022
Accepted: 17 August 2022
Published: 26 August 2022



## 1. Introduction

Sharing health data creates value for clinical care, trials, and case studies, as well as an improved knowledge base [1–3] for healthcare researchers and healthcare organizations. Furthermore, it is crucial for advancing health ecosystems [4]. Health data also have immense commercial value [5] for other parties such as the pharmaceutical industry, data analytics providers, insurers, data markets, or business intelligence. It is also relevant for patients who want to control and share their data (e.g., the service digi.me, the crowd-sourced project wiki.p2pfoundation.net/Category:Health, etc.) in their interests, e.g., monitoring of health status, independent health data analysis, or experience sharing in a patient community.

The huge value associated with health data can lead to data misuse, for example, targeted use of ransomware, participation in the black market [6–8], and other cybercrimes. The conventional health data infrastructure was not designed for anticipating value-driven data mobility and the associated cyber threats. There is a structural deficiency in the conventional infrastructure on which patch-like remedies only add to the complexity of the challenge.

Obstacles for health data sharing are data silos, lack of appropriate tooling and lack of needed trust. Rather than reinforcing the infrastructure from a traditional view of vulnerability identification, protection, detection and response, in this project, we address the health data infrastructure's structural and functional deficiency to facilitate data mobility across trust boundaries through the concept of data democratization and a corresponding set of theories and technologies to implement the concept. Data democratization is a process of making data accessible to everybody and easying the understanding of that data for expediting decision making and supporting the business process [9,10]. Data democratization requires a strong governance for data and process management as well as a related culture, education, training, and tooling to enable this process irrespective of the actors' domain of expertise and technical know-how. Different contexts and objectives of actors as well as trust antecedents of the actors' environments establish trust boundaries to be overcome by harmonization/mapping of the related policies [11]. A policy is set of legal, political, organizational, functional, and technical obligations for communication and cooperation, defining the intended behavior of a system [4].

Our work aims at defining, architecting, implementing and evaluating a democratic health data infrastructure that is expected to incentivize all parties, including individuals, to prove, negotiate, and configure their rights and duties associated with health data. The conflicts of interest among different parties can be reconciled through a set of automated mechanisms so that data can be mobilized across trust boundaries.

A burgeoning health data sharing scenario could be more integrated and multifaceted than it used to be. Different parties could have different concerns towards sharing health data, e.g., privacy leakage, technical complexity of interoperability and security, lack of incentives, lack of resources and tools, and high cost of multilateral negotiation. The conventional health data infrastructure is insufficient in coping with data protection in an era of data mobility, e.g., accountability across trust boundaries. Moreover, the plan of future health data infrastructure usually only insufficiently considers fundamental logics and rationales (e.g., risk and incentive modeling, rights negotiation, cognitive modeling, etc.) of data mobility besides technical and regulatory compliance. The complexity attributed to a multitude of social and technical factors makes it difficult to make informed decisions to minimize the risk of a data breach while facilitating data mobility.

We are dedicated to architecting and constructing a data transaction model by strikingly practicing the concept of Data Democratization (or say, democratic data sharing). Formally, this indicates two core ideas, which will be followed throughout the design of our HD platform:

- All stakeholders are treated identically without discrimination. The platform and any constructed protocol would not take into account any player's distinguishing attributes (e.g., size, market volume, profitability, proprietary technology and knowledge, dominance in administrative power or market influence, information sources, etc.) and therefore each player can be treated equally in our platform;
- The promotion of fairness as a complementary. Based on the first fundamental, this is also essential when facing the inequivalence reality among each party, especially quite often seen between the individual data subject (DS) and the so-called "digital oligarchs".

State-of-the-art research and ethical and legal efforts have paid extensive attention to the first idea. However, we argue that fairness promotion is also critical concerning data democratization, due to the extremely unequal reality that exists between the individuals and the colossus entity.

For properly responding to the aforementioned challenges and solution weaknesses, we also consider architectural standards as well as related security and privacy specifications from the International Standards Organization (ISO), the European Committee for Standardization (CEN) and Health Level Seven International (HL7). In that context, we have to first mention ISO 23903:2021 [12], the interoperability and integration reference architecture model and framework, but also ISO 22600:2014 [13]. Privilege management and access control, Part 1–3, ISO 21298:2017 [14]. Functional and structural roles, but also the HL7 Privacy and Security Logical Data Model, Release 1, June 2021 [15], all using the ISO 23903 models and principles.

In this paper, we concentrate on a high-level architecture that will meet our design intention. We first provide a brief overview on related works in Section 2. In Section 3, we distinguish different types of stakeholders that would be concerned in our platform based on the differences in motivations, privacy tendencies, functionalities, etc. The definition and description of each derived role are presented in Section 3.1. To improve the universal understanding, in Section 3.2, we provide a mapping between the roles defined in our platform and the roles presented in the European General Data Protection Regulation (GDPR). We deeply consider the hierarchical perspective of our platform and propose, in

Section 4, a conceptual architecture to achieve our goal of data democratization. Section 5 illustrates democratic-promoting designs. One of our essential design primitives is a token-based approach to fairness promoting mechanism which focuses on facilitating a "reverse onus" during negotiation between two stakeholders with great disparity. We conclude our work in Section 6.

## 2. Related Works

The national eHealth infrastructure (e.g., local health authorities' Electronic Medical Record (EMR) systems, north Norway telemedicine infrastructure, and Norsk Helsenett) [16] in Norway has been built since the middle 1990s and is in its design intended for an organization's internal use, which emphasizes localized data retention and confidentiality. The "one citizen–one journal" plan was proposed in 2012 with the laws regarding medical records and health registers, updated in 2015 to facilitate data mobility. The national pilots Helseplattformen and Helseanalyseplattformen [17] were launched in recent years to technically implement connectivity and coordination in data sharing. On the EU level, the effort has so far mainly focused on the technical (e.g., the epSOS project), policy [18–20] and legal [21] interoperability towards the EU eHealth strategy 2020 [22]. As regulations are evolving and national laws always differ, the current health data infrastructure builds segregated silos, differing in purposes, data sharing methods, regulatory compliance practice, and the users' roles.

The trend towards preventive and personalized healthcare implies that health data can be collected from non-conventional health data sources, such as patients' devices, living environments [23], and the healthcare industry [24–27]. These patient-generated health data (PGHD) have frequently not yet been integrated into the national health data infrastructure. We also note that there, so far, exists a trend towards a patient-to-patient [28] crowd-sourced information-sharing community, where the generated new health knowledge may be regarded as PGHD too. However, such platforms are usually plagued by insufficient consideration of privacy.

The data breach caused by health IT outsourcing from Helse Sør-Øst [29] in Norway 2017 received massive public attention. Important concerns have been: the lack of risk management for decision making, lack of diligence from local health authorities regarding data protection of outsourced IT operation, and the lack of technical control (effective rights management in this case). The local municipalities may have an even worse situation [30] due to the fact that they have not adopted the national health data infrastructure. In addition to managerial and technical challenges, we may find it hard to consolidate an unambiguous set of "standard" rules and policies patching up all loopholes or fuzzy zones in laws [31], forcing all organizations and states to unanimous consensus [32]. The complexity attributed to legal, ethical, economic, managerial, interoperability, and technical factors makes security policy and decision making a great burden for all parties dealing with health data mobility, which can be seen from cases such as health record selling [33], data sharing with the government [34] bypassing patients, or patient safety endangered by health data access control in emergency [35,36]. An advanced solution for meeting those challenges is the deployment of ISO 23903 with the ontological representation of policies including ethical ones.

## 3. Classification of Stakeholders and Matching with Roles Defined in GDPR

The prior task for our work is to distinguish discrepant stakeholders with significant behavior characteristics and interest relationships. We first classify our HD platform-relevant stakeholders into seven types. Then, we present a sample of matching between these types of roles and the roles defined in GDPR.

### 3.1. Stakeholders Classification

The HD platform will "circulate" among diverse stakeholders. Some stakeholders participating in the Health Democratization (HD) project intend to get the health data to enable their service provision, while some others have the right of disposal of the health data. Other stakeholders may tend to provide data processing/storage/analyzing facilities. As follows, we classify these stakeholders into sveen different types according to their contexts, objectives and functions, ruled by related policies. A policy is set of legal, political, organizational, functional, and technical obligations for communication and cooperation, defining the intended behavior of a system [4].

- Computing resource manager (CRM)

The service provider assists each actor in managing computing, storage, and communication resources in facilitating data sharing with other actors.

The CRM service is provided through general computing infrastructure layers to support data sharing activities on the logic and operation layers, and is neither intended nor supposed to have any interest in the semantics layer (e.g., the content or utility of the data).

The actor is supposed to fully represent the interest of the stakeholders it serves. Depending on trust models and other factors, one CRM may serve one single or multiple actors. In the latter case, the CRM may have a conflict of interest when it comes to security and privacy aspects.

- Data consumer (DC)

The actor can access data directly, query a database, or receive data from DS, DG, or DSP to exploit the value of the shared data. It is a destination with which the data are shared.

- Data generator (DG)

The actor directly generates data from a DS or converts sensed signals into formatted data, through biomedical sensing, human recording/reporting, social media, human observation, questionnaire, interview, and other technical or non-technical means. A typical DG can be for instance a health or medical sensor, personal mobile device, speech-to-text generator, online questionnaire, a human being, etc.

- Data manager (DM)

The service provider assists each actor in processing, managing, and exchanging the data with other players.

The DM processes, manages, and exchanges data up to the operation layers, and is neither intended nor supposed to have any interest in the semantics layer (e.g., the content or utility of the data). At the syntax level (data structure, data models, database structure, dataset structure, etc.), operations such as formatting, encoding, decoding, transforming, indexing, pseudonymizing, access controlling, encrypting, decrypting, differential privacy-enhancing, content-dependent encryption/decryption, machine learning, data analysis, etc., are included At the binary level (file structure, file management system, etc.), operations such as storing, copying, appending, deleting, encoding, decoding, transmitting, logging, encrypting, decrypting, file format conversion, etc., are included.

DM is supposed to fully represent the interest of the actor/customer served. Depending on applied trust models and other factors, one DM may serve one single or multiple actors. In the latter case, the DM may have a conflict of interest when it comes to security and privacy aspects due to possible trust boundaries.

- Dataset provider (DSP)

The DSP creates and maintains-under the consent given by DS, and possibly the agreement with DG-one or several both syntactically and semantically structured datasets sourced from DS or/and DG, and shares the data with other stakeholders for a data-semantics-dependent purpose consented (in advance or real-time) by DS and harmonized by other involved parties with their rights and obligations. It is a possible source of data provided for sharing. It can also be a destination of shared data.

The DSP differs from DM, as DSP has an interest concerning the content or utility of the data for sharing, while DM does not.

A typical DSP can be: (1) an end dataset provider (e.g., hospital, an Electronic Health Record (EHR) operator, a research institute, etc.); or (2) a proxy dataset provider (e.g., a data portal, a data cache service provider, etc.).

The DSP processes data, not exclusively, on the semantic (content) level, such as appending, deleting, editing, combining, decomposing, transforming, structuring, sanitizing, summarizing, searching, retrieving, anonymizing, content-aware or content-dependent encrypting/decrypting, analyzing, etc., the data.

- Data rights manager (DRM)

The DRM assists each actor in managing his/her rights in relation to other actors, i.e., proving, negotiating, and recording the terms and conditions describing the rights and obligations regarding the data to be shared.

The DRM processes data up to the logic layers and is intended or supposed to have an interest in the data semantics (e.g., the content or utility of the data). This can include activities such as risk and benefit analysis, ethic and socioeconomic constraints, multi-party policy reconciliation, computational strategizing and negotiation, rights and obligations updating and recording, etc.

The DRM is supposed to fully represent the interest of the actor/customer served. Depending on trust models and other factors, one DRM may serve one single or multiple players. In the latter case, the DRM may have a conflict of interest when it comes to security and privacy aspects.

- Data analysis service provider (DASP)

The actor provides data analysis as a service to DS, DG, DC, or DSP.

### *3.2. Relation with Roles Defined in GDPRSubsection*

The relation between the participants or stakeholders (DS, DG, DC, DSP, DASP, DRM, DM, and CRM), defined in the Health Democratization (HD) project, and the three roles ("data subject", "data controller", and "data processor"), defined in GDPR, is understood in the following way.

The Data Controller is defined in GDPR as the party which determines the purposes and means by which personal data are processed. An organization can be a Joint Data Controller when, together with one or more organizations, it jointly determines 'why' and 'how' personal data should be processed. Such a joint controller relation must result in an agreement defining the respective responsibilities. The Data Processor processes personal data only on behalf of the controller.

The three roles in GDRP were defined as a legal status to clarify rights and obligations.

The participants in HD are defined in a way taking into account their functional roles in data sharing as well as their interest and rights in the shared data. Thereby, they are defined to facilitate understanding the various data sharing types, models, and scenarios through their independency and dependency relation among each other in function and interest in a specific data sharing transaction.

The data subject defined in HD is equivalent to that in GDPR.

A virtual example for illustrating the relation described above is given as follows:

- **Example**: A general practitioner (GP) can provide a value-added service for his/her patients who have their own Personal Health Record (PHR) system which is technically provided and maintained by a PHR service provider who builds their service on infrastructure provided by the public cloud from Amazon. The GP can specify what data are needed for a health monitoring process for purpose of a specific longitudinal study to personalize the care plan for a specific patient. The GP sets up the longitudinal study plan, collects data from a PHR which has the data sourced from different independent wearable sensor data vault used by the patient, outsources part of the collected data to a data analytics service provider for data analysis purpose, accumulate the data, and finally design a new care plan for the patient. To provide legitimate, auditable, and efficient service information and contract management, the GP uses a contract management App to communicate with the patient for negotiating the rights, obligations, prices, and other issues concerning the offering of the service.

We have developed the following mapping between the aforementioned HD project stakeholder types (GP, patient, PHR service provider, sensor service provider, data analytics service provider) and the GDPR roles, listed in Table 1.

**Table 1.** A sample mapping between stakeholders defined above and the GDPR-defined roles.

| Party | Participant Defined in HD | Role Defined in GDPR |
|---|---|---|
| Patient | data subject | data subject |
| GP | data consumer | joint data controller |
| PHR portal managed by the patient | data manager | data processor |
| PHR service provider | dataset provider | joint data controller, data processor |
| Amazon cloud | computing resource manager | data processor |
| Sensor service provider | data generator | data processor |
| Data analytics service provider | data analytics service provider | data processor |
| Contract management App | data rights manager | data processor |

## 4. Conceptual Layered Architecture of HD Platform

To meet the principle of data democratization and the promised capabilities, we gazed deep into the platform from a hierarchical perspective. The HD platform enables developing and managing the democratic negotiation procedures during the healthcare data business, for use in, and exchange of, clinical and individual health information between the potential DS/DM and the potential DC.

For each principle and the potentially promissing scenario, the executive process could be considered as a correlation between the data sharing participants and an affair-related data sharing function at different executive levels, defining the business system's behavior. The objective must be to adjust the system's behavior in its structure and function according to the multiple applicable policies from legal, procedural, contextual up to ethical policies and principles including individual policies of the stakeholders involved.

Guided by ISO 23903, which standardized the model and framework of an interoperability and integration reference architecture, but also by ISO 22600 and ISO 21298 (all those standards have also been approved as CEN standards and and re-used in the HL7 security and privacy specifications), as well as the eHealth standardization in the Nordic countries [37] concerning the interoperability [38,39], our HD platform represents the proposed the stakeholders' classification and related functions. The data sharing function ranges from the incipient data provenance to the rights and obligation tracking according to the agreement. We stratify our platform into four conceptual layers, named "Computing Infrastructure Layer", "Data Sharing Operation Layer", "Data Sharing Logic" and "Healthcare Business Layer". Each layer is eligible for interoperability with its adjacent layers. Our Architecture also obtains references from the peer work on diverse eHealth networking and healthcare data sharing solutions [40–42].

Figure 1 presents our conceptual architecture in detail. The architectural three-dimensional model describes the data sharing hierarchical structure, the data sharing participants, and the data sharing functions for achieving the business objectives. It outlines a thorough view of related implications of democratic data sharing with our platform. Each square implicates a potential relevance at the practical level. The main systematic-level functions required in our platform include:

- **Data provenance**: providing backward traceability of medical devices, the personal device in the homecare environment, etc., and the health data sourced from these devices to be audited in a trusted way regarding rights and operation status;

- **Risk Assessment**: enabling each data subject to have different risk acceptance tolerance and incentive degrees when they are entitled to rights and benefits from data;
- **Computational negotiation**: negotiating agents can operate and negotiate decisions. The requirements will be developed in compliance with the GDPR, healthcare regulations, and other relevant policies. When processing and exchanging personal data between the agents, the design of the infrastructure will address such key requirements of the GDPR as data protection by design and by default, accountability, pseudonymization, right of access, and right to be informed, to rectify, to erasure, and to be forgotten;
- **Multi-lateral security policing**: enabling individuals to be able to share and control access to health data without having to place extensive trust in entities, and institutions must also be able to share data responsibly for research, innovation, and quality assurance across institutional boundaries.

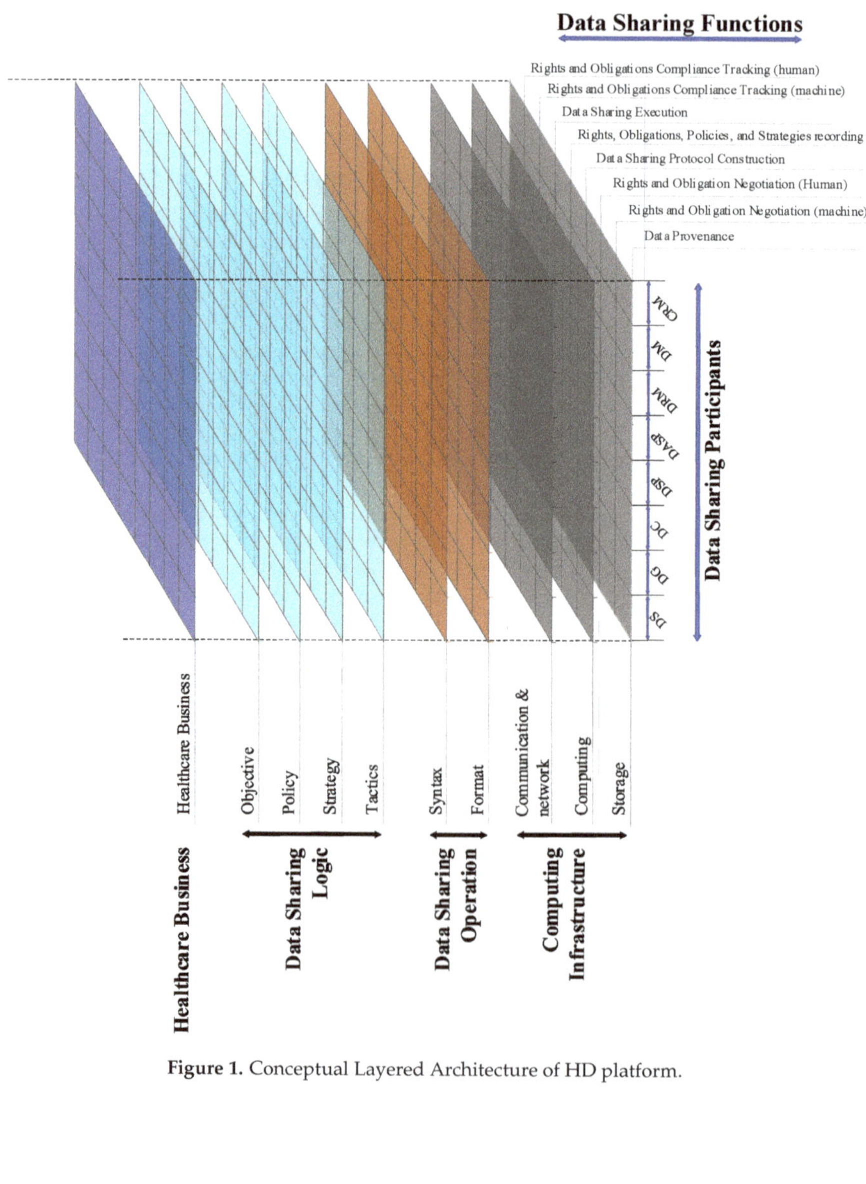


**Figure 1.** Conceptual Layered Architecture of HD platform.

A dynamic data sharing transaction could consist of the following steps:

- A data provenance process that clarifies among the concerned players the history of the parties with their rights regarding the data to be shared;
- If a default (pre-defined) right and obligation setting is not unanimously agreed upon by the involved players, a knowledge-driven negotiation process must be performed where each player takes into account different factors such as ethical and legal contexts, risk assessment of data breach/privacy breach, benefit from data sharing, etc., based on risk models, and AI-based inference. As business systems are frequently highly dynamic regarding their objectives, context, processes, etc., a dynamic policy management and mapping in consistency with legal and ethical requirements and principles is inevitable;
- The computational negotiation mechanism takes as inputs the risk assessment result from individual players as well as the multi-party security policy logical representation and reconciliation solution, and generates a new recommendation to all the involved parties for achieving an agreement. This process could iterate in several rounds;
- The outcome of the computational negotiation determines the data sharing protocol and the security and privacy-enhancing technical methods for data sharing (e.g., homomorphic encryption, secure multi-party computation, differential privacy methods, federated machine learning, etc.);
- The new configuration of rights of the involved players is recorded using blockchain technology, and the execution of data sharing is encoded into a smart contract which could trigger the automated data sharing now or in the future.

The aforementioned design could be merged into a democratic design. Figure 2 shows a function-level relational architecture between the defined roles and the functions.

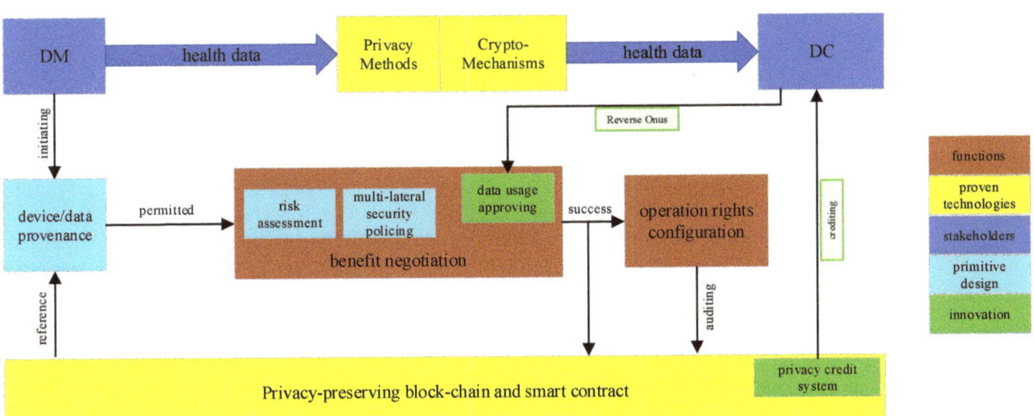


**Figure 2.** Function-level relational architecture.

We illustrated several proven enabling technologies which could be used as a mature solution in the counterpart functions, such as the blockchain-based data provenance mechanism, the conventional privacy-enhancing methods, and crypto-based solutions such as the operable contract enforcement. Our primitive design series for enabling data democratization, such as the risk assessment and multi-lateral security policing, focus on the the negotiating part, which ensures that the backward traceable health data could be traded or shared under an equipotent situation.

In addition, the green part shown in Figure 2 represents one of our innovations, which moves forward to a more democratic vision in the principle of fairness promotion. The next section will provide a brief overview on this part.

## 5. Democratization-Promoting Primitive Design

Numerous state-of-the-art proven technologies and solutions could be utilized for realizing our HD platform. However, a gap still exists between the current solutions and the data democratization vision [43,44]. Our vital task is to design promising technical and procedural solutions that can promote democratic data sharing. For integrating different specifications and solutions, that way enabling comprehensive interoperability, it is inevitable to harmonize the different representation styles and languages by properly re-engineering them on the basis of ISO 23903:2021. Thereby, the axes of the ISO 23903 Reference Model correspond to those in Figure 1 as follows: the ISO 23903 Domain dimension summarizes both the Data Sharing Participants and the Data Sharing Function; the ISO 23903 Development Process dimension is represented by the process-related components; while the ISO 23903 Granularity dimension representing the composition/decomposition of the systems elements is completely missing.

In this section, we will introduce one of the critical data-democratization-promoting designs.

### *5.1. Token-Economy-Powered Incentive Mechanism for Promoting Reverse Onus*

In our HD platform, each DC may have the right to claim how much privacy they need to perform a certain healthcare service, whereas the DM may lack the knowledge to assess the validity of the claim. Our HD platform seeks to provide an incentive mechanism to help improve the privacy level of health data. This also could play a role when considering the principle of "data minimization" defined in GDPR.

Considering a vulnerable DS (and his/her DM) with insufficient knowledge to engage in a beneficiary negotiation with the data user, this mechanism will assist this negotiation for achieving a more reasonable scheme or contract from a privacy perspective. It will also cover the execution of the agreement-based contract, especially when the real-world scenario goes beyond the contract's coverage, by a token-economy-based mechanism and a virtual credit system. The incentive component is expected to restrain the "grey gap" of privacy leakage.

The objectives of the incentive demo include: (1) to provide a "reverse onus" mechanism between data collector and data manager; (2) to promote the faithful execution of the contract; and (3) to inhibit potential incompliant/illegal data user.

In our mechanism shown in Figure 2, the data usage approving helps build the privacy-enhancing consistency between data collector and data manager. After the mutual agreement was achieved and the contract was built, the private credit system will monitor the execution of the protocol to stimulate the data collector to follow the privacy terms, build a token currency system on encouraging privacy-friendly behaviors, and generate the virtual credit of privacy integrity of data collector based on its history log. This credit will be further used to consult the future negotiations.

### *5.2. Data Usage Approval*

The negotiation procedure is protected by requiring the data collector to apply form (*appFm*) on the usage of the health data, including:

1. Usage purpose;
2. Data precision upper limit in percentage;
3. Data requesting schedule instant/time period/data manager triggered/etc;
4. Requiring a pattern in the frequency distribution;

The *appFm* will be assessed by the platform, based on the usage log, considering:

1. Purposes to precision. The required data precision should be in accordance with the purposes of the data usage;
2. Purposes to schedule. To assess whether the data accesses conform to the purposes.
3. Purposes to the pattern. To assess whether the data requesting is coherent with the purposes;
4. History comparison across entities.

The *appFm* will always be approved by our incentive component. Here, we only assess the privacy-leakage risk and register the *appFm* in the token currency credit system.

### 5.3. Token Economy Rules

The incentive component organized all the data transmission into a "purchase" behavior in the token-economy system. Here, the component will use a token named "healthcoin", inherited from our previous work [45], to build a token balance and transaction system. The rules of this token system are as follows:

**Rule 1** (coin creation): For each time the data collector registers the *appFm*, the system will create some healthcoin and transfer them to the data collector's balance. The amount of the health coin is determined by the details of *appFm* and the credit level of the data collector. By default, for each time the data piece is requested, there will be 1 $ healthcoin generated and transferred to the data collector;

**Rule 2** (health data purchase): Each time a data transmission in the platform happens, the token system will consider it as a purchase behavior of the data collector by using its healthcoin. By default, the price of the health data will be 1 $ as long as it is following the *appFm* claimed by the data collector. The component will always satisfy the purchase if the data collector can afford the price. In combination with **Rule 1**, it is clear that an honest data collector will always work well in our system;

**Rule 3** (credit score): The incentive component will set a credit score for each data collector, denoted as $\alpha \in [0, 1]$, where 1 means data collector has the highest credit score. The credit score will be adjusted based on the simple idea that the more balance of healthcoins it has, the more dangerous the data collector will be, since the credit score will always be satisfied when the data collector has enough healthcoins to obtain whatever data he wants;

**Rule 4** (credit-based coin creation): Based on **Rule 1**, for each *appFm*, the healthcoin DC will gain is (amount $\times$ $\alpha$) $, where the amount is calculated by **Rule 1**;

**Rule 5** (discount): DC can claim a discount by reducing the data requirement (e.g., precision, amount, frequency) to get a discount, the discount strategy is simply following the ratio of data distortion.

### 5.4. Behavior Analysis

An honest and stable DC can be adapted into this system very well, because it always has a low balance, i.e., a high credit score, and earned enough healthcoin for his claimed *appFm*. When a greedy data collector performs:

1. Excessive data transmission, the balance cannot be enough for him to afford the rest of the data, and hence go against his plan of *appFm*;
2. Hoarding the healthcoin (e.g., by utilizing **Rule 5** to save healthcoin on purpose) to perform potential privacy data transmission. However, when the balance becomes high, the gain from the new *appFm* will decrease, and the balance will be exhausted soon since the payments it gets barely cover his expenses.

When an embarrassed DC cannot afford a regular data transmission claimed by himself, he can choose to use the discount to make up for the loss, regain his credit and normal balance in the future.

### 5.5. Incentive Mechanism

Based on the aforementioned token-based mechanism, it will be a choice put in front of DC, which is either to break the balance, be bankrupt, but collect some more health data and then receive profit from it; or to honestly behave as a normal stakeholder, with no gain from extra health data, but also without loss from being bankrupt and leading to harm to the profit from the contract.

The incentive mechanism's job is to maintain the platform always in a configuration status, which encourage DC to always being the honest part rather than harming DS and DM. Here we use a policy toolkit to configure the global parameters to incentive honest behaviors.

1. The credit parameter

This is the aforementioned parameter to decide how acutely the credit score will decrease with the increase of the healthcoin balance. The incentive mechanism could use this parameter to adjust the balance in the system. For example, when DC finds not enough income and decides to ask for more data, the incentive mechanism can turn up this parameter to achieve a more severe balance reaction;

2. Gain/loss ratio $\theta$

This is a parameter that reflects the gain (from the privacy stealing) and loss (from the regular business). Both gain and loss are inherited from outside information, e.g., the domain expert advice, or the market analysis. Notice that this is not the gain/loss of the virtual healthcoin, but the real-world profit;

3. Discount ratio $\delta$

When the data collector finds it acceptable to discount the data transmission every time to achieve the profit, the incentive mechanism will use discount ratio $\delta$ to ensure the discount is no longer cost-effective. For example, obtaining a 50% decrease in data precision with only a 10% discount.

## 6. Conclusions

In this paper, we raised the concept of data democratization, which will reinforce health data-sharing concerning privacy enhancement and benefits insurance. Based on current standards, an overall conceptual layered architecture was proposed which aims to enable such a vision. We illustrated the key components that lead to a democratic data-sharing scenario regarding data provenance, risk assessment, multi-lateral security policing, and computational negotiation. Some proven technologies are also illustrated to cope with the corresponding functions. The output of our HD platform is an executable and auditable contract, democratically signed between well-defined stakeholders. The contract could also be a configuration instruction for conventional privacy-enhancing technologies (e.g., differential privacy) and the crypto-based solutions (e.g., ABE access policies).

We further introduced an advanced concept of data democratization, which emphasized fairness promotion in the HD platform. A token-economy-powered incentive mechanism for promoting "Reverse Onus" on data usage was proposed. This mechanism rebalances inequitable situations among the stakeholders.

Future work will keep on implementing and integrating the proposed conceptual designs. Several landing case studies will be put into consideration to improve the practicability of our work. In that context, we have to harmonize our approach by correctly and comprehensively deploying ISO 23903:2021. ISO 23903:2021 provides a model and framework for a system-theoretical, architecture-centric, ontology-based and policy-driven approach to formally and correctly represent any living or non-living system including its evolution/development [4]. Policies considered ranged from legal, procedural and contextual up to ethical policies and principles. Details will be presented in our paper to pHealth 2022.

**Author Contributions:** Writing—original draft, Y.W. and B.Y.; Writing—review & editing, B.B. All authors have read and agreed to the published version of the manuscript.

**Funding:** This research work was funded by the project Reinforcing the Health Data Infrastructure in Mobility and Assurance through Data Democratization under the IKTPLUSS program of Research Council of Norway (grant number 288856).

**Institutional Review Board Statement:** Not applicable.

**Informed Consent Statement:** Informed consent was obtained from all subjects involved in the study.

**Data Availability Statement:** Not applicable.

**Conflicts of Interest:** The authors declare no conflict of interest.

## References


1. *Sharing Clinical Research Data: Workshop Summary*; The National Academies Press: Washington, DC, USA, 2013.
2. Walport, M.; Brest, P. Sharing research data to improve public health. *Lancet* **2011**, *377*, 537–539. [CrossRef]
3. Blobel, B.; Lopez, D.M.; Gonzalez, C. Patient privacy and 12 security concerns on big data for personalized medicine. *Health Technol.* **2016**, *6*, 75–81. [CrossRef]
4. Blobel, B.; Oemig, F.; Ruotsalainen, P.; Lopez, D.M. Transformation of Health and Social Care Systems—An Interdisciplinary Approach Toward a Foundational Architecture. *Front. Med.* **2022**, *9*, 802487. [CrossRef] [PubMed]
5. Scientific American. Available online: https://www.scientificamerican.com/article/how-data-brokers-make-money-off-your-medical-records/ (accessed on 5 August 2022).
6. Czeschik, C. Black Market Value of Patient Data. In *Digital Marketplaces Unleashed*; Springer: Berlin/Heidelberg, Germany, 2018; pp. 883–893.
7. Ruotsalainen, P.S.; Blobel, B.; Seppälä, A.; Nykänen, P. Trust Information-Based Privacy Architecture for Ubiquitous Health. *JMIR mHealth uHealth* **2013**, *1*, e23. [CrossRef] [PubMed]
8. Blobel, B.; Nordberg, R.; Davis, J.M.; Pharow, P. Modelling privilege management and access control. *Int. J. Med. Inform.* **2006**, *75*, 597–623. [CrossRef] [PubMed]
9. Mallik, P. Data Democratization. Towards Data Science. 18 July 2019. Available online: https://towardsdatascience.com (accessed on 5 August 2022).
10. Marr, B. What Is Data Democratization? A Super Simple Explanation and The Key Pros and Cons. 24 July 2017. Available online: https://www.forbes.com (accessed on 5 August 2022).
11. Ruotsalainen, P.; Blobel, B. How a service user knows the level of privacy and to whom trust in pHealth systems? *Stud. Health Technol. Inform.* **2021**, *285*, 39–48. [PubMed]
12. *ISO 23903:2021*; Health Informatics—Interoperability and Integration Reference Architecture—Model and Framework. International Organisation for Standardisation (ISO): Geneva, Switzerland, 2021.
13. *ISO 22600:2014*; Health Informatics—Privilege Management and Access Control. International Organisation for Standardisation (ISO): Geneva, Switzerland, 2014.
14. *ISO 21298:2017*; Health Informatics—Funtional and Structural Roles. International Organisation for Standardisation (ISO): Geneva, Switzerland, 2017.
15. HL7 International. *HL7 Privacy and Security Logical Data Model, Release 1, June 2021*; HL7 International: Ann Arbor, MI, USA, 2021.
16. Hartvigsen, G.; Pedersen, S. *Lessons Learned from 25 Years with Telemedicine in Northern Norway*; NST-Rapportserie: Tromso, Norway, 2015; pp. 6–16.
17. Helseanalyseplattformen. Available online: https://ehelse.no/helsedataprogrammet/helseanalyseplattformen (accessed on 5 August 2022).
18. Blobel, B.; Davis, M.; Ruotsalainen, P. Policy Management Standards Enabling Trustworthy pHealth. *Stud. Health Technol. Inform.* **2014**, *200*, 8–21. [PubMed]
19. Ruotsalainen, P.; Blobel, B. Trust Information and Privacy Policies—Enablers for pHealth and Ubiquitous Health. *Stud. Health Technol. Inform.* **2014**, *200*, 133–139. [PubMed]
20. Ruotsalainen, P.; Blobel, B. Trust Model for Protection of Personal Health Data in a Global Environment. *Stud. Health Technol. Inform.* **2017**, *245*, 202–206. [PubMed]
21. Directive 2011/24/EU on Patients' Rights in Cross-Border Healthcare. Available online: https://ec.europa.eu/health/cross_border_care/policy_en (accessed on 5 August 2022).
22. European eHealth. Available online: https://ec.europa.eu/health/sites/health/files/ehealth/docs/ev_20161121_co01_en.pdf (accessed on 5 August 2022).
23. Facebook Life Trajectory. Available online: https://www.technologyreview.com/s/514186/lifes-trajectory-seen-through-facebook-data/ (accessed on 5 August 2022).
24. Google Clinical Care. Available online: https://theconversation.com/google-is-now-involved-with-healthcare-data-is-that-a-good-thing-58901 (accessed on 5 August 2022).
25. Blobel, B.; Ruotsalainen, P. How Does GDPR Support Healthcare Transformation to 5P Medicine? *Stud. Health Technol. Inform.* **2019**, *264*, 1135–1339. [PubMed]
26. Blobel, B.; Ruotsalainen, P. Healthcare Transformation Towards Personalized Medicine—Chances and Challenges. *Stud. Health Technol. Inform.* **2019**, *261*, 3–21. [PubMed]
27. Ruotsalainen, P.; Blobel, B. Digital pHealth—Problems and Solutions for Ethics, Trust and Privacy. *Stud. Health Technol. Inform.* **2019**, *261*, 31–46. [PubMed]
28. The Patient Information Sharing Platform. Available online: https://www.patientslikeme.com/ (accessed on 5 August 2022).
29. Helse Sør-Øst Outsourcing Health IT. Available online: https://www.nrk.no/norge/helse-sor-ost_-outsourcing-stoppes-1.13578806 (accessed on 5 August 2022).
30. NRK Nordland. Available online: https://www.nrk.no/nordland/irenes-private-helseopplysninger-la-apent-ute-pa-nett_-_-sjokkerende-og-ekkelt-1.13693173 (accessed on 5 August 2022).
31. Madge, R. Five Loopholes in the GDPR. Available online: https://medium.com/mydata/five-loopholes-in-the-gdpr-367443c4248b (accessed on 5 August 2022).

32. Dette Kan Ramme Viljen Til å Delta i Forskning. Available online: https://forskning.no/2018/04/dette-kan-ramme-viljen-til-delta-i-forskning/produsert-og-finansiert-av/de-nasjonale-forskningsetiske-komiteene (accessed on 5 August 2022).
33. Millions of NHS Records Sold to Insurance Firms. Available online: http://www.telegraph.co.uk/news/health/news/10906390/Millions-of-NHS-records-sold-to-insurance-firms.html (accessed on 5 August 2022).
34. Patients Will Resist Medical Record Sharing if NHS Bosses Ignore Their Privacy Fears. Available online: https://theconversation.com/patients-will-resist-medical-record-sharing-if-nhs-bosses-ignore-their-privacy-fears-46147 (accessed on 5 August 2022).
35. Informasjonssikkerhet er Mer enn Bare Personvern. Hurlen og Gulbrandsen. Available online: https://www.aftenposten.no/meninger/kronikk/i/WV2Vg/Hvor-trygg-kan-pasientjournalen-egentlig-vare-Informasjonssikkerhet-er-mer-enn-bare-personvern--Hurlen-og-Gulbrandsen (accessed on 5 August 2022).
36. Ruotsalainen, P.; Blobel, B. Transformed Health Ecosystems—Challenges for Security, Privacy, and Trust. *Front. Med.* **2022**, *9*, 827253. [CrossRef] [PubMed]
37. Nasjonal e-Helsestrategi og Mål 2017–2022. Available online: https://ehelse.no/publikasjoner/nasjonal-e-helsestrategi-og-mal-2017-2022-oppdatert-2019 (accessed on 5 August 2022).
38. ANTILOPE Refinement Definition Document. Available online: https://www.antilope-project.eu/wp-content/uploads/2013/05/D1.1-Refinement_of_Antilope_Use_Cases_v1.2.pdf (accessed on 5 August 2022).
39. Europe eHealth ev. Available online: https://ec.europa.eu/health/sites/default/files/ehealth/docs/ev_20151123_co03_en.pdf (accessed on 5 August 2022).
40. Cole, A.M.; Stephens, K.A.; Keppel, G.A.; Lin, C.-P.; Baldwin, L.-M. Implementation of a health data-sharing infrastructure across diverse primary care organizations. *J. Ambul. Care Manag.* **2014**, *37*, 164–170. [CrossRef]
41. Explaining the Technical Architecture of Health Information Exchange. Available online: https://www.colleaga.org/sites/default/files/attachments/ExplainingTheTechnicalArchitectureOfHIE.pdf (accessed on 5 August 2022).
42. Meng, S.; Zhu, L.; Xu, K. Layered Data Sharing Architecture with Blockchain. In *Blockchain: Empowering Secure Data Sharing*; Springer: Singapore, 2020; pp. 29–37.
43. Ruotsalainen, P.; Blobel, B. A Model for Calculated Privacy and Trust in pHealth Ecosystems. *Stud. Health Technol. Inform.* **2018**, *249*, 29–37.
44. Ruotsalainen, P.; Blobel, B. Privacy Is Dead—Solutions for Privacy-Enabled Collections and Use of Personal Health Information in Digital Era. *Stud. Health Technol. Inform.* **2020**, *273*, 63–74. [PubMed]
45. Wang, Y.; Tian, Z.; Sun, Y.; Du, X.; Guizani, N. LocJury: An IBN-based location privacy preserving scheme for IoCV. *IEEE Trans. Intell. Transp. Syst.* **2020**, *22*, 5028–5037. [CrossRef]

Journal of *Personalized Medicine*

MDPI

*Article*

# Aortic Risks Prediction Models after Cardiac Surgeries Using Integrated Data

**Iuliia Lenivtceva [1,*], Dmitri Panfilov [2], Georgy Kopanitsa [1,3] and Boris Kozlov [2]**

1 National Center for Cognitive Research, ITMO University, 49 Kronverskiy Prospect, 197101 Saint-Petersburg, Russia; georgy.kopanitsa@gmail.com
2 Cardiology Research Institute, Tomsk National Research Medical Center of the Russian Academy of Science, 634012 Tomsk, Russia; pand2006@yandex.ru (D.P.); bnkozlov@yandex.ru (B.K.)
3 Almazov National Medical Research Center, 2 Akkuratova Street, 197341 Saint-Petersburg, Russia
* Correspondence: lenivezzki@gmail.com

**Abstract:** The complications of thoracic aortic disease include aortic dissection and aneurysm. The risks are frequently compounded by many cardiovascular comorbidities, which makes the process of clinical decision making complicated. The purpose of this study is to develop risk predictive models for patients after thoracic aneurysm surgeries, using integrated data from different medical institutions. Seven risk features were formulated for prediction. The CatBoost classifier performed best and provided an ROC AUC of 0.94–0.98 and an F-score of 0.95–0.98. The obtained results are widely in line with the current literature. The obtained findings provide additional support for clinical decision making, guiding a patient care team prior to surgical treatment, and promoting a safe postoperative period.

**Keywords:** postoperative risks; aortic aneurysm; integrated data; predictive modeling; feature extraction; machine learning



**Citation:** Lenivtceva, I.; Panfilov, D.; Kopanitsa, G.; Kozlov, B. Aortic Risks Prediction Models after Cardiac Surgeries Using Integrated Data. *J. Pers. Med.* **2022**, *12*, 637. https://doi.org/10.3390/jpm12040637

Academic Editors: Bernd Blobel and Mauro Giacomini

Received: 21 March 2022
Accepted: 12 April 2022
Published: 15 April 2022



## 1. Introduction

The complications of thoracic aortic disease include aortic dissection and aneurysm. These pathologies are common for elderly patients, males, smokers, and those with a family history of aneurysms. More than 20% of patients with aortic disease, suffering from acute aortic events, have no symptoms and die at home, without receiving medical help [1].

The causes of death include not only aortic rupture, but also myocardial infarction, renal insufficiency, and stroke [2]. In combination with several cardiovascular comorbidities, these factors complicate clinical decision making. One of the ways to decrease a patient's risk is to ensure a timely prognosis of complications.

Despite the fact that various risk scales (Euroscore, Euroscore II, STS score) are successfully used in cardiac surgery, there is still no single prognostic risk assessment scale for patients with thoracic aortic pathology. Currently, there are several attempts being made to design specific predictive models for thoracic aortic pathology risk assessment [3,4]. However, extension of the dataset is required to identify the most significant risk factors, due to the heterogeneity in the obtained predictors in all studies. The significant risk factors are used to create a scale that is correct for assessing perioperative risk in patients with thoracic aorta.

Machine learning (ML) can provide tools for personalized risk prediction based on real-world data and the clinical history of a patient [5]. It employs collected routine clinical data to implement mathematical models that can forecast risks [6]. The ML models can predict the expansion of aortic aneurysm based on the anatomical features extracted from CT scans and textual documents. The ML algorithm developed by Hirata et al. [7] could predict an expansion of an aneurysm with high accuracy. Another study used ML techniques to make a prognosis on the risk of aortic aneurysm growth in 85% and 71% of patients at 12 and 24 months, respectively [8].

The incidence of adverse events is not the same in each patient. The evaluation of risk factors for adverse events in patients after such a complex procedure is crucial. To date, some authors have attempted to identify predictors of early postoperative complications [4,9–11]. However, searching the predictors for perioperative and postoperative complications and mortality after thoracic aortic surgery is still an issue. Recent studies have investigated the problem of TAA and related risks.

Table 1 summarizes the results of the review performed for cardiovascular predictive modelling.

**Table 1.** Recent studies for cardiovascular predictive modelling.

| Scheme | Algorithm | AUC-ROC | Data | Target |
|---|---|---|---|---|
| Lee, 2018 [12] | XGBoost | 0.78 | Open heart and TAA surgery | Acute kidney injury |
| Zhong, 2021 [13] | XGBoost | 0.93 | Coronary artery bypass surgery, aortic valve replacement and other heart surgeries | 30-day mortality, septic shock, liver dysfunction, and thrombocytopenia |
| Allyn, 2017 [14] | Model ensemble | 0.78 | Elective heart surgery | Postoperative mortality |
| Fernandes, 2021 [15] | XGBoost | 0.88 | Intraoperative open heart surgery data | Postoperative mortality |
| Coulson, 2020 [16] | Logistic regression | 0.78–0.85 | Open heart surgery | Acute kidney injury |

The algorithms most frequently used for cardiovascular predictive modelling are logistic regression (LR), ensemble models and tree models (random forest and decision tree classifiers), and boosting strategies, such as XGBoost. The most frequent metric for the evaluation of predictive models is the area under the receiver operating characteristic curve (AUC-ROC). Thereby, a higher value corresponds to better discrimination [17].

The goal of the presented study is to develop predictive models for significant risk factor identification in patients after thoracic aneurysm surgeries, using integrated data from different medical institutions.

## 2. Materials and Methods

The model for risk prognosis was developed using two datasets from two clinical providers. The first dataset contains 97 structured records for 137 patients with clinical records on aortic operations. The second dataset contains 56,929 text documents from the years 2008–2019 for the 343 TAA operations of 319 patients.

We formulated seven target features: in-hospital mortality; temporary neurological deficit (TND); permanent neurological deficit (PND); prolonged (>7 days) lung ventilation (LV); renal replacement therapy (RRT); myocardial infarction (MI); multiple organ failure (MOF). In total, 61 input parameters were used for the risk prediction model. The features were organized in the following categories: anthropometric data (6 features), comorbidities (8 features), laboratory tests (5 features), coronary angiographic data (4 features), echocardiographic data (8 features), computed tomographic data (14 features), intraoperative data (15 features), and concomitant cardiac procedures (3 features). The full feature list is available in Appendix A.

The pipeline for the model development is represented in Figure 1.

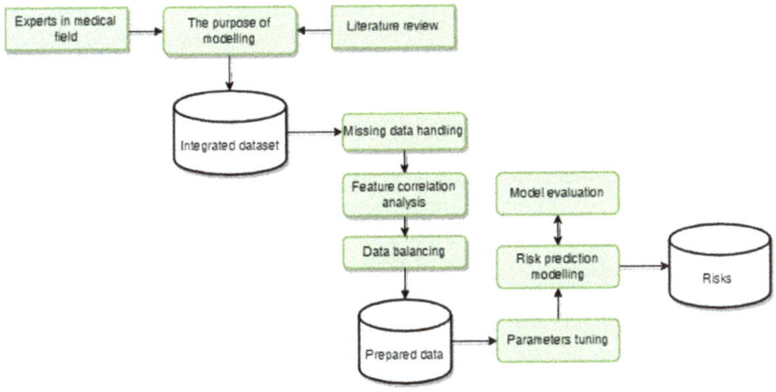


**Figure 1.** The pipeline for medical risk model development.

The features in the dataset with >30% missing values were eliminated. For managing features with up to 30% missing values, the k nearest neighbors (KNN) imputation technique was applied. The Pearson's correlation method was used for feature correlation analysis. Features with a high correlation coefficient were eliminated. The synthetic minority over-sampling technique (SMOTE) was employed for balancing the dataset. The classification was conducted using the two most important features, and all of the features were used to compare performances. The feature selection was organized through the voting of several techniques: univariate feature selection with a chi-squared test, recursive feature elimination (RFE), extra trees classifier, and Lasso.

We used logistic regression (LR), random forest (RF) and CatBoost (CC) classifiers for experiments. The parameters were tuned through the grid search, and the F-score was used as the optimization metric.

LR is expressed by the following equation:

$$Z = \frac{1}{1 + e^{-(\beta_0 + \beta_1 x)}} \tag{1}$$

LR is the most frequently used machine learning model in medical applications, due to its high interpretability. Its sensitivity to the multicollinearity problem is one of the disadvantages of the LR model. Thus, highly correlated features should not be included in the predictive model.

RF is an ensemble model based on decision trees. During classification, each tree assigns the most likely target to each patient with a set of predictors. The averaging function is expressed by the following equation:

$$Z = argmax \frac{1}{T} \sum_{t=1}^{T} p_t(y|x) \tag{2}$$

where $p_t\,(y\,|\,x)$ is the probability distribution for each tree. RF is also a widespread algorithm for medical applications.

CatBoost is an ordered gradient boosting algorithm that addresses the problem of target leakage. CC is effective on small datasets. Binary decision trees are used in the CC classifier. The CC output can be expressed as follows:

$$Z = H(x_i) = \sum_{j=1}^{J} c_j 1_{\{x \in R_j\}} \tag{3}$$

$H(x_i)$ is a decision tree function and $R_j$ is a disjoint region corresponding to the leaves of the tree.

The experiments were conducted with the following Python 3 packages: scikit-learn [18] and CatBoost [19] for machine learning model implementation; seaborn [20] and matplotlib [21] for data visualization; SMOTE [22] for dataset balancing; and SHapley Additive exPlanations (SHAP) [23] for the interpretation of black-box results. The discrimination was evaluated using ROC curves.

Table 2 lists the machine learning models and parameters used in the research.

**Table 2.** Models and parameters.

| Model | Parameters |
|---|---|
| LR* (imp. feat.) | 'C': 2.83, 'solver': 'newton-cg' |
| LR + SMOTE (imp. feat.) | 'C': 0.5, 'solver': 'newton-cg' |
| LR + SMOTE (all feat.) | 'C': 4.0, 'solver': 'liblinear' |
| RF (imp. feat.) | 'criterion': 'gini', 'max_features': 'auto' |
| RF + SMOTE (imp. feat.) | 'criterion': 'gini', 'max_features': 'auto' |
| RF + SMOTE (all feat.) | 'criterion': 'gini', 'max_features': 'log2' |
| CC * (all. feat.) | 'depth': 4, 'l2_leaf_reg': 3, 'learning_rate': 0.6 |
| CC + SMOTE (imp. feat.) | 'depth': 5, 'l2_leaf_reg': 2, 'learning_rate': 0.9 |
| CC + SMOTE (all feat.) | 'depth': 4, 'l2_leaf_reg': 1, 'learning_rate': 0.2 |

* LR–logistic regression, RF—random forest, CC—CatBoost classifier; imp. feat.—the model is composed using only important features, all feat.—the model is composed using all available features.

## 3. Results

Table 3 shows the best performances for each classification target.

**Table 3.** Performance of the classifiers for each target.

| Target | Best Classifier | ROC AUC | F-Score | Recall | Precision |
|---|---|---|---|---|---|
| In-hospital mortality | CC * + SMOTE (all feat.) | 0.965 | 0.966 | 0.992 | 0.942 |
| Temporary neurological deficit (TND) | CC + SMOTE (all feat.) | 0.960 | 0.959 | 0.936 | 0.983 |
| Permanent neurological deficit (PND) | CC + SMOTE (all feat.) | 0.946 | 0.947 | 0.969 | 0.926 |
| Prolonged lung ventilation (>7 days) | CC + SMOTE (all feat.) | 0.957 | 0.958 | 0.984 | 0.934 |
| Renal replacement therapy (RRT) | CC + SMOTE (all feat.) | 0.985 | 0.984 | 0.992 | 0.978 |
| Myocardial infarction (MI) | CC + SMOTE (imp. feat.) | 0.986 | 0.984 | 0.993 | 0.979 |
| Multiple organ failure (MOF) | CC + SMOTE (all feat.) | 0.952 | 0.950 | 0.964 | 0.958 |

* CC—CatBoost classifier; imp. feat.—the model is composed using only important features, all feat.—the model is composed using all available features.

Figure 2 represents the interpretation of the CatBoost classifier results for each target variable. The diagram shows the impact of each feature on the model output.

The red color in Figure 2 relates to a higher value of the feature (for binary features, it corresponds to one), while the blue color corresponds to a lower feature value. The negative SHAP value corresponds to a negative impact on prediction, leading the model to predict zero, and a positive SHAP value corresponds to a positive impact on prediction, leading the model to predict one. For instance, a higher intraoperative hematocrit leads to a lower mortality risk, and a lower intraoperative hematocrit leads to a higher mortality risk. A decreased level of red blood cells leads to lower risks of TND cases, but a decreased level of red blood cells does not necessarily lead to higher risks of TND cases.

Figure 3 represents the plot, showing the most powerful predictors for a particular patient from the dataset for in-hospital mortality.

The bold value in Figure 3 indicates the model's output value. The red features increase the prediction and the blue features decrease the prediction. Aortic valve insufficiency has a positive impact on the output value and the red blood cell feature has a negative impact on the output value.

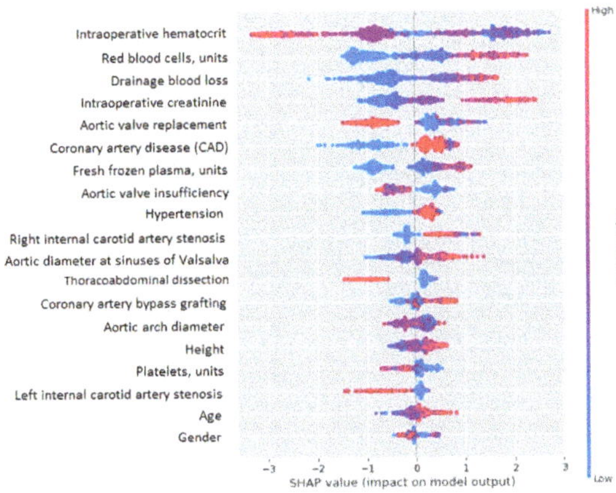


(a)

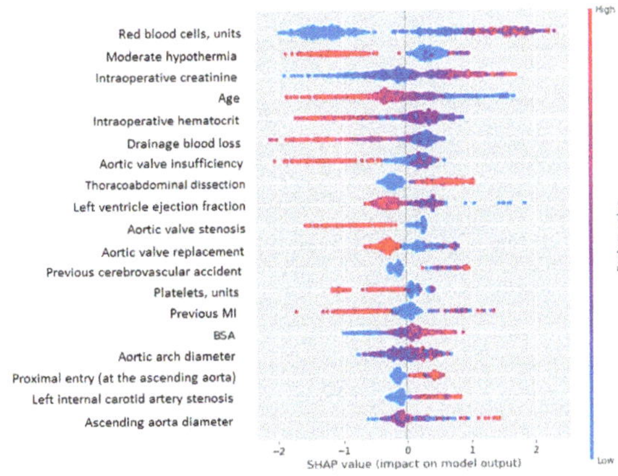


(b)

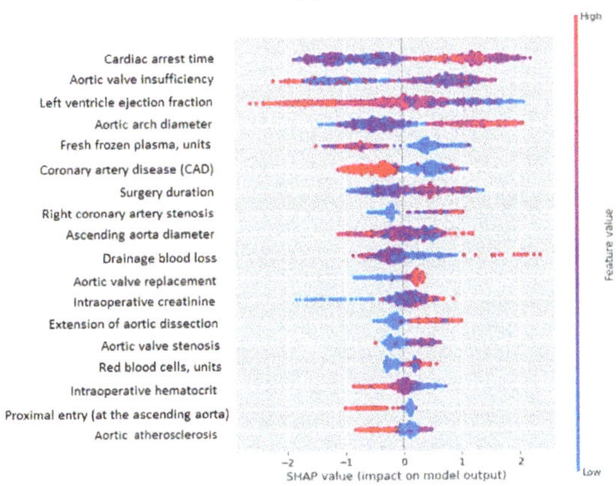


(c)

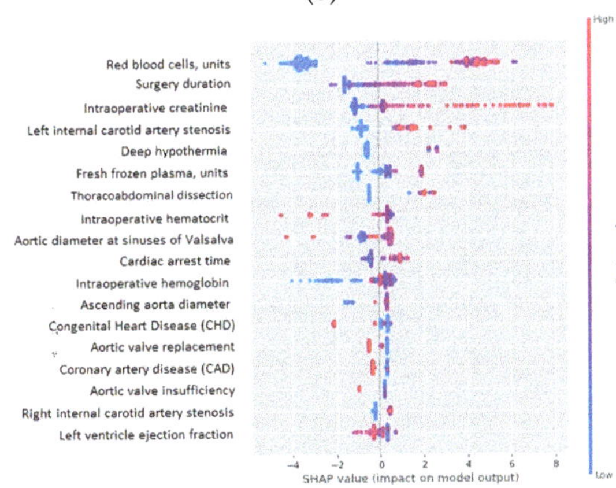


(d)

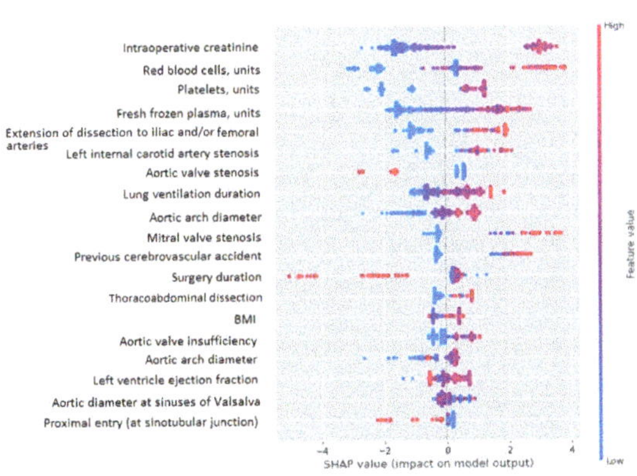


(e)

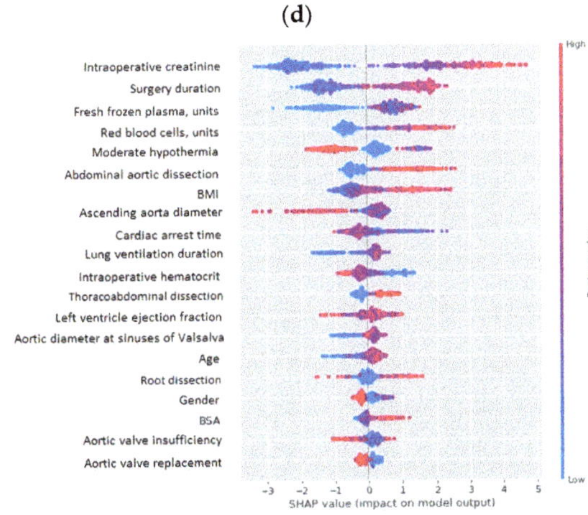


(f)

**Figure 2.** *Cont.*

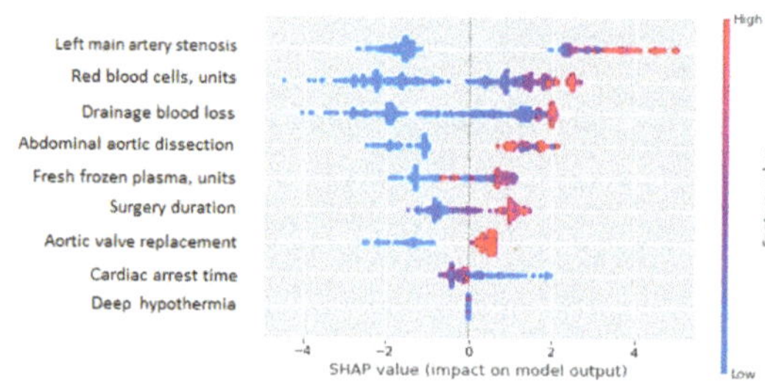


(**g**)

**Figure 2.** Feature importance diagrams for target variables: (**a**) in-hospital mortality; (**b**) TND; (**c**) PND; (**d**) prolonged lung ventilation; (**e**) RRT; (**f**) MOF; (**g**) MI.

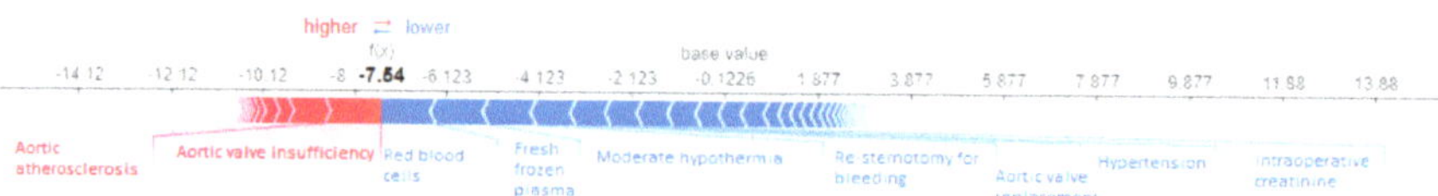


**Figure 3.** The example of a single patient's prediction.

## 4. Discussion

Despite the fact that a number of scoring systems for cardiac risk assessment have been developed and successfully applied in practice, they do not take into account the specificity of thoracic aortic pathology. More and more medicine-related studies concentrate on building machine learning models to learn from historical experience [24], and to identify specific risk factors.

Currently, there are a number of studies devoted to the identification of prognostic factors for postoperative outcomes in patients with thoracic aortic pathology. Age, NYHA III–IV class of heart failure, renal insufficiency, ascending aorta dilatation, involvement of the aortic arch in the pathological process, lower limb malperfusion, and emergent/urgent aortic surgery are the most common risk factors that affect the survival and development of postoperative complications. In addition, the likelihood of a favorable prognosis decreases, due to reoperations, combined cardiac surgery (e.g., coronary artery bypass grafting), and a prolonged cardiopulmonary bypass duration [4,11]. Some studies have emphasized the negative role of increased blood components in transfusions (packed red blood cells, fresh frozen plasma, and platelets) [4,9,10].

Great attention is paid to the prognostic criteria for thoracic aortic surgery; however, there are few studies that aim to identify the relationship between risk factors and adverse outcomes. This study is dedicated to the development of a predictive model based on integrated medical data, using two datasets from high-throughput aortic centers.

Feature selection plays an important role in medical risk prediction using machine learning models. We removed six features due to discrepancies in the data storage formats and in the diagnostic methods applied in the participating clinics, and because of the missing values. The exploratory data analysis resulted in the removal of weight, due to the high correlation with two other features. The circulatory arrest time, cardioplegic arrest time, and cardiopulmonary bypass time were eliminated because of the large number of missing values, as shown in [25], acknowledging that the application of imputation methods can distinctly affect the performance of the predictive model.

We tested three machine learning algorithms to develop a predictive model: (1) LR; (2) RF; (3) CatBoost. CatBoost, with the SMOTE balancing technique, demonstrated the best performance for the most targets.

We demonstrated several tools for CatBoost evaluation and interpretation: featuring importance scores, which are summarized using summary plots for each target variable

(Figure 2); comparison with other well-known machine learning models (LR and RF), using metrics such as ROC AUC, F-score, Recall, and Precision (Table 3). An accuracy measurement can be misleading, due to the fact that higher metric values indicate overfitting, especially on imbalanced datasets [26]. Precision is the ratio between correctly classified patients and all patients assigned to the class. Recall is the rate of correctly classified patients. If recall equals one, the prediction of positive classes is perfect. This metric is crucial to evaluate medical prediction models, as it is important to identify as many cases of the pathological event as possible. A low recall value corresponds to a high rate of positive cases of medical risk missed. F-score is the harmonic mean of recall and precision. The use of F-score in parameter tuning helps to penalize models for extreme values [27].

The SHAP value was used to ensure interpretability of the model. SHAP covers two aspects: global and local interpretability. Global interpretability explains the relationships of predictors with target variables, i.e., risk factors with risks, and allows the consistency of the model to be analyzed with the current practices. Local interpretability helps to understand why a particular case or patient obtains a particular prediction.

Figure 2 illustrates the summary plots for each target variable, showing negative and positive relationships of predictors with targets. These plots take into account the feature importance, the impact of each feature on the final prediction, the initial value of the feature (lower values are blue and higher values are red), and the correlation of the feature with the target (lower intraoperative creatinine correlates with a lower risk of multiple organ failure). The SHAP value provides the correlation, but not causation.

Figure 3 illustrates an example of a force plot for a single patient from the dataset. It helps to understand the influence of each predictor on the final output. Such a plot might be useful for future decision making.

The performance of the developed models could be compared to the results of other studies in predicting postoperative cardiovascular complications. Coulson et al. [16] set an aim to develop models to predict the risks of acute kidney injury and the need for renal replacement therapy after cardiac surgery, using as few predictors as possible. The simplicity and interpretability of the models, and the few predictors used, ensure the accessability of prediction models for clinicians. Thus, a careful analysis of the literature and accumulated practical experience is needed to stratify risk factors. The AUC ROC for the acute kidney injury postoperative prediction was 0.70, and the AUC ROC for the need for renal replacement therapy postoperative prediction was 0.85.

Fernandes et al. [15] investigated machine learning models to predict mortality after cardiac surgery. The best results were shown by boosting classifiers and random forest, showing 0.87 AUC ROC and up to 0.91 recall.

Czerny et al. [3] showed that logistic regression outperformed the other investigated classifiers, with a mean AUC of 0.712 for predicting mortality rate in acute aortic dissection.

The CatBoost classifier performs better in comparison with the results from the literature.

In most cases, the obtained results are in line with the current literature. Thus, the independent risk factors for postoperative acute kidney injury requiring RRT are impaired preoperative renal function, reduced left ventricle ejection fraction, and transfusion of a large volume of blood components, as well as being overweight [28–30]. In our model, these factors contribute significantly to the postoperative acute kidney injury.

Additionally, Wang et al. [11] demonstrated that the large extent of aortic dissection was an independent risk factor for early mortality. In another study, a significant negative role of primary fenestration with aortic dissection, especially with type B, was revealed as an important factor for mortality [31]. Moreover, the presence of this type of aortic dissection led to an increase in postoperative renal complications [32]. In another study, an enlarged abdominal aortic diameter was shown to be a risk factor for complications in the postoperative period [33].

Nevertheless, we should point out that, from a clinical perspective, the impact of many features in the predictive model is obscure. However, most of the features have a logical clinical explanation. The example of such clinical significance is a direct relation of the aortic diameter at the sinuses of Valsalva to temporal neurological deficit, which is still indistinct. To reveal the answer, one needs to resolve a logical chain. A large aortic root is an indication that it has been replaced. This naturally prolongs the cardiopulmonary bypass time and, successively, increases the risk of neurological deficiency.

Despite the successful implementation of surgical risk calculators (Euroscore, Euroscore II, and STS score), a standardized prognostic risk assessment scale for patients with thoracic aortic pathology has not yet been adopted. In the current literature, there have been a few attempts to compile prognostic models [4]. However, due to the heterogeneity of the predictors obtained in each particular study, the accumulation of more data is needed, in order to identify the significant risk factors. Elaboration of the correct risk score calculation for prognosis assessment in patients with thoracic aortic diseases is crucial. Our findings provide additional support for clinical decision making, guiding a patient care team prior to a surgical treatment, and promoting a safe postoperative period.

The presented study has certain limitations. Despite the integration of medical records from the datasets of two different clinics, the number of patients and clinical cases (operations) is relatively small. We are planning to extend it in the future. The study faced a problem of unbalanced data, which is a traditional concern for medical data [12]. This leads to situations where machine learning algorithms tend to classify the data into predominant classes. SMOTE for data balancing, and F-measure as the optimization metric, which is less sensitive to data imbalance, were applied to address the problem. However, the study still has limitations due to the imbalanced medical datasets. Another limitation is related to the loss of data during the integration process. We had to compare and map not only the logical data structures and contents, but also diagnostic methods and treatment approaches in different institutions. This reduced the amount of data we could include in the study.

## 5. Conclusions

This study has implemented models for postoperative risk prognosis for patients with thoracic aortic disease, using real-world data from two different medical institutions, comprising from both structured data and free-text medical records. The obtained findings provide additional support for clinical decision making, guiding a patient care team prior to surgical treatment, and promoting a safe postoperative period. Future studies may address the current limitations of the study, such as relevant synthetic patients' generation, model validation in a medical practice, and the development of applied risk stratification scales based on the obtained results.

**Author Contributions:** Conceptualization, D.P. and I.L.; methodology, I.L. and D.P.; validation, I.L., D.P., G.K. and B.K.; formal analysis, I.L.; investigation, I.L.; data curation, B.K. and D.P.; writing—original draft preparation, I.L.; writing—review and editing, D.P.; visualization, I.L.; supervision, G.K.; project administration G.K. and B.K. All authors have read and agreed to the published version of the manuscript.

**Funding:** The work was funded by the Ministry of Science and Higher Education of the Russian Federation (Agreement No. 075-15-2020-901).

**Institutional Review Board Statement:** Not applicable.

**Informed Consent Statement:** Patient consent was waived due to the use of anonymized medical data, without any possibility to identify patients.

**Data Availability Statement:** Not applicable.

**Acknowledgments:** This work is financially supported by National Center for Cognitive Research of ITMO University.

**Conflicts of Interest:** The authors declare no conflict of interest.

## Appendix A

Endpoints:
1 In-hospital mortality;
2 Temporary neurological deficit (TND);
3 Permanent neurological deficit (PND);
4 Prolonged lung ventilation (LV) (>7 days);
5 Renal replacement therapy (RRT);
6 Myocardial infarction (MI);
7 Multiple organ failure (MOF).

Anthropometric data:
1 Gender;
2 Age;
3 Height;
4 Weight;
5 Body mass index (BMI);
6 Body surface area (BSA).

Comorbidities:
1 Congenital heart disease (CHD);
2 Hypertension;
3 Coronary artery disease (CAD);
4 Previous MI;
5 Previous cerebrovascular accident;
6 Chronic obstructive pulmonary disease (COPD);
7 Marfan syndrome;
8 Aortic atherosclerosis.

Laboratory tests:
1 Preoperative hematocrit;
2 Preoperative urea;
3 Preoperative creatinine;
4 Preoperative glomerular filtration rate (GFR).

Coronary angiographic data:
1 Left main artery stenosis (LMA);
2 Right coronary artery stenosis (RCA);
3 Obtuse margin artery stenosis (OMA);
4 Left anterior descending artery (LAD).

Echocardiographic data:
1 Left internal carotid artery stenosis;
2 Right internal carotid artery stenosis;
3 Left ventricle ejection fraction;
4 Aortic valve stenosis;
5 Aortic valve insufficiency;
6 Mitral valve stenosis;
7 Mitral valve insufficiency;
8 Aortic diameter at sinuses of Valsalva.

Computed tomographic data:
1 Ascending aorta diameter;
2 Aortic arch diameter;
3 Segment A diameter = proximal descending aortic diameter;
4 Segment B diameter = distal descending aortic diameter;
5 Segment C diameter = abdominal aortic diameter;
6 Proximal entry (at sinotubular junction);
7 Proximal entry (at the ascending aorta);
8 Proximal entry (at the aortic arch);
9 Proximal entry behind the left subclavian artery = type B aortic dissection;

10 Involvement aortic root in dissection;
11 Involvement ascending aortic in dissection;
12 Involvement aortic arch in dissection;
13 Thoracoabdominal dissection;
14 Abdominal aortic dissection;
15 Extension of aortic dissection down to iliac and/or femoral arteries.

Intraoperative data:

1 Cardiac arrest time;
2 Antegrade cerebral perfusion time;
3 Circulatory arrest time;
4 Deep hypothermia;
5 Moderate hypothermia;
6 Re-sternotomy for bleeding;
7 Surgery duration;
8 Red blood cells, units;
9 Fresh frozen plasma, units;
10 Platelets, units;
11 Drainage blood loss;
12 Intraoperative hematocrit.
13 Intraoperative creatinine.

Concomitant cardiac procedures:

1 Coronary artery bypass grafting;
2 Aortic valve replacement;
3 Mitral valve replacement.

## References


1. Saeyeldin, A.A.; Velasquez, C.A.; Mahmood, S.U.B.; Brownstein, A.J.; Zafar, M.A.; Ziganshin, B.A.; Elefteriades, J.A. Thoracic aortic aneurysm: Unlocking the "silent killer" secrets. *Gen. Thorac. Cardiovasc. Surg.* **2019**, *67*, 1–11. [CrossRef] [PubMed]
2. Orandi, B.J.; Dimick, J.B.; Deeb, G.M.; Patel, H.J.; Upchurch, G.R. A population-based analysis of endovascular versus open thoracic aortic aneurysm repair. *J. Vasc. Surg.* **2009**, *49*, 1112–1116. [CrossRef] [PubMed]
3. Czerny, M.; Siepe, M.; Beyersdorf, F.; Feisst, M.; Gabel, M.; Pilz, M.; Pöling, J.; Dohle, D.S.; Sarvanakis, K.; Luehr, M.; et al. Prediction of mortality rate in acute type A dissection: The German Registry for Acute Type A Aortic Dissection score. *Eur. J. Cardiothorac. Surg.* **2020**, *58*, 700–706. [CrossRef] [PubMed]
4. Wagner, M.A.; Wang, H.; Benrashid, E.; Keenan, J.E.; Ganapathi, A.M.; Englum, B.R.; Hughes, G.C. Risk Prediction Model for Major Adverse Outcome in Proximal Thoracic Aortic Surgery. *Ann. Thorac. Surg.* **2019**, *107*, 795–801. [CrossRef] [PubMed]
5. Weng, S.F.; Reps, J.; Kai, J.; Garibaldi, J.M.; Qureshi, N. Can Machine-learning improve cardiovascular risk prediction using routine clinical data? *PLoS ONE* **2017**, *12*, e0174944. [CrossRef]
6. Lareyre, F.; Adam, C.; Carrier, M.; Raffort, J. Prediction of Abdominal Aortic Aneurysm Growth and Risk of Rupture in the Era of Machine Learning. *Angiology* **2020**, *71*, 767. [CrossRef]
7. Hirata, K.; Nakaura, T.; Nakagawa, M.; Kidoh, M.; Oda, S.; Utsunomiya, D.; Yamashita, Y. Machine Learning to Predict the Rapid Growth of Small Abdominal Aortic Aneurysm. *J. Comput. Assist. Tomogr.* **2020**, *44*, 37–42. [CrossRef]
8. Lee, R.; Jarchi, D.; Perera, R.; Jones, A.; Cassimjee, I.; Handa, A.; Clifton, D.A.; Bellamkonda, K.; Woodgate, F.; Killough, N.; et al. Applied Machine Learning for the Prediction of Growth of Abdominal Aortic Aneurysm in Humans. *EJVES Short Rep.* **2018**, *39*, 24–28. [CrossRef]
9. Estrera, A.L.; Miller, C.C.; Lee, T.Y.; Shah, P.; Safi, H.J. Ascending and transverse aortic arch repair: The impact of retrograde cerebral perfusion. *Circulation* **2008**, *118*, S160–S166. [CrossRef]
10. Ghincea, C.V.; Reece, T.B.; Eldeiry, M.; Roda, G.F.; Bronsert, M.R.; Jarrett, M.J.; Pal, J.D.; Cleveland, J.C.; Fullerton, D.A.; Aftab, M. Predictors of Acute Kidney Injury Following Aortic Arch Surgery. *J. Surg. Res.* **2019**, *242*, 40–46. [CrossRef]
11. Wang, X.; Yang, F.; Zhu, J.; Liu, Y.; Sun, L.; Hou, X. Aortic arch surgery with hypothermic circulatory arrest and unilateral antegrade cerebral perfusion: Perioperative outcomes. *J. Thorac. Cardiovasc. Surg.* **2020**, *159*, 374–387.e4. [CrossRef] [PubMed]
12. Lee, H.; Yoon, H.; Nam, K.; Cho, Y.; Kim, T.; Kim, W.; Bahk, J. Derivation and Validation of Machine Learning Approaches to Predict Acute Kidney Injury after Cardiac Surgery. *J. Clin. Med.* **2018**, *7*, 322. [CrossRef] [PubMed]
13. Zhong, Z.; Yuan, X.; Liu, S.; Yang, Y.; Liu, F.F. Machine learning prediction models for prognosis of critically ill patients after open-heart surgery. *Sci. Rep.* **2021**, *11*, 3384. [CrossRef] [PubMed]
14. Allyn, J.; Allou, N.; Augustin, P.; Philip, I.; Martinet, O.; Belghiti, M.; Provenchere, S.; Montravers, P.; Ferdynus, C. A comparison of a machine learning model with EuroSCORE II in predicting mortality after elective cardiac surgery: A decision curve analysis. *PLoS ONE* **2017**, *12*, e169772. [CrossRef] [PubMed]

15. Fernandes, M.P.B.; Armengol de la Hoz, M.; Rangasamy, V.; Subramaniam, B. Machine Learning Models with Preoperative Risk Factors and Intraoperative Hypotension Parameters Predict Mortality After Cardiac Surgery. *J. Cardiothorac. Vasc. Anesth.* **2021**, *35*, 857–865. [CrossRef] [PubMed]
16. Coulson, T.; Bailey, M.; Pilcher, D.; Reid, C.M.; Seevanayagam, S.; Williams-Spence, J.; Bellomo, R. Predicting Acute Kidney Injury After Cardiac Surgery Using a Simpler Model. *J. Cardiothorac. Vasc. Anesth.* **2021**, *35*, 866–873. [CrossRef]
17. Hanley, J.A.; McNeil, B.J. The meaning and use of the area under a receiver operating characteristic (ROC) curve. *Radiology* **1982**, *143*, 29–36. [CrossRef]
18. Pedregosa Fabianpedregosa, F.; Michel, V.; Grisel Oliviergrisel, O.; Blondel, M.; Prettenhofer, P.; Weiss, R.; Vanderplas, J.; Cournapeau, D.; Pedregosa, F.; Varoquaux, G.; et al. Scikit-learn: Machine Learning in Python. *J. Mach. Learn. Res.* **2011**, *12*, 2825–2830.
19. Prokhorenkova, L.; Gusev, G.; Vorobev, A.; Dorogush, A.V.; Gulin, A. CatBoost: Unbiased boosting with categorical features. In Proceedings of the NIPS'18: Proceedings of the 32nd International Conference on Neural Information Processing Systems, Montréal, QC, Canada, 3–8 December 2018; pp. 6639–6649. [CrossRef]
20. Waskom, M.L. seaborn: Statistical data visualization. *J. Open Source Softw.* **2021**, *6*, 3021. [CrossRef]
21. Hunter, J.D. Matplotlib: A 2D graphics environment. *Comput. Sci. Eng.* **2007**, *9*, 90–95. [CrossRef]
22. Chawla, N.V.; Bowyer, K.W.; Hall, L.O.; Kegelmeyer, W.P. SMOTE: Synthetic minority over-sampling technique. *J. Artif. Intell. Res.* **2002**, *16*, 321–357. [CrossRef]
23. Lundberg, S.M.; Lee, S.-I. A Unified Approach to Interpreting Model Predictions. In Proceedings of the NIPS'17: Proceedings of the 31st International Conference on Neural Information Processing Systems, Long Beach, CA, USA, 4–9 December 2017; pp. 4768–4777. [CrossRef]
24. Kartal, E.; Balaban, M.E. Machine learning techniques in cardiac risk assessment. *Turkish J. Thorac. Cardiovasc. Surg.* **2018**, *26*, 394. [CrossRef] [PubMed]
25. Lenivtceva, I.; Grechishcheva, S.; Kopanitsa, G.; Panfilov, D.; Kozlov, B. Predicting the Aortic Aneurysm Postoperative Risks Based on Russian Integrated Data. *Stud. Health Technol. Inform.* **2021**, *285*, 88–93. [CrossRef] [PubMed]
26. Cabitza, F.; Campagner, A. Who wants accurate models? Arguing for a different metrics to take classification models seriously. *arXiv* **2019**, arXiv:1910.09246. [CrossRef]
27. Hicks, S.A.; Strümke, I.; Strümke, S.; Thambawita, V.; Hammou, M.; Riegler, M.A.; Al Halvorsen, P.; Parasa, S. On evaluation metrics for medical applications of artificial intelligence. *medRxiv* **2021**, *12*, 5979. [CrossRef]
28. Kim, W.H.; Park, M.H.; Kim, H.J.; Lim, H.Y.; Shim, H.S.; Sohn, J.T.; Kim, C.S.; Lee, S.M. Potentially modifiable risk factors for acute kidney injury after surgery on the thoracic aorta: A propensity score matched case-control study. *Medicine* **2015**, *94*, e273. [CrossRef]
29. Zhou, H.; Wang, G.; Yang, L.; Shi, S.; Li, J.; Wang, M.; Zhang, C.; Li, H.; Qian, X.; Sun, X.; et al. Acute Kidney Injury After Total Arch Replacement Combined With Frozen Elephant Trunk Implantation: Incidence, Risk Factors, and Outcome. *J. Cardiothorac. Vasc. Anesth.* **2018**, *32*, 2210–2217. [CrossRef]
30. Nota, H.; Asai, T.; Suzuki, T.; Kinoshita, T.; Ikegami, H.; Takashima, N. Risk factors for acute kidney injury in aortic arch surgery with selective cerebral perfusion and mild hypothermic lower body circulatory arrest. *Interact. Cardiovasc. Thorac. Surg.* **2014**, *19*, 955–961. [CrossRef]
31. Codner, J.A.; Lou, X.; Duwayri, Y.M.; Chen, E.P.; Binongo, J.N.; Moon, R.; Jordan, W.D.; Leshnower, B.G. The distance of the primary intimal tear from the left subclavian artery predicts aortic growth in uncomplicated type B aortic dissection. *J. Vasc. Surg.* **2019**, *69*, 692–700. [CrossRef]
32. Hoogmoed, R.C.; Patel, H.J.; Kim, K.M.; Williams, D.M.; Deeb, G.M.; Yang, B. Acute Kidney Injury in Acute Type B Aortic Dissection: Outcomes Over 20 Years. *Ann. Thorac. Surg.* **2019**, *107*, 486–492. [CrossRef]
33. Heo, W.; Song, S.W.; Lee, S.Y.; Kim, T.H.; Lee, J.S.; Yoo, K.J.; Cho, B.K. Locational impact of luminal communication on aortic diameter changes and reintervention in acute type I aortic dissection. *Eur. J. Cardiothorac. Surg.* **2019**, *55*, 1037–1044. [CrossRef] [PubMed]

MDPI
St. Alban-Anlage 66
4052 Basel
Switzerland
www.mdpi.com

*Journal of Personalized Medicine* Editorial Office
E-mail: jpm@mdpi.com
www.mdpi.com/journal/jpm

www.ingramcontent.com/pod-product-compliance
Lightning Source LLC
Chambersburg PA
CBHW042013200926
51615CB00030B/9
*9783036592572*